The
Neuropsychology
of
Learning Disorders
Theoretical
Approaches

Proceedings of the International Conference on Neuropsychology of Learning Disorders, held at Korsør, Denmark, June 15–18, 1975. Sponsored by the North Atlantic Treaty Organization, Scientific Affairs Division, and Carleton University, The Pickering Fund

The Neuropsychology of Learning Disorders
Theoretical Approaches

Edited by

Robert M. Knights, Ph.D.
Psychology Department
Carleton University
and
Dirk J. Bakker, Ph.D.
Pedagogical Institute

University Park Press
Baltimore · London · Tokyo

UNIVERSITY PARK PRESS
International Publishers in Science and Medicine
Chamber of Commerce Building
Baltimore, Maryland 21202

Typeset by The Composing Room of Michigan, Inc.
Manufactured in the United States of America by Universal Lithographers,
Inc., and the Maple Press Co.

Library of Congress Cataloging in Publication Data
Main entry under title:
The Neuropsychology of learning disorders.
  Bibliography: p.
  Includes index.
  1. Learning disabilities. I. Knights, Robert M.
II. Bakker, Dirk J. III. North Atlantic Treaty
Organization. Division of Scientific Affairs.
IV. Carleton University. V. Pickering Foundation.
[DNLM: 1. Neurophysiology—Congresses. 2. Minimal
brain dysfunction—Congresses. 3. Learning disorders—
Congresses. LC4704 N494 1975]
LC4704.N48   371.9   76-29072
ISBN 0-8391-0951-2

Contents

Contributors

Dirk J. Bakker, Ph.D. Head, Department of Developmental and Educational Neuropsychology, Pedagogical Institute, Koningslaan 22, Amsterdam (Z), The Netherlands

Joop Bosch, M.A. Department of Child Psychology, Free University, Koningslaan 22, Amsterdam (Z), The Netherlands

Anthony W. H. Buffery, Ph.D., Senior Lecturer in Psychology, Institute of Psychiatry, University of London, De Crespigny Park, Denmark Hill, London, SE5 8AF, England

C. Keith Conners, Ph.D., Associate Professor of Psychiatry, Western Psychiatric Institute and Clinic, University of Pittsburgh School of Medicine, Pittsburgh, Pennsylvania 15261

Stuart J. Dimond, Ph.D., Senior Lecturer in Psychology, University College, P.O. Box 96, Cardiff, CF1 1BX, Wales

Donald G. Doehring, Ph.D., Professor of Human Communication Disorders, Psychology and Otolaryngology, McGill University, School of Human Communication Disorders, Beatty Hall, 1266 Pine Avenue West, Montreal, Quebec, H3G 1A8, Canada

Virginia I. Douglas, Ph.D., Senior Psychologist, Montreal Children's Hospital, Montreal, and Professor, Department of Psychology, McGill University, P.O. Box 6070, Station A, Montreal, Quebec, H3C 3G1, Canada

Henry G. Dunn, M.B., F.R.C.P., F.R.C.P.(C), Department of Paediatrics, University of British Columbia, 715 West 12th Avenue, Vancouver, B.C., V5Z 1M9, Canada

H. Bruce Ferguson, Ph.D., Assistant Professor of Psychology, Carleton University, Ottawa, Ontario, K1S 5B6, Canada

Christine Fiedorowicz, B.A., Neuropsychometrist, Neuropsychology Laboratory, Royal Ottawa Hospital, 1145 Carling Avenue, Ottawa, Ontario, K1Z 7K4, Canada

Morton P. Friedman, Ph.D., Professor of Psychology, Department of Psychology, University of California at Los Angeles, Los Angeles, California 90024

William H. Gaddes, Ph.D., Professor, Department of Psychology, University of Victoria, and Consulting Psychologist, Department of Neurology and Neurosurgery, Royal Jubilee Hospital, Victoria, B.C., Canada

B. LaRue Guyer-Christie, M.A., Research Associate, Department of Psychology, University of California at Los Angeles, Los Angeles, California 90024

John R. Hughes, D.M. (Oxon.), M.D., Ph.D., Professor of Neurology, Northwestern University Medical Center, Searle 11-473, 303 E. Chicago Ave., Chicago, Illinois 60611

Alex F. Kalverboer, Ph.D., Reader in Experimental Clinical Psychology, Laboratory of Experimental Clinical Psychology, Department of Clinical Psychology, State University, Groningen, The Netherlands

Gerald Leisman, M.D., Ph.D., Professor, Department of Health Science, Brooklyn College, CUNY, Brooklyn, New York 11210, and Coordinator, Clinical Neurophysiology Laboratory, Veterans Administration Hospital, East Orange, New Jersey 07019

Che K. Leong, Dip. Ed. Psych., Ph.D., Associate Professor, Institute of Child Guidance and Development, University of Saskatchewan, Saskatoon, Saskatchewan, S7N 0W0, Canada

Maureen Julianne Levine, Ph.D., Assistant Professor, Department of Psychology, Central Michigan University, Mount Pleasant, Michigan 48859

Isabelle Y. Liberman, Ph.D., School of Education, University of Connecticut, Storrs, Connecticut 06268, and Research Associate, Haskins Laboratories, New Haven, Connecticut 06510

Annetta Karâa McBurney, Acad. Dip. Ed., Ph.D., Department of Paediatrics, University of British Columbia, 715 West 12th Avenue, Vancouver, B.D., V5Z 1M9, Canada

Donald Meichenbaum, Ph.D., Professor of Psychology, University of Waterloo, Waterloo, Ontario, N2L 3G1, Canada

Hazel E. Nelson, M. Phil., A.B.Ps.S., Senior Psychologist, The National Hospital for Nervous and Mental Diseases, Queen Square, London, England

Luigi Pizzamiglio, Full Professor of Psychology, Department of Psychology, State University of Rome, V. del Sardi 70, 00185 Rome, Italy, and Researcher, Institute of Psychology C.N.R., V. del Monti Tiburtini 509, 00100 Rome, Italy

Byron P. Rourke, Ph.D., Department of Psychology, University of Windsor, Windsor, Ontario, N9B 3P4, Canada, and Windsor Western Hospital Centre, Windsor, Ontario, Canada

Michael Rutter, M.D., F.R.C.P., F.R.C. Psych., D.P.M., Professor of Child Psychiatry and Consultant of Child Psychiatry, Consultant Physician, The Bethlem Royal and Mudsley Hospital, University of London, Institute of Psychiatry, De Crespigny Park, Denmark Hill, London SE5 8AF, England

Paul Satz, Ph.D., Professor of Psychology and Clinical Psychology, Director, Neuropsychology Laboratory, Shands Teaching Hospital, University of Florida, Gainesville, Florida 32601

Joddy Schwartz, M.S., Department of Health Science, Brooklyn College, CUNY, Brooklyn, New York 11210, and Research Assistant, Clinical Neurophysiology Laboratory, Veterans Administration Hospital, East Orange, New Jersey 07019

Donald Shankweiler, Ph.D., Department of Psychology, University of Connecticut, Storrs, Connecticut 06268 and Research Associate, Haskins Laboratories, New Haven, Connecticut 06510

Daniel E. Sheer, Ph.D., Professor of Psychology, Director, Psychology Laboratory, University of Houston, Houston, Texas 77004

Suzanne Simpson, M.A., Department of Psychology, University of Ottawa, Ottawa, Ontario, K1N 6N5, Canada

Esther K. Sleator, M.D., Research Pediatrician, Institute for Child Behavior and Development, University of Illinois, 51 Gerty Drive, Champaign, Illinois 61820

Robert L. Sprague, Ph.D. Director and Professor of Psychology, Institute for Child Behavior and Development, University of Illinois, 51 Gerty Drive, Champaign, Illinois 61820

Otfried Spreen, Ph.D., Professor of Psychology, University of Victoria, and Consulting Psychologist, Department of Neurology and Neurosurgery, Royal Jubilee Hospital, Victoria, B.C., V8W 2Y2, Canada

Paula Tallal, Ph.D., Instructor in Pediatrics, The Johns Hopkins University School of Medicine, 725 N. Wolfe Street, and Coordinator of Research in Special Education, the John F. Kennedy Institute, 707 N. Broadway, Baltimore, Maryland 21205

David C. Taylor, M.D., M.R.C.P., F.R.C. Psych., D.P.M., Clinical Lecturer in Psychiatry, University of Oxford, and Consultant in Developmental Psychiatry, Park Hospital for Children, Old Road, Headington, Oxford OX3 7LQ, England

Jetty Teunissen, M.A., Psychotherapist, Haarlem, The Netherlands

Ronald L. Trites, Ph.D., Associate Professor of Psychology and Psychiatry, and Head, Neuropsychology Laboratory, Royal Ottawa Hospital, 1145 Carling Avenue, Ottawa, Ontario, K1Z 7K4, Canada

Alexander Tymchuk, Ph.D., Assistant Professor of Psychiatry and Psychology, Department of Psychiatry, University of California at Los Angeles, Los Angeles, California 90024

H. John van Duyne, STB, Ed.D., Director, Learning and Cognition Laboratory, and Associate Professor, Educational Psychology, 143-145 Graham Hall, Northern Illinois University, DeKalb, Illinois 60115

Elizabeth K. Warrington, Ph.D., D.Sc., Top Grade Psychologist, The National Hospital for Nervous and Mental Diseases, Queen Square, London, England

Paul H. Wender, M.D., Professor of Psychiatry, University of Utah College of Medicine, 50 North Medical Drive, Salt Lake City, Utah 84132

Sandra F. Witelson, Ph.D., Associate Professor of Psychiatry (in Psychology), Department of Psychiatry, Chedoke Hospitals, McMaster University, Hamilton, Ontario, L8S 4J9, Canada

William Yule, M.A., Dipl. Psych., Senior Lecturer in Psychology and in Child and Adolescent Psychiatry, and Principal Psychologist, The Bethlem Royal and Maudsley Hospital, University of London, Institute of Psychiatry, De Crespigny Park, Denmark Hill, London, SE5 8AF, England

Acknowledgments

We would like to express our appreciation to the NATO Scientific Affairs Division, Human Factors Panel whose support made this conference possible. In addition, we express our thanks to the Pickering Foundation, Psychology Department, Carleton University, the Paedologisch Instituut, Amsterdam, and Carleton University, Ottawa for their support.

In Denmark, Professor Rolf Willanger and Lector Mogens Brun of the Psychology Laboratory, University of Copenhagen, arranged for the site of the conference and helped in many ways to organize the proceedings. The success of the conference was the result in large part of their assistance, and we thank them for their efforts.

The conference was held at Klarskovgaard, six kilometers from Korsør in the south of Denmark. The modern Danish architecture blended with the surrounding fields and forest to provide an ideal countryside setting. The warmth and easy friendliness of the atmosphere as well as the excellent meeting facilities promoted stimulating discussion, an important factor in the success of the conference. We would like to thank Lillian Anderson and the staff of Klarskovgaard for all their help and kind hospitality.

The opening ceremonies took place the first evening with addresses from three distinguished guests. Mr. Asger Baunsbak-Jensen, Director General of the Directorate for Secondary Education and Teacher Training of Denmark, welcomed the conference on behalf of the Ministry of Education and hosted a delightful wine and cheese reception. Mr. Peter Drenth of the Psychology Department, Free University of Amsterdam, and chairman of the NATO Human Factors Panel, described the various NATO research and scholarship programs. The country of Denmark has produced some pioneer work in the area of brain behavior studies, and Professor Willanger of Copenhagen University reviewed the studies of K. Hermann on dyslexia and aphasia as well as the more recent work of other neuropsychologists in his country.

Six of the participants were kind enough to record and transcribe the evening discussion sessions. This transcription was a difficult task, and we would like to acknowledge the work of Ann Altman, Department of Psychology, University of Florida, Gainesville; Darla Drader, Royal Ottawa Hospital, Ottawa; Bruce Ferguson, Department of Psychology, Carleton University, Ottawa; William Gaddes, Department of Psychology, University of Victoria, Victoria; Sandra Witelson, Department of Psychiatry, Chedoke Hospital, Hamilton; and Ronald Trites, Royal Ottawa Hospital, Ottawa. Unfortunately, because of an editorial decision we were unable to include this material.

Finally, a special note of gratitude to our students and colleagues Freeke Bruijn, Mary Grenier, Peter Reitsma, Jetty Teunissen, June Cunningham, Louis Dumontier, Darla Drader, Jan Norwood, and Jinny McNaughton for their good-natured assistance and support throughout the conference.

R.M.K.
D.J.B.

Preface

For centuries the proper education of children has been of great concern to all peoples of the world. It has always been known that some children learn more readily than others, but only during the last century have differences in learning ability come under scientific study. These investigations have shown that there are children who appear normal physically and mentally who still encounter great problems in learning reading, writing, spelling, and arithmetic.

The early studies of learning disorders were concerned with the relationship between nervous system disorders and learning abilities, and it was generally assumed that the basic cause of many learning disorders had to do with brain injury, generally of a mild type. Subsequent research suggested that the learning disorder may be caused by an unusual or abnormal functioning of the brain in the absence of gross brain damage. The idea was advanced that these children had minimal brain dysfunction. Scientists in such fields as neurology, pediatrics, physiology, biochemistry, and neuropsychology began a variety of investigations in an attempt to deliniate the nature of the differences in brain structure and function found in children with learning disabilities.

Another approach to the study of children with learning disorders has been concerned with behavioral measures. Descriptive studies have classified the behavioral characteristics of these children and attempted to show how they differ from normal children in the incidence of abnormal maturational conditions, activity level, impulsiveness, emotional stability, classroom behavior, and many other factors.

Only recently have there been several attempts to integrate information from a variety of areas of research in order to provide a comprehensive theory of the etiology of learning disorders. The increasing number of diverse findings about these children indicates the complexity of the problem. In spite of this, there is a large amount of clinical and research data that should provide a basis for the development and extension of theories in this area.

The study of neuropsychology attempts to relate what is known about the functioning of the brain to what is known about the behavior of people. Over the last few decades a great deal of information has been gathered about the brain and about children's behavior, but is has been accumulated as small chunks or isolated bits of information. As a result it has been difficult to make use of this knowledge in explaining the learning problems experienced by youngsters. Recently there have been several attempts to weave these knots of information into a network of variables to provide appropriate theories for the generation of testable hypotheses. At the present stage of knowledge in neuropsychology, we feel it is time to encourage the development of new questions and hypotheses for the extension of these theories.

These proceedings provide a variety of theoretical positions and ideas which will stimulate future research. As Dr. Spreen suggests in his post-conference review, theories implicating such features as developmental lag, hemispheric asymmetry, cognitive or perceptual deficit, sustained attention or focused arousal are not necessarily incompatible but, rather, function as building blocks in the integration of a neuropsychology of learning disorders.

The
Neuropsychology
of
Learning Disorders
Theoretical
Approaches

Part I

Epidemiology and
Social Implications
of Learning Disabilities

Prevalence Estimates and the Need for Definition of Learning Disabilities

William H. Gaddes

A number of attempts have been made in recent years in Britain and North America to make prevalence studies of learning-disabled children (CELDIC Report, 1970; Minskoff, 1973; Walzer and Richmond, 1973), but all of these, with possibly the exception of the Isle of Wight Study (Rutter, Tizard, and Whitmore, 1970), have been incomplete or seriously limited because of the debilitating methodological problems inherent in the task. This chapter examines the problem of identification of the learning-disabled child and attempts a generic definition of learning disabilities. To reach that goal, the validity of the term "epidemiology" for viewing populations of academically underachieving children is questioned, the basic etiological factors are briefly reviewed, and the psychometric problems inherent in the task are discussed. All of these topics are prerequisite conditions for producing a workable definition.

EPIDEMIOLOGY

Epidemiology is a medical term dating back to the time of Hippocrates, who devoted one of his treatises to the subject of epidemics (Skinner, 1961). The word was revived during the sixteenth century and has been used generally since then by the medical profession to refer to the scientific study of factors influencing the distribution and frequency of infectious diseases in man (MacMahon and Pugh, 1970; Miller and Keane, 1972; Oxford English Dictionary, 1933; Black's Medical Dictionary, 1971; Blakiston's New Gould Medical Dictionary, 1956; McGraw-Hill Encyclopedia of Science and Technology, 1971; Chambers's Encyclopaedia, 1966); however, in recent years it has been extended to include, as well, noninfectious diseases, physical defects, accidents, and death rates in

This manuscript was prepared during study leave from the University of Victoria and supported by a Leave Fellowship from the Canada Council during the academic year 1974–1975.

specific groups (Encyclopedia Canadiana, 1970; McGraw-Hill Encyclopedia of Science and Technology, 1971). In the last two years, attempts have been made to extend the term to include more subtle, non-life-threatening conditions, such as chronic impairment of the ability to learn the regularly expected academic material of our public school systems (Minskoff, 1973; Walzer and Richmond, 1973). One difficulty that is created by this attempt to broaden a medical term to cover a specific behavioral syndrome is that the functions are numerous and varied, and only some are transferrable from medical surveys to behavioral studies. Gruenberg in his epidemiological review of mental retardation (Stevens and Heber, 1965, pp. 259–306) has suggested several purposes for epidemiological studies in the field of health care and medical problems. From Gruenberg's list and other sources, nine functions of an epidemiological study can be identified. Let us examine each of these and their usefulness in studying learning disabilities.

(1) To study the distribution and prevalence of a particular disease or clinical syndrome, using frequency of cases, mortality rates, morbidity rates, incidence rates, and case fatality ratios. This would be applicable for using frequency and incidence rates, but obviously not for mortality and morbidity rates and fatality ratios.

The next three points, 2, 3, and 4, are directly transferrable to studies of learning disorders. They are: (2) to imply and develop a professional definition of the disease, (3) to identify and locate special high-risk populations, (4) to define the need for and direction of corrective and preventive programs. However, the remaining five points have little or no use for non-health-threatening behavioral conditions. They are: (5) to estimate the degree of success of the health services in dealing with the observed disease, (6) to compute the risk of chances of infection by it, (7) to provide knowledge about a particular disease, and to change public attitudes to it through health education, (8) to allocate the same causes for two or more clinical illnesses, and (9) to study the factors that influence the frequency and distribution of diseases in man. Since all nine of these functions are useful for population studies of physical disease conditions and less than half are transferrable to group studies of academic failure, this is a major difficulty created by attempting to apply a medical concept to a behavioral syndrome.

BASIC PROBLEM

Psychology in the past has been both helped and hindered by the acceptance of the medical model in diagnosis and treatment. Methods of psychotherapy during the past thirty years have been more varied and innovative and generally more useful since researchers have freed themselves from the restrictive concept of illness and pathology. In studying or treating behavioral syndromes, it is necessary to select operationally valid concepts and definitions in order to ensure a successful diagnosis and remedial prescription. Since clinical psychology grew out of subordinate cooperation with professional medicine, it was more likely, thirty years ago, that psychologists were willing to accept blindly a medical diagnostic concept and apply it to a behavioral problem. No doubt many patients gained when this procedure was appropriate, but many more suffered when its theoretical and practical incongruities punished them. The medical model, both with its knowledge and techniques, is best for dealing with cases of conclusive traumatic brain damage and dysfunction. But by contrast the psychological-special-educational model is more useful for treating trainable mentally retarded subjects or the learning problems of the brain damaged.

Epidemiological studies are particularly suited to physical syndromes, such as the presence of congenital malformations (Gentry, Parkhurst, and Bulin, 1959), because of their "all-or-none" nature. They are suitable also for some behavioral syndromes like suicide, alcoholism, neurosis, and epilepsy. Note that most of these syndromes, in contrast with learning disabilities, have discrete behavioral definitions (e.g., suicide, epilepsy) or they have readily recognized organic parameters, and hence may be relatively easily isolated, observed, and counted. One behavioral syndrome that lends itself particularly well to epidemiological study is mental retardation, as Gruenberg (1964), Heber (1970), and Sorel (1974) have shown. In this syndrome there are nearly always conclusive and measurable signs such as clearly indicated IQ cutoff points, measures of impaired adaptive behavior, and sometimes some unequivocal physical signs. It is interesting that while medical study and care of the mentally retarded are essential, the current definitions of mental retardation stress behavioral rather than organic criteria (Heber, 1970) or social and mental competence and development (Sorel, 1974). Because he stresses behavioral rather than medical criteria, Sorel has chosen to title his book "Prevalences of Mental Retardation" rather than "Epidemiology," and this would seem to be a logical move away from medical and toward a behavioral terminology.

It seems evident that the concept of epidemiology is an inappropriate model for dealing with the problems of learning disabilities as they are generally defined in the United States and Canada, and because of this, no complete North American epidemiological study has yet been carried out. In those few cases where it has been attempted (Minskoff, 1973; Walzer and Richmond, 1973) the writers have commented on the great difficulty of the task, and the ideational chaos and complexity it presents.

In searching the *Psychological Abstracts* of the last five years, the author noted that the term "epidemiology" did not even appear until 1973. In 1973 there were 43 articles listed under this classification, and in 1974 there were 54. Of all of the 97 papers, only one included the topic of learning disabilities, but it provided no information about their prevalence.

Since learning disabilities do not imply disease, but a level or quality of deficit behavior, "prevalence" rather than "epidemiology" seems to be a better term to describe them, even though about half of the underachievers in some settings appear to suffer from organic causes (Myklebust and Boshes, 1969). Etiological studies of children who are underachieving at school suggest that their inferior performances may result from abnormal deficits in one or more of the three major causal areas, (1) constitutional, (2) psychological, and (3) social. This means that since most abnormal psychological and behavioral syndromes lack a sophisticated taxonomy with universally accepted and operationally defined criteria for assignment to each diagnostic category, a systematic compilation is extremely difficult if not impossible. Since there is no generic definition, we cannot recognize the cases with reliability. At present the learning-disabled child is diagnostically almost faceless, unless his symptoms are so extreme or his abilities to learn so refractory that there is general and immediate agreement on his condition.

PROBLEM OF DEFINITION OF LEARNING DISORDER

Many definitions in the past have been plagued by the difficulty of trying to dichotomize behavior as physical and psychosocial. Frierson and Barbe (1967) tried to resolve this by defining "learning disorder" as "a known impairment in the nervous system" and a "learning disability" as a "demonstrated inability to perform a task normally found within the capability range of individuals of comparable mental ability" (Frierson and Barbe, 1967, p. 4). This type of approach, since it defines different aspects of the problem, is more likely to confound the issue than resolve it, since the first definition is exclusive and the second inclusive.

It is necessary to recognize the various spheres of influence, the different professional disciplines involved in the diagnosis and treatment, and the significant problem areas; any successful definition must include all of these.

Before attempting a definition let us look very briefly at: (1) the etiological factors, (2) the concerned professional and lay groups, (3) the educational psychometric problems, (4) the psychological and (5) the sociological aspects of learning disabilities. Once we have examined all aspects of the problem, we shall strive to produce a definition to include all of these determinants.

Regardless of the etiology or professional problems of a child's deficient learning, it is reflected by his classroom achievement and the evaluation by his teachers. Therefore, the definition that we will ultimately construct will describe the level of his psychosocial adaptation within a circumscribed educational environment.

ETIOLOGICAL FACTORS

Biological Factors

I have discussed at greater length elsewhere (Gaddes, 1975) the neurological implications of learning and the inextricable relationship of organic functions (chiefly those of the central nervous system) and learning behavior. Philosophers characteristically have wrestled with the mind—body problem, but more recently and particularly during the last 40 years other disciplines such as neurology, neurosurgery, neuropsychology, biochemistry, nutrition, gynecology and obstetrics, environmental medicine, and special education have all contributed to improving and clarifying the understanding of this obscure relationship. There is no doubt that mental functions and brain activities are highly correlated (Hebb, 1949; Sherrington, 1951), and neurologists, psychiatrists, neuropsychologists, and special educators are beginning to relate the significance of these correlations to the better understanding and remediation of learning disorders (Adams, 1973; Bannatyne, 1971; Benson and Geschwind, 1969; Benton, 1962a, 1964; Boder, 1971; Chalfant and Scheffelin, 1969; Critchley, 1970; Cruickshank, 1966; Drake, 1968; Duane, 1974; Kinsbourne, 1972; Myklebust and Boshes, 1969; Penfield and Roberts, 1959; Reed, 1968; Reitan, 1966; Reitan and Heineman, 1968; Tymchuk, Knights, and Hinton,1970c; Wada, 1969b). While not all children with learning disorders suffer from brain damage and/or dysfunction, a huge literature has appeared on the diagnosis and management of those who do (Birch, 1964; Clements, 1966; Clements and Paine, 1969; Conners, 1967; De La Cruz et al., 1973; Gaddes, 1972; Kirk and Becker, 1963; Myklebust and Boshes, 1969; Paine, 1962, 1965; Rutter, Graham, and Yule, 1970; Rutter, Tizard, and Whitmore, 1970; Wender, 1971, 1973; Wikler, Dixon, and Parker, 1970) and, in some studies, the terms "minimal brain dysfunction" and "learning disorder" have been used synonymously. In this paper they are not used synonymously, however; where the two conditions evidently coexist it is important to know how the possible organic damage correlates with deficits in perceptual, cognitive, motor, serial order, and sensori-motor behavior, and how it influences emotional development and interpersonal relationships. Much evidence exists of mental impairment following traumatic brain injury (Benson and Geschwind, 1969; Kinsbourne, 1967; Reitan, 1967; Russell and Espir, 1961; Teuber, 1962) and less but equally convincing evidence exists on "developmental" impairments resulting from conditions of cerebral agenesis and other malformations and brain dysfunctions (Benton, 1964; Drake, 1968).

Hallahan and Cruickshank (1973) have shown that while malnutrition has been known for a long time to limit physical growth, its relation to learning impairment has enjoyed only recent study. They have provided an interesting review of current research studies made of children who are economically and socially underprivileged, and in it they find the theory of Scrimshaw and Gordon (1968) the most acceptable of present theories relating malnutrition and delayed mental development. This view proposes that "both social and nutritional factors can affect mental development independently, yet also interact strongly," so that in slum areas of Harlem in New York only one child in sixteen was able to reach his average grade level (Birch and Gussow, 1970). Hallahan and Cruickshank extend this hypothesis "to include learning disability as a manifestation of affected 'mental development' " (p. 18), although they are careful to point out that evidence for this is still limited owing to the complex methodological problems in such studies.

In the past decade there has been a growing research interest in the relation between neural growth and nutrition. Studies have shown that malnutrition in animals (Cravioto, De Licardie, and Birch, 1966; Stewart and Platt, 1968) and in humans at critical periods of their early growth (Stoch and Smythe, 1968) appears to result in reduced brain size and impaired intellectual development. This critical period in humans is believed to include the last trimester of intrauterine life and the first year, or possibly the first thirty months, of life postnatally (Birch, 1970).

Damage to the central nervous system due to malnutrition during this critical period is usually permanent and irretrievable even with restored adequate nutrition. Studies of children suffering prolonged early malnutrition showed them to be subnormal in verbal and nonverbal intelligence, auditory-visual integration, and visual-kinesthetic intersensory integration, and relatively inferior to their siblings who had grown up in the same disadvantaged environment but had not experienced the same degree of severe malnutrition (Cravioto, De Licardie, and Birch, 1966; Cravioto, 1972).

Psychological Factors

Studies of children with learning disorders suggest that a basic emotional pattern of behavioral maladaptability is the most common correlate. In fact, it has been reported that "the commonest single immediate cause for referral to our guidance clinics today is behavioral, academic, or social difficulty experienced by children at school" (Rabinovitch, 1959). The child with minimal brain dysfunction may be socially adjusted until he enters school, at which time his cognitive handicaps first become evident. Such children frequently suffer secondary emotional problems related to severe frustrations from mediocre or unsuccessful school performance (Kurland and Colodny, 1969), and remedial teaching may be the first step to restoring a better level of mental health. Poor general intelligence will nearly always result in learning problems, as will deficits in specific abilities. The child with adequate perceptual-spatial constructional abilities but poor verbal skills will likely suffer, since our school systems are usually designed to cater more to the child's left hemisphere skills, and deemphasize the importance of right hemisphere skills. Social and mental maturity for learning readiness is essential to academic success, and the child showing a maturational lag will suffer in the school learning situation. The seriously emotionally disturbed child may project his anxieties by destructiveness, aggression, depression, masochistic behavior, refusal to attend school, and devious methods of trying to manipulate the parents. This will also interfere with his ability to give attention to intellectual and concrete facts and may suppress his motivation through fear of competition, counteraggression, or lack of support and direction.

Many studies of the psychiatric aspects (Eisenberg, 1966) and discussions stressing the need for love, self-worth, and successful achievement (Glasser, 1969) have indicated this relationship. Rabinovitch (1962) has stressed the need to avoid "negativism, anxiety, depression, emotional blocking, psychosis, limited schooling opportunity, or other external influence" in order to promote normal learning. The child who is academically somewhat ineffective, regardless of whether the cause is organic, intrinsically psychological, or social, may resort to various strategies such as hostility or helplessness in order to gain control over or protect himself from the adults in his life-space.

Sociological Factors

It is difficult if not impossible to uncover selectively the effects of social factors on learning, since the environmental determinants, the inner biological, the outer physical, and the experiential are unaccountably and dynamically fused. The children of the ghettos are at highest risk both for pathological social environment and for biological insult (Walzer and Richmond, 1973) and as Hallahan and Cruickshank have aptly pointed out, "The incidence of a great many diseases and physical disabilities varies inversely with socioeconomic status" (1973, p. 55). The imposed living conditions of the poor promote ill health and its deprivations in all spheres—physical, psychological, and social. The disadvantaged child is more likely to suffer from poor teaching, greater absenteeism, deficient mental stimulation, less competent adult models to follow, and hence poorer motivation and personal direction. Large-scale studies have shown a pattern of reading retardation for the majority of children in large urban centers, and a reverse pattern of advanced reading level for most of those children in city private schools or suburban neighborhoods of better than average socioeconomic status (Eisenberg, 1966). Although there is evidence to suggest that, provided nutrition is adequate, development during the first fifteen months of life shows no obvious impact from various socioeconomic influences, "there is also ample evidence that mental-test scores after 3 or 4 years of age are correlated with a number of variables which are customarily used as indicators of socioeconomic status" (Bayley, 1965). This evidence and the discrepant performance of school-age children suggest strongly that sociological influences begin to stimulate forces during the second year of life that increase and vary, and account for the relatively better mental achievements of the socially advantaged child.

CONCERNED PROFESSIONAL AND LAY GROUPS

The 1960s were the decade when neurology, psychology, and special education began to collaborate in their attempts to help children of normal intelligence with specific learning problems. In January 1963 a conference was called at the University of Illinois to discuss the learning problems of children with cerebral dysfunctions; the participants included neurologists, neuropsychologists, and special educators. New journals in neuropsychology and in learning disabilities began to appear about that time, and conferences devoted to these problems included major speakers from all three disciplines. This was a welcome development from the professional isolation and interprofessional ignorance that had previously existed, but it brought with it a semantic chaos and a confusion of cross-professional communication. For example, neurologists, with their medical training, sometimes preferred to define alexia as reading disability resulting from a brain lesion and dyslexia as an innate inability to read (Benson and Geschwind, 1969). Psychologists and educators, with their liberal arts training, were more likely to stress the linguistic derivations and use the terms to express degrees of reading retardation from moderate to complete. A pediatric neurologist in discussing the interhemispheric rivalry and collaboration might write, "Damage to one polar element of the system will cause imbalances that generate symptomatology which does not occur when both elements are approximately equally impaired" (Kinsbourne, 1974), but this statement might convey little or no meaning to a teacher or educator or psychologist accustomed to dealing completely with behavioral phenomena. Many professional educators and psychologists were not only resistant to the use of neurological knowledge but they advised against it (Englemann, 1967; Gallagher, 1957, 1966; Reger, 1965). This issue has been examined at some length elsewhere (Gaddes, 1969). Psychologists and educators, with no training in neuroanatomy and neural function, tended to stress the behavioral aspects of learning disorders, and neurologists have bemoaned the fact that "Virtually all definitions of learning disabilities exclude children whose learning problems are due to neurological handicaps" (Schain, 1972). At the same time many educators have written at length regarding the importance of neurological knowledge in understanding learning deficits in children (Hallahan and Cruickshank, 1973; Myklebust and Boshes, 1969) and numerous psychologists have advocated its use (Adams, 1973; Bakker and Satz, 1970; Bannatyne, 1971; Benton, 1962a; Chalfant and Scheffelin, 1969; Gaddes, 1968, 1969, 1975; Kinsbourne, 1972; Knights, 1970, 1973b; Reed, 1963; Reitan, 1966; Reitan and Heinemann, 1968), and most definitions refer to the possibility of an underlying neurological condition (Bateman, 1964; Clements, 1966; Kirk and Bateman, 1962; Myklebust, 1963; National Advisory Committee, 1967; Strauss and Lehtinen, 1947). However, for purposes of classification and remedial allocation, only the behavioral aspects of the child's psychosocial adaptation are usually included, and the neurological factors are recognized as essential correlates (Benton, 1973) that include uniquely valuable information for a diagnostic understanding of the learning-disabled child.

In addition to the professional groups, with their varying terminology and concepts, are the parents of the affected children, who want professional clarification for themselves and competent remedial attention for their children. They constitute a powerful pressure group who have frequently been successful in persuading their respective governments to provide special classes and extra teaching services where such resources had not previously existed. Parent groups are effective allies in developing new services for their learning-disabled children, but frequently there is a mutual difficulty between them and the various professional groups in fully understanding the aims, the concepts, and the language of the other. Books that appeal to parents are sometimes simplistic and even inaccurate, and these differences of knowledge, communication, and emotional involvement can be troublesome obstacles in reducing the distance between the lay groups and the professionals.

PREVALENCE OF LEARNING DISORDERS

In the mid-1960s a number of private national agencies in Canada appointed The Commission on Emotional and Learning Disorders in Children (CELDIC). It was made up of a large committee of medical men (child psychiatrists and pediatricians), psychologists, educators, social workers, and parents. In 1970 the Commission published its report, which they called "One Million Children," the estimated number of exceptional children in Canada believed to need specific diagnostic and remedial help. This count included between 10 and 16% of Canada's population of school-age children. The writers warned of the difficulties of making prevalence estimates. "Definitions differ and classifications differ, depending upon whether they are based upon a medical or an educational model; or whether they are based primarily on cause, symptoms or treatment" (CELDIC Report, 1970, p. 51). They collected incidence studies that indicate that in Great Britain 14% of children had special needs (Kellmer Pringle, Butler, and Davie, 1966), in France 12–14%, in the United States 10–15%, and in Canada 10–16%. They concluded that "Perhaps, in view of the lack of definition of what is included in exceptionality we should be more surprised at the consistency of the estimates in recent years . . . than dismayed by their variability" (p. 55).

Data provided by the Canadian Dominion Bureau of Statistics show that in 1966 a little less than 2% of children between the ages of 5 and 19 were enrolled in special classes (*Statistics of Special Education, 1966,* Catalogue 81-537, Table 5, and *Population 1921–1971,* Catalogue 91-512, p. 55). Service statistics, since they are largely determined by budgetary restrictions and educational policy, are a minimum estimate and indicate nothing about the number of neglected needy.

In Canada in 1966 there were 6,232,000 school-age children. Of these, 120,720 were receiving special education instead of the needy 623,200 to 997,120 if the 10–16% estimate was correct. It was this alarming discovery of possible educational neglect that directed the authors of the CELDIC Report to recommend an organization of services to meet the needs of these one million children.

A service statistical survey of children with learning disabilities in the United States in 1970 (Silverman and Metz, 1973) showed an estimate of 1.4–2.6% of all school-age children in special classes, an estimate that matches the same statistic in Canada. If the real need is between 10 and 15%, a figure supported by empirical investigation by Myklebust and Boshes (1969), then the proportionate neglect in the United States and Canada may be very close. However, this figure in the United States is probably spuriously low since in many states a learning-disabled child is not categorized as being in a special class unless he is there full time. "Mainstreaming" has been operant for about five years and most schools strive to keep the number of special-class children at a minimum by providing intermittent remedial help to those in regular classes who need it.

PSYCHOMETRIC PROBLEMS OF DEFINITION

Probably the most common definition in North America of severe reading retardation recommends the selection of children who are reading 1½ to 2 or more grades below expected grade level (Eisenberg, 1966; Newbrough and Kelley, 1962; Schain, 1972; Walzer and Richmond, 1973), a method more likely to produce stereotypes than descriptions of the dynamic and qualitative subtleties inherent in any kind of behavior. Such broad definitions, used commonly in the 1950s and 1960s, and still recommended by some, identified the severely retarded readers but they provided no discriminative designations of those in the middle or borderline groups. In addition they produced some psychometric incongruities that bear examining.

To review the validity of the two-year-retarded cutoff method, three commonly used tests of reading ability were compared. The Wide Range Achievement Test (Jastak and Jastak, 1965) measures only single word recognition, the Canadian Tests of Basic Skills (Thomas Nelson Ltd., Canada, 1968) measure among other skills reading comprehension, and two subtests from the Gates Basic Reading Tests (1958) measure comprehension and what the authors call General Significance. Table 1, derived from the test norms in each case, shows that when two years are subtracted from the average reading level of six year olds on the W.R.A.T., less than 1% of the population is considered retarded. At age 7, 2% would be allocated to this classification, and so on until the age of 19 when 25% would be so categorized. This suggests a developmental pattern of increasing recognition of reading problems with age and greater complexity. The Canadian Tests of Basic Skills show the same inherent

Table 1. Percentile Ranks of Children Two Years Retarded in Reading as Measured by Three Widely Used Achievement Tests

Age (yr-mo)	WRAT (%)	Can. Basic Sk. (%)	Gates: 1958 General Significance (%)	Gates: 1958 Comprehension (%)	Range of Differences (%)
6 - 0	0.2				
6 - 6	1				
7 - 0	2				
7 - 6	4				
8 - 0	7	<1			
8 - 6	6	<1	1	1	6
9 - 0	9	2	3		5
9 - 6	13	3	5	5	7
10 - 0	13	5	11		10
10 - 6	14	6	14		8
11 - 0	16	6	18	15	9
11 - 6	16	6	20		12
12 - 0	18	7	20	21	15
12 - 6	19	8	20		13
13 - 0	19	8	21	21	13
13 - 6	21	9	21		13
14 - 0	21			20	12
14 - 6	23			22	1
15 - 0	21				
15 - 6	23			23	0
16 - 0	25				
18 - 0	25				

The *Canadian Tests of Basic Skills* are edited by Ethel M. King in cooperation with E. F. Lindquist and A. N. Hieronymus. They are basically similar to the *Iowa Tests of Basic Skills*, Houghton Mifflin, New York, 1956 and developmental pattern for reading comprehension, except that it is about two years slower in reaching the same percentages of impaired readers for ages 8 and 9, but the lag increases with age beyond that point. The two subtests from the Gates Basic Reading Tests show the same developmental pattern, and the trend is evident in all four tests, showing more agreement at the younger and older ages. The greatest discrepancies of measurement appear to be between about ages 8 and 13, the age range with which the school is most concerned regarding learning problems.

An up-dated version of the Gates earlier tests was examined (Gates-McKillop Reading Diagnostic Tests, 1962) but it could not be included in the comparisons on Table 1 since no percentile ranks were supplied. This battery includes a series of 17 subtests designed to measure a large number of different perceptual and language functions involved in reading. For discriminating levels of reading retardation, tables are provided of raw scores that can be converted into grade score norms and final achievement ratings of High, Medium, Low, or Very Low. "Normal progress" includes raw scores in the middle 50% of the range of scores made by all pupils at a particular level of reading. Instead of using the fixed two-year lag as a cutoff for children at all ages, Gates and McKillop have provided a developmental scale of increasing cutoff points with age (see Table 2). The data produced by these four Reading Achievement tests indicate that using a fixed academic retardation lag at all school ages to define educationally impaired children is illogical and scientifically untenable.

Table 2. Gates–McKillop Cutoff Points for Ratings of "Low" and "Very Low" Readers

Actual Grade	Low: A Lag of	Very Low: A Lag of
2.0	0.5–0.8[a]	1.0 or more[a]
2.5	0.7–1.1	1.2 or more
3.0	0.8–1.3	1.4 or more
3.5	0.9–1.5	1.6 or more
4.0	1.0–1.6	1.7 or more
4.5	1.2–1.8	1.9 or more
5.0	1.5–1.9	2.0 or more
5.5	1.5–2.1	2.2 or more
6.0	1.5–2.1	2.2 or more

[a]The values in columns 2 and 3 are grade score norms.

The Canadian Tests of Basic Skills use the same tables for converting grade point scores to percentile ranks for tests of reading, vocabulary, spelling, arithmetic, and several language and work-study skills, but the two-year lag model is equally unsatisfactory for these subjects.

This makes it clear that the two-year-retarded cutoff method is rough and varies markedly with the level of development of the child and the particular academic skill a test is designed to measure. A more sophisticated method must be sought if a workable definition of learning disabilities is to be established. Two attempts to use more sensitive criteria will be examined. The first of these was developed by Myklebust and his colleagues.

Myklebust argues (1967) that diagnosis and classification rest upon three fundamental criteria: generalized integrity, a deficit in learning, and a brain dysfunction. The first two of these can be measured operationally and compared quantitatively so as to produce a Learning Quotient, that is, a measured relation between learning potential and achievement. Myklebust emphasizes the importance of including both verbal and nonverbal abilities in evaluating a child's potential. A child's "expectancy age" is the average of his mental age, his chronological age, and his grade age. Since the Wechsler Intelligence Scale for Children was used to derive his mental age, both verbal and nonverbal measures are involved in producing his expectancy age. When this measure is divided into an age score for a particular type of learning, a quotient is produced which, like the IQ, will indicate whether the child is performing in that particular academic skill above or below average for his age and learning potential.

$$\text{In reading, a child's Learning Quotient} = \frac{\text{Reading Age}}{\text{Expectancy Age}}.$$

Similar Learning Quotients (LQ) may be calculated for perception, conception, motor function, language, and nonverbal skills where normative data have been collected.

While the Learning Quotient provides a useful measure of learning competence of children in the mid-IQ range, there is still the question of choosing a cutoff point between those with normal learning abilities and the disabled. In a large study of 2,767 third and fourth graders, Myklebust and Boshes (1969) selected an LQ of 90 as the pass—fail criterion for choosing the underachievers. LQs were computed on verbal and nonverbal intelligence, reading, arithmetic, spelling, and written language portions of the screening test battery. A child obtaining an LQ of at least 90 on all these areas was classified as passing the Screening Battery. Those were classified as failing the Battery if they obtained an LQ of 89 or less on one or more of the areas. Any child with an LQ of less than 90 on both the verbal and nonverbal tests was considered to be mentally impaired and was eliminated from the study, as were those with serious physical or sensory deficits. This selection produced 410 underachievers (or about 15% of the studied sample), and about two-thirds of these were studied exhaustively with educational, psychological, and neurological examinations. The underachievers were further divided into a Borderline group (LQ = 85 to 89 inclusive) and a severe Learning-Disabled group (LQ = 84 and below), and Myklebust found that both groups were inferior to the Controls (LQ = 90 and above) on measures of educational achievement. As well, both experimental groups showed many more signs of neurological disturbance than the Controls; the Borderline group exhibited more "soft signs," and the Learning-Disabled group more clearly exhibited abnormal or "hard" signs. Forty-nine different psychoeducational tests were found to discriminate between the normal Controls and the two experimental groups. Of these the Gates-McKillop Syllabication Test and the Pupil Behavior Rating Scale were most powerful in discriminating both experimental groups from the Controls.

The Myklebust and Boshes study is, to my knowledge, the most thorough-going North American attempt to examine large numbers of learning-disabled children and to provide direction for definition and classification. Unfortunately, the reader is submerged in endless tables, and the authors make no attempt to summarize their findings in general conclusions.

From my reading, the Isle of Wight Study (Rutter, Tizard, and Whitmore, 1970) seems to be the only genuine epidemiological study of handicapped children in the English-speaking world. Three related surveys were carried out in 1964 and 1965 in which almost 2,300 children, aged 9 to 12, were studied exhaustively on neurological, medical, educational, psychological, and psychiatric tests and examinations. The original publication in 1970 is detailed, comprehensive, and sizable, and it has spawned an excellent further report on the neurological and psychiatric impairments of the children in their studied population (Rutter, Graham, and Yule, 1970) and a large number of journal articles that are still issuing from its stimulation. While this study is most impressive, and merits strenuous attention, I shall comment only briefly on it because it is more fully explained in Dr. Yule's chapter.

To understand the form and content of the Isle of Wight Study it will be profitable to compare and contrast it with the only large North American study, by Myklebust and Boshes (1969). In the first place, its aim is different; it is an epidemiological study of intellectual, physical, psychiatric, and educational impairment, rather than a study of children of normal intelligence level with academic learning problems. Hence, like any medically planned epidemiological study it includes all cases of low intellect, and the arbitrary cutoff point to delineate the category of "intellectual retardation" was an IQ of 70 or less (Rutter, Tizard, and Whitmore, 1970, p. 23). In fact, this means that the Isle of Wight Study included all grades of mental retardation, where Myklebust and Boshes deliberately excluded mentally retarded subjects by studying only those children with an IQ of 90 or higher on either the verbal or performance scale of the WISC, or both. In other words, the British study includes children impaired both mentally and educationally; the American study only children in the second category. In addition, the criteria for selecting children with educational retardation and/or learning disabilities are quite different.

In Rutter's study the evaluation of academic competence was based on reading skills only, particularly accuracy and/or comprehension as measured by the Neale Analysis of Reading Ability (Neale, 1958). Children reading 28 months below their expected level relative to their chronological age were classified as suffering "Reading Backwardness." Those who fell 28 months or more below the level predicted on the basis of chronological age and WISC IQ were classified as falling in the "Reading Retardation" group. To avoid the "regression effect" of achievement quotients such as Myklebust's Learning Quotient, Yule has advised the use of a multiple regression formula (Rutter, Tizard, and Whitmore, 1970, p. 35; Yule, Rutter, Berger, and Thompson, 1974).

By contrast, in Myklebust and Boshes's study (1969) children were selected as learning disabled if their LQ fell below 90 on one or more of the screening tests. These included 11 measures, specifically verbal IQ, nonverbal IQ, perceptual speed, spatial relations, reading (word knowledge, word discrimination, comprehension), spelling, arithmetic problem solving, auditory receptive language, and nonverbal learning (pp. 12 and 13). Any combination of two or more deficit scores on this list was possible for keeping the child in the study except the WISC Verbal IQ and Performance IQ. If, as already stated, both of these measured less than 90, the child was eliminated from the learning disabled category as being globally mentally impaired.

While the Isle of Wight Study was inclusive and broad in terms of health, behavior, and education as measured by reading competence, the Myklebust study was broader and more detailed in its educational screening procedures. Where the Rutter study included all levels of intellectual and educational impairment and superiority, Myklebust's formula selected those children of average or better intelligence level, with a specific learning disability in one or more of the basic academic skills. Because of the different emphasis, the British study might be described as a model of public health and education epidemiology, whereas the American study is not epidemiological but more specific in providing a technique for identifying reliably the normal child with a specific academic learning problem.

In spite of the differences of the two studies, their conclusions regarding the prevalence of educational problems show some similarities. Rutter and his colleagues concluded that of the 9–12-year-old population, 7.9% were mentally impaired and educationally retarded, and 16.1% were multiply handicapped (i.e., mentally, educationally, psychiatrically, and physically, p. 348). Myklebust found that 7.5% of third and fourth graders showed signs of neurological involvement (i.e., one-half of 15% who were underachievers, p. 68), and that using the cutoff point of LQ 85, 7.4% were underachievers (p. 22). Because of the selection criteria, Rutter's sample includes some mentally retarded children (actually 2.5%, p. 348) and hence fewer purely learning-disabled children, in Myklebust's concept.

DEFINITION OF LEARNING DISABILITY

At the outset let us look at a number of definitions already in use and observe the most common characteristics.

1. California State Educational Code 6750: "Educationally handicapped minors are minors who by reason of marked learning or behavior disorder or both cannot benefit from the regular educational program and who as a result thereof require the special educational programs authorized by this chapter. Such learning or behavior disorders shall be associated with a neurological handicap or emotional disturbance and shall not be attributable to mental retardation."

#3230 (a) (1) "The learning or behavior disorders are specific learning disabilities in the psychological processes involved in understanding or in using spoken or written language. Such learning disabilities include, but are not limited to, those sometimes referred to as perceptual handicaps, minimal brain dysfunction, dyslexia, dyscalculia, dysgraphia, or communication disorders, except aphasia as defined in Section 3600 (g).

#3230 (a) (2) "The specific learning disabilities are of such severity that the pupils' level of functioning in basic learning skills is significantly below the range of functioning expected from pupils of similar age and ability and evidence is presented for a favorable prognosis for the reduction of the discrepancy between ability and achievement.

(3) "Where the general level of academic functioning is retarded, such retardation shall not be attributable to limited intellectual capacity for academic learning.

(4) "The specific learning disabilities shall be determined by complete evaluation accompanied by recommendations for the amelioration of the learning disorder that can be carried out within the class or program recommended." (Special Education Memorandum, EH 72-3, (Buff), March 3, 1972, Department of Education, State of California, Sacramento, Calif.)

2. The National Advisory Committee on Handicapped Children (1967), United States Office of Education, Washington, D.C.:

"Children with Specific Learning Disabilities exhibit a disorder in one or more of the basic psychological processes involved in understanding or in using spoken or written language. These may be manifested in disorders of listening, thinking, talking, reading, writing, spelling or arithmetic. They include conditions which have been referred to as perceptual handicaps, brain injury, minimal brain dysfunction, dyslexia, developmental aphasia, etc. They do not include learning problems which are due primarily to visual, hearing, or motor handicaps, to mental retardation, emotional disturbance, or to environmental disadvantage."

The State of Arkansas adheres to the above Federal Government definition, and the general rule regarding intellectual functioning level for this group is that the child must achieve an IQ of 90 or above on either the Verbal or the Performance Scale of the WISC in order to be eligible for the special remedial programs (Clements, 1975). Numerous other states, including Pennsylvania (Wary, 1975), also have adopted the Federal Government definition quoted above.

Several definitions of learning disabilities or educational retardation from various states of the United States have been proposed, which, when they are compared, include the following points: They include children (1) of near-normal, average, or above average intelligence, (2) who have a disorder in one or more of the primary psychological processes involved in learning the basic school subjects, e.g., perception, cognition, motor response, and/or serial order behavior, (3) who are of school age, (4) whose language development is retarded and/or impaired, (5) whose learning disability may or may not be correlated with medically documented brain damage and dysfunction, or may be supposed to be related to minimal cerebral dysfunctions and/or genetic abnormalities or growth anomalies, (6) whose learning problems are not primarily due to sensory or motor handicaps, mental retardation, emotional disturbance, or environmental deprivation, (7) whose disability may show a shifting pattern increasing with educational neglect, and reducing or disappearing with successful remedial help, and (8) whose learning deficits require "special educational programs and services for educational progress" (State of Iowa, Department of Public Instruction, Des Moines, 1974).

Chalfant and King (1975) also have attempted to provide an operational definition of learning disabilities by proposing five component parts identified as (a) task failure, (b) exclusion factors, (c) physiological correlates, (d) discrepancy or extreme intra-individual differences in performance, and (e) psychological processes such as memory, discrimination, perceptual integration, concept formation, and reasoning. They make the point that of all five components, the last is the most difficult to operationalize, "because psychological correlates are not clearly understood."

PROPOSED DEFINITION

The two major studies cited above have proposed two basically different definitions of learning disabled children. The Rutter study includes all children showing "reading retardation," an achievement level calculated by using a regression formula including a WISC IQ and the child's chronological age, and "reading backwardness," a reading level 28 months or more below the child's chronological age. These classifications yielded 7.9% of the children in the 9–12-year-old range. This selection technique recommended by Yule, and the Learning Quotient of Myklebust, are designed to set apart the borderline or minimal cases that have always provided the difficult problems of identification. It is these children who previously have been misdiagnosed, neglected, or blamed.

Yule has made some logical objections to the use of achievement quotients both on conceptual and statistical grounds. He has made it clear (Yule, Rutter, Berger, and Thompson, 1974, p. 3) that when correlation coefficients are less than unity, for example with mental age and reading age, children who are well above average on one measure will be underestimated on the other, and those who are well below average on the first measure will be less inferior on the second. He illustrates this distortion in both tails of the normal distribution curve. However, IQ and reading show similar measures when IQ falls between −1SD and +1SD (Yule et al., 1974, p. 3) and since this is where Myklebust has chosen his IQs (either verbal or nonverbal or both) then it would seem that Yule's objection would not cover this particular LQ.

Because some children with learning disabilities do have high IQs, Yule's multiple regression method is preferable to an achievement quotient approach. So as not to frighten off teachers with the name, simple conversion tables could be supplied that would enable teachers to read off a child's predicted level of achievement, knowing his or her mental age and chronological age.

Since both of the large studies described above have covered ages 8–12 inclusive, we are not yet sure how a selection formula would work with 6 and 7 year olds. A large-scale research study is needed to investigate this and to derive the best values for intelligence or mental age, and to derive the academic skills or psychological performances that are most relevant. One such study (Silver and Hagin, 1975) has found one-third of kindergarten children in four Manhattan schools vulnerable to learning failure.

Once a task force or research committee has decided on the values to be included in a formula (possibly a multiple regression equation), they can then derive and apply the resulting impairment index to each child suspected of an intrinsic chronic or recurrent learning handicap. Such values will emerge from answers to the following questions:

1. IQ cutoff point. Is 90, as suggested by Myklebust, the most productive cutoff point for discriminating normal control subjects from those with subtle learning deficits?
2. Is the IQ cutoff point similar for all age levels, or does it show developmental differences?
3. Is a discrepancy between verbal and nonverbal intelligence a significant indicator of subtle learning problems, as suggested by Myklebust (1969, p. 68), or nonsignificant, as suggested by Rutter, Tizard, and Whitmore (1970, p. 49)?
4. Should achievement measures be obtained on reading, spelling, and arithmetic, and if so, what particular aspects of each? Should these include a few skills from age 6 to 9 and be increased after that? Should other academic skills be included?
5. Is it desirable to have a brief annual retesting to examine the possibility that the child's learning problem has been resolved or is retaining a stable chronicity? If so, what nature or format will such a test take?

Once all of these decisions have been made, a Learning Formula can be derived for each age level beginning at age 6. This will be the first step in selecting children with learning problems. But a second step will also be necessary to pick up those children who may be missed by the formula. Any test battery, no matter how carefully constructed, will produce a number of false negatives and false positives. To ensure a process of identification as complete as possible, a carefully prepared pupil behavior rating scale (Myklebust and Boshes, 1969, pp. 271 and 294–302) and/or questionnaires completed by parents, teachers, and the children themselves (Rutter, Tizard, and Whitmore, 1970, p. 5) may be used. Such a combination of a selection formula possessing a comprehensive choice of academic learning skills, a number of educational achievement tests, and the descriptive material from those privileged to observe the child's learning behavior over an extended period of time, would seem to be the most sensitive screening procedure.

It is almost certain that all children with severe learning disorders (those with LQs of less than 85 in Myklebust's system) will be identified by such a method. All of those children with superior IQs who are underachieving (+1SD to +2SD in Yule's IQ bands; Yule et al., 1974, p. 3) can be identified by a multiple regression equation, and can be placed in enriched learning programs with superior teachers if their problem is purely motivational, or in diagnostically arranged learning situations if their problem results from a specific learning deficit. This latter example is likely to be rare, but arrangements should be made to meet it when it occurs.

The group of children who should benefit most from a sensitive screening procedure are Myklebust's Borderline group (LQ 85–89). These are children with potentially normal or above average IQs who, because of specific and subtle cognitive dysfunctions, cannot meet the academic demands of school except with great difficulty and frustration. This group may make up as many as 7–17% of the public school population in the United States (Myklebust and Boshes, 1969, pp. 1 and 22).

DEFINITION

A child of school age is identified as suffering from a learning disability if his Learning Index, as derived from the formula officially accepted in his school district, state, or country, falls below the cutoff point officially recognized. This formula should be used for selecting diagnostically those children likely to be missed by informal observation of their teachers, because of the subtle or minimal nature of their educational impairments. More severe or obvious cases of learning problems may be identified by administrative selection or the application of the officially accepted formula.

CONCLUSIONS

A brief discussion of the possible etiological factors of learning disabilities has been presented. These are biological, neuropsychological, psychological, and/or social. Since prevalence studies must depend on a definition possessing wide acceptance, an examination of a number of official definitions from the United States were examined and compared for common elements. A definition has been proposed which is socially determined by the authorities of the child's educational system and which will assess the level of his psychosocial adaptation using measures of his learning potential and educational achievement. Because deficient learning is not a disease condition and its evaluation is socially based rather than always organically determined, prevalence rather than epidemiological studies are more appropriate to its study.

To arrive at an official definition a task force or an official committee in each country or national subdivision will have to devise a selection procedure to include all of the educational and psychosocial determinants, and to produce a functional structure to identify the learning-disabled child. In understanding the learning problem and devising a remedial program, all knowledge of the physiological, psychological, social, and cultural correlates must be recognized. When such a definition is evolved, prevalence studies may be made in the areas where the definition is recognized.

ACKNOWLEDGMENTS

I am indebted to Dr. Dorothea Ross, Associate Research Psychologist, Department of Pediatrics, University of California, San Francisco, for a detailed reading of the text, and for many valuable suggestions about content, emphasis, and style. Dr. Janet Bavelas, Dr. R. Leslie D. Wright, and Dr. Otfried Spreen of the University of Victoria have made useful suggestions about the discussion of the psychometric problems.

Epidemiology and Social Implications of Specific Reading Retardation

William Yule and Michael Rutter

The study of children with learning disorders has been bedeviled by a number of methodological problems that have been repeated in numerous investigations. More particularly, these problems can be seen in the published studies of children with reading difficulties. In the first place, there is a lack of agreement on the definition of what constitutes a reading difficulty. This disagreement is apparent at both the conceptual level and at the level of operationalizing the definition. In the second place, too many small-scale studies have been conducted with highly selected groups of children. Insufficient attention has been paid to the bias introduced by careless selection, and the result has been confusion and contradictions in the published findings.

This chapter addresses the problem of finding a satisfactory definition of reading difficulty. The psychometric and statistical problems involved in operationalizing the concept of severe underachievement in reading are discussed and one suggested definition is advanced. This definition is then applied in a series of large-scale epidemiological studies, and the substantive findings from these studies are briefly described. Finally, the similarities between specific reading retardation and more traditional views of dyslexia are examined.

TERMINOLOGY AND CRITICAL CONCEPTS

The number of different terms enployed in referring to difficulties in learning to read is sufficient testimony to the confused state of knowledge.

The studies upon which this chapter is based were supported by grants from the Department of Education and Science, The Nuffield Foundation, and the Social Science Research Council. They were carried out in collaboration with Professor J. Tizard, Professor P. Graham, Mr. L. Rigley, Mr. M. Berger, Dr. K. Whitmore, and Mr. J. Thompson.

25

Descriptive words such as backwardness, illiteracy, disability, impairment, and difficulty are used by educationalists, while medical investigators employ terms such as word-blindness or dyslexia. In more recent times, American investigators tend to talk more broadly of "learning disability." This chaotic situation arises in part because of a traditional vagueness of definitions in educational research, and in part because of more fundamental disputes concerning the nature of reading problems (Pilliner and Reid, 1972; Rutter and Yule, 1975). Consider some widely used definitions.

Dyslexia has been defined by the Research Group on Developmental Dyslexia of the World Foundation of Neurology as "A disorder manifested by difficulty in learning to read despite conventional instruction, adequate intelligence, and socio-cultural opportunity. It is dependent upon fundamental cognitive disabilities which are frequently of constitutional origin" (Critchley, 1970).

Myklebust, Bannonchie, and Killen (1971) propose that "A learning disability assumes a discrepancy between potential and achievement," and elsewhere Myklebust (1968) attempts to measure this discrepancy through his "learning quotient."

Boder (1971) reflects the state of affairs when she notes that ". . . no definitive diagnostic criteria for specific dyslexia have been established." Despite this, she attempts a definition that, in many ways, summarizes the sort of thinking to be found in many research papers:

> "In the presence of significant reading retardation—usually two or more years below grade level or mental age, though a retardation of even one year may be regarded as diagnostically significant—developmental dyslexia is diagnosed in one or more of the following ways: (1) by a process of exclusion, (2) indirectly, on the basis of its neurological or psychometric concomitants, (3) directly on the basis of the frequency and persistence of certain types of errors in reading and spelling. In all diagnostic approaches poor response to standard remedial techniques and a familial history of reading disability are viewed as important corroborative evidence" (Boder, 1971).

These may well be regarded as rich clinical descriptions of conditions of interest, but they are unacceptable as definitions, largely because in their present form they cannot be operationalized. Reid (1969) points out that this type of definition is negative rather than positive—that is, children are classified as "dyslexic" by a process of elimination rather than by noting the presence of any single or multiple pathognomonic signs. By ruling out of the dyslexic category all children whose reading difficulty is associated with one of the major groups of factors presumably underlying the condition, then one is left with a rag-bag of reading disorders of unknown origin (Eisenberg, 1962) rather than a carefully selected group of potentially homogeneous cases.

Underlying these attempted definitions is the assumption that there are different types of reading difficulties. Implicitly, it is assumed that it is necessary to segregate a small group of children who are having unexpectedly severe difficulties of a qualitatively different sort from the larger group of children whose problems are more readily understood in terms of a more general difficulty in all developmental and academic areas. In other words, interest is often focused on a small group of children who appear to be grossly underachieving in reading.

Despite all the terminological problems, there does appear to be general agreement on the need to differentiate between those children who, irrespective of their ability, are at the bottom end of a continuum of reading attainment (backward readers) and those children who are underachieving in relation to their chronological age and their level of general intelligence. It is customary to use the term specific reading retardation to describe children who are underachieving in reading in the latter sense (Rutter and Yule, 1973; Pilliner and Reid, 1972).

The need to differentiate between backward and retarded readers has been expressed for many years (Schonell, 1935; Department of Education and Science, 1964). However, the method whereby this differentiation could be made has been the subject of much controversy in the past (Burt, 1959; Crane, 1959). In order to understand more fully the problems involved in the definition of reading disability, it is necessary to look at the controversy surrounding the measurement of underachievement.

MEASUREMENT OF UNDERACHIEVEMENT

Underachievement is, in many ways, a simple, attractive, and common-sense notion. Unfortunately, there are many statistical pit-falls between the concept and its operationalization.

Among the earliest attempts was that of Franzen (1920). Franzen's "Accomplishment Quotient," being the ratio of Attainment Age to Mental Age, is the historical and conceptual forerunner of Myklebust's (1968) "Learning Quotient." In the 1920s, intelligence was largely seen as a fixed, inherited entity, and so Mental Age was regarded as an index of the upper limit to scholastic attainment. It therefore came as an embarrassment to find children whose Attainment Age exceeded their Mental Age, and who thereby obtained Accomplishment Quotients in excess of 100.

Such embarrassing findings were regarded as rare exceptions, explicable either on the grounds that the tests were inaccurate, or that ". . . . they occur sporadically in a few young bookworms who show an extra zeal or talent in academic work, but less practical shrewdness and common sense. They occur rather more frequently in dull youngsters who have been assiduously coached by a good teacher. . . ." (Burt, 1937, 1950).

However old fashioned these ideas may seem today, Accomplishment Quotients, Accomplishment Ratios, and the like are still to be found on the pages of learned journals (e.g., Myklebust, 1968). The most important of the statistical objections to such ratios stems from the operation of the "regression effect" (Crane, 1959; Thorndike, 1963). The use of accomplishment ratios assumes that there is almost a one-to-one correlation between reading age and mental age, whereas the value is more often in the region of +0.6. Now, wherever the correlation between two measures is less than perfect, the children who are well above average on one measure will be less superior on the second measure, and, at the other end of the continuum, those who are well below average on the first measure (say, Mental Age) will be less inferior on the second (say, Reading Age). Thus, the average reading age of 10 year olds with an average mental age of 13 years will not be 13 years; the average reading age will be more like 12 years. Only in the middle of the distribution will the two values be nearly equal.

Thus, any measure of underachievement that fails to allow for the statistical effects of regression will end up with a group of "underachievers" in whom bright children are overrepresented and dull children are underrepresented. Many of the bright underachievers will, in fact, not be underachieving at all. Even taking differences between standard scores does nothing to avoid the regression effects.

In a much neglected monograph, Thorndike (1963) argues as follows:

> "If a simple difference between aptitude and achievement standard scores, or a ratio of achievement to aptitude measures, is computed, the high aptitude group will appear primarily to be underachievers and the low aptitude groups to be overachievers. For this reason, it is necessary to define underachievement as discrepancy of actual achievement from the predicted value, predicted upon the basis of the regression equation between aptitude and achievement. A failure to recognize this regression effect has rendered questionable, if not meaningless, much of the research on 'underachievement.' "

Knowing the correlation between a predictor variable (such as mental age or score on an intelligence test) and a criterion variable (such as reading age, reading grade, or standardized reading score), it is possible to calculate the expected value of reading for any particular level of the predictor variable. Thus, one can determine whether the child scores above, at, or below this predicted value, and more importantly the statistical probability of any deviation from the expected value can be computed (Yule, 1967; Yule, Rutter, Berger, and Thompson, 1974). Severe degrees of underachievement in reading can then be defined in terms of the empirically determined relationship between intelligence and attainment, while avoiding the errors of classification associated with the regression effect.

This prediction technique has been used to define specific reading retardation in a series of five epidemiological total population studies on reading difficulties (Rutter, Tizard, and Whitmore, 1970; Yule, 1973; Berger, Yule, and Rutter, 1975). The results of these studies are presented below to examine the validity and usefulness of the differentiation between specific reading retardation and general reading backwardness. Prevalence estimates for specific reading retardation are presented, and by drawing from the descriptive findings, it is argued that the type of definition discussed in this chapter contributes substantially to the selection of appropriate cases for neuropsychological study.

NEED FOR EPIDEMIOLOGICAL STUDIES

Much of the confusion in the literature on reading retardation stems from the fact that most investigators have examined highly selected groups of children. The type of problems seen at any one clinic naturally reflects the biases influencing referral to that clinic and the kind of services that it provides. It is hardly surprising that the children retarded in reading who are referred to a neurologist are rather different from those referred to a child psychiatrist or those seen by a remedial teacher, a speech therapist, or an educational psychologist. These kinds of biases can only be avoided by epidemiological investigations of total child populations (Rutter, Tizard, and Whitmore, 1970). Two examples will illustrate the problems encountered by clinic-based studies.

On the basis of a study of a small, selected group of children attending a neurological clinic, Kinsbourne and Warrington (1963) suggested that visuospatial difficulties commonly accompany reading difficulty. A later larger study of a somewhat more representative group showed that, on the contrary, visual spatial difficulties are quite uncommon among retarded readers, and at most account for a very small proportion of children with reading difficulties (Warrington, 1967).

Again, take the question of handedness among retarded readers. Vernon (1971) claims that, "With clinic cases of dyslexia, left or mixed handedness seems to occur more frequently." From the amount of space she devotes to the matter, it is clear that the idea that left handedness is more common among retarded readers is still widely held. Yet, four independent studies of total populations—Belmont and Birch (1965) in Aberdeen; Malmquist (1958) in Sweden; Clark (1970) in Dumbartonshire; and ourselves (Rutter, Tizard, and Whitmore, 1970) on the Isle of Wight— are unanimous in failing to find any excess of left handers among the poor readers.

Clinic-based studies may be invaluable sources suggesting hypotheses about the nature of reading disability. Such hypotheses can often only be tested in total population studies. These, then, are some of the reasons for our selecting an epidemiological approach in our studies of children's handicaps.

POPULATIONS STUDIED

The results to which this paper refers come from five studies of total child populations which employed group tests of intelligence and reading, and three epidemiological studies of the same populations which utilized individual testing of the children. The groups are:

1. Approximately 1,100 children in each of three age groups, 9, 10, and 11 years, whose homes were on the Isle of Wight (Rutter, Tizard, and Whitmore, 1970).
2. Some 2,100 children aged 14 years. These were the two youngest age-cohorts previously seen at 9 and 10 years, and followed up to their final year of compulsory schooling (Yule, 1973).
3. 1,634 ten-year-old nonimmigrant children in an inner London borough (Berger, Yule, and Rutter, 1975).

OUTLINE OF METHODOLOGY

All children in each of these five populations were tested on similar group tests of nonverbal intelligence and reading attainment. This constituted the first stage of a two-stage methodology. In the second stage of each study, children who scored two standard deviations or more below the appropriate group mean on the reading test were selected, together with a randomly selected group, for further detailed examination. The precise sort of further examination varied between studies, and the data most relevant to describing characteristics of retarded readers come from the detailed investigations of 9 and 10 year olds on the Isle of Wight. These children were seen individually by psychologists, school doctors, and psychiatrists. They were given audiometric assessments and neurological examinations, and their mothers were interviewed by social scientists about the children's developmental and social histories, as well as their current behavioral adjustment. Details of the assessments and findings are given elsewhere (Rutter, Tizard, and Whitmore, 1970; Rutter, Graham, and Yule, 1970).

QUESTIONS POSED BY THE READING RETARDATION MODEL

The data from these studies will now be used to examine the following key questions posed by the concept of specific reading retardation:

1. Are over- and underachievement in reading equally distributed in the general population, or is there an excess of underachievers?
2. Are retarded readers different from generally backward readers?
3. In particular, do the two groups have different educational prognoses?
4. Are "specific reading retardation" and "dyslexia" synonymous?

1. Is There an Excess of Underachievers?

On theoretical grounds (Thorndike, 1963), the distribution of discrepancies between predicted attainment and actual attainment should be normal. Most children should show little discrepancy while a few will show extreme degrees of underachievement and a few will show extreme degrees of overachievement. The extreme underachievers could, therefore, merely represent the lower end of a continuum and have nothing else remarkable about them (Department of Education and Science, 1972). On the other hand, if an excess of severe underachievers is found, this would suggest that severe underachievement or specific reading retardation constitutes a qualitatively different category.

The data from the five population studies using group tests and the three more intensive studies were used to examine this question (Yule, Rutter, Berger, and Thompson, 1974). In all eight cases, the rate of severe specific retardation in reading (defined in terms of underachievement of at least two standard errors below prediction) was above the predicted level, the difference being statistically significant in all but two instances.

To give some idea of the magnitude of underachievement being considered in this chapter, at age 10 years a child's obtained reading age has to be at least 2.5 years below the level predicted on the basis of his age and IQ score before he is classified as a specifically retarded reader.

When the distribution of differences between actual and predicted levels of reading is examined (Yule, Rutter, Berger, and Thompson, 1974), the general symmetry of each distribution is striking. However, in each case there is a noticeably prolonged "tail" of severe underachievers. When the proportion of children falling below the two standard errors of prediction cutoff in the tail is examined, significant excesses of severe underachievers are discovered. On theoretical grounds, one expects to find only 2.28% having such large discrepancies. In fact, one finds about 3.5% of Isle of Wight 10 year olds, about 4.5% of Isle of Wight 14 year olds, and no less than 6% of London 10 year olds showing specific reading retardation.

We know from subsidiary studies and accuracy checks that these observed rates for specific reading retardation must be regarded as minimum estimates. It must therefore be concluded that there *is* an excess at the lower end of the distribution, and that extreme degrees of specific reading retardation *do* occur at a rate above that expected if the distribution of over- and underachievement were entirely normal.

2. Specific Reading Retardation
Compared with General Reading Backwardness

The next question to be investigated is whether the distinction between specific reading retardation and general reading backwardness has any meaning medically or educationally? This is examined in the data from the studies of 9 and 10 year olds on the Isle of Wight.

Psychologists administered a shortened form of the Wechsler Intelligence Scale for Children (Wechsler, 1949; Yule, 1967) and the Neale Analysis of Reading Ability (Neale, 1958) to suspected poor readers and a randomly selected control group. Reading backwardness was defined as "an attainment on reading accuracy or reading comprehension on the Neale Test which was 2 years 4 months or more below the child's chronological age." Specific reading retardation was defined as "an attainment on either reading accuracy or reading comprehension which was 2 years 4 months or more below the level predicted on the basis of the child's age and short WISC IQ." In these studies, a prediction was made on the basis of multiple regression equations (Yule, 1967).

The total population of 9 and 10 year olds amounted to 2,300 children. These definitions yielded 155 backward readers and 86 retarded readers. However, the two groups overlapped considerably, having no less than 76 children in common. In order to determine whether there were any meaningful differences between the two varieties of reading disability, the 86 children with specific reading retardation were systematically compared with the remaining 79 children who displayed general reading backwardness alone.

As expected from the definition, the two groups differed in terms of their average intelligence. The mean IQ of the retarded readers was 102.5, while that of the backward readers was only 80. This merely confirms that our selection procedures have been reasonably effective. In order to make valid distinctions between the two types of reading disability, it is necessary to compare the groups on variables other than those used in the selection procedure (Davis and Cashdan, 1963).

Sex Distribution The two groups differ markedly in sex ratio. Only 54.4% of the backward readers were boys, whereas 76.7% of the retarded readers were boys (χ^2 = 8.18, 1 df, $p < 0.01$). Put another way, in the group with general reading backwardness the ratio of boys to girls was only 1.3 to 1, while it was no less than 3.3 to 1 in the group with specific reading retardation. This finding has since been cross-validated in the study of children in an inner London borough (Berger, Yule, and Rutter, 1975).

Neurological Disorder Definite organic disorders such as cerebral palsy were found in no less than 11.4% of the generally backward readers, whereas none of the retarded group had such a condition. Differences in the same direction were also found on more dubious neurological abnormalities.

Motor and Praxic Abnormalities Motor and praxic abnormalities were assessed on a variety of tasks, some clinical and some standardized (Rutter, Graham, and Yule, 1970). Constructional difficulties, as assessed by requiring the child to copy various shapes in match sticks, were noted in three-fifths of the backward readers, compared with only one-quarter of the retarded readers.

Clumsiness, assessed both clinically and on a modified version of the Lincoln–Oseretsky motor proficiency scale, was twice as common in the reading backward group (20.2% versus 8.1% on clinical judgment, and 24.1% versus 12.8% on psychometric testing). Likewise, motor impersistence (Garfield, 1964) was twice as common in the group of backward readers.

Right–left differentiation was assessed following the five items suggested by Williams and Jambor (1964); 28% of the backward readers had errors on this task, compared with only 15% of the retarded readers.

Speech and Language Difficulties A family history was obtained by a school medical officer during a standardized interview with the parents. In both groups, about a third of the children had parents or sibs who were reported to have had reading difficulties, and about one in ten had parents or siblings who were delayed in their acquisition of speech. The groups did not differ in this respect, and in both cases the rate was about three times that found in the general population control group.

A similar finding comes from the history of the child's own speech development. In both groups, about a third of the children had been delayed in speech, either not using meaningful single words until after 18 months, or not using three-word phrases until after 24 months. Again, this rate is three times that in the general population.

Summary of Differences   It may be concluded that general reading backwardness is associated with overt neurological disorder and with abnormalities on a wide range of motor, praxic, speech, and other developmental functions. Specific reading retardation, on the other hand, was found to be associated to a marked degree only with abnormalities of speech and language development. The rate of other developmental abnormalities was in some cases above that in the control group (cf. Rutter, Tizard, and Whitmore, 1970), but the differences were both less marked and less differentiating than was the case with speech and language delay.

It is clear from these findings that there are marked differences between the two types of reading disability on characteristics that may be of aetiological importance. General reading backwardness is a disorder present in both boys and girls; it is sometimes associated with overt neurological disorder and is usually accompanied by abnormalities on a wide range of neuro-developmental functions including motor coordination, constructional abilities, right–left differentiation, motor impersistence, speech delay, and language impairment. It is more commonly found in children from large families and it is also more frequent in children whose fathers have a job of very low social status (Rutter and Yule, 1973, 1975). On the other hand, specific reading retardation is very much commoner in boys, is not often found with overt neurological disorder, and is more specifically associated with delays in the development of speech and language. It, too, is commoner in children from large families, but it is no more frequent in those from families of very low social status.

Thus, on both contemporaneous and developmental measures, the two types of reading disorder are sufficiently differentiated to argue for the validity of the conceptual distinction.

3. Differential Prognosis

Despite these interesting findings, it could be that the distinction between backwardness and retardation has little educational relevance. Ultimately, it will be of immense importance to investigate whether the two groups respond differently to various remedial techniques. More immediately, it was possible to use data from a 4–5-year follow-up study to check whether the groups made different educational progress.

On a priori grounds, one could make two mutually contradictory predictions (Yule, 1973). First, one might argue that because retarded readers are so much more intelligent than backward readers, they will not need extra help to catch up but will do so on their own accord. Second, one might argue that because the retarded readers are so much brighter, their unexpected failure in learning to read suggests some sort of specific handicap. A third prediction would be that there would be no difference at follow-up, the distinction being theoretical, having no practical significance.

To ascertain how the poor readers progressed, they were all followed up until they reached what was then their final year of compulsory schooling. At age 10 years, each group was some 33 months below the general population control group on the measure of reading. At follow-up, the children were again individually tested, this time on the Neale Analysis of Reading Ability, the Schonell spelling test, and the Vernon Arithmetic-mathematics test (see Yule, 1973 for details). The findings clearly indicated that the two groups had progressed somewhat differently.

In spite of their much better intelligence, the retarded readers had made significantly less progress in reading during the 4–5-year follow-up period. Thus, their attainment on reading accuracy was over six months below the level achieved by the duller, backward readers. The retarded readers had also made less progress in spelling, attaining scores some eight months behind the backward readers. Despite the contrary prediction expected from the regression effect, in both groups of readers, the children's spelling was even more impaired than their reading. This strongly reinforces the suggestion that there is a specific association between reading and spelling.

The differences on the arithmetic test stand in marked contrast. Questions had been presented orally so that poor readers would not be automatically penalized on the test. The findings show that the children with specific reading retardation had made more progress than the reading backward children. Even so, both groups were still performing below age level.

Thus it can be concluded that the distinction between specific reading retardation and general reading backwardness did have educational implications. The reading retarded children made less progress in reading and spelling but more progress in arithmetic and mathematics than did the duller, backward readers. Educators cannot assume any longer that bright children with reading difficulties will catch up. Good intelligence in a disabled reader is no talisman against long-lasting reading failure.

4. "Specific Reading Retardation" or "Dyslexia"?

The concept of specific reading retardation carried no implications concerning type of aetiology, nor does it imply any type of unitary causation. Nevertheless, the many similarities between the characteristics of children with specific reading retardation (Rutter and Yule, 1973) and those attributed to "dyslexia" immediately raise the question as to whether specific reading retardation and "dyslexia" are the same thing.

As noted earlier, current attempts at defining dyslexia leave much to be desired (Reid, 1969; Rutter, 1969). If the problems of case identification are ignored for the moment, then a review of the literature on dyslexia yields a rich, but varied, description of the cognitive disabilities that are commonly thought to be associated with dyslexia. The following characteristics are usually included: disorders in speech and language, clumsiness and lack of coordination, difficulties in the perception of space relationships, directional confusion, right—left confusion, disordered temporal orientation, difficulties in naming colors and in recognizing the meaning of pictures, inadequate, inconsistent, or mixed cerebral dominance, bizarre spelling errors, and a family history of reading difficulties.

Elsewhere (Rutter and Yule, 1973) we have reviewed the evidence on the importance of features such as these in specific reading retardation. Briefly, we concluded that, with the exception of mixed handedness noted earlier, most of the characteristics have been found to be associated with specific reading retardation. However, they are not all equally strongly associated. It seems that speech and language difficulties and problems in sequencing are those most strongly and consistently associated with reading retardation.

These findings in many ways parallel the changing ideas of those who apply the label "dyslexic" in clinical settings. Originally, the term was used to describe a very specific and qualitatively inexplicable inability to read words—so-called "word blindness." In recent years the emphasis on mechanisms underlying the disability has shifted from considering a visuospatial deficit to be primary to implicating language functions (Yule, 1976). Some investigators emphasize the children's difficulties with auditory-phonic decoding tasks (Boder, 1971), while others lay heavier emphasis on the bizarre spelling errors that seem to persist into adult life (Miles, 1974). Both views are consistent with the hypothesis that language difficulties are the unifying factor underlying specific reading retardation.

The question of the constitutional component in dyslexia is far from being answered. As always, the problem is to disentangle genetically transmitted predispositions from socially transmitted disadvantages. Clearly, both operate simultaneously, but the evidence for there being any simple mode of biological inheritance is very scanty (Rutter and Yule,

1975). There is good evidence in favor of the view that reading skills in general have a hereditary basis or important genetic component (cf. Jensen, 1969), but there is no convincing evidence that a specific condition (i.e., dyslexia) is inherited.

By contrast, there is mounting evidence for the concept of social transmission, in that a family history of reading retardation is much commoner in children from large families. Moreover, it is known that, even within the British Isles, children's reading attainment varies both according to the area of the country in which they live and with the amount of interest their parents take in academic matters (Davie, Butler, and Goldstein, 1972). These observations, together with the findings reported above of a greater prevalence of specific reading retardation in inner London compared with the Isle of Wight, point strongly to the comparatively greater importance of social and environmental factors in the aetiology of reading retardation.

Thus, it is argued that specific reading retardation is usually multifactorially determined, whereas it is claimed that dyslexia is a unitary condition. It is suggested that the developmental impairment in reading retardation may be due to a relative failure in the normal maturation of certain specific functions of the cerebral cortex, or some neurological damage, or a lack of suitable environmental stimulation, or a combination of all three. These factors interact with school influences, temperamental features, motivation, and family circumstances. In particular, it appears that language impairment (due either to some biological factor or to some environmental privation) renders the child at risk, and whether he actually shows reading retardation will depend also on his personality characteristics, the nature of his home environment, and the quality of his schooling.

Such an interactionist, multifactorially determined view of specific reading retardation is quite different from that associated with dyslexia. Attempts to separate out a dyslexic core from within the broader group of specific reading retardation have failed. Neither in a population study of children with specific reading retardation (Rutter, 1969) nor in an investigation of a highly selected clinic sample of children widely regarded as dyslexic (Naidoo, 1972) was it possible to demonstrate any clustering of the developmental anomalies said to characterize dyslexia. In short, there has been a complete failure to show that the signs of dyslexia constitute any meaningful pattern. There is no evidence for the validity of a single special syndrome of dyslexia. It may therefore be concluded that the term "dyslexia" . . . "serves little useful purpose other than to draw attention to the fact that the problem of these children can be chronic and severe. It is not susceptible to precise operational definition; nor does it indicate any clearly defined course of treatment. . . . A more helpful term to describe the situation of these children is 'specific reading retardation' " (Department of Education and Science, 1975).

SOME SOCIAL AND EDUCATIONAL IMPLICATIONS

It can be concluded that the traditional distinction between general reading backwardness and specific reading retardation has been shown to have validity. Specific reading retardation constitutes more than just the lower end of a normal distribution in that its frequency significantly exceeds that predicted on statistical grounds. The disorder differs from reading backwardness in terms of sex distribution, neurological disorder, and pattern of neuro-developmental deficit, demonstrating the clinical validity of the distinction. It also differs in terms of a worse prognosis for reading and spelling but a better prognosis for mathematics, demonstrating the educational usefulness of the differentiation.

One of the major implications of these findings is that future research into learning disability in general, and specific reading retardation in particular, can proceed on a firmer scientific basis by employing more sophisticated and valid measures of underachievement. By studying more carefully defined groups, one can confidently predict that many apparent controversies will be settled, while more fruitful areas of investigation are brought into focus.

In the field of remedial education, one can also look forward to significant advances. At present, the literature on the efficacy of remedial reading programs shows that in most cases only very limited benefits have been obtained (Carroll, 1972). However, distinctions have rarely been drawn between backward and (properly identified) retarded readers. It might well be the case that the two groups respond to different remedial approaches. As long as undifferentiated groups of poor readers are used in remedial experiments, gains and losses will cancel each other out. Better definition of cases could lead to significant advances in remedial work.

The differentiation of the two types of poor readers may also have implications for the prediction of reading failure, or at least the early identification of poor readers. Using data from yet another of our Isle of Wight studies, this time a predictive study of 5 year olds (Yule, Berger, Butler, Newham, and Tizard, 1969), Maxwell (1972) discovered that children who later (at age 7 years) turned out to be poor readers showed a different cognitive structure on the Wechsler Pre-School and Primary Scale of Intelligence from good readers. The WPPSI had been administered two years earlier at age 5.5 years. The children who became poor readers appeared to make less efficient use of their cognitive skills. Unfortunately, the number of children was too small, and the children were too young, to separate out retarded readers from backward readers.

At the other end of the school age spectrum, the follow-up study of young adolescents revealed some disturbing findings about the reading habits and vocational aspirations of the retarded readers. It will be recalled that, as a group, these children are of average intelligence. About half the retarded readers, compared with only one in five of the general population, never read a morning newspaper, despite the fact that 80% of the homes had a morning newspaper delivered. Sixty percent of retarded readers had not read any books outside their school curriculum in the month prior to interview. Only about 30% of the general control group admitted to this lack of book reading. While it is understandable that poor readers will not read as much as good readers, it must be remembered that we are here emphasizing the lowered quality of life of a group of teenagers of otherwise average intelligence.

Perhaps even more worrying were the findings on the retarded readers' vocational aspirations. Almost 70% of them expected to leave school at the earliest opportunity, compared with only 30% of the controls who held such low academic aspirations. While 60% of the control group hoped to take some form of examinations before leaving school, less than 15% of the retarded readers had such aims. None anticipated going on to professional or university training.

Overall, the retarded readers in adolescence had vocational aspirations more like their generally backward peers than like peers of like ability. It may be realistic of these adolescents to expect that their poor attainment in reading will debar them from pursuing interesting careers, but it is a sad commentary on the present educational system that a group of children of at least average intelligence can experience ten years of schooling and still emerge with major handicaps in reading and spelling.

Again, we would argue that in the long run more careful definition of reading difficulties will improve the quality of research that bears on these social and educational issues. It is sometimes forgotten in arguments over terminology that we are really talking about children whose reading difficulties are educationally, emotionally, and socially very handicapping. While it is to be hoped that improved definitions and sounder conceptual frameworks will lead to better understanding of the neurological, developmental, and psychological processes underlying specific reading retardation, it is also to be hoped that more careful studies will be undertaken in the areas of preventing reading failure and remedial education. It is clear from our epidemiological studies that, at present, if a child is a retarded reader by 10 years of age, one can only be pessimistic about his educational future.

Follow-up Study of Children with Specific (or Primary) Reading Disability

Ronald L. Trites[1] and Christine Fiedorowicz

Research studies on children with learning disabilities are not only plagued with the problems of definition, measurement, and treatment choice, but estimates of the prevalence vary to an extreme degree. As a result of these and other factors, meaningful follow-up data are virtually nonexistent. With respect to reading disability, in particular, Spreen stated in 1970 that "at the present time, we know nothing about the further development of poor readers, treated or untreated, beyond Elementary School and Junior High School level" (Spreen, 1970). Although some promising studies have appeared since 1970, this statement can still be taken as largely valid.

The follow-up studies of children with reading disability that have been reported have generally given results that support one of two extreme positions: (a) those that conclude that there is a very favorable outcome in adulthood, and (b) those that point to a persistence of the reading disability over time. Among the favorable outcome studies, Robinson and Smith (1962) and Rawson (1968) both point to generally high educational and vocational achievement among their samples of retarded readers. However, in both studies the subjects had very high levels of intelligence (mean IQ of 120 in the Robinson and Smith study and a phenomenal mean IQ of 131 in the Rawson study). Balow and Blomquist (1965) reported that their group, which had a more modest IQ, also did well educationally and vocationally. On the one hand they found that their subjects did not like school, did not read for pleasure, and generally had a negative and defeatist attitude. In spite of these negative findings, however, only 17% did not graduate from high school. One's curiosity as to the reason behind this very favorable outcome is hardly satisfied since the

---

[1] Research Scholar of the Ontario Mental Health Foundation.

authors attributed the academic success to a "minor miracle." Unfortunately, although this was reportedly a follow-up study, only 9 of the 32 subjects were actually brought in for follow-up testing and even the data on these subjects were not reported. In a somewhat equivocal study, Preston and Yarington (1967) found a much higher failure rate among retarded readers (over 66% as compared to 16% in the normal population). In general, they found that retarded reading limits academic aspiration and ultimate achievement and narrows vocational possibilities. However, they did find that the percentage of retarded readers who complete high school was the same as in the general population. The problem in this and virtually all of the other follow-up studies is that academic achievement scores obtained on well-standardized tests and expressed in grade equivalent scores for reading, spelling, and arithmetic are not presented. Even when initial and follow-up reading tests were administered, the group means have not been presented. Hence, the reader has no idea as to the actual change in academic achievement levels over time among the subjects. Among the studies showing persisting deficits in retarded readers, Silver and Hagin (1964, 1966) found a persistence of right—left confusion along with reading and spelling problems that continued into adulthood. This conclusion has been supported by the work of Yule and his colleagues (1973, 1974). Koppitz (1971) concluded, based on her experience, that if a child is still reading at the grade one or two level by age 10 or 11, reading will not be fluent by age 16 and the subject will not likely have progressed beyond an approximate reading grade level of two or three as an adult. However, again this observation was not quantified.

The purposes of the present study were (a) to obtain retest information on well-standardized academic achievement tests on a group of boys who were diagnosed during elementary school as having a specific reading disability; (b) to obtain similar follow-up data on a group of girls with reading disability; and (c) to compare these groups with a group of boys with reading disability presumably secondary to neurological disease. The aim was primarily to gather follow-up data on group (a) but also to assess the comparative rates of progress in acquisition of reading, spelling, and arithmetic skills in the three groups.

METHOD

Subjects

All boys with a diagnosis of primary reading disability who had been examined in the Neuropsychology Laboratory during the years 1970 to

1973 were selected for study. If they had not already been brought in for a follow-up assessment, they were requested to do so for the purpose of this study. Follow-up testing was obtained on 27 of a total possible 28 subjects. The criteria for specific or primary reading disability generally included, in addition to the lag in reading, a family history of reading disability, no evidence of gross or focal brain damage, average intelligence or greater, and no evidence of severe emotional disturbance. For comparison purposes, a group of 10 girls with a reading disability that generally met the above criteria were retested. Ten boys with a reading disability presumably secondary to neurological disease were examined in a similar test-retest fashion. The various neurological diagnoses included cases of prenatal or perinatal injury (3), epilepsy (3), head injury with brain contusion (2), encephalitis (1), and cyst (1). The age, grade placement, grade at which the reading problem was recognized, and lateral dominance information is presented in Table 1.

It is clear that the reading problems were recognized in the girls at a much earlier age than in the boys. Consequently, the girls were younger when first examined. The two groups of boys were very similar in age and grade placement. With respect to the cerebral lateralization of dysfunction in the brain-damaged group, the right and left hemispheres appeared to be implicated about equally.

Test Procedures

All subjects were, on the first testing, given a 6–8-hour battery of neuropsychological tests. The test battery included widely used measures of intelligence such as the Wechsler Intelligence Scale for Children (WISC) and Peabody Picture Vocabulary Test (PPVT) along with tests of auditory perceptual abilities such as the Boston University Speech-Sound Discrimination Picture Test. The Wide Range Achievement Test (WRAT) (Jastak and Jastak, 1965) was used to obtain grade equivalent scores for reading, spelling, and arithmetic. In addition, the Halstead–Reitan Tests and the Wisconsin Motor Steadiness Battery, which have been well described elsewhere (Kløve, 1963), were used. This battery of tests has proved to be highly sensitive to mild deficits in subjects with specific reading disability (Doehring, 1968) and, in particular, is extremely useful in ruling out the presence of gross or focal neurological impairment in subjects with reading disability.

Subjects who had not been routinely retested were brought in for retesting on the vocabulary and academic achievement tests. At the same time, their educational history was updated and type and extent of special help for their reading disability recorded.

Table 1. Descriptive Data for the Three Groups of Retarded Readers

Groups	N	Age	Grade Placement	Grade in Which Reading Problem Was Recognized	Lateral Dominance R	L
Specific reading disability						
First testing	27	11.6	5.08	2.2	21	6
Second testing		14.1	7.0			
Neurologically impaired						
First testing	10	11.5	5.3	3.1	8	2
Second testing		14.3	7.2			
Girls with reading disability						
First testing	10	8.9	2.8	1.2	7	3
Second testing		11.5	5.7			

RESULTS

The WISC was administered to all of the subjects on first testing only. The results are presented in Table 2. The Verbal IQ, Performance IQ, Full Scale IQ, and subtest scores are very similar for the group of boys with primary reading disability and the group of girls. Both these groups are significantly higher on a number of the scores as compared to the brain-damaged group. All groups had a lower Verbal IQ as compared to Performance IQ and tended to have a low score on the Digit Span Subtest (an auditory attention span measure). In addition, all groups tended to have consider-able difficulty (mean of 6 errors, which is in the lowest quartile for age) on the Boston University Speech-Sound Discrimination Picture Test (ability to discriminate between similar sounding words presented auditorily) along with moderate right−left orientation confusion and difficulty in accurately perceiving numbers written to the fingertips. Generally speak-ing, there were no other consistent deficits within the three groups on the sensory tests or on the motor tests nor were there any other striking group differences. There was a tendency, however, for the brain-damaged group to perform more poorly on the coordination tests. Correlations between the academic achievement scores, vocabulary scores, auditory perceptual test, and IQ scores are presented in Table 3.

The correlation between Verbal IQ and academic achievement level, although significant, was smaller than the usual 0.60 reported in other studies (Hinton and Knights, 1971; Yule, 1973). Of considerable interest, the magnitude of the discrepancy between recognition vocabulary and

Table 2. Wechsler Intelligence Scale for Children Data for the Three Groups of Retarded Readers at the Time of First Test

Groups	Age	VIQ	PIQ	FSIQ	Inf	Comp	Sim	Vocab	D Sp	PA	PC	BD	OA	Code	Maze
1. Specific reading disability	11.6	101	110	106	9	11	11	10	9	12	11	12	12	9	11
2. Neurologically impaired	11.5	90	96	92	9	7	10	7	7	9	10	10	12	7	8
3. Girls with reading disability	8.9	98	107	103	9	10	11	9	9	10	10	10	12	13	10
Significance:															
groups: 1–2		.03	.01	.001		.008		.01	.01	.01		.03		.01	.001
1–3			.01	.01								.05		.05	
2–3		.01				.03		.04	.05					.005	.05

Table 3. Correlations Between Selected Achievement, IQ, Vocabulary, and Perceptual Measures

	WRAT Reading	WRAT Spelling	WRAT Arith.	PPVT B-A	PPVT IQ	Boston	VIQ	PIQ
WRAT spelling	.88[a]							
WRAT arithmetic	.86[a]	.84[a]						
PPVT B-A[b]	-.67[a]	-.53[a]	.61[a]					
PPVT IQ	.16	.18	.02	-.08				
Boston	-.17	-.36[a]	-.31[a]	.08	-.14			
VIQ	.35[a]	.35[a]	.31[a]	.08	.59[a]	-.11		
PIQ	.02	.02	.01	.10	.44[a]	.09	.56[a]	
FSIQ	.22	.22	.19	.11	.59[a]	-.21	.91[a]	.86[a]

[a] $p < .05$.
[b] Score denotes difference between recognition vocabulary and reading vocabulary. Higher score equals more severe reading disability.

reading vocabulary (PPVT B-A) was highly related to reading, spelling, and also arithmetic levels, while the recognition vocabulary only (PPVT IQ) was unrelated to academic achievement levels but highly correlated with VIQ and PIQ. Although there was a tendency toward slightly higher scores on arithmetic as compared to reading and spelling tests, there was a consistent, high intercorrelation among the three measures. The children with reading disabilities had considerable difficulty on arithmetic tasks even though the questions are presented in numerical form.

The average test-retest interval on the academic achievement testing was 2.6 years. Age, grade placement, test, and retest PPVT IQ scores along with reading, spelling, and arithmetic grade scores and the corresponding percentile placements are presented in Table 4.

There was an improvement in reading, spelling, and arithmetic grade scores for all three groups on retesting. However, the increase did not keep pace with the time interval between first and second testing; thus, there generally was a drop in percentile placement.

To further assess the relative standing of the three groups, discrepancy scores between grade placement and achievement levels were computed for first and second testing. In addition, the discrepancy between "normal" expected grade placement for age (i.e., age 6 = grade 1, age 7 = grade 2, etc.) and actual achievement scores was calculated. The two types of discrepancy scores are presented in Table 5.

It can be seen that for all groups and for all academic achievement skills measured, the discrepancy between grade placement and actual level of achievement becomes larger as the subjects grow older. The discrepancies are smaller in the "actual" than in the "normal" comparison since most subjects had failed at least one grade. Thus, although the academic difficulties were usually recognized in the early grades, the subjects were behind their classmates in all areas and this gap grew larger over time in spite of remedial help in all cases. Students in the top quartile and the bottom quartile on first testing retained their relative position on second testing. The outcome was the same irrespective of sex and whether or not the reading disability was congenital-familial in origin or presumably related to brain damage.

DISCUSSION

Results of this study point strongly toward the conclusion that, in subjects with specific reading disabilities, the deficits not only persist with age but tend to grow larger relative to their age and grade placement. However, it must be emphasized that this conclusion is based on the study of a sample of very carefully screened subjects who all met stringent criteria of specific

Table 4. Group Means on the Vocabulary and Achievement Tests for First Testing and Follow-Up

Groups	Age	Grade	PPVT IQ	Wide Range Achievement Test							
				Reading		Spelling		Arithmetic			
				Grade	%ile	Grade	%ile	Grade	%ile		
Specific reading disability											
First testing	11.6	5.1	106	3.3	13	2.9	10	4.6	36		
Second testing	14.1	7.0	105	4.6	14	3.6	8	5.2	21		
Neurologically impaired											
First testing	11.5	5.3	90	3.3	9	2.8	6	4.3	20		
Second testing	14.3	7.2	91	4.0	8	4.1	6	5.3	15		
Girls with reading disability											
First testing	8.9	2.8	98	2.3	26	2.3	36	3.1	40		
Second testing	11.5	5.7	97	3.6	15	4.0	27	4.4	20		

Table 5. Discrepancy Between Grade Placement and Achievement Level

Groups	Actual Grade Placement Minus Achievement Level			Normal (for Age) Grade Placement Minus Achievement Level		
	Reading	Spelling	Arithmetic	Reading	Spelling	Arithmetic
Specific reading disability						
First testing	1.8	2.2	0.5	2.8	3.3	1.5
Second testing	2.4	3.4	1.8	3.7	4.6	3.0
Neurologically impaired						
First testing	2.0	2.5	1.0	2.7	3.2	1.9
Second testing	3.2	3.1	1.9	4.2	4.3	3.2
Girls with reading disability						
First testing	0.5	0.5	0.3	1.1	1.1	0.3
Second testing	2.1	1.7	1.3	2.6	2.1	1.7

reading disability. If there was any doubt that other factors such as mixed language background, poor motivation, lack of stimulation in the home, etc. were implicated, the subject was not included in the study. Individuals in the latter groups may have a better prognosis with respect to literacy acquisition. Given the stability of the deficit in reading in these groups, the maturational lag hypothesis put forward by many as the predisposing factor to reading disability (e.g., Bender and Yarnell, 1941; Koppitz, 1971; Satz and Sparrow, 1970), viewed simply, would not provide an adequate explanation for the persistence of the deficits into adulthood. If the origin of the reading disability was simply a delayed maturation, the subjects should eventually develop reading skills more in keeping with their general abilities. However, if one also considers a "critical stage" for the acquisition of reading skills, then one could consider that the subject with delayed maturation is not ready to acquire reading skills at the critical time.

The specific reading disability group and neurologically impaired group had similar outcomes on the achievement tests. This does not necessarily mean that they can be lumped together in studies of etiology or in studies of methods of remedial teaching. There are differences in IQ scores between the groups, and pattern of reading subskill deficits may similarly prove to be quite different.

Although many deficits have been found in groups of retarded readers, such as right-left confusion (Belmont and Birch, 1965), fingertip recognition deficit (Rabinovitch et al., 1954), impairment of form perception (Benton, 1962c), spatial orientation difficulties (Kinsbourne and Warrington, 1966), etc., a specific syndrome for identifying each individual case has not yet been established. Indeed, the difficulty in finding a reliable syndrome is not surprising since this is not at all rare in the behavioral sciences (Money, 1962). Should a reliable pattern of reading subskill deficits be identified, one would expect that this pattern of deficits would remain very stable in the individual over time in view of the persistence of the reading deficit itself.

Lastly, in follow-up studies of children with reading disabilities, completion of high school should not be used by itself as the criterion of reading proficiency. There were subjects in this study who were either in their final year of high school or who had completed high school but who obtained scores at the sixth grade and as low as the fourth grade on the academic achievement tests.

ACKNOWLEDGMENTS

The authors express appreciation to Jennifer Brooks, who gave help in collecting data for a pilot version of this study.

Part II

Physiological and Biochemical Correlates of Learning Disabilities

Biochemical and Electroencephalographic Correlates of Learning Disabilities

John R. Hughes

One of the great controversies in early neurophysiological circles was whether synaptic transmission between neurones was essentially chemical or electrical. These discussions were often said to be arguments over "soup" versus "sparks." It soon became evident that both sides of the controversy were correct to some degree; the events that occurred during synaptic transmission not only had a distinctive chemical basis, but also had definite electrical manifestations. The present discussion of the essential nature of learning disabilities in some ways reflects this controversy and thus part of this presentation will be a short review of biochemical correlates, followed by a longer review of electrophysiological correlates, which will feature the findings from the human EEG. No attempt will be made to be exhaustive in giving this account, which at this point must derive its data from studies of both learning and memory. Only selected works that illustrate certain major points will be mentioned in the section on biochemical changes. In the part dealing with EEG, certain themes will be emphasized that seem to offer the most promise for present understanding and future research.

BIOCHEMICAL CORRELATES

The story of the biochemical changes associated with learning and memory can be briefly told in various steps. The first of these steps, following the suggestion of Essman and Nakajima (1973), deals with the chemical "improvement" of intelligence before 1960. The major compound investigated at this time was glutamic acid. This compound, with glutamine, makes up one-half of the nonprotein nitrogen of the brain, and has, therefore, an important role in brain metabolism. In addition, glutamic acid is one of the very active compounds in the donation of an amino group in an important biochemical event called transamination. In 1944 Zimmerman and Ross provided evidence that glutamic acid and other amino acids enhanced intelligence in white rats, but there were questions regarding the controls and, most importantly, there were negative reports in man. The second phase of these first steps was the suggestion from Rosensweig, Krech, and Bennett (1960) that the ability for learning may be related to the concentration of acetylcholine (ACh) relative to that of cholinesterase (ChE). Acetylcholine is, of course, the transmitter stored at the endplate of a muscle, released by an electrical impulse, to act on the membrane of the muscle to permit contraction. Cholinesterase is the protein enzyme that destroys the ACh. The important question among neurochemists has been to what extent this model of neuromuscular transmission also applies within the central nervous system (CNS), and, with regard to the experiments of Rosensweig et al., to what extent do the experiments on rats apply to the human. The third and last phase of these first steps was the suggestion by McGaugh and Petrinovich (1959) that weak strychnine had a stimulating effect on maze learning.

The second step can be entitled the emergence of macromolecular theories. In 1961 Gerard pointed out that the neurone, engaged in high rates of metabolism, likely would show its enduring modification associated with learning and memory in the form of changes in nucleic acids or proteins (Gerard, 1961). At that same time Hydén (1961) specified ribonucleic acid (RNA) as the basis of memory and during the same year Gaito (1961) added the possibility that DNA, our controller of protein synthesis, may also be involved.

The third steps can be called the era of discoveries and features the years 1961–1963. The goal of these investigations was to search for compounds that affected RNA synthesis in some way. Egyhazi and Hydén (1961) reported that tricyano-amino-propene (TCAP) augmented RNA synthesis, Dingman and Sporn (1961) reported that 8-azaguanine interfered with antimetabolites, and Flexner, Flexner, and Stellar (1963) indicated that puromycin interfered with the RNA synthesis. At that same time, Rosensweig and his colleagues (1962) were progressing with their experiments on ACh and ChE and reported that an enriched environment produced a heavier brain from an increase in the ChE.

The fourth step deals with the chemical analysis of learning. Hydén and Egyhazi (1964) showed that neurones from a trained cortex, compared to the untrained side, contained more RNA with more adenine and less cytosine (the former a purine and the latter a pyrimidine, both forming nucleotides that are the units for nuclei acids). Three other studies during this era featured leucine, one of our essential amino acids. In 1966 Altman and Das showed an increase in the incorporation of radioactive leucine into the neuronal protein after motor exercise. Four years later Hydén and Lange (1970) showed an increase in leucine in hippocampal neurones after handedness transfer training, and Beach et al. (1969) showed similar results after shock avoidance training.

The fifth step can be entitled the behavioral assay of memory substances or transfer of training. McConnell (1962) showed transfer of training to planaria after having eaten pieces of other planaria that had learned a given task. Nissen, Roigaard-Petersen, and Fjerdingstad (1965) showed a transfer of light–dark discrimination by intracisternal injection of RNA, but others could not confirm this finding. In 1966 Bohus and de Wied reported that ACTH was the substance effective in the transfer of avoidance responses.

The penultimate step in this account of biochemical changes associated with learning and memory is the pharmacological facilitation of learning and memory. In 1966 Glasky and Simon reported that some magnesium pemoline increased an important enzyme in protein metabolism, namely, RNA polymerase, and also facilitated learning. During the same year Essman (1966) showed that the injection of TCAP resulted in higher RNA concentration with greater resistance to the amnesic effect of electro-convulsive shocks, but other investigators, like Buckholtz and Bowman (1970), failed to confirm these results. Certain substances, all stimulators for the CNS, were said to facilitate the consolidation of memory and included strychnine (McGaugh and Petrinovich, 1959), picrotoxin (Garg and Holland, 1968), caffeine (Paré, 1961) and finally metrazol (Irwin and Benuazizi, 1966). Note that all of the latter substances are actually convulsants, some even at relatively low concentration. Because ACh has often been assumed to be the transmitter within the CNS, cholinergic drugs, like DFP (diisopropylfluorophosphate), were said to increase learning by prolonging the effect of ACh, if injected into the rat's hippocampus. Another cholinergic drug, physostigmine, had a similar effect, while anti-cholinergic drugs, like scopolomine, had an opposite effect. Drachman and Leavitt (1974) have shown that in man scopolamine produced an impairment in memory storage, but no change in memory function was noted from physostigmine. Later (1975) these same investigators showed a slight improvement in cognitive and memory functions with d-amphetamine alone, but if the latter drug was used after scopolamine, a further impairment was noted to the "scopolamine dementia." On the other hand, physostigmine used after scopolamine improved the memory function. These studies are significant in providing evidence of a specific relationship between central pharmacosystems and certain memory-cognitive functions rather than a nonspecific change that would have been indicated if d-amphetamine had reversed the scopolamine dementia.

A few years ago, Deutsch (1971) proposed that cholinergic drugs at the height of synaptic excitation actually block transmission by flooding the synapse with ACh, but if given at normal levels the same cholinergic drugs may improve performance.

The final step in this account deals with the interference of memory transfer. An antibiotic, actinomycin D, is isolated from a Streptomyces culture and is used in treating Wilm's tumor, certain sarcomas, testicular tumors, and trophoblastic malignancies. This drug forms a stable complex with DNA and thereby inhibits DNA-dependent synthesis of RNA. In 1967 Agranoff and his colleagues showed that actinomycin D produced a deficit in learning in goldfish and Nakajima (1969) reported that the same compound injected into the hippocampus may produce epileptic activity. Three other compounds that inhibit protein synthesis have been shown to affect memory. They are puromycin (Flexner, Flexner, and Roberts, 1967), acetoxycycloheximide, and cycloheximide (Cohen and Barondes, 1968 a,b). Finally, Essman (1972) reported that 5-hydroxytryptamine (5HT, serotonin), considered a putative transmitter, has amnesic effects, possibly by inhibiting cerebral protein synthesis.

After dealing with these seven steps on the biochemical changes associated with learning and memory, what general conclusions can be drawn? Many studies have been mentioned that suggest that certain substances improve learning and others interfere with the cognitive state. However, the conclusions of Essman and Nakajima (1973) seem appropriate: it is obvious that some electrolytes and transmitter substances in the CNS are involved in learning, and there is no behavior that does not involve these chemicals. However, no one has found a method for facilitating the specific synthesis of RNA or proteins in the brain of man, and no substance has been available to disrupt macromolecular synthesis without producing multiple effects. This latter point is most important and emphasizes one of the major problems in this area of investigation, namely, that substances affecting cognitive function may produce only a general nonspecific change rather than a specific effect on learning and memory. Neurochemists will continue to investigate the mechanisms with which various chemicals contribute to a lasting change of behavior. The search for the engram continues and neurochemists have helped to chart methodological and conceptual maps, but the exact pathways for the mechanism and site of action remain to be ascertained.

The process of learning to read is undoubtedly related to the activation of aminergic systems, which appear to be a component of the biochemical correlates of all learning. Park, Bieber, and Zeller (1975) have begun investigations into the possibility that, in dyslexia, amine metabolism may be abnormal. One way to investigate this matter is to explore the amines, like norepinephrine or epinephrine, compounds likely used in all learning tasks. The enzyme used for the regulation of amine metabolism is mono-amine oxidase (MAO). Park and his colleagues investigated the only in vivo available MAO, namely, the MAO in platelets. The rationale was that, if the active site of platelet MAO is altered in dyslexia, then the degradation rate of various substrates may be affected differentially between dyslexia patients and control subjects.

The method used was to isolate platelets by centrifugation and sonic oscillation and then to determine the degradation products of p-methoxy-benzylamine (pMBA), tyramine, and m-iodobenzylamine (mIBA) by spec-trophotometrical and spectrofluorometric procedures. The experimental group consisted of children 8–13 years of age, of normal or above normal IQ (as determined by the WISC, Stanford-Binet, and Peabody Picture Vocabulary Tests), with a reading ability at least 1.5 years below expec-tancy, as measured by the Stanford Reading Test and Gilmore Oral Reading Test. The controls were a group of age- and sex-matched subjects. As can be seen from Table 1, the degradation rates of all three substrates were consistently increased for the dyslexics over the controls. With pMBA, the difference is statistically significant. There is another differ-

Table 1. Degradation Rates of Three Substrates by Platelet MAO from Dyslexics (D) and Controls (C)

Substrate	Group	No.	Mean (nmoles/10^9 plat/hr.)	SD	VD/VC
mIBA	C	11	51	17.0	100%
	D	17	59	30.8[a]	116%
Tyramine	C	11	32	9.8	100%
	D	9	37	18.8[b]	116%
pMBA	C	11	114	36.0	100%
	D	13	148	37.0	130%[c]

[a] $F = 2.62; p < 0.05.$
[b] $F = 4.00; p < 0.05.$
[c] $T = 2.16; p < 0.05.$

ence, referring to the range of variation of mIBA and tyramine, that is statistically larger in dyslexic children as compared to the controls. Thus, in the probing of MAO activity by checking the degradation rate of various substrates, dyslexics are different from their controls.

These studies suggest that dyslexia is a disorder with systematic manifestations. It remains for further investigation whether changes occur for brain MAO similar to those for the platelet enzyme and whether these changes are of importance in the etiology or pathogenesis of dyslexia, rather than relating to some effect of the disorder.

Another very recent study on dyslexics relates to another important biochemical change. Park and Schneider (1975) investigated thyroid function of 53 dyslexic children (47 boys and 6 girls) from 7 to 15 years of age. The control group of 18 was similar in age, but with normal reading ability. All laboratory determinations were made without knowledge from which group a given sample had come. Thyroxine determinations were prepared by passing the serum through ion-exchange columns and were measured in an autoanalyzer. The results are seen in Table 2. This table shows a highly significant difference between the dyslexics and controls. The control group had values similar to those found in healthy adults with a normal range of 5.73–9.65 μg/dl. On the other hand, in the dyslexic group, 43 of the 53 children had serum thyroxine values greater than 9.65.

This report by Park and Schneider is intended to call attention to an association between dyslexia and thyroid function. Since free thyroxine values have not been analyzed, it is possible that the increased thyroxine may be due to increased thyroid binding globulin levels. Since only the free form can be used, it is this form that regulates thyroid function, and the present study serves only as an important stimulus for further investigations. This study does provide one more association between dyslexia and a systemic change in metabolism. In a study by Hughes and Park (1968) on the EEGs of dyslexics, a definite trend was noted for higher thyroid (PBI) values to be found in dyslexics with abnormal EEGs com-

Table 2. Thyroxine Determinations in Dyslexics and Controls

Group	Mean Serum Thyroxine (μg/dl)	SD
Control	7.69	0.978
Dyslexic	11.44[a]	2.493

[a]$t = 6.35; p < 0.001$.

pared to those with normal records. The highest PBI values were found in dyslexics with epileptiform discharges and those with positive spikes.

These two latter reports on dyslexics, involving MAO and thyroid activity, can possibly fit together in a unifying hypothesis. At least it is worth speculating that dyslexics with high thyroxine levels may tend to have hypermetabolic rates, which may be related to high levels of MAO activity that usually parallel high levels of aminergic compounds, like epinephrine and norepinephrine. Future research will determine whether dyslexics actually tend to have hypermetabolic states or whether medical treatment directed against such a state may be therapeutic.

ELECTROENCEPHALOGRAPHIC CORRELATES

Problems

The usefulness of the electroencephalogram in dealing with children with learning and/or behavioral disorders has been controversial. The reasons for the controversy include (1) the difficulty of precisely defining the groups under study and the overlapping of these groups, (2) the presence of questionable EEG findings in many of these children, and (3) the relatively high incidence of "abnormal" EEG findings in control groups of similar age. Regarding the different kinds of groups studied, an attempt will be made in this presentation to collate the data from very similar groups and then to compare those results with those from other groups. The presence of questionable and controversial EEG findings is a reflection of the need for further research in a field that otherwise makes a strong contribution in today's clinical setting. The high incidence of "abnormal" EEG findings in control groups is also a reflection of the latter point, but statistically significant differences between these control and experimental groups will be clearly evident in many studies.

Clinical Entities

Although considerable overlap exists, the major conclusion in dealing with different clinical entities is that the EEG tends to be more abnormal with more clinical disturbance. Table 3 summarizes the findings of many different studies and demonstrates this point. Most children classified as hyperkinetic (89%) have a more severe disturbance than those considered as a behavior disorder (59%). Patients with clear mental retardation (63%), of course, have a more significant disturbance than those with a learning disability (45%) or with a specific dyslexia (44%), the latter two groups having a similar incidence of EEG abnormality. The studies on hyper-

Table 3. EEG Abnormality in Different Behavior-Learning Disorders

Clinical Entity	No. of Patients	% Abn. EEG (Weighted Mean)
Hyperkinetic	383	89%
Behavior disorder	208	59%
Mental retardation	1,592	63%
Learning disability	622	45%
Dyslexia	312	44%

kinetic children included the 90% of Klinkerfuss et al. (1965) and 87% of Anderson (1963). In the former study, the patients were divided into two groups, hyperkinetic children with (I) convulsive disorder or definite neurological findings and those (II) with only minimal neurological signs. Consistent with the general point that the EEG tends to be more abnormal in the patients with a greater clinical disability, in Group I 50% had a definite EEG abnormality (40% mild) compared to Group II with 30% (60% mild). The behavior disorders included the 71% of Jasper, Bradley, and Saloman (1938), 63% of Knobel, Wolman, and Mason (1959), and 47% of Stevens, Sachdev, and Milstein (1968). Table 4 shows the studies dealing with mental defectives.

Learning disability studies included the 95% incidence of EEG abnormality in the study by Gubray et al. (1965), 88% of Paine (1962), 62% of Hughes (1967), 50% of Capute, Niedermeyer, and Richardson (1968), 41% of Hughes (1971), and 25% of Koppitz (1971). The studies that dealt with a specific dyslexia involved the 63% incidence of EEG abnormality in the study by Muehl, Knott, and Benton (1965), 49% of Torres and Ayers (1968), and 36% of Hughes and Park (1968), 35% of Bryant and Friedlander (1965), and 34% of Ingram et al. (1970). Also consistent with the general point that greater clinical disability is associated with a higher incidence of EEG abnormality, the study of Ingram, Mason, and Blackburn (1970) showed that 34% of patients, with a specific disorder in reading and spelling only, had an abnormal record, contrasted to 84% of children with a general learning disorder, in addition to a reading and spelling deficit. Furthermore, only 12% of those with a specific defect had a definite increase in slow waves and 7% had spikes, contrasted to 50% and 25%, respectively, among those with a general deficit.

The reviewer is aware that these latter studies, summarized in Table 3, show a range of (1) variability of time when the investigation was performed, (2) criteria of what was considered abnormal in the EEG, (3)

Table 4. Incidence of EEG Abnormality in Mental Defectives

N	% Abnormal	Investigator
200	43.0	Brandt (1957)
84 (without seizures)	54.0	Walter (1964)
401	58.9	Fugslang-Frederiksen (1961)
74	59.9	Beckett et al. (1956)
578	65.9	LaVeck and De la Cruz (1963)
40	70.0	Posey (1951)
55 (mongolian idiots)	78.2	Fugslang-Frederiksen (1961)
85	78.6	Landucci and Piantossi (1961)
75 (with seizures)	90.7	Walter (1964)
1,592—Total	62.7—Average	

criteria of the clinical entity under investigation, and all of the other reasons that collating data from different studies on cognitive disorders cannot offer precise conclusions. However, a trend seems indicated from these data.

Types of EEG Abnormality Found in Learning-Behavior Disabilities

Schain (1972) has emphasized that some of the abnormalities frequently reported in children with learning or behavioral disorders are controversial or questionable. Into that group Schain has placed the 6—7 and 14 per second positive spikes, occipital or posterior temporal slow waves, non-focal sporadic sharp wave, excessive slowing, increase (slowing) with hyperventilation and mild diffuse dysrhythmias. The reviewer is in agreement that some of these patterns are questionable, e.g., increase slowing with hyperventilation, and that some of the others are very controversial, e.g., 6—7 and 14 per second positive spikes. However, in dealing with clinical entities like learning disabilities, a disorder unrecognized by professional psychologists or neurologists until only very recently, the predicted EEG patterns would not likely be gross abnormalities like a focus of delta (slow) waves. Instead, the more subtle patterns would be expected, like excessive posterior slowing or possibly positive spikes.

The most controversial pattern is likely the 6—7 and 14 per second positive spike pattern. This pattern has aroused the greatest of debate, but ten years ago more than 100 papers had been written about their probable clinical significance (Hughes, 1965). However, certain studies, especially that of Lombroso et al. (1966), have reported such high incidence in asymptomatic children that many electroencephalographers now have considered this pattern normal. The great difference in the incidence of positive spikes in normals reported by Lombroso and his colleagues (58%) and by others, like Hughes (17%, 1971), has never been resolved, but the sample size or clinical setting (private boarding school versus public school) may prove to be important. It seems possible that positive spikes in the adolescent may be similar in their clinical significance to temporal slow waves in the aged. The latter slow waves may appear so commonly in the aged that they are noted in the majority of certain older age groups. On the basis of one definition of "normal," namely, a condition found in the majority of a given population, these slow waves could then be called "normal." However, some aged subjects do not have these slow waves and careful study of various clinical subtleties, with like tests measuring cognitive function, has revealed that these temporal lobe slow waves do, in fact, correlate with a cognitive disorder in aged subjects, who are considered well and remain active in the community (Drachman and Hughes, 1971). A similar situation may pertain to positive spikes, which are commonly found among adolescents. Like almost all other EEG waveforms, positive spikes are found in subjects who are asymptomatic, but as a relatively "benign" waveform, they are found with a higher incidence than most EEG abnormalities. Like temporal slow waves in the aged, they may be found even in the majority of certain groups, but labeling them "normal" ignores the huge number of papers that argue strongly for a correlation with neurovegetative or behavioral disorders (Hughes, 1965). One relevant philosophical question here is whether negative evidence ever proves anything, i.e., whether studies that fail to find correlations provide the ultimate "truth" about a given phenomenon in the face of other investigations with positive results.

Positive spikes have been reported in many different investigations dealing with learning or behavioral disorders. This waveform was found in 36% of behavior disorders (Stevens, Sachdev, and Milstein, 1968) and in 20% of learning disorders (Hughes, 1971).

A range of incidence has been reported for positive spikes in dyslexics; Hughes and Park (1968) reported 21%, Knott et al. (1965) 30%, Bryant and Friedlander (1965) 35%, and Muehl, Knott, and Benton (1965) 55%. The problem of control groups must be mentioned here. Stevens and her colleagues indicated that, compared to the behavior disorders, a similar incidence of positive spikes was found in one control group, but significantly lower incidence was noted in another control group (26%). Torres and Ayers (1968) found no significant differences between dyslexics and controls for positive spikes, nor did Bryant and Friedlander, who reported a 28% incidence in their control group of 18 subjects. Clearly the number of subjects in the latter study was far too small for any definite conclusions to be made. In the study by Hughes on learning disorders, a 15% incidence was found in the control group of 214 subjects (compared to 20% of 214 underachievers); the p value of 0.099 shows that statistical significance (0.05) was not quite achieved, but a clear trend was indicated.

Excessive occipital slowing is one other abnormality commonly mentioned in these studies and previously emphasized by Cohn and Nardini (1958) in their study on children with aggressive behavior disorders. Knobel, Wolman, and Mason (1959) indicated that 47% of hyperkinetic children showed this pattern, constituting over 75% of the abnormal patterns found. In learning disorders in general and dyslexics in particular a lower incidence has been reported. Hughes (1971) found a statistically significant difference ($p = 0.008$) for slow waves in underachievers versus controls, but it was the temporal slowing that was significantly different ($p = 0.03$) and not that on the occipitals (10% in underachievers). However, when the underachievers were divided into two different groups (clinically determined), the one group that showed the greatest difference from the controls had significantly more abnormal slow waves in general and nearly half of these were on the occipital areas. In dyslexics the incidence of occipital slowing seems similar to that of learning disorders in that Hughes and Park (1968) reported a 10% incidence constituting 27% of those with some type of abnormality. Knott et al. (1965) had a higher value (50%) for the incidence of posterior slowing among dyslexics with abnormal EEGs.

Another type of abnormality mentioned in these children is diffuse or generalized slowing. In hyperkinetic children Anderson (1963) reported that two-thirds showed this pattern constituting three-fourths of the abnormality found. In the study by Gubray et al. (1965) on apraxia and agnosia, diffuse slowing was also the major abnormality found, accounting for nearly three-fourths of the subjects tested. Capute, Niedermeyer, and Richardson (1968) reported on minimal brain dysfunction or learning disabilities and found that one-half of these children had abnormal slowing. This slowing was usually nonfocal or diffuse, and therefore the authors concluded that a nonspecific disturbance was indicated.

The last abnormal pattern to be mentioned here is the sharp wave, spike, or spike and wave complex, usually called an epileptiform discharge. In the very early study by Jasper, Bradley, and Saloman (1938), a 39% incidence of this type of pattern was reported in behavior disorders, but the definition of epileptiform at that time was definitely broader than now and the incidence in this study is likely too high. Green (1961) called attention to the presence of spikes in behavior disorders and found that in certain cases (especially occipital spikes) anticonvulsants were helpful. Stevens et al. also found spikes in some behavior disorders. In learning disabilities, Paine (1962) reported that one-third of those with abnormalities had epileptiform patterns (three with clinical seizures) and exactly the same incidence (one-third) was found by Gubray et al. among the children with apraxia or agnosia. In Hughes' study (1971) less than 6% of underachievers showed this type of waveform. In dyslexics less than 4% were found by Hughes and Park (1968), accounting for only 11% of abnormality found in these children, but Torres and Ayers (1968) claimed that focal spikes on the temporal areas were the most common abnormality found. Finally, Laufer and Denhoff (1957) found that hyperkinetic children had a low photometrazol threshold, suggesting a seizure tendency, but this test has now fallen into disfavor.

The general conclusions that can be drawn from this section are that positive spikes have been more frequently mentioned in these studies than any other waveform, but a definite conclusion regarding their incidence in different groups seems impossible at this time in view of the variation, especially within the control groups. It is unfortunate that this waveform has become so controversial that further studies designed to resolve some of these questions may not ever be done. The data from some dyslexia studies, however, are very suggestive, ranging in incidence from 20 to 50% of the children tested. Excessive occipital slowing is a waveform that is likely found more often in behavior disorders than learning disorders. The general conclusion for this EEG pattern is similar to that of positive spikes, and these two waveforms do have a relationship to each other (Kellaway, Crawley, and Kagawa, 1959); the data on posterior slowing are suggestive, likely with at least a 10% incidence in learning disorders, but further studies are needed. The other two waveforms mentioned have in common that they have been found with a relatively high incidence by some investigators, but not by others. Thus, when diffuse slowing or epileptiform activity is reported, it is prominently mentioned in these studies. Possibly, these waveforms constitute distinctive patterns to be found in certain children, like the diffuse slowing in some hyperkinetics and apraxics or agnosics and the spikes in certain behavior or learning disorders. Thus, when found, these two patterns may be more significant than other waveforms, but various investigators have not found the high incidence reported by others.

Correlation of Specific EEG Waveforms with Clinical Conditions

Positive spikes were found by Stevens et al., especially in behavior disorders who were both clumsy and poor in arithmetic. In the investigation by Muehl et al. this waveform did not correlate with any psychological test score. In their study on dyslexics, Hughes and Park found that those with positive spikes were the brightest of four different EEG groups, but with the greatest difference between their potential and actual achievement in reading; also, they scored high on different tests measuring tension and metabolic rate. These latter findings may be consistent with the finding that positive spikes are often seen in behavior disorders with impulsivity (Hughes, 1965).

Excessive occipital slowing was found more frequently in deaf children than learning disorders, and the deaf child also tends to have diminished photic responses (Hughes, 1971). In a study on speech disorders (Pavy and Metcalfe, 1965) this EEG pattern was associated with abnormal results on a visual motor performance test. Dyslexic children with occipital slowing were the poorest readers with poor potential and with decreased visual responsivity, especially in the form of poor visual duction (Hughes and Park). These latter studies emphasize that occipital slowing may, at times, be associated with visual disabilities, as might be predicted by neuro-anatomy. However, the same waveform may be seen in patients whose primary clinical disorder seems to be behavioral (Cohn and Nardini) rather than visual.

Specific clinical correlations with diffuse or generalized slowing have rarely been made. Only the study by Stevens et al. provides evidence on this point, and these investigators reported that diffuse EEG abnormalities were associated with antisocial activities, aggressiveness, low tolerance, clumsiness, and variability of behavior.

Correlations with epileptiform activity were also made by Stevens and her colleagues, who found that children with these spikes had defects in attention and ideation. Some of Green's patients with discharges also showed a short attention span, especially those with spikes on the temporal or occipital areas. In the dyslexic group Hughes and Park found that the small group with sharp wave or spike discharges showed evidence of "organicity" in the form of the highest thyroid (PBI) values and also low neutrophil counts. Perhaps the most suggestive organic aspects of this group were the visual deficiencies in the form of the abnormal duction tests, with nearly half of these children with weak or absent stereopsis. Thus, the presence of spikes or sharp wave discharges seems associated with both visual disorders and also with defects of attention among children with learning-behavioral disabilities.

Two Points of Emphasis Relating to Future Research

1. In a study on learning disabilities with double-blind controls (Hughes,

1971), the most effective way to separate the underachievers from the controls was on the basis of aspects of the record, usually not considered or categorized as abnormal. In particular, the presence of poor rhythmicity (organization) and low amplitude (development) of the background rhythm, in addition to asymmetrical photic driving responses with depression on the left side, permitted surprising prediction of the group in which a given child belonged. The abnormal EEGs were placed into the underachiever group if any of these three variables were found. In this way 79% of the abnormal records were correctly placed into the underachiever group and one could account for 62% of all of the underachievers by using these three variables. If the EEGs were normal, the success rate was less in that 62% were correctly placed into the underachievers, accounting for 63% of underachievers with normal records. The depressed photic responses on the left side, found to be significantly different ($p = 0.02$) between the underachiever and control groups (Hughes, 1971), find confirmation in an excellent study by Conners (1971a). The latter investigator studied a family of poor readers and found a decreased amplitude in the late components of the visual evoked response on the left parietal area. Also, in children with learning disabilities there was a significant relationship on the left parietal area with the late wave VI. It was the amplitude of wave VI from the left parietal area that showed the highest correlation with achievement.

The results from the latter study by Conners (1971a) and the investigation by Hughes (1971) emphasize that all aspects of electrophysiological recordings must be evaluated rather than emphasizing only the intermixed, specific focal or diffuse abnormal patterns. Future EEG studies on learning disabilities must evaluate aspects of the record that are not traditionally considered as constituting abnormality.

2. The results of a number of studies on children with various learning-behavioral disorders have led to conclusions opposite to what would be expected based on traditional concepts in electroencephalography. Morin (1965) found that stutterers who failed to show improvement with training had normal EEGs, while those who improved usually had abnormal records. Bergés, Harrison, and Lairy (1965) found that there was a favorable prognosis in children with a speech disorder who had an abnormal EEG and an unfavorable prognosis for those with normal records. In the study by Knobel et al. some of the most severely involved hyperkinetic children had normal EEGs, although others had the most abnormal records. In two different articles, Tymchuk, Knights, and Hinton (1970 a,b) have shown that in the comparison between a normal and an abnormal EEG group, the normal EEG group performed at a lower level

than the abnormal subjects in seven out of nine tests that showed a significant difference (1970a). In the second report, the normal EEG group's poorest performance was shown to be on tests measuring fine motor function (1970b). Finally, Hughes (1971) found that when under-achievers were clinically divided into the less and the more abnormal group, the less abnormal group, called borderline, had a greater incidence of EEG abnormality. These findings indicate that we may need to look upon some EEG abnormalities in quite a different way than is traditional. For example, in the case of the spike and wave complex of petit mal epilepsy, this discharge is traditionally considered to be related to the cause of the epilepsy, not to the effect. However, in the case of learning disabilities, the significance of positive EEG findings may be that at times they may represent the effect, not the cause, of the disorder. Following a suggestion of Lairy and Harrison (1968), one may presume that a child with a learning disability has become maladjusted to the scholastic environment, that the central nervous system has reacted to this maladjustment and the positive EEG findings represent the electrical manifestations of this reactivity or compensation. In these cases improvement in the scholastic situation is possible and likely, because the CNS is reacting or compensating. However, in some children with a learning disability, the CNS does not react to correct the maladjustment and, therefore, there are fewer positive EEG findings as the manifestation of the brain's reactivity, and little improvement occurs. In Hughes' study the borderline group showed more positive EEG findings because of the greater reactivity of the CNS to the scholastic maladjustment, and accordingly these individuals showed only a minimal academic deficit. On the other hand, the more severely involved learning disorders in that study would be considered as a group with less reactivity of the CNS to the scholastic difficulties and, therefore, with a greater clinical deficit, and fewer EEG findings would appear as a manifestation of this diminished reactivity. Thus, normal EEGs are found not only in individuals with normal function, but also may be found in abnormal subjects in whom there is no more reactivity of the central nervous system to a maladjusted environment. It seems, therefore, that positive or abnormal EEG findings may, at times, represent the reaction of the brain to stress.

SUMMARY

This review deals with biochemical and electroencephalographic correlates of learning disabilities. The story of the biochemical studies is divided into seven short steps (Essman and Nakajima):

1. Chemical improvement of intelligence, especially involving glutamic acid and strychnine.
2. Emergence of macromolecular theories—RNA and DNA.
3. Era of discoveries 1961–1963—emphasizing various compounds either augmenting or interfering with RNA synthesis, in addition to quantification of acetylcholine and cholinesterase content of the brain.
4. Chemical analysis of learning, involving adenine, cytosine, and leucine.
5. Behavioral assay of memory substances or transfer of training by ingestion or injection of RNA.
6. Pharmacological facilitation of learning and memory, especially with TCAP, strychnine, picrotoxin, and caffeine in addition to the effects of scopolamine, amphetamine, and physostigmine.
7. Interference of memory transfer with actinomycin D, puromycin, acetoxycycloheximide, and cycloheximide.

The general conclusion was that some electrolytes and transmitter substances in the CNS are involved in learning, but the search continues for a method for facilitating the specific synthesis of RNA and for substances disrupting macromolecular synthesis without producing multiple effects.

Recent studies have shown that dyslexia may be a disorder with systemic manifestations, suggested by high levels of monoamine oxidase, as indicated by degradation rates of three different substrates. Also, dyslexics have significantly higher thyroxine levels than controls.

The section on EEG correlates begins with the clarification of the major problems: precisely defining the groups under study, the presence of questionable EEG findings, and abnormal EEGs in control groups.

Generally, the more disordered behavior or learning is associated with a higher incidence of EEG abnormality, as exemplified by higher values in hyperkinetic children than behavior disorders.

The types of EEG abnormality found in learning disorders include the controversial 6–7 and 14 per second positive spike phenomenon and excessive occipital slowing. Both waveforms have been frequently mentioned in a number of reports, but definite conclusions regarding their average incidence cannot be made until further data are forthcoming, although some of the evidence is most suggestive for an association with learning disabilities. Diffuse slowing and epileptiform activity seem to be more specific patterns and, when found, may have more clinical significance.

In the correlation of specific EEG waveforms with clinical conditions, positive spikes may be seen especially in bright children with high levels of tension or with a behavior disorder. Excessive occipital slowing is associated, at times, with various forms of visual disabilities. Generalized slowing can be seen in aggressive, antisocial children, and epileptiform activity may be noted in learning disorders with defects of attention.

Two points of emphasis relating to future research are that all aspects of the EEG, including characteristics of the background rhythm and of photic responses, must be evaluated, and these characteristics of the EEG may have the closest relationship to learning disabilities. Finally, considerable evidence exists to suggest that positive EEG findings may, at times, represent the electrical manifestation of the reactivity or compensation of the central nervous system to a maladjusted environment. Thus, abnormal or positive EEG findings may, at times, represent the reaction of the brain to stress.

Focused Arousal
and 40-Hz EEG

Daniel E. Sheer

Learning disability in children is a complex, multidetermined problem. The predisposed child, developing in a highly reactive social environment, must necessarily build up a superstructure of secondary behavioral effects interactive with primary ones. Given such a set of conditions, it is no wonder that we have a broad nosology, widely ranging symptoms, and considerable variance in prognosis. Clinical management and treatment must obviously be focused on the individual child, his social setting, specific deficits, and major assets. But all of this does not relieve us of the responsibility to search for etiological abnormalities. And it is equally true that, no matter what generalizations we may come up with, someone can always point to individual cases or to specific behaviors that do not quite fit.

In this chapter, the author proposes a brain function etiology for at least one subgrouping of the learning disability classification. The proposal is that these children have a primary deficit in "focused arousal," a high-order behavioral abstraction, overlapping with the concepts of "sustained attention" by Douglas (1974a), "attentional deficit" of Dykman et al. (1971), "selective attention" of Kinsbourne (1973), and the "poorly modulated activation" of Wender (1971). Perhaps more important than the different words is an electrophysiological measurement operation for the concept and empirical data showing significant differences between learning disability children and normal controls during problem-solving behavior. Before the discussion of brain measurement, the behaviors that provide observational referents for focused arousal are briefly examined.

Along with a behavioral picture of general hyperactivity, Wender (1971) has noted: "The most striking and constant perceptual-cognitive abnormality of the MBD child is shortness of attention span and poor concentration ability." Performance on objective testing procedures demonstrates the effects of this abnormality on a wide range of reaction time, perceptual-motor, sensory discrimination, vigilance, and memory

Supported in part under NIE Grant No. NE-G-00-3-0012.

71

tasks (Conners, 1971c; Douglas, 1974a; Dykman et al., 1971; Senf and Freundl, 1971; Stevens et al., 1967; Sykes et al., 1971). Of equal significance are the varying deficits for different children in motor patterns (the clumsy child), reading, and language. The point to be made here is that in the initial learning of these skills, focusing arousal on relevant associations and sequencing is an important part of the processing.

In language, naming has to occur before the complexities of grammar. The child first learns to name by pointing excitedly to an object as he says "mommy," "doggy," and so on.[1] In the process of assigning "verbal mediation" to some stimulus in the environment, the child must learn to sequence the motor patterns that reproduce the heard sound sequences of speech. As the child proceeds with connected speech, a continuous short-term storage process is necessary for comprehension. The meaning of connected speech is a function not only of the individual constituent words but also of their subsequent organization. Information presented early in the sequence has to be retained to modify and illuminate the significance of subsequent items.

In reading, the child must further learn and remember correct associations between the verbal responses and dimensions of visual stimuli differing in form, orientation, and sequential arrangement. He must focus arousal on these different dimensions of the visual stimuli as they are appropriate to the verbal associates. In a series of analytical studies, Kinsbourne (1971) found that a major source of confusion by backward readers is their failure to "focus attention" on the relevant dimensions. In motor behavior, in forming skilled motor patterns and fine coordinated movements out of segmental units, focused arousal is needed to fit together the motor sequences (Keele, 1973).

In their progressive development of proficiency in motor skills, language, and reading, children who have maturational deficiency in focused arousal may lag behind in some specific area as a consequence of environmental interactions. Thus one child with marginal arousal mechanisms, interactive with environmental stress and unsatisfactory models during critical periods in language development, may show up as having a more specific deficit in language. Another child with marginal arousal may develop a specific reading problem because of poor teaching techniques during his first training period in reading. Aside from negative environmental feedback, in some children there could very well be a marginal

---

[1] I am indebted to Dr. Marcel Kinsbourne for pointing out this connection to me, and I am sure he would want me to add that he is not responsible for the further use I have made of it.

brain condition in a sense modality channel or in specific functional areas such as perceptual-motor or speech—interactive with the deficiency in focused arousal.

The distinction between focused arousal and various concepts of attention should be made clearer. There is, in the mainstream of cognitive psychology, a considerable body of information on attention (Kintsch, 1970; Kornblum, 1973; Norman, 1969). It is clear from the behavioral data that any concept of attention must include, in addition to selective facilitatory processing, inhibitory processing that does not function simply as an on—off switch but incrementally attenuates input stimuli. In addition, attention must also include some comparison or match—mismatch processing that feeds back to the input stimuli in order to account for expectancies. Focused arousal is much more limited; it refers only to selective facilitatory processing. In a comprehensive theoretical network it may actually represent a part function of attention.

The distinction here is important because with a more limited behavioral concept, it allows us to specify more definitively the brain mechanisms involved, and thus the abnormality. If we say a learning disability child has a deficit in attention, it can be any one of a number of combinations of function and brain mechanisms. When we say he has a deficit in focused arousal, it narrows the field considerably.

The general behavioral picture associated with learning disability is hyperactivity, which would indicate that the problem may be overarousal, distractability and so on, but this need not be the case. The data available on distractability indicate that it is not. Distractors introduced in discrimination problems (Whitman and Sprague, 1968), color and color-word distraction tests (Campbell, Douglas, and Morgenstern, 1971), a continuous performance task (Sykes et al., 1971), and a choice reaction time procedure (Douglas, 1974a) do not result in differential performance by learning disability children as compared with normal controls.

It is also true that, although the hyperactivity is prominent, children with learning disabilities can also be normoactive or hypoactive (Dykman et al., 1971; Wender, 1971). When we look at peripheral autonomic and other measures of arousal a fairly consistent picture emerges. Learning disability children, compared with normal controls during baseline conditions, exhibited no significant differences in skin resistance, heart rate, and muscle action potentials in one study (Boydstrum et al., 1968), or in skin conductance in another (Cohen and Douglas, 1972). In the first study, the controls were significantly more reactive during an operant conditioning procedure designed to discriminate and generalize to tones. In the second, when required to respond in a delayed reaction time task where a warning signal was given at the onset of each reaction time trial, the signal was significantly less effective in alerting the learning disability children.

In another study (Dykman et al., 1971), responding to a series of ten tones, learning disability children were significantly more labile in skin resistance during the series of orienting tones and less responsive in heart rate to the first and tenth tones, which were novel. In the study by Satterfield and Dawson (1971), a group of 24 hyperactive children showed a lower basal skin conductance in response to a series of 50-decibel sounds, but with a high degree of variability in which half of the LD subjects matched or exceeded the controls.

Learning-disabled children, on peripheral autonomic measures of arousal, do not show an overarousal or hyperactivity, but they do show a good deal of lability and an inability to mobilize or focus this arousal on relevant stimuli in specific tasks. The general behavioral hyperactivity may actually be an attempt by some children to increase their level of arousal through motor feedback. On measures of brain electricity, Cohen (1970) recorded the contingent negative variation (CNV) in 65 controls and 42 learning disability children. The CNV is a negative DC potential, triggered by a ready signal and terminated by the respond signal in a reaction-time task and appears to reflect cortical excitability (Walter, 1967). Cohen found a normal CNV in all 65 normals but in only 16 of the 42 LD children, and Dykman et al. (1971) also found a lower CNV in LD children as compared with controls. On EEG measures, Grunewald-Zuberbier, Grunewald, and Rasche (1975) report that hyperactive children with attention disorders as compared with nonhyperactive behavior problem children had significantly lower EEG arousal to tones in a tone–light conditioning situation. Thus, on central physiological measures of arousal, the LD children are again not hyperactive. Instead, as compared with control children, they appear to be less responsive to the task at hand.

An additional factor of some significance is the so-called paradoxical effect of amphetamines. These drugs produce their central effects via their interactions with noradrenergic and dopaminergic receptor systems within the brain (Ban, 1969; Fuxe and Ungerstedt, 1970). The noradrenergic interaction of amphetamines stimulates the ascending reticular activating system, which produces a state of increased cortical arousal (Baldessarini, 1972).

After considerable dispute with many questions still unanswered (Grinspoon and Singer, 1973), some effects of amphetamines on selected groups of hyperactive learning disability children are clear-cut. They decrease hyperactivity and reaction times and increase correct responding in reaction-time tasks (Sprague, Barnes, and Werry, 1970). They improve reaction times and decrease variability on the delayed-reaction-time test (Cohen, Douglas, and Morgenstern, 1971). They increase correct responses and decrease incorrect responses on a continuous-performance test, requiring maintenance of attention in detection of significant stimuli (Sykes et al., 1971). They improve performance on tasks requiring rapid response rates in the isolation of relevant stimuli from a confusing backgroup (Campbell, Douglas, and Morgenstern, 1971). The prediction of drug response appears to be best for functions involving sustained attention, such as the Porteus Mazes and vigilant tasks (Conners, 1971a).

Amphetamines help the appropriate learning disability child to fix and maintain his attention so that he can learn and perform more effectively. This particularly shows up in tasks and testing situations that are sensitive enough to overcome other interacting variances. The problem with the learning disability child is that he cannot focus arousal—as efficiently as his normal peer—in order to maintain sequences in short-term store and fix memories in long-term store.

Elsewhere, the present author has reviewed the propositions that learning and problem-solving behavior must depend upon short-term memory processing and, second, that memory traces in short-term store— dynamic organizations which are time dependent, state dependent, and context dependent—must take the form of patterned electrical brain activity (Sheer, 1970, 1972). With the recording techniques and computer resolution now available, it is time that we took a much closer look at the low-amplitude, fast-frequency "desynchronized" EEG usually represented in charts as irregularly thickened black lines.

The single designation "desynchronized" or "arousal" EEG clearly refers to a number of different electrical patterns. Morrell and Jasper (1956), in their study of conditioning in monkeys, found that a generalized desynchronization was diffusely present cortically only during the first stage of sensory—sensory conditioning. When conditioning was just being established, a "stable, well-localized desynchronization" was limited to relevant cortical areas. Further, Morrell (1961) reported differences in units recorded from the brainstem reticular formation, hippocampus, and visual cortex during generalized cortical desynchronization as compared with the localized desynchronization in visual cortex.

General arousal, diffuse cortical EEG desynchronization, represents initial responding to novel stimuli within the complex matrix of irrelevant environmental stimuli. It is an oscillatory, unstable state of the organism, in which many different subassemblies of the intrinsic electrical activity are firing in different spatio-temporal patterns, i.e., nonsynchronously. When connections are becoming established, through spatio-temporal patterning of inputs—as in CS—UCS pairings, associations, and sequencing—subassemblies of the electrical activity now fire in synchronous organizations restricted to the relevant circuitry. The desynchronized EEG is no longer diffuse, but it still may appear as desynchronized without finer-grained analysis because the synchronous subassemblies restricted to limited cortical areas are submerged within the total ongoing electrical activity. The limited subassemblies, defined by the relevant environmental inputs and the contingent reinforcement or arousal, are now firing at a synchronous frequency "optimal" for consolidation into long-term store.

A narrow frequency band in the EEG, centering at 40 Hz, reflects this limited cortical excitability for maintaining sequences in short-term store. The maintenance of short-term memory is necessary both for problem-solving and for consolidation in long-term store. The association of this focused arousal with 40 Hz represents an extension of the continuum of psychophysiological states from sleep-delta, through wakefulness-alpha, and general arousal-beta.

Our interest in 40-Hz EEG had its beginnings in the large-amplitude, highly synchronous bursts recorded from the olfactory bulbs and other rhinencephalic structures during sniffing, exploring, and orienting behaviors, through a range of species from catfish to man (Sheer and Grandstaff, 1970). At the olfactory bulb in the cat, the essential and sufficient stimulus is airflow; at the amygdala, airflow is essential but a certain level of arousal is now necessary (Pagano, 1966; Sheer, Benignus, and Grandstaff, 1966); and at prepyriform cortex, 40 Hz can be conditioned to neutral stimuli (Freeman, 1963). All this is very interesting, because, in quadruped animals particularly, olfaction is an important distance receptor, and sniffing is a highly adaptive orienting response for exploratory, food, and sex behavior.

At the neocortical level, where laminar structure is far more complex, the 40-Hz rhythm is now at a much lower amplitude in a more complicated electrical background, but it can still be observed visually from epidural leads at fast paper speeds on the oscillograph. However, for systematic reliable data, computer analysis is clearly necessary. In a series of studies with the cat in a successive visual discrimination task (Sheer, 1970; Sheer and Grandstaff, 1970), consistent relationships were obtained between 40 Hz and the acquisition phase of learning. In the 10-sec epoch of a 7/sec S_D flickering light, a burst of 40 Hz occurred in visual and motor cortex about 0.5 sec before, and remained continuous for about 1.5 sec after, a correct barpress response.

Recording 40-Hz EEG from the intact scalp in humans with attendant muscle artifact is by no means a simple task. The meditation state provides a unique situation in which subjects are relatively immobile. Das and

Gastaut (1955), recording from occipital leads in seven trained yogis, reported rather high-amplitude levels of 40-Hz activity during the samadhi state, the final most intense concentration stage in this form of meditation. Recently, Banquet (1973), studying 12 subjects practicing transcendental meditation with recordings from left occipital and frontal leads, also observed 40 Hz during the third deep stage of meditation in subjects with advanced training.

Other references in the literature on 40 Hz and behavior, in both animals and humans, present a rather consistent picture of correlations with learning and attention to input stimuli (Dumenko, 1961; Galambos, 1958; Giannitrapani, 1969; Hess, Koella, and Akert, 1953; Itil, 1970; Killam and Killam, 1967; Motokizawa and Fujimori, 1964; Parmeggiani and Zanocco, 1963; Perez-Borja et al., 1961; Rowland, 1958; Sakakura and Doty, 1969; Sakhuilina, 1961). In our original work with learning disability children, significant decrements were obtained in the 40-Hz EEG band during problem-solving tasks in a carefully selected group of such children, as compared with matched children at normal grade level (Sheer, 1974; Sheer and Hix, 1971).

EXPERIMENTAL RESULTS

Some experimental data are briefly presented to reinforce the point that learning disability children show a deficit in 40-Hz EEG activity during problem-solving behavior. Reliable, consistent EEG recording of 40 Hz from the intact scalp is the first essential procedure that has to be accomplished. This low-amplitude, fast-frequency part of the EEG spectrum, recorded from the human scalp, is of the order of 5 μV. In addition, it completely overlaps with the muscle spectrum, which is broad and highly polyphasic, with generally a peak at 50 Hz (Chaffin, 1969). Thus one must contend, at the same time, with a low signal level and muscle artifact at a much higher amplitude, both in the same frequency range. Over the past several years, we have developed recording and computer analysis procedures for use in the laboratory situation and portable hardware for biofeedback training in the field situation[2] (Sheer, 1975).

---

[2] A special-purpose computer for this analysis was designed and built by Dr. Jack Smith, Department of Electrical Engineering, University of Florida, following our original design used in on-line biofeedback training (Sheer, 1975). A compact portable unit that can be used for biofeedback training under unshielded conditions has been designed and built by the Bioscan Co., Houston, Texas. It includes a FET electrode configuration to provide low-impedance conduction to the first amplification stage, filter and logic circuitry, audio feedback reinforcement provided through a hearing aid device, and a digital counter to keep a cumulative record of reinforcements.

The control for muscle, both with computer analysis and on-line, is essentially nonparametric contingency detection of the coincidence between EEG and muscle digital counts from filter outputs, within the threshold limits specified. It is based on a correction for muscle using a parametric analysis of covariance developed with analog and hybrid computer techniques. Electrical activity in the 23% frequency range from 62 to 78 Hz with a center frequency at 70 Hz is specified as muscle (Σx^2) and, from the same leads, activity in the 23% frequency range from 36 to 44 Hz with a center at 40 Hz is specified as EEG (Σy^2). The corrected power function $[\Sigma y^2 = (\Sigma xy)^2/\Sigma x^2]$ represents the variance or power of the EEG independent of muscle.

In the computer analysis, an additional control is used with two bordering 23% frequency bands, centering at 31.5 and 50 Hz. Outputs from these three frequency windows, 31.5, 40, and 50 Hz, are compared across subjects, across conditions, and across subjects $\times$ conditions. There is no reason why polyphasic muscle, with a relatively higher amplitude at 50 Hz, should differentially show up in the 40-Hz band, but not in the 31.5- and 50-Hz bands. The threshold limits for digit counts are set at a three cycle time constant or burst duration and a 3.1 μV amplitude level. With different time delays in the different center frequency filters, the muscle inhibit window is adjusted to be $\pm$100 msec from a muscle burst.

The electrical placements during the behavioral testing consisted of C_z as a reference with O_1 and O_2, P_3 and P_4, and F_3 and F_4 recorded on a ten-channel Grass EEG unit and seven-channel Ampex tape recorder. Leads between the temporal and neck muscles, on both the right and left sides, were also monitored as visual controls. The procedure for the behavioral testing situation is shown in Figure 1. The subject sits in a chair holding a response button and facing an easel and the examiner. The testing situation is automatically programmed as shown and consists of visually presented, orally presented, or tactually presented items behind a screen.

The problem-solving tasks are divided into three major sets, Verbal-Visual, Verbal-Auditory, and Tactile-Kinesthetic. There are three subtests in each set with five items in each subtest. The subtests in the Verbal-Visual set include (1) Picture Arithmetic, (2) Visual Classifications, and (3) Visual Rhyming. The subtests in the Verbal-Auditory set include (1) Word Arithmetic Problems, (2) Auditory Classifications, and (3) Auditory Rhyming. The subtests in the Tactile-Kinesthetic set include (1) Modified Seguin Formboard, (2) Dot Outline Comparisons, and (3) Wire Form Comparisons.

The data to be reported here were obtained on a control group of 20 children and two learning disability groups of 30 each. Age, IQ, and

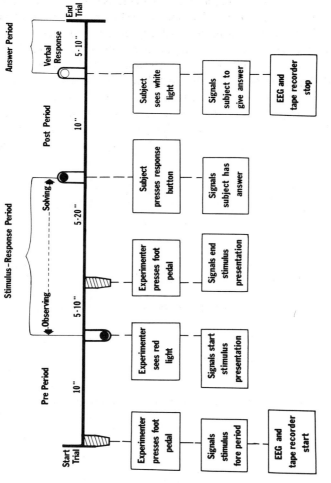

Figure 1. Diagram of the automatic sequencing of events in the behavioral testing and EEG recording sessions.

behavioral testing results for these groups are presented in Table 1. Learning disability Group II was rated as more severe than I on the basis of school performance. There were no significant differences on age and IQ, but it should be noted that the variance on IQ was about twice as high for LD I and three times as high for LD II as compared with the controls. On the three sets of problem-solving tasks, there were significant differences between both learning disability groups and the control children. These special tasks seemed to be relatively sensitive in differentiating learning disability children as a group from control children.

A sample EEG record obtained during the behavioral testing situation is shown in Figure 2. On the Grass, the channels are run at maximum or near maximum gain on the EEG leads, with the 60-Hz notch filter out and the high-pass filter at 10 Hz in. The paper speed during test trials is run at 100 mm/sec. Reliable extraction of 40 Hz from these records requires

Table 1. Means and Standard Deviations on Age, IQ, and Problem-Solving Tasks for the Normal Grade Level and the Moderate (I) and More Severe (II) Learning Disability Groups

Groups	N	Age			IQ	
		Mean	SD		Mean	SD
Normal grade level	20	10.11	0.85		100.30	4.80
Learning disability I	30	9.87	1.03		99.03	8.35
Learning disability II	30	10.62	1.40		94.21	12.75

Groups	N	Verbal-Visual Errors		Verbal-Auditory Errors		Tactile-Kinesthetic Errors	
		Mean	SD	Mean	SD	Mean	SD
Normal grade level	20	2.20	1.03	2.05	1.50	3.60	1.24
Learning disability I	30	4.83[a]	2.90	5.43[a]	2.56	5.40[a]	1.96
Learning disability II	30	5.83[a]	2.82	6.70[a]	3.16	4.83[b]	2.33

[a]Significant beyond 0.01 compared with Normal Grade Level.
[b]Significant beyond 0.02 compared with Normal Grade Level.

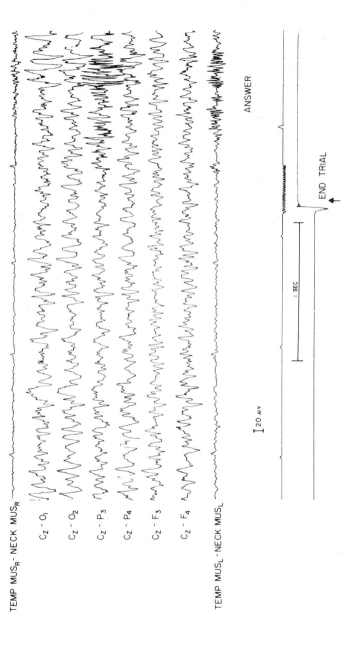

Figure 2. An EEG record of a testing trial just before an answer is given, showing the EEG and muscle leads recorded. The EEG is not recorded on tape for computer analysis after "End Trial" to avoid muscle artifact during the verbal response.

computer analysis, but some 40 Hz can be seen in the C_2-P_4 lead from the second quarter to the middle of the record.

Computer data on the parietal and occipital leads for the normal and learning disability children during control and testing sessions are presented in Table 2. The computer output is in digital counts, that is, the number of times per successive 0.1-sec epochs that the specified criteria have been met. The criteria are a three cycle burst above 3.1 μV not contingent, within ±100 msec, with a muscle signal. By multiplying the digital count by 0.1 sec we can obtain the time the particular EEG signal was on; dividing this time by total trial time we can obtain the percent time per trial for that EEG signal.

A comparison of the means between each set of test trials and the control trials shows significant increases in 40 Hz on right and left parietal leads during problem-solving for the normal children but not the learning disability groups. There were no significant changes in the 31.5- and 50-Hz bands and none in the occipital leads. The analyses of the frontal leads have not been completed and temporal leads are not possible to record because of excessive muscle artifact from the temporal muscle. On the basis of these data, it would appear that cortex bordering the parietal-occipital-temporal junction region, the angular and supramarginal language area on the left and homologous cortex on the right, are both important in solving these sets of problems. Learning disability children do not seem to mobilize these cortical regions as well.

BRAIN MECHANISMS

There is a unique value in the cerebral activity termed EEG because it provides an index of the combined activity of masses of cells; it is precisely this combination that is of major interest in the analysis of molar brain function. The effective use of EEG data lies in synthesizing the framework within which molecular analysis can be carried on, in the fashion that Sherrington reflex physiology provided the essential molar concepts on which the analysis of the electrical properties of the spinal motor neuron has been based. There still remains the problem of specifying the mechanisms in the brain that generate 40 Hz and, thus, the mechanisms that may be abnormal in learning disability children.

In the olfactory bulb, laminar structure is first encountered in a much simpler form than in neocortex and an analysis of mechanisms should be easier to come by. The evidence is strong that the 40-Hz waves in the olfactory bulb are standing potentials derived from synaptic and post-synaptic events, with the synchrony attributable to successive trains of

Table 2. Means of the Percent Time Per Trial for 30, 40, and 50 Hz EEG from Parietal and Occipital Leads During Control and Problem-Solving Conditions for the Normal and Learning Disability Groups

	Mean % Time per Trial					
	30 Hz	40 Hz	50 Hz	30 Hz	40 Hz	50 Hz
	$Cz-P_3$			$Cz-P_4$		
Normal ($N = 20$)						
Control	1.62	1.03	0.02	2.11	1.05	0.02
VV trials	1.42	1.55[a]	0.04	1.69	1.97[a]	0.04
VA trials	1.45	1.87[a]	0.04	1.84	1.77[a]	0.03
TK trials	1.41	2.32[a]	0.06	1.65	2.47[a]	0.05
LDI ($N = 30$)						
Control	1.74	1.15	0.03	1.48	0.67	0.02
VV trials	1.46	1.09	0.02	1.26	0.95	0.03
VA trials	1.52	1.10	0.02	1.35	0.72	0.02
TK trials	1.63	1.20	0.04	1.50	0.83	0.03
LDII ($N = 30$)						
Control	1.57	1.02	0.01	1.46	0.43	0.01
VV trials	1.25	0.99	0.02	0.84	0.70	0.02
VA trials	1.24	0.88	0.02	1.09	0.30	0.01
TK trials	1.22	1.30	0.03	0.63	0.66	0.02
	$Cz-O_1$			$Cz-O_2$		
Normal ($N = 20$)						
Control	1.68	1.80	0.06	1.54	1.17	0.04
VV trials	1.34	1.67	0.03	1.58	1.73	0.05
VA trials	1.32	1.63	0.02	1.75	1.13	0.03
TK trials	1.25	1.57	0.02	1.72	1.80	0.03
LDI ($N = 30$)						
Control	1.69	1.80	0.03	1.39	1.05	0.02
VV trials	1.41	1.50	0.02	1.18	1.10	0.02
VA trials	1.27	1.62	0.03	1.10	1.02	0.03
TK trials	1.49	1.23	0.04	1.25	1.08	0.03
LDII ($N = 30$)						
Control	1.70	1.62	0.03	1.48	0.83	0.01
VV trials	1.40	1.25	0.03	0.92	0.80	0.02
VA trials	1.28	1.35	0.04	1.09	0.73	0.02
TK trials	1.81	1.28	0.04	0.63	0.70	0.03

[a]Significant beyond 0.05 compared with Control.

excitation and recurrent inhibition. The property of recurrent inhibition is essentially negative feedback, which functionally contributes to the phasing of rhythmic discharges (Anderson and Andersen, 1968; Anderson, Eccles, and Loyning, 1963; Eccles, 1965; Granit, 1963).

Rall and Shepherd (1968) and Shepherd (1970) have made an elegant detailed analysis of a dendro-dendritic synaptic interaction as a mechanism for this rhythmic activity in the olfactory bulb. Airflow excites bipolar receptor cells in the olfactory mucosa, whose axons form the olfactory nerves synapsing within encapsulated glomeruli with dendrites of tuffed and mitral cells. Impulse discharge in mitral cells results in synaptic excitation of granule cells; these granule cells then deliver graded inhibition to mitral cells. This inhibition cuts off the source of synaptic excitatory input to the granule cells. As the granule-cell activity subsides, the amount of inhibition delivered to the mitral cells is reduced, which permits the mitral cells to respond again to excitatory input from the glomeruli. In this way a sustained excitatory input to the mitral cells would be converted into a rhythmic sequence of excitation followed by inhibition, locked in timing to a rhythmic activation of the granule cell pool.

At the neocortex, there is a more complicated situation where comparable details on mechanisms are lacking. Stefanis and Jasper (1964) and Jasper and Stefanis (1965) have reported that the axon collaterals of cortical pyramidal cells in cats become particularly effective at relatively high frequencies of repetitive excitation. The negative feedback of recurrent inhibition provides an automatic control of level of excitation: the greater the excitation, the more the feedback of inhibition.

The point to be made here is that the 40-Hz EEG reflects repetitive stimulation at a constant frequency for a limited time over a limited circuitry. The circuitry is defined behaviorally by the spatial-temporal patterning of sensory inputs, motor outputs, and reinforcement contingencies. It is "optimal" for consolidation because repetitive synchronous excitation of cells maximizes the efficiency of synaptic transmission over the limited circuitry.

Eccles (1964) has well documented this property of frequency potentiation by measuring the size of EPSPs that develop with repetitive activation at different frequencies. The duration of constant repetitive discharges is probably as significant in the transfer of information as the intensity of neuronal firing or the number of cells involved. From quantitative studies in the spinal cord, Granit (1963) concluded that frequency of firing was the main code determining rate of continuous discharge in control of tonic motoneurons. At the human somatosensory cortex, Libet et al. (1967) have shown that subthreshold stimulus pulses could elicit conscious sensory experience only if they are delivered repetitively at 20–60 pulses per second.

A significant outcome of this feedback loop—wherein frequency potentiation sets up recurrent inhibition, which sets up synchrony, which sets up frequency potentiation—is the property of contrast. The negative feedback of recurrent inhibition particularly depresses those synapses that are weakly excited in the "surround" and so serves to further sharpen the focus of excitation. Behaviorally it is reflected on the input side in sharpening of attention toward relevant stimuli; and on the output side, in decreasing extraneous responses and greater precision of relevant movements. The operation of contrast as a function of surround inhibition has been detailed for the somesthetic system (Mountcastle, 1961), visual system (Hubel and Wiesel, 1962), and audition (Whitfield, 1965).

There is evidence that this repetitive synchronous excitation of cortical cells is dependent upon cholinergic pathways approaching the pyramidal cells of layer V. These pathways provide the final stage in the ascending reticular activating system arising from the tegmental and reticuli nuclei of the brain stem (Montplaisir, 1975; Shute and Lewis, 1967). Direct stimulation of the mesencephalic reticular formation enhances the release of acetylcholine and is correlated with an EEG activation pattern (Celesia and Jasper, 1966).

Behaviorally, the importance of the reticular activating system in the consolidation process has been detailed by Block and his colleagues (Block, 1970). They showed that direct reticular stimulation, when applied immediately after registration of information, considerably facilitates learning; the effect is less when the stimulation is delayed until 90 sec after the learning trial. Also, under certain conditions, post-trial reticular stimulation annuls the effect of fluothane anesthesia which, by itself, prevents consolidation.

Central administration of norepinephrine in animals (Stein, Belluzzi, and Wise, 1975) and systemic amphetamines in humans (Hurst et al., 1969) enhances memory. An active site for cortical arousal by amphetamines is in the midbrain (Masamoto, Bost, and Himwich, 1971). With the evidence from amphetamine administration in LD children, one possibility that presents itself is an abnormality in norepinephrine operation at the subcortical level. This may be partly the case or it may be significant in certain cases, but the important inference that could be drawn from the behavioral data is that there was not a deficit in arousal per se, but in the focusing of the arousal at the cortex.

As already noted, the final stage in the ascending reticular activating system is cholinergic. With the exception of its nicotinic action on Renshaw cells, the effects of acetylcholine (ACh) on neurons in the cortex has a slow onset and offset, not suitable for rapid "detonation" transmission, but functional in the modulation of the excitability of cortical input cells (Krnjevic, 1969). The early work of Dempsey and his colleagues (Chatfield and Dempsey, 1942; Morrison and Dempsey, 1943) reported that repetitive excitation after single stimulation of a peripheral nerve was greatly increased after application of ACh to the cortex of cats. This work has been extended by Krnjevic and Phillis (1965), who found that ACh enhances rhythmic after-discharge following sensory volleys, and by Spehlman (1971), who found that ACh facilitates the firing rate of cortical units activated by reticular stimulation.

A series of animal studies have shown that learning may be impaired by drugs that inhibit and facilitated by drugs that increase ACh action. Atropine blocks the cortical postsynaptic effects of ACh release and induces a slow-wave, high-voltage EEG pattern. Although behaviorally there is no concomitant appearance of drowsiness or sleep, atropine does affect learning. It depressed the rat's performance of learned avoidance responses (Herz, 1959) and auditory discrimination learning (Michelson, 1961), but in both only when administered in the early stages of training. Other impaired tasks include successive discrimination learning (Whitehouse, 1964) and learned alternation and complex multiple-choice discrimination (Carlton, 1963). On the other hand, physostigmine, which increases ACh action, facilitated one-trial avoidance by rats when administered a few minutes before training trials (Bures, Bohdanecky, and Weiss, 1962). It also improved the learning of a Lashley III maze when given 30 sec after each daily trial (Stratton and Petrinovich, 1963).

At the human level, the anticholinergic scopolamine has marked effects on attention and the storing of new information (Ostfeld, Machme, and Unna, 1960; Safer and Allen, 1971). Perhaps a better possibility for mechanism in the learning disabled child is an abnormality in acetylcholine operation at the cortical level. Or there may be a number of other ways in which this complicated cortical circuitry may become deficient. We simply do not know now.

SUMMARY

In at least one subgrouping of the broad classification "learning disability," a primary deficit in focused arousal is hypothesized. The behavioral referents for this high-order concept include short attention span, poor concentration, and performance decrements on a wide range of reaction-time, perceptual motor, sensory discrimination, vigilance, and memory tasks. Of equal significance, focusing arousal on relevant associations and sequencing is an important part of the processing in the development of motor, language, and reading skills.

Focused arousal, referring only to selective facilitatory functions, is distinguished from attention, which must include both incremental inhibitory and match¬mismatch processing. This distinction is important because it allows one to specify more definitively the brain mechanisms involved, and thus the abnormality.

Autonomic peripheral and central electrical potential measures of arousal indicate that learning disability children, as compared with normal controls, show a good deal of lability and an inability to mobilize or focus arousal on relevant stimuli in specific tasks. Amphetamines help the appropriate learning disability child to fix and maintain his attention so that he can learn and perform more effectively.

The problem with the learning disability child is that he cannot focus arousal—as efficiently as his normal peer—in order to maintain sequences in short-term store and fix memories in long-term store. A narrow frequency band in the EEG, centering at 40 Hz, reflects this limited cortical excitability or focused arousal, "optimal" for consolidation into long-term store.

With computer analysis and control for muscle artifacts, learning disability children, as compared with normal controls, showed significant decrements in 40 Hz in parietal regions during problem solving, as compared with bordering EEG frequencies and control conditions.

The brain mechanisms specified for the generation of this rhythm depend upon repetitive synchronous excitation of cortical cells as a property of recurrent inhibition. The latter is set up by cortical interactions with the cholinergic pathways of the ascending reticular activating system. A possible abnormal mechanism in the learning-disabled child might be in acetylcholine operation at the cortical level or there may be other ways in which this complicated circuitry may become deficient.

ACKNOWLEDGMENTS

I would like to acknowledge the collaboration of Dr. Lyllian Hix in the computer analysis and the subject testing and EEG recording with the help of Mary Ellen Hayden and Patricia Johnson, and also William Ellis for technical assistance.

Psychophysiological Study of Methylphenidate Responders and Nonresponders

H. Bruce Ferguson,
Suzanne Simpson, and Ronald L. Trites

Grinspoon and Singer (1973) have argued that, despite the large research literature, the etiology and physiological mechanisms of hyperkinesis are no better understood than when Laufer and Denhoff (1957) proposed an organic basis for the syndrome. Furthermore, our ignorance of the mechanisms underlying treatment with stimulant drugs, together with the inability to reliably predict drug response, has come under repeated attack (Fish, 1971; Grinspoon and Singer, 1973; Walker, 1974). However, newly developed research approaches using psychophysiological measures promise to shed more light on both of these issues.

Much of the momentum in the present research approach originated with Wender's (1971, 1973b) speculations that hyperactive (or minimal brain dysfunction, MBD) children are underaroused. This proposal contradicted the traditional concept of these children being overaroused and hyperreactive. The experimental evidence accumulated thus far, combined with the widespread "good" response to stimulant medication, suggests that Wender's postulated centrally mediated underarousal may apply to some hyperactive children.

The first step is to operationalize "arousal" in terms of selected psychophysiological measures. Initial investigations contrasted hyperactive and normal samples. Satterfield and Dawson (1971) reported that hyperactive children had lower basal skin conductance (SC) and gave fewer and smaller SC orienting responses (ORs) to tones. Cohen and Douglas (1972) found a similar lack of tonic and phasic SC responsivity in hyperactive

This study was part of a thesis submitted by Suzanne Simpson in partial fulfillment of the requirements for the Master of Arts degree at Carleton University.

children engaged in a task but no difference when no task was involved. Satterfield et al. (1973) reported that cortical evoked potentials to auditory stimuli showed lower amplitude and longer latencies for MBD than for normal boys. Buchsbaum and Wender (1973) also found reliable differences in the cortical evoked potentials of MBD and normal boys to visual flash stimuli but in the opposite direction, i.e., higher amplitude and shorter latencies for MBD subjects. They argued that MBD children typically showed immature patterns of evoked potential responding. Recent reports by Sroufe et al. (1973) and Spring et al. (1974) have provided additional evidence that hyperactive children are physiologically less responsive than normals. There are obvious contradictions in the evidence; however, a clear definition of physiological differences between hyperactive and normal subjects would represent an important advance in the search for mechanisms to explain the syndrome.

Comparisons also have been made between hyperactive children whose responses to stimulant drugs differed. Satterfield et al. (1972) studied 31 "hyperkinetic" boys and compared the six "best responders" to methylphenidate treatment with the five "worst responders." Off the drug, EEG measures indicated that the good responders were underaroused in comparison to the worst responders. When methylphenidate was administered, the best responders showed an increase in EEG arousal while the worst responders tended to show a decrease. Although there are difficulties with this study, it pointed the way to a potentially productive research strategy. Buchsbaum and Wender (1973) compared the average evoked cortical responses of MBD subjects who were "responders" and "nonresponders" to amphetamine treatment. Off the drug, responders showed patterns of evoked potential responding that tended to deviate from the norm more than those of the nonresponders. While taking amphetamine, the responders became more like normals while the nonresponders moved in the opposite direction. In another preliminary study, Knopp et al. (1973) examined the extent of pupillary contraction to a light stimulus before and after a test dose of amphetamine. They tentatively differentiated the 22 "hyperkinetic" children into four groups: "hypoaroused responders" (23%); "physiologically paradoxical responders" (36%); "physiologically normal nonresponders" (27%); and a "worse" group (9%). This pupillary response measure also showed some promise of being a useful predictor of the children's clinical response to chronic administration of amphetamine.

While the evidence is not without conflicts and methodological problems, the following tentative hypotheses were constructed to provide direction for the present study: (1) At least some subset of hyperactive (MBD, hyperkinetic) children are underaroused compared to normal controls. (2) Two subgroups of hyperactive responders and nonresponders to stimulant drug treatment may be differentiated on the basis of psychophysiological measures. (3) It may be possible to predict response to drug treatment from psychophysiological measures taken before and after a trial dose.

The present study was designed to examine differences in arousal levels between hyperactive "good" and "poor" responders to methylphenidate and a control group of nonhyperactive reading-disabled children. Arousal levels were assessed by comparing basal levels of heart rate (HR) and skin conductance (SC) both at rest and during a reaction-time (RT) task. Level of physiological responsivity was examined by measuring orienting responses to signal and nonsignal tones. In addition, the effects of loud white noise on arousal levels and task performance were assessed. This latter manipulation was prompted by Berlyne and Lewis' (1963) report that loud white noise raised arousal levels (decreased skin resistance).

METHOD

The subjects (Ss) were boys from 7 to 12 years of age who had been referred to the Neuropsychology Laboratory, Royal Ottawa Hospital for assessment. "Good" (GDRs) and "poor" (PDRs) responders to methylphenidate treatment were selected from the files of diagnosed hyperactive children. The judgment as to drug response was made by parents, physician, or both. The GDRs were taken off methylphenidate one week before being tested. The reading-disability (RD) group was screened to rule out any history of hyperactivity. An effort was made to exclude children with histories of neurological problems. However, the RD group had one S having had febrile convulsions while each hyperactive group had one epileptic and one child who had suffered a traumatic head injury resulting in seizures. The groups did not differ in age or IQ.

All Ss were tested in a single session. Skin resistance and HR were recorded throughout the experiment. Subjects were in the test situation at least 15 minutes before recording commenced. The test session consisted of five phases termed TASKs, each approximately 6 minutes in duration. To assess basal arousal levels at rest, Ss were instructed to sit quietly through TASKs 1–3. During each of these periods, three nonsignal tones (500 Hz, 85 db, linear scale) were presented for 5 seconds at random intervals. Between TASKs 3 and 4, Ss were introduced to the RT apparatus and instructed to respond "as fast as they could." The two-choice RT task incorporated a 500-Hz tone (85 db) as a warning signal and an 8.5-second preparatory interval. At the tone Ss depressed a start button until the response was signaled by the onset of a light directly behind the correct response button. Measures for start time and full reaction time were recorded in milliseconds. Each TASK level contained 12 trials with an intertrial interval of 21 seconds. Loud white noise (79 db, linear scale) was presented continuously during TASKs 2 and 5.

Basal HR was assessed by averaging five beats at 30-second intervals throughout the first three TASKs and by averaging the five beats preceding a point 4 seconds prior to the onset of the tone during the RT task. Heart rate ORs were assessed by subtracting the average of the three beats following tone onset from the average of the three beats preceding tone onset. To compare the HR orienting responses to random variability, an equivalent number of "dummy" ORs was scored 8 seconds before tone onset. During the RT task, HR anticipatory responses were scored by subtracting the rate for the beat occurring at light onset from the rate of the third antecedent beat.

Skin resistance measures were converted to conductance before being transformed and analyzed. Basal resistance was measured at the same time points as HR. Skin resistance ORs were measured by scoring the maximum and minimum resistance as they occurred in the period 0.5—4 seconds after tone onset. These measures were converted to conductance and a difference score was obtained by subtracting the first from the second. These change scores were then transformed to range-corrected difference scores (Lykken and Venables, 1971). Skin conductance "dummy" ORs were scored at the same points as those for HR. During the RT task, SC orienting responses to the warning tone were measured.

RESULTS

Basal measures (TASKs 1—5), ORs (TASKs 1—3), and RT task measures (TASKs 4 and 5) were analyzed separately using multivariate analyses of variance. In addition, since all designs involved within-subject repeated measures, a specialized analysis described by McCall and Appelbaum (1973) was used.

Basal Measures

Each of the TASKs was divided into three blocks (TIME). To overcome heterogeneity of within-group variances, the basal SC measures were transformed into natural logarithm scores for analysis.

There were no significant group effects. Both the TIME effect and the TIME X TASK interaction were significant at the multivariate level. Interpreting the results at the univariate level, a significant contrast for HR indicated that basal rate increased during the average of TASK 2 but did not change across TIME for TASKs 1 and 3.

Significant contrasts at the univariate level indicated that basal SC decreased over time for TASKs 1–3 while during the RT phases (TASKs 4 and 5) basal SC increased.

The TASK effect was significant at the multivariate level and for several HR and SC contrasts at the univariate level. Basal HR during rest (TASKs 1–3) was higher than during the RT task (TASKs 4 and 5). Within these groupings HR was lower for TASK 1 than TASK 3 and lower for TASK 4 than TASK 5. Basal SC was lower during TASK 2 than the average of TASKs 1 and 3 and lower during TASK 4 than TASK 5.

In summary, there were no group differences evident. The two indices of arousal level showed different patterns. Heart rate was faster in the resting phases than in the on-task situation. Basal SC decreased while Ss were at rest but increased with involvement in the task. While subjects were resting, white noise increased basal HR and depressed basal SC. When white noise was presented during task performance basal levels of both measures were elevated.

Orienting Response Measures

The HR and SC difference scores were first compared to their corresponding "dummy" ORs. The OR "dummy" factor was significant at the multivariate level and for both HR and SC at the univariate level. Thus, the ORs for both measures were significant phenomena.

When the HR and SC orienting responses were analyzed separately, there were no significant group effects. There was a significant multivariate TASK effect but at the univariate level only two SC contrasts were significant. These indicated that SC orienting responses were larger during TASK 1 than TASK 3 and the ORs for TASK 1 and 3 averaged were larger than those for TASK 2.

These results indicated that SC orienting responses habituated across the three levels of TASK. Since habituation may have masked differences between groups, SC orienting responses for TASK 1 alone were analyzed. A significant overall correlation between OR magnitude and prestimulus skin conductance was eliminated by a natural logarithm transformation; however, when checked separately for each group, the correlation remained significant for the GDRs. The analysis revealed a significant GROUP effect. Paired comparisons revealed that the GDRs had smaller ORs than the PDRs. Thus there is tentative evidence that GDRs are less responsive than PDRs on the SC measure. This parallels the finding of Spring et al. (1974) for a hyperactive good responder versus normal control comparison. It is of interest that both group differences and habituation were present only in the SC responses.

Reaction-Time Task Measures

In this analysis the dependent measures were the start RT scores, the full RT scores, the HR anticipatory differences, and the SC difference scores. Only the last 10 trials of TASK were scored. These were divided into two equal blocks and analyzed as a factor labeled TRIALS. Reaction time scores were transformed into common logarithms in an attempt to satisfy the normality assumption.

At the multivariate level, only the TASK effect was significant. Full RT was significant at the univariate level. Consideration of the significant contrasts indicated that the full RTs were faster for TASK 4 than TASK 5. The main effects for TRIALS and Groups were significant at the univariate level for full RT but not the multivariate level. The former reflected the faster responses for the first half of each level of TASK. Paired-comparison follow-up of the Group effect revealed that the GDRs showed faster full reaction times than the PDRs. A posteriori analysis of movement RTs (full RT minus start RT) duplicated the results for full RT.

To test the hypothesis that group differences in motor coordination may have accounted for the RT results, the full RT scores were reanalyzed with three speed and coordination measures from the neuropsychological test battery as covariates. Adjusting for all three covariates together or one at a time did not change the significance of the Group effect. No significant differences were found for the HR anticipatory responses or the SC orienting responses to the warning tone.

Thus the on-task results showed no evidence of group differences in physiological responsivity to the signal stimuli of the RT task. There was, however, some evidence that the PDRs did not perform as well on the RT task as the GDRs.

DISCUSSION

This study extensively examined SC and HR indicators of resting and on-task arousal levels in "good" drug responders, "poor" drug responders, and boys with reading problems. No consistent pattern of group differences emerged. The sole significant finding was that the hyperactive "good" responders gave lower-amplitude SC orienting responses to the first non-signal tones than did the "poor" responders. This difference in responsivity is consistent with the interpretation of Satterfield et al. (1972) that responders are underaroused compared to nonresponders. Unfortunately, statistical problems necessitated that the present result be interpreted with caution. The failure to find basal level on-task arousal differences between either hyperactive group and controls contradicts earlier studies (Satterfield and Dawson, 1971; Cohen and Douglas, 1972; Spring et al., 1974). White noise did not alter group relationships on the arousal measures and its overall effect was ambiguous. When white noise accompanied the RT task, both basal HR and SC increased. However, both measures had started to increase during the preceding task and RT performance deteriorated over time, as Cohen and Douglas (1972) had found. This suggests that the increased arousal measures shown for Task 5 probably result from a factor such as fatigue rather than being caused by the white noise itself.

In the RT task, there was some evidence that the "good" responders were faster than the "poor" responders. Also, performance clearly deteriorated over time in all groups. The lack of hyperactive–control group differences failed to replicate the results of Cohen and Douglas (1972). In addition, previous work in our laboratory had found normal controls to be faster than hyperactives on the task used in this study. The use of different control groups may account for the disparity between present and previous findings.

Our general failure to find consistent group effects in arousal measures is surprising. A major difference between this and previous studies was the method of group definition. Satterfield et al. (1972) and Buchsbaum and Wender (1973) used behavior rating measures evaluating response to drug treatment to divide subjects into responder and nonresponder groups. Subjects in this study were assigned to groups on the basis of clinical histories. Furthermore, a clinic control group of reading-disabled boys was used in this experiment. While the use of a clinic group is essential to control for such factors as testing experience, it may account for our failure to find hyperactive–control differences. Future investigations should include both clinic and normal control samples. Finally, our study can be critized on the grounds of the small group sizes. However, small group sizes have been typical of past studies and the present nonsignificant differences were often in directions other than those predicted. Thus inadequate group size does not appear to explain lack of significant differences.

Close examination of the subjects' medical histories produced interesting results. Appropriate events in subjects' lives were categorized as physical (e.g., eye operation) or emotional (e.g., divorce, death of a parent) traumas. More of the reading-disability group had experienced physical trauma, while significantly more "poor" responders had emotional or emotional and physical traumas. Fewer of the "good" responders experienced traumas of any kind. This suggests that the "poor" responders' hyperactivity might have had a psychological rather than an organic basis. This analysis was a posteriori and, therefore, the results are merely suggestive, but they certainly merit follow-up work.

These results, taken with the sum of the experimental findings to this time, suggest that theories proposing generalized arousal level differences between hyperatives and normals, or between subgroups of hyperactive children, may be oversimplifications. In fact, inconsistencies in the reported psychophysiological data question the utility of such a vaguely defined dimension as arousal in classifying hyperactive children. However, if differences in arousal level do exist, much more needs to be specified about the conditions under which they can be measured before such differences can be used as a basis for speculating about altered physiological mechanisms or deficits in psychological function. This goal requires that in the future investigators be extremely careful in the definition of subject groups and include a range of experimental tasks.

A number of our observations on data treatment and analysis warrant mention. The first relates to the transformation of the TASK 1 SC orienting responses in order to statistically eliminate the significant relationship between OR amplitude and prestimulus level of SC. This procedure was successful for the overall relationship but the correlation remained significant for one group. The remaining correlation has an uncertain effect on the validity of the subsequent analysis. It does indicate that similar individual group checks should be carried out as well as a correlation across all subjects.

The remaining points relate to the choice of analytic techniques. The specialized analysis developed by McCall and Appelbaum (1973), and used in this study, was complex and time consuming. Using this method, each repeated measures factor (k levels) is analyzed by selecting $k - 1$ orthogonal contrasts and using these to generate $k - 1$ new dependent variables. These new dependent variables are then analyzed by multivariate analysis of variance techniques. The model can readily be extended to cases having more than one within-subject factor and more than one dependent measure. This method has the advantage of avoiding the positive bias produced by violation of the assumption of homogeneity of covariance between levels of the within-subjects factors. Also, it permits exact probability determination rather than applying corrections that may be too conservative.

The specialized analysis used here demonstrates the value of more general multivariate statistical analysis to psychophysiological studies. Psychophysiological experiments often have involved measurement of several related dependent variables. Typically each dependent variable has been subjected to a separate univariate analysis. This approach greatly enhances the probability of obtaining spurious significance. The multivariate analysis of variance controls experiment-wise error rate for correlated dependent measures considered simultaneously. For those interested in prediction, this technique also determines appropriate weights for combining a set of dependent variables to maximize correct assignment to designated clinical groups.

Multivariate statistical procedures have been available for some time. A variety of texts and computer programs are available for each technique. Van Egeren (1973) provided psychophysiologists with an excellent introduction to the rationale and application of several methods (multivariate analysis of variance, canonical correlation analysis, factor analysis). He emphasized the opportunity these statistical methods hold for the study of both the structural relationships between dependent measures and the functional relationships between independent and dependent variables. Such an approach might allow us to set aside ill-defined concepts such as "arousal" and provide us with a logic and mathematics to construct relationships between specified experimental conditions and dependent variables arising from complex and interdependent physiological response systems. Certainly these analytic tools hold potential value for our attempt to establish the important differences between groups of hyperactive children and the conditions necessary to measure these differences.

Physiological Responses in Intrasensory and Intersensory Integration of Auditory and Visual Signals by Normal and Deficit Readers

Maureen Julianne Levine

The most consistent overall finding from the literature on sensory integration suggests that children with reading deficits have a less efficient capacity to integrate information from auditory and visual channels than do normal readers (Birch, 1962; Senf and Freundl, 1971; Shipley and Jones, 1969). A number of interpretations have been offered to explain these results in reading deficient groups: notably, a failure of dominant visual system; dominance of auditory over visual modality; and an inability to reject auditory distraction with visual stimuli. A common feature of these results is that the attentional element is inferred from other measured variables. Attention would be expected to be functional in these studies since observing the relevant stimulus parameters and approaching the correct cue in that dimension are minimum requisites for processing of sensory information. An understanding of the function of attention in the study of sensory integration as related to reading problems would require that this factor be independently and directly estimated.

A neurophysiological theory that elucidates the physiological parameters of attention in information processing has been formulated by Sokolov (1963). This theory proposes that reaction to a stimulus elicits a cortical, neuronal model of the stimulus parameters. A subsequent stimulus is compared to the neuronal model and if a match exists then response decrement occurs, whereas a lack of correspondence produces the orienting response. Sokolov's theory has generated a substantial body of psychophysiological investigations that have produced considerable evidence that attentional and cognitive factors appear to be associated with physiological changes.

Cardiovascular and electrodermal responses to stimulation have been the focus of a number of recent investigations. In these studies heart rate deceleration and increased galvanic skin responses (GSR) have been reported to occur during stimulus presentation (Lacey et al., 1963). An extensive review of the experimental evidence related to heart rate change shows that heart rate deceleration occurs with presentation of nonpainful stimuli (Graham and Clifton, 1966). Heart rate acceleration and GSR responsivity were also found to occur in association with cognitive activity (Steele and Lewis, 1968). Specifically, these studies suggest that heart rate deceleration and GSR responsivity will occur during periods of stimulus presentation, whereas heart rate acceleration and GSR responsivity take place during periods of recall or cognitive activity. As noted, previous work on sensory integration in reading deficiencies, the theoretical models of which incorporated the attentional factor, generally inferred its estimation from other variables. In view of the psychophysiological findings, the concomitant determination of physiological variables during the processing and recall of bisensory integration tasks should provide a direct estimate of the attentional factor in children with reading problems. The confounding variable of linguistic competence in sensory integration studies also supports the view that psychophysiological paradigms be used with children having linguistic incompetence (Allen and Fitzgerald, 1974).

Physiological and reading deficit models of attention and cognitive processing that have been formulated recently have generally overlooked differences in subjects who are in the normal IQ range. In the present study, subject differentiation was obtained on the basis of a reading classification scheme (Rabinovitch et al., 1954) that has been incorporated into a quantitative measure of visual-motor stability, the Minnesota-Percepto Diagnostic Test (MPD; Fuller, 1969). This test was used to classify the reading-deficient group into two of the three reading constructs, primary and secondary, proposed by Rabinovitch. Judgment of visual-motor stability is based on the degree of rotation and distortion that occurs when a subject reproduces Wertheimer designs (Bender, 1938). On the MPD test, normal and primary readers rotate $25°$ or less, secondary readers rotate figures $26°$ to $54°$ and the third classification, organic readers, more than $55°$. Primary readers, who score in the normal range, are considered to have adequate visual motor functions. Secondary readers produce a moderate degree of rotation and distortion on the MPD test and experience defects in visual motor stability. The capacity to read is impaired in both groups, primary and secondary readers. The third reading classification group, organic readers, appear to have severe problems in visual motor stability. Rotation and distortions scores on the MPD are extremely high, well beyond that expected for age and IQ values. The organic group differs significantly from primary and secondary groups on all measures of performance (Fuller, 1974) and the case history of these children is suggestive of neurological damage. In view of the severity of the performance of organic readers, an experimental investigation would have to be designed specifically to fit their low tolerance level. Therefore, children classified as organic readers were not included, and only primary and secondary categories were subject to investigation in the present study.

A fruitful approach for the investigation of bisensory integration in deficit readers appears to be one that incorporates the results from the three areas discussed. The study reported in this paper was designed to reflect such an approach by comparing the psychophysiological parameters of attention involved in the processing and recall of bisensory tasks in groups of deficient readers classified as primary and secondary readers and in a control group of normal readers.

METHOD

Subjects

The subjects were 48 males with a mean age of 11 years (range 9–13 years) and a mean IQ of 112 (range 90–135 IQ). Of the total sample, 16 children who were reading at expected grade level or above composed the control group of normal readers (NR). The remaining 32 children had a reading level of one or more years below expected grade level for age and IQ (mean reading lag = 3.0 grades). Of these, 16 met the criteria for primary readers group (PRD) and 16 met the criteria for secondary readers (SRD). Statistical summary of ages and IQ of reading classification groups is shown in Table 1.

Procedure

In the experiment proper, the child was asked to sit in front of a Bell & Howell Language Master. The stimulus display area and procedures were described to the child and the electrodes were attached. All electrodes were applied with sodium chloride electrode paste. Heart rate was recorded from standard leads I, II, and III (active electrodes on left arm and right wrist and ground electrodes on left leg). EKG-R waves were used to trigger input signals to the cardiotach, which measured the rate as the reciprocal of the average R-R time interval. The change in GSR was measured using the "Record AC" mode of the E & M physiograph

Table 1. Statistical Summary of the Ages and IQ of the Reading Classification Group and for Total Sample

| Reading Group | N | Chronological Age | | | Performance IQ[a] | | |
		Mean	Range	SD	Mean	Range	SD
Normals	16	11 yr, 3 mo	9–13 yr	12.6 mo	119	99–133	11.3
Primary	16	11 yr, 5 mo	9–13 yr	13.9 mo	106	90–135	13.8
Secondary	16	11 yr, 0 mo	9–13 yr	12.0 mo	111	92–128	7.8
Total	48	11 yr, 2 mo	9–13 yr	12.9 mo	112	90–135	11.2

[a]Wechsler Intelligence Scale for Children Performance Scales were administered to total sample.

preamplifier. A constant DC of 20 μA was applied across the electrodes attached to finger and wrist. Changes in resistance amplitude and frequency were recorded on a strip chart. Responses of resistance change of 750 ohms or more were counted. Continuous monitoring of cardiac acitivity and GSR responsivity was maintained throughout the entire experiment.

Experimental Conditions

Auditory and visual stimulus pairs composed of digits that incorporated intersensory and intrasensory conditions were administered simultaneously. The same digits were not paired and the presentation was balanced using a Latin square design.

Eight experimental conditions (four intersensory and four intrasensory) that required paired and serial verbal recall with alteration of first recalled modality (auditory or visual) were used. Four different tasks were employed in the intersensory (four visual and auditory) conditions using verbal recall. The tasks used in the four intrasensory (two visual and two auditory) conditions paralleled those in the intersensory conditions. All subjects participated in the same intersensory and intrasensory conditions.

Ten trials of each of the eight experimental conditions (four intersensory and four intrasensory) were given. Each trial was divided into three 6-second periods, preperiod, stimulus presentation, and recall. On each trial, three pairs of stimuli were presented 2 seconds apart during stimulus period. A three-variable multifactor design with repeated measures on two variables was chosen for all the experiments (Winer, 1962, p. 319).

RESULTS AND DISCUSSION

The results of the present study are consistent with previous measurable physiological changes that occur under specific conditions indicative of attentional processes. Both heart rate deceleration and heart rate variability are observed to accompany an increase in attention (Porges, 1972). The cardiovascular data indicate that heart rate deceleration and heart rate variability are attributes of the differences in attentional mechanisms found among the reading classification groups used in this experiment. As shown in Figure 1, heart rate deceleration occurred only in the normal readers groups. The absence of heart rate deceleration in deficient readers groups is evidence of a defective attentional mechanism.

However, a high level of attention that is ineffective is indicated for the secondary readers group by the significant decrease in heart rate

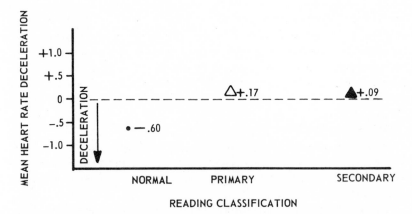

Figure 1. Mean heart rate deceleration [from minimum HR (bpm) in preperiod] for reading classification groups for total data. •, normal readers; △, primary readers; ▲, secondary readers.

variability as shown in Figure 2. The analysis of the data, presented in Figure 2, showed that heart rate variability decreases from preperiod to stimulus period and then increases in recall period for intersensory conditions for the total sample, but only the secondary reading group followed this pattern. An increase in heart rate variability in the recall period from stimulus period was found in the normal readers group and secondary readers group.

The effects of the tasks on heart rate variability for the reading classification groups are presented in Figure 3. Change in heart rate variability occurred in normal readers across the tasks, but not in the primary or secondary readers group.

Consideration of these results in association with the characteristic of the reading classification groups suggests that a regulatory mechanism controls the physiological parameters of attention and produces an optimal level that facilitates cognitive processing.

The secondary readers group, whose etiology contains an element of emotional stress, apparently overattend during stimulus presentation. Although this group can relax attention during the recall period, the excessive attention during stimulus presentation prevents the early initiation of cognitive processing (in stimulus period).

In the primary readers group, a stable level of heart rate variability across the periods occurred with no evidence of heart rate deceleration. These results suggest that the primary readers do not attend at a sufficient level to promote adequate information processing.

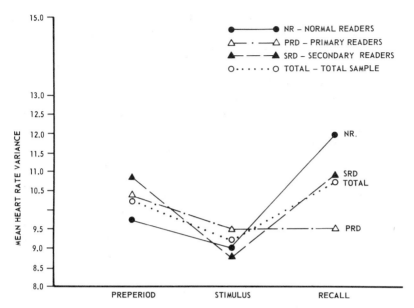

Figure 2. Mean heart rate variability of reading classification across periods for intersensory tasks.

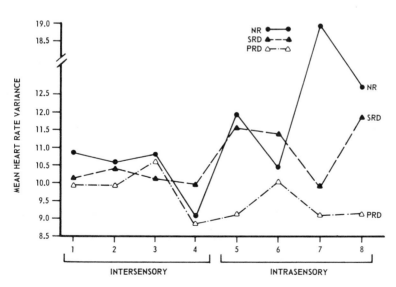

Figure 3. The effect of tasks on the mean heart rate variability of the three reading classifications. NR, normal readers; SRD, secondary readers; PRD, primary readers.

The capacity for adjustment of attention levels was present in the normal readers group since greater plasticity in heart rate variability across all experimental conditions was found. The normal readers group whose heart rate variability increased in recall can apparently "switch off" attention to pursue cognition without the disturbing interference of attention. The normal readers group maintain a moderate and apparently adequate attentional level during stimulus presentation and initiate cognitive activity during this period. These subjects then relax the attentional elements during the recall period for more effective, final cognitive processing.

Stress or increased cognitive activity is each interpreted in the literature to result in electrodermal responsivity. In the present study, for the total sample, increased GSR activity was obtained for all the tasks during the recall period, but not for the stimulus period. These results, considered with the finding of no heart rate acceleration during recall periods, suggest that the increased GSR may be due to cognitive activity rather than stress during this period. Thus, the expected increased cognitive activity was found for all subjects in the recall period. As illustrated in Figure 4, greater capacity of the normal readers group to regulate levels of physiological activity was observed since GSR responsivity for intrasensory, auditory tasks was higher than for the intrasensory, visual ones. Similar capacity for adjustment was not indicated for the deficient readers group.

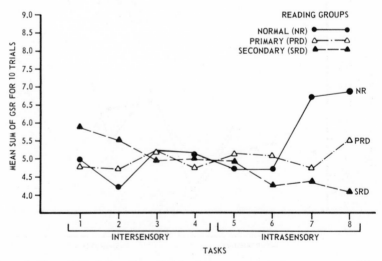

Figure 4. Mean GSR for reading classification groups across intersensory and intrasensory tasks.

As expected, the level of recall errors was related to the reading classification groups in support of the view that reading ability is dependent upon a complex set of attentional and cognitive factors. As shown in Figure 5, the mean total errors for the secondary reader group exceeded those of the normal and primary readers group and the mean errors of the primary group exceeded those of the normal readers. These results support the validity of the reading classification system (Rabinovitch et al., 1954) for differentiating groups of deficit readers. Gross errors were scored for omission of correct digit or substitution by another digit, and order errors were scored for digits properly recalled but out of sequence. Interchange errors were counted for pairs of digits properly recalled, but in which inversion occurred, i.e., in a VA pair, the auditory digit was recalled as a visual digit. Comparison of intersensory and intrasensory conditions for mean, gross, and order errors showed that more errors of both types occurred in intrasensory conditions than in intersensory ones. These results do not necessarily contradict the frequently reported findings in the literature that the performance of deficit readers is inferior on inter-sensory tasks since most of the studies reviewed (Berry, 1967; Birch and Belmont, 1964; Senf and Freundl, 1971) did not incorporate an intra-sensory comparative base in their experimental designs.

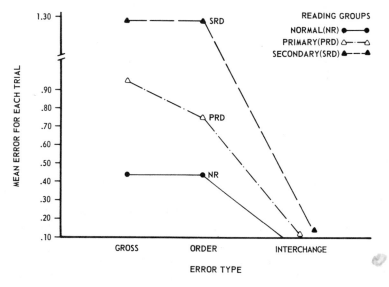

Figure 5. Mean errors of reading classification groups across error types (gross, order, and interchange).

In the treatment of intersensory tasks, the error types, gross and order, were analyzed for modality (auditory or visual) type. Mean errors of reading classification groups across error types in intersensory tasks are shown in Figure 6. The analysis of variance indicated that the normal readers group made fewer errors than both reading-deficit groups across all error types except for visual and auditory order errors, where differences were not significant between normal and primary readers.

The order errors reflect an incapacity to use cues to process a sequential memory task. For the pairing tasks, the secondary readers group made fewer intrasensory than intersensory gross errors, indicating modality confounding, but made the same amount of order errors in both intrasensory and intersensory experimental conditions, whereas the normal and primary readers made fewer order than gross errors on intrasensory tasks. The secondary readers appear to have a more deficient capability for processing visual information and the sequential recall of auditory and visual stimuli. Whether these are separate, independent factors or are related to the quality of attentivity–cognitive interaction has not been determined in the present study.

Pribram and McGuinness (1975) in a recent review proposed that psychophysiological and neuropsychological data support a model of interacting neural systems that controls attentional components identified as arousal, activation, and effort. Accordingly, arousal, the phasic (initial) response to stimuli, is monitored by a reciprocal mechanism in the amygdala. The second control system operates in the basal ganglia of the forebrain and regulates activation, a readiness response. The third process, centered in the hippocampus, coordinates the amygdala and basal ganglia and produces cortical representation defined as state changes, set, and attitude, all of which demand the process of effort.

A model that is analogous to the three factors (arousal, activation, and effort) of Pribram and McGuinness has been formulated to explain the results of the present study. An attentional parameter is functional during the initial stimulus presentation. A cognitive parameter that reaches its maximum during recall is impeded in its effectiveness if the attention factor is inadequate, excessive, or is not sufficiently relaxed after the encoding of the stimulus cues. The "activation" of the Pribram and McGuinness model would be approximated here by the interaction of the attention and cognition parameter. The optimum condition for task performance is related to quality of the factors, the capacity for fine tuning of both factors, and the "start-up" of cognition before the completion of the stimulus period.

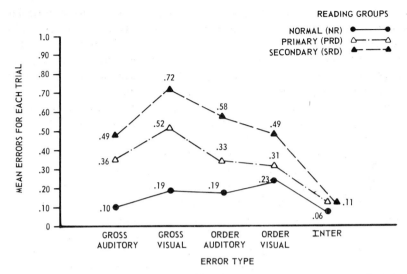

Figure 6. Mean errors of reading classification groups across error types in intersensory tasks.

Physiological support for the interaction phenomena between attention and cognition is afforded by the observed findings in the study of Schell and Catania (1975) that greater sensory acuity was associated with heart rate deceleration, as well as the findings of Berdina et al. (1972) and Obrist, Webb, and Sutterer (1970) that somatic muscular activity is associated with cardiac responses. Berdina and his co-workers found that somatic muscular reactions increased with associated cardiac acceleration during mental activity. Obrist et al. (1970) found a decrease in task-irrelevant somatic activity with a concomitant decrease in heart rate in a study using reaction-time tasks with a foreperiod. The neuronal, structural models relating heart rate change and cortical activity are limited by the lack of an adequate functional element that deals directly with the quality of cognitive processing. The model presented below provides this element by proposing that the quality of cortical functioning is related to the level of available oxygen in the blood.

As noted, recent reports in the literature suggest that changes in heart rate that accompany stimulus processing and/or cognitive activity are associated with somatic muscular activity. In their review, Pribram and McGuinness have stated that work (energy utilization) occurs during cortical activity. Certainly, the "work" (energy utilization) by the cortical centers is negligible; however, the "work" done by the somatic muscular reactions is significant and measurable by cardiovascular techniques. On the basis of presently available evidence, it appears unlikely that anaerobic metabolism occurs in the cortical centers. Therefore, the level of available oxygen in the blood should directly effect cortical activity. This level would not change as the result of cortical activity since the amount used is negligible, but would be determined by the somatic muscular reactions, which are the major oxygen consumers during aerobic modes of metabolism. It would be of interest to determine if the large biosystems might switch to anaerobic modes during intensive mental activity to maintain a high level of available oxygen in the cortical centers. Alternatively, it is possible that increased availability of oxygen to the cortical centers may be afforded by the increased pumping action of the skeletal muscles. The significance of somatic muscular reaction for reading deficiencies is supported by the finding that poor readers have a weaker grip strength than normal readers (Doehring, 1968; Levine and Fuller, 1972).

In the present study, differences in psychophysiological parameters of attention in the processing and recall of sensory integration information have been found between reading-deficient and normal readers as well as between two reading-deficient groups, primary and secondary. A hypothetical model based on attentional and cognitive factors and their interaction is proposed. Whereas recent analysis of psychophysiological and neuropsychological data emphasizes structural, neural mechanisms, the present paper suggests oxygen metabolism as a valuable indicator of the source of the psychophysiological responses. Overall, there presently exists a substantial basis for the increased application of psychophysiological methodology to the elucidation of factors related to reading problems.

ACKNOWLEDGMENTS

This chapter is based on a dissertation submitted in partial fulfillment of the requirement for the Ph.D. degree in Psychology from Michigan State University under the direction of Hiram E. Fitzgerald. The author is most grateful to Dr. William Sleeper, Director of the Fancher School Reading Clinic, Mt. Pleasant, Michigan and to Dr. Leo Kipfmueller, Director of Central Michigan University Reading Clinic and the staff of both reading clinics for their generous cooperation. Presentation of the paper at the NATO Conference was supported by a Central Michigan University Faculty Research and Creative Endeavors grant.

Hypothesis for a Possible Biochemical Basis of Minimal Brain Dysfunction

Paul H. Wender

The syndrome of minimal brain dysfunction (MBD) bears a close relationship to and may perhaps include the syndrome of learning disabilities. It is not known exactly what MBD is. It is defined as a cluster of signs and symptoms with no known and specifiable underlying biological abnormality. The absence of a pathognomonic "lesion" is a characteristic it shares with many other psychiatric conditions which, there is good reason to believe, are genuine nosological entities. The absence of any defining symptomatic attributes and the absence of any underlying "basic" abnormality make the boundaries unclear; in many instances the diagnostic inclusion or exclusion of a particular individual is difficult.

MBD is one of a number of designations for a common behavioral syndrome of childhood for which a variety of other terms and phrases have previously been employed, including the hyperactive child syndrome, hyperactivity, hyperkinesis, minimal brain damage, minimal cerebral dysfunction, etc. Although the boundaries are, as mentioned, unclear, there is general consensus regarding the signs and symptoms of typical MBD children. These signs fall into two major realms: (1) behavioral and (2) perceptual and cognitive (learning disabilities). These signs occur in MBD children in all three logical combinations: (1) children with behavioral problems alone; (2) children with learning disabilities alone; (3) children with both behavioral problems and learning disabilities. The proportions of children falling into each of these three categories are not known.

A good summary of the behavioral abnormalities is given by Laufer and Denhoff (1957) in their description of the "Hyperkinetic Behavior Syndrome." Among the characteristic features described are: hyperactivity—"involuntary and constant over-activity that completely surpasses the normal . . . and may already be present during early infancy"; a short attention span and poor powers of concentration with the children generally being unable to persist for long in an activity whether at play or at school; impulsivity and "inability to delay gratification"—the child is described as "doing things on the spur of the moment, without thinking"; anhedonia—the child "despite the mother(s) best efforts is tense, unhappy and demanding"; "poor school work which seems to be a compound of problems in the visual motor perception (mentioned below) and concentration areas." In addition to the attentional deficit and the diminished ability to experience pleasure, there is another characteristic that has been found to be particularly prominent among MBD children and that deserves special emphasis: that is, their refractoriness to discipline of any sort. With regard to the latter, parents frequently state that attempting to make the child comply with the shoulds and shouldn'ts of ordinary family existence is an overwhelming task. Punishment is described as rolling off the child's back and reward as ineffective. The child thus refutes Skinner and Pavlov. The other area in which many MBD children manifest deficits is in perceptual-cognitive functioning. In excessive abbreviation, these deficits include problems with orientation in space (manifested by right—left confusion, by reversals in reading and writing and poor performance on the Bender Gestalt), difficulties in auditory discrimination (confusing similar sounds); difficulties in auditory synthesis (so that phonemes cannot be combined to sound out a word); and difficulties in transferring information from one sensory modality to another (e.g., recognizing equivalence between the printed Morse code and its sounding out).

Together with the two other combinations, perceptual-cognitive problems alone have been grouped under minimal brain dysfunction. In other words, by force of definition, learning disabilities have been included as one manifestation of MBD. Are there reasons for believing learning disabilities are related to the behavioral problems? Yes, but whether the evidence is sufficient is uncertain. The first piece of evidence comes from clinical observation and consists of the finding that perceptual cognitive problems and behavioral problems exist in the same individual with apparently greater than expected frequency. The second suggestive clinical finding is an apparently increased frequency of "pure dyslexia" among the sibs of children with behavioral problems. Moving in the opposite direction, one study (Hallgren, 1950), which began with dyslexic index cases, found an increased prevalence of oppositional, aggressive, restless, childish, labile behavior and concentration difficulties among the nondyslexic siblings. These data may be suggestive but they are certainly not conclusive. They suggest a relationship between the behavioral problems and learning disabilities; they do not prove it. Systematic family studies exploring both behavioral characteristics and learning disabilities must be carried out.

POSSIBLE CAUSES OF MBD

One of the major explanatory hints into the possible causes of MBD comes from an event that is now only of historical interest: the pandemic of Von Economo's encephalitis that occurred during and after World War I. This encephalitis produced a postencephalitic Parkinsonian syndrome in adults and a postencephalitic behavior disorder in children. The now 50-year-old descriptions of the postencephalitic behavior disorder sound very much like typical MBD. That a phenocopy of typical MBD could be produced by this viral infection is relevant. We know that the virus destroyed dopamine-containing neurons in adults and would tend to infer that it attacked similar neurons in children. If this were so, it is obviously unclear as to why different syndromes were caused in different age groups, but it does leave us with a suggestion that specific destruction of dopaminergic, or perhaps catecholaminergic, neurons will produce signs and symptoms of MBD. In succeeding years MBD was shown to be associated with a variety of agents that are noxious to growing brains, including head trauma, lead poisoning, various infections in infancy, and difficulties of pregnancy and delivery. Of these various organic noxae, perhaps the most interesting—for environmental reasons—is lead poisoning, which was associated with MBD many years ago and which has recently received revitalized interest. Lead poisoning is of theoretical interest because in experimental animals it produces damage to the basal ganglia, structures particularly rich in dopamine-containing neurons. The most interesting findings concerning the etiology of MBD are recent ones that strongly indict the role of genetic factors. Clinicians had long noted what seemed to be an increased prevalence of various forms of psychopathology among the parents of MBD children and what was certainly an increased probability of MBD-like behavior among their siblings. The increased frequency of psychopathology among parents of MBD children was documented by Cantwell (1975) who found an increased prevalence of sociopathy and alcoholism among the fathers and of hysteria among the mothers. Such an association between psychopathology in parent and offspring is obviously subject to two interpretations: that the disorder is transmitted psychogenically or that the disorder is transmitted genetically. Until recent years this recurring problem has been the bane of those who have tried to understand the causation of psychiatric illnesses. Recently, however, the technique of adoption has been employed to resolve the thorny nature—nurture dilemma and it has been applied to the area of MBD as well. There are two relevant studies. The first is that of Safer (1973), who studied full and half-siblings of "hyperactive" children all of whom had been placed in foster care. Of concern to Safer was that all of the subjects in his study had been subjected to a number of psychological and social traumata in the early years of life. Accordingly, it is possible that the siblings and the half-siblings of the hyperactive index cases would have shown an increased frequency of hyperactivity but that this increase was due solely to the psychological maltreatment that the index cases as well as the siblings and half-siblings had received in early years. Safer hypothesized that if there were a genetic component to "hyperactivity," he would find an increased frequency of hyperactive symptoms in the siblings of his hyperactive children and an increased but lesser degree of hyperactive symptoms among the half-siblings (because the full siblings share half their genetic complement with the index cases, whereas the half-siblings share only one-quarter of their genetic complement with the index case). Thus, the existence of full and half-siblings permitted him to distinguish between psychological traumata and genetic factors. Safer found that approximately 50% of the full siblings and 20% of the half-siblings of the hyperactive index cases in foster care had been independently diagnosed as hyperactive, a finding compatible with genetic transmission. Unfortunately, since all the children had been traumatized, such trauma may have raised the prevalence in the group of both full and half-siblings. Nonetheless, it indicates the existence of a genetic component. A complementary study was combined by Cantwell (1975). In this research design, one studies the parents of adopted hyperactive children and compares them with parents who had reared their own hyperactive children. In addition, one employs a nondisturbed control group, in Cantwell's case the parents of pediatric patients. What Cantwell found was, as mentioned, an increased prevalence of psychopathology in the natural parents of hyperactive children and a prevalence of psychopathology in the adoptive parents of hyperactive children that was the same as that of the pediatric controls. These data, taken together, support the hypothesis that at least some MBD children develop their disorder on a genetic basis.

CAUSATION BY BIOCHEMICAL DEFICIT

If MBD does occur on a genetic basis, what aspect of brain function is being genetically transmitted? Using a computer analogy, the genetically transmitted abnormality might be manifested either in the components (tubes, transistors, or neurons), the wiring, or the programs. Given our present neurological knowledge and techniques, one must hope that the genetic abnormality is in the elements. Furthermore, one must hope that the elements affected involve enzymes rather than protein structures. This is simply because we can much more easily measure enzymes and their products. In short, one hopes that the defects will be in enzymatic function in certain portions of the nervous system. To what evidence may we appeal in order to determine which enzymes might be involved? The first is the naturalistic evidence already cited relating to the effects of Von Economo's encephalitis and lead poisoning, both of which produced an MBD-like picture and both of which are associated with damage to dopamine-containing structures. Therefore, it is tenable that what is transmitted is a biochemical abnormality involving catecholaminergic functioning.

The second piece of evidence that suggests a biochemical deficit in certain MBD children is the response of such children to drugs. The present author used the argument of drug responsiveness frequently in the past, and is aware of its logical pitfalls. The response of cardiac failure to digitalis does not imply that heart failure is caused by an absence of normally present digitalis. The amelioration of pain by morphine does not imply that pain is produced by a deficiency in the body's normal secretion of morphine. On the other hand, of course, response of beri beri or pellagra to B vitamins or certain microcytic anemias to iron does tell us something about the etiology of these disorders. With this in mind, the nature of the response of MBD children to stimulant, and sometimes to antidepressant medication, should be examined: Is this response like that of pain to morphine or of pellagra to B vitamins? Anyone who has treated MBD children with these medications is aware that in an appreciable fraction of instances these medications produce very specific and dramatic effects. In these instances, drugs produce changes in behavior far more wide reaching than simply reducing motor activity and increasing attention. The effect of these drugs on some MBD children is remarkable: for the duration of the drug's action, these drugs can produce immediate psychological growth. During such periods the children may display more mature cognitive, social, and interpersonal behavior than they have ever shown. Such treatment response suggests the correction of abnormalities that lie at the beginning of the causal chain. What is particularly intriguing is that we now know something of the mechanism of action of these drugs, and from their similarities and differences can infer what the possible biochemical lesions might be in the brains of MBD children.

During the last 20 years, a mass of evidence has accumulated indicating that interneural transmission in the central nervous system is mediated by chemicals, so-called neurotransmitters. The evidence, which is still circumstantial and not direct, is that one cell (the presynaptic cell) transmits its impulses to the next cell (the postsynaptic cell) by releasing small amounts of chemicals, the neurotransmitters, which attach themselves to portions of the membrane of the second cell and cause it to fire. The impulse is terminated when the neurotransmitter is released from the second cell and either metabolized (broken down) or taken up by the first cell, which can then use the same chemical to transmit another impulse. The second finding of considerable importance is that there is "chemical coding" within the central nervous system. In different portions of the central nervous system, different chemicals are employed as neurotransmitters. Attention during the past twenty years has focused on a group of simple chemicals, used in perhaps 1% of the brain, which share a chemical attribute, the possession of a single amine group. This group of neurotransmitters is referred to as the monoamines and comprises serotonin, dopamine, and norepinephrine. One of the most exciting discoveries of recent years has been that of the mechanisms by which drugs effective in treating depression, mania, and schizophrenia, and drugs capable of producing psychosis act to influence functioning of nerve cells utilizing the monoamines as transmitters. This knowledge is still provisional but allows one to make certain inferences nonetheless. The stimulant drugs, the agents most effective in MBD children, probably act upon all three monoamines. They have multiple actions, causing the cells to release their stored monoamines, preventing their reuptake by the cell that has released them, and preventing the breakdown of stored monoamines in the releasing cells. All of these actions act to increase the amount that is released from the presynaptic cells and free to stimulate the postsynaptic cell. In addition, these drugs are probably chemical mimics of norepinephrine and dopamine, and have a direct action on the postsynaptic cell. The tricyclic antidepressants, the drugs most useful in treatment of physiological depressions in adults, have a simpler mechanism of action. It is believed that their efficacy is due to their prevention of the reuptake of norepinephrine and, for some compounds, serotonin as well, into the presynaptic cell. This leaves, so to speak, free monoamines "floating around" in the intersynaptic space and free to adhere to the postsynaptic membrane.

DRUG RESPONSE OF MBD CHILDREN

Mention has not been made of the issue, but it is apparent clinically that MBD children respond differentially to treatment with different drugs: One child responds better to one drug, another child to a second one. This suggests that there may be a number of, perhaps related, underlying biochemical lesions. That certainly is to be expected since there are a number of causal pathways that produce MBD such as familial transmission, brain damage, lead poisoning, etc. With this in mind, we now turn to the question of the inferences we can make concerning drug responsiveness. An appreciable fraction of MBD children respond better to stimulant medication than they do to tricyclic antidepressants. Since some do respond to the tricyclic antidepressants and of those some very well, we must assume this subgroup has some abnormality in the functional utilization of norepinephrine and/or serotonin. On the other hand, many MBD children respond appreciably better to stimulant medication than they do to treatment with the tricyclic antidepressants. The major difference between these two classes of drugs is that the stimulant drugs facilitate the action of dopamine-containing neurons. Therefore, in these children dopaminergic function would seem to be important. There is another way to check this inference. This involves the differences between the stereoisomers of d- and l-amphetamine. The author and colleagues conducted a study in which he compared the efficacy of these two isomers of amphetamine versus placebo on a group of MBD children (Arnold et al., 1972). It was found that one subgroup of children did as well on l-amphetamine as on d-amphetamine whereas a larger group did well only on d-amphetamine. This experiment was undertaken because of the known differential effects of these two isomers on neurotransmitter function. Both d- and l-amphetamine are equally effective on norepinephrine-containing systems, but d-amphetamine is ten times as potent on dopamine-containing systems. The division of children into these groups implies that one group has a deficiency only in norepinephrine-containing systems while the group who responded to d-amphetamine presumably had a lesion largely affecting dopamine-containing systems of the brain. The conclusion to be drawn from the evidence of drug responsiveness, together with the evidence from the natural accidents producing MBD, is that dopamine-containing systems play an appreciable role in the genesis of the syndrome, although the role of the other monoamines cannot be ruled out.

CLINICALLY OBSERVED PSYCHOLOGICAL ABNORMALITIES

Two cardinal, clinically observed, psychological abnormalities of MBD children are lack of attentiveness and refractoriness to reinforcement. What is known about these characteristics in MBD children?

Measures of Attention

What about direct measures of attention in MBD children? Attentiveness can be measured by a number of tests, but a serious difficulty is that attentiveness often cannot be separated from interest and motivation to perform. What about arousal? Attention appears to be a U-shaped function of arousal, being decreased at very low and very high levels of arousal. What is the arousal level of MBD children? MBD children appear to be overaroused and then their cognitive characteristics resemble those seen in ostensibly highly aroused adults. Such characteristics include decreased attentiveness, inability to focus on the relevant, and increased difficulty in figure–ground discrimination. These are characteristics similar to those seen in early schizophrenic excitement and mania. Another datum suggesting hyperarousal comes from the reported characteristics of MBD children, particularly when younger. The author knows of no controlled studies, but it appears that MBD children have more than their share of sleep difficulties, including early awakening and difficulties in falling and in remaining asleep. Determination of arousal level demands its operational definition. Using a variety of EEG measures, a number of authors have found evidence that some MBD children appear to be underaroused, and using the GSR as a measure of arousal, Satterfield and Dawson (1971) found that a significant fraction of MBD children manifested low physiological measures of arousal. Unfortunately, other studies utilizing both the GSR and other physiological measures have failed to confirm these results. Also in conflict with the underarousal hypothesis is the clinical observation that some young MBD children sleep better while receiving stimulant drugs and some MBD children grow up who remain symptomatic and describe becoming more sleepy on stimulant medication.

The question of arousal level in MBD children is therefore unresolved. What is known about the relationship of monoamines to arousal in animals (Wender, 1972)? The answer is that the two seem intimately related; the question is how? There is a rapidly growing mass of confusing data. Confusion stems from the possibility that the same substance may exert different effects on different parts of the brain, that species response may vary, and that attention in man may have little to do with the excitement and hyperactivity we generally measure in animals. An example that illustrates some of the difficulties is the fact that norepinephrine injected intraventricularly produces sedation, while injected intrahypothylamically it produces excitation. A crude overview would suggest that serotonin appears to decrease motor activity, whereas dopamine, and particularly norepinephrine, appear to increase activity and decrease sedation. In regard to the effect of drugs on animals, the results are somewhat clearer. Normal animals show increased motor activity with low to moderate doses of stimulants and stereotyped behavior with higher doses. What of animal models for hyperactivity (and it should be remembered that hyperactivity is not a necessary condition for MBD)? Hyperactivity can be produced in rodents by nursing them on lead-poisoned mothers or by the intraventricular administration of 6-hydroxydopamine and imipramine (Shaywitz, Yager, and Klopper, 1976), a technique that selectively destroys dopaminergic tracts. Hyperactivity also occurs spontaneously in certain strains of dogs. Stimulant drugs decrease activity levels in lead-poisoned mice and the hyperactive dogs (Corson, Corson, and Kerelcuk, 1973). In the latter, the underlying brain abnormalities have not yet been reported.

Decreased Sensitivity to Reinforcement

The second hypothesized deficiency in MBD children was a decreased sensitivity to reinforcement. Considerable experimental data with animals exist documenting a relationship between reinforceability and mono-aminergic function. The behaviors that have been more frequently studied are positive reinforcement via electrical stimulation of the brain and two-way (active) avoidance conditioning. The relevance of these data depends on how closely one feels such behavioral paradigms are analogous to the behavior of MBD children. Electrical stimulation of the brain may not be too close to praise, and the two-way avoidance tasks may not provide a good model for social compliance and nonimpulsivity. Two-way avoidance is employed most frequently because its technology is simple; however, it entails an animal's returning to an area where he has been shocked and this may be a greater measure of disinhibition than "animal caution." With these warnings in mind, a brief review of the data follows (Wender, 1972). Animal experimentation suggests that reinforcement produced by electrical stimulation of the brain is potentiated by drugs such as amphetamines which facilitate the activity of monoaminergic systems and is decreased by agents that decrease the activities of such systems. Depending on the locus of stimulation, dopamine or norepinephrine seems to mediate reinforcement. Active, two-way avoidance is diminished by drugs that decrease dopaminergic and noradrenergic functioning, and the most recent data would seem to indicate that dopamine is the more important neurotransmitter of the two. Most recently, Hill has performed some ingenious experiments elucidating the effects of stimulant drugs and their mechanisms of action on positive and negatively reinforced operant behavior. Ordinarily, stimulant medication cannot be used in operant experiments with food as a reinforcer since stimulant medication diminishes appetite. Hill (1974) employed a secondary reinforcer (a click that had been paired with milk) in the operant situation. It was found that animals for which such a click was a secondary reinforcer would not bar press for the click unless they received stimulant medication. When they did receive stimulant medication, they would bar press for the secondary reinforcer almost indefinitely and showed very little extinction. Using a tone as a CS for a negative reinforcer, an electric shock, Hill found stimulant drugs potentiated the effect of the aversive conditioned stimulus in suppressing bar pressing. Thus, in an operant situation it was demonstrated that stimulant drugs potentiated the effects of both positive and negative reinforcement. Proceeding further, he examined the effect of dopaminergic and noradrenergic blockade on these effects of stimulant medication. Noradrenergic blockers inhibited the effect of stimulant medication upon negative reinforcement and dopaminergic blockage blocked the effects of positive reinforcement. Thus, each catecholamine seemed to play a separate role in the maintenance of these behaviors. By analogy, one would hypothesize that *l*-amphetamine would sensitize a child to blame but not to praise, whereas *d*-amphetamine would sensitize him to both.

All this is circumstantial evidence supporting the hypothesis. What more direct methods are available? The best would be to study the animal models already mentioned. Probably the best of these is a strain of dogs obtained by Corson, Corson, and Kerelcuk (1973). These animals were found to be not only restless but also difficult to condition classically. When amphetamine was administered not only did the restlessness disappear but conditioning was also made possible.

TESTING ANIMAL-MODEL HYPOTHESES IN HUMANS

The animal models can be suggestive but not conclusive. Is there any way of testing the hypothesis in humans? The hypothesis asserts that there are abnormalities of monoamine metabolism in the brains of MBD children. Unfortunately, direct measures of such metabolism are not available and only indirect tests can be employed. This places the theory in the same category as the monoamine hypothesis of depression. One may suppose that the abnormality is confined to the brain alone or that it is a generalized abnormality of monoamine metabolism. One may assume that the fundamental underactivity is due to decreased synthesis, decreased release, or decreased receptor sensitivity. With these suppositions in mind, we may: (1) measure urinary monoamine metabolites in MBD children. An initial experiment has been performed Wender et al. (1971) with a fairly heterogeneous group, and failed to show any difference between the MBD group and control group. Since the variances in the MBD group were larger—although not significantly so—than those of the comparison group, it is possible that one subgroup of MBD children does exist with such an abnormality. (2) A more direct test is to measure the levels of monoamine metabolites in the CSF. If an abnormality of metabolism does exist but is confined to the brain, one would not expect to find such differences reflected in urinary metabolites since the brain contributes only approximately 10% of the total of such metabolites. Measuring monoamine metabolites in the CSF appears to be a more direct test. There are difficulties with this method too, since there is some concern that metabolites measured in the CSF may come from the spinal cord rather than from the brain. One way of circumventing this difficulty is to administer probenecid to block the egress of metabolites from the CSF, allowing accumulation, perhaps allowing better mixing, and therefore providing a better reflection of brain metabolism. Shaywitz (1975) has performed such an experiment on six MBD children and found that, compared to the normals, the MBD group had spinal fluid HVA (the principal metabolite of dopamine) which was half that of the controls. The sample is exceedingly small and there are a number of possible interpretations but, nonetheless, the finding is exciting and compatible with the other suggestions that dopaminergic functioning is decreased in MBD children. (3) Tests of altered autonomic nervous system reactivity. If MBD children do have a generalized abnormality of monoamine metabolism, it might be evidenced in abnormalities of autonomic nervous system reactivity. Two possibilities exist. If there were diminished production and/or release, peripheral receptors might exhibit increased sensitivity to exogenous amines (analogous to supersensitivity in denervated receptors). Presumably, from the one urinary metabolic study performed, production and release are normal, so that this possibility is unlikely. Another possibility is that MBD children might have adequate production and release of amines with decreased receptor sensitivity. In that event, one would anticipate less cardiovascular responsiveness to exogenously administered sympathomimetic drugs. The test of these hypotheses is the administration of sympathomimetic drugs to MBD and normal children and the determination of their degree of cardiovascular responsiveness. (4) Administration of drugs with known mechanisms of action. Employing this technique, one administers different drugs to the same child or group of children, sees which drugs are beneficial, and infers the biochemical lesion from the known action of the drugs. To repeat the example given: The author (Wender, 1974) administered the two stereoisomers of amphetamine to a small group of MBD children. d-Amphetamine is known to have ten times as great an effect on dopamine as l-amphetamine, while both have equal effects on norepinephrine. From the finding that some children benefited only from d-amphetamine while others did satisfactorily with l-amphetamine, it was inferred that some children had a biochemical lesion of the noradrenergic system where others had a lesion of the dopaminergic system and possibly the noradrenergic system as well. Similar chemical dissection might be performed by comparing the relative efficacy of the tertiary and secondary tricyclic antidepressants on MBD children. Since the former affect both norepinephrine and serotonin while the latter affect only norepinephrine, a response to the former compounds but not the latter would indicate the relevance of serotonin to MBD behavior. (5) Finally, one may administer precursor amines and blockers of amine synthesis. From the data adduced so far, there is a strong suggestion that a dopamine deficiency plays an etiological role in a large number of MBD children, and the logical amine precursor to employ would be L-dopa. These strategies have been employed in the study of depression and are subject to the same interpretive limitations. As a result, even if one found that precursor amines were effective therapeutic agents, one could still not be completely certain that they were simply compensating for an underlying deficiency.

SUMMARY

To recapitulate, the major hypotheses presented in this chapter are that MBD's signal characteristics are a deficiency in the attention mechanism and a relative insensitivity to reinforcement. Furthermore, it is hypothesized that these abnormalities are frequently mediated by an abnormality in monoamine metabolism that is genetically transmitted. The author is not entirely satisfied with these hypotheses: They are incomplete and, like the monoamine theory of depression, they generate no predictions, failure of confirmation of which would disprove the hypotheses. Such susceptibility to disproof constitutes the mark of a good scientific hypothesis. At this point, the author will be content if the hypotheses advanced prove to be useful and suggest to other workers fruitful lines of inquiry.

Part III

Genetic and Maturational Variables in Relation to Learning Disabilities

Reading Retardation in Children: Developmental Lag or Deficit?

Byron P. Rourke

Several cross-sectional studies conducted in our laboratory (e.g., Rourke, Dietrich, and Young, 1973) have been carried out with a view to the elucidation of age differences in the patterns of neuropsychological abilities exhibited by children with learning disabilities. These studies were related to and, to some extent, arose out of an interest in the age differences that had been demonstrated in the attentional abilities of brain-damaged children (Czudner and Rourke, 1972; Rourke and Czudner, 1972).

Other studies (e.g., Rourke and Finlayson, 1975; Rourke, Yanni, MacDonald, and Young, 1973) have been designed to demonstrate whether and to what extent the patterns of abilities and deficits exhibited by children with learning disabilities may be the result of dysfunction at the level of the cerebral hemispheres. A summary of our efforts in this regard has been presented recently (Rourke, 1975). Currently, we are focusing our efforts on the genetic (developmental) dimensions of disabilities in learning and perceptual development.

Because of the theme of this conference—namely, the elucidation of theoretical models and the implications of data for theories of brain functioning—this presentation is confined to a consideration of the relative merits of the "developmental lag" position and the "deficit" position vis-à-vis the explanation of one particular learning disability (reading retardation) in children. First, a brief explanation of these two theoretical

The investigations conducted in our laboratory and reported herein were supported by Grant No. 195 from the Ontario Mental Health Foundation and by a grant received from the Province of Ontario Ministry of Education Grants-in-aid of Educational Research and Development. Funds were also received from the Research Division, Windsor Western Hospital Centre.

positions will be presented, followed by an elucidation of several "developmental lag" and "deficit" paradigms. Finally, the results of a study conducted in our laboratory will be compared with those of Satz, Friel, and Rudegeair (1974a) in an attempt to deal with this issue. Both of these studies involved longitudinal comparisons of the performance of children who were making adequate or above-average progress in reading with that of children who were experiencing difficulties in the acquisition of this complex ability.

DEVELOPMENTAL LAG VERSUS DEFICIT

Satz and Van Nostrand (1973) and de Hirsch, Jansky, and Langford (1966) have postulated a "lag mechanism" in brain maturation that is thought to underlie and forecast the later onset of dyslexia. According to Satz and Van Nostrand, developmental dyslexia is seen as due to a lag in the maturation of the cerebral cortex (primarily that of the left hemisphere). Thus, they see their theory as an attempt to conceptualize dyslexia within the framework of a developmental model rather than within that of a "disease" or "deficit" model. They postulate that the underlying lag in brain maturation causes a delay in the rate of acquisition of developmental skills rather than a loss or impairment—that is, a deficit—in these skills. According to this view, it is predicted that those children who, during the preschool years, are delayed developmentally in the acquisition of skills that are in primary ascendency at that stage will eventually fail in acquiring reading proficiency.

As do Doehring (1968), Reed (1968), and Reitan (1964), Satz and Van Nostrand (1973) conceptualize dyslexia as more than a reading disorder per se. Satz and Van Nostrand view dyslexia as the result of a delay in sensory-motor abilities (primarily during the preschool years) and conceptual-linguistic abilities (primarily during the early and middle school years) which are crucial for the acquisition of reading skills and which are, in turn, the result of a lag in the maturation of the cerebral cortex. In all of this, it is assumed that the dyslexic child is developmentally similar to a younger normal child and that eventually he will "catch up" to his age-mates in those skills that are crucial for the development of reading.

The "deficit" model with respect to developmental dyslexia—a view more akin to that espoused by Doehring (1968), Reed (1968), and Reitan (1964)—suggests that there is some sort of cerebral dysfunction underlying the acquisition of age-appropriate reading skills. This view differs from the "developmental lag" position in that there is no necessary expectation that the children who suffer from the deficit(s) will ever catch up with their normal age-mates in those skills required for age-appropriate reading. It is similar to the "developmental lag" view in that it predicts a less than age-appropriate level of reading performance throughout the elementary school years. (Precisely how long the deficiency in reading is expected to persist is a moot point for both theoretical positions.) From the point of view of the deficit position, it is possible that children will exhibit a deficit in the cerebral structures or systems that subserve some of the abilities necessary for reading from which they will never fully recover. However, it should also be noted that this position allows for adaptation to and/or compensation for the deficits in question, possibly by the enlisting of other neuronal structures or systems which, in the ordinary course of events, would not subserve these abilities (see Luria, 1966b; Wepman, 1951, 1964). It is not clear whether the developmental lag position espoused by Satz and Van Nostrand would provide for these sorts of compensatory mechanisms.

DEVELOPMENTAL LAG–DEFICIT PARADIGMS

In order to explain seven of the main possible sets of results that can be obtained in developmental studies (in this case, of reading retardation) of either a cross-sectional or a longitudinal nature, the graphs in Figure 1 have been constructed. Although the paradigms presented are not meant to be completely exhaustive, it is felt that they encompass the principal sorts of

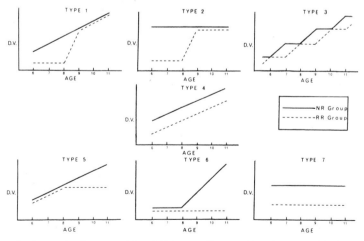

Figure 1. Seven developmental lag-deficit paradigms. Abbreviations: DV, dependent variable; NR, normal reading; RR, retarded reading.

results that are obtained in the types of studies under consideration. Each of these seven "types" is couched in a two-way analysis of variance design. For purposes of illustration, two-way designs with repeated measures across the factor of age, as employed by Satz et al. (1974a), are used as examples.

The hypothetical paradigms illustrated by the schematic graphs in Figure 1 are arranged such that age (6–11 years) is represented along the abscissa, and the scale for any particular dependent variable (e.g., verbal fluency) is represented along the ordinate. The curves in each graph reflect the hypothetical performance of a normal reading (NR) group and a retarded reading (RR) group. Results obtained that approximate those situations designated as Types 1, 2, and 3 would tend to support the "developmental lag" view as outlined by Satz and Van Nostrand (1973). Results coinciding with those designated as Types 5, 6, and 7 would lend support to a "deficit" position. Results most adequately characterized by Type 4 could be viewed as support for either position. The following is a description of each of the seven paradigms.

Type 1

In this situation, the within-subjects term is significant; the significant increment in performance for the RR group occurs only between ages 9 and 11. The between-subjects term is also significant, but the between-groups differences are significant only at ages 6, 7, and 8. The interaction term is significant. This type of relationship would be expected in the case where there is a clear developmental lag in an ability, and the lag is made up in a relatively short time. Thereafter, the NR and RR groups continue to improve their performance over time.

Type 2

In this instance, the within-subjects term is significant for the RR group only. The between-subjects term is significant, but the between-groups differences are significant only at ages 6, 7, and 8. The interaction term is significant. This is also a clear example of a developmental lag. It differs from Type 1 in that the ability develops relatively early and reaches its maximum for normal subjects at a relatively early developmental period. This is the sort of relationship that one would expect to see, for example, in the reaction-time performance of younger (6- to 8-year-old) and older (9- to 11-year-old) brain-damaged and normal children. That is, there is no difference in reaction time among the younger normal, older normal, and older brain-damaged children, but the performance of these three groups is significantly superior to that of younger brain-damaged subjects (e.g., Czudner and Rourke, 1972; Rourke and Czudner, 1972).

Type 3

In this situation, the within-subjects and the between-subjects terms are significant, but the between-groups differences are significant only at ages 7, 9, and 11. The interaction term is significant. This is an example of an ability that exhibits, alternately, spurts and plateaus in development. Thus, the RR group is seen to follow the same course of development, and differences are in evidence only when there is a simultaneous "spurt" for the NR group and "plateau" for the RR group. This type of developmental paradigm may help to explain the seemingly contradictory results that can be obtained in cross-sectional developmental studies (e.g., of dichotic listening) wherein the performances of (say) boys and girls are compared at different age levels. That is, one may find significant or nonsignificant differences at progressively advanced age levels as a function of the presence or absence of ongoing spurts or plateaus. It should be noted that this Type 3 situation may very well be a combination of Type 2, mentioned above, and Type 6 to be described below.

Type 4

In this type, the within-subjects and between-subjects terms are significant, whereas the interaction term is not significant. This sort of situation is ambiguous with respect to its support for the developmental lag position as opposed to the deficit mode of interpretation. On the one hand, this type of relationship could be viewed as similar to the first part of the Type 1 situation: that is, perhaps the RR group, if followed long enough, will eventually "catch up" to the NR group in this particular ability. On the other hand, this situation may be an example of the last part of Type 5 (to be discussed next) in which the performances of the NR and RR groups begin to diverge.

Type 5

In this instance, the within-subjects term is significant. However, in the case of the RR group, advancement in this ability declines or ceases at age 8. The between-subjects term is significant, but the between-groups differences are significant only at ages 9, 10, and 11. The interaction term is significant. It should be noted that Type 5 is the reverse of Type 1. In the Type 5 situation, the deficit does not "express itself" until well into the developmental sequence. After that point, the members of the RR group fall progressively further behind in this ability.

Type 6

In this situation, the within-subjects term is significant, but only for the NR group. The between-subjects term is also significant, but the between-groups differences are significant only at ages 9, 10, and 11. The interaction term is significant. This is an example of a relatively "late-blooming" ability that is not seen as a deficit in the RR group until relatively late in development (in this case, at age 9 and beyond). Thereafter, the deficit in the RR group is clearly in evidence. It should be noted that Type 6 is the reverse of Type 2.

Type 7

In this instance, the within-subjects term and the interaction term are not significant. The between-subjects term is significant, and the between-groups differences are significant across the age span in question. This is an example of a clear deficit in the RR group in an ability that is salient and matures at a very early developmental stage. However, it should also be noted that there is a possibility that this may be an example of the sort of situation that obtains in the first part of Type 2.

Now we are in a position to cite the data of Satz et al. (1974a) and some of those from our own longitudinal study of reading retardation in an attempt to determine the relative merits of these two positions.

COMPARISONS OF THE DATA

The Satz et al. (1974a) investigation is well known and need not be described at any great length here. For our purposes, it is sufficient to note that the study employed two groups of elementary school children, a "dyslexic" group and a control group of average to superior readers, both of whom were tested at the beginning of kindergarten and at the end of Grade 2. The dyslexic group was selected from a larger group of disabled readers in the very large population tested. This group was retarded in reading on three criterion measures administered at the end of Grade 2. These children were required to have a Peabody Picture Vocabulary Test (PPVT; Dunn, 1965) IQ of 90 or above and no evidence of gross neurological, sensory, or emotional handicap. A control group of average readers was selected from the same population; this group obtained grade levels consistent with or above their chronological age on the three criterion reading measures. The groups were matched for chronological age, socio-economic level, and attendance at rural versus urban schools. The dyslexic group had a mean PPVT IQ of 99.8; the control group had a mean PPVT IQ of 114.3.

Sixteen dependent measures were employed. These comprised a fairly broad spectrum of fine motor, perceptual-motor, somato-sensory, and cognitive-language skills. In terms of the paradigms outlined above, the results of the study can be categorized as follows:

Type 1. The Finger Localization Test; the Recognition-Discrimination Test; the Similarities subtest of the Wechsler Intelligence Scale for Children (WISC; Wechsler, 1949).
Type 2. The Alphabet Recitation Test.
Type 4. The Auditory Discrimination Test; the Right—Left Discrimination Test; the Embedded Figures Test; the Verbal Fluency Test; the PPVT.
Type 5. The Auditory-Visual Integration Test; the Beery Development Test of Visual-Motor Integration.

The results for the Finger Tapping Test (for both preferred and nonpreferred hands) were of the Type 4 variety, but the between-groups differences and the interaction term were not statistically significant.

Some data from an ongoing study of reading retardation have been reported previously (Ridgley and Rourke, 1970; Rourke, Orr, and Ridgley, 1974). In the initial phase of this investigation (Study 1), there were 30 subjects in the NR Group and 29 subjects in the RR Group. The subjects were drawn from a population of Grade 1 and Grade 2 male students from seven schools in an urban school system in Ontario, Canada. The schools were selected because of their geographical proximity and relatively homogeneous socio-economic make-up (lower-middle to middle-middle class).

Normal readers were selected on the basis of the following criteria: a centile score of 50 or above on the Reading subtest of the Metropolitan Achievement Test (MAT) and a score of 60 or above on either the Word Knowledge or the Word Discrimination subtests of the MAT. Subjects in the RR Group all had a centile score of 20 or below on the Reading subtest of the MAT and 35 or below on either the Word Knowledge or the Word Discrimination subtests. All subjects in both groups obtained a Full Scale Intelligence Quotient (FSIQ) of between 91 and 117 on the WISC. An attempt was made to include only those subjects who fell close to the normal FSIQ range on the WISC. The exclusion of subjects who fell outside of this roughly normal range was considered desirable for two reasons: (1) it would be reasonable to assume that "dull" and "bright" children, quite apart from differences in reading ability, would differ markedly on a large number of the dependent variables employed in this study, and (2) the results of this investigation were intended to apply to groups of "average" children at the age levels in question, not to subjects for whom special class placement was being considered. In Study 1, the groups were matched for age; the age range for subjects in the NR Group was 88–100 months ($\overline{X}$ = 92.87); for those in the RR Group, 87–100 months ($\overline{X}$ = 92.10). The groups were also tested at intervals of 2 years (Study 2), 3 years (Study 3), and 4 years (Study 4) after this initial examination.

In Study 4, 24 NR subjects and 20 RR subjects from the original groups were still in the school system and available for retesting. In this study, the age range for subjects in the NR Group was 133–148 months ($\overline{X}$ = 139.07), and for subjects in the RR Group it was 133–146 months ($\overline{X}$ = 139.28). In this study, the WISC FSIQ scores ranged from 101 to 125 for subjects in the NR Group and from 82 to 120 for subjects in the RR Group.

The following tests were administered to all of the subjects by psychometrists trained extensively in the administration of neuropsychological test batteries to children. (A more complete, detailed description of the tests used is available from the author upon request.)

In Studies 1, 2, 3, and 4 the following tests were used: WISC; PPVT; the Reading, Spelling, and Arithmetic subtests of the Wide Range Achievement Test (WRAT; Jastak and Jastak, 1965); tests for sensory-perceptual disturbances (tactile perception, auditory perception, visual perception; Reitan and Davison, 1974); Thurstone Reversals Test (Doehring, 1968); Underlining Test (Doehring, 1968); Seashore Rhythm Test (Reitan and Davison, 1974); Speech-Sounds Perception Test (Reitan and Davison, 1974); Auditory Closure Test (Kass, 1964); Sentence Memory Test (Benton, 1965a); a Verbal Fluency Test; Word Finding: Rhymes (Doehring, 1968); tests for lateral dominance (Harris, 1958; Miles, 1929); Right–Left Awareness Test (Piaget, 1926a); Strength of Grip (Reitan and Davison, 1974); Writing Speed (Reitan and Davison, 1974); Finger Tapping Test (Reitan and Davison, 1974); Foot Tapping Test (Knights and Moule, 1967); Maze Test (Kløve, 1963); Target Test (Reitan and Davison, 1974).

The following tests, all of which are described in Reitan and Davison (1974), were used in all four studies, but differ somewhat for older and younger children: Tactile Form Recognition Test; Halstead-Wepman Aphasia Screening Test; Graduated Holes Test; Grooved Pegboard Test; Tactual Performance Test; Halstead Category Test. The Trail Making Test (Reitan and Davison, 1974) was administered only in Studies 2, 3, and 4.

In terms of the paradigms outlined above, the results of this study can be categorized as follows. (The results for the Underlining Test, the Right—Left Awareness Test, and the tests for lateral dominance are not included here for the sake of brevity and because they form the basis of a separate presentation.)

Type 1. The Object Assembly subtest of the WISC; the Sentence Memory Test; the Verbal Fluency Test; the Target Test; left-hand speed on the Finger Tapping Test; the right- and left-hand scores on the Mazes Test; the left-hand time score on the Grooved Pegboard Test.

Type 3. The Comprehension and Picture Completion subtests of the WISC; the Seashore Rhythm Test; the Word Finding: Rhymes Test; the Thurstone Reversals Test; the right-hand time score on the Grooved Pegboard Test; right-foot speed on the Foot Tapping Test.

Type 4. The Information, Arithmetic, Digit Span, and Coding subtests of the WISC; the Speech Sounds Perception Test; the Auditory Closure Test; the Aphasia Screening Test; Part B of the Trail Making Test; the Reading, Spelling, and Arithmetic subtests of the WRAT.

Type 5. The Similarities, Vocabulary, and Block Design subtests of the WISC; the PPVT; left-foot speed on the Foot Tapping Test; the Halstead Category Test.

The tests that approximated the Type 4 paradigm, but for which no between-groups differences were obtained, were as follows: the Picture Arrangement subtest of the WISC; Part A of the Trail Making Test; strength of grip with the right and left hand; right-hand speed on the Finger Tapping Test; right- and left-hand scores on the Graduated Holes Test. It should be noted that these results may be examples of the patterns of performance exhibited by the groups in the last half of the Type 1 paradigm or the first half of the Type 5 paradigm.

The results that approximated the Type 7 paradigm, but for which no between-groups differences were obtained, were as follows: tests for sensory-perceptual disturbances (tactile perception, auditory perception, visual perception, finger agnosia, finger-tip symbol- or number-writing recognition); the Tactile Form Recognition Test; the Tactual Performance Test. It should be noted that these results may possibly be examples of the type of relationship evident in the last half of the Type 2 paradigm. It is possible that significant differences would have been obtained on these types of measures at an earlier age level, as was the case in the Satz et al. (1974a) study.

There are several very obvious differences between the Satz et al.

(1974a) investigation and the study conducted in our own laboratory. In the first place, the subjects in the former study were drawn from a much larger population of kindergarten students (aged 5—6 years) who at the end of Grade 2 (aged 7—8 years) were considered to be either "dyslexic" or average or above-average in reading ability. Our own study covered the age range from 7—8 years to 11—12 years, and the subjects were divided initially into NR and RR groups. Moreover, although there were certain similarities in the dependent measures used in both studies, our own investigation involved a larger number of dependent variables. Nevertheless, there are several conclusions, with respect to the principal theoretical issue to which this paper is addressed, that can be made on the basis of a comparison of the results of these two investigations. These are as follows.

(1) There were four dependent measures in the Satz et al. study that fell within the Type 1 and Type 2 paradigms. The results for the Finger Localization Test were classified as Type 1, although an argument could be made for classifying them as Type 2, along with the results of the Alphabet Recitation Test. The results for the Recognition Discrimination Test and the WISC Similarities Test were classified as Type 1, although it is possible, especially in the case of WISC Similarities subtest, that these results could be included within the Type 4 paradigm. In any case, these results would tend to support the developmental lag position. However, it should be noted that, especially in the case of the Finger Localization and Alphabet Recitation results, there was an obvious "ceiling effect" coming into play with respect to these results. In other words, there is an almost built-in assurance that the interaction term will be significant, thereby virtually ensuring that a developmental lag interpretation of the results would be tenable.

(2) The results for the Auditory Discrimination Test, Right—Left Discrimination Test, Embedded Figures Test, Verbal Fluency Test, and the PPVT in the Satz et al. (1974a) investigation were of the Type 4 variety. As mentioned above, insofar as one can rule out a ceiling effect for performance on these tests during the elementary school years, they lend as much support to a deficit position as they do to the developmental lag viewpoint.

(3) The results for the Auditory-Visual Integration Test and the Beery Developmental Test of Visual-Motor Integration in the Satz et al. (1974a) study fell within the Type 5 paradigm. These results would tend to support a deficit position with respect to these abilities.

(4) Those tests that fell within the Type 1 paradigm in our own investigation could be characterized as fairly simple (in the sense of being homogeneous) measures of visual-spatial, visual-motor, and verbal expres-

sive abilities. The only exception to this was performance on the Sentence Memory Test.

(5) Those tests that fell within the Type 3 paradigm in our investigation were, in general, somewhat more complex (e.g., the Word Finding: Rhymes Test, the Thurstone Reversals Test) measures of verbal encoding and visual-spatial skills. It is possible for these results to be interpreted within the developmental lag framework.

(6) The test results that fell within the Type 4 paradigm in our own study (e.g., the Arithmetic and Coding subtests of the WISC, the Auditory Closure Test, the Aphasia Screening Test, Part B of the Trail Making Test) required, in general, more complex abilities than did those which fell within Types 1 and 3.

(7) The results for the WISC Similarities, Vocabulary, and Block Design subtests, together with those for the PPVT and the Halstead Category Test, fell within the Type 5 paradigm. It is clear that performance on these tests requires rather "high-order" skills, and it is these test results that offer fairly clear support for the deficit position.

(8) It should be noted that the tests that fall within Types 1 and 2 in the Satz et al. (1974a) study and our own investigation do not, in general, involve abilities that are ordinarily thought to be subserved primarily by the left cerebral hemisphere. On the other hand, the majority that fall within Types 4 and 5 in both investigations do involve abilities ordinarily thought to be subserved primarily by the left cerebral hemisphere. What this may mean is that those abilities that "catch up" are not subserved primarily by the left cerebral hemisphere, and those that either emerge as significant differentiating variables or continue to be significant differentiating variables are those that are. This would lend support to the deficit position: specifically, deficit(s) that are the result of disordered functioning of the structures or systems primarily localized within the left cerebral hemisphere.

Finally, it should be noted that Reed (1968) found a high degree of concordance between the sets of rank-order distributions of the standardized mean differences for his two age groups (6 and 10 years). The $\rho = .76$ was of the same order as those which we have obtained in the rankings of the mean differences for the NR and RR groups across Studies 1, 2, 3, and 4 in our own investigation, as well as those between each of our four studies and Doehring's (1968) results. Thus it would seem that those variables that serve to differentiate between NR and RR groups at the initial phases of learning to read (age 6) are, by and large, those variables that differentiate the groups at much more advanced levels of reading requirements (at ages 10–14). However, it is also the case that Reed's

(1968) data would lend support to the contention that, relative to verbal skills, visuo-motor abilities may be somewhat more important for learning to read (age 6) than they are at more advanced reading levels (age 10).

CONCLUSION

The main purpose of the current presentation was to determine the relative merits of the "developmental lag" position and the "deficit" position vis-à-vis the explanation of reading retardation in children. Viewed in the light of the seven paradigms presented, it would appear that, in general, the developmental lag position is tenable in the case of fairly simple, early-emerging abilities. However, it should be emphasized that the lack of adequate "ceilings" for the tests that are most differentiating at this early level makes for spurious interactions which, if not interpreted with caution, can lend equally spurious support to the developmental lag position. It is also clear that inadequate "floors" for measures of auditory-verbal and concept-formation abilities or—of even more concern—the absence or paucity of such measures in the battery of tests employed can have untoward results, viz., spurious support may be afforded the position that sensori-motor abilities are more crucial during the early stages of learning to read, whereas higher-order conceptual and linguistic abilities are more salient at more advanced reading levels.

The specific developmental lag position espoused by Satz and Von Nostrand (1973) postulates a particular lag in the development of the left cerebral hemisphere. The current structuring of the results of the studies under consideration would lend some support to the notion that dysfunction of the left cerebral hemisphere is particularly involved in the genesis of reading retardation. However, until it is shown that retarded readers, either as a group or individually, eventually "catch up" in those abilities thought to subserve the reading function—and, for that matter, until it is actually shown that they "catch up" in reading ability itself—the weight of the evidence would appear to favor a deficit rather than a developmental lag position. That some children initially classified as "retarded readers" in our investigation did make fairly substantial gains in reading (an analysis of which forms the basis for another study in this series) would lend support to the developmental lag position. However, the results of the group-wise comparisons in both investigations under consideration certainly indicate that at least some, if not most, of the retarded readers studied suffered from a deficit or deficits in at least some of those abilities ordinarily thought to be subserved primarily by the left cerebral hemisphere. And, although this group of retarded readers can be expected to exhibit advances in those skills crucial for reading and in reading ability itself over the years, there is little or no reason, on the basis of the data available, to predict that they will ever either catch up to or closely approximate the performance of their normal reading age-mates in these particular abilities.

Finally, it should be noted that the "developmental lag-deficit" paradigms described herein are not exhaustive: they do not embrace all possible variations in the rates and levels of acquisition of the skills in question across the age span of interest. However, it is felt that these paradigms, taken together, can be employed to characterize changes over time for a fairly substantial segment of the abilities in question, as is clear from the relative ease with which the results of the two investigations reviewed could be classified in terms of them. This being the case, it would also seem likely that these paradigms could be applied rather more generally—that is, to data from groups of cross-sectional or longitudinal investigations in areas other than reading retardation.

Handedness, Footedness, Eyedness: A Prospective Study with Special Reference to the Development of Speech and Language Skills

Annetta Karâa McBurney and
Henry G. Dunn

Developmental patterns in the establishment of laterality have not yet been fully documented. Evidence from related areas also still appears to be inadequate to support any one firm theory concerning the relationship between laterality and cerebral control of language function.

Developmental studies of laterality are few in number and limited to specific aspects of the problem. Gesell and Ames (1947), for example, documented the handedness of seven children up to the age of 10 years and included other cases in their analyses at each age level. Considerable bilaterality was observed from 2.5 to 3.5 years, right-handedness in general predominating from 4 to 10 years. Subirana (1964), on the contrary, finding relatively few 6–14-year-old subjects to be fully right- or left-handed in manual skill tests, emphasized the varying degrees of hand preference observed. Sinclair (1971) reexamined, after an interval of 3 years, the preferential use of hand, foot, eye, and ear in 27 children whose ages ranged from 5 to 7 years. Twelve of the children (44%) showed a change in dominance pattern over the period. While none of the various patterns of "dominance" seemed to be significantly related to school success as determined by the Metropolitan Reading scores, further studies were considered indicated. Coren's study (1974) of ocular dominance in 68 infants, 62 elementary school children, and 86 adults found little change in sighting dominance from the age of 44 weeks up to adulthood, with about 64% of each group right-eyed. Recent work also shows that some asymmetry of development affecting the cerebral hemispheres is already demonstrable in infants and is related to dominance (Wada and Dolman, 1974).

Most laterality investigations in which children have been the subject of study tend to focus on correlates of classical cerebral specialization and contralaterality theory. For instance Fagan-Dubin (1974), interested in the question of incompatibility between processes within each hemisphere in left-handers, looked for disparities in verbal and nonverbal abilities between right- and left-handed kindergarten children and incidentally did not find any. Most reports concern groups exhibiting disorders such as aphasia, epilepsy, mental retardation, low achievement, poor perceptual-motor functioning, stuttering, and impaired learning, particularly in the area of reading failure. Findings have been contradictory. The "breadth and timeliness" of a study, as Culton and Mueller (1971) point out, have often determined the author's concept of cerebral dominance since each generation and profession has had its own peculiar methods of study. Less adequate functioning observed in left-handers or in children with inconsistent laterality has frequently been interpreted as indicating that the usual pattern of left cerebral dominance for language function has not been established (e.g., Wusser and Barclay, 1970). However, the need for a more complex concept of the cerebral control for speech is indicated by evidence from studies using improved clinical research methods. The predominance of the left cerebral hemisphere in many sinistrals as well as in most dextrals has been demonstrated (e.g., Branch, Milner, and Rasmussen, 1964). The theory of incomplete lateralization of speech functions in children with impaired learning is further challenged by findings in dichotic listening tests. For example, in one verbal dichotic listening examination of children with auditory linguistic deficits, it appeared that the impaired children had definite lateralization of speech functions but with a higher incidence of right hemispheric superiority for speech than might be expected in a normal population (Witelson and Rabinovitch, 1972).

EXPERIMENTAL STUDY

The authors have been engaged since 1958 in a prospective study of neurological and ophthalmic disorders in 480 infants with a birth weight below 2,041 g (4.5 lb) and 204 control infants with a full birth weight of more than 2,500 g (5.5 lb). Of the former group 319 and of the latter 136 have been followed to the age of 6.5 years. The present investigation attempts to determine any associations between the development of language skills and laterality. Those children were excluded in whom speech and language difficulties might be attributed to any of the following factors: mental retardation (Full Scale WISC IQ below 70), more than minimal cerebral palsy, visual or hearing defects, gross emotional disturbance, bilingual background, plurality of birth. A total of 390 children remained, of whom about 49% were boys and 74% were of low birth weight (below 2,041 g).

Language skills were assessed by performance on the Griffiths Mental Development Scale, Division C (Hearing and Speech) at the ages of 3, 6, 12, and 18 months, by medical examinations at 4 and 6.5 years, by developmental speech and language assessment at 4 years, and then at 6.5 years by the Benton sentence repetition test, the ITPA vocal encoding test, the WISC vocabulary subtest and verbal IQ. These data were examined in relation to laterality ratings at 6½ years (see Table 1): (1) Handedness: strong right (76%), strong left (13%), slight preference for right (3%), slight preference for left (2%), ambidextrous or inconstant (6%). For the purposes of analysis children who had been judged as ambidextrous, inconstant, or as showing slight preference for the right or left hand were considered together to be a group whose handedness was weak. (2) Hand, foot, eye: homolateral (67%), both hand and foot different from eye (26%), both eye and hand different from foot (4%), both eye and foot different from hand (3%). Some consideration was also given to the question of stability of the handedness and lateral congruity variables as recorded at the ages of 4 and 6.5 years.

Laterality ratings were based on the following tests: Handedness: pencil work, ball throwing, knob turning, cutting with scissors, winding a watch. When the same hand was used for four or all of these five tasks, a rating of strong handedness was obtained. Footedness: ball kicking, chair

Table 1. Laterality at 6.5 Years ($N = 390$)

Hand	
Strong right	76%
Strong left	13%
Slight preference for right	3%
Slight preference for left	2%
Ambidextrous or inconstant	6%
Hand, foot, eye	
Homolateral	67%
Hand and foot different from eye	26%
Eye and hand different from foot	4%
Eye and foot different from hand	3%

climbing, jumping. Eyedness: looking through a hole, pointing at the examiner's nose, shooting an imaginary gun, looking into a kaleidoscope.

Since no significant sex/birth weight-gestation group differences in laterality ratings were found at 4 or 6.5 years, results reported here refer to the total cohort of 390 children.

When children were grouped according to strength of handedness, right or left, scores differed significantly in Griffiths Mental Development Scale Division C (Hearing and Speech) at 9 months, and in a number of tests given at the 4-year speech and language assessment: articulation: vowels and diphthongs, initial consonants, final consonants, connected speech; vocabulary: verbs, nouns, prepositions, conjunctions; rote counting. Significant differences appeared at 6.5 years in the medical examination of language development and in the Benton Sentence Repetition Test, and the Wechsler VIQ, PIQ and FSIQ. Differences consistently favored right-handers (see Table 2).

Table 2. Significant Association Found in Analyses of Speech and Language Variables versus Laterality Variables. Strength of Handedness ($N = 390$)

Age at Time of Testing	Speech and Language Variable	Test of Significance
	Griffiths Mental Development Scale	
9 mo	Division C (hearing and speech)	$F = 2.61^a$
	Tests of articulation:	
4 yr	vowels and diphthongs	$\chi^2 = 20.45^a$
4 yr	initial consonants	$\chi^2 = 21.53^a$
4 yr	final consonants	$\chi^2 = 20.90^a$
4 yr	connected speech	$\chi^2 = 22.54^a$
	Test of vocabulary:	
4 yr	verbs	$\chi^2 = 22.44^a$
4 yr	nouns	$\chi^2 = 18.39^a$
4 yr	prepositions	$\chi^2 = 24.15^b$
4 yr	conjunctions	$\chi^2 = 22.69^a$
	Medical examination:	
6.5 yr	language development	$\chi^2 = 88.31^c$
6.5 yr	Benton Sentence Repetition Test	$F = 2.82^a$
6.5 yr	VIQ (WISC)	$F = 2.88^a$
6.5 yr	PIQ (WISC)	$F = 4.64^c$
6.5 yr	FSIQ (WISC)	$F = 4.41^c$

[a] $p < 0.05$.
[b] $p < 0.01$.
[c] $p < 0.001$.

When the grouping criterion of lateral congruity was used (Table 3), a condition of inclusion in either of the two groups was strength of handedness, right or left. Children who were homolateral (right and left) had significantly better ratings in the Griffiths hearing and speech subscale at 9 months, in the 4-year medical examination of language development, and in the 4-year speech and language assessment where significant differences were found in a somewhat different set of scores from those of the strength of handedness analyses: speech mechanisms: lip retraction, lip protrusion, with phonation and with various measures of receptive and expressive language. At 6.5 years a significant difference, again in favor of the laterally congruous, was found in WISC Performance IQ. Of all groups in this lateral congruity part of the analysis, those children whose eyedness and footedness differed from their handedness tended to be the least successful. Those whose handedness and footedness differed from their

Table 3. Significant Association Found in Analyses of Speech and Language Variables versus Laterality Variables. Lateral Congruity (right + left) ($N = 214$) versus Lateral Noncongruity ($N = 117$)

Age at Time of Testing	Speech and Language Variable	Test of Significance
	Griffiths Mental Development Scale	
9 mo	Division C (hearing and speech)	$F = 4.81^a$
	Medical examination:	
4 yr	language development	$\chi^2 = 36.69^b$
	Speech mechanism:	
4 yr	lip retraction	$\chi^2 = 15.98^b$
4 yr	lip protrusion	$\chi^2 = 17.01^a$
	Phonation:	
4 yr	pitch	$\chi^2 = 47.94^a$
	Receptive language:	
4 yr	points to named pictures	$\chi^2 = 19.97^b$
4 yr	follows gesture directions	$\chi^2 = 11.53^b$
	Expressive language:	
4 yr	names objects	$\chi^2 = 27.26^b$
4 yr	names pictures	$\chi^2 = 29.65^b$
4 yr	names animals	$\chi^2 = 22.56^c$
4 yr	Intelligibility of speech	$\chi^2 = 17.32^c$
6.5 yr	PIQ (WISC)	$F = 2.96^c$

[a] $p < 0.001$.
[b] $p < 0.01$.
[c] $p < 0.05$.

eyedness performed only a little better. Thus, for these measures it seemed that children whose dominant feet and eyes were homolateral with their hands, whether right or left, had an advantage.

The homolaterals were then categorized as uniformly dextral or uniformly sinistral for further comparison of scores (Table 4). The uniformly dextral group performed significantly better than the sinistral at the 4-year speech and language examination in articulation: vowels and diphthongs; vocabulary: nouns, verbs, conjunctions, articles, and in overall classification of language development. At 6.5 years the dextrals obtained significantly higher scores in the Benton Sentence Repetition Test and in Verbal, Performance, and Full Scale IQ. These indications of better performance by the right congruous children were supported by inspection of the data. In each of the 4-year speech and language tests, even where differences were not statistically significant, a higher percentage of uniformly sinistrals obtained ratings which placed them in categories below what might be expected for that age level (Table 5). Furthermore, again in marked contrast to the dextrals, not one uniformly sinistral child received above

Table 4. Significant Association Found in Analyses of Speech and Language Variables versus Laterality Variables. Right Congruous ($N = 187$) versus Left Congruous ($N = 27$)

Age at Time of Testing	Speech and Language Variable	Test of Significance
	Tests of articulation[a]	
4 yr	vowels and diphthongs	$\chi^2 = 7.51^b$
	Tests of vocabulary[a]	
4 yr	nouns	$\chi^2 = 6.79^c$
4 yr	verbs	$\chi^2 = 7.64^b$
4 yr	conjunctions	$\chi^2 = 6.47^c$
4 yr	articles	$\chi^2 = 8.20^b$
	Speech and language examination[a]	
4 yr	overall classification	$\chi^2 = 8.54^b$
6.5 yr	Benton Sentence Repetition Test	$F = 3.95^c$
6.5 yr	VIQ (WISC)	$F = 4.31^c$
6.5 yr	PIQ (WISC)	$F = 11.69^d$
6.5 yr	FSIQ (WISC)	$F = 7.04^b$

[a]N.B. In *left congruous group,* no child obtained ratings above age level, and a higher percentage was in all below-age-level categories than among right congruous children.

[b]$p < 0.01$.
[c]$p < 0.05$.
[d]$p < 0.001$.

Table 5. Right Congruous ($N = 187$) versus Left Congruous ($N = 27$). In these tests no significant differences were found, but in the left congruous group no child obtained ratings above age level and a higher percentage was in all below-age-level categories than among right congruous children

---

Tests of articulation
   Initial consonants
   Final consonants
   Connected speech
Tests of vocabulary
   Adjectives
   Prepositions
   Describing picture
   Relating event

---

age-level ratings. It appeared, therefore, that the significant difference found in mean VIQ was between dextrals who were laterally uniform and those who were not.

Looking at the Verbal and Performance IQ data in another way, there appears to be no confirmation of the hypotheses that there are inherent disparities associated with sinistrality between verbal and nonverbal abilities, at least as determined by WISC, VIQ, and PIQ.

In respect of stability from the 4-year to the 6.5-year examination for both strength of handedness and lateral congruity–incongruity, there were many individual changes not reflected in the overall totals, and these changes were not necessarily in the direction of dexterity or homolaterality.

INTERPRETATION OF DATA

Interpretation of the data in their present form would be hazardous, but the results do indicate that in certain aspects of language development at 9 months, 4 years, and 6.5 years and in Verbal and Performance IQ at 6.5 years, children whose handedness is other than strongly right or whose handedness, footedness, and eyedness are not uniformly dextral are less likely to be achieving above age level and are more likely to be achieving below.

The further finding that for a considerable number of children the years from 4 to 6.5 see various shifts in laterality would appear to have relevance in any attempt to understand the etiology of learning problems in the early school years; that in these 4- and 6.5-year measures uniform dexterity bestowed fairly pervasive additional advantages over and above those of uniform laterality of hand, foot, and eye.

Because lateral noncongruity in relation to various disabilities has figured prominently in the literature and since we had found so many differences between the laterally congruous children, right or left, and the laterally noncongruous, the analysis was extended to include right congruous—right noncongruous and left congruous—left noncongruous groups, respectively. From these series of comparisons only one area of significant difference was found. In the Verbal IQ at 6.5 years right-handed, right-footed, right-eyed children obtained a significantly higher mean score than the right-handed noncongruous children.

Since the uniformly dextrals had differed significantly from the uniformly sinistrals in a number of measures but in only one measure (VIQ) from dextrals not correspondingly right-footed and right-eyed, further work documenting noncongruous laterality and its correlates would seem to be indicated. Figure 1, for instance, depicting VIQ and PIQ means of the several laterality groupings, shows most sinistral groups obtaining lower mean scores than the dextrals. The single area of overlap appeared in VIQ means, where noncongruous sinistrals did slightly better than noncongruous dextrals. Dextrality appears to be a weighty factor here, but that it is not an unconfounded one is seen in the significant difference found in mean VIQ between dextrals who were laterally uniform and those who were not.

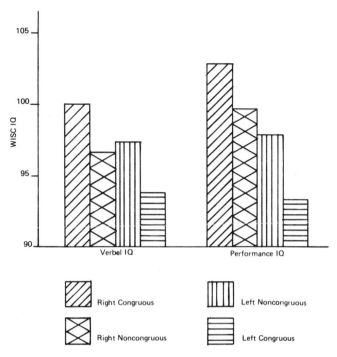

Figure 1. Mean VIQ and PIQ in various laterality groupings.

Developmental Stratagems Organizing Intellectual Skills: Evidence from Studies of Temporal Lobectomy for Epilepsy

David C. Taylor

This chapter considers some of the ways in which the development and organization of intelligence, as measured by the Wechsler tests, are modified by events that take place within the brain. The premise is that the pattern of adult intelligence has been modified by such things as the presence of small developmental anomalies, damage sustained by viral infection or by anoxia, and by the occurrence of cerebral dysrhythmia. A detailed analysis of the patterns of Wechsler scale scores, and changes of scores over time, could thus reveal useful information about the basic mechanisms by which loss of skills and compensation for loss of skills come about. Such an analysis should show not only the pattern of skills in these epileptic patients, but should reveal something of the parts usually played by either cerebral hemisphere, or the effect of sex differences, or the role of developmental changes in the brain.

It is not intended as a clinical exercise. In the main body of this chapter are presented new data analyzed in a manner that highlights these fundamental issues and that is undertaken in a way which the author hopes, meets the objections of Reitan (1974):

> "Many if not most of the psychological studies in this area have failed to indicate specifically the various types of brain disorders that characterise the patients investigated. Previous research has indicated clearly the pronounced influence on psychological test findings of various factors such as area of cerebral involvement, type of lesion, age

This work was supported by the Research Fund of the British Epilepsy Association.

at which the cerebral lesion was sustained, and duration of cerebral lesion."

The scientific aspects of epileptology are valuable insofar as the findings are generalizable. Paradoxically, it happens that the greatest chance of finding basic rules worth generalizing is likely to come from studying phenomena of great specificity. Thus it would be wrong to regard the hypotheses generated or the phenomena studied here as obscure because the population was highly selected and the treatment recherché.

In fact the patients used in this study come from a series that has generated a large literature. They are a considerably distressed population. The physical, psychological, and social effects of their illness, either severally or jointly, create very serious life predicaments. For the psychiatrist or neuropsychologist, the prospect of correlating brain anomalies with behavioral abnormalities compels serious attention to these data. Yet the difficulties are formidable. The time of origin of brain insults is difficult to determine, the mechanisms of brain maturation mostly unknown. The biological basis of sex differences, only a year or so ago, was disputed by some psychologists who confused the need for sexual equality with biological sameness. Hitherto, the effects of lateralized cerebral lesions upon the verbal and performance scale scores of the Wechsler tests have been belittled as revealing much information about the lateralization strategy in the brain, mainly because the effects were small in degree.

From a study of patients with temporal lobe epilepsy, the author proposed a radical theory of cerebral maturation (Taylor, 1969). Male cerebral maturation proceeded slower than in the female, and right hemisphere maturation proceeded faster than in the left. Thus, that area of brain exposed for the longest period of time to risk of damage during its basic development was the left brain of males. Thus most cerebral developmental problems would concern males with left brain disorders. However, the fewer number of females with left brain disorders would suffer most severely since the brief period of vulnerability occurs when the child is very young, and damage done when the whole organism is young is generally the most destructive.

Specifically, going back to the same case material from which the hypothesis was raised, it predicts that those females with left temporal lesions who sustained anoxic sclerosis in early childhood should have the lowest levels of intelligence, especially verbal intelligence. The interaction between the side of the operation, sex, the nature of the lesion, the age at onset of epilepsy, and the Wechsler scale scores are omnipresent in previous studies of these patients. IQ superiority of patients who were well adjusted before temporal lobectomy over those who were poorly adjusted has previously been described (Taylor and Falconer, 1968). This correlation was lost in the postoperative assessment because both bright and dull patients were much improved. Thus, intelligence predicted social adjustment in the one condition but not in another.

In a later study (Taylor, 1972), the author described the mental state of these patients more fully. Higher intelligence correlated with neurosis and with lesions in the right temporal lobe; lower intelligence correlated with psychopathy, with maleness, and with left-sided lesions.

Recently, using exactly the same cases that are used in this study, it was shown that the schizophrenia-like psychosis that occurs in temporal lobe epilepsy follows more frequently in females than in males, where the lesion is in the left temporal lobe and its nature is tumor-like (Taylor, 1975). The present study, too, clearly indicated that the cognitive data should be explored to see whether these patients showed evidence of a different "brain stratagem" that might help explain these interesting findings.

At the Human Development Research Unit in Oxford, under the aegis of the Department of Education and Science, the author has been exploring the learning problems of epileptic children. Most problems stem from relative poverty of verbal skills in children with early onset epilepsy. In their time a large proportion of these adults had suffered such learning difficulties. What we can learn from them may help us understand the problems of the children.

BACKGROUND

It is necessary to understand the rationale and something of the history of temporal lobectomy for epilepsy in order to avoid erroneous interpretations of its apparently variable effects. Originally the surgical treatment of epilepsy was confined to the removal of superficial cortical scars produced by trauma. Of the chronic intractable focal epilepsies, the largest proportion arose from the temporal lobe. The development of electroencephalography allowed the detection of abnormalities in the lobe, despite the absence of a history of trauma or apparent scarring. The results of temporal lobectomy, in terms of relief from fits, improved as the surgeons learned to excise more tissue than they had formerly when dealing with surface lesions, and included removal of the mesial structures, especially the hippocampus and amygdala (Rasmussen and Branch, 1962). Where the style of the lobectomy allows, and where they have been looked for, pathological changes in the lobe are found in over 80% of cases (Falconer, Serafetinides, and Corsellis, 1964). Thus, variations in neurosurgical technique, both over time and between neurosurgeons, may account for some of the different psychological effects that have been reported in the literature.

Mr. Murray Falconer performed the first temporal lobectomy in his series at the Neurosurgical Unit of Guys and the Maudsley Hospitals in February, 1951. His technique has been standard (Falconer, 1953, 1973). The anterior portion of the temporal lobe is removed enbloc from about seven centimeters back from the pole (usually marked by the vein of Labbé), retaining at least the posterior part of the superior temporal gyrus on the left. This bloc of tissue is then examined in detail by the neuropathologists.

The selection of patients for surgery is made from those patients presented by a wide variety of referring physicians who treat large numbers of patients with epilepsy. Intractable psychomotor seizures, a clear cut focus in the EEG limited to one temporal lobe, and sufficient social and intellectual ability to profit from rehabilitation are the main criteria of selection. Experience has modified the selection process so that over the years the age at operation has become less, the ratio of males has increased, and schizophrenic patients have not been operated upon since 1964. Patients are admitted to hospital several weeks before operation for extensive investigations that include psychological testing, using the Wechsler Tests among others. Nearly all patients are readmitted 1 year after operation and the psychological tests are repeated at that time. Each review is conducted by a psychiatrist as well as the neurosurgeon. Patients in this series are kept in regular follow-up for at least 10 years. Several surveys of the effects of lobectomy have been made. These have been clinical evaluations of outcome of increasing scope and sophistication (Falconer et al., 1955; Falconer and Serafetinides, 1963; Taylor, 1972, 1975; Taylor and Falconer, 1968).

The neuropathological changes in the resected temporal lobes are classified into four main groups:

Group 1	50%	Mesial temporal sclerosis	i.e.,	Incisural sclerosis
				Ammon's horn sclerosis
Group 2	20%	Alien tissue	i.e.,	Small "focal" tumors
				Hamartomas
				Focal dysplasia
Group 3	20%	No specific lesion	i.e.,	Inadequate tissue
				No changes
				Changes not believed
				to be significant
Group 4	10%	Miscellaneous	i.e.,	Scars
				Infarcts
				Abscesses

These figures have recently been well supported (Brown, 1973).

Our experience has been that the nature of the pathological changes in the resected lobe is of paramount importance in almost every sphere of outcome (Falconer and Taylor, 1968; Taylor and Falconer, 1968).

METHOD

Subjects

In the study to be reported here, only patients with one of two sorts of pathological changes were considered:

Group 1: Mesial Temporal Sclerosis; 41 Patients This is a gliotic cerebral scarring, also called Ammon's Horn Sclerosis or Incisural Sclerosis. It is most prominent in the mesial temporal areas but is associated with a general reduction in the size of the lobe. Other areas of the brain, the thalamus and cerebellum, are also but more mildly affected. While a variety of "triggers" may be involved, the damage usually results from local, consumptive, cellular hypoxia caused during prolonged febrile fits in early childhood. It is a postnatal insult to the brain having a maximum incidence between 6 months and 4 years of life. It can be mimicked in animals (McLardy, 1969; Meldrum and Brierley, 1972).

Group 2: Alien Tissue; 47 Patients This rubric covers that group of patients previously referred to in our papers as hamartomas, small focal tumors, and focal dysplasia. These lesions were "unsuspected" and were only revealed in the course of the surgical treatment of epilepsy. The term "alien tissue" encompasses all those cases where the surgical approach to treatment brought to light the existence of a small locus of cells alien from their context. Patients who are treated by lobectomy because they present with obvious signs of a cerebral tumor involving the temporal lobe are excluded from this series.

The age of onset of epilepsy in these patients is considerably later than for those with mesial temporal sclerosis. Nevertheless, many of the alien tissue lesions are probably failures in embryogenesis and are incorporated in the temporal lobe before birth.

Procedure

This study compares the verbal and performance scale IQs of two groups of patients selected on the basis of the pathological changes in the resected temporal lobes. There were 47 patients with alien tissue lesions and 41 patients with mesial temporal sclerosis.

Verbal and performance scale scores on the Wechsler Intelligence Tests were available for 39 of the alien tissue and 40 of the mesial temporal sclerosis patients before operation and 40 alien tissue and 36 mesial temporal sclerosis patients afterwards. Seventy-three sets of scores were complete for both tests on both occasions.

Preoperative tests refer to those made immediately before the lobectomy. Postoperative tests refer to those made nearest to 1 year afterwards. [Testing 1 month after operation reflects some acute losses of skills rather than the residual capacity of the brain to reorganize and compensate (Meyer and Jones, 1957; Meyer and Yates, 1955)].

RESULTS

Two important tactics were employed in the analysis of the data. First was the maintenance of each individual so as to reveal their particular outcome among the general effects. Second was to regard the nature of the lesion (in virtue of the different developmental stages in brain maturation where they exert influence), the sex of the individual (in view of the difference in the rate of development between the sexes), and the side of the lesion (as generally agreed) as each being liable to exert a considerable influence and to create from them eight principal groups in analyzing the effects.

The patients in the two pathological groups (alien tissue and mesial temporal sclerosis) do not differ in the distribution of their age at operation (Table 1). There are no significant differences in the mean age at operation between any of the eight main sex/side lesion groups although there is a trend for females operated on the left who had alien tissue to be older.

An interaction between the side operated, sex, and pathological group achieves the 0.10 level of significance ($z = 3.68$, df = 1, $0.05 < p < 0.10$). It is possible that some groups have been preferentially regarded as suitable for, or in need of, operative treatment (Table 2).

Two within-subject conditions, verbal and performance IQ, and pre- and postoperative testing, create a total of 32 subgroups in all. The mean and standard deviation of the IQ in these groups is shown in Table 3. All

Table 1. Age at Operation

Group	0–9	10–19	20–29	30–39	40+	Total
Alien tissue	2	15	10	11	9	47
Mesial temporal sclerosis	1	15	11	10	4	41

Table 2. Interaction Between Side Operated, Sex, and Pathological Findings in the Resected Temporal Lobe

	Alien Tissue		Mesial Temporal Sclerosis	
	Male	Female	Male	Female
Left operation	10	10	16	5
Right operation	18	9	10	10

the available figures were used to calculate these mean values so that the N values may differ pre- and postoperatively.

Considering the preoperative testing only, the difference between each of the mean IQ scores (mesial temporal sclerosis⁻alien tissue; female⁻male; left⁻right; verbal⁻performance) can be considered in turn, in terms of the other three variables (Table 4). The difference between pre- and postoperative testing can be shown in terms of each of the other four variables (Table 5). For between-subject differences, pathological group, sex, and side of operation, the greatest differences between the subgroup means extend to 25⁻30 IQ points, or two standard deviations of the mean of the test. The differences in the within-subject groups achieve only about 15 points or one standard deviation.

These difference scores highlight the issues raised above (Reitan, 1974). Thus, the mean performance scale score for females operated on the right is 9.4 points higher where the lesion found was mesial temporal sclerosis than where it was alien tissue. But the reverse obtains (−13.1) for male subjects.

Male⁻female differences are at their greatest extremes as between favoring female performance scores for right operated mesial temporal sclerosis, and male verbal scores for left operated mesial temporal sclerosis. Similarly the extremes of right⁻left difference were female verbal scores and male performance scores, both for mesial temporal sclerosis lesions.

In Figure 1, the preoperative performance (abscissa) and verbal scale scores (ordinate) of each individual are represented by a single point. This also provides a visual display of the correlation between verbal and performance scale scores. The main axis of the new measure, which combines verbal and performance, is the diagonal. This new vector can be designated F.

The scores of patients with left lesions tend to be located above the diagonal (where P is greater than V) and those with right lesions below it

Table 3. Mean Verbal and Performance Scale Scores by Side, Sex, and Pathological Group Pre- and Postoperatively

	Preoperative Scores				Postoperative Scores			
	Performance Female	Performance Male	Verbal Female	Verbal Male	Performance Female	Performance Male	Verbal Female	Verbal Male
Right sided operations								
Alien tissue								
N	7	16	7	16	7	15	7	15
Mean	96.3	106.4	101.4	113.8	95.0	108.7	100.7	114.0
S.D.	21.0	17.1	18.4	15.8	18.0	16.7	19.3	17.3
Mesial temporal sclerosis								
N	9	10	9	10	8	8	8	8
Mean	105.7	93.3	108.1	101.3	105.9	98.9	110.8	108.1
S.D.	9.1	21.3	12.7	20.3	13.3	18.0	14.8	19.2
Left sided operations								
Alien tissue								
N	8	9	8	8	8	10	8	10
Mean	104.0	95.8	101.0	94.8	106.4	105.9	96.6	98.6
S.D.	10.4	18.9	13.8	21.0	7.4	16.9	9.9	23.1
Mesial temporal sclerosis								
N	5	16	5	16	4	16	4	16
Mean	94.4	103.8	87.8	102.4	102.5	106.0	92.0	102.9
S.D.	11.6	11.7	6.0	9.1	15.3	13.7	7.7	12.7

Table 4. Difference Scores Ranked in Order of Magnitude

(a) Mesial Temporal Sclerosis—Alien Tissue

+ 9.4	PRF	− 9.6	PLF
+ 8.0	PLM	−12.5	VRM
+ 7.6	VLM	−13.1	PRM
+ 6.7	VRF	−13.2	VLF

(b) Female—Male

+12.4	MTS	RP	− 9.4	MTS	LP
+ 8.2	AT	LP	−10.1	AT	RP
+ 6.8	MTS	RV	−12.4	AT	RV
+ 6.2	AT	LV	−14.6	MTS	LV

(c) Right—Left

+20.3	MTS	FV	+ 0.4	AT	FV
+19.0	AT	MV	− 1.1	MTS	MV
+11.3	MTS	FP	− 7.7	AT	FP
+10.6	AT	MP	−10.5	MTS	MP

(d) Verbal—Performance

+ 8.0	MTS	RM	− 1.0	AT	LM
+ 7.4	AT	RM	− 1.4	MTS	LM
+ 5.1	AT	RF	− 3.0	AT	LF
+ 2.4	MTS	RF	− 6.6	MTS	LF

Code: MTS = Mesial temporal sclerosis; AT = Alien tissue; F = Female; M = Male; L = Left operation; R = Right operation; P = Performance scale IQ; V = Verbal scale IQ.

In this table the figures refer to the difference between the preoperative mean scores (shown in Table 3) of 16 subgroups produced by four factors. Eight difference scores are produced by the subtraction in turn of alien tissue from mesial temporal sclerosis (e.g., 105.7 − 96.3 = +9.4), male from female (e.g., 105.7 − 93.3 = +12.4), left from right (e.g., 108.1 − 87.8 = +20.3), and performance from verbal (e.g., 101.3 − 93.3 = +8.0).

Table 5. Difference Scores Ranked in Order of Magnitude

Postoperative–Preoperative

+10.1	AT	LPM	+2.3	AT	RPM
+ 8.1	MTS	LPF	+2.2	MTS	LPM
+ 6.8	MTS	RVM	+0.5	MTS	LVM
+ 5.6	MTS	RPM	+0.2	MTS	RPF
+ 4.2	MTS	LVF	−0.2	AT	RVM
+ 3.8	AT	LVM	−0.7	AT	RVF
+ 2.7	MTS	RVF	−1.3	AT	RPF
+ 2.4	AT	LPF	−4.4	AT	LVF

Code: MTS = Mesial temporal sclerosis; AT = Alien tissue; F = Female; M = Male; L = Left operation; R = Right operation; P = Performance scale IQ; V = Verbal scale IQ.

In this table the figures refer to the differences produced by subtracting the preoperative scores from the postoperative scores. This manipulation defines the greatest extent of the differences produced by one factor in terms of the other three.

(where V is greater than P). If considered without regard to the size of these differences the effect would be highly significant (Table 6) ($\chi^2 = 17.8, p < 0.001$).

Analysis of variance, however, shows that the verbal-performance difference is significant for the right lesion group but not for the left lesion group ($z = 2.97, p < 0.005, z = 1.20, p < 0.25$). Figure 1 indicates that the left lesioned group differs from the right on verbal, but not on performance, IQ both before ($F = 6.31$, df = 1, 260, $p < 0.025$, and $F < 1$) and after operation ($F = 9.37$, df = 1, 260, $p < 0.005$, and $F < 1$).

After operation (Figure 2 and Table 7) the finding that left operated patients show performance scores greater than verbal, and right operated patients show verbal scores greater than performance, is significant both by nonparametric and parametric tests ($\chi^2 = 14.9, p < 0.001; z = 3.54, p < 0.001, z = 4.82, p < 0.001$). Obviously some patients operated on the left have changed since before the operation.

The changes in performance and verbal scores made by any individual from before to after operation can be described on the performance-verbal correlation diagram by one of four classes of change: gain in both performance and verbal scores, loss of both, increased performance but loss on the verbal scale, and decreased performance and gain on the verbal scale. Figure 3 illustrates these changes theoretically. Losses or gains on both

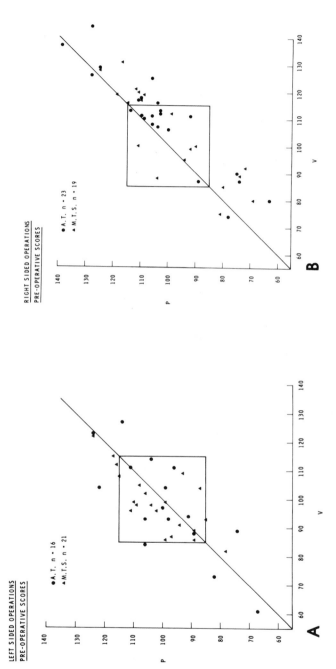

Figure 1.   Scattergram showing performance and verbal scale score of each patient before operation. This diagram is a visual correlation of P and V. A, left operations; B, right operations.

Table 6. Number of Patients Preoperatively with $P > V$ or $V > P$ by Side of Lesion

	$P > V$	$V > P$	Total
Left lesion	24	10	34
Right lesion	8	33	41
Total	32	43	75

Four patients where $P = V$ were excluded.

scales (P+V+; P−V−) are shifts along the F axis; they result in increased or decreased F but are not strongly "lateralizing." Changes in performance and verbal scores of unlike sign (P+V−; P−V+) are lateralizing since they occur at right angles to the F axis.

These functions are illustrated in Table 8, where all 64 patients who changed on both scales are represented. Of these 64 changes, 41 were along the F axis and 23 at right angles to it. The least frequently occurring change was P−V+. Considered as changes of either performance or verbal scores there were 43 P+, 21 P−, 36 V+, and 28 V−.

Table 9 is extracted from Table 8 to show the effects of side, sex, and pathology on these functions. The side operated is without influence on the number of changes that occur along the F axis; the functions P+V+ and P−V− occur equally after operation on either side. P+V− changes occur most often after left operation, and P−V+ after right operations. Sex has no significant effect on the distribution of these functions. The effect of type of pathology is that 12 of 15 P+V− moves occurred in the alien tissue group, but there was no other notable effect.

Tables 10 and 11 display only those 34 patients who changed on both performance and verbal scores after operation and whose change in either

Table 7. Number of Patients Postoperatively with $P > V$ or $V > P$ by Side of Operation

	$P > V$	$V > P$	Total
Left operation	10	26	36
Right operation	28	9	37
Total	38	35	73

Three patients where $P = V$ were excluded.

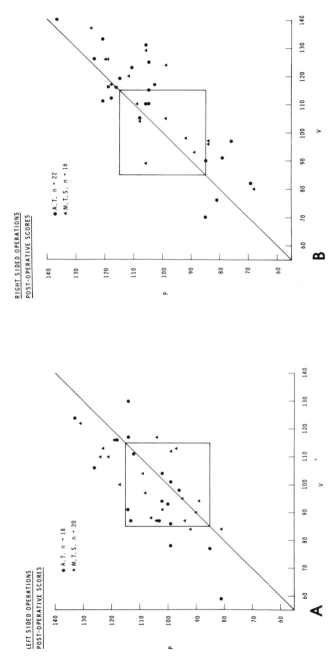

Figure 2. Scattergram showing performance and verbal score of each patient after operation. This diagram is a visual correlation of P and V. A, left operations; B, right operations.

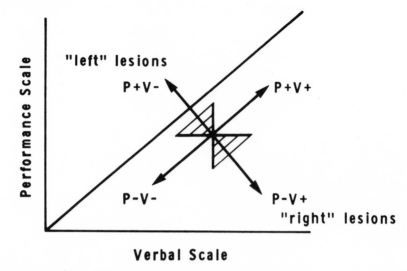

Figure 3. Gains and losses on verbal and performance scale scores produce shifts in the locus of points on the V-P correlation diagram.

performance or verbal scores was ten or more points. Table 10 shows the size of the changes in each of these 34 patients. No significant difference between the side operated on can be shown in the number of patients who made any particular form of change on the performance or verbal scales independently when either any degree of change, or only a change of ten points or more, was considered.

In Table 11, the joint performance and verbal changes are illustrated for this reduced group of 34 patients. It remains true that there are twice as many changes along the F axis as at right angles to it.

All eight P+V− moves occurred in the alien tissue group and seven of the eight followed operations on the left temporal lobe in the alien tissue group. The only four P−V+ moves were in the mesial temporal sclerosis group.

These changes are shown diagrammatically in Figures 4–7. The figures reinforce the mathematical data by showing that the majority of changes are fairly well in the line of the F axis even though they may involve crossing the diagonal and changing the sign of the verbal-performance difference. Such changes occur equally in all four figures. The only group that shows consistent changes, at variance to the general rule, was the left alien tissue group (Figure 7).

Table 8. Total Number of Patients Changing on Both Performance and Verbal Scales after Operation

Group		P+ V+	P− V−	P+ V−	P− V+	Total	Total with P or V > 10	Total N of Group
Mesial temporal sclerosis								
Left operation	Female	3	1	0	0	4	2	5
	Male	4	5	3	1	13	6	16
Right operation	Female	3	1	0	3	7	4	10
	Male	5	1	0	1	7	4	10
Alien tissue								
Left operation	Female	1	1	4	0	6	5	10
	Male	4	0	4	0	8	4	10
Right operation	Female	4	2	1	0	7	3	9
	Male	4	2	3	3	12	6	18
Total		28	13	15	8	64	34	88

Table 9. Total Number of Patients Changing after Operation on Both Performance and Verbal Scales by at Least Ten Points on Either Scale

Group	P+ V+	P− V−	P+ V−	P− V+	Total
Left operation	12	7	11	1	31
Right operation	16	6	4	7	33
Female	11	5	5	3	24
Male	11	8	10	5	40
Mesial temporal sclerosis	15	8	3	5	31
Alien tissue	13	5	12	3	33

Table 10. Actual Scale Score Changes for the 34 Patients with Performance or Verbal More Than Ten Scale Points Changed after Operation

	Left Operations				Right Operations			
Group	P+	V+	P−	V−	P+	V+	P−	V−
Mesial temporal sclerosis								
Female	11	10			11	7		
	26	5			19	15		
						10	2	
						4	12	
Male			13	2	8	18		
			18	15	10	8		
	13	14				1	19	
	12	8					7	12
	28	1						
		8	11					
Alien tissue								
Female	14			6	19	10		
	4			11			23	1
	6			17			25	27
	14			1				
			23	3				
Male	1			15	12	4		
	14			2	11	3		
	22			8	21	13		
	22	9					22	13
							8	11
					16			6
N	13	7	4	10	9	11	8	6
N 10+ points	10	2	4	4	8	4	5	4

Table 11. Total Number of Patients Changing Either Performance or Verbal Scores More Than Ten Points after Operation

Group		P+ V+	P− V−	P+ V−	P− V+	Total
Mesial temporal	Left	5	2	0	1	8
sclerosis	Right	4	1	0	3	8
Alien tissue	Left	1	1	7	0	9
	Right	4	4	1	0	9
Total		14	8	8	4	34
Both groups	Left	6	3	7	1	17
	Right	8	5	1	3	17

DISCUSSION

Two types of influence on performance and verbal abilities are considered in this study. First, the influence that the epileptogenic lesion had upon the acquisition, development, and deployment of skills. Second, the effect of lobectomy upon skills as they had been influenced by the lesion.

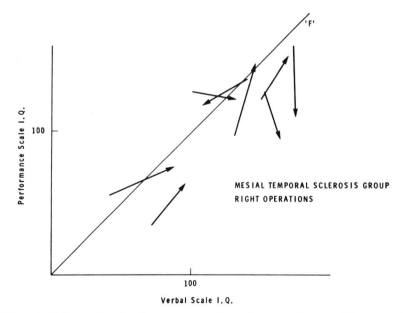

Figure 4. Patients changing ten or more points after operation: mesial temporal sclerosis group. Right operations.

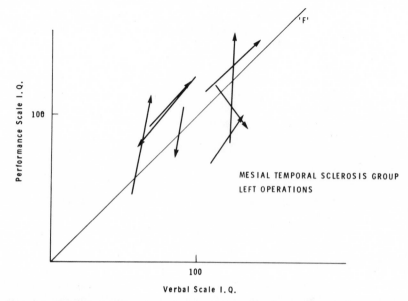

Figure 5. Patients changing ten or more points after operation: mesial temporal sclerosis group. Left operations.

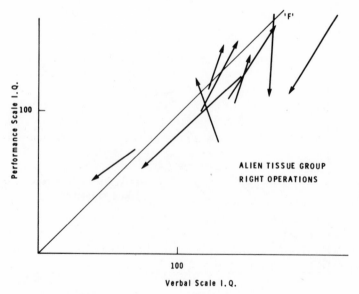

Figure 6. Patients changing ten or more points after operation: alien tissue group. Right operations.

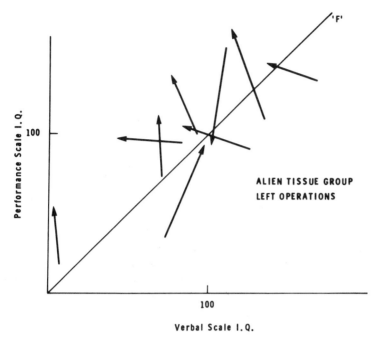

Figure 7. Patients changing ten or more points after operation: alien tissue group. Left operations.

Two types of epileptogenic lesions are considered: alien tissue whose time of origin is probably mostly prenatal, and mesial temporal sclerosis whose time of origin is mainly from 9 months to 3 years postnatally. Our expectation that these lesions will have exerted different influences upon the developing brain seems justified by the results of preoperative testing. As predicted by an earlier hypothesis (Taylor, 1969), scale scores of females with mesial temporal sclerosis in the left temporal lobe are lowest. Patients with right temporal alien tissue lesions have elevated verbal scale scores, a feature that had been noted previously in association with neurosis (Taylor, 1972). Nevertheless, the difference between verbal and performance scale scores is generally modest. The situation that obtains before operation, illustrated in Figure 1, is best regarded as reflecting the compromise between the deleterious effects of the epileptogenic lesion on verbal or performance abilities and the best compensation that could be achieved. There seems to be a tendency to approximate V and P to reduce the "lateralizing" effect of the lesion. Nor are the residual discrepancies all due to deficits; they may be enhancements. As has been shown previously by others (Benton, 1962b), the right and left lesioned groups in this study differed in verbal IQ but not in performance IQ. The left lesioned group had inferior verbal ability. But the left lesioned group showed no statistical difference between their verbal and performance scores, whereas the right lesioned group showed superior verbal ability. Thus if the right lesioned group show superior verbal skills, but similar performance skills to the left lesioned group, this must be due to relative enhancement of the verbal abilities of the right lesioned group. This supports the suggestion that increased early exploratory drive might lead to increased intelligence (Ounsted, 1970). Figure 8 illustrates an ideal model of the situation.

The difference scores shown in Table 4 illustrate the interactions between side of lesion, sex of subject, and nature of lesion. The author has been interested in the development of sex differences, especially in the different organization of male and female brains (Ounsted and Taylor, 1972; Taylor, 1974; Taylor and Ounsted, 1972), and believes that developmental pace is, itself, a sexually differentiating mechanism. Pace differences are a function of the Y chromosome. Thus, brain lesions occurring at any given age produce regular and consistent but different patterns of effect as between the sexes, since the cerebral substrate will already be sexually differentiated and, age for age, will be at a different developmental stage.

After the operation, a sufficient number of left operated patients have had their verbal-performance difference modified for the left operated group to show a significant verbal-performance discrepancy. There was no material change in the right operated group who had shown this previously. It was clear that in analyzing the effects of operation it was insufficient to consider verbal and performance abilities separately. An important theoretical aspect of this study was to derive a tactic that explores their joint effect. It is also possible to study changes in these conjoined scores as "moves" across the correlation diagram.

Gain in performance and verbal ability was the most common effect. There have been reports of psychological benefit resulting from cerebral damage (Storey, 1967), but in the case of removing epileptogenic foci it must be recognized that lobectomy might enhance cerebral function by improving its performance generally; however, it might also reduce performance by the excising of tissue. This point has been previously emphasized (Milner, 1954). Two-thirds of all changes of P and V were in the F axis and thus only weakly lateralizing by increasing the verbal-performance differences. Thus, even when a large surgical lesion is made, verbal and performance skills stay approximate to each other so that changes in one usually determine a like sign change in the other. The effects, P+V− and P−V+, did occur but they were clearly special instances. All the P+V− changes that

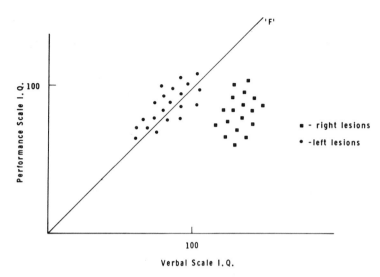

Figure 8. Ideal model of the effects of left and right cerebral lesions on verbal and performance scores.

included one change of ten or more points, and the entire excess of all P+V− over all P−V+, were due to operations on alien tissue patients. Milner (1975) attributes this effect to age, without explaining the means by which "age" accounts for the finding. The only instance of a P+V− change in the right alien tissue group was in the case of the only male, operated on the right, who had developed a schizophrenia-like psychosis. He was left handed. No general effect of left handedness was noted except that it was common in the alien tissue series (Taylor, 1975). Overall, 20.4% of the 88 patients were left handed as compared with Satz's figure of 17% for patients with epilepsy (Satz, 1972).

Granted the effects shown here, there may be a tendency to regard both V and P in Wechsler Tests as themselves lateralized. This temptation should be resisted. It is better to consider the evidence as supportive of the viewpoint of Semmes (1968), that the two hemispheres work to a different strategy; the left containing some localized, point-specific skills, the right hemisphere skills being more diffusely represented. There is some anatomical evidence of different organization in the left and right cerebral hemisphere (Geschwind and Levitsky, 1968; Lansdell, 1964; Wada, Clarke, and Hamm, 1975; Witelson and Pallie, 1973). Left hemisphere lesions, then, may or may not disrupt measured skills, but whether they do or not may be quite anatomically precise. Right lesions may cause losses by reducing the general functional efficiency of the lobe and their removal may produce greater gains than losses; whereas, if lesions in the left temporal lobe are already producing problems, then their removal may increase them.

Alien tissue lesions in the left temporal lobe are a special case. Lobectomy leads to verbal deficits. This was not so for left sided lobectomy revealing mesial temporal sclerosis. It seems that the lobe with alien tissue in it was functional up to the operation whereas the lobe with mesial temporal sclerosis had previously reorganized so that the surgical ablation produced no further significant deficit to general verbal skills. The effect of infantile hemiplegia treated by hemispherectomy provides an analogy. Hence, it seems that patients with alien tissue lesions in the left temporal lobe, the group most vulnerable to schizophrenia-like psychosis (Taylor, 1975), suffered a dysfunctional, irritative, epileptogenic lesion in a lobe that was still functioning. Perhaps that was part of their problem.

At least this study strongly suggests that within the large and mixed group of patients who suffer psychomotor epilepsy of temporal lobe origin, there are some with small, alien tissue lesions of the left temporal lobe who are peculiarly susceptible to schizophrenia-like psychosis and who also show evidence of cognitive effects that separate them from the rest. For future studies the more precise the clinical, neuropathological, and psychological data are, the easier it will be to avoid empty pointless wrangling about population sampling. The population of patients with temporal lobe epilepsy contains almost as much variety as the rest of the population.

Our knowledge of the effects on intelligence of temporal lobe lesions in man has grown slowly from single case studies, through studies of small groups of patients. It was necessary at first, in order to reach any conclusions at all, to consider together, as ostensibly homogeneous, patients who differed widely in the development of their disorder. Only now has a sufficiently large series of patients, with known lesions in the temporal lobe adequately described, become available to enable the tactics of research to change from aggregating information to sorting it out; to deduce the varieties of effect and relate them to relevant variables. We need to approach the new possibilities with an open mind. As Semmes (1968) observed, the hemispheric specialization cannot be too rigid in early life since each can compensate for the loss of the other; children's recovery from aphasia was shown by Guttman (1942). Thus, early hemispheric organization is superseded. Some of the epileptogenic lesions found in the temporal lobes will have been incorporated in the brain before this reorgnization. Others (Taylor, 1969) will be located in the brain partly as determined by that reorganization. We cannot continue to regard "brain lesions" nor indeed "temporal lobectomies" as all of a piece.

This is, partly, the purpose of bringing this study to the attention of neuropsychologists interested in learning problems. The verbal and performance scales of the Wechsler tests are relatively crude, but well-validated measures. An estimate of intelligence is always made before subjects are included in complex testing for "learning problems." Yet relatively little has emerged by way of understanding the neurological basis of the most commonly used intelligence tests themselves. It is also necessary to understand, since we deal mainly with individuals who are surviving in society, that reparative processes are dominant, and that the brain is plastic and optimistic—it is doing its best and, by definition, securing survival.

What have been studied are not "the effects of temporal lobe lesions," but the results of what a series of brains have made of their own particular lesion. Between the small areas of imperfection in the brain and the patients' measurable functions and predicaments are vast modifications made by innumerable factors mostly unknown and largely unaccounted for. The more reason to respect such associations as we can manage to glimpse! For, I believe, and it is an article of faith, that what happens is governed by rules.

ACKNOWLEDGMENTS

This study was made possible by the painstaking work of Mr. Murray Falconer over a period of 20 years. Dr. J.A.N. Corsellis and Dr. C. Bruton at Runwell Hospital provided the neuropathological evidence from which the alien tissue group derived. It was greatly assisted by Mrs. Susan Marsh. I am indebted to my colleagues Dr. Janet Lindsay and Dr. Christopher Ounsted. I am grateful to John Richardson of the Neuropsychology Unit at the Churchill Hospital for the statistical analysis.

Neurobehavioral Relationships in Young Children: Some Remarks on Concepts and Methods

Alex F. Kalverboer

Once, Beach gave a lecture on the Ramstergig, an animal species, in which all relationships between anatomical, psychological, and behavioral characteristics were completely known and never subject to controversy (Tobach et al., 1971). Relationships between hormonal action, brain processes, and behavior followed precisely current theories. This mysterious animal turned out to be a composition of the rat, the hamster, and the guinea pig, animals at the very basis of human psychology, in which these relationships were much less unequivocal than in the ramstergig.

Undoubtedly, structure−function relationships are far more complicated in humans than in any lower animal species. This is particularly true in young children. Quite minor changes in the environment can alter the behavior dramatically, regardless of the child's neurological status. Results of studies on neurobehavioral relationships in young children (Kalverboer, 1975) show the complete fallacy of opinions suggesting simple one-to-one relationships between children's neurological status and behavior. Labels such as learning disorders, hyperactivity, minimal brain dysfunction, etc., each cover an enormous variety of very complex neurological and behavioral phenomena.

Before speculating about the determination of neurobehavioral problems in children, we have to consider what we mean by the labels we use. Data obtained from my studies on neurobehavioral relationships in young children are reported here in order to:

1. Present a method of direct observation and quantitative analysis of behavior that seems promising for the study of problems of the MBD type.
2. Make some general remarks on the neurobehavioral relationships in young children.

173

The work was triggered by the problem of learning and behavior disorders in children; these disorders are supposedly related to a nonoptimal condition of the nervous system and are described in the literature under headings such as minimal brain dysfunction (MBD) or special learning disorders. Such terms generally stand for a conglomerate of very complex learning and behavioral disturbances that are sometimes linked to functional disorders of the central nervous system (CNS), as indicated in so-called soft neurological signs. But even children without any neurological signs have been considered to suffer from MBD, solely on the basis of behavioral phenomena. In general, the concept is applied for school-age children (6–13 years of age) in whom learning and/or behavioral disorders have already developed.

METHOD

This study examines relationships between neurological findings and free-field behavior at the preschool age.[1] The material was collected during one of a series of follow-up studies, carried out at the Department of Developmental Neurology in Groningen since 1956 (for details see Kalverboer, 1975; see Figure 1). This study concerns 147 preschool children (age range 4–5 years), randomly selected from the hospital population of full-term newborns in 1962–1963, on whom complete obstetrical and neonatal neurological data were available. The group carries a somewhat higher risk for minor neurological dysfunctions than the population in general, because of medical or social indication for hospital delivery. All children lived in their homes at preschool age and none of them was included in this group on the basis of the presence of behavior problems. Two children presenting serious neurological problems (spastic hemiplegia and oligophrenia) at preschool age were excluded from the analysis, because of our focus on the implications of *minor* neurological conditions for the child's behavior.

At 5 years of age, standardized neurological assessments were related to systematic and detailed observations of the child's behavior. The study was "blind" in that the examinations were conducted independently. The neurological examination was based on techniques of Touwen and Prechtl (1970). Each child obtained measures for six neurological

---

[1] In a strict sense the term "free-field" behavior should be applied only to behavior in a natural environment. In human as well as in animal research this term is also used for the behavior shown by a freely moving subject in a laboratory setting where the subject is only limited by the specific structure of the environment. In this chapter the term is mainly used in this last connotation.

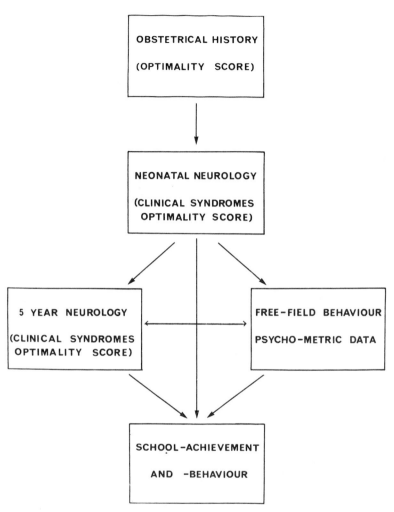

Figure 1. Flow diagram of studies performed in the Department of Developmental Neurology during the last 20 years.

categories (Table 1), labeled as sensorimotor, posture, coordination, chore-iform movements, maturation of functions, and maturation of response. Free-field behavior was studied in relation to these measures. Behavioral observation took place in a specially designed play-room with a block pattern on the floor (Figure 2).

Behavior was video-recorded through a one-way screen and from a corner of the room and analyzed from video recordings by two cooperat-

Table 1. Neurological Categories*

Sensorimotor	Posture	Coordination
Resistance to passive movements	Posture of the feet, standing	Romberg
Tendon reflexes of the arms	Posture, walking	Kicking against examiner's hand
Tendon reflexes of the legs	Body posture, standing	Following object, sitting
Abnormal skin reflex	Posture of the legs, standing	Response to push, standing
Threshold tendon reflexes of the arms	Posture of the feet, sitting	Fingertip–nose test
Active power		Rebound
Skin reflexes of the leg on the toes		
Threshold tendon reflexes of the legs		
Position of the arms in forward extension		
Plantar response		

Choreiformity	Maturation of Functions (Gross Motor Functions)	Maturation of Responses
Choreiformity in finger muscles	Heel–toe gait	Planter grasp
Choreiformity in eye, tongue, and face musculature	Raising into sitting	Mayer
Choreiformity in arm and trunk muscles	Walking on heels	Lery
	Walking on tiptoe	Galant
	Hopping	
	Standing on one leg	
	Diadochokinesis	

*Details on assessment and evaluation in Touwen and Prechtl: The Neurological Examination of the Child with Minor Nervous Dysfunction, Heinemann, London, 1970.

ROOM – PLAN

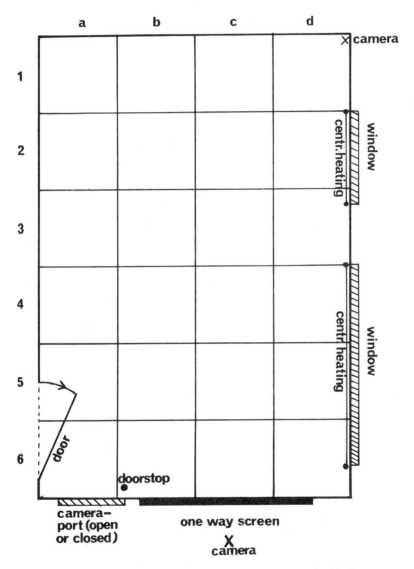

Figure 2. Plan of the observation room. The squares represent the block pattern on the floor. Each square is 80 × 80 cm.

ing observers. Children were observed in six differently structured environments, always in the same sequence:

1. Together with mother in the novel empty room (3 min)
2. Alone in the empty room for the first time (3 min)
3. With blocks and a passive observer (10 min)
4. Alone in the empty room for the second time (3 min)
5. Alone with a variety of toys (15 min)
6. Alone with one "non-motivating" toy (5 min).

These environments were selected because they differed with respect to a number of aspects important for the structuring of the behavior at preschool age: the novelty of the environment, the presence of a social figure, and the amount and variety of material.

Behavior was described in terms of predefined categories, partly derived from systems of Hutt, Hutt, and Ounsted (1965), Berkson (1969), and McGrew (1972), and partly developed in pilot studies preliminary to this study. These categories allowed for a detailed description of the behavior of the child in relation to the social environment (mother, observer), the physical environment (fixtures in the room, play material), and the child's body. Aspects of the motor, visual, and verbal activity were scored. The procedures of registration, observation, scoring, and coding of behavior were standardized as much as possible. Details of design, categorization, and modes of analysis are given in Kalverboer (1975). Reliability studies indicated that measures were sufficiently high for a study in which a group of children are compared, most coefficients reaching values of 0.80 or higher.

RESULTS AND DISCUSSION

One of the most striking findings in this study was the enormous *intra-individual variability* in children's behavior, depending on the situation in which the children were observed. Most of the significant correlations between identical behavior patterns in the six observational situations ranged from 0.20 to 0.35, indicating that scores had only 4–12% variance in common; one would have little success in trying to predict behavior in one situation by knowledge of that in another. With an interest in the generality of so-called "hyperactive" behavior, a separate analysis was performed on the amount of gross motor activity of children in the various observational conditions. Each child obtained a compound score for the amount of locomotion, changes in body postures and locomotion patterns, and number of times fixtures in the room were manipulated. In each situation

20% of the children were taken with the highest "motor-activity" scores. Remarkably enough, only 1 out of the 117 children included in this analysis belonged to the 20% highest in all six observational situations. This finding deserves some attention from those interested in the so-called hyperactivity syndrome and is highly relevant for the MBD discussion. These and other findings in this study indicate the complete fallacy of stereotyped opinions about neurobehavioral relationships in so-called MBD children.

In the present study, the differences in behavior between neurologically optimal and nonoptimal children were generally more apparent in mildly distressing than in more stimulating situations. Especially in the case of girls, the first situation (together with mother in the novel room) distinguished between the children with a favorable and a nonfavorable neurological status. Those with unfavorable neurological scores showed a high amount of room exploration in the unfamiliar room, while girls with a more favorable neurological status showed signs of discomfort and kept close to their mothers. In the boys, on the other hand, behavior was most strongly affected by neurological dysfunctions in situations with a low amount of stimulating input, e.g., in the empty, familiar room. After a high amount of room exploration, paying much attention to the one-way mirror, boys with unfavorable neurological scores dropped to a disinterested sort of behavior, waiting passively or showing random motor activity until the end of the observation period. Most intriguing were differences between boys with and without mild neurological impairment when a variety of toys was available. In contrast to results in other play conditions, where children with unfavorable neurological scores played at a low level, in this condition with a variety of toys, boys with unfavorable neurological scores showed more constructive play at a high level than the boys with a good neurological status.

The data indicate that neurological dysfunctions may have quite different effects on the organization of the behavior in stimulating and nonstimulating environments. They show that children with mild neurological impairment may function quite well in a moderately stimulating, but not too distracting, environment. Such data have implications for educational practice; they call for carefully designed observational studies of neurobehavioral problems in children. By systematic variations of the complexity and motivating value of observational conditions, one can try to define for each child the environments in which he functions optimally. These findings indicate that even a mildly impaired system has a large amount of freedom to vary behavior. This view of the variability of behavior is very similar to that advanced by writers such as Waddington (1971), whose view of the genetic control of behavior is far less restrictive than that of some earlier geneticists. Waddington's conception is of "chreods" or "pathways of development" that allow many factors to influence behavior but do, nevertheless, put some genetic limitation on the organism's adaptability. Waddington postulates that there are genetically based differences in the organism's capacity to maintain its functional integrity in the presence of external stress. Hence one may take Waddington's concept and use it to state that, despite the neurological impairment, the organism has a great deal of freedom and is able to display a wide variety of behaviors, but that the impairment does imply some limits on the organism's ability to adapt. One should, therefore, be most careful in selecting educational environments for children with neurological impairment. Those environments that cause stress to the child will be most sensitive in distinguishing between children with and without neurological problems.

These results further show the gross oversimplification in studies in which groups of children labeled as children with learning disorders, hyperactives, MBD cases, etc., are compared with controls. Such studies suggest behavioral and neurological "homogenity" within such groups and simple one-to-one relationships between neurological factors on the one hand and behavioral and learning problems on the other hand. Often such relationships owe more to the perceptual and cognitive schemata of the observer than to the factual behavior of the child.

Many MBD studies show fallacies, such as the following:

1. Biased groups; groups of children referred to outpatient clinics because of behavioral and/or learning disorders.
2. Dubious criteria for brain damage or brain dysfunction.
3. Lack of standardization of methods for neurological and behavioral assessment.
4. Built-in correlations between data from different assessments.
5. Relating poorly defined so-called "soft" neurological signs to complex behavior disorders.

Clinical descriptions and psychometric data almost exclusively concern school-aged children presenting learning and behavioral problems. Data are lacking relating children's free-field behavior to their neurological condition, although problems reported by parents often concern daily life adaptation. In the light of the above discussion, the best strategy in MBD studies in children seems to be to analyze in detail the behavioral repertoire in relevant situations and to relate findings to those obtained in comprehensive neurological assessments.

Often, relationships at the behavioral level are obscured by the application of "sophisticated" statistical techniques. Many psychologists try to "reconstruct" behavior by inspecting factor matrices. Complicated techniques can be useful and even necessary, but only when we proceed step by step from what is really going on, carefully considering the consequences of successive reductions. Very often, sophistication is applied at the wrong place; e.g., when people spend much energy and money in precisely measuring all sorts of physiological parameters, relating outcomes to very crude clinical impressions of the behavior.

Although meaningful relations between children's neurological status and behavior were found in all six experimental environments, in general the relationships were rather weak. Differences in neurological status account for no more than 5% of the variance in the free-field behavior. There are large numbers of children with an unfavorable neurological status who deviate from the general picture. This implies that detailed behavioral assessments are necessary in young children who are suspected of being at risk for developing neurobehavioral problems.

Some restrictions must also be placed on the interpretation of neurological findings in young children in general; particularly in the evaluation of minor signs of nervous dysfunction that are frequently reported in children with learning or behavioral problems, structural evidence for a diagnosis of brain damage is generally lacking. Such signs are considered indicative of an unfavorable condition of the nervous system, primarily on the basis of "indirect" evidence: empirical data showing that such signs relate to generally accepted "risk factors" or are more common in children with problem behavior than in controls; on similarities between such minor dysfunctions and signs in children with unequivocal evidence of brain damage; and on results of experimental studies on early brain lesions in animals. Problems are compounded in children by the functional changes throughout development. There is still a serious lack of normative data about the neurological repertoire of children at various age levels.

Results of the present study confirmed the opinions of several authors (e.g., Bell, Weller, and Waldrop, 1971; Wolff and Hurwitz, 1973) who stress the necessity of analyzing neurobehavioral data separately for boys and girls. Neurobehavioral relationships are stronger in boys than in girls, and the kinds of relationships are different. In boys, minor neurological dysfunctions seemed to affect the behavioral organization particularly in nonstimulating environments, whereas in girls contact and exploratory activity in an unfamiliar environment distinguished between neurological groups (for details see Kalverboer, 1975). An interesting finding was that in girls signs of *dysmaturity* of the nervous system related most strongly to free-field behavior, whereas in boys signs of neurological *dysfunction* (such as choreiform dyskinesia, lack of motor coordination) had the strongest effects on the behavior. Although no conclusions about MBD can be drawn from these data, one might speculate that Kinsbourne's (1973) view that "all indicators of MBD represent the normal state of affairs in younger children" does not hold equally for boys and girls. In girls the dysmaturity aspect may be predominant, whereas in boys the aspect of neurological dysfunction may play a more prominent role in the genesis of the typical MBD case. Because learning and behavioral problems of the MBD type are much more common in boys than in girls, one might speculate that at school age the dysfunctions of the CNS are more important in the determination of such difficulties than dysmaturity of the CNS.

Neither the genetic make-up nor the neurological status accounts to any very great extent for the variability in behavior. From the very beginning of extra-uterine life, there exists a complex interaction between the individual and his environment. Certain behaviors of the infant may trigger specific reactions in the caregiver, and vice versa. For example, newborns who adapt their movements and body posture smoothly to those of the mother may give her less difficulty in handling than infants who are motorically inconsistent. So-called "apathetics" possibly get less attention from parents than alert newborns who react spontaneously. Also, the initial reaction tendencies of the child may be strengthened by his social environment (Sameroff, 1974).

As the human newborn is increasingly studied, precise observation of developing social interaction in children of varying biological and neurological make-up will be needed in order to reach a better understanding of the determination of behavioral differences. Clearly, behavioral differences between young children have at least partly developed as a result of such complex interactions.

All findings in this study point to the very complex determination of behavioral differences and suggest that linking any behavior directly to an implication of brain damage is dangerous and unrealistic. One must define precisely the situation in which a child shows a particular behavior. Appropriately used, the method of free-field observation allows for a refined analysis of complex behavior. Making allowance for the limitations of the method, free-field observation can provide valuable information about problem behavior in young children and is therefore particularly suited to neurobehavioral studies.

Part IV

Cerebral Dominance and Learning Disabilities

Sex Differences in the Neuropsychological Development of Verbal and Spatial Skills

Anthony W. H. Buffery

Developmental neuropsychology should not begin and end with childhood. A neuropsychological theory must place a learning disorder within a developmental perspective and in relation to normal ability if it is to have both heuristic and practical value.

This chapter describes two studies, one of normal children and another of normal adults. Each study was concerned with sex differences in the cerebral lateralization of verbal and spatial function. The "child study" investigated sex differences in the cross-modal matching of auditory–visual pairs of verbal or spatial stimuli both within and between the cerebral hemispheres of the 5–9-year-old brain—a prerequisite for the normal development of certain linguistic and perceptual skills. The "adult study" investigated sex differences in the relationships between the direction and degree of the cerebral lateralization of verbal and spatial function in the 18–25-year-old brain and the direction and degree of eye dominance and hand preference—relationships that are more frequently assumed than assessed.

It is hoped that these data from normal people, who were not suffering from any discernable intellectual difficulty or physical incapacity, will serve as a cautionary tale for any neuropsychologist who has ever been tempted to create an elaborate theory of learning disorder, or indeed of the whole of cognitive development, from nothing more than a cursory glance at the mistakes and laterality of a few children who were suffering from either a severe neurological dysfunction or from the enigma of "minimal brain damage" and variations on that theme.

This research was supported in part by the Medical Research Council and the Department of Education and Science.

CHILD STUDY

Neuropsychology has yet to identify the neural substrata that subserve a child's ability to associate seen events with heard descriptions—an ability basic to the normal acquisition of certain language skills. However, because cerebral hemispheres primarily subserve their contralateral visual hemifield, ear and limb, research into such questions has begun through the introduction of techniques of stimulus presentation that utilize these neuroanatomical relationships. By combining the technique of tachistoscopic presentation to a visual hemifield with that of "dichotic listening" it has proved possible to present a printed word to one cerebral hemisphere for comparison with a spoken word presented to either the same or a different cerebral hemisphere, same—different responses being made by right- or left-hand button presses (Buffery, 1971). The present technique replaces the printed words with easily named drawings but is otherwise similar to that used in the earlier experiment. In both investigations dichotic listening was modified so as to permit the presentation of one word at a time to either ear. Instead of the simultaneous presentation of a different word to each ear, a word to one ear coincided with a burst of white noise to the other. Since the white noise was of the same duration and loudness as the word, a binaural conflict was maintained that was sufficient to dampen transmission via the ipsilateral auditory pathways and thereby facilitate a primarily contralateral cerebral representation (reviewed by Milner, 1962).

METHOD

Subjects

The children were 32 girls and 32 boys of at least average intelligence, aged from 5 to 9 years of age and from a broadly middle-class background. All had normal vision and hearing, and were strongly right-handed as determined by their performance on a modified version of the Annett (1967) questionnaire. All children were tested on Raven's Coloured Progressive Matrices (Raven's) and on an age-appropriate version of the English Picture Vocabulary Test (EPVT) as a guide to their level of spatial and verbal skill, respectively. Eight girls and eight boys made up each of four age groups, viz., 5 years to 5 years 11 months, 6 to 6.11, 7 to 7.11, and 8 to 8.11, within each of which a close cross-sex pairing was attempted on the basis of chronological age and performance on the Raven's and EPVT. Eye dominance was also determined for each child by methods similar to those described in the adult study, but no relationship was found between it and any other data in the child study (24 of the 32 girls and 20 of the 32 boys were right eye dominant, 8 of the girls and 10 of the boys were left eye dominant, and 2 of the boys, both from the youngest age group, were of mixed or indeterminate eye dominance).

Apparatus and Materials

In the verbal task the Easy to Verbalize (EV) stimuli were four monosyllabic nouns chosen from an age-appropriate list of self-generated words (Edwards and Gibbon, 1964). A different set of four words was used for each of the four age groups in an attempt to keep the degree of familiarity constant. The EV visual stimuli were simple drawings of these nouns and the EV auditory stimuli were the same nouns spoken. The drawing of each noun was prepared in black ink on a 8 × 5 in. (20.3 × 12.7 cm) white index card for presentation in a tachistoscope (Electronic Developments). When viewed binocularly by a child, each drawing subtended 4° of visual angle both horizontally and vertically upon a hemiretina and was centered on the horizontal meridian at 4° of visual angle either to the left or to the right of the central fixation point. The spoken names of the drawings were recorded onto a stereophonic tape deck (Brenell 3 Star) and transmitted for dichotic listening (Broadbent, 1954) through stereophonic earphones (Amplivox Jetlite).

In the spatial task the Difficult to Verbalize (DV) visual stimulus was a black dot placed in any one of four positions, i.e., high or low and to the left or right of the central fixation point. The dot was presented at 2° of visual angle, either above or below a point on the horizontal meridian set at 4° of visual angle either to the left or to the right of the central fixation point. The DV auditory stimulus was a tone of either one of two frequencies, viz., 1,200 or 400 Hz. The DV visual and auditory stimuli were presented by the same apparatus as that used for the EV stimuli (see Figure 1).

The child sat in a quiet and darkened room, wearing earphones, looking at the central fixation point on the screen of the tachistoscope and with each thumb resting upon a response button set into an arm of the chair. The children were happy and worked well in this situation and many described it as "like being in a space ship."

A duration of exposure for the visual stimuli and a level of loudness for the auditory stimuli, each compatible with a 90% accuracy of recognition within a sensory modality, were "titrated" (Buffery, 1974) independently for each child with a control set of nouns. Any child who titrated to a tachistoscopic exposure greater than 180 msec or to a level of

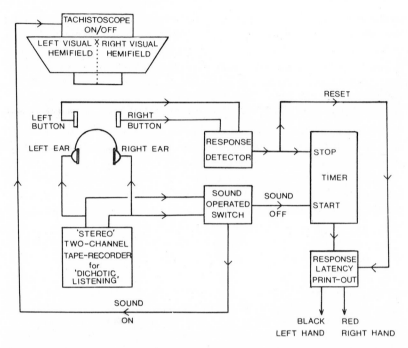

Figure 1. Block diagram of apparatus for testing the ability to compare a visual stimulus with an auditory stimulus when they are presented simultaneously to either the same or to different cerebral hemispheres.

loudness above 70 dB re 20 μN/m^2 was excluded from the subsequent experimental tasks. Where a child's titrated values met these criteria they were used for that child throughout the subsequent experimental tasks. Thus the 64 children who met these criteria not only had equated levels of performance on intramodal recognition prior to cross-modal matching, but also shared the 180-msec constraint upon eye movements, which would limit them to less than 3° of visual angle scan to the left or right of the central fixation point. If eye movements were observed the trial was discounted and repeated later.

After this titration each child was told to fixate the central point and to be ready to see and hear either the EV or DV stimuli. If what was seen was the same as what was simultaneously heard, e.g., in the EV task a drawing of a dog with the spoken word dog, or, in the DV task, a high dot with a 1,200-Hz tone, a child had to press whichever button meant "same." If what was seen was different from what was simultaneously heard, e.g., in the EV task a drawing of a car with the spoken word pig, or, in the DV task, a high dot with a 400-Hz tone, then a child had to press whichever button meant "different." Half the girls and boys in each age group performed the EV task before the DV task and half the reverse. Half of each of these sub-groups made "same" responses with the right-hand button (red print out) and "different" responses with the left-hand button (black print out) and half the reverse.

The onset of the taped auditory stimulus triggered the tachistoscopic exposure of the visual stimulus. Response latencies were measured from the cessation of the auditory stimulus, which was approximately 200–400 msec longer than the visual stimulus. An intertrial interval of 15 sec was started by pressing either button. The EV task and the DV task each consisted of 96 trials; 12 "same" and 12 "different" cross-modal stimulus pairs presented at random for comparison in each of four conditions:

1. Auditory to Left cerebral hemisphere/Visual to Left cerebral hemisphere.
2. Auditory to Left cerebral hemisphere/Visual to Right cerebral hemisphere.
3. Auditory to Right cerebral hemisphere/Visual to Left cerebral hemisphere.
4. Auditory to Right cerebral hemisphere/Visual to Right cerebral hemisphere.

For example, on 12 trials, in either the EV or DV task, a child was presented with an auditory stimulus to the left cerebral hemisphere for comparison with a different visual stimulus presented simultaneously to the right cerebral hemisphere.

RESULTS

No significant interaction was found between task order and performance level but response latencies await analysis. Figure 2 summarizes the performance of the 32 girls and 32 boys on the EV and DV task, respectively. The abscissa divides each set of histograms into the four conditions of stimulus presentation; the upper line indicates whether it was to the left (L) or to the right (R) cerebral hemisphere that the auditory stimulus was initially presented, and the lower line indicates the same for the simultaneously presented visual stimulus. The ordinate is the mean percentage trials correct and consequently the four histograms of a particular age–sex subgroup show the mean percentage distribution of the total trials correct between the four conditions of stimulus presentation. The degree to which the histogram bars deviate from the 25% level of equal distribution may be

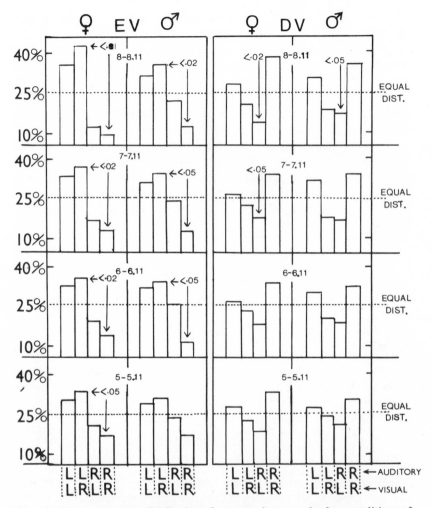

Figure 2. Mean percentage distribution of accuracy between the four conditions of presentation (L, Left cerebral hemisphere; R, Right cerebral hemisphere) for auditory–visual stimulus pairs in the easy to verbalize (EV) and difficult to verbalize (DV) tasks by 5+, 6+, 7+, and 8+ year old, right handed girls (♀) and boys (♂)—8 in each age/sex sub group; *p* values for two-tailed t tests.

taken as an indication of the degree to which the verbal and spatial functioning required by these cross-modal matching tasks have asymmetrical cerebral representation.

In the EV task, for both sexes and at all ages, the greatest accuracy was achieved when an auditory word was presented to the left cerebral hemisphere for comparison with a visual drawing presented simultaneously to the right. This is an example of a "split-load" condition (Buffery, 1971) in which each stimulus of a pair is presented to a different cerebral hemisphere. The condition in which the auditory and visual EV stimuli were both presented to the left cerebral hemisphere was the next easiest with the reversed "split-load" condition being considerably more difficult (i.e., auditory word presented to the right cerebral hemisphere, visual picture to the left). The most difficult condition was when the auditory and visual EV stimuli were both presented to the right cerebral hemisphere. This pattern emerged earlier and was more marked in the girls than in the boys. A statistically significant difference between the four conditions of stimulus presentation was observed in girls of 5+ years ($p < 0.05$); of 6+ and 7+ years ($p < 0.02$); and 8+ years ($p < 0.01$) compared with boys of 6+ and 7+ years ($p < 0.05$); and of 8+ years ($p < 0.02$), where p values are for two-tailed t tests throughout.

In the DV task, for both sexes and at all ages, the greatest accuracy was achieved when the auditory tone and the visual dot were both presented to the right cerebral hemisphere. The condition in which the auditory and visual DV stimuli were both presented to the left cerebral hemisphere was the next easiest, followed by the "split-load" condition in which the auditory and visual stimuli were presented to the left and right cerebral hemispheres, respectively. The remaining "split-load" condition was the most difficult of all (i.e., auditory tone presented to the right cerebral hemisphere, visual dot to the left). The pattern emerged earlier and was slightly more marked in the girls than in the boys, but statistically significant differences (two-tailed t tests) were not as prevalent in the DV task as in the EV task, i.e., in girls at 7+ years ($p < 0.05$) and 8+ years ($p < 0.02$), and in boys only at 8+ years ($p < 0.05$).

DISCUSSION

Although the profiles of the histograms for the EV task (Figure 2) are similar for both sexes of the strongly right-handed children, they do show that cerebral asymmetry for the cross-modal analysis of verbal material emerges later in boys (i.e., around 6 years) than in girls (i.e., present at 5 years). Under this condition of the simultaneous presentation of an auditory and of a visual verbal stimulus, greatest accuracy for same–different judgments was achieved when the word was spoken to the right, i.e., the "split-load" condition of same time, different place. In a similar study (Buffery, 1971) conditions of successive presentation of cross-modal stimuli were included, and the greatest accuracy was then achieved when the two verbal stimuli were presented one after the other to the left cerebral hemisphere, i.e., the "split-load" condition of same place, different time; this is the case whether auditory preceded visual or vice versa. In both studies greater accuracy ensued from the left cerebral hemisphere initially receiving the auditory verbal stimulus. These findings supplement other evidence of sex differences in the development of cerebral dominance (Buffery, 1970; reviewed by Buffery and Gray, 1972) and are in keeping with the known specialization of, usually, the left cerebral hemisphere for the perception of spoken language (Studdert-Kennedy and Shankweiler, 1970).

The profiles of the histograms for the DV task (Figure 2) are also similar for both sexes, although very different from those of the EV task. Again, cerebral asymmetry for cross-modal analysis, this time of spatial material, emerges later in boys (i.e., around 8 years) than in girls (i.e., around 7 years). Under this condition of simultaneous presentation, greater accuracy for same–different judgments was achieved when the tone and the dot were initially received by the same cerebral hemisphere, and in particular when received by the right cerebral hemisphere. Indeed, unlike the EV task, the two "split-load" conditions of the DV task were the more difficult.

These data from the child study indicate greater lateralization of cerebral functions in the brain of the female than in that of the male of the same age. The implication of this to a theory of sex differences in verbal and spatial ability (Buffery and Gray, 1972), and to the question of whether we are observing an omnipresent sex difference or merely a transient lag in male development (reviewed in Ounsted and Taylor, 1972), will be discussed in the light of data from the adult study.

ADULT STUDY

Is a sex difference in cerebral asymmetry of function present in adulthood?

Are there sex differences in the direction and degree of eye dominance or hand preference?

What is the relationship of eye dominance and hand preference to each other and to the lateralization of cerebral function? Can we predict the degree of cerebral lateralization of verbal function from knowledge of the degree of cerebral lateralization of spatial function and vice versa?

Do the levels of performance on verbal and spatial tasks relate to the degree of cerebral lateralization of these functions?

Upon these and related questions the following investigation was designed to shed light.

METHOD

Subjects

The young adults who took part in this study were 100 female and 100 male students at Cambridge or Oxford University from 18 to 25 years of age. All were tested for degree of eye dominance and handedness prior to the experimental tests for degree of verbal or spatial "brainedness."

Apparatus and Materials

Eye dominance was measured at the beginning and end of a testing session by the following five tasks (making ten in all), which are similar to those used by Money (1972).

1. Cone test:	Sighting a target set between the feet through the narrow end of a cone held at waist height.
2. Paper test:	Sighting a target set 5 m away through a small hole in a large piece of paper held initially at arm's length and then drawn close to the face.
3. Preferred finger test:	Aligning the tip of the preferred hand's index finger when held close to the nose with a target set 5 m away.
4. Nonpreferred finger test:	The same as 3, but using the nonpreferred hand's index finger.
5. Ruler test:	Aligning a ruler held by both hands and at arm's length with a target set 5 m away.

Hand preference was measured by performance of the ten tasks on Oldfield's (1971) Edinburgh Handedness Inventory:

1. Writing
2. Drawing
3. Throwing
4. Scissors
5. Toothbrush
6. Knife (without fork)
7. Spoon
8. Broom (upper hand)

9. Striking match (match)

10. Opening box (lid)

Data concerning the task of threading a needle and its relationship to eye dominance, hand preference, and "brainedness" were collected and analyzed separately and are not included in the present report.

The direction and degree of asymmetry in cerebral functioning were determined by analyses of performance on two visual matching tasks, one verbal (EV) and one spatial (DV), each of 80 trials. Eighty pairs of stimuli were tachistoscopically presented at random to the left or right visual hemifield for monocular comparison; 40 trials with one eye followed by 40 trials with the other. Each EV stimulus was a pair of words printed one above the other. Half of these word pairs were similar in meaning, e.g., **GOOD FINE** , and half were not, e.g., **LARGE SMALL** . Each DV stimulus was a pair of abstract designs concocted from the rearranged letters of the words used in the EV task. Half these design-pairs were the same, e.g., and half were different, e.g., . Consequently, in the EV task stimulus pairs had to be judged as being the same or different in meaning but in the DV task they had to be judged as being the same or different in configuration. All the visual stimuli were printed in black Letraset 28 point Futura Demibold capital letters on plain 8 × 5 inch (20.3 × 12.7 cm) white index cards for presentation in the tachistoscope (Electronic Developments).

When viewed, each stimulus pair subtended 3° of visual angle vertically upon a hemiretina and between 3° and 5° of visual angle horizontally, while being centered on the horizontal meridian at 4° of visual angle to the left or right of the central fixation point.

Procedure

In both the EV and DV visual matching tasks, same–different judgments were communicated by right- or left-hand button presses. Similar methods were used to those described in the child study for measuring response accuracy and latency and for controlling for possible order effects.

In a preliminary test a tachistoscopic exposure was titrated for each person that was compatible with 90% accuracy for identifying single words presented under the same constraints of visual angle as those described for the experimental stimuli. Any person titrating to an exposure greater than 180 msec was excluded from the study. These titrated exposures were used by the individual for all the subsequent EV and DV visual stimuli. As in the child study, the preliminary titration of exposure length equated the levels of performance of all the subjects before the experiment and helped to prevent scanning of the stimulus, given its degree of eccentric visual angle and lateral uncertainty. If eye movements were observed the trial was discounted and repeated later.

RESULTS

The *A* parts of Figures 3 to 10 show the direction and degree of eye dominance (ED), hand preference (HP), verbal brainedness (VB), and spatial brainedness (SB) for 100 women; the *B* parts of Figures 3 to 10 show the same for 100 men. The five-point scales for the degrees of laterality used for the ordinates and abscissae in the figures were derived as follows.

In eye dominance the incidence of left eye dominance was subtracted from the incidence of right and divided by the total number of tests, i.e., $(R-L)/10$. Scores of $+1.00$ and $+0.80$ were designated as strongly right ($+R$); $+0.60$ and $+0.40$ as right to some degree (R); $+0.20$, 0.00, or -0.20 as mixed or ambi-eyed (M); -0.40 and -0.60 as left to some degree (L); and -0.80 and -1.00 as strongly left ($+L$).

In hand preference the number of left-hand responses were subtracted from the number of right and divided by the total number of tests, i.e., $(R-L)/10$. The distribution of hand preference across the five-point scale was determined by the same method as that used for eye dominance, with M, in the case of hand preference, representing mixed or ambidextrous handedness.

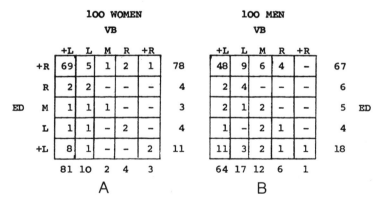

Figure 3. Verbal brainedness vs. eye dominance. VB = Verbal Brainedness; ED = Eye Dominance; SB = Spatial Brainedness; HP = Hand Preference; +R = strongly right; R = Right to some degree; M = mixed or bilateral; L = left to some degree; +L = strongly left.

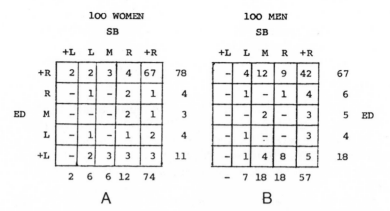

Figure 4. Spatial brainedness vs. eye dominance. Abbreviations as for Figure 3.

The distribution of scores across the five-point scale measuring the direction and degree of laterality in cerebral functioning—whether by the EV task as Verbal Brainedness (VB) or by the DV task as Spatial Brainedness (SB)—was determined from the amount of disparity between the performance levels of the left and right cerebral hemisphere. Since, within each task, 40 stimulus pairs were presented for comparison via the left visual hemifield to the contralateral right cerebral hemisphere, and 40 via the right visual hemifield to the contralateral left cerebral hemisphere, chance level for accuracy of same—different judgments on each side was 20 trials correct. Consequently, the disparity between the performance levels of the left and right cerebral hemisphere could range from approximately

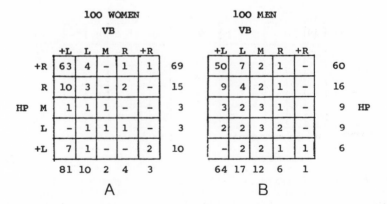

Figure 5. Verbal brainedness vs. hand preference. Abbreviations as for Figure 3.

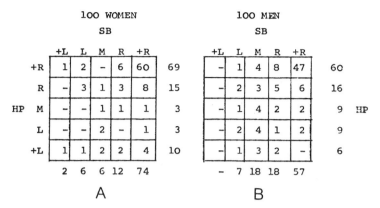

Figure 6. Spatial brainedness vs. hand preference. Abbreviations as for Figure 3.

0 to 20. A disparity of 0 to 5 trials correct was taken as evidence of mixed or bilateral brainedness for either visual-verbal or visual-spatial function (M); a disparity of 6 to 10 trials correct of left or right brainedness to some degree (L or R); and a disparity of 11 to 20 or more trials correct of strong left or right brainedness (+L or +R).

Eye Dominance (ED) Figure 3 shows that 11% of the women and 15% of the men were neither +R nor +L eye dominant. However, whereas 78% of the women had +R eye dominance compared with 67% of the men, 18% of the men had +L eye dominance compared with 11% of the women.

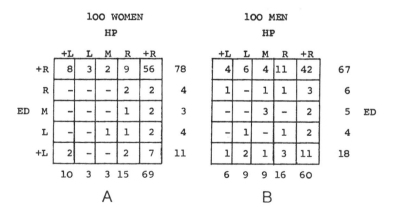

Figure 7. Hand preference vs. eye dominance. Abbreviations as for Figure 3.

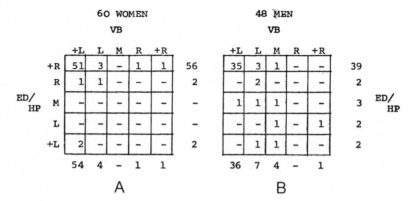

Figure 8. Verbal brainedness vs. eye dominance/hand preference. Abbreviations as for Figure 3.

Hand Preference (HP) Figure 5 shows that more women than men had a strong hand preference, 69% being +R compared with 60% of the men, and 10% being +L compared with 6% of the men. A strong hand preference was not exhibited by 34% of the men, compared with only 21% of the women.

Brainedness Figure 3 shows the degree and laterality of Verbal Brainedness (VB) for the 100 women and 100 men, respectively, and Figure 4 the Spatial Brainedness (SB). Figure 3 shows that 84% of the women had strong cerebral lateralization for visual-verbal functioning, i.e., 81% +L and 3% +R, compared with only 65% of the men, i.e., 64% +L and 1% +R. A

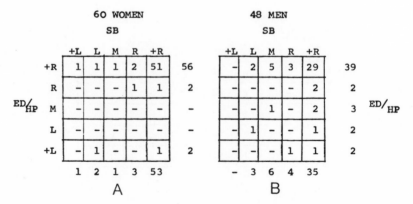

Figure 9. Spatial brainedness vs. eye dominance/hand preference. Abbreviations as for Figure 3.

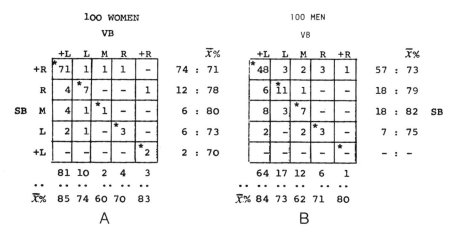

Figure 10. Verbal brainedness vs. spatial brainedness. Asterisks indicate the relationship of verbal to spatial "brainedness" in keeping with the Buffery and Gray (1972) hypothesis of sex differences in the degree of asymmetry of cerebral functions. $\bar{X}\%$ = mean percentage correct. Other abbreviations as for Figure 3.

higher percentage of men than women showed only some degree of cerebral lateralization (R and L) for visual-verbal functioning, i.e., 23% of the men compared with 14% of the women, and 12% of the men showed mixed or bilateral brainedness (M) compared with only 2% of the women. Figure 4 shows that 76% of the women had a strong cerebral lateralization for visual-spatial functioning, i.e., 74% +R and 2% +L, compared with only 57% of the men, i.e., 57% +R and no man with +L. A higher percentage of men than women showed only some degree of cerebral lateralization (R and L) for visual-spatial functioning, i.e., 25% of the men compared with 18% of the women, and 18% of the men showed mixed or bilateral brainedness (M) compared with only 6% of the women.

Eye Dominance and Brainedness Figure 3 shows that contralateral congruity between the degree of Eye Dominance (ED) and of Verbal Brainedness (VB) occurred in 76% of the women but only in 56% of the men (i.e., the sum of the subsquares forming the top left to bottom right diagonal of each figure). Figure 4 shows ipsilateral congruity between the degree of Eye Dominance (ED) and of Spatial Brainedness (SB) occurred in 70% of the women but in only 46% of the men (i.e., the sum of the subsquares forming the top right to bottom left diagonal of each figure).

Hand Preference and Brainedness Figure 5 shows that contralateral congruity between the degree of Hand Preference (HP) and of Verbal Brainedness (VB) occurred in 70% of the women but in only 60% of the men (i.e., the sum of the subsquares forming the top left to bottom right diagonal of each figure). Figure 6 shows that ipsilateral congruity between the degree of Hand Preference (HP) and of Spatial Brainedness (SB) occurred in 65% of the women and in 58% of the men (i.e., the sum of the subsquares forming the top right to bottom left diagonal of each figure).

Eye Dominance and Hand Preference Figure 7 shows that ipsilateral congruity between the degree of Eye Dominance (ED) and of Hand Preference (HP) occurred in 60% of the women but in only 48% of the men (i.e., the sum of the subsquares forming the top right to bottom left diagonal of each figure).

Eye Dominance, Hand Preference, and Brainedness Taking only the 60 women and 48 men who showed an ipsilateral congruity between their degree of eye dominance and hand preference, Figure 8 shows the relationship of this congruity (ED/HP) to Verbal Brainedness (VB) and Figure 9 the relationship of ED/HP to Spatial Brainedness (SB). Figure 8 shows that contralateral congruity between degree of ED/HP and of VB occurred in 52 of the 60 women (86.7%) and in 38 of the 48 men (79.2%). Figure 9 shows that ipsilateral congruity between degree of ED/HP and of SB occurred in 52 of the 60 women (86.7%) but in only 31 of the 48 men (64.6%).

Verbal Brainedness and Spatial Brainedness The incidence and nature of the congruity between the degree of Verbal Brainedness (VB) and of Spatial Brainedness (SB) are shown in Figure 10 for women and men, respectively. Contralateral congruity between the degree of cerebral lateralization of visual-verbal function (VB) and of visual-spatial function (SB) occurred in 84% of the women but in only 69% of the men (i.e., the sum of the subsquares forming the top left to bottom right diagonal of each figure—also marked by asterisks as the predicted relationship from the Buffery and Gray, 1972, hypothesis of sex differences in the degree of asymmetry of cerebral functions).

Accuracy of performance is also summarized in Figure 10. The $\overline{X}\%$ row is the mean percent of trials correct in the visual-verbal task (EV) for each of the five degrees of VB, and the $\overline{X}\%$ column is the mean percent of trials correct in the visual-spatial task (DV) for each of the five degrees of SB. Those women and men with strong cerebral lateralization of visual-verbal functioning (+L or +R for VB) had a higher $\overline{X}\%$ accuracy on the EV task than those with less clear cerebral lateralization (L, M, or R for VB). Figure 10*A* shows that, on the EV task, 81 women who were +L for VB and 3 who were +R for VB had the relatively high mean accuracy scores of 85% and 83% respectively. Similarly, Figure 10*B* shows that, on the EV task, 64 men who were +L for VB had the relatively high mean accuracy score of 84%, and the 1 man who was +R for VB scored with 80% accuracy. However, the reverse was true for the DV task. Those women and men with less clear cerebral lateralization of visual-spatial functioning (L, M, or R for SB) had a higher $\bar{X}\%$ accuracy on the DV task than those with strong cerebral lateralization (+L or +R for SB). Figure 10 shows that 6 women with M for SB and 18 men with M for SB had relatively high mean accuracy scores of 80% and 82%, respectively.

Hemiretinae Only one statistically significant finding emerged from comparison of the levels of performance between different hemiretinae. In the EV task the monocular presentation of word pairs in the right visual hemifield to the nasal hemiretina of the right eye and thence, via a crossing visual pathway, to the contralateral left cerebral hemisphere, was superior to all other routes [$p < 0.05$, t test; a one-tailed test since the direction was predicted from the work on the cat by Hubel and Wiesel (1959), who found that contralateral (nasal) afferent projections activate more striate cortical units than do ipsilateral (temporal) projections]. This finding was particularly clear for those people who combined a strong right eye dominance (+R ED) with a strong left brainedness for visual-verbal function (+L VB), i.e., 69 women in Figure 3*A* and 48 men in Figure 3*B*. The suggestion that the most influential visual pathway is that which connects a dominant eye to the contralateral cerebral hemisphere was made by Kershner (1971), but in relation to the visual-spatial skill of children not the visual-verbal skill of adults. Since only two women and one man combined strong left eye dominance (+L ED) with strong right brainedness for visual-verbal function (ER VB), it is not possible to judge whether the hypothesis of a prepotent visual pathway can be generalized to people with atypical cerebral dominance. It is somewhat surprising that the Kershner (1971) hypothesis for the "acquisition of visuo-spatial dimensionality" should prove so seminal to the analysis of the visual-verbal task (EV) and yet find no support from the analysis of the visual-spatial task (DV).

DISCUSSION

As individuals, these 200 normal, intelligent young adults exhibited a wide variety of degree of lateral congruity and noncongruity among dominant eye, preferred hand, and verbal or spatial cerebral hemisphere. Certainly, such idiosyncratic patterns of laterality in a university population are contrary to any simplistic hypothesis of crossed laterality being a sufficient condition for learning disorder (e.g., Delacato, 1963). This is particu-

larly so when such an hypothesis is without reference to assessed brainedness, i.e., without knowledge of the functional nature of whichever
cerebral hemisphere is in the influential contralateral relationship to the
favored eye, hand, ear, or, indeed, foot (e.g., Delacato, 1967).

Women showed stronger lateralization of hand preference and of verbal
and spatial cerebral functioning than men. The one exception was eye
dominance, where men showed a higher incidence of strong left eye
dominance (18%) than women (11%). Whereas a strong cerebral lateralization of visual-verbal function was associated with a high level of performance
in the EV task and was characteristic of women, a more bilateral
cerebral representation of visual-spatial function was associated with a high
level of performance in the DV task and was characteristic of men. This is
in keeping with the Buffery and Gray (1972) hypothesis of a sex difference in cerebral asymmetry of function. So too is the high incidence of a
lateral counterbalancing of the verbal and spatial cerebral functions, e.g.,
strong left verbal brainedness (+L VB) combined with strong right spatial
brainedness (+R SB), or bilateral verbal brainedness (M VB) combined
with bilateral spatial brainedness (M SB), etc. Figures 10A and 10B show that
a lateral counterbalance of cerebral functions occurred in 84% of the women
and in 69% of the men (i.e., the sum of the subsquares marked with an
asterisk in each table). Since Buffery and Gray (1972) claim that the
degree of lateralization of cerebral function has different implications for
verbal and spatial skill, then the women's advantage in the visual-verbal
task and the men's advantage in the visual-spatial task may reflect a sex
difference in the incidence of the various degrees of lateralization of
function rather than a sex difference in performance level per se.

Finally, now that a sex difference in cerebral asymmetry of function
has been demonstrated in adults which is similar to that found in children
(reviewed by Buffery and Gray, 1972), an explanation in terms of a
transient lag in male development is not appropriate.

SUMMARY AND CONCLUSIONS

The investigation of cerebral functions by techniques derived from experimental psychology has been reviewed by Dimond and Beaumont (1974),
and recent advances in the study of laterality (e.g., Marshall, Caplan, and
Holmes, 1975) and of cross-modal asymmetries (e.g., Hines and Satz,
1974) suggest that this is at least one area of behavioral science where
expansion is accompanied by improvement. The techniques and theories,
however, are not becoming ends in themselves. Their applications to the
problems of neurosurgical patients (Milner, 1971) and deaf children (Luki-

anowicz, 1975) exemplify bastions against such phenomena as a Quarterly Journal of Tachistoscopic Exposure or an International Congress of Dichotic Listening.

The present studies have used tachistoscopic and dichotic techniques to demonstrate a sex difference in cerebral asymmetry for the auditory–visual integration of verbal and spatial stimuli in childhood, and for the visual comparison of verbal and spatial stimuli in adulthood. The implications of these differences for a neuropsychological explanation of female verbal superiority and male spatial superiority have been considered. Buffery and Gray (1972) envisaged the asymmetry of cerebral function in the child and adult human brain as subsequent upon the asymmetry of cerebral structure in the human fetus and newborn brain as first observed by Wada (1969a) and reviewed by Geschwind (1974). Buffery and Gray (1972) also hypothesized a sex difference in the degree of asymmetry of cerebral structure in the human neonate brain such that the tendency for the left temporal planum to be more developed than the right should be more marked in the female than in the male. This prediction was confirmed in a small sample by Witelson and Pallie (1973), but a much larger study is awaited.

The relationship of various patterns of lateral congruity to learning disorder in general remains enigmatic. But in those learning disorders with a clear sex difference (e.g., poor reading where "dyslexia" is much more common in boys than girls) the observed sex differences in patterns of laterality and of cerebral functioning may have relevance (Zangwill, 1962), provided they are seen within the context of such wide normal variations as those described in the present studies.

Two things remain outstanding: analyses of response latencies from the child and adult studies in the light of a recent investigation, i.e., Berlucchi et al. (1971), and an explanation for the disparity between the incidence of strongly left-handed men in the present study (6%) and that found in the "children of Benjamin" and "inhabitants of Gibeah" (2.7%) as determined by the ability to "sling stones at an hair breadth, and not miss."

ACKNOWLEDGMENTS

These data were collected between 1967 and 1972 when the author was a Fellow of Corpus Christi College at the University of Cambridge and later a Senior Research Officer at the University of Oxford. I am most grateful to Mrs. E. Maloney, who typed the manuscript at International Hall, University of London.

Development of Laterality-Reading Patterns

Dirk J. Bakker, Jetty Teunissen, and Joop Bosch

Reproduction of dichotically or monaurally presented stimuli ordinarily results in ear asymmetry. The right ear is usually better in perceiving verbal stimuli, the left ear in nonverbal stimuli (Bakker, 1970a; Doehring, 1972; Frankfurter and Honeck, 1973; Kimura, 1967; Milner, 1962; Milner, Taylor, and Sperry, 1968). The superiority of the right ear in perceiving speech stimuli is ascribed to the dominance of the left hemisphere in processing verbal information (Kimura, 1961a). Since written language, as well as spoken language, is considered dependent on the integrity of the left hemisphere it seems obvious to assume a relation between right ear dominance and reading ability.

In a study (Bakker, 1969) of 10-year-old girls of a normal reading level, the author found a positive correlation between ear difference scores and performance on a word naming test. Zurif and Carson (1970) compared poor and normal readers, fourth grade primary school boys. The normal readers tended to obtain better right ear scores, the poor readers better left ear scores. Sparrow and Satz (1970) found a more frequent left ear preference in below-normal readers than in above-normal readers in the ages 9–12. Satz, Rardin, and Ross (1971) and Leong (1975d) demonstrated a difference in right ear performance between normal readers and reading-disturbed subjects in a study of older school children: the performances of normal readers were significantly higher. DeHaas (1972) compared above-average and below-average readers in a group of reading-disturbed boys in the ages 9–14. In the above-average group greater right minus left differences were noted than in the below-average group. In a recent study by Witelson and Rabinovitch (1972), 8–13-year-old children who attended a learning clinic were compared with normal readers of approximately the same age. Just as in Zurif and Carson's study, the normal readers tended to right ear superiority and the reading disturbed to left ear superiority. Bryden (1970) investigated the relationship between uncrossed dominance and reading ability. A greater percentage of the "good readers" had a same hand and ear preference (uncrossed dominance) than was found with the "poor readers."

The investigations on the relation between ear asymmetry and reading ability reviewed to this point have in common that the subjects were older school children. Although different groupings were used, the results point in the same direction: retarded and below-average readers demonstrate less right ear superiority than do normal and above-average readers. In our laboratory, the relations between ear asymmetry and reading ability have been investigated in groups of normal and disturbed readers at ages 7–13. In three experiments (Bakker, Smink, and Reitsma, 1973) right–left differences subsequent to monaural stimulation were analyzed in relation to reading ability. At an older age (9–11 years), relatively large right–left differences are associated with high reading ability. This result corroborates the findings of earlier studies. At a younger age (7–8 years), on the other hand, it was found that the best readers had the smallest between-ear differences are associated with high reading ability. This result corroborates the findings of earlier studies. At a younger age (7–8 years), on the younger (9–10 years) reading disturbed, relatively large right–left differences were found to be associated with high and low reading scores, respectively. These subjects were retarded 2 years in reading. Thus both their reading level and their asymmetry-reading ability pattern correspond to those of normal readers in the investigation by Bakker et al. On the basis of these results it can be concluded that the nature of the relation between ear asymmetry and reading ability is dependent on the phase of the learning-to-read process. It has been argued that this phase effect is due to the prominence of perceptual discrimination and analysis in early reading (Bakker, Smink, and Reitsma, 1973; Bakker, 1973).

SEX DIFFERENCES IN LATERALITY–READING PATTERNS

A recent investigation was set up primarily to demonstrate the influence of perceptual complexity on the laterality–reading relationship. Eight-year-old elementary schoolchildren were presented a Word Naming Test (WNT) and a Masked-Word Naming Test (M-WNT). The WNT and M-WNT were comprised of the same words, which were to be read aloud. In the Masked-Word Naming Test the words were made perceptually complex by masking the letter shapes. It has been shown that in adults the recognition of perceptually complex letters and words may be dependent on the integrity of the right hemisphere (Faglioni, Scotti, and Spinnler, 1969; Gibson, Dimond, and Gazzaniga, 1972). A similar dependency may emerge more strongly in schoolchildren since in early reading perceptual operations are prominent (Fries, 1963; Smith, 1971). Proficiency on the Masked-Word Naming Test was consequently predicted to show more right hemisphere dependence than proficiency on the ordinary Word Naming Test. Hemisphere dominance was deduced from ear asymmetry subsequent to dichotic stimulation. There is evidence to show that boys and girls of the same age differ markedly in their laterality—reading ability patterns (Bryden, 1970). The ear asymmetry—reading relations were therefore analyzed separately for boys and girls in the present study.

EXPERIMENT 1

Method

Subjects The investigation was conducted with 23 boys aged 8.2–9.2 years (mean 8.6 years) and 22 girls aged 8.0–9.1 years (mean 8.6 years) from the third grade of a normal elementary school (socio-economic middle class). No subject had repeated a class. All subjects used the right hand for writing. No auditory or uncorrected visual defects were reported for any of the children.

Dichotic Listening Test (DLT) Thirty series of four digit pairs were presented at a speed of two pairs per second by means of a Ferrograph Model 722 H/P stereo tape recorder and a set of Beyer DT 480 stereophonic earphones, at an intensity of approximately 70 dB (SPL). The tape was made by the Neuropsychology Laboratory of the University of Florida. Since the first four series were regarded as practice trials, these were not included in the final analysis. The earphones were exchanged interindividually in order to counterbalance possible channel effects. Subjects were asked to reproduce as many digits as possible in any order. Recently Hines and Satz (1974) applied a similar Dichotic Listening Test and reported a split half reliability coefficient of 0.86.

Word Naming Test (WNT) The WNT is form B of a standard reading test (Brus and Voeten, 1972) with two parallel forms A and B. S has to read as many words as possible within a minute. The number of words wrongly read is subtracted from the number of words read. The difference is converted into a grade-norm being one of the values between 1 and 10 of a decile scale. The reported parallel-forms reliability coefficients of this test are above 0.90 and the test—retest coefficients for the A and B forms above 0.80.

Masked-Word Naming Test (M-WNT) The M-WNT was comprised of the words of the A form of the reading test by Brus and Voeten (1972). In order to effect perceptual complexity, parts of the words were sifted out. The subject had to read as many words as possible within a minute. A raw score was obtained by subtracting the number of mistakes from the number of words read. Since it was an experimental version of a standard reading test, no grade norms of the M-WNT were available. The Dichotic Listening Test was administered first, followed by the WNT and the M-WNT. Testing was done in a quiet room of the school building.

Results and Discussion

Regression analyses up to third-degree polynomials were applied to the asymmetry and reading scores. In order to correct for total recall, ear asymmetry is expressed in the proportion of total information processed by the left ear. Thus values of L/R+L smaller than 0.50 reflect right ear advantage, and values greater than 0.50 reflect left ear advantage. The mean L/R+L values of boys (M = 40.04, SD = 11.17) and girls (M = 45.68, SD = 11.95) did not differ significantly (t = 1.64, df = 43, $p > 0.10$, two-tailed). Regression curves of significant trends are presented in Figures 1 and 2.

In girls, only the linear components of the regressions of Word Naming and Masked-Word Naming on ear asymmetry are significant (WNT: F = 4.45, df = 1/20, $p < 0.05$, R = 0.43; M-WNT: F = 5.91, df = 1/20, $p < 0.025$, R = 0.48). In boys only the quadratic components of these regressions reach significance (WNT: F = 3.78, df = 1/21, $p < 0.10$, R = 0.39; M-WNT: F = 4.91, df = 1/21, $p < 0.05$, R = 0.43).

Thus the results show a sex but no task effect: Word Naming and Masked-Word Naming proficiency are similarly associated with ear advantage. The nondifferential effect of Word Naming and Masked-Word Naming may be due to common factors underlying both tasks. In that case, one would predict a correlation between the WNT and M-WNT scores. A correlation coefficient of +0.28 (df = 43, $p < 0.05$) was found. It is felt that the common variance of both reading tasks partly accounts for their similar regression on ear asymmetry. The sex effect suggests that third grade girls read well only with their left hemisphere while third grade boys may be equally proficient with either hemisphere.

It could be that the asymmetry—reading pattern of the boys reflect a transitional stage already passed by the girls. Earlier studies (Bakker, Smink, and Reitsma, 1973; Bakker, 1973) suggest that the nature of dominance—reading patterns depends on the stage of the learning-to-read process. In the present study girls appear to read significantly better than boys: the mean Word Naming scores of girls and boys are 6.77 and 4.70 respectively (t = 2.21, df = 43, $p < 0.05$, two-tailed). The difference in reading ability may indicate that these girls and boys are in different stages of the learning-to-read process.

The proposed explanation for the sex effect would imply that lower

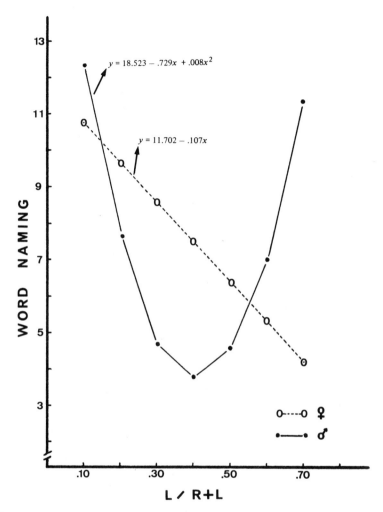

Figure 1. Regression of Word Naming (WNT) on ear asymmetry in normal third grade boys and girls.

grade girls and higher grade boys would show asymmetry–reading patterns similar to those of the present third grade boys and girls, respectively. Girls below the third grade level are not likely in a more advanced learning-to-read stage than third grade boys, and boys above the third grade level should at some point have reached the stage of third grade girls. A second experiment was set up to test these hypotheses.

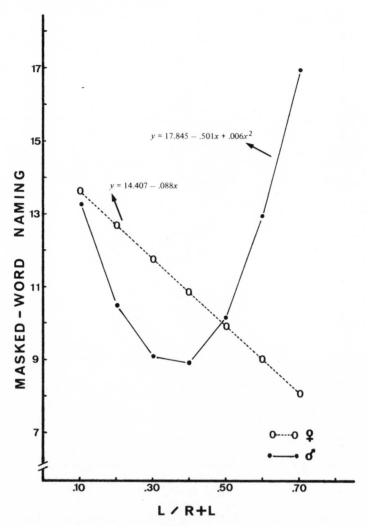

Figure 2. Regression of Masked-Word Naming (M-WNT) on ear asymmetry in normal third grade boys and girls.

EXPERIMENT 2

Method

Subjects One hundred and nineteen children from a normal elementary school (socio-economic middle class) participated in the experiment. They were 20 boys aged 10.7–11.4 years (mean 11.0 years) and 20 girls aged 10.6–11.3 years (mean 11.0 years) from the fifth and sixth grade; 20 boys aged 8.5–9.6 years (mean 9.1 years) and 20 girls aged 8.5–9.4 years (mean 9.0 years) from the third and fourth grade; and 20 boys aged 7.3–8.1 years (mean 7.6 years) and 19 girls aged 7.3–8.1 years (mean 7.6 years) from the second grade. No subject had repeated a class. No auditory or uncorrected visual defects were reported for any of the children. All subjects from the third to sixth grade were 100% right handed as measured with subtest 2 of the Harris Tests of Lateral Dominance (1958). Subjects of the second grade were at least 90% right handed. The 90% cutoff was chosen because one of the ten items of Harris' subtest 2 ("wind a watch") seems unreliable for young Dutch children: most second grade children do not wear a watch and if they do it is sometimes worn on the left and sometimes on the right wrist.

Tests   All subjects were presented the Dichotic Listening Test (DLT) and the Word Naming Test (WNT). Administration and scoring procedures were the same as in the first experiment. The Masked-Word Naming Test (M-WNT) was not presented since this test and the WNT were similarly related to ear asymmetry in the first experiment.

Results and Discussion

Ear asymmetry was again expressed in L/R+L proportions. A 2 × 3 analysis of variance was applied to these proportions with sex and grade as factors. Neither of the main factors nor their interaction were significant (p values > 0.10). The mean L/R+L values of boys and girls appeared to be 44.28 (SD = 12.04) and 43.35 (SD = 10.36), respectively. Regression analyses applied to the L/R+L and standard reading scores showed a significant cubic trend in second-grade girls (F = 4.46, df = 1/17, p < 0.05, R = 0.46) and a significant linear trend in fifth- to sixth-grade boys (F = 4.89, df = 1/18, p < 0.05, R = 0.46). These trends are represented in Figure 3.

Reading proficiency in second grade girls tends to go with both (moderate) right ear and left ear advantage. Reading proficiency in fifth to sixth grade boys is associated with right ear advantage only. Thus the reading–asymmetry patterns of the present second grade girls and fifth to sixth grade boys resemble the patterns of the third grade boys and the third grade girls of the first experiment, respectively. These findings support the hypotheses.

Older schoolchildren, especially the older girls, did not show significant ear asymmetry—reading relations in the present experiment. This may be due partly to variance reduction of the laterality and/or the reading scores at older ages. As to the laterality score, no significant variance differences between grades could be found (F max. = 2.04, k = 3, df = 39, p > 0.05). The variances of the reading scores were not homogeneous across

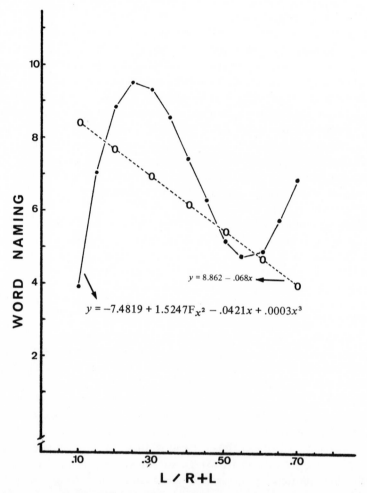

Figure 3. Regression of Word Naming (WNT) on ear asymmetry in normal second grade girls (*solid line*) and normal fifth to sixth grade boys (*broken line*).

grades (F max. = 2.40, $k = 3$, df = 39, $p < 0.05$). The reading scores within the group of the third to fourth grade children varied to a smaller degree than those within the group of the second and the group of fifth to sixth grade children. It is clear that these findings do not give an adequate explanation of the less frequent laterality—reading relations at older ages. The present laterality measure evidently is not sensitive enough to differentiate between reading performances toward the end of the normal learning-to-read process.

GENERAL DISCUSSION

Considering the results of the two experiments one can conclude that reading proficiency goes with right ear advantage in fifth to sixth grade boys and third grade girls and with either right ear or left ear advantage in third grade boys and second grade girls. Similar results were obtained by Bakker and Steenis (in preparation) in a recent replication study with second, fourth, and sixth grade boys and girls from a normal elementary school. These children were presented two reading tasks including the present Word Naming Test (WNT). In second grade boys and girls, high reading performance appeared to be associated with either right or left ear advantage. In fourth grade girls, on the other hand, a significant linear trend was found indicating an association between reading proficiency and right ear advantage only. Thus the results consistently suggest that in early stages of the learning-to-read process both hemispheres possess the capacity to mediate written language and that in later stages only the left hemisphere has that capacity.

Bakker, Smink, and Reitsma (1973), applying a monaural listening technique and using absolute values of right minus left ear differences, found positive relations between these differences and reading ability at later school ages. As to the younger school ages they found a negative correlation between the right—left differences and reading ability, suggesting that proficiency in reading at these ages goes with lack of ear advantage. In the present experiments nonlinear relations between ear asymmetry and reading ability emerged in young schoolchildren, indicating that reading proficiency is associated with either right or left ear advantage. The apparently diverging results may be due partly to the different laterality measures used. The results of both studies would be more reconcilable if the absolute values of the small right minus left ear differences that were associated with reading proficiency in the Bakker et al. study would appear to be at least partly negative differences. Upon closer examination about 50% of the small absolute between-ear differences in the younger schoolchildren of the Bakker et al. study were in fact negative differences reflecting left ear advantage. Thus the small positive and the small negative ear differences in the younger schoolchildren of our former study may both be associated with reading proficiency, suggesting that slight left and slight right hemispheric dominance are both compatible with efficient early reading. The present experiments, especially the second, warrant a similar conclusion.

There is additional evidence that right hemisphere dominance is appropriate in early phases of the learning-to-read process. Van Duyne, Scanlan, and Faltynsky (in preparation) report smaller degrees of ear asymmetry in above-average than in below-average readers from the first grade of the elementary school. The preliminary results of a current investigation implemented by Northern Illinois University and our laboratory similarly show that young primary schoolchildren with a left ear advantage are better readers than children having a right ear preference.

In conclusion, there is growing evidence that whereas right hemisphere dominance is appropriate for early reading, only left hemisphere dominance favors advanced reading.

TWO HEMISPHERES—TWO READING STRATEGIES?

It would be valuable to know whether cerebrally left and right dominant young children use similar reading strategies or not. Equal reading proficiencies may result from quite different reading strategies. One could speculate that young schoolchildren showing right hemispheric dominance are more sensitive to the perceptual features of the stimuli; they explore the visual configuration carefully. They could be relatively slow readers making few errors. Cerebrally left dominant children may explore the visual configuration less intensively. Like fluent readers they may quickly compare hypothetical word meanings with the words on the page (Smith, 1971). These subjects will read at relatively fast rates with the risk of making many errors because they are still at a stage of the learning-to-read process that requires close attention to the perceptual features of the text.

These hypotheses can be tested by splitting the reading proficiency score up in a reading accuracy and a reading speed score. The reading proficiency scores used so far were obtained by the total number of words read diminished by the number of errors made. Thus reading speed, reading accuracy, and reading proficiency are reflected respectively by the number of words read, the number of errors made, and the difference between these measures. Consideration of the number of words read and errors made permits a reformulation of the hypothesis: Children with right hemisphere dominance and children with left hemisphere dominance, equally proficient in reading, differ in that right dominant children read slower but make less errors than left dominant children.

Unfortunately, the speed and accuracy components of the reading tests used in the experiments described above are inappropriate for analysis in relation to left and right cerebral dominance. The test instructions of both the Word Naming Test and the Masked-Word Naming Test stress speed of reading, preventing the readers from choosing their preferred reading strategy. Moreover, the Word Naming Test is constructed in such a way that only a very few errors will be made.

Bakker and Steenis (in preparation) administered a Word Matching Test (WMT) in addition to this standardized Word Naming Test (WNT), to children of the second, fourth, and sixth grade of the elementary school. The Word Matching Test (WMT) requires the child to compare a masked meaningful word on the left side of a card with three normally printed meaningful words on the right side, of which one matches. The one, two, or three syllabic masked words are composed of partially sifted out letters. Figure 4 represents some of the 30 items. Though time to complete the series was limited, speed was no more stressed than accuracy. The Word Matching Test (WMT) was administered to all children at the same time. The subject was asked to underline the correct match. In addition to the reading test the earlier described Dichotic Listening Test (DLT) was applied. The phi coefficients (Kuhn, 1973) of each child's between-ear difference were calculated (90% level of confidence). Performance on the Word Matching Test (WMT) was split into total number of items attempted (speed), number of errors made (accuracy), and the difference between these measures (proficiency). The error rate was approximately 12% of the total number of words attempted. Proficiency, speed, and accuracy were analyzed in relation to left and right hemisphere dominance as reflected by right ($N = 28$) and left ($N = 13$) ear advantage, respectively. No differences in proficiency between left and right dominant subjects were found (p values > 0.20).

Within each grade the numbers of items attempted were transformed to z scores, as were the numbers of errors made. These two z scores were summed for each subject. Thus high summed z values indicate high speed–low accuracy and low summed z values indicate low speed–high

GROEP	GREEP	GROEF	GROEP
SLEPEN	SLEPEN	SLAPEN	SLOPEN
GEBIT	GEBED	GEBIT	DEBET
BEVER	BOVEN	BEVEN	BEVER
GEEUW	LEEUW	ZEEUW	GEEUW
KELDER	MELKER	KELDER	HELDER

Figure 4. Some items of the Word Matching Test (WMT).

accuracy. The results are summarized in Table 1. Across grades children with right hemisphere dominance show significantly lower z values than children with left hemisphere dominance. The difference is most marked in second grade children. Thus right and left dominant young children, while equally proficient, differ in the strategy used to reach this equal proficiency; right dominant subjects are slow but accurate, left dominant subjects are fast but careless.

One may argue that word matching is not word naming, suggesting that the relations found may not hold for ordinary reading. Although the standard Word Naming Test, as explained above, is not suitable for splitting up into a speed and accuracy component, we (Bakker and Steenis, in preparation) found trends between dominance and these components similar to the relations between dominance and the components of the Word Matching Test. Moreover, speed and accuracy of the Word Matching Test were low but significantly correlated with speed and accuracy of the Word Naming Test ($r = 0.26, p < 0.05$).

CONCLUSION

Proficient reading at an advanced stage of the learning-to-read process goes with left himisphere dominance only (Bakker, 1969; Bakker, Smink, and Reitsma, 1973; Satz and Sparrow, 1970). However, the dominance–reading patterns are different at early stages of the learning-to-read process: Proficient early reading may go with either left or right hemisphere dominance. Reading proficiency in right dominant subjects is achieved differently from reading proficiency in left dominant subjects. Young left dominant children, like fluent readers, read rapidly at the risk of making many errors. Young right dominant children read slowly but accurately.

The slow but accurate strategy, while appropriate at early stages of the learning-to-read process, may be unfavorable at later stages. The results suggest that girls pass through the successive laterality–reading stages faster than boys. As a consequence, boys more than girls may run the risk of getting stuck in early reading strategies generated by the right hemisphere. Such a stagnation may result in the reading retardation that is found more frequently in boys than in girls. Several writers (Sparrow and Satz, 1970; Witelson and Rabinovitch, 1972; Zurif and Carson, 1970) report a higher incidence of left ear advantage in older retarded than in older normal readers. This finding may disclose older reading retarded children still relying on right hemispheric reading strategies that were appropriate in early stages of the learning-to-read process only.

Table 1. Reading Strategy as a Function of Cerebral Dominance; Positive Values Indicate High Speed–Low Accuracy, Negative Values Indicate Low Speed–High Accuracy

	Second Grade	Fourth Grade	Sixth Grade	Across Grades
Left hemisphere dominance (Right ear advantage)	+.83	+.37	+.19	+.44
Right hemisphere dominance (Left ear advantage)	−1.32	−.82	−.55	−.95
t	2.39	1.30	.55	2.47
df	11	14	10	39
p (one-tailed)	<.025	>.10	>.25	<.01

ACKNOWLEDGMENTS

We would like to thank Mr. P. Borgman and the Staff of the Johannes School in Amsterdam-Osdorp for their pleasant cooperation. Our thanks also to our colleagues Dr. Miny and Dr. Nicholas Den Hartog for the critical reading of the manuscript.

Lateralization in Severely Disabled Readers in Relation to Functional Cerebral Development and Synthesis of Information

Che K. Leong

One feature that distinguishes the human brain from that of lower species is the development of hemispheric specialization. Some time ago Hughlings Jackson (1874, 1876) held that speech processes are represented in both hemispheres with the right hemisphere responsible for the "automatic" use of words and the left hemisphere for the creative use of language. Cerebral dominance is now seen as relative to the complementary functions of the two hemispheres. Benton (1965b) provided a qualitative and quantitative interpretation of the differential and reciprocal functions of the "major" and "minor" hemispheres: the left hemisphere mediates language and the right hemisphere "specializes" in perceptual, constructional, or motoric functions. Masland (1967) suggested the left hemisphere acts as a "trigger mechanism" or "primary initiator of activity" for language functioning. The double-dissociation experiments that are possible in split-brain adult humans (Bogen and Gazzaniga, 1965; Sperry, 1968, 1970) are not seen in infrahuman species. In man, the "complementary–different" relationship between the hemispheres is necessary, while for infrahumans a "complementary–same" relationship could be obtained.

The "symbiotic relationship" of the two hemispheres with the left being dominant for conceptual categories and the right for auditory and visual Gestalts, as it is succinctly explained by Levy (1974), is that the two hemispheres may be "logically incompatible," with the right hemisphere synthesizing over space and the left hemisphere analyzing over time. A possible clue to the mechanism of cerebral lateralization in man is the "basic incompatibility of language functions on the one hand and synthetic perceptual functions on the other" (Levy-Agresti and Sperry,

1968, p. 1151). With these findings as the backdrop, this chapter further explores the meaning of "dominance" or lateralization in children with specific reading disability. The emphasis is on the theoretical postulates from which the study is predicated, and only salient points from relevant experiments are described to buttress the postulates. These are the functional cerebral development with the implicit maturational lag in severely disabled readers and the simultaneous—successive syntheses of information.

THEORETICAL POSTULATES

Functional Cerebral Development

Functional cerebral development with the implicit developmental lag in disabled readers invokes the concept of hemispheric specialization, in which the differentiation of brain function proceeds from the lateralization of gross and fine motor skills followed by the lateralization of sensori-motor functions to the lateralization of speech and language. This concept of progressive differentiation in lateralization finds support from diverse sources. Lenneberg (1967) suggests that the hemispheric organization of speech evolves from a state of diffuse and bilateral representation in infancy to one of increased lateralization by puberty. Geschwind (1968) has discussed the relationship between brain maturation and ontogenetic development and points out the "terminal" zones (left angular gyri) with intercortical connections, necessary for the mediation of more complex language and cross-modal integration skills, myelinate the latest. Semmes and associates (Semmes, 1968; Semmes et al., 1960) state that hierarchical functions from somatosensory to language activities are more focally represented within the left hemisphere and more diffusely organized in the right hemisphere in man. The focal representation of elementary functions in the left hemisphere favors integration of similar units and consequently specialization for behaviors that demand fine sensori-motor control, such as manual skills and speech. Conversely, diffuse representation of elementary functions in the right hemisphere may lead to integration of dissimilar units and hence specialization for behaviors requiring multimodal coordination, such as various spatial abilities. Semmes further suggests that focal representation, in bringing about a more precise coding of the input of stimuli and making possible a more finely modulated control of the output, is the basis of hemispheric dominance.

From the convergence of the different perspectives on language, including reading, maturation is seen as the process of successive and overlapping neurological and psychological changes that take place in the individual. Maturational lag refers to a delayed or undifferentiated pattern of functional cerebral development especially in areas of the left hemisphere mediating the acquisition of developmental skills. Satz and associates (Satz and Friel, 1974; Satz, Friel, and Rudegeair, 1974b; Satz and Sparrow, 1970; Satz and Van Nostrand, 1973; Sparrow and Satz, 1970) have critically evaluated the postulate of functional cerebral developmental lag in dyslexics and have offered empirical evidence to support their formulation. The present study further examines the formulation of maturational lag and adduces evidence to show the importance of developmental skills as antecedents to the initial reading process.

Syntheses of Information

A related postulate underpinning reading dysfunction and initial reading is Luria's (1966a, 1966b, 1970, 1973) two basic forms of integrative activities of the cerebral cortex: simultaneous (primarily spatial, groups) and successive (primarily temporally organized series) syntheses at the perceptual, mnestic, and intellectual levels. Very briefly, simultaneous synthesis involves the synthesis of separate elements into simultaneous groups while successive synthesis relates to the ability of the cerebral apparatus to integrate external influences or their traces into successive series, distinguishable in time. Luria identifies broad areas in the cortex mainly responsible for the different syntheses. In general, disturbance in the parieto-occipital area leads to difficulties with simultaneous-spatial groups, while damage to the fronto-temporal area, which forms part of the motor and acoustic analyzers, is primarily associated with analysis of stimuli separated from each other in time and with their syntheses into successive series. Luria (1966b) mentions specific tasks at different levels of each mode of synthesis. For example, simultaneous synthesis at the perceptual level may be manifested in copying of geometric figures, drawing of a map, performance on Koh's Block; and at the mnestic level in "arithmetic difficulties" and "grammatical structure involving arrangement of elements into one simultaneous scheme." In successive synthesis, examples are counting sequences of tapping, digit span, and serial learning such as drawing " o + + − " while keeping the correct order. The Luria model has been operationalized by Das (1972, 1973a, 1973b; Das, Kirby, and Jarman, 1975). Das proposes that the simultaneous and successive syntheses of information provide a more parsimonious explanation of the traditional reasoning and memory factors in cognitive tasks and, to buttress his proposal, offers findings from principal component analyses of "simultaneous" and "successive" tasks with different groups of children.

The postulate of functional cerebral development in disabled readers was tested with a dichotic listening experiment while the related postulate of simultaneous–successive syntheses of information was verified with a correlational study involving a number of perceptual-cognitive tasks.

DICHOTIC EXPERIMENT

Subjects

The subjects for the study were 58 dyslexic boys in 16 schools with mean chronological age of 111.07 months and mean Lorge-Thorndike nonverbal IQ of 102.45. These boys had all been diagnosed as "retarded" in reading by 2.5 grades or more, but were otherwise of average intelligence and free from gross emotional, visual, and auditory disabilities. These children were further screened for normal hearing (25 dB ± ISO, 0.25 to 8kHz). This experimental group was compared with a control group of 58 above-average readers drawn from the same schools and equated on age (mean chronological age of 110.93 months), sex (boys only), and general ability (mean Lorge-Thorndike nonverbal IQ of 107.57).

Materials and Procedure

The stimulus material consisted of a dichotic list of three sets of digits drawn from 0 or zero to 9 with five series in each set ranging from two-digit pair to four-digit pair series. The dichotic tape was prepared with a specially devised system of instrumentation (Leong, 1975b) with verification of both onset synchrony of individual pairs of stimuli (to within 5 msec difference) and of interstimulus intervals (two-digit per second). All playback was via a Sony 777-4J dual-channel tape recorder with a pair of Sony earphones. A counterbalanced design was used in testing the children, who were asked to report all the digits heard. The main scoring method was that of ear order scoring where the first digit reported is taken to denote the half-span recalled first, taking into account the correct serial position of the stimuli. A variation of the ear order scoring was the attempted ear order scoring. This takes into account digits correctly reported for each channel but disregards serial positions.

Results and Discussion

It was hypothesized that the experimental and the control groups would show an overall right-ear effect, with the latter group showing significantly higher ear scores. This hypothesis of overall lateralization effect was tested with a 2 (group) × 2 (half-span) repeated measures analysis of variance with left/right ear scores as the repeated measure.

The main effects for group are highly significant for both ear order reporting ($F = 14.761$, df = 1/114, $p < 0.001$) and attempted ear reporting ($F = 37.247$, df = 1/114, $p < 0.001$). Similarly, the main effects for half-span are highly significant for both ear order reporting ($F = 26.269$, df = 1/114, $p < 0.001$) and attempted ear reporting ($F = 39.537$, df = 1/114, $p < 0.001$). Both the experimental group and the control group performed better in the right ear, with the latter group obtaining higher scores than the former. The results are shown graphically in Figure 1. A subsidiary 2 (group) X 2 (half-span) X 3 (series length) repeated measures analysis of variance was performed, with half-span and series length as the repeated measures on each subject. All main effects were significant; however, the three-digit pair series was found to be the most discriminating. The main ANOVA results demonstrate the overall right-ear dichotic effect for both disabled and nondisabled reader groups; however, disabled readers perform significantly worse in the overall right-ear superiority vis-à-vis their coun-

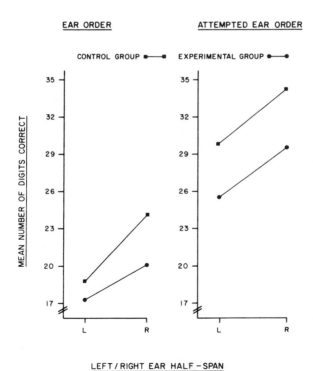

Figure 1. Mean number of digits (collapsed across series lengths) recalled by experimental and control groups for each half-span for two methods of scoring.

terparts equated for age, sex, and general ability (as measured by Lorge-Thorndike nonverbal IQ). This differential performance is taken as prima facie evidence of a lag in functional cerebral development of the disabled readers. This explanation of slightly poorer right-ear performance, without implying that disabled readers have better left-ear scores or that readers with better left-ear performance are necessarily at risk, is consonant with the cerebral maturation lag postulate (Bakker, 1973; Satz and Sparrow, 1970; Satz and Van Nostrand, 1973).

CORRELATIONAL STUDY

Subjects, Tasks, and Procedure

The same groups of 58 disabled readers and 58 nondisabled readers were used to examine the different modes of information-processing. Of the eight main tasks used to tap the Luria–Das paradigm of information syntheses, six tasks with minor modifications were from the battery consistently used by Das (1972, 1973a, 1973b) and the remaining two tasks were subtests from the Revised Illinois Test of Psycholinguistic Abilities (ITPA) (Kirk, McCarthy, and Kirk, 1968). These eight tasks were (a) Raven's Colored Progressive Matrices, (b) Figure Copying Test, (c) Memory-for-Designs Test, (d) Auditory-Visual Coding, (e) Visual Short-Term Memory Task, (f) Auditory Serial Recall Task, (g) ITPA Visual Sequential Memory Subtest, (h) ITPA Auditory Sequential Memory Subtest. The Figure Copying Test and Raven's were given to small groups of about four children at a time. All the other tasks were administered individually.

Results and Discussion

Performance of the experimental and control groups on the perceptual-cognitive tasks was tested by Hotelling T^2 (Tatsuoka, 1971). The vectors of the eight variables, with the exception of the ITPA Visual Sequential Memory Subtest, were all significantly different. When the eight tasks were considered simultaneously in linear combination the Hotelling T^2 of 154.186 and the F ratio of 18.090 were highly significant ($p < 0.001$ for 8/107 df). This divergence points to the fact that in respect of the perceptual-cognitive tasks tapping different modes of information-processing the experimental and control groups do not come from the same population despite their equivalence in age, sex, and general ability (as measured by Lorge-Thorndike nonverbal IQ). Two separate principal component analyses and two alpha factor analyses were carried out for each of the two groups. Table 1 shows the dimensions of the eight tasks.

Without loss of generality, the patterns in the two different analyses for the experimental group are similar. Briefly, Raven's Colored Progressive Matrices, Figure Copying, and Memory-for-Designs loaded on Component/Factor I as found with other groups of children by Das (1972, 1973a, 1973b). This may be labeled according to the Luria–Das terminology as the simultaneous component/factor. Auditory Serial Recall and ITPA Auditory Sequential Memory loaded on Component/Factor II with Auditory Visual Coding straddling the first two component/factors. This second dimension confirms the Das' successive component. The low communality of the ITPA Visual Sequential Memory subtest might be due to the ceiling effect or the earlier maturing of this ability. The Visual Short-Term Memory task with a loading of 0.934 for the principal component analysis and of 0.593 for the alpha factor analysis may be measuring some unique quality and this is labeled as Perceptual Organization. The consistency of the two methods of analyses was tested with the Schonemann (1966) procedure and the average sum of squares for the error matrix of 0.0107 showed that the patterns for the experimental group are similar.

With the control group, again both component and alpha factor analyses were carried out and the loadings for the separate analyses were tested with the Schonemann procedure and shown to be consistent (average trace value of 0.0092). As with the experimental group, the basic marker tasks of Raven's, Figure-Copying, and Memory-for-Designs all occupied the simultaneous dimension, while the marker tasks of Auditory Serial Recall and ITPA Auditory Sequential Memory all loaded in the expected successive dimension. However, with this analysis Visual Short-Term Memory also loaded appreciably on the latter dimension with Auditory-Visual Coding almost straddling the three dimensions and the ITPA Visual Sequential Memory occupying a unique position.

While the generality of the simultaneous–successive syntheses is demonstrated in separate analyses, the specificity of the dimensions should be interpreted with caution. In other words, as the magnitude of the loadings differs and as some variables shift from one factor to the other, the psychological reality of the simultaneous–successive syntheses found with the experimental group is similar but not identical to the matrix found with the control group. This is shown by Visual Short-Term Memory occupying a "unique" vector space with the experimental group, whereas it shifts to the successive dimension with the control group. Similarly, with

Table 1. Dimensions of Eight Tasks for Experimental and Control Groups ($N = 58$ each) by Principal Component Analysis and Alpha Factor Analysis

Tasks	Experimental Group								Control Group							
	Varimax Rotated Components from Principal Component Analysis				Varimax Rotated Factors from Alpha Factor Analysis				Varimax Rotated Components from Principal Component Analysis				Varimax Rotated Factors from Alpha Factor Analysis			
	I	II	III	h²	I	II	III	h²	I	II	III	h²	I	II	III	h²
Raven's Colored Progressive Matrices (RCPM)	.802	.138	-.149	.684	.697	.121	-.051	.503	-.079	.817	.190	.710	-.078	.754	.262	.643
Figure Copying (FCT)	.694	-.095	.378	.633	.561	-.041	.308	.411	.210	.739	-.350	.713	.169	.552	-.146	.354
Memory-for-Designs (MFD)[a]	-.808	-.073	-.012	.658	-.742	-.095	-.079	.566	.185	-.585	-.514	.640	.126	-.443	-.476	.438
Auditory-Visual Coding (AVC)	.424	.526	.212	.502	.372	.377	.236	.336	.387	.420	.399	.485	.345	.294	.335	.318
Visual Short-Term Memory (VSTM)	.052	.142	.934	.895	.090	.134	.593	.378	.620	-.098	.386	.543	.500	-.041	.269	.324
Auditory Serial Recall (ASR)	.105	.888	-.047	.802	.113	.929	-.018	.877	.817	.009	-.016	.667	.635	.019	.002	.404
ITPA Visual Memory (VM)	.408	.272	.158	.266	.303	.207	.157	.159	.040	.032	.834	.699	.057	-.009	.621	.389
ITPA Auditory Memory (AM)	-.010	.824	.129	.696	.050	.625	.196	.432	.863	.083	-.138	.770	.862	.096	-.157	.777
% Total Variance	26.71	23.41	14.08	64.21	20.05	18.54	7.18	45.76	25.38	21.89	18.08	65.34	19.61	14.58	11.40	45.59
% Common Variance	41.60	36.46	21.92		43.83	40.50	15.67		38.82	33.49	27.67		43.02	31.97	24.99	
Eigenvalues[b]	2.687	1.459	.991		5.195	1.842	0.978		2.202	1.802	1.224		3.846	2.583	1.576	

[a]Error scores for Memory-for-Designs.

[b]Eigenvalues for alpha factor analysis to 15th iteration with tolerance level = 0.005.

the latter group the ITPA Visual Sequential Memory takes on what may again be termed a visual perceptual dimension. Statistically, the disparity in the dimensions of the two groups is confirmed with the Schonemann procedure. The average sum of squares for the error matrix was 0.0895, which, according to the Skakun, Maguire, and Hakstian (1972) guideline of 0.0145 (95th percentile) and 0.0232 (99th percentile), is highly significant. One explanation of the disparity in the loadings of the dimensions interpreted within the simultaneous–successive syntheses framework is the heterogeneity of the two groups with respect to the tasks. The other and more important explanation is the "double dissociation principle," which suggests that "apparently, identical psychological processes can be distinguished and apparently different forms of mental activity can be reconciled" (Luria, 1973, p. 41).

GENERAL DISCUSSION

The formulation of maturational lag in functional cerebral development holds the attraction of being consonant with the positions of developmental psychologists (Hunt, 1961; Piaget, 1926a). The dichotic experiment and the factorial structure of the perceptual-cognitive tasks applied to a cross section of dyslexic boys confirm the findings of Satz (Satz and Sparrow, 1970; Satz and Van Nostrand, 1973; Sparrow and Satz, 1970). The keynote in both the present and the Satz investigations is that "retardation" is in the acquisition of various skills rather than in the loss of abilities. Thus the Satz studies validate the earlier suggestion by Benton (1962c) that perceptual deficiencies are found more in younger retarded readers and that conceptual deficiencies are found in older retarded readers. The perceptual and conceptual aspects, however, merge imperceptibly, because even perceptual tasks are verbally mediated and require for their successful performance a large conceptual component.

The maturation lag formulation also carries the implicit assumption that disabled readers considered as individuals rather than as groups may show a slight increase in sinistral tendencies without implicating the left-ear effect as indicative of reading disability. There is some circumstantial evidence for this from inspection of right-left dichotic scores for individual children in the dichotic experiment. Studdert-Kennedy and Shankweiler (1970, p. 592) emphasize that:

> "The absence of an ear advantage is not inconsistent with complete lateralization of some portion of the perceptual function, since the outcome may simply indicate that the acoustic materials being studied are not susceptible to information loss under certain experimental conditions."

The assertion that the left-ear effect does not accentuate reading disability is well argued by Bakker and associates (Bakker, 1973; Bakker, Smink, and Reitsma, 1973). Their suggestion that cerebral dominance interacts with the learning-to-read process and that every stage in this process is characterized by an optimal lateralization pattern merits more careful attention. The cautiously stated rider that "it is even possible to think that early reading profits by a bilateral representation of functions" (Bakker, 1973, p. 17) may apply in some cases. This seems to echo the earlier and equally cautious view stated in the obverse by Geschwind (1962) that bilateral mal-development of the angular gyrus would be the minimum substrate for difficulty in learning to read—bilateral, according to Geschwind, because of the tremendous ability for the nervous system of the young child to find alternative means of compensating for dysfunction to localized areas. Might not the bilateral representation suggested by Bakker explain the impaired performance of the present experimental group in the perceptual-cognitive tasks as well? In any case, the Bakker explanation can be accommodated within the hypothesis of a lag in cerebral maturation.

In the inquiry into modes of information processing in disabled readers, results of the present correlational study and of an extended study reported in detail elsewhere (Leong, 1975a) demonstrate the statistical and psychological realities of the Luria–Das simultaneous–successive dimensions. Recently, Das, Kirby, and Jarman (1975), in a synthesis of a number of principal component analyses of cognitive abilities, related the Luria model to studies of memory, imagery as well as language. From his study of 9-year-old children, Leong (in press) reaffirms the realities of the two modes of integrative activities, simultaneous–successive syntheses, and further explicates these dimensions. Drawing from statistical, epistemological, psychological, and neuropsychological sources, Leong argues for a flexible, interchangeable spatial-temporal order or integrated "analytico-synthetical" activity as a possible clue to the understanding of reading dysfunction. With the dichotic task tapping mainly temporal, analytical functions and the perceptual-cognitive tasks "concrete-active" as well as "verbal-logical" dimensions, the complementary–different functions reflect current views of cerebral mechanisms.

In a detailed delineation of the role of the right hemisphere or the "appositional mind," Bogen (1969) draws attention to Luria's dichotomy of simultaneous and successive syntheses without reference to lateralization and hints that the distinction might well be an important one between left and right hemisphere modes. Further insight into the mechanisms of reading dysfunction may come from reconciling lateralization and the interchangeable simultaneous—successive syntheses as modes of information processing.

ACKNOWLEDGMENTS

I wish to thank Dr. Dirk J. Bakker of the Paedologisch Instituut, Amsterdam and Dr. J. P. Das of the University of Alberta for their helpful suggestions.

Abnormal Right Hemisphere Specialization in Developmental Dyslexia

Sandra F. Witelson

The relationship between brain and behavior has long intrigued philosophers and scientists. One dimension of brain–behavior relationships that is now relatively well documented is hemisphere specialization of function, originally labeled cerebral dominance and first inferred by Das and by Broca on the basis of their observation that aphasic deficits occurred only in patients with left-sided brain damage (Benton, 1965b). Now, more than a century later and after abundant study of various types of brain-damaged patients and of normal individuals with the use of biologically noninvasive techniques, it is generally established that in most adults the left hemisphere is the major hemisphere for mediating linguistic, analytic, sequential processing; and that the right hemisphere is the major hemisphere for mediating nonlinguistic, spatial, holistic processing (e.g., Dimond and Beaumont, 1974; Kinsbourne and Smith, 1974).

Some of the most fruitful strategies used for the study of hemisphere specialization in adults include methods such as the study of the behavioral sequelae of unilateral brain damage, of various types of brain surgery, and of intracarotid sodium amytal injections (Wada and Rasmussen, 1960). These strategies have limited possibility in the study of children and, accordingly, our knowledge of hemisphere specialization is less complete for the period of childhood.

This work has been supported since its inception in 1970 by the Ontario Mental Health Foundation Research Grant No. 322. I also acknowledge support from the U.S. National Institute of Mental Health Research Training Grant in Biological Psychiatry at New York University School of Medicine (No. MH 08638) for the Postdoctoral Research Fellowship during which many of the issues of this research were formulated.

233

HEMISPHERE SPECIALIZATION IN CHILDHOOD

On the basis of the available evidence it appears that left hemisphere specialization for linguistic processing is present at least by 5 years of age according to studies of brain-damaged children (e.g., Annett, 1973; Basser, 1962) and of normal children (e.g., Kimura, 1963; Porter and Berlin, 1975). Very recent evidence indicates that left hemisphere specialization for linguistic processing is probably present at birth, at least for those aspects of linguistic processing of which infants are capable such as phonemic discrimination (Eimas, Siqueland, Jusczyk, and Vigorito, 1971). The data to support specialization at birth come from several diverse sources: asymmetry in ear scores on an adaptation of the dichotic listening test applicable to infants (Entus, 1975); hemispheric asymmetry in cortical evoked responses to speech and nonspeech stimuli in infants (Molfese, Freeman, and Palermo, 1975); and perhaps somewhat less directly by the finding that gross anatomical asymmetry between the hemispheres in a language-mediating area exists in newborns (Wada, Clarke, and Hamm, 1975; Witelson and Pallie, 1973) as it does in adults (Geschwind and Levitsky, 1968).

There is less information concerning right hemisphere specialization in children. The little available evidence again indicates specialization at birth: the right hemisphere appears more efficient even in infancy for the processing of nonlinguistic auditory information such as musical sounds (Entus, 1975; Molfese et al., 1975). However, there is virtually no information concerning right hemisphere specialization for the processing of spatial information in childhood.

HEMISPHERE SPECIALIZATION IN DYSLEXIA

Despite the fact that our knowledge of hemisphere specialization in childhood is limited and recent, there has been a long-standing nonspecific hypothesis, originally suggested by Orton (1937), that there is some lack of cerebral dominance in at least one group of children with learning problems, those with reading problems or "strephosymbolia," subsequently labeled specific reading disability or developmental dyslexia. This hypothesis was originally based and maintained (Critchley, 1970; Zangwill, 1962) on tenuously relevant clinical observations of frequent mirror-image errors in the reading of letters and words, of a higher incidence of nonconcordant hand and eye preference, and of a greater incidence of lack of definite hand preference or of more frequent left hand preference in children with reading problems than in normal children.

This hypothesis of abnormal cerebral dominance remained untested until the last decade when several biologically noninvasive methods (behavioral, electrophysiological) became available for the study of hemisphere specialization in neurologically intact individuals, including children. One type of behavioral method involves the use of various perceptual tests, the rationale of which depends upon the fact that different types of stimuli (linguistic or nonlinguistic-spatial) may be presented in the left or right sensory fields. Given the predominance of crossed anatomical connections between sensory field and the brain, lateralized stimulation is initially transmitted, either predominantly, as in the auditory and somesthetic modalities, or completely, as in the visual modality, to the contralateral (opposite) hemisphere. Consequently, any asymmetry in hemisphere processing of particular stimuli may be reflected in response asymmetry to left versus right stimulation as measured in accuracy or reaction time.

One example is the dichotic listening paradigm, originally devised by Broadbent (1954) for the study of auditory attention and memory, and subsequently observed by Kimura (1961a) to be a possible index of speech lateralization. In this test, pairs of different "competing" stimuli are presented simultaneously, one to each ear, and the subject has to report or recognize what he heard. Because each ear is predominantly connected to the opposite hemisphere, when linguistic stimuli are presented, a right ear advantage is typically observed for adults (Milner, 1971) and for children (Porter and Berlin, 1975) and is considered to reflect the left hemisphere's specialization for language functions. Conversely when nonlinguistic stimuli are used, adults (Milner, 1971) and children (Knox and Kimura, 1970) show a left ear advantage, which is considered to reflect right hemisphere specialization for nonlinguistic auditory processing.

Another such experimental paradigm is in the visual modality which involves tachistoscopic presentation of linguistic or spatial stimuli in the lateral visual fields. This procedure was first indicated as a means of studying hemisphere specialization (Bryden and Rainey, 1963; Goodglass and Barton, 1963; Kimura, 1961b) only after it was devised and extensively used to study the neural effects of acquired reading habits and directional scanning (Heron, 1957). Again, because of the crossed anatomical connections in the visual system, when linguistic processing of stimuli is required, perception is better for right field stimulation and is considered to reflect left hemisphere specialization. When spatial processing is required, perception is better for left field stimulation and is considered to reflect right hemisphere specialization (Milner, 1971). Little, if any, data are available with this test paradigm and nonlinguistic spatial processing for children.

More recently a new behavioral procedure (dichotomous tactual stimulation) has been described in the haptic modality; it was developed specifically to study right hemisphere specialization for spatial processing in neurologically intact individuals (Witelson, 1974). In this test, pairs of different "competing" stimuli are presented simultaneously, one to each hand, for the subject to examine by touch. When the stimuli are not readily encoded linguistically and depend on spatial perception, a left hand superiority has been observed for boys, interpreted as reflecting right hemisphere specialization for spatial processing. When the stimuli involve a linguistic component, the left hand superiority is attenuated, which may indicate the use of both spatial and linguistic processing for this task.

There have been several recent reports using the more established test procedures of dichotic listening and tachistoscopic stimulation that have studied hemisphere specialization in variously defined groups of learning-impaired children. The few reports that do support some abnormality of cerebral dominance in children with reading problems have been suggestive at most, and usually involve statistically nonsignificant differences between the poor reading and control groups (e.g., Bryden, 1970; Zurif and Carson, 1970). The studies that report the most statistically significant data indicative of abnormal left hemisphere specialization for language functions in impaired children involved children with more pervasive language or dysphasic disorders rather than children with specific reading problems (e.g., Sommers and Taylor, 1972; Witelson, 1962; Witelson and Rabinovitch, 1972). Contrary to much discussion and the widely held belief of either delayed, diminished, or lacking left hemisphere specialization for language in dyslexics, in general the results of most of the studies reveal a right field superiority for dyslexics and support the conclusion that children with reading problems do have left hemisphere specialization for language functions as do normal children (e.g., Leong, 1975c; McKeever and Huling, 1970; Satz and Van Nostrand, 1973; Yeni-Komshian, Isenberg, and Goldberg, 1975).

RIGHT HEMISPHERE SPECIALIZATION AND DYSLEXIA

All these studies focused exclusively on the possiblity of abnormal left hemisphere specialization for language in dyslexia. Not one report questioned right hemisphere specialization for the processing of nonlinguistic auditory information or of spatial information. This situation may result from an implicit assumption by the researchers of the importance of linguistic processing in reading, or it may result from an implicit assumption that the basic cognitive deficit in dyslexia is a language deficit. It may also stem from the simple practical fact that there has been a lack of methods and of data relevant to right hemisphere specialization in chil-dren, particularly for spatial processing.

If the general hypothesis that dyslexic children have atypical hemisphere specialization is to be tested, then the functional specialization of the right hemisphere as well as that of the left hemisphere merits study. So far most of the evidence suggests that dyslexic children have normal left hemisphere specialization. With the use of the new dichotomous touch test as an index of right hemisphere specialization for spatial processing as observed in normal boys, it is now possible to study right hemisphere specialization for spatial processing in dyslexics.

Although right hemisphere specialization in dyslexia has not been studied, theoretically there are at least two lines of reasoning why abnormal right hemisphere specialization for spatial processing may be involved in dyslexia. First, the act of reading likely involves aspects of spatial processing such as shape discrimination of letters and words, and memory of the visual images of words (Gibson, 1971; Smith, 1971), as well as aspects of phonetic and linguistic encoding of the words (Conrad, 1972). Several authors have interpreted some of the reading errors of dyslexic children as reflecting difficulties in visual-spatial processing (Boder, 1973; Johnson and Myklebust, 1967). In fact, Orton (1937) was so impressed with the visual-spatial errors of the children he studied that he coined the diagnostic label "strephosymbolia" to indicate "twisted symbols." Moreover, his hypothesis of abnormal cerebral dominance in dyslexia may be interpreted as implying that the right hemisphere has relatively too strong a role in processing the visual-spatial aspects of linguistic information.

Second, several studies (Levy, 1969; Miller, 1971; Milner, 1969) have suggested that atypical language representation, as in left-handed individuals and in individuals with early brain damage, may be associated, not with lower verbal ability, but with lower spatial ability. Levy (1969) suggests that it is spatial ability which suffers because it is mediated by the right hemisphere, which is also occupied with linguistic processing in these individuals. Levy's case could be applied in reverse to atypical spatial representation in dyslexia. It is possible that in dyslexics there is atypical spatial representation and that the left hemisphere is more involved in spatial processing than in normals. Such a neural organization could result in interference with the linguistic processing of the left hemisphere in dyslexics. This would be consistent with the dyslexics' poor reading, poor spelling, and often deficient oral language, all of which involve linguistic processing.

Hence, there were two main purposes of the present research: one, to begin the study of right hemisphere specialization for spatial processing in dyslexics, mainly with the use of the dichotomous tactual test; and two, to further study left hemisphere specialization for linguistic processing in the same group.

METHODOLOGICAL CONSIDERATIONS

Neural processing and organization are not observed directly in this study but are inferred on the basis of observed test performance. Interpretation and inference of hypothetical constructs are too likely to be equivocal when based on only one set of data. This is especially true when group differences are involved and variables such as different levels of overall ability, motivation, and attention may warrant consideration. Moreover, there is an imperfect correlation between neurologically determined hemisphere specialization and inferred specialization on the basis of behavioral test performance (Satz, 1976, in press). It is for these reasons that it is important to use several methods to test the same neural processes. The present research used the method of converging operations by employing several different test methods (dichotomous tactual stimulation, lateral tachistoscopic stimulation, and dichotic listening) to study the same theoretical neural organization and to allow for the possible observation of converging patterns of performance from different sets of data. If evidence from all these different tests were found to be consistent, then any inferences of neural organization could be more definite than if based on a single observation.

It was expected that a pattern of hemisphere specialization in dyslexics might emerge indicating typical left hemisphere specialization for language functions on the basis of a verbal dichotic listening test. In addition, it was thought that possibly some abnormality in right hemisphere specialization for spatial processing might be observed for dyslexics on the basis of their performance on the spatial dichotomous touch test and on a visual spatial test. A "linguistic" dichotomous touch test, unique in the respect that it may require both types of cognitive processes as does reading, the real-life problem of dyslexics, was also used as a possible fruitful probe without any specific predictions.

A second methodological consideration of the study concerns subject selection. Careful attention was given to objectively defining the criteria of developmental dyslexia and subsequently selecting a homogeneous group of dyslexic children, given the constraints of present clinical knowledge and available diagnostic tools. This approach provides not only a clear description of the group studied, which has been lacking in much of the research in this area, but also provides sufficient objective information about the children to allow comparison with and possible replication by other studies.

In summary, the purpose of the present research is to study left hemisphere specialization for linguistic processing and right hemisphere specialization for spatial processing in children with developmental dyslexia. It was hypothesized that some abnormal neural organization for higher mental processes may be associated with this cognitive disorder. Given the results of earlier reports, it was particularly suspected that if any abnormality in the pattern of hemisphere specialization were to be found, it might be for right hemisphere specialization for spatial processing.

GENERAL PROCEDURE

Subject Selection

The children were tested over a period of 5 years. All were referred as possible subjects to the study from various clinical sources, were first assessed medically and psychiatrically, and were then tested with a battery of standardized psychological tests. The only children included in the sample were those who had a Performance IQ of at least 85 on the Wechsler Intelligence Scale for Children (Wechsler, 1949), documented difficulty in reading since Grade 1, and a difference of at least 1.5 grade levels between their actual reading grade level on the Reading Subtest of the Wide Range Achievement Test (Jastak and Jastak, 1965) and that expected on the basis of their chronological age at the time of testing. For the younger children whose expected reading level was below Grade 3 the criterion was that they were virtually nonreaders on the test. Each child also had no detectable brain damage, no prescribed medication for behavioral problems, no primary emotional disturbance, adequate visual and auditory sensory acuity, the usual educational opportunities, and English as his first and main language. The author considers these children to be a different type of learning-impaired child than those described as "hyperactive" (Douglas, 1972) or as having "minimal brain dysfunction" (Wender, 1971).

Of a total of approximately 200 referrals, 113 children were found to meet the criteria. No one refused to participate in the study. There were 98 boys and only 15 girls, a ratio of about 6:1 in favor of boys. This finding is consistent with many previous results indicating a markedly greater incidence of dyslexia in males than in females (Critchley, 1970). Of the 98 dyslexic boys, 85 were strongly right-handed, defined as right hand preference for writing and right hand preference on at least seven of the ten unimanual tasks of the Harris Tests of Lateral Dominance (Harris, 1958). Not one of the 15 dyslexic girls was left-handed, making 88% of the total dyslexic sample right-handed. Handedness (Hécaen and Sauguet,

1971) and more recently sex (Lansdell, 1968; McGlone and Kertesz, 1973; Witelson, 1976) have been suggested as relevant factors in patterns of hemisphere specialization. Since the present samples of dyslexic girls and of left-handed dyslexic boys were so small, the present report will be restricted to the group of 85 right-handed dyslexic boys, who ranged in age from 6 to 14 years. Their mean reading lag was 2.6 grade levels. Their mean Full Scale IQ was 102; mean Performance IQ, 107; and mean Verbal IQ, 97.4, which was significantly lower than their mean Performance IQ (t = 5.49, df = 84, $p < 0.001$). Lower Verbal than Performance IQ scores were found in 71% of the dyslexic group ($p = 0.0002$, binomial test). This finding of lower Verbal than Performance IQ in dyslexics is consistent with many other reports (Rabinovitch et al., 1956; Warrington, 1967).

A total of 156 normal boys obtained from city public schools and ranging in age from 6 to 14 years were studied and used as control groups. They were drawn from the same general population and socio-economic levels as the dyslexics. All were strongly right-handed by the same criteria as were the dyslexics, had at least a Full Scale IQ of 85 (mean IQ = 111.2) on a short-form of the Wechsler Test [Arithmetic, Vocabulary, and Block Design Subtests (Glasser and Zimmerman, 1967)], were in the appropriate grade level was at least at the expected level according to chronological age. None had any history of academic, behavioral, or relevant medical difficulties.

Tests

Each child was given several perceptual tests specifically chosen for their relevance in making inferences of hemisphere specialization for cognitive processing: (1) dichotomous tactual stimulation: two forms, a nonsense shapes test and a letters test (the latter always given approximately one month later); (2) lateralized tachistoscopic stimulation: pictures of people; and (3) a dichotic listening test: digits. These tests are described in more detail in the following section. The perceptual tests plus the standardized clinical tests were administered to each child individually in three to four sessions each consisting of 2–3 hours.

DESCRIPTION OF TESTS, RESULTS, AND IMPLICATIONS

Right Hemisphere Specialization

Dichotomous Tactual Stimulation: Nonsense Shapes   The main method used to study right hemisphere specialization for spatial processing employed a version of the dichotomous tactual stimulation paradigm that required spatial perception of pairs of competing nonsense shapes through touch. The subject was required to feel, out of view, two different nonsense shapes (3.8 cm^2) simultaneously for 10 seconds, one with each hand using the index and middle fingers. Many pretest trials were given to provide practice in simultaneously feeling two stimuli. The response required that the subject choose the two stimuli he felt from a visual recognition display of six shapes. There were ten trials and the scores obtained were the number of left and of right hand objects correctly chosen. This test has been previously described in more detail (Witelson, 1974).

Since this is an unfamiliar test procedure, the main aspects of its rationale follow. First, shape discrimination that is not readily amenable to linguistic encoding has been shown to be mainly dependent on right hemisphere functioning in adults (Milner and Taylor, 1972; Nebes, 1971, 1972). For this reason, shape discrimination was used as the cognitive task, and the entire test was designed to be as nonlinguistic and right-hemisphere dependent as possible. The stimuli were meaningless shapes, not readily labeled. The alternate items in the recognition display were designed to have spatial details similar to those of the palpated stimuli, so that a correct choice depended on a gestalt perception of the whole stimulus, considered a right hemisphere function, rather than on analysis of details, possibly a left hemisphere function. The response of pointing to a visual match with the left hand also ensured that verbal processing was not required in the cognitive process.

Second, tactual shape discrimination has been shown to depend on only the contralateral or crossed somesthetic pathways (Sperry, Gazzaniga, and Bogen, 1969). In the present test situation two different stimuli were presented simultaneously, one to each hand. The consequence of this, it was hoped, would be the production of a competing situation between the processing of left and right inputs at some level in the central nervous system. If the right hemisphere is more effective in processing nonlinguistic spatial information in children as it is in adults, then this perceptual task might confer some advantage to the stimuli presented to the contralateral (left) hand. This result was predicted because only left hand information would be initially transmitted to the right hemisphere, the one specialized for the spatial processing required in the task. The predicted result was observed in a previous study: greater accuracy was found for left hand shapes for normal boys ranging in age from 6 to 14 years. The greater left hand accuracy is interpreted as indicating right hemisphere specialization for spatial processing in boys at least as young as 6 years of age (Witelson, 1974).

This test was given to 49 of the dyslexic boys, only a portion of the total group studied because the test was devised and introduced into the study after it had started, and to a comparable group of 100 normal boys. Table 1 gives the mean accuracy scores for the left and right hands at different age levels for the dyslexic and normal groups. Figure 1 presents the data graphically. A mixed design analysis of variance was carried out with two between factors, Group and Age, and one within factor, Side. The results are summarized in Table 1. No significant Group effect was found, which indicates that the dyslexics did not differ from the normals in overall accuracy. Accuracy increased with age similarly for both groups. Side was a significant main effect, indicating that left hand objects were recognized more accurately than right hand objects. The Group X Side interaction term was significant. Individual comparisons were made using the Duncan Multiple Range Test (Duncan, 1955). For the normal group the left hand score was significantly greater than the right hand score (df = 141, $p < 0.01$). The difference between left and right hand scores for the dyslexics was not significant. The right hand score of the dyslexics was significantly greater than the right hand score of the normals (df = 141, $p < 0.01$). Left hand scores did not differ significantly between groups.

An analysis was also done to determine whether the number of individuals with greater left or right hand scores was different for the two

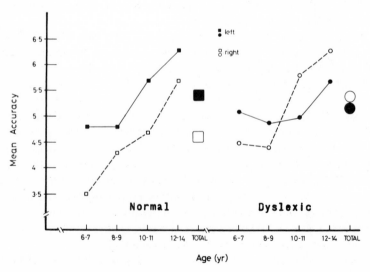

Figure 1. Mean accuracy scores for left and right hands on nonsense shape dichotomous tactual stimulation test for normal and dyslexic boys.

Table 1. Mean Accuracy Scores for Left and Right Hands for Dichotomous Tactual Stimulation with Nonsense Shapes

Age (yr)		Normal					Dyslexic		
			Accuracy					Accuracy	
	n	L	R	Σ	n	L	R	Σ	
6–7	25	4.8	3.5	8.3	8	5.1	4.5	9.6	
8–9	25	4.8	4.3	9.2	11	4.9	4.4	9.3	
10–11	25	5.7	4.7	10.4	15	5.0	5.8	10.8	
12–14	25	6.3	5.7	12.0	15	5.7	6.3	11.9	
Total	100	5.4	4.6	10.0	49	5.2	5.4	10.6	

Maximum possible score for each hand is 10.

Summary of Analysis of Variance
Significant main factors and interaction terms

Age	$F = 14.22$	df = 3/141	$p < 0.001$
Side	$F = 7.27$	df = 1/141	$p < 0.01$
Group × Side	$F = 6.99$	df = 1/141	$p < 0.01$

groups. A χ^2 test again indicated a significant group difference ($\chi^2 = 6.29$, $p < 0.02$).

These results clearly indicate a significant behavioral difference between the groups. It is suggested that the finding of greater accuracy for left than for right hand objects in the normal boys again indicates the greater role of the right hemisphere in spatial processing in normal boys, at least for those aspects of spatial processing required by this task. The lack of behavioral asymmetry observed for the dyslexics may indicate a lack of right hemisphere specialization for spatial processing or bilateral spatial representation in dyslexic boys compared to normal boys. Greater left hemisphere involvement in spatial processing in dyslexics compared to normals is suggested not only by the dyslexics' lack of left hand superiority, but also by their significantly greater right hand score compared to normals.

Tachistoscopic Presentation of Lateralized Pictures of People The tachistoscopic paradigm was used as a second method to study right hemisphere specialization for spatial processing, but this time in the visual modality. The anatomy of the visual system is such that stimulation in each lateral visual hemifield is transmitted initially only to the contralateral (opposite) primary visual cortex. Since the right hemisphere is specialized for spatial processing, one might predict that stimuli which require the perception of spatial relationships (such as faces, slanted lines, dot patterns) would be better perceived when presented in the left than in the right visual field. This result has been frequently reported for adults (Kimura and Durnford, 1974) although so far there are no reports for children.

A specific test was designed that involved a set of stimuli composed of unfamiliar pictures of figures of people that were approximately 6 mm^2. This particular type of stimulus was chosen because verbal encoding of the stimuli seemed difficult and unlikely, and only spatial processing was necessary for the task. Each stimulus card presented either two identical or two different pictures of people in a vertical array in either the left or right visual field. Binocular viewing in a two-channel Scientific Prototype tachistoscope (Model 800-F) was used and the subject fixated on a central dot before each stimulus presentation. The distance from the fixation point to the near edge of the stimulus was 3.2 cm, which subtends a visual angle of 2°, 12′, placing the stimulus outside the field of possible bilateral cortical representation. For each stimulus card the subject had to indicate orally whether the two stimuli were the same or different. Twenty such stimulus cards were presented and the scores obtained were the number of left and of right stimulus pairs correctly discriminated.

Since pilot work indicated that children, unlike adults, vary greatly in the stimulus exposure time needed for such visual discriminations, exposure time was determined for each child by the psychophysical method of limits to yield approximately 75% accuracy. However, stimulus exposure was never allowed to exceed 150 msec, since exposure beyond this duration may allow eye movements that could bring the peripheral stimulus into central vision. The only children used as subjects for this test were those who indicated on ophthalmological screening (WIRT Stereopsis Test, 1960) that they had fine stereopsis (at least six correct out of the nine WIRT dots) and therefore fusion, and hence were viewing the tachistoscopic stimuli with homologous peripheral areas of the retinae of both eyes.

The normal group of 85 boys obtained mean accuracy scores for the left and right visual field stimuli of 6.0 and 5.5, respectively, which are significantly different ($t = 2.28$, df = 84, $p < 0.05$). The dyslexic group ($N = 82$) obtained left and right mean accuracy scores of 5.8 and 5.6, respectively, which are not significantly different ($t = 0.96$, df = 81). Although total accuracy was similar for the normal and dyslexic groups, the mean stimulus exposure for the dyslexics ($\overline{X}$ = 55.0 msec) was significantly greater than that for the normals ($\overline{X}$ = 41.3; t = 2.07, df = 165, p < 0.05). Performance asymmetry in the normal group and between groups is less clear in this case than in the nonsense shapes touch test. One possible reason is that this visual test was too difficult as administered. The overall accuracy for each group was considerably less than the planned 75% level.

The significantly greater accuracy for left field spatial stimuli in the normal group provides evidence of right hemisphere specialization for spatial processing in the visual modality in children as in adults. This may be the first report of right hemisphere specialization for visual-spatial processing in children. The lack of significant behavioral asymmetry for the dyslexic group could be suggestive of a lack of right hemisphere specialization for spatial processing. These data derived from a completely different test in a different sense modality corroborate the hypothesis based on the nonsense shapes touch data, namely, a lack of right hemisphere specialization for spatial processing or bilateral spatial representation in dyslexic boys compared to normal boys.

Left Hemisphere Specialization

Dichotic Listening: Digits   To study left hemisphere specialization for language each child was given a verbal dichotic listening test. On such tests, right ear superiority is well documented and is considered to reflect left hemisphere specialization for linguistic functions. The specific test used in this study involved the simultaneous presentation of pairs of different digits (1 to 10, excluding the two-syllable digit, 7), one to each ear via Sharpe HA-10 Mark II headphones and a two-channel Tandberg tape recorder (Model 1200X). The stimuli were presented at the rate of two pairs per second, in ten sets each of two and of three pairs, making a maximum possible score of 50 per ear. A free recall method of response was used in which the subject was asked to report as many numbers as he could. The scores obtained were the number of right and of left ear digits correctly reported, regardless of order. Order or response was not random, but almost always involved the ear order of report, in which numbers from one ear are reported first, followed by those from the other ear. This is the typical strategy used by children as well as adults at this fast rate of presentation (Witelson and Rabinovitch, 1971).

The intensity of the stimuli measured as sound pressure level at the earphones was 60 dB SPL, which was a subjectively comfortable loudness level for all subjects. All children were screened audiologically. Only those children whose pure tone thresholds for each ear were within the normal range and which did not differ by more than 5 dB in favor of one ear on two or more of the four tested frequencies (0.25, 0.5, 1, 2 kHz) were used as subjects for dichotic listening.

Table 2 presents the mean accuracy scores for the left and right ears for the dyslexics and a group of normal children. The results are shown graphically in Figure 2. A mixed design analysis of variance as before (Group × Age × Side) indicated (see Table 2) that overall accuracy increased with age for both groups. However, the overall accuracy for the normal group was significantly greater than for the dyslexic group at all age levels. Side was also a significant main effect indicating that the right ear score was greater than the left ear score. Neither the Group × Side nor the Group × Age × Side interaction term was significant, indicating no difference between the groups in relative accuracy of left and right ear scores at different age levels.

The Group × Side interaction term was not significant. However, since one of the main purposes of the study was to determine whether dyslexics do in fact show a significant right ear effect on dichotic listening comparable to normals, two Duncan Multiple Range Tests were done to test left versus right ear accuracy for the normal and dyslexic groups separately. For each group the right ear score was significantly greater than the left ear score (df = 233, $p < 0.001$).

An analysis of the data in terms of the number of individuals with greater right or left ear superiority also indicated no difference in ear

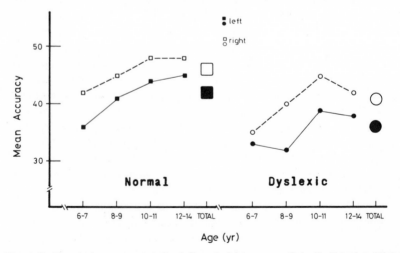

Figure 2. Mean accuracy scores for left and right ears on dichotic listening (digits) test for normal and dyslexic boys.

Table 2. Mean Accuracy Scores for Left and Right Ears for Dichotic Listening of Digits

| Age (yr) | | Normal | | | | Dyslexic | | |
| | | | Accuracy | | | | Accuracy | |
	n	L	R	Σ	n	L	R	Σ
6–7	25	36.4	41.5	77.9	12	32.6	34.5	67.1
8–9	48	41.0	45.2	86.2	25	31.9	40.0	71.9
10–11	45	44.4	47.8	92.2	26	38.8	44.9	83.7
12–14	38	44.6	48.0	92.6	22	37.6	41.6	79.3
Total	156	42.1	46.0	88.2	85	35.6	41.1	76.7

Maximum possible score for each ear is 50.

Summary of Analysis of Variance
Significant main factors and interaction

Group	$F = 105.76$	df = 1/233	$p < 0.01$
Age	$F = 33.95$	df = 3/233	$p < 0.01$
Side	$F = 76.91$	df = 1/233	$p < 0.01$

asymmetry between groups. Approximately 70% of each group showed a right ear superiority, defined as a difference of at least one point between left and right ear scores ($\chi^2 = 0.02$).

On the basis of these results it is suggested that the left hemisphere is the major hemisphere for linguistic processing in normal children; this is consistent with the numerous other reports. It is also suggested that the left hemisphere is the major hemisphere for linguistic processing in dyslexic boys. However, the level of ability of processing the linguistic information required in this task is markedly lower in the dyslexic children. This finding could suggest a disorder in left hemisphere functioning in dyslexics. The implications of this suggestion will be discussed more fully in a later section.

Dual Hemisphere Participation

Dichotomous Tactual Stimulation: Letters A second dichotomous tactual stimulation test was used analogous to the one described with nonsense shapes. In this case the stimuli were two-dimensional letters (approximately 2 × 2.5 cm) that were presented in ten sets of two dichotomous pairs, each pair presented for 2 seconds with a 1-second interpair interval. The subject's task was to orally report the names of the four letters he just felt.

Previous work with normal boys indicated that in contrast to left hand superiority on a dichotomous touch test with nonsense shapes, no left hand superiority was observed with letters, but rather a trend in favor of the right hand. It was suggested that the lack of superiority for either right or left hand letters indicated a lack of either left or right hemisphere superiority in the processing of this task. This may be because this test requires participation of both hemispheres: spatial processing by the right hemisphere to initially recognize the shape of the stimuli, and linguistic processing by the left hemisphere to linguistically encode the stimuli in order to name them for the response (Witelson, 1974).

If this task does require both types of cognitive processing, the question arises of how dyslexic children might perform on this task in view of the findings of this study so far. Language functions appear to be lateralized to the left hemisphere in dyslexics, although processed very poorly. In addition, spatial processing appears to involve more left hemisphere functioning in dyslexics than in normals since the data indicate a lack of right hemisphere specialization for spatial processing. If the left hemisphere is involved in mediating both cognitive processes in dyslexics, this suggests the possibility that this task may overload the capacity of the left hemisphere in dyslexics. Any behavioral asymmetry that dyslexics may show on this task that differs from normal performance may indicate a difference in hemisphere participation and in choice of cognitive strategy compared to normal boys. The results may be of particular interest since dyslexics' difficulties are precisely on tasks such as reading and spelling which, like this letters touch test, may involve both types of cognitive processes and the possibility for bias in use of cognitive strategy.

The results of the performance of dyslexic and normal boys on this task are presented in Table 3 and in Figure 3. A mixed design analysis of variance (Group × Age × Side) indicated (see Table 3) that the groups did not differ significantly in overall accuracy. Again accuracy increased with age for both groups. There was a significant Group × Side interaction, which was further analyzed by individual comparisons using Duncan Multiple Range Tests. It was found that in this case for the normal group the right hand score was significantly greater than the left hand score ($df = 68$, $p < 0.05$). For the dyslexic group a significant difference was found in the opposite direction: the left hand score was significantly greater than the right hand score ($df = 68$, $p < 0.05$). It was also found that the left hand score of the dyslexics was significantly greater than the left hand score of the normals ($df = 68$, $p < 0.001$). Right hand scores did not differ significantly between groups.

Table 3. Mean Accuracy Scores for Left and Right Hands for Dichotomous Tactual Stimulation with Letters

| Age (yr) | | Normal | | | | Dyslexic | | |
| | | Accuracy | | | | Accuracy | | |
	n	L	R	Σ	n	L	R	Σ
6–7	7	3.3	5.3	8.6	7	4.9	6.4	11.3
8–11	7	5.4	6.4	11.9	26	7.2	5.7	12.9
12–14	14	6.9	7.8	14.7	13	10.1	8.2	18.2
Total	28	5.6	6.8	12.5	46	7.7	6.5	14.2

Maximum possible score for each hand is 20.

Summary of Analysis of Variance
Significant main factors and interaction terms

Age	$F = 6.11$	df = 2/68	$p < 0.005$
Group $\times$ Side	$F = 9.97$	df = 1/68	$p < 0.005$

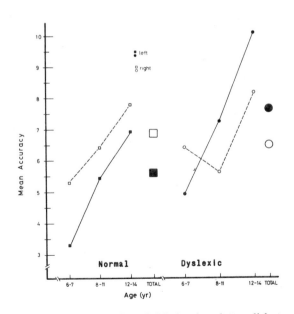

Figure 3. Mean accuracy scores for left and right hands on letters dichotomous tactual stimulation test for normal and dyslexic boys.

A χ^2 analysis of the number of individuals with greater left or right hand scores in the two groups also indicated a significant group difference ($\chi^2 = 7.62, p < 0.01$).

The difference in behavioral asymmetry between the groups is very clear, and may reflect differences in hemisphere specialization and/or in cognitive strategy. In this study the normal group showed a significantly greater right than left hand score, which might suggest relatively greater participation of the left hemisphere and use of a linguistic-analytic approach in this task. The reverse behavioral pattern observed for the dyslexics could suggest a different neural substrate and a different preferred cognitive strategy for this task, one favoring the right hemisphere and spatial-holistic processing.

In isolation, these data might raise the possibility that in dyslexic boys both spatial and linguistic processing are predominantly mediated by the right hemisphere, thus resulting in the observed left hand superiority on the letters touch test. However, this hypothesis is unlikely in view of the two other sets of data observed for the dyslexic boys which suggest that, first, the left hemisphere is specialized for linguistic processing and, second, the right hemisphere is not the major hemisphere for spatial processing. The following very tenuous line of speculation is offered, if only to serve as hypotheses for future studies. When dyslexics are presented with a task that requires both cognitive processes, the left hemisphere mediates the linguistic processing and it appears to have limited capacity to do this. This situation may necessitate the right hemisphere to mediate the spatial processing. This may occur even though the right hemisphere may not function as the main spatial processor in other circumstances, such as with relatively pure spatial tasks that require no linguistic processing. These results taken together support the specific hypothesis of bilateral spatial representation in dyslexics. In addition, when tasks requiring both cognitive strategies are involved, dyslexic children may tend to favor spatial-holistic strategies. This suggestion is supported not only by the dyslexics' greater left than right hand score, but also by their greater left hand score compared to normals. Hence, if in dyslexics the right hemisphere is forced to be the spatial mediator and a spatial-holistic strategy is preferred, a left hand superiority on this letters touch test would be explicable.

GENERAL DISCUSSION

Several sets of data of left–right behavioral asymmetries have been observed for a group of right-handed dyslexic boys in comparison to those for matched normal boys. The behavioral asymmetries observed for the normal boys are all consistent with previous reports or expectations as reviewed earlier. The behavioral asymmetries observed for the dyslexics appear to emerge into a consistent pattern but different from that of the normals. These data do not prove, but they strongly suggest a pattern of hemisphere functional specialization associated with developmental dyslexia that is different from that observed in normal boys. Specifically, it is suggested that dyslexic boys have an atypical pattern of hemisphere specialization compared to normal boys, but only in respect to right hemisphere specialization for spatial processing.

Left Hemisphere Specialization for Language in Dyslexia

On the basis of the dichotic listening data it is hypothesized that dyslexic boys have left hemisphere specialization for linguistic processing as do normal boys. This conclusion is consistent with the data of many other reports of children with reading problems, as previously indicated. This hypothesis, however, must be restricted to functional specialization for that level of linguistic processing tested in the present dichotic task (Porter and Berlin, 1975), which required analyses at the mnemonic and semantic levels of the perceptual process as well as at the earlier levels of acoustic and phonetic analyses.

This conclusion of the normal pattern of left hemisphere specialization for language in dyslexia does not rule out the possibility that left hemisphere functioning per se may be deficient in dyslexics even though it is mediating the typical cognitive process. The dyslexics were markedly impaired on total recall on the dichotic digits task, a left hemisphere task. This result is consistent with the data of many other studies (Leong, 1975c; Witelson, 1962; Yeni-Komshian et al., 1975; Zurif and Carson, 1970). This markedly poor total recall for verbal dichotic stimulation is similar to that observed for preoperative as well as postoperative brain-damaged patients with left (language dominant) hemisphere lesions (Kimura, 1961a, 1961b).

Bilateral Spatial Representation in Dyslexia

In contrast to the normal pattern of right hemisphere specialization for spatial processing, it is suggested that dyslexics have bilateral representation of spatial functions. This is the first report suggesting abnormal right hemisphere specialization for spatial processing in dyslexics. This hypothesis is based on the dyslexics' lack of left field superiority on the spatial touch test and the visual spatial test, and on their atypical pattern of left hand superiority on the "linguistic" touch test. Despite possible abnormal lateralization of spatial processing, it is noted that the dyslexics' overall performance on these tests was not at all deficient compared to the performance of the normal boys.

Spatial Strategy Bias in Dyslexia

On the basis of the dyslexic boys' performance on the "linguistic" touch test, it is hypothesized that on tasks in which both cognitive processes are required, dyslexics tend to use spatial-holistic strategies more than do normals. The same hypothesis also emerges from a completely different line of reasoning. Individuals who are deficient in linguistic processing, as may be the case for dyslexics, might necessarily rely more on spatial-holistic strategies. This suggestion of greater use of spatial strategies in dyslexics is consistent with recent reports which indicate that poor readers are less able than normal readers to use phonetic analyses in reading (Shankweiler and Liberman, 1975), and that normal readers tend to pass from a visual-holistic strategy to a phonetic-analytic strategy in reading (Bakker, Teunissen, and Bosch, 1975).

Perhaps dependence on spatial strategies for reading is one immediate factor hindering dyslexics' progress in reading. This hypothesis may have relevance for devising theoretically based teaching methods for dyslexics. Of all the tests in the present study, the letters touch test appears most similar to reading in that both may require spatial and linguistic processing. Although dyslexic children appear predominantly to use a different cognitive strategy and neural substrate on this test than do normals, their overall accuracy was similar to normal performance. These results suggest that one teaching method of possible benefit for dyslexics might be to foster use of phonetic analyses in reading and/or activity in related linguistic tasks such as reading or repeating some words orally. This procedure might prevent the left hemisphere from engaging in spatial processing and leave only the right hemisphere to spatially process the written material.

Pattern of Hemisphere Specialization and Level of Cognitive Ability

If this proposed atypical pattern of neural organization is in fact associated with, or is the neurological substrate of, developmental dyslexia, it may be important to ask what relationship lateralization of function has to the level of cognitive skills. The present study provides some data relevant to this issue. A pattern was observed for dyslexics in which performance was impaired on those tasks associated with the normal pattern of hemisphere specialization, but, in contrast, performance was adequate, even somewhat higher, on those tasks associated with an abnormal pattern of specialization.

On all the laterality tests involving at least some spatial processing (shapes touch test, visual "people" test, letters touch test), the overall accuracy of the dyslexic boys was at least equal to that of the normal boys. Normal spatial ability for the dyslexics is corroborated by their performance on the WISC Block Design subtest for which the normal and dyslexic groups obtained mean scaled scores of 11.9 and 11.3, respectively (t = 1.30, df = 239, p < 0.20). However, it is precisely on tasks involving spatial processing that atypical laterality in performance was observed and abnormal hemisphere specialization was suggested.

In contrast, on the one laterality test involving only linguistic processing, the typical pattern of right ear superiority indicative of left hemisphere specialization for language was observed for both dyslexics and normals. However, in this test the overall performance level of the dyslexics was significantly lower than that of the normal boys. Their mean WISC Vocabulary scaled score ($\overline{X}$ = 10.2) was also significantly lower than that of the normals ($\overline{X}$ = 11.4, t = 3.44, df = 239, p < 0.001). Moreover, the dyslexic boys had significantly lower Verbal than Performance IQ scores, as indicated previously.

This pattern of impaired ability on cognitive tasks involving processes associated with normal lateralization has a precedent in another domain, although in reverse pattern. Levy (1969) found that a lack of left hemisphere lateralization of verbal functions is associated not with lower verbal ability but with lower spatial ability. It was suggested that spatial ability suffered because the right hemisphere was responsible for mediating both cognitive functions. The impaired left-hemisphere linguistic skills of the dyslexics may be considered in terms of this type of speculation, namely, that in dyslexics the left hemisphere may mediate both linguistic and spatial processing as hypothesized above, and consequently linguistic functions suffer.

Neural Substrate of Dyslexia

It may be that for some reason there is bilateral representation of spatial processing in dyslexia that interferes with the left hemisphere's processing of linguistic functions. Or alternatively it may be that there is left hemisphere dysfunction per se in dyslexics that results in poor linguistic functioning. This left hemisphere dysfunction may somehow cause the lack of right hemisphere specialization for spatial processing, or possibly both abnormalities are manifestations of some more antecedent dysfunction. Either situation would be consistent with the suggested preference of dyslexics for spatial-holistic strategies, and this may be the most immediate factor in their poor reading. Maybe one cannot read fluently by spatial processing alone.

The question arises whether a lack of right hemisphere specialization for spatial processing and deficient left hemisphere processing of linguistic functions are both necessary correlates of developmental dyslexia or whether either alone is a sufficient correlate. This may be an important question for future research. The results of the present study suggest that perhaps much of the research in this area has not been asking the right questions. The prevalent question has been whether dyslexics have left hemisphere specialization for linguistic processing. On the basis of the present data, in conjunction with those of many previous studies, it is strongly suggested that left hemisphere specialization for language is present in dyslexia. It appears that more fruitful questions may be: do dyslexics show abnormal right hemisphere specialization for various aspects of spatial processing in perception and memory; do they show abnormal right hemisphere specialization for nonlinguistic auditory processing, an issue not yet studied at all; and what is the level of right and left hemisphere cognitive functions in relation to observed patterns of hemisphere specialization. It may be that answers to these questions will be of more help in elucidating the neural and cognitive deficits of dyslexia.

The lack of right hemisphere specialization for spatial processing is hypothesized for dyslexic boys in late childhood and adolescence. In view of the literature reviewed earlier suggesting the existence of at least some left and right hemisphere functional specialization at birth, the present results favor a neural deficit or dysfunction correlate of dyslexia, rather than a neural maturational lag as suggested by several authors (Kinsbourne, 1973; Satz and Sparrow, 1970). It is noted, however, that a neural deficit hypothesis does not preclude the observation of a lag in the development of cognitive skills, the data upon which the neural maturational lag hypothesis is based.

In summary, the present study suggests an association between the syndrome of developmental dyslexia and two possible neural abnormalities; a lack of right hemisphere specialization for spatial processing and a dysfunction in left hemisphere processing of linguistic functions. The broader implication of this association is that there may be a biological correlate or substrate of developmental dyslexia that may be elucidated, at least at the gross level of neurological organization and function, despite present technological limitations. This postulated association, however, does not necessarily imply a causal relationship. In fact, the abnormal neural and cognitive manifestations in dyslexia may both be the result of more antecedent conditions involving genetics, biochemistry, or neural trauma, which may themselves be the etiological factors of developmental dyslexia.

ACKNOWLEDGMENTS

My appreciation is extended to the members of the Wentworth County Roman Catholic Separate School Board, with special appreciation to Principal R. Peet, for their unlimited cooperation in providing so many students for such extensive testing; to the many clinicians who cared enough to refer their patients to this research project; and to the families and particularly the dyslexic children who so willingly gave of their time and effort. I am indebted to Lois Cohen, Jeri Lee, Diane Clews, Hope Evenden, Marilyn Irvine, Chris Crowley-Anderson, Janice Swallow, Gerald Chan, and Mike Dismatsek for their generous technical assistance in many stages and in various aspects of the project, and to many individuals, particularly Dr. Morris Moscovitch, for their thoughtful discussions of this work and for critical comments on earlier drafts of this paper. And finally I thank and dedicate this work to my husband, Henry Witelson, without whom this work would never have come to be.

Cognitive Style and Specialized Hemispheric Processing in Learning Disability

Morton P. Friedman,
B. LaRue Guyer-Christie, and Alexander Tymchuk

The relationship of brain structure and function to cognitive processing has been a fruitful area of research in recent years. The rapidly accumulating data and theoretical conjectures on the development and differentiation of brain function have been of particular value in the understanding of Learning Disability (LD). However, these analyses have mainly focused on understanding reading deficits in terms of disorders of brain development. This chapter will attempt to take a broader view, and consider how some of the overall problem-solving and perceptual strategies of the LD child, that is, his "cognitive style," and his personality characteristics, might be interpreted and understood in terms of brain function and structure.

Two theoretical notions of importance related to this argument are, first, the development and differentiation of cerebral function, and second, the concept of "cognitive style," in particular, Witkin's (1962) construct of "Field Articulation."

CEREBRAL FUNCTION

Some basic (but certainly oversimplified) notions of hemispheric function that are important here are: (1) There appear to be at least two semi-independent processing systems operating on the same input information: The right cerebral hemisphere appears to be specialized for holistic functioning and sensory coding, while the left hemisphere may be specialized

This research was supported in part by National Institutes of Health Grant MH-7809 and Maternal and Child Project 927. Address reprint requests to Morton P. Friedman, Department of Psychology, University of California, Los Angeles, California 90024.

for language coding and propositional forms of thinking. Also, the left hemisphere may be dominant, and have attentional and executive control in integrating the activities of the different processing systems (Gazzaniga, 1974). This attentional function of the left hemisphere has not received the attention it deserves in the analysis of LD. (2) The preceding generalizations apply to normal adult functioning. In the child, as cognitive structure develops, there is a parallel development of greater differentiation in brain function organization, with increasing lateralization of language function and executive control to the left hemisphere.

The most popular theories of LD are variations of the "Maturational Lag" hypothesis. (See Satz and Sparrow, 1970, for a review and definitive statement of the theory.) This theory suggests that LD is due to "incomplete dominance"—slower and less complete differentiation of brain function in some children. Thus, as compared with a normal child of the same age (say, age 7 or older), the LD child typically is deficient in verbal and attentional skills—both of which are left hemisphere functions—but not in many nonverbal right hemisphere skills (Guyer and Friedman, 1975).

CEREBRAL DOMINANCE

The notion of cerebral dominance is important and deserves some additional comment here. There are two points of view to consider. One view stresses the verbal functions of the left hemisphere (Vygotsky, 1962), while the second view (Gazzaniga, 1974) stresses the decision-making and integrative functions necessary to coordinate the various cerebral systems.

According to the first point of view, the attentional or executive function of the left and more verbal hemisphere can be understood in terms of work on language development by Vygotsky (1962) and other Soviet workers. These workers argue that language and thought develop from preverbal thought through a series of stages, beginning with the use of language for communication and social purposes and then to a stage of egocentric speech where language acquires its "second signal properties." It seems reasonable to assume that it is during this stage that self-speech begins to obtain control over attentional processes. In the final level of development, logical propositions dominate language. In this view, language dominates cognition, and as a second signaling system or newer phylogenetic ability, it inhibits control by older phylogenetic systems.

An alternative view of cerebral dominance (Gazzaniga, 1974) is that dominance is not strictly verbal control. Gazzaniga suggests that the brain consists of a number of semi-independent information processing systems all operating on the same data, trying to make sense of experience and reach decisions. "Dominance" is the decision or central control system that brings order and attentional control to these various information-processing activities and leads to a "final cognitive path." In Gazzaniga's view, this central control system "involves itself in language activity but at the same time is a superordinate system that is independent of the natural language mechanism per se" (Gazzaniga, 1974, p. 368).

The available data make it difficult to choose between these alternative views of dominance.

COGNITIVE STYLE

The "maturational lag" and/or "incomplete dominance" theories of LD presented above suggest the following: It was noted earlier that in many LD children, verbal and attentional skills are impaired, while nonverbal skills are normal. If cognitive processing systems are not synchronous in their development, continued use of the better developed system could be expected to result in a "cognitive style" of information processing that would inhibit responding by the other system and would affect performance over a wide range of perceptual, learning, and problem-solving tasks. Thus, when task requirements and cognitive style are incompatible, a "deficit" in performance should be detectable. The construct of cognitive style has emerged in recent years as an important theoretical concept in child development, and is presently the focus of much research (Keogh, 1973).

The cognitive style literature suggests that Witkin's (1962) "Field Articulation" construct might be important for an understanding of LD. One of the principal tasks used to define the concept is the Rod and Frame Test (Witkin, 1962; Nickel, 1971). This task requires the subject to align a rod vertically in the presence of a distorting tilted frame with no other visual cues available. Those subjects who are able to ignore the frame and make few errors in aligning the rod are said to be "Field-Independent." According to Witkin, Field-Independent people show a high degree of field articulation and are generally analytic in their approach to cognitive tasks. On the other hand, the "Field-Dependent" or "Field-Sensitive" person cannot ignore the distorting effect of the tilted frame and tends to make more errors in setting the rod vertically. The Field-Sensitive person tends to respond to the total field and to use a more global and perhaps less verbal information-processing style. [Although the term "Field-Dependent" is better known than the more recent "Field-Sensitive"

(Ramirez and Castaneda, 1974), the latter term maintains better value equivalence with "Field-Independent" and will be used in this chapter.]

There is a large body of evidence linking field articulation styles with behavior over a broad range of tasks. For example, Field-Independent people are better able to attend to a digit recitation task under distracting auditory stimuli (Bloomberg, 1965), are more task and achievement oriented (Ruble and Nakamura, 1972), perform better than Field-Sensitive people on tests of verbal learning (but not visual pattern learning) (Berent and Silverman, 1973), and are superior to Field-Sensitive people in verbal prediction and fluency (DeFazio, 1973). Developmental studies of field articulation indicate that Field-Independence tends to increase with age until adulthood, but relative differences in its extent are reasonably stable (Witkin, Goodenough, and Karp, 1967).

COGNITIVE STYLE AND BRAIN FUNCTION

The characteristics attributed by these research findings to Field-Independent and to Field-Sensitive people show a similarity with reports of specialized brain hemisphere function. Memory for faces (Geffen, Bradshaw, and Wallace, 1971), memory for forms (Milner, 1971), and perception of human emotion (Carmon and Nachson, 1973) have been associated with right hemisphere brain function; these abilities are also characteristic of Field-Sensitive people. On the other hand, many verbal abilities as well as some measures of body articulation (Kinsbourne and Warrington, 1963b) have been related to left hemisphere function; Field-Independent people are more likely to demonstrate superior performance on measures of these constructs.

Some recent experiments by Cohen, Berent, and Silverman (1973) also suggest important relationships between field articulation and specialized hemispheric processing. They studied the effect of electroconvulsive shock treatments on Rod and Frame Test scores of adult women hospital patients diagnosed as depressed. Different groups of patients received electroconvulsive shock to the left hemisphere, right hemisphere, or received no shock. The patients who received shock to the left hemisphere increased their error scores on the Rod and Frame Test and became more Field-Sensitive, while the patients who received right hemisphere shock decreased their error scores and became more Field-Independent. These results suggest that although the Rod and Frame Test appears to be a perceptual spatial task, it is the attentional or executive control function of the left hemisphere that is important to successful performance. As noted earlier, the task requires attention to the cues from the rod and proprioceptive stimuli, and inhibition of responding to cues from the frame.

COGNITIVE STYLE AND LEARNING DISABILITY

The evidence reviewed above suggests that Witkin's Field Articulation concept can be related to differential hemispheric function, with Field-Sensitivity being associated with "incomplete dominance" of left hemisphere systems on cognitive behavior.

There is substantial support for the "maturational lag" and/or "incomplete dominance" theories of LD based on analyses of the development of different information-processing skills (Satz and Sparrow, 1970). Is it also the case that the LD child tends to be Field-Sensitive?

There is some evidence that the LD child tends to be Field-Sensitive (Keogh and Donlon, 1972), and a recent study by Guyer and Friedman (1975) has explored the relationship between field articulation styles and differential hemispheric processing skills in LD children in some detail. This study compared a group of 41 LD boys and normal control boys matched for age (7.7–12.7 years) and Peabody Picture Vocabulary Test IQ (90–146 range). All of the boys were administered the Rod and Frame Test of field articulation, a set of tests chosen for their association with specialized hemispheric processing, and standard achievement tests. The test battery included measures of visual and auditory-verbal short and long-term memory, visual and verbal closure, verbal concepts, and hand awareness and laterality. The main results of interest to the present discussion were that the LD boys were considerably more Field-Sensitive than the controls, and also performed poorly on certain other left hemisphere tests of verbal ability and hand awareness.

The Rod and Frame Test measures cognitive style on a continuous scale. Using the median error score to classify children as Field-Sensitive or Field-Independent, 63% of the LD group were Field-Sensitive as compared with 37% of the normal control group. In agreement with other studies, there were no differences between the groups on visual pattern long- and short-term memory tests designed to measure right hemisphere function. Using three measures of left hemisphere function—Field Articulation, verbal long-term recognition memory, and verbal closure (a "Cloze" test)—it was possible to correctly classify 82% of the boys as good or poor readers. These tests do not require reading or writing skills or exposure to academic material and so may be useful for further research on prediction and diagnosis.

Another result relating to cognitive style differences between the LD and normal groups was that Visual Closure scores (which may be taken as indicants of right hemisphere skills) were positively related to Reading Vocabulary and Mathematics Calculation for the LD group, but not for the normal controls. The importance of Visual Closure for the LD group suggests the use of this right hemisphere ability as a strategy, albeit a not very successful one, in coping with academic tasks.

These results indicate that the field articulation concept can be of value in the analysis of the behavior of LD children. Another aspect of field articulation that may be of equal value to the understanding of the behavior of LD children is the relationship of this variable to personality characteristics and social behavior. For example, the literature on field articulation suggests that although the Field-Independent person with his analytic and verbal skills may be more suited to the traditional academic environment than the Field-Sensitive person, he also tends to be more hostile, more demanding, more unconventional, more inclined to blame others when things go wrong, and more resistant to authority (Elliot, 1961). In adult groups seeking mental health services, Field-Independent people are more severely disordered than the Field-Sensitive people as measured by the MMPI (Berent, 1975). Field-Sensitive people view themselves and are viewed by others as more reliant on social cues (Gordon, 1953). Indeed, when social cues have been made relevant to task accomplishment, Field-Sensitive children have performed better than Field-Independent children (Ruble and Nakamura, 1972). Painting with rather broad strokes, the overall picture that emerges is that the Field-Independent person attends better to task requirements—perhaps to the detriment of his social relationships—while the Field-Sensitive person is concerned with the social situation to the detriment of task performance. Although there does not appear to be much experimental evidence on this point, clinical experience suggests that the above characterization of the Field-Sensitive personality would be an apt description of many LD children.

COGNITIVE STYLE AND THE "DEPRIVED" CHILD

It is argued here that the Field-Sensitivity shown by the LD child is, like his reading deficit, attributable to maturational lag, e.g., slower development of language function and the associated attentional and executive processes of the left hemisphere. In actuality, the LD category contains only a very small proportion of the total population of poor readers. Children whose reading deficit may be a function of membership in certain ethnic and social groups and/or environmental and economic deprivation are usually excluded from the LD classification. However, many of the environmentally deprived children who have difficulty in learning to read have similar characteristics to the traditional LD group—including a language deficit and the tendency to Field-Sensitivity. Although an extensive analysis cannot be presented here, it is possible to interpret field articulation style and associated learning difficulties in the environmentally deprived child in terms of hemispheric processing. It can be argued that certain socialization practices and reinforcement patterns in different cultural situations can lead to cognitive styles which emphasize particular processing systems and deemphasize others (Witkin, 1967).

IMPLICATIONS FOR REMEDIATION

This analysis of cognitive style and its relationship to hemispheric processing has some interesting implications for remediation programs. First, it was argued in this chapter that there is an attentional control deficit associated with the LD child's verbal deficit. This suggests that it is important to work not only on the child's verbal skills, but also on his attention to verbal stimuli and his own use of verbal stimuli in attentional control. The techniques used by Meichenbaum and Goodman (1969) to teach attentional control to the impulsive child seem to be potentially useful here. Second, the Guyer and Friedman (1975) study and many other results show that many LD children have intact right hemisphere spatial or holistic processing skills. There is good evidence that imagery training can enhance verbal memory in both normal and retarded children with pronounced verbal deficits. The use of this technique with the LD population deserves some careful research. Finally, it is important to take into account the personality pattern of the LD Field-Sensitive child in planning a program of remediation. Research is needed to determine whether the LD child fits the pattern of the Field-Sensitive child described in the literature. If so, he would tend to be more responsive to immediate social rewards and punishments, more sensitive to the needs of his peers, more able to learn by modeling and imitation, and more able to work cooperatively than the Field-Independent child. It would seem to be important to fit the instructional strategy to the cognitive style of the child.

Cognitive Approach to Hemispheric Dominance

Luigi Pizzamiglio

Evidence for differentiation in brain function organization comes from several sources. Observations on unilaterally brain damaged patients and on commissurotomized patients have provided researchers with invaluable information concerning the functional asymmetry of the brain (Milner, 1971).

Studies devised for testing the functional asymmetry of the brain in normal subjects substantially support the research findings on the brain damaged. Such investigations have studied behavioral responses under particular conditions of stimulation such as dichotic listening, monoaural stimulation, and tachistoscopic presentation of different stimuli in the two hemifields. In other cases more neurophysiological responses have been studied under specified environmental conditions, such as EEG and evoked potentials.

In a recent report on hemispheric function, it was pointed out that when we are dealing with language or speech production or perception and with closely related functions, we observe systematically large and consistent differences, calling for a clear dominance of one hemisphere over the other (usually the left in the right handed); on the other side, when one moves toward the field of perceptual functioning, in different sensory modalities, we do find significative differences between the two hemispheres, usually calling for the right superiority, but the differences we observe are of smaller intensity and not so consistent as in the previous case (Benton, 1973).

RIGHT HEMISPHERIC FUNCTION

Several studies have attempted to investigate right hemispheric function. Patients with damage to the right hemisphere of the brain were observed to be more impaired than patients with left hemisphere damage on tasks

This work was supported by a grant from Consiglio Nazionale Delle Ricerche.

such as identification of faces (De Renzi and Spinnler, 1966a; Hécaen and Angelergues, 1963), sketch completion and identification of overlapping figures (De Renzi and Spinnler, 1966b), and perception of spatial exploration (De Renzi, Faglioni, and Spinnler, 1970). In patients with hemispheric disconnection the right hemisphere becomes dominant when the task is to immediately recognize and memorize visual shapes (Levy, Trevarthen, and Sperry, 1972). In normal subjects faces or rod rotation are better perceived when presented in the left hemifield and when no verbal mediation is possible (Umilta et al., 1974). Is there any general ability underlying all of these tasks that may be helpful in defining the functional capacity of the right hemisphere?

The response to this question differs according to whether one stresses the "quality" of the operation performed, or the "operative principles and strategies" of the two hemispheres.

De Renzi (1967) suggests that the role of the right hemisphere may be a visuospatial orientation ability, referring to the fact that many of the impaired abilities of patients with damage to the right hemisphere are in the area of perception and organization of space. It has been suggested that the left hemisphere operates analytically and searches for "distinctive subordinate features that could be handled verbally; whereas the right hemisphere functions for gestalt perception" synthesizing in a global way the information input (Levy-Agresti and Sperry, 1968; Levy, Trevarthen, and Sperry, 1972). Another way of formulating the same concept is that one hemisphere processes input "simultaneously" and the other "sequentially." Clearly, these and similar other interpretations have to be intended as heuristics. One characteristic of these attempts is that all of them are dichotomic.

MAPPING COGNITIVE CAPACITIES

A quite different approach to investigating the contributions of the two hemispheres could be to utilize a set of cognitive abilities and see if one could account for a sufficient number of performances that have been observed as predominantly subserved by different neurophysiological structures of either hemisphere. In other words, one could borrow from psychology different models to map the cognitive capacities and look for their usefulness in explaining the variety of acquisitions on interhemispheric differences.

An attempt of this kind would provide powerful tools for describing a great number of behavioral observations, but could also transfer previously acquired knowledge about the interelationship between different cognitive abilities and their developmental mechanisms to the problem of hemispheric specialization.

The primary objection to this approach is that psychologists are far from agreement about cognitive structures and one is faced with a great variety of different "cognitive traits."

In spite of these objective difficulties, it seems desirable to find a way to utilize some of the basic concepts in the field of cognitive psychology. Which kind of cognitive models can be used? A possible answer to this question may be found in focusing attention upon some cognitive dimensions, the biological correlates of which have already been studied. It seems to the author that this approach provides researchers with the assurance that what they are dealing with are not simply technical or mathematical artifacts, as are many "factors" identified by cluster analysis, but basic psychological processes that may affect a variety of complex performances.

Biological Correlates of Three Cognitive Dimensions

The above idea will be illustrated with three cognitive dimensions the author has been working with; however, it should be stressed that the intention is not to suggest that by using these dimensions one can explain exhaustively the problems connected with hemispheric dominance. The author simply wishes to exemplify the kind of biological characteristics one may look at before trying to use a cognitive model in this area, and to discuss how such a framework may be used to explain some of the abilities that neuropsychologists have indicated as being linked to the functions of one or the other hemisphere.

The first cognitive dimension is that of field dependence–independence, the second dimension is space rotation, and the third dimension is space visualization. None of these three dimensions need to be described, since they are widely used. For the field dependence–independence one may refer to the "Psychological Differentiation" by Witkin et al. (1962); for both space rotation and space visualization and the relative testing procedures, one may refer to the KIT Manual (1963).

The first attempt to study biological correlates of these dimensions comes from the field of behavioral genetics. Stafford (1961), utilizing tasks of space visualization, studied family correlation patterns. The correlations mother–son and father–daughter were significant, e.g., while the father–son correlation was around zero.

The author has advanced the hypothesis that this cognitive ability can be sustained by a recessive gene located on the X chromosome. Similar findings were confirmed by Hartlage (1970) and Bock and Kolakowsky (1973). Corah (1965), again using a family correlation study, found evidence for the same pattern; using a different methodology, a population of subjects with the X chromosome marked for the XGa factor was studied (Goodenough et al., 1975). Families with three brothers, two identical and one different for the X chromosome, according to the biological marker (for instance, two brothers XGa+ and one XGa−), were included in the study. All subjects were tested for field dependence–independence, space rotation, and space visualization. Brothers with identical X chromosomes had significantly higher correlations in their measures of field dependence than did the nonidentical brothers.

This result supports the idea that this cognitive dimension may be, at least partly, genetically determined, and more particularly X-linked.

Following the same line of research (Serra, Pizzamiglio, and Boari, 1976), the same cognitive abilities were examined in a population with numerical abnormalities of the X chromosome, the Turner's syndrome. The results show that the Turner's syndrome group (45XO) were significantly lower in both space rotation and space visualization when compared with a group of normal and of sterile females with 56XX. On the field dependence–independence dimension the results were in the same direction, although the differences did not reach significance.

In addition, the difference between the 45XO and 46XX sterile females tends to be against an interpretation of cognitive characteristics of the Turner's syndrome as mediated by the hormones, while supporting the idea of an X-linked genetic mechanism.

The next question is: Can knowledge of ability levels be of any use in understanding hemispheric dominance?

Marcel, Katz, and Smith (1974) stated, "an interesting hypothesis is that hemispheric specialization leads to an improvement in the functions concerned." On the cognitive side the hypothesis of differentiation, applied to the field-dependence dimension, stimulated several investigations aimed to show any possible connection between hemispheric specialization and degree of differentiation in this cognitive style."

Silverman, Adevais, and McGough (1960) found that left-handed people, including subjects with some degree of ambilaterality, were more field dependent, that is, less differentiated, than right-handed people. Oltman and Capobianco (1967) found mixed eye-dominant subjects. Similar findings are presented by Goodenough et al. (1971), who used binocular rivalry techniques.

In a recent study (Pizzamiglio, 1974) right-handed subjects were more field independent than were ambidextrous subjects. It was also shown that subjects who demonstrated a strong ear preference in dichotic listening were more field independent, that is, more differentiated, than mixed ear-preferent subjects. In another work (Pizzamiglio and Cecchini, 1971), investigating the development in children of both acoustic lateralization and field dependence, a significant correlation for 8- to 10-year-old children was found between the performance on a dichotic listening task and measures of field dependence. In view of the above studies, the possibility exists that the differentiation hypothesis in the field of cognitive style and the concept of brain specialization may be linked. More specifically it may be said that a cerebral ambilaterality is significantly linked to a less differentiated cognitive style. Is there any evidence for hypothesizing that field dependence, space rotation, and space visualization are predominantly supported by the left or right hemispheric function?

Relevant to the field dependence dimension is the observation by Russo and Vignolo (1967) that relates to the performances of unilateral brain damaged patients on the visual embedded figures test. Performance on this test appeared to be selectively disturbed in aphasic patients. However, it was pointed out that the association with aphasia cannot completely explain the patients' failure, since right brain damaged patients performed significantly worse than left brain damaged patients without aphasia.

In a recent paper it was shown that right brain damaged patients performed significantly worse than a left-nonaphasic group on the tactile embedded figures test (Pizzamiglio and Carli, 1974). The results on the equivalent visual test did not reach the significance, although they were in the same direction.

Basso, Bisiach, and Faglioni (1975) studied the susceptibility to Muller-Lyer illusion in left and right brain damaged patients. Their hypothesis was that "right hemisphere damage, by impairing a holistic attitude, should lessen susceptibility to the illusion, and the left hemispheric damage should produce the opposite effect." Contrary to the expectation, the left brain damaged showed a reduced susceptibility as compared to the right brain damaged patients. Since it is well known that the resistance to the Muller-Lyer illusion in normals is positively correlated with a good performance in the embedded figures test (Immergluck, 1966), this paper as well as the two previously quoted provides evidence for a connection between right hemisphere functions and ability to single out embedded figures (i.e., field dependence–independence). It should be pointed out that the many visual tasks developed in this research area are difficult to interpret as being strictly connected with the specific abilities of spatial rotation and visualization. In order to further investigate this point, the author is completing a study on a group of neurosurgical patients with unilateral lesions to whom a large battery of tests is applied to measure the above-mentioned three cognitive abilities. In addition, tasks measuring visuo-spatial abilities were used; they had been selected from the literature as being clearly discriminant between left and right brain damaged. The objectives are: (1) to attempt to verify associations that appear to exist between specific cognitive abilities and the right hemisphere, and (2) to investigate if some of the tasks that are sensitive to the right hemispheric impairment are correlated with one or more of the three dimensions discussed in this paper. This approach is advantageous in that it allows one to describe some of the hemisphere functions by utilizing conceptual models developed by cognitive psychology.

Up to this point the author has attempted to stress the practicality of approaching the problem of hemispheric dominance through the employment of cognitive constructs, specifically delineating three such constructs.

The main points of such reasoning are: (1) research has indicated a possible genetic basis for all three cognitive dimensions; (2) the degree of differentiation along the field dependence–independence dimension appears to be correlated with the degree of cerebral specialization; and (3) there is preliminary evidence to support the idea that field dependence is connected with right hemisphere functions.

APPLICATION TO LEARNING DISABILITIES

How can this proposal be applied to learning disabilities? Particularly in the field of dyslexia, there have been several attempts to connect this developmental abnormality with hemispheric specialization. The latter has been measured either by traditional hand-eye-foot preference or by speech perception, using dichotic listening (Bryden, 1970; Zurif and Carson, 1970). The support for greater ambilaterality in dyslexic children has been rather weak. Attempts have been made to study the degree of asymmetry for the perception of words presented tachistoscopically to the two hemifields. Such studies have produced convincing evidence for less lateralization of linguistic functions in poor readers.

Utilizing the first approach, the assumption has too often been made that one type of performance (e.g., handedness, speech) can be taken as an indicator of cerebral specialization in general. This assumption is far from being proved. The second approach seems to be more direct in the manner in which one measures the degree of lateralization of a complex ability, as in the above-mentioned case of word perception.

Learning to read and write may be connected to other abilities that are not strictly linguistic, for instance the capacity to connect visual and linguistic information. In fact, Zangwill (1960), in his excellent monograph, observes that reading and writing disorders often coexist with difficulties in spatial judgment and directional control. Parenthetically, it is interesting to note that one out of four patients whom he described had difficulty with Block Design and with spatial tasks on Thurstone's PMA; the former test is highly correlated with field-dependence measures and the second with the space rotation dimension.

In summary, the following two assumptions are stated:

1. Learning disabilities result as a consequence of a complex cognitive disorder.
2. Cerebral development implies a progressive specialization and lateralization of a net of different cognitive abilities.

If both assumptions can be taken, it would seem to be appropriate, in the research area of learning disabilities, to investigate the degree of lateralization reached for each of the cognitive dimensions for which there is evidence of asymmetry.

The availability of techniques for presenting a variety of stimuli in different modalities to either hemisphere makes the suggestion quite feasible.

Although the author is aware that many of the previous considerations are rather speculative, it is interesting to underline some advantages in studying the cerebral organization, using as tools different cognitive dimensions: linguistic, spatial and others. The first gain is that, along with the improvement of our knowledge in behavior genetics, we may increase the feasibility of investigating possible genetic components of learning disorders.

In this field, as well as in other areas of pathology, the difficulty in defining the phenotype in a quantitative way has always been a hindrance. The possibility of describing the cognitive dimensions (which have already been shown to be genetically determined as well as sustained by cerebral organization) would produce great advantages.

The second point, on a completely different side, is that, interacting with biological factors, a number of environmental conditions are known to have relevance in the development of the cognitive abilities we are talking about. Once a certain disorder has been described in terms of a set of cognitive deficits, the knowledge about the environmental conditions relevant to these cognitive areas can be directly transferred to therapeutic purposes.

In concluding, the author's effort was to justify the possibility of approaching the problem of hemispheric dominance in general and particularly in learning disabilities, utilizing certain cognitive constructs. An attempt was also made to specify some of the desirable conditions to look for. The stress on field dependence–independence, space rotation, and visualization is by no means a suggestion for an exhaustive explanation of, for example, nonverbal behavior. The intention was simply to exemplify how the suggested general approach can be followed.

Cerebral Dominance and Reading Disability: An Old Problem Revisited

Paul Satz

It was Samuel T. Orton who first postulated a relationship between cerebral dominance and specific reading disability. His writings on this subject spanned the years from 1925 to 1945 and represent a scholarly attempt to bridge the disciplines of education and psychology with neurology. His contributions are particularly noteworthy because they were made during a period in which interest in higher cortical functions, especially the neuroanatomical substrates of aphasia, was unfashionable, due largely, according to Geschwind (1974), to the intemperate polemics of Head (1926) and the dynamic psychiatry of the 1930s. Briefly, this period witnessed an extreme reaction to the classical localization school that dominated neurology from 1860 to 1918 and which attempted to tie changes in the brain, after damage, to selective disturbances in behavior.

A review of Orton's papers (1966) clearly shows an awareness of modern concepts of hemispheric dominance and its relationship to numerous gnostic functions including speech, reading, writing, spelling, vocabulary competence, and skilled motor movements. In other words, he conceptualized the reading process as only one of the many complex linguistic-cognitive functions subserved by the left cerebral hemisphere. He also revealed an astute grasp of the relationship between the tertiary or overlapping zones of the cortex (i.e., left angular gyrus) and the alexias. In this respect, he antedated current attempts to correlate the acquired disorders of reading and writing with selective lesions in the posterior regions of the left cerebral hemisphere (Benson, 1974; Geschwind, 1962). However, there is little evidence to suggest that he was aware of the more connectionistic-localization theory of Dejerine (1892), who first postulated the specific lesions underlying cases of pure word blindness without

This research was supported in part by funds from the National Institutes of Health (NS08208) and the National Institutes of Mental Health (MH19415).

273

agraphia. It was not until Geschwind's paper (1962) that the mechanisms for this disorder were more fully explained within the context of the aphasias and alexias.

Undoubtedly, Orton's greatest contribution lies in his distinction between the acquired disorders of reading, seen in adults following unilateral injury to the left hemisphere, and those specific disorders of reading seen in children with no demonstrable pathology of the CNS. Noting the similarity or parallelism in the reading errors between both groups, he postulated a differential etiology, the mechanisms of which were nevertheless referable to the left cerebral hemisphere. With acquired disorders of reading he postulated a pathological defect (i.e., lesion) that resulted in a loss or impairment in reading skill. With specific disorders of reading in children, by contrast, he postulated a physiological defect that prevented the normal establishment of unilateral cerebral dominance and the acquisition of reading proficiency.

The explanation for this physiological theory of reading disability is presented as follows in his 1928 paper:

> "In skeleton, then, my theory of the obstacle to the acquisition of reading in children of normal intelligence which results in the varying grades of reading disability is a failure to establish the physiological habit of working exclusively from the engrams of one hemisphere. As a result there is incomplete elision of one set of antitropic engrams and there results confusion as to the direction of reading which serves as an impediment to facile associative linkage with the auditory engrams, which during the learning years at least, carry the meaning" (1966, p. 96).

In other words, Orton postulated that the reversals and mirror images of letters and words in these children were due to confusion of competing images in both hemispheres because of a failure in the establishment of unilateral cerebral dominance. Orton referred to this disorder as strephosymbolia (i.e., "twisted symbols") to differentiate it from Hinshlewood's concept of "congenital word blindness," which implied an underlying neuroanatomical defect. This distinction between a pathological and physiological defect is particularly relevant because it postulates a reversible process in the latter condition, especially with educational training and perhaps with maturation of the brain—although Orton was vague on this latter point. As such, the theory is optimistic with respect to prognosis, and compatible with contemporary positions that view these children as having a specific reading or language impairment in the absence of gross intellectual, sensory, or neurological handicap (Waites, 1968).

However, the theory remains vague with respect to the etiology and mechanism underlying specific reading disability. The basis for the concept of incomplete unilateral dominance (i.e., hypothetical construct) is still unclear in Orton's writings. The construct, in effect, proposes little more than a label to describe unobservable events referable to these children. The construct seems to inhere in the fact that language, speech, and writing disturbances systematically result from lesions to the left rather than the right hemisphere in right-handed adults, suggesting less complete unilateral representation of speech in sinistrals. Therefore, the fact that children with specific reading disability and average intelligence have often been reported to have a variety of speech (stuttering) and language (naming) disabilities in the absence of gross neurological impairment may have suggested to Orton that a nonpathological mechanism underlies the functional organization of the cerebral hemisphere. However, the primary clue to an incomplete or faulty lateralization of the speech mechanisms is based largely on the behavioral reports of an increased incidence of left handedness, incomplete handedness, and/or crossed hand and eye dominance in these children. In fact, Orton (1937, 1966) made frequent reference to the high incidence of deviant hand and eye preference in these children, particularly the raised incidence of incomplete hand preference, often left sided, in which abnormal clumsiness, motor inaptitude, and speech disturbances symptomatically converged. These mixed lateral preferences apparently led Orton to postulate a similar ambilaterality at the level of the cortex (tertiary zones) which, in effect, would facilitate competition between the hemispheres in the perception of images and lead to reversals of letters and words. Thus, the theory is based on unobservable events postulated to occur in the left hemisphere that represent indirect inferences from adults with alexia and from dyslexic children who show speech disturbances and ambiguous handedness.

This formulation, while loose and speculative, has a ring of truth as evidenced in the writings of theorists concerned with the development of perception and cognition. For example, Tschirgi (1958) and Mach (1959) have suggested that the awareness of spatial position and directionality in space (an ability required for reading mastery) is dependent upon asymmetry of the perceiving system. These authors contend that an animal whose brain is bilaterally symmetrical cannot differentiate between stimuli arriving at homologous points. Also, Kephart (1960) argues that a spatial coordinate system must be established—primarily through motor activity—within the body before directionality in objective space can be appreciated. In this view, according to Palmer (1964), the absence of a consistent laterality, primarily in motor spheres, should lead to a greater directional confusion than would be the case in strong right or left handedness.

The occurrence of reversal errors and mirror imaging (i.e., twisted symbols), in the absence of brain damage or intellectual retardation, represents necessary symptoms in Orton's theory of specific reading disability (i.e., strephosymbolia). The presence of directional confusion, incomplete handedness, and mixed hand–eye preference represents additional symptoms that have been adduced as support for the construct (unobservable) of incomplete cerebral dominance.

It is the contention of this paper that the second group of symptoms (especially deviant hand and/or eye preference), while traditionally the basis of evaluation of the theory, are not essential, if even relevant, to the theory. First, research in the past decade has generally failed to show a relationship between left handedness or deviant hand–eye preference and specific reading disability (Balow, 1963; Belmont and Birch, 1965; Coleman and Deutsch, 1964; de Hirsch, Jansky, and Langford, 1966; Satz and Friel, 1974; Shankweiler, 1963; Sparrow and Satz, 1970; Zurif and Carson, 1970). Second, the process of induction from these behavioral symptoms to the construct of "faulty dominance" in disabled readers is speculative at best. Third, knowledge is still lacking on the relationship between handedness and cerebral speech dominance in adults (Altman, Sutker, and Satz, 1974; Levy, 1974; Satz, 1975a). Fourth, the relationship between handedness and cerebral speech dominance, while less clear in left-handed adults, is virtually unknown in children (Satz, Bakker, Teunissen, Goeber, and Van der Vlugt, 1975). Consequently, extrapolations from this construct to reading-disabled children further obscures the problem.

LATERALITY AND READING DISABILITY: A REVIEW

More direct evaluation of Orton's theory was not undertaken until the development of special laterality assessment procedures in audition (dichotic listening) and vision (visual half-field perception) in the early 1960s. However, it was almost a decade before these methods were applied to learning-disabled children.

To date, there has been no comprehensive review of these laterality studies to determine what light they shed, if any, on the problem of cerebral dominance and reading disability. A recent review of cerebral dominance and developmental dyslexia (Benton, 1975) mentions only four studies (all dichotic listening), two of which were never published (Kimura, 1967; Taylor, 1962), and two of which ostensibly revealed an attenuated ear asymmetry in the disabled reading groups—a conclusion that will be shown to be unsupported by the original data (Bryden, 1970; Zurif and Carson, 1970).

The author's review of this literature reveals that 19 published and unpublished studies have been reported, 15 of which have employed at least a dichotic verbal task and four of which have employed a visual half-field verbal task. These studies are reviewed separately.

Dichotic Listening Studies (Verbal)

The first two studies employing dichotic listening with disabled readers were reported as incidental unpublished findings by Kimura (1967). Kimura referred to an earlier study by Taylor (1962) which found a right ear advantage (REA) in both poor readers and good readers who were female (ages 7–11) but no REA in the poor readers who were male— suggesting a developmental lag in left hemisphere speech in the latter group. However, when older boys with reading disability were tested (ages not specified), Kimura (1967) reported finding a REA, from which she concluded that ". . . the normal developmental lag is simply accentuated in boys with reading problems" (p. 169). Unfortunately, these two early studies (summary reports) cannot be critically evaluated without additional statistical or procedural information. Also, Kimura did not state whether a control group was used to determine whether the magnitude of the REA varied as a function of reading group.

The first published study was reported by Sparrow (1969) and elaborated by Sparrow and Satz (1970). A dichotic listening task (four-pair digits) was administered (including a battery of manual laterality and cognitive tasks) to a large group ($N = 40$) of boys (ages 9–12) who were carefully selected for specific reading disability. An equal number of average readers were then selected as matched controls on age, sex, race, social class, and WISC Performance IQ. An analysis of variance revealed a similar REA for both groups of children, although a χ^2 analysis revealed that almost four times as many dyslexic subjects had a left ear advantage (28% versus 8%, $p < 0.025$).

This study was followed by two studies (Bryden, 1970; Zurif and Carson, 1970), both of which employed a dichotic digit task. Bryden (1970) administered a two- and three-pair task to an unspecified number of good readers and poor readers. The poor readers were defined as children (ages 8–12) whose intelligence scores (Otis) were higher than their reading scores (Gates-MacGinitie)—a method that would tend to misclassify some good readers as poor readers (i.e., false positives). The results, contrary to Benton (1975), revealed a REA for both groups (69% goods versus 58% poors). Failing to demonstrate a group difference on this task, the author proceeded to compare the percentage of crossed versus uncrossed hand–ear dominance on this task. No significant group differences emerged.

The study by Zurif and Carson (1970), by contrast, reported no REA in their small group ($N = 14$) of poor readers (boys, age 10). In fact, there was a nonsignificant trend in favor of the left ear. This led them, along with others, to conclude that the weak perceptual asymmetry score in their small group of boys ". . . is perhaps best explained in terms of incomplete cerebral dominance" (p. 358). Unfortunately, this conclusion is not supported by the data because their normal readers also failed to show a significant right ear asymmetry. Surely, the authors would not want to imply a lack of cerebral dominance in their normal readers too!

This study was followed by an attempt to examine whether the ear asymmetry, in reading disabled children, might vary as a function of age (Satz, Rardin, and Ross, 1971). The study represented a test of a theory advanced by Satz and Sparrow (1970) concerning the role of developmental factors in specific reading disability. The dichotic digit task (three pairs) comprised just one of several developmental-cognitive measures administered to a younger group of disabled male readers (ages 7–8) and an older group of disabled readers (ages 11–12), both of which were individually matched with a normal control group on age, sex, race, and WISC IQ. The results revealed a significant REA in both the younger and older age groups (dyslexic and control), but the magnitude of the REA was significantly greater in the older normal reading group. This finding was adduced as support for the theory that postulates that the brain evidences increasing maturation and functional lateralization with age, but at a slower rate in disabled readers. Consequently, measures of verbal-cognitive function, which are known to develop ontogenetically later in development (Bloom, 1964; Piaget, 1926a; Thurstone, 1955) would be expected to show their primary delays in older dyslexic children who are postulated to be lagging maturationally. Despite the cross-sectional design and small sample size used in this study, the results at least provided additional information on the crucial role of developmental factors in specific reading disability.

Witelson and Rabinovitch (1972), in a later study, administered a two- and three-pair dichotic digit task (at three different rates) to an older group (ages 8–13) of 24 linguistically impaired children and 24 normal children without any behavioral or academic difficulty. The majority of children in both groups were males (N = 21 and 17, respectively). The results were similar to the earlier study by Zurif and Carson (1970); i.e., no significant REA was found in the learning disabled group. In fact, a nonsignificant trend in favor of the left ear again emerged. This led the authors to the sweeping conclusion that ". . . the clinic children have some dysfunction in the left hemisphere, and that some cases have speech functions lateralized to the right hemisphere" (p. 422). They also concluded that ". . . Left hemisphere dysfunction may be a factor in all the learning-impaired children of the present study, but the time of onset of dysfunction, the extent, and/or localization of the lesions may differ" (p. 423). This conclusion is also not supported by the data because their normal reading group also failed to show a significant ear asymmetry in all of the list-length by rate conditions. Moreover, speculation on deviant hemispheric dominance and early brain injury, in their learning disabled group, was made despite the fact that subjects with mental retardation, sensory handicaps, and known brain damage were excluded from the study! The authors' conclusion is not even reasonable if they postulated a similar hemispheric dysfunction in their normal group—who also failed to show an REA. The latter finding is probably due to ceiling effects in the recording procedures that made the tasks too easy for this group of older children. For example, the administration of two- and three-pair digit tasks, especially at two of the slower rates (<2 pairs per second) would increase overall task recall and thus decrease the likelihood of obtaining differences in recall between ears (Satz, 1968).

The role of developmental factors in the ear asymmetry—particularly as it relates to reading ability—was studied more directly in two studies by Bakker and associates (Bakker, 1973; Bakker, Smink, and Reitsma, 1973). Based on the theory of Satz and Sparrow (1970), and two later tests of the theory (Sparrow and Satz, 1970; Satz, Rardin, and Ross, 1971), they noted a relationship between the ear asymmetry and reading ability only at later school ages—a period in which language functions are postulated to be more fully lateralized in normal children (Lenneberg, 1967).

They reasoned that because formal reading begins at age 6, before hemispheric lateralization is complete, perhaps early reading may proceed without complete lateralization, but not so for fluent later reading, which may require complete hemispheric lateralization of speech. The authors, citing Smith (1971), hypothesized that, in early reading, considerable weight is given to perceptual operations from which meaning is deduced from surface structure. By contrast, in later stages fluent reading is aided more by linguistic operations that sample the visual information to conform to prior expectations concerning meaning. Thus, Bakker and associates predicted that efficient reading would be associated with an attenuated ear asymmetry (left or right) at younger ages and with a significant REA at older ages. As stated, this prediction is compatible with those developmental positions that view the brain as undergoing increased maturation and functional lateralization with age (Satz and Sparrow, 1970). However, Bakker et al. (1973) and Bakker (1973) introduced a corollary hypothesis which predicted that, in cases of advanced early functional lateralization of the brain, perceptual strategies would be compromised, which would then interfere with efficient reading. Defining precocious lateralization in terms of large REA scores on the dichotic listening task, the authors found that such scores (large REA) were associated with poor reading at younger ages and with fluent reading at older ages.

This corollary hypothesis has subsequently been modified by Bakker,

Teunissen, and Bosch (1976, this volume) because of problems in replication (see below). The basic problem concerns the implication that the disabled child (ages 7–8) possesses an advanced degree of hemispheric specialization that attenuates by puberty. This explanation makes sense neither in the context of theories of hemispheric dominance, nor with respect to developmental parameters of the ear asymmetry (Satz, Bakker, Teunissen, Goebel, and Van der Vlugt, 1975). Moreover, Bakker and associates presented neither information on the frequency of these large REA scores at younger ages nor repeat measurements on the same subjects at later ages. By excluding this corollary hypothesis, their data are more in line with developmental theory—i.e., no relationship between the ear asymmetry and reading at younger ages when speech lateralization is presumed to be less complete for all children, but a relationship between the ear asymmetry and reading ability at older ages when speech lateralization is presumed to be more complete—especially in normal readers (Satz and Sparrow, 1970). If the magnitude of the ear asymmetry is presumed to be smaller or more unstable at younger ages, then this might reflect an artifact of task complexity at these ages. If so, it could produce a floor effect that would mask an association between reading and the ear asymmetry at younger ages.

More recently Bakker, Teunissen, and Bosch (1976, this volume) revised their position, stating:

"... proficient reading at an advanced stage of the learning to read process goes with left hemisphere dominance only (i.e., REA). However, the dominance-reading patterns are different at early stages of the learning to read process: proficient early reading may go with either left or right hemisphere dominance (i.e., LEA or REA). Young left (speech) dominant children, like (older) fluent readers, read rapidly at the risk of making many errors. Young right (speech) dominant children read slowly but accurately."

This reformulation, while heuristic with respect to proficient younger readers, still fails to explain the dominance-reading patterns for younger disabled readers. This problem may still reflect confusion with respect to the ear asymmetry and reading ability at younger ages, regardless of reading level. Moreover, if a floor effect exists in the ear asymmetry at these younger ages, then it would tend, in part, to obscure this earlier dominance-reading relationship in Bakker's reformulation; this point again highlights the crucial importance of information on the development of the ear asymmetry in normal children before embarking on extrapolations to disabled readers.

A final problem in Bakker, Teunissen, and Bosch (1976, this volume) concerns the classification of younger children into predicted left and right dominant speech groups based on the ear asymmetry scores. This inductive inference seems contradictory to the author's a priori assumption that speech lateralization is more diffusely represented in younger children. This inductive problem is discussed separately in the final critique.

The most rigorous attempt to examine developmental parameters of the ear asymmetry in reading was conducted by Darby (1974). Darby selected a group of severely retarded male readers identified at the end of Grade 1 (age 7) who were originally tested 2 years earlier at the beginning of kindergarten (age 5.5) on a number of developmental-cognitive measures, including dichotic listening. The subjects were selected from the total population of white boys ($N = 497$) who began kindergarten in 1970 in Alachua County, Florida as part of a longitudinal-predictive study of dyslexia (Satz and Friel, 1974; Satz, Friel, and Rudegeair, 1976, in press).

The disabled readers were selected exclusively for evidence of dyslexia. That is, no male child with a low socio-economic rating, low emotional maturity level, sensory handicap, or Peabody IQ under 90 was included. Moreover, each child had to be rated as a severe high-risk reader concurrently at the end of kindergarten and first grade (criterion outcomes). Similarly, each child had to be predicted as severe high risk, based on the initial tests against the criterion outcomes at the end of kindergarten and first grade (test predictions). Finally, each child had to be reading at or below preprimer level at the end of Grade 1.

The control readers were then selected from the remaining population of children who had no evidence of predicted or assessed reading problems during the first 2 years of the follow-up project. Final selection was then made on age (within 1 month) and absence of low SES, sensory handicaps, emotional immaturity, or low IQ (< 90).

A third group of older dyslexic children (ages 11–12) was then selected from the Vanguard School in Lake Wales, Florida in order to conduct the full range of age comparisons on the ear asymmetry. Similar SES, sex, and IQ considerations were used in the selection phase. Moreover, the children had to show evidence of severe reading disability (> 2 years) in the absence of sensory handicaps or brain damage. The control children for this older group were selected from the Alachua County School System under similar matching conditions employed for the younger and older dyslexic subjects.

Multiple linear regression methods were then used to compare the left and right ear scores for each group (D, C) separately at ages 5 (20 D, 20 C), 7 (16 D, 20 C), and 12 (15 D, 15 C). The dichotic listening task (3-pair digits) was readministered to the 7-year-old group (D and C) and administered for the first time to the older group (D and C). The results for the control group are presented in Figure 1 and reveal that the magnitude of

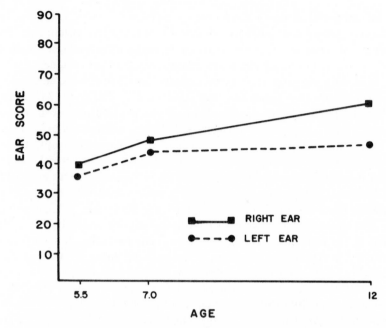

Figure 1. Mean dichotic listening scores by ear and age for good readers.

the ear asymmetry increased with age with a significant REA evident only in the older group (age 12). However, the trend was evident as early as age 5. These results are compatible with the development of the ear asymmetry in normal Dutch children (Satz et al., 1975) where a significant REA was first seen at age 9.

By contrast, the results for the dyslexic children (Figure 2) reveal a lag in the development of the ear asymmetry with no significant REA at any age level. Although overall recall (R + L) increased with age, the rate of improvement between ears was not significantly different over years, despite a trend as such. This finding is again compatible with the theory of Satz and Sparrow (1970), which predicts an age relationship between reading ability and the ear asymmetry—especially at older ages when lateralization of speech is assumed to be more complete.

Two recent studies provide additional information on the relationship between the ear asymmetry and reading ability at older ages (Leong, 1975c; Yeni-Komshian, Isenberg, and Goldberg, 1975). A significant REA was reported in disabled and control readers in both studies, although Leong (1975c) found a larger magnitude in the REA in his control male readers (age 9) when an ear order of report (EOR) was employed. While

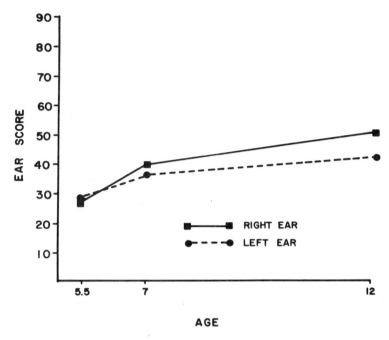

Figure 2. Mean dichotic listening scores by ear and age for poor readers.

the Leong study lends support to the developmental lag theory of Satz and Sparrow (1970) and Satz and Van Nostrand (1973), the results may have been influenced by a floor effect for this task condition. For example, when an attempted EOR was employed, overall recall improved, revealing a similar REA for both groups.

The Yeni-Komshian et al. study (1975), by contrast, revealed a similar REA in both recall conditions for older disabled and control readers (ages 11–15). This study, however, is more difficult to interpret for the following reasons. First, the digits (3 pairs) were presented at a much slower rate (1 pair per second), which would tend to increase overall recall, particularly at older ages, and attenuate the ear asymmetry (i.e., ceiling effect). Inspection of their data revealed high overall recall for digits presented to the right and left ears in both groups under the attended ear condition. In fact, the asymmetry recall between ears was negligible for the control group (93% versus 92%) despite the fact that a significant overall REA was reported for the good readers! Second, all subjects were requested to report six digits on every trial, which would tend to increase guessing and correct responses when only eight total digits were used (1–10, excluding

6 and 7). Third, sample size was small in both groups of subjects (black) and included approximately equal numbers of boys and girls; this makes it difficult to extrapolate to other studies that have largely focused on white boys from middle to upper SES levels.

The problem of ceiling effects, in developmental studies employing the dichotic listening paradigm, has been reviewed recently by Satz et al. (1975). The effect, when it occurs, is bound to wash out developmental age changes, especially in older subjects who perform better in these recall tasks. Consequently, one is unable to evaluate those developmental hypotheses that postulate a lag in hemispheric lateralization of speech in older dyslexic children. This problem surfaced again in a recent attempt to investigate developmental changes in hemispheric lateralization in dyslexia (Witelson, 1975b). The author, using a carefully selected group of normal (N = 156) and disabled readers (N = 85) between the ages of 6 and 14, examined the asymmetry scores on a number of verbal and nonverbal laterality tasks. A two- and three-pair dichotic digit task (2 pairs per second) comprised part of the test battery. The results revealed a significant REA in both groups of children at all ages (6, 8, 10, 12) with the exception of the youngest dyslexic group. Unfortunately, her older normal subjects (ages 10–14) showed almost errorless recall for digits presented to the right ear (95%) which, in effect, prevented assessment of possible magnitude differences in the REA between reading groups at the older ages. This ceiling effect was undoubtedly influenced by the two-pair condition which, like slower presentation rates, tends to increase overall recall and wash out asymmetry differences in older subjects (Yeni-Komshian et al., 1975; Zurif and Carson, 1970; Witelson and Rabinovitch, 1972). Leong (1975c) examined the effect of list length on the ear asymmetry and found that the two-pair condition attenuated the REA in older subjects.

The most recent developmental study addressed to the ear asymmetry and reading ability was derived from the ongoing longitudinal-predictive study of Satz and associates (Satz and Friel, 1974; Satz, Friel, and Goebel, 1975; Satz, Friel, and Rudegeair, 1976, in press). This study (Satz, 1975a) selected all those boys (right-handers) who became severe reading casualties by the end of Grade 2 (N = 86) from a population of white boys who were followed since kindergarten 3 years earlier (N = 678). Criterion reading evaluations were based on the Iota Word Recognition Test, Gates-McGinitie Test (Reading and Comprehension) and Classroom Reading Level (Satz, Friel, and Rudegeair, 1974). The population comprised the total group of white boys who started kindergarten in 1970 in Alachua County, Florida (validation group) plus the total group of white boys who started kindergarten in 1971 in seven of the urban elementary schools (cross-validation group). The validation group comprised the population from which Darby (1974) selected his younger subjects (experimental and control) for the 2-year follow-up from kindergarten to the end of Grade 1. The control readers (right-handers) were matched on age (within 1 month), SES, and school (rural versus urban). No match on IQ was used between groups although subjects with IQs under 85 were excluded.

The power of this study is that identical tests were given to all subjects at the beginning of kindergarten (mean age = 5.5) and at the end of Grade 2 (mean age = 8.0) in order to evaluate developmental changes, if any, between and within reading groups with age. A battery of cognitive, perceptual, and mnemonic tests was administered, including the dichotic listening digit task (3 pairs per trial at 2 pairs per second). Only the results of the dichotic listening test are presented below; however, the reader is referred to an earlier paper for discussion of the overall findings (Satz, Friel, and Rudegeair, 1974).

The results are depicted in Figure 3. An analysis of variance, based on each group separately, revealed a significant REA in both poor readers and good readers, although the ear by age interaction was significant only in the good readers. The ear by age interaction in the disabled reading group, while showing the same trend, was not significant. These findings are compatible with the study by Darby (1974), based on dichotic listening

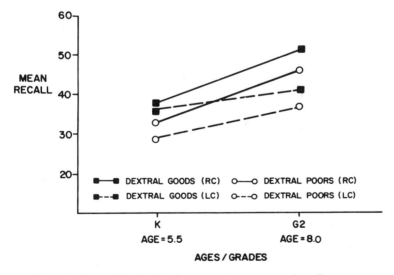

Figure 3. Mean dichotic listening scores by ear, age, and reading group.

scores obtained at ages 5.5 and 7 years on many of the same subjects, and suggest an encroaching lag in the magnitude of the ear asymmetry with age in the disabled readers (Satz and Van Nostrand, 1973).

The preceding study, however, should be viewed with caution even though the results were based on repeat measurements on a large number of the same subjects over time. First, the ear by age interaction in the disabled reading group was just short of significance. Second, the possibility of a floor effect at the younger ages may have depressed overall recall and thereby masked an earlier appearance of the ear asymmetry. Third, the subjects in the older groups (mean age = 8.0) are still too young to provide a critical test of the developmental lag hypothesis predicted to occur in the older dyslexic age groups (Satz and Van Nostrand, 1973). This definitive test will not be carried out until spring 1976, at which time the validation group will be 11 years of age. Because of these limitations, the present study should be viewed as providing only tentative support at best for the theory of delayed hemispheric lateralization of speech in older dyslexic children.

Visual Half-Field Studies (Verbal)

In contrast to the dichotic listening studies, only four studies have been conducted, with disabled readers, using the tachistoscopic verbal paradigm. The first study was reported by McKeever and Huling (1970) on a small group of older children (mean age = 13) half of whom were severely retarded in reading (≥ four grades). No information on sex was given. The task involved presentation of a four-letter noun to one visual half-field (VHF); the noun was simultaneously paired with a fixation digit. Subjects were required to correctly report the fixation digit before identifying the VHF word in order to control for random eye movements. A decreasing method of limits was also employed at exposure durations ranging from 100 to 20 msec as a further control for unwanted eye movements. The results showed superior recognition of words presented to the right visual half-field (RVHF) for both reading groups under both monocular and binocular conditions. No interaction between fields and groups was found, suggesting that the magnitude of the asymmetry was similar in both reading groups. The results, in summary, provided no support for the construct of incomplete or delayed hemispheric speech dominance in disabled readers, at least as assessed by this VHF task.

Somewhat similar findings were reported in a later study by Marcel, Katz, and Smith (1974). The authors selected a younger group of boys and girls (ages 7.6–8.7), half of whom (N = 20) were retarded readers as measured by the National Foundation for Educational Research Reading

Test. All subjects were right-handed except two boys who were disabled readers. The task involved random unilateral VHF presentation of five-letter concrete nouns at varying exposure durations. During the procedure a central fixation point appeared for 650 msec followed by a word to the right or left of fixation (VHF) for that subject's assessed exposure duration. This presentation was immediately followed by a bilateral mask field for 1 second. Subjects were instructed to report the word if they saw it or, if not, to report as many of the letters as possible. Thus, analyses were made on correct word and letter responses. The results revealed a significant RVHF asymmetry for word and letter reports in both the good and poor readers, which is consistent with the findings of McKeever and Huling (1970). However, an analysis of the hemifield difference scores, within subjects, revealed that the magnitude of the RVHF asymmetry was greater in the good readers for both letters and words although the difference scores were significant only for letters. The authors, after careful consideration of possible eye movement or attentional artifacts in their data, concluded that ". . . the relevant linguistic information is more asymmetrically stored in the good reader" (p. 136).

Just the opposite conclusion was reached in another study by Yeni-Komshian et al. (1975), which was discussed earlier with respect to dichotic listening. The authors administered a digit numeral and word tachistoscopic task to a small group of older black children (ages 11–13), boys and girls, half of whom were retarded in reading. The results revealed a significant RVHF asymmetry for both numerals and words (vertically presented) only in the poor readers. This finding led them to conclude, erroneously, that hemispheric lateralization was greater in children with reading disability. This conclusion is not supported by their data because their normal reading group failed to show a reliable right or left VHF asymmetry under both conditions. Procedural problems must have produced this artifact which suggests, ironically, that normal older readers are incompletely lateralized for speech. An additional finding of lower LVHF scores in the poor reading group, which undoubtedly increased the magnitude of their VHF asymmetry scores, led the authors to further speculations concerning a right hemisphere deficit in dyslexia. This interpretation is discussed below (Critique) with respect to the inductive problem in laterality research.

The final VHF study to be discussed in this review concerns the important chapter by Witelson (1976, this volume), which was also evaluated earlier under dichotic listening. The author, using a carefully selected group of normal (N = 156) and disabled readers (N = 85) between the ages of 6 and 14, examined the asymmetry scores on a number of verbal and spatial laterality tasks in audition, vision, and somesthesis. The general findings, particularly on the bilateral simultaneous tactual tasks, pointed to atypical hemispheric lateralization in the dyslexic children, the vast majority of whom were boys. The results on the tachistoscopic VHF letter task, however, were difficult to interpret because of the type of response paradigm used. The stimuli presented were two capital or upper case letters that were either the same or different. The response required that the subject indicate whether the two letters were the same or different, but not name the letters. Witelson utilized this response mode to circumvent the letter naming defect that dyslexic children have been reported to have. This task was administered to a smaller group of dyslexic (N = 83) and normal boys (N = 86). The results failed to demonstrate a RVHF asymmetry for both reading groups, which Witelson explained as an artifact of the response mode employed. That is, the fact that judgments of name identity were not used may have minimized the role of linguistic encoders in the left hemisphere on this task. More difficult to explain, however, is why a left visual half-field asymmetry was not obtained when the task required judgments of physical identity which have been shown to be processed faster when such stimuli are presented to the left field—right hemisphere.

LATERALITY AND READING DISABILITY: A CRITIQUE

One might ask what light the preceding review of laterality studies sheds, if any, on the problem of cerebral dominance and reading disability. The answer should be—not much. The reason for this somewhat discouraging view lies in the numerous methodological and conceptual problems that continue to plague research efforts in this area. With the advent of binaural rivalry procedures in audition and tachistoscopic procedures in vision during the 1960s, it was hoped that more direct assessment of functional hemispheric mechanisms in normal and disabled readers would result. Unfortunately, the preceding review indicates that answers to this question—and the one posed by Samuel Orton four decades ago—will not be available until further progress is made in both methodology and theory.

Before discussing these problems, a brief review of the preceding studies should be made to highlight directions for future research. The review indicates that the hypothesis of delayed or incomplete hemispheric speech representation in disabled readers, as measured by the dichotic or VHF asymmetry scores, is only partially supported by the data. The reason for this is that most studies have reported a significant REA or

RVHF in both normal and disabled readers (box score = 13), but only a few of the studies have conducted the critical test of asymmetry differences between groups.

Most of the studies that revealed no perceptual asymmetry in disabled readers and/or controls were marred by procedural artifacts (Witelson and Rabinovitch, 1972; Yeni-Komshian et al., 1975; Zurif and Carson, 1970). Furthermore, in those studies that assessed possible differences in the magnitude of the asymmetry, the tests were at times invalidated by ceiling effects, particularly in the older age groups (Witelson, 1976, this volume; Witelson and Rabinovitch, 1972; Yeni-Komshian et al., 1975). However, those studies in which ceiling artifacts were controlled have shown a lag in the magnitude of the ear asymmetry in disabled readers, but not at all ages. The lag was shown, with one exception (Marcel et al., 1974), only in older groups of dyslexic children for whom left hemispheric speech representation was postulated to be less complete (Bakker, 1973; Bakker and Steenis, 1975; Darby, 1974; Leong, 1975a; Satz, 1975a; Satz, Rardin, and Ross, 1971). This lag effect, however, has been neither robust nor reliable and has sometimes been seen only in terms of frequency scores (Sparrow, 1969). In fact, more studies have reported a significant REA or RVHF asymmetry in disabled readers than an attenuated asymmetry, even at older ages.

More troublesome to explain is the relationship between the asymmetry measures and reading disability at younger ages. Most studies have not even addressed this problem. By contrast, those that have, have demonstrated variable results. The Florida studies (Darby, 1974; Satz, 1975a; Satz, Rardin, and Ross, 1971) indicate that the magnitude of the ear asymmetry undergoes increasing lateralization with age in normal children and that therefore the lag phenomenon will not be seen in disabled readers until early puberty, at which time hemispheric speech lateralization is almost complete in normal children (Satz and Van Nostrand, 1973). The Amsterdam studies (Bakker, 1973; Bakker, Smink, and Reitsma, 1973; Bakker and Steenis, 1975) differ primarily with respect to the ear asymmetry and reading at earlier ages. Bakker's most recent position, while revised from his earlier papers, suggests that the direction of the ear asymmetry in younger control children may be differentially related to reading ability. That is, young normal children who show an REA (presumed left-brained speech) on the dichotic listening tasks are like older fluent readers, but read rapidly at the risk of making many errors. Conversely, young normal children who show an LEA (presumed right-brained speech) on the dichotic listening tasks are inclined to read more slowly but with fewer errors. This reformulation, while heuristic with respect to proficient younger readers, still fails to explain the ear dominance-reading patterns for younger disabled readers. Also, the classification of children into predicted left and right hemisphere speech groups seems contradictory to Bakker's a priori assumption of more diffuse bilateral speech representation in younger children (ages 5–7). We shall return to this inductive problem shortly. Another problem that confronts both the Florida and Amsterdam studies is the possibility of floor effects in the recording procedures used for younger children (ages 5–7). While the use of three- and four-pair digit trials may represent optimal measures of the ear asymmetry in older children (ages 7–12), they may be too difficult for younger children, which could mask asymmetry scores at these ages. This problem has recently been discussed as a major issue confronting developmental laterality studies in normal children (Satz, Friel, and Rudegeair, 1974).

It should be apparent from this summary, and the preceding review, why information is still lacking on the crucial issue of cerebral dominance and reading disability. Under closer examination, the problems converge on issues remote from reading disability per se.

A major problem concerns the concept of cerebral dominance itself. It was stated earlier that the concept, as used by Orton (1926) and others, represents a hypothetical construct that refers to unobservable events postulated to exist in the brain. Some authors, however, have argued that the concept is essentially useless for it proposes nothing about mechanism. According to Semmes (1968), the concept of cerebral dominance ". . . is little worse than a label, a restatement of the finding that lesions of one hemisphere produce deficits that lesions of the other hemisphere do not" (p. 11). Semmes proposed that milestones in language development be conceptualized within an ontogenetic context emerging from earlier milestones in sensorimotor development. For example, perhaps hemispheric specialization of speech stems from a basic difference in sensorimotor organization that has already been differentiated within the left hemisphere:

> "It is proposed that focal representation of elementary functions in the left hemisphere favors integration of similar units and consequently specialization for behaviors which demand fine sensorimotor control, such as manual skills and speech. Conversely, diffuse representation of elementary functions in the right hemisphere may lead to integration of dissimilar units and hence specialization for behaviors requiring multimodal coordination, such as the various spatial abilities. . ." (Semmes, 1968, p. 11).

This position at least attempts to account for differences in hemispheric organization of a complex function (e.g., speech) as an outgrowth or synthesis of elementary sensorimotor functions whose neural organization already favors specialization on the left.

A major advantage with Semmes' formulation is that it provides a theoretical explanation of cerebral dominance in terms of mechanism and function—and within the context of normal development. This brings us to a second problem. The preceding review of laterality studies revealed only a few studies that addressed themselves to developmental parameters of the ear or visual half-field asymmetry. It was shown that most of the studies were concerned with teasing out differences on these tasks between normal and clinical groups without any understanding of how performance might vary as a function of age in normal children generally. Failure to isolate specific age effects on these tasks could easily mask both within- and between-group differences and hence retard developmental theory in this area. This problem has already been reviewed critically for dichotic listening tasks (Satz et al., 1975).

A third problem concerns the validity of these laterality tests as measures of cerebral speech dominance. The issue of test validity has been implicitly assumed to be true because of the relationship (contralateral) that has been observed between these laterality measures (EA, VHF) and the hemisphere postulated to be dominant for the task (Kimura, 1967). This research, whether intentional or not, has also promulgated the rather simplified concept of the brain as a dual hemispheric processor—the left for analysis of speech and language and the right for analysis of Gestalt laws of perception (Levy, 1974). The problem more specifically concerns the assumption that, because a relationship exists between two variables (e.g., ear asymmetry and hemispheric speech dominance), therefore inductive inferences can be made on individual subjects to classify them into respective hemispheric dominant groups. This assumption, concerning predictive validity, has been shown to be both unwarranted and reckless when the lateral measures are themselves unreliable or when the antecedent probabilities (i.e., base rates) concerning hemispheric lateralization are markedly asymmetric in the population (Satz, 1976, in press). The author examined the inductive inferences on hemispheric speech dominance, based on the dichotic listening digit tasks. A Bayesean analysis was conducted using the estimated base rates for left- and right-brain speech in the normal population of right-handed adults (p = 0.95 and 0.05, respectively) and the estimated frequencies for the right- and left-ear asymmetry in this same population (p = 0.70 and 0.30, respectively). This inductive analysis, which was applied to hypothetical data, revealed that the probability of left-brain speech, given a right ear advantage (REA), is extremely high (p = 0.97). In fact, the results showed that the probability of left-brain speech, given a left ear advantage (LEA), is almost as high (p = 0.90). The hooker is related to the probability of right-brain speech, given a left ear advantage (LEA)— the probability value is only p = 0.10. This means that when subjects are grouped into a predicted right-brain speech group, based on an LEA in a dichotic verbal task, the probability of misclassification is on the order of 90%! This outcome, while sobering, is intuitively reasonable when one considers the small likelihood of selecting a right-hander with right-brain speech in the population (antecedent probability). The population base rates for speech lateralization are markedly asymmetric in favor of left-sided representation; hence, the strong likelihood of left-brain speech, given either a REA or LEA (p = 0.97 and 0.90, respectively).

It should be apparent from this study (Satz, 1976, in press) that extreme caution should be exercised whenever inferences are made concerning predicted right hemisphere speech dominance in right-handed adults. This problem, moreover, is substantially increased whenever similar inferences are made concerning children for whom base rate information on hemispheric dominance is unknown. Yet it was shown in the preceding review that inferences concerning right hemisphere dysfunction in dyslexic children continue to be made (Witelson and Rabinovitch, 1972; Yeni-Komshian et al., 1975). Similarly, other authors continue to speculate on differential reading strategies between predicted left and right hemisphere speech dominant normal younger children (Bakker and Steenis, 1975). The inductive inference concerning right hemisphere speech in younger children is bound to obscure any relationship between cerebral dominance and reading ability because the validity of the inference is grossly inaccurate for adults for whom at least base rate information is known.

Similar inferential traps inhere in those studies that attempt to examine differences in hemispheric dominance between dyslexic and control readers on a variety of verbal and nonverbal laterality measures. The ingenious and potentially fruitful study by Witelson (1976, this volume) represents such an example. Inferences concerning atypical right hemisphere organization in dyslexic children, based on manual asymmetry scores on a bilateral tactual shape discrimination task, are probably incorrect. The reason is that virtually 40% of the normal control group showed a similar asymmetric pattern. Also, if the base rates for nonverbal shape discrimination are markedly asymmetric in the population, then the inferences would be further in error. Unfortunately, such information is currently lacking, which should therefore argue for greater caution in the interpretation of these results.

A final problem concerns the potential usefulness of these laterality measures in the study of hemispheric dominance and reading ability. This issue is again related, in part, to the validity problem previously discussed. Although research has consistently shown a relationship between these behavioral measures and hemispheric lateralization of function, the strength of this predictive relationship in adults has been small, particularly as it relates to right hemisphere dominance. This finding might well explain why the results with children, especially disabled readers, remain unclear, if not obscure. More research is urgently needed with normal children, at specified ages, before extrapolations are made to clinical groups.

Two incidental findings might clarify this point as it relates to specific reading disability. First, in the longitudinal-predictive study by Satz and associates, a large battery of cognitive and perceptual tests (including the dichotic digit task) was administered to the total population of white boys (validation group) who began kindergarten in Alachua County in 1970. This battery, moreover, was readminstered to all children three years later (end of Grade 2), at which time reading criterion measures were also obtained. An identical procedure was used for a cross-validation sample of boys who began kindergarten in 1971 and who were retested three years later at the end of Grade 2 (1974). The point is that while substantial differences were found in the tests before (predictive) and after reading ability was assessed for both validation groups of children, not once were these differences related to performance on the ear asymmetry (Satz, Friel, and Rudegeair, 1974; Satz, Friel, and Rudegeair, 1976, in press). In fact, the step-wise regression analyses have consistently ranked the ear asymmetry measure last for both predictive and concurrent validity.

These negligible results between the ear asymmetry and reading disability, however, stand in marked contrast to a second incidental finding in this longitudinal project. When the ear asymmetry measures were compared for all left handers ($N = 85$) in both validation groups who became average–superior readers at the end of Grade 2, the results failed to show a significant REA at ages 5 or 8. Despite an increasing trend in the ear asymmetry with age (Figure 4), the difference was not significant. The puzzling, if not sobering, fact is that developmental differences in the ear asymmetry seem more related to handedness (Figure 4) than to reading disability (Figure 3). That is, no major differences in the ear asymmetry were found between right-handed good readers and poor readers at ages 5 or 8 (Figure 3). By 8 years of age, both groups revealed a significant REA, although the magnitude of the asymmetry was greater in the right-handed good readers. Yet, when the ear asymmetry scores were compared across ages for left-handed boys who were average readers, a lag in the development of the ear asymmetry emerged. The crux of the problem is that if

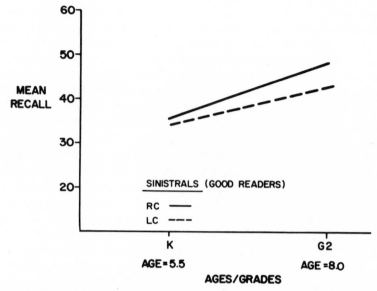

Figure 4. Mean dichotic listening scores by ear and age for left-handed good readers.

this lag is construed as a lag in the functional lateralization of the brain in left-handed children, then why did they not reveal a pattern of reading disability?

These results further illustrate the magnitude of the problem concerning hemispheric dominance and reading disability. The present paper has attempted to identify some of the problems in hopes that subsequent research will shed additional light on these still unanswered questions, the first of which was posed by Samuel Orton over four decades ago.

Part V

Perceptual Factors as Determinants of Learning Disabilities

Exploring the Relations between Reading and Speech

Donald Shankweiler and Isabelle Y. Liberman

Given so little agreement on how best to teach children to read, it is perhaps not surprising to find divergent conceptions of the nature of reading itself. Among these, we find two contrasting positions concerning the relationships between reading and speech. On the one hand, some writers (e.g., Goodman, 1968; Smith, 1973) have tended to ignore the relationship, choosing instead to emphasize the relative autonomy of reading and writing. Their counsel is, in effect, to forget about speech when teaching reading. A major target of their criticism has been the advocate of the so-called phonic approach to reading instruction who stresses the letter-to-sound mappings while failing to appreciate that we cannot read simply by concatenating individual letter sounds. On the other hand, we and a few other investigators (Huey, 1908; Mattingly, 1972; Rozin and Gleitman, 1976; Shankweiler and Liberman, 1972) have emphasized the importance of the derivative nature of reading and writing and the intimate connection between speech and the alphabet. In defending this aspect of the study of reading, however, we give due weight to the complexity of the relationship. We believe that many of the criticisms that have been offered would apply only to a very simplistic view of how spoken sounds and alphabetic characters are related.

Central to the problem of understanding how reading is acquired, in our view, is the question of how reading builds on the speech processes of the child. We know, of course, that spoken language is historically prior to reading and writing in the development of the race, ontogenetically prior in the life of the individual, and logically prior in the relation of written symbols to their speech referents. Further evidence of the derivative status of writing and reading and the practical importance of the priority of

The preparation of this chapter and some of the research reported in it was supported in part by a grant to Haskins Laboratories from the National Institute of Child Health and Human Development, Bethesda, Maryland.

speech is readily at hand. Consider the contrasting situations of the congenitally blind and the congenitally deaf. The blind acquire spoken language normally; the profoundly deaf, even under the most favorable conditions, are so effectively isolated from language that they show severe deficiencies in every aspect of language development (Furth, 1966). Since the blind child learns to read by means of the substitute sense of touch, we may ask why can the deaf child not effectively exploit his intact visual channel for reading? Presumably he cannot do so because deafness blocks the development of a foundation in primary language so necessary as a basis for learning to read. If reading were, as some have argued, an alternative and co-equal language reception system, then it becomes hard to explain why the deaf could not learn language by eye as readily as the hearing learn it by ear. Our interest, of course, is to understand the acquisition of reading in children with intact sensory capacities. We make reference to reading in the blind and the deaf only to emphasize how closely reading is tied to speech.

If reading and speech are so closely linked, we would expect them to share much of the same neural machinery. As Halwes (1968) has pointed out, it is unparsimonious to imagine a completely parallel language understanding system (for reading) that borrowed nothing from the primary speech system. Rather than developing a separate device for reading, it would be more parsimonous to expect that the would-be reader modifies the speech perception system to accept optical information. We assume that the speech system works by mapping the acoustic signal into progressively more abstract representations, and we assume that the reading device must tie in with that system at some level. How much visual processing must be done before script can be represented in the common language processing system (as though the input had been speech rather than script)? To put the question another way, what is the level of representation at which script is recoded?

Certain facts about the writing system must constrain how we conceive of the reading process. All writing systems make contact at some point with the spoken language. Some, like Chinese and Japanese logographs, tie in at the level of words, others at the level of the syllable. Some, the alphabets, link their primary symbols to distinctive aspects of the sound structure of the language. In the case of English, there is good reason to believe that script makes contact with the primary language system at more than one level. At times, similarity of spelling may denote not similarity of sound, but similarities of origin and root meaning, as in such word pairs as "sign" and "signal." Such cases are not uncommon. Moreover, the assignment of grammatical class is sometimes preliminary to determining the correct phonetic form. To use an example of Rozin and Gleitman (1976), the written word "contract" is ambiguous until we know whether it functions as a noun or as a verb. The correct phonetic representation of such ambiguous words cannot be fully attained without reference to more molar representations. These observations obviously constrain our choices when we attempt to model the perceptual system in reading. Thus, we do not assume that the reader is tied to a rigid hierarchy of successive processing stages. Rather, we suppose that the transformation of script into speech occurs at a number of levels concurrently and in parallel.

To recapitulate, the fundamental task of the beginning reader is to construct a link between speech and the arbitrary signs of script. Although the alphabet is roughly a cipher on the phonemes of speech, this does not imply that learning to read is merely a matter of acquiring letter-to-sound correspondences. English spelling does not fully reflect the phonetic facts of the language, and at times seems deliberately to ignore them in order to convey other kinds of information helpful to the easy comprehension of what is read. We assume that the experienced reader learns to detect and to exploit such mutileveled representation, though the complexity of the orthography is surely an added source of difficulty for the beginning reader.

FUNCTIONS OF THE PHONETIC REPRESENTATION

Although English spelling is not a faithful phonetic transcription, there is reason to suppose that the phonetic level of representation plays an especially significant role in the acquisition of reading in the young child. Even in English the alphabet is largely keyed to the sound structure. Hence, new words can be given at least an approximate pronunciation on first encounter if the reader understands how the alphabet works. Obviously, the reader must recode phonetically if he is to obtain the phonetic realization of a new word. But what does he do with words and phrases he has read many times? Does he in these cases construct a phonetic representation, or does he, as some believe, by-pass the phonetic level and go directly from visual shape to meaning?

It seems likely that phonetic recoding might occur even with frequently read materials, and that its persistence in older, more experienced readers is not to be regarded merely as a habit that has ceased to be functional. The possibility we are proposing is that the reader needs a phonetic base on which to extract the message from its encipherment in script; that is, the normal primary language processes of storing, indexing, and retrieving from the dictionary in our heads are carried out by means of a phonetic code. Moreover, in addition to the possibility that the dictionary may be indexed phonetically, consider what cues we use to decode the syntax of the message. Here we are aided by the rise and fall of the speech melody and its pattern of rhythms and stresses. These are not given directly in script, and it may require the mediation of an internal phonetic representation to enable the reader to construct those prosodic features so necessary to comprehension (Liberman et al., 1976).

Since the perceiver cannot process each message unit fully at the time of its arrival, we may be sure that short-term memory is one of the primary linguistic processes essential to comprehension of both written and spoken language. The perceiver, whether functioning as reader or hearer, must hold a sufficient number of shorter segments (words) in memory in order to apprehend the longer segments (sentences). Obviously, if he had a span of only two words, the perceiver's comprehension of connected discourse would be extremely limited. But does the reader form a different kind of memory representation than the hearer? Although we do not rule out the possibility that read words can be held temporarily in some visual form, we have indicated reasons above for supposing that the reader typically engages in recoding from script to some phonetic form. (See A. Liberman, Mattingly, and Turvey, 1972, for a fuller exploration of the suggestion that the phonetic representation is uniquely suited to the short-term storage requirements of language.)

Apart from these speculations, there is much relevant experimental evidence for phonetic recoding. In a large number of investigations it has been found that when lists of letters or alphabetically written words are presented orthographically to be read and remembered, the confusions in short-term memory are based on phonetic rather than visual similarity (Baddeley, 1966, 1968, 1970; Conrad, 1964, 1972; Hintzman, 1967; Kintsch and Buschke, 1969; Sperling, 1963). From these findings it has been inferred that the stimulus items had been stored in phonetic form rather than in visual form. Conrad (1972) has emphasized that the tendency to recode visually presented items into phonetic form is so strong that subjects do this even in experimental situations in which to do so penalizes recall.

There is evidence from a similar kind of experiment (Erickson, Mattingly, and Turvey, 1973) that phonetic recoding occurs even when the linguistic stimuli are not presented in an alphabetic form that represents the phonetic structure, but in a form (the Japanese kanji characters) that represents the semantic message more directly. Moreover, under some circumstances, even nonlinguistic stimuli may be recoded into phonetic form and stored in that form in short-term memory. In this connection,

Conrad (1972) found that in recall of pictures of common objects, the confusions of children age 6 and over were clearly based on the phonetic forms of the names of the objects rather than on their visual or semantic characteristics.

To be sure, none of these experiments dealt with wholly natural reading situations, since most involved the reading of isolated words and syllables rather than connected text. They are nevertheless relevant to the assumption that even the skilled reader might recode phonetically in order to gain an advantage in short-term memory and to utilize the primary language processes he already has available to him. It remains to be determined whether good and poor readers among children in the early stages of reading acquisition are distinguished by greater or lesser tendencies toward phonetic recoding.

PHONETIC RECODING IN GOOD AND POOR BEGINNING READERS

In view of the short-term memory requirements of the reading task and evidence for the involvement of phonetic coding in short-term memory, we might expect to find that those beginning readers who are progressing well and those who are doing poorly will be further distinguished by the degree to which they rely on phonetic recoding.

In exploring this possibility, we used a procedure similar to one devised by Conrad (1972) in which the subject's performance is compared on recall of phonetically confusable (rhyming) and nonconfusable (nonrhyming) letters. The expectation was that phonetically similar items would maximize phonetic confusability and thus penalize recall in subjects who use the phonetic code in short-term memory. Strings of five uppercase letters were presented tachistoscopically in a simultaneous 3-second exposure. Half were composed of rhyming consonants (drawn from the set B C D G P T V Z) and half were composed of nonrhyming consonants (drawn from the set H K L Q R S W Y).

The test was given twice: first with immediate recall, then with delayed recall. In the first condition recall was tested immediately after presentation by having subjects print as many letters as could be recalled in each letter string, in the order given. To make the task maximally sensitive to the recall strategy, we then imposed a 15-second delay between tachistoscopic presentation and the response of writing down the string of letters. The children were requested to sit quietly during the delay interval; no intervening task was imposed. We have reason to believe that the subjects used this period for rehearsal, as many were observed mouthing the syllables silently.

The subjects were three groups of school children nearing completion of the second year of elementary school who differed in level of reading achievement as measured by the word recognition subtest of the Wide Range Achievement Test (Jastak, Bijou, and Jastak, 1965). The first group, the superior readers, comprised 17 children reading about 2 years above their grade placement. The other two groups (whom we originally designated marginal and poor readers) can be considered together as the "poor readers" since their performances in these experiments were not significantly different from each other. Together the poor readers included 29 children averaging from one-half to a full year of reading retardation and roughly equated with the superior readers in mean age and IQ.

The responses were scored in two ways, with and without regard to serial position. In the first scoring procedure, only those items listed in the correct serial position were counted correct. The second scoring procedure credited any items that occurred in the stimulus set regardless of the order in which they were written down. The pattern of results was remarkably similar from data derived for each method of scoring. Ability to recall in correct serial order is apparently not the major factor that distinguishes good and poor readers on this task.

As was to be expected, the phonetic characteristics of the items influenced the rate of correct recall. This may be seen in Figure 1, which shows the results summed over serial positions. The circles give the error rates for strings of rhyming items (labeled "confusable"); the triangles give errors on recall of the nonrhyming ("nonconfusable") strings. In all groups, there were significantly more errors on recall of the confusable items. However, there were notable differences in the effects of phonetic similarity on the recall of children who differed in reading level. It is apparent from the figure that the main differences are between superior readers and the other groups.

The net effect of phonetic confusability on recall was much greater in the superior readers than in the others. It would be difficult to explain this result by assuming that the groups differ merely in general memory capacity. Superior readers were clearly better at recall on nonconfusable items than were the poor readers, while, at the same time, failing to show a clear advantage on the confusable items. This is an interesting result. It is a relatively easy matter to demonstrate that poor readers do less well than good readers on a variety of language-dependent tasks. But here, by manipulation of the phonetic characteristics of the items, we have virtually eliminated the advantage of the superior readers.

Recall was measured on half the trials immediately after presentation of the display, and on the other half after a 15-second delay. Turning back to

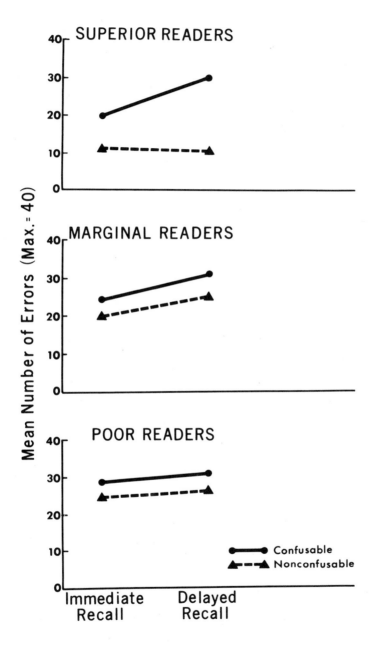

Figure 1. Mean recall errors summed over serial positions.

Figure 1, we see that delay magnified the penal effect of phonetic confusability, but only in the superior readers. Figure 2 shows plots of the error rates at each serial position. Viewing the results of the delay condition (shown in the lower portion), we see that the superior readers are sharply distinguished from the others in recall of nonconfusable items and nearly indistinguishable in their recall of confusable items. Why should imposing a delay between stimulation and recall affect good and poor readers differently? Is it simply the case that good readers try harder and rehearse the items more vigorously? Although we cannot be sure, we do not think that vigor or rate of rehearsal is a factor that chiefly distinguishes good and poor readers on this task. Certainly we know that the poor readers were attempting to rehearse because they so often mouthed the items during the interval (Liberman et al., 1976).

The authors considered and rejected other explanations of the pattern of results obtained by good and poor readers. (1) The difference between the groups cannot easily be attributed to briefer memory span in the poor readers. Even if it were generally true that poor readers have briefer spans, the differential effect of phonetic similarity on recall performance by the two groups would still require explanation. (2) To suppose that the poor readers suffer mainly from a difficulty in reproducing the order of the items in the memory set encounters the same difficulty. Moreover, the pattern of results is much the same when the scoring credited the correct items in each string regardless of serial position.

The interpretation we find most plausible and interesting is that the results reflect genuine differences between good and poor readers in their use of a phonetic code. Of course we cannot argue that phonetic coding is entirely absent in the poor readers, since they demonstrated significant effects of confusability, though of lesser magnitude. A weak or defective phonetic representation in the poor readers could account for the failure of rehearsal to be effective.

AN AUDITORY ANALOGUE AND ITS VISUAL COUNTERPART

In light of the foregoing results, it seemed reasonable to suppose that poor readers may have a specific difficulty in constructing a phonetic representation from script. Before we could accept this hypothesis, however, we needed to find out what would happen when confusable and nonconfusable items were presented by ear. Since phonetic coding is presumably inescapable when speech material arrives auditorily, presentation by ear should force the poor reader into a phonetic mode of information processing. If an important component of his difficulty is that he is deficient in recoding visual symbolic material into phonetic form, then the phonetic

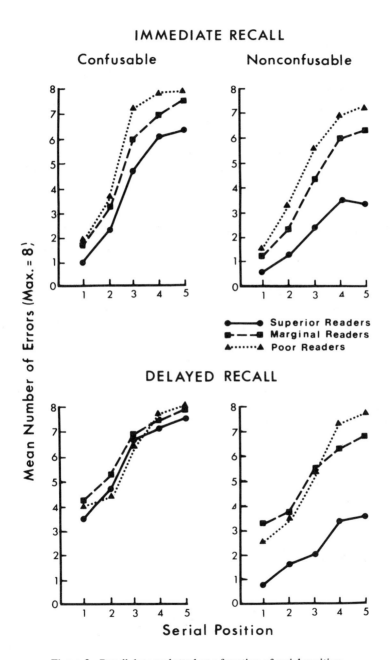

Figure 2. Recall data replotted as a function of serial position.

similarity of auditorily presented rhyming items should affect him as much (or as little) as it does the superior readers. Quantitative differences in memory capacity between the two groups may still show up in the general level of recall on the auditory presentation, but the statistical interaction of reading level and phonetic confusability should be diminished. If, on the other hand, the interaction remained, then it would follow that the difference between good and poor readers in regard to the use of a phonetic representation is not specifically linked to the visual information channel.

Two new experiments were carried out on the same subjects in order to clarify this important point. Since auditory presentation requires successive input, a parallel experiment was designed with visual serial presentation. Except in minor details, the results are like those previously obtained for simultaneous presentation of the letters, and, surprisingly, the visual and auditory experiments differed hardly at all in their results. The findings of each experiment are displayed in Figure 3, which gives serial position curves for recall of auditorily presented and visually presented items. As in the earlier experiment, the performances of the groups representing the extremes of reading ability differed mainly on the phonetically dissimilar items. Once again, phonetic similarity produced a greater impact on the superior readers than on the poor ones. It made practically no difference to the results whether the items to be recalled were presented to the eye or to the ear. Apparently, the crux of the difficulty for the poor reader on these tasks cannot be pinpointed as specifically as we originally believed. Although poor readers may indeed experience difficulty in the transformation of visual features into phonetic ones, the root problem is more general.

These new experiments lead us to expect that differences between good and poor readers will turn on their ability to determine and use a phonetic representation and not merely on their ability to recode from script. We suspect that individual differences in the availability of phonetic recoding strategies on recall tasks may indicate limits of the reader's active awareness of those aspects of language structure to which the alphabet is most directly keyed. This is a possibility that we shall wish to explore directly. We turn now to those aspects of cognitive development that are most relevant to the use of an alphabet.

WHAT A CHILD NEEDS TO "KNOW"
IN ORDER TO USE AN ALPHABET TO FULL ADVANTAGE

The preliterate child brings to the task of learning to read considerable competence in his spoken language. Our concern is to discover what

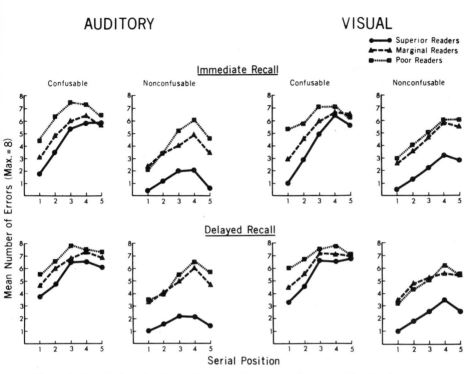

Figure 3. Recall data for the auditory analogue experiment and its visual counterpart.

additional abilities he needs in order to become a reader. Bolinger (1968) places the problem of the learner and the teacher of reading in proper perspective:

"When a child who is already almost fully equipped with a language comes to the task of reading, anything that will help him transfer what he already knows to what he is expected to write and read is priceless" (p. 177).

The authors have argued that an efficient short-term memory system is a requirement for good comprehension of language, both by eye and by ear, and that this requirement is most efficiently met by a phonetic representation. Reading, however, poses an additional requirement. The child must also have ready conscious access to certain aspects of the contents of that memory; he must have, in Mattingly's (1972) phrase, a degree of "linguistic awareness." In order to fully realize the advantages of an alphabet, the user, child or adult, must know quite explicitly what speech segments are represented by the strings of letters (I. Y. Liberman, 1973; Liberman et al., 1976).

It is appropriate at this point to remind ourselves of the benefits that alphabets confer. A unique advantage is that each new word does not have to be learned as if it were an ideographic character before it can be read. That is, given a word that is already in his mental word store, the reader can apprehend the word without specific instruction, although he has never seen it before in print; or, given a word that he has never before seen or heard, he can closely approximate its spoken form until its meaning can be inferred from context or discovered later by asking someone about it. By functioning, however roughly, as a surrogate for phonemes, the alphabet gives its users immediate access to all items in a vast word store by means of a highly economical symbol set.

The savings may be had, however, only by the user who knows how the alphabet works. As in all complex cognitive skills, alternative strategies are possible. The very diversity of the orthographies that have developed during the course of evolution of writing is testimony to the flexibility of the perceptual apparatus. It is possible to read words written by an alphabet as though they were logograms. Many children undoubtedly begin reading acquisition in this way. However, the unique advantages of the alphabet are closed to the child who cannot use it analytically; although he may translate the logograms into phonetic representation, this will not help him to apprehend new words. In order to make the alphabet work for him the child has first to be able to make an explicit analysis of the segments of spoken language. He has to be able to analyze speech into words, syllables, and phonemes. The last mentioned is of particular importance for users of an alphabet, because the phoneme is the principal point at which the writing system meshes with the speech system.

When we speak of explicit knowledge of the segments in the spoken message we wish to make it very clear that something more is involved than the ordinary competence required in language use. That is to say, a person may be a completely adequate speaker–hearer of his language without having the dimmest awareness that the spoken word "bed" contains three phoneme segments and "bend" contains four. The immediate recognition of these as different words, failing the ability to indicate that /n/ is the unshared segment, is an example of what Polanyi (1964) has called "tacit knowledge." Such knowledge is sufficient, of course, for comprehension of the spoken message. Writing and reading, on the other hand, demand an additional analytic capability. Even before the advent of writing, those who used speech poetically must have been able to count syllables in order to form the meter, and to be aware of the phonemic level in order to make rhymes. Some such explicit knowledge of these properties of speech is a precondition for understanding the alphabetic principle.

DIFFICULTIES IN MAKING SPEECH SEGMENTS EXPLICIT

Elsewhere (Liberman, 1971, 1973; Liberman et al., 1974) we have considered reasons why awareness of the phoneme might be rather difficult to attain. In brief, we referred to a fact about the acoustic structure of speech. Consonants and vowels are not discreetly present in the signal, but overlappingly represented in the syllable, a condition that has been called "encodedness" (Liberman et al., 1967). As a consequence, the word "dig," for example, has three phonetic segments but only one acoustic segment. Analyzing an utterance into syllables, on the other hand, may present a different and easier problem. We expect this to be so because in most cases each syllable has a distinctive peak in acoustic energy. The cue of auditory amplitude is a crude one that could not be used to locate exact syllable boundaries, but it can serve to indicate to the listener how many syllables there are in an utterance.

The merging of phones in the sound stream complicates the process of discovery of the phonemic level of speech for the would-be reader. This is not to say, of course, that the young child has difficulty differentiating word pairs, such as "bad" and "bat," that differ in only one phoneme. There is evidence (Read, 1971) that children hear these differences quite as acutely as adults. The problem is not, as many believe, to get the child to discriminate such word pairs, but rather to lead him to appreciate that each of these words contains three segments, and that they are alike in the first two and differ in the third. This is a further example of the distinction we drew earlier between tacit and explicit knowledge of the phonetic structure of language.

The encoded nature of the phonemes has another consequence that surely contributes to the difficulty of learning to read analytically. It makes it impossible to read by sounding out the letters one by one. In the example of "dig," used above, reading letter by letter gives, not "dig," but "duhiguh." In order to learn to read analytically, one must instead discover how many of the letter segments must be taken simultaneously into account in order to arrive at the correct phonetic rendition. In the case of the word "dig," there is reason to believe the number would be three. But, in fact, there is no simple rule for arriving at that number and we suspect that learning to group the letters for the purpose of proper phonetic recoding is one of the really significant skills one must acquire. Thus, even in languages such as Finnish and Spanish in which the writing system closely approximates one-to-one correspondences between letters and phonemes, reading cannot be a simple matter of association between alphabetic characters and spoken sounds. In order to recover the spoken form, the reader must still "chunk" all the letters that represent the phonetic segments encoded into each syllable. In the case of reading a word in isolation, the coding unit is probably the syllable. In reading connected text, the number of letters that must be apprehended before recovery of the spoken form may at times be quite large, for reasons we have discussed. We do not know how the coding unit may vary with the prosody of the text and the reader's experience, but we may be sure that such units almost always exceed one letter in length. Therefore, we would stress that making analytic use of an alphabet does not mean reading letter by letter.

The foregoing discussion has stressed that explicit awareness of the phonetic structure of utterances is a very different thing from the ability to distinguish words whose phonetic structure differs minimally. The latter is easy for every normal child of school age, whereas the difficulty of explicit analysis has been noted by a number of researchers (Bloomfield, 1942; Calfee, Chapman, and Venezky, 1972; Elkonin, 1973; Gleitman and Rozin, 1973; Rosner and Simon, 1971; Savin, 1972). However, there had been no experiments designed to demonstrate directly that phonetic segmentation is more difficult for young children than syllabic segmentation, and that the ability to do it might develop later.

DEVELOPMENT OF THE AWARENESS
OF SPEECH SEGMENTS IN THE YOUNG CHILD

A recent study (Liberman et al., 1974) investigated the development of the ability to explicitly analyze words in syllables and phonemes. The task was posed to the child subjects in the guise of a tapping game, in which segments had to be indicated by the number of taps. We found steep age trends for analysis of words into each kind of segment, but, at each age, test words were more readily segmented into syllables than into phonemes. At age 4, none of the children in our sample could segment by phoneme (according to the criterion we adopted), while nearly 50% could segment by syllable. Even at age 6, only 70% succeeded in phoneme segmentation, whereas 90% were successful in the syllable task.

Further research is needed to confirm and generalize these results. Since the syllable is also the unit of metric scan, it is conceivable that the motor response of tapping is more compatible with analysis by syllable than with analysis by phoneme. An alternative procedure, designed by Goldstein (1974), asks the child to indicate the number of segments in test words by counting out tokens, thus limiting rhythmic motor responses that might bias the outcome in favor of the syllable. Goldstein's prelim-

inary work with this alternative procedure confirmed that phoneme segmentation is genuinely more difficult than syllable segmentation.

We hope eventually to clarify the meaning of these age trends. On the
one hand, the increase in ability to segment phonetically might result from
the reading instruction that typically begins between ages 5 and 6. Alternatively, it might be a manifestation of cognitive growth not specifically
dependent on training. The latter possibility could be tested by a developmental study of segmentation skills in a language community such as the
Chinese, where the orthographic unit is the word and where reading
instruction therefore does not demand the kind of phonetic analysis
needed in an alphabetic system.

SEGMENTATION AND READING ACQUISITION

There is some evidence that the difficulties of phoneme segmentation may
be related to problems of early reading acquisition. Such a relation can be
inferred from the observation that children who are resistant to early
reading instruction have problems even with spoken language when they
are required to perform tasks demanding some rather explicit understanding of phonetic structure. Such children are reported (Monroe, 1932;
Savin, 1972) to be deficient in rhyming, in recognizing that two different
monosyllables may share the same first (or last) phoneme segment, and
also in playing certain speech games that require a shift of the initial
consonant segment of a word to a nonsense syllable suffix.

In the segmentation experiment, a sharp increase in the number of
children passing the phoneme-segmentation task was noted, from only
17% at age 5 to 70% at age 6. Hence, the steepest rise in segmentation
ability coincides with the first intensive concentration on reading-related
skills in the schooling of the child. This result, together with the observations on the lack of "transparency" of the phoneme, suggests a connection
between phonetic segmentation ability and early reading acquisition. In a
pilot study, the authors have begun to explore this relation. We measured
the reading achievement of the children who had taken part in our
experiment on phonemic segmentation described above. Testing at the
beginning of the second school year, we found that half the children in the
lowest third of the class in reading achievement, as measured by the
word-recognition task of the Wide Range Achievement Test (Jastak,
Bijou, and Jastak, 1965), had failed the phoneme segmentation task the
previous June; on the other hand, there were no failures in phoneme
segmentation among the children who scored in the top third in reading
ability.

It is hoped that studies of preschool children's ability to segment speech may shed some light on the matter of reading readiness. The authors plan to examine the pattern of reading errors in children at different levels of reading ability in relation to their ability to indicate the segments of spoken speech. If the indications of our pilot work are borne out, failure on both the syllable and the phoneme tasks at the first grade level will be prognostic of extreme reading difficulty.

SUMMARY AND CONCLUSIONS

The priority of spoken language and the derivative nature of reading and writing are the starting points for any understanding of the nature of writing systems and their acquisition. Reading, however, presents special problems for the perceiver, the nature of which reflects the manner in which the writing system makes contact with the primary speech system. In the case of English, the ties between the language and its spelling are based only partly on the sound structure. Nevertheless, it is particularly appropriate to direct the child's attention to the phonemic level, because the phonemic correspondences are the entry points to any alphabetic writing system.

This chapter considered that a primary function of a phonetic representation, whether for the listener or the reader, is to yield an adequate span in working memory to permit linguistic interpretation of the temporally arrayed segments of the message. Results of our studies of short-term memory in good and poor readers suggested that the poor reader is deficient in forming a phonetic representation from speech as well as from script.

In order to learn to read an alphabetically written language, the availability of a phonetically organized short-term memory is not sufficient. In addition the child must have the ability to make explicit the segmentation of his own speech, particularly at the level of the phoneme. Data were presented that indicate that explicit knowledge of the phonetic level is difficult to attain in contrast to the tacit appreciation of phonemic differences reflected in ordinary language use. We and others have noted that phonemic awareness is lacking in many children when they start to learn to read, and may be a cause of reading failure. In sum, the relations between speech and reading are both intimate and subtle. It would seem appropriate for the early instruction in reading to place initial stress on making the child aware of the speech segments he will eventually learn to represent by written signs.

ACKNOWLEDGMENTS

This chapter reflects the joint efforts of several individuals. The data were obtained by F. W. Fischer, C. Fowler, L. Mark, and M. Zifcak, who also assumed responsibility for their tabulation and statistical analysis. We are also indebted to A. M. Liberman, who suggested the hypothesis concerning the functions of the phonetic representation.

Full details of the experiments on phonetic coding in recall will be presented in a paper in preparation.

Auditory Perceptual Factors in Language and Learning Disabilities

Paula Tallal

Diagnoses of developmental language or learning disorders are, at present, primarily diagnoses by exclusion. That is, such diagnoses are based on excluding those factors that do not appear to be related to the developmental disorder, rather than identifying those that are involved. Whereas such diagnoses are a preliminary step towards delineating developmental syndromes, they fail to suggest specific etiological, therapeutic, or prognostic implications. If we are eventually to understand the precise etiology of developmental language and learning disabilities, and hence to improve diagnostic and therapeutic techniques, it is imperative to investigate, in a systematic and detailed manner, the underlying sensory, perceptual, and cognitive mechanisms involved in these developmental disabilities.

Various research approaches have been utilized in studying children with language and/or learning disabilities. One approach, which has significantly increased our understanding of these syndromes, has been to investigate the development of basic perceptual mechanisms that are thought to be involved in language or learning processes. Orton suggested as early as 1937 that children with developmental communication disorders may be perceptually impaired, particularly in their ability to perceive sequences of events. He concluded that it may be this sequencing disability that underlies developmental communicative disorders. Since Orton's time clinical reports have continued to stress the predominance of auditory temporal processing and memory disabilities in children with communicative disorders (Benton, 1964; Eisenson, 1972; Hardy, 1965; Monsees, 1961).

Lowe and Campbell (1965) experimentally investigated the sequencing abilities of children they classified as "aphasoid." They used methods originally employed by Hirsh (1959) in the study of temporal order

This work was funded by the Grant Foundation, New York.

perception in normal adults, and later by Efron (1963) in the study of temporal order perception in adult aphasics. Lowe and Campbell found that, compared with normal children, "aphasoid" children were impaired in their ability to indicate which of two rapidly presented tones occurred first. Efron (1963) found similar disabilities in adult aphasics with left temporal lobe lesions and suggested that the left temporal lobe plays a primary role in temporal analysis and that the disruption of this function results in the language impairment of brain-damaged adult aphasic patients.

There is also evidence suggesting impairment of visual sequencing and visual memory in language-impaired children (Stark, 1966; Withrow, 1964). Poppen et al. (1969) claim that aphasic children exhibit a general sequencing disability and a pervasive memory impairment that is not limited to the auditory modality. They suggest that these deficits may explain these children's language disorder.

Recently, we have experimentally examined a well-defined group of developmental dysphasic children and demonstrated, by use of nonverbal operant conditioning techniques, not only an impairment in perceiving the temporal order of rapidly presented auditory stimuli, but also equally inferior discrimination of sound quality to which a sequencing difficulty could be secondary (Tallal and Piercy, 1973b). In further studies the same subjects were tested for their ability to perceive binary sequences of nonverbal stimuli in the visual as well as the auditory modalities, using the same nonverbal operant techniques. Performance was studied in relation to duration of stimulus elements, interval between elements, and the number of elements in a sequence pattern. No significant differences between the dysphasic and control children's performance were observed on the visual tests. In sharp contrast, on the auditory tests the dysphasics but not the controls were adversely effected by decreases in duration of stimulus elements and intervals between elements, and by increases in the number of elements in the stimulus pattern. The total duration of stimulus patterns correlated significantly ($r_s = 0.89$, Spearman rank correlation) with the percentage correct performance of dysphasic children (Tallal and Piercy, 1973b).

The results of these studies demonstrate that developmental dysphasic children are incapable of responding correctly to nonverbal acoustic information that is presented rapidly. How could this basic perceptual impairment in processing rapidly changing acoustic information affect the speech perception abilities of language-disordered children?

Recent work in speech synthesis and perception has demonstrated that vowels and certain consonants are processed differently by normal subjects. These basic differences in phoneme perception can be attributed to the differential duration of the critical formant information of these two classes of speech sounds, as well as their differently shaped formants. For the stop consonants there appears to be a relatively complex relationship between the phoneme and its representation as sound. The essential acoustic cue is a rapidly changing spectrum provided by the second and third formant transitions. These are not only transitional in character, but also of a relatively short duration (approximately 40 msec). On the other hand, the major cue for the synthetic vowels used in perceptual experiments is the steady-state frequencies of the first three formants, which have a relatively long duration (approximately 250 msec) and remain constant over the entire length of the stimulus (Fry et al., 1962; Liberman et al., 1967).

The results of our previous experiments demonstrated that, unlike normals, children with developmental language delay are incapable of processing nonverbal stimuli presented at rapid rates, but can process the same stimuli at slower rates of presentation. In one experiment it was demonstrated that, provided the duration of the complex tones was at least 250 msec, language delayed subjects performed as well as matched controls when nonverbally indicating which two- and three-element patterns they perceived.

On the hypothesis that impaired auditory processing of rapidly changing acoustic cues in speech is a primary disability of language-impaired children, it was predicted that (1) these children would show no impairment in discriminating steady-state vowels (e.g., /ɛ/ and /æ/) of the same duration (250 msec) as the nonverbal steady-state tones studied previously, but (2) they would show impaired discrimination of synthesized stop-consonants (e.g., /ba/ and /da/) which have the same total duration (250 msec), but with an initial transitional component of only 40 msec in duration, which is critical for discrimination.

This hypothesis was examined by using the same subjects and procedures as were used in the previous experiments, but with substitution in one instance of computer synthesized vowels, and in another of computer synthesized stop-consonants, for the previously studied computer synthesized complex nonverbal stimuli of the same total duration (Tallal and Piercy, 1974).

The results of these experiments were striking. The language-impaired subjects' discrimination of vowel stimuli did not differ significantly from their discrimination of nonverbal auditory stimuli of the same duration on any of the perceptual or serial memory tasks studied. Clearly, these children's discrimination performance does not deteriorate simply as a consequence of changing from nonverbal to verbal auditory stimuli, when both are of a steady-state character. However, the results with synthesized stop-consonants were entirely different. On all tasks studied, the language-impaired subjects' discrimination of consonant stimuli was significantly inferior both to their own discrimination of vowel and nonverbal stimuli of the same duration, and to that of their matched controls.

Further experiments showed that the limiting factor underlying the inferior performance of these language-disordered children on the consonant tasks was the total duration of the rapidly changing initial portion of the acoustic spectrum. In these experiments the initial formant transitions of the same stop-consonants (/ba/ and /da/) were extended (by use of a speech synthesizer) from 43 to 95 msec, while maintaining the total length of the stop-consonant at 250 msec. The ability of language-disordered children to discriminate transitions of this longer duration was now found to be unimpaired. It is important to note that normal children still perceived these "extended" consonants as /ba/ and /da/. The language-disordered children were able to perform as well as the controls on both the discrimination and sequencing of these same stop-consonants, once the formant transition had been extended in time (Tallal and Piercy, 1975). The potential therapeutic value of this specialized "stretching" technique, which allows these children to discriminate previously indiscriminable speech sounds, is an exciting area now under study.

This finding has led us to conclude that some language disorders may result from a primary impairment in auditory temporal processing. This hypothesis is supported further by our recent investigations into the speech production abilities of these children with perceptual impairments (Stark, Tallal, and Curtiss, 1975; Tallal, Stark, and Curtiss, 1976). The same speech sounds that incorporate rapidly changing acoustic spectra, and hence are the most difficult for these children to perceive, are also the most difficult ones for them to produce correctly.

It has also been reported that some types of specific reading disorders (developmental dyslexia) may result, at least in part, from the inability to analyze the acoustic-phonetic components of written language that are essential in learning to read. More specifically, it has been noted that dyslexic children are impaired in their sequential processing abilities (Bakker, 1967; see Bakker for review, 1971). In a study of the patterns of impairments characterizing children with specific reading disabilities, Doehring (1968) found deficits of sequential processing to be an important factor underlying reading disorders. Such deficits were particularly marked when items were presented rapidly.

However, there are also many reports in the literature indicating that some dyslexic children are unable to analyze the visual-spatial aspects of written language (see Doehring for review, 1968). Thus, Myklebust (1965) suggested that we think of dyslexic children as forming a heterogeneous rather than a homogeneous group, comprising both "visual dyslexics" as well as "auditory dyslexics." Other authors have also delineated these two subgroups of dyslexics and have reported that the difficulties of children within these groups reflect deficiencies of either central visual or central auditory processing (Bateman, 1968; Quiros, 1964). In her excellent review article on diagnostic concepts pertaining to developmental dyslexia, Boder (1973) pointed out that in addition to the "visual dyslexic" subgroup, which basically manifests visual-spatial processing deficits, and the "auditory dyslexic" subgroup, which manifests auditory-temporal processing deficits, a third subgroup exists that has a more general pervasive deficit incorporating both auditory and visual processing difficulties. Boder concluded that, in essence, reading may be a two-channel function requiring the integration of intact visual and auditory processes, peripheral and central. It is precisely these two processes underlying reading that are basic to the two standard methods of reading instruction. The whole-word, or look-and-say technique, requires the reader to experience the printed word globally as a visual Gestalt, while the phonetic technique requires the reader to analyze and segment words into phonetic elements. Hence, for the two subgroups of dyslexics these two methods of teaching reading would not be equally appropriate. Presumably, the whole-word teaching method (which relies heavily on visual processing) would be a more appropriate teaching approach to use with the auditorily impaired dyslexic child than the phonetic approach (which relies more on auditory processing) would be, and vice versa for the visually impaired dyslexic child.

However, before this hypothesis can be investigated experimentally, it is essential first to establish which dyslexic children's reading disabilities stem primarily from auditorially based dysfunction, which from visual, and which from general or combined dysfunctions. Furthermore, it is of both theoretical as well as clinical importance to delineate more precisely the patterns of perceptual dysfunction that are characteristic of various subgroups of reading-impaired children.

The research techniques that we have developed to investigate a hierarchy of nonverbal and verbal auditory processing capabilities of language-impaired children have been employed recently to investigate similar processes in reading-impaired children (Tallal, 1976b, 1976c). The preliminary results of these studies indicate that a subgroup of the children studied with reading disabilities have an auditory perceptual deficit similar to that of the language-disordered children previously studied, although to a lesser extent. However, the remaining children studied, with equally impaired reading skills, performed as well on these auditory tasks as did normal children their same age (see Tallal, 1976a for normative developmental data for these tasks).

All of the reading-disabled subjects were also tested for their ability to read nonsense words. It was hypothesized that those dyslexic children who had the greatest difficulty on the auditory perceptual tasks would also have the most difficulty in reading nonsense words correctly, since this task relies heavily on phonetic analysis. This hypothesis was sustained by experimental test, and is presently being investigated in further detail. The degree of impairment on the auditory perceptual test correlated significantly ($r_s = 0.80$, Spearman) with the number of errors made in reading nonsense words. This finding suggests that the phonics teaching method may not be the most appropriate one to use when remediating dyslexic children who have auditory perceptual impairments.

These same tasks have not, as yet, been presented visually to dyslexic children. It will be important to assess the visual processing abilities of dyslexic children both with and without auditory perceptual impairments, to ascertain whether positive correlations exist between patterns of performance on these auditory and visual perceptual measures and measures of specific reading skills.

The results of these studies demonstrate that children with severe developmental language disorders are severely impaired in their ability to analyze rapidly changing acoustic information. Furthermore, a subgroup of children with specific reading disabilities are also impaired in this same aspect of acoustic processing, although to a lesser extent. Using the same experimental procedures, we have also found the same pattern of impairment in analyzing rapidly changing acoustic nonverbal and verbal information in adult patients with residual receptive aphasia, resulting from left hemisphere lesions. The degree of impairment in analyzing rapidly changing acoustic information was highly correlated ($r_s = 0.83$, Spearman) with the degree of receptive language impairment in these subjects, as measured by the Token Test (De Renzi and Vignolo, 1962). Nonaphasic patients with right hemisphere lesions were unimpaired on these perceptual tasks (Tallal and Newcombe, 1976).

Thus, it appears that not only is this rate specific auditory processing deficit related to communicative disorders, but it is positively correlated with the degree of communication impairment. Furthermore, both communicative abilities and the ability to analyze rapidly changing acoustic information are disrupted by damage to the left cerebral hemisphere of the brain, but not by similar damage to the right hemisphere. The basic question that emerges from these studies, then, is what is the precise relationship between auditory temporal processing, language, and hemispheric asymmetry?

TEMPORAL PROCESSING, SPEECH PERCEPTION, AND HEMISPHERIC ASYMMETRY

It is generally agreed that the human brain is functionally asymmetric. One of the most basic assumptions related to hemispheric asymmetries is that the left cerebral hemisphere is predominantly involved in language processing, for most normal people. The dichotic stimulation technique has been used to show that when two different acoustic signals are presented simultaneously to a listener, one to each ear, most normal listeners are more accurate in perceiving verbal stimuli when they are presented to the right ear than when they are presented to the left ear. Kimura suggested that the right ear advantage (REA) for dichotically presented verbal material indicates that this material is being processed in the left hemisphere (see Kimura, 1967 for a discussion of this phenomenon).

New computerized techniques, which allow for synthesizing speech while selectively controlling various acoustic variables, have been used in an attempt to understand how speech is distinguished from nonspeech and why it is processed in the left hemisphere. It has been demonstrated that not all classes of speech sounds produce an equally strong REA when they are presented dichotically. Cutting (1973) demonstrated that the largest REA was produced when stop consonants (b,d,g,p,t,k) were presented in pairs dichotically, while liquids (such as l and r) produce a less strong REA, and steady-state isolated vowel (such as ϵ and æ) did not produce a right ear advantage.

The magnitude of the right ear advantage has been directly related to the degree of verbal encodedness, in other words, the degree to which speech sounds undergo context-dependent acoustic variation (Haggard, 1971). Furthermore, the degree of encodedness of classes of speech sounds has also been shown to be related to the extent to which these sounds are perceived categorically, that is, the degree to which two acoustically different speech sounds, identified as belonging to the same speech category, can be discriminated (see Liberman et al., 1967 for review).

Interestingly, highly encoded phonemes are also characterized by very abrupt changes in frequency over time. Thus the magnitude of the REA Cutting described for stop consonants, liquids, and vowels in addition to correlating with the degree of encodedness of these classes of speech sounds also correlates with the rapidity of frequency changes in these speech sounds. Fujisaki and Kawashima (1970) demonstrated in a series of elegant experiments that the degree to which vowels were perceived categorically depended on their duration; whereas relatively long-duration, isolated, steady-state vowels, used most often in speech perception experiments, were shown not to be perceived categorically, the same vowels were perceived categorically if they were very brief in duration (about 20 msec) or presented in a fixed phonemic context. These experiments indicate that the degrees of lateralization of speech may be related to the duration over which the critical acoustic aspects occur within certain sounds. Recently, Halperin, Nackshon, and Carmon (1973) were able to demonstrate a REA for nonverbal dichotically presented tone sequences containing abrupt changes in frequency or duration. However, despite these few excellent studies, most evidence continues to favor the hypothesis that the REA indicates that specific verbal material must be processed in the left hemisphere and that this lateralization results from processing that occurs beyond the level of acoustic analysis (A. Liberman, 1973).

Our recent finding that subjects with communicative disorders are unable to discriminate speech sounds that incorporate rapidly changing acoustic spectra, but can discriminate these same speech sounds when the duration over which the critical acoustic information occurs is extended (Tallal and Piercy, 1975) indicates that processing rapidly occurring acoustic information may be a critical feature for speech perception.

In collaboration with Dr. Grace Yeni-Komshian, we are presently investigating the effect on normal adult speech perception of extending the duration of the formant transitions within stop consonants. Studies of categorical perception and dichotic perception using standard duration (about 40-msec) as well as extended duration (50–80-msec) transitions within stop consonants are presently underway. It is hoped that these studies will indicate whether functions that are presently considered to reflect specifically phonetic analysis, such as categorical perception and the REA for dichotic presentation, may be reflecting, at least in part, analysis at the acoustic level of speech processing, which is directly related to the rate of change of acoustic information within certain speech sounds. Our studies with children and adults with and without communication disorders indicate that the processing of rapidly occurring acoustic information is critically involved in the development and maintenance of language. Several other authors have arrived at a similar conclusion, using different experimental techniques, that the dominant hemisphere must play a primary role in the analysis of rapid temporal acoustic information.

Hence speech, which requires such acoustic analysis, is also laterilized to this hemisphere (Efron, 1963; Lackner and Teuber, 1973). Our results would strongly support this hypothesis. Hopefully, these new techniques will be a useful means of further delineating the role of auditory temporal processing in normal and disordered communication.

ACKNOWLEDGMENT

I would like to thank Dr. Michael Bender, Director of Special Education at the Kennedy Institute, and his staff for allowing me to study the dyslexic children at the Kennedy School and for their continued cooperation with this project.

Developmental Spelling Retardation

Hazel E. Nelson and Elizabeth K. Warrington

As knowledge of learning disorders in children has increased, so it has become increasingly possible to distinguish different types of disorders within this general category: disorders that differ in their qualitative characteristics and in their associated cognitive disorders or weaknesses and that, by implication at least, differ in their aetiologies. For many decades the term "specific developmental dyslexia" has been applied to certain cases of retardation in literacy skills, but the singular lack of success in obtaining an agreed definition of this term, or even in formulating a set of "characteristic" symptoms, is but one indication that more than one type of disorder is involved. Although most so-called "dyslexic" children are retarded in both reading and spelling attainments, there are a number of children who experience great difficulty in learning to spell while having relatively little or no corresponding difficulty in learning to read. The authors should like to argue that these two groups of children, namely, the reading plus spelling retardates and the spelling-only retardates, are exhibiting different disorders, disorders that differ in their quality and in their associated pattern of cognitive abilities. Furthermore, it is proposed that a closer analysis of the quality of the spelling errors made by these children may provide valuable indications as to the possible cognitive mechanisms and deficits underlying these different forms of "dyslexic" difficulties.

RETARDATION OF READING AND SPELLING

Dyslexic children who manifest both reading and spelling retardation are considered here first. Delayed speech and language development is frequently reported in the case histories of these children (e.g., Ewing, 1930; Warrington, 1967). Naidoo (1972) specifically noted that the early language difficulties reported in her series of dyslexic children occurred predominantly in the reading plus spelling retardates as compared to the spelling-only retardates. Several authors (e.g., Ingram, 1959; McCready,

325

1910) have stressed the similarities between the retarded speech development of the dyslexic child and the acquired speech difficulties of the dysphasic adult, but such comparisons are generally at only a qualitative level and therefore difficult to evaluate from the written descriptions alone. It is undoubtedly true that in clinical practice one can usually detect the early stages of an acquired dysphasia at a qualitative level long before the language disturbance is severe enough to be detected on quantitative tests. Consequently we should certainly not wish to reject out of hand these qualitative comparisons made by clinically experienced researchers. Nevertheless, quantitative data are most welcome in this area.

Specific dyslexic difficulties are not usually detected by the teachers or parents until the child is 7 or more years of age, and often not until he is 9–10 years of age. By the time the child is referred to a specialist, his speech rarely shows any definite abnormalities of the sort that would be directly comparable to those found in adult dysphasic speech. Nevertheless, indications of a general language "weakness" may be evident, for example, in a significantly poorer Verbal than Performance IQ on the Wechsler Intelligence Scale for Children (WISC).

Warrington (1967) demonstrated an abnormally high incidence of Verbal–Performance IQ discrepancies (in the direction of lowered Verbal IQs) in her series of 76 children. These findings were confirmed in a later retrospective study of some 121 children with specific reading and/or spelling retardation. Furthermore, it was demonstrated in this later study that the size of the Verbal IQ decrement is much more strongly associated with the degree of reading retardation than it is with the degree of spelling retardation. Thus, whereas our group of reading plus spelling retardates had a mean Verbal IQ 14 points lower than the mean Performance IQ, there was no significant difference between the mean Verbal and Performance IQs in the spelling-only retardates.

It is often argued that the general language weakness, so measured for example on the WISC, is secondary to the child's inability to read, resulting from his reduced experience with words in the written media. However, several factors mitigate against the sufficiency of this explanation for the general verbal weakness. First, it is difficult to see why failure to read should result in the nominal difficulties mentioned earlier. Second, the development of language and verbal skills in primary school children is influenced to a far greater extent by the spoken word than by the written word. In part this is because the child spends so much more of his time surrounded by the spoken word than he spends with the written word; but also it is because at these early stages the child's efforts are concentrated in learning to read some of the very many words with which he is already familiar, and that are already well established in his spoken vocabulary. Indeed, it is not until the reading skill is well developed that written material can be used as a source of information to extend vocabulary.

Yet in the analysis of WISC subtest score patterns in our retrospective study, the mean Vocabulary score of the reading plus spelling retardates was as much as three scaled points below that of the spelling-only retardates. It is perhaps interesting to notice that this was the largest subtest score difference between the two groups, and that it was obtained on the subtest that is usually considered to be the most purely "Verbal" of all the WISC subtests; see for example Maxwell's (1959) factorial study. Third, the histories of delayed speech and language development prior to the child's attendance at school indicate that the more general language weakness precedes the reading difficulties.

Regarding the quality of the spelling errors made by the reading plus spelling retardates, in a retrospective study (Nelson and Warrington, 1974) these authors analyzed the first ten errors made by children on the Schonell Graded Word Spelling Test according to three major error categories. First was the Order error category: this included all errors that contained all and only the letters of the stimulus word itself, but in an incorrect order. Second was the Phonetically Inaccurate error category: this included all errors that involved the addition of a phoneme not included in the stimulus word and/or the omission of a necessary phoneme. For example, if the word "land" were rendered as l.a.n.d.e.d. or l.a.d. or l.a.r.n. these would be scored as phonetically inaccurate errors. Third was the Phonetically Accurate error category: this included all errors in which the phonetic structure had been maintained but in which the child had used the inappropriate graphemes to represent the phonemes. For example, if the word "brain" were rendered as b.r.a.n.e. or b.r.a.y.n., these would be scored as phonetically accurate errors. Analysis of the errors in this qualitative way showed that the reading plus spelling retardates made a significantly higher proportion of phonetically inaccurate errors than did the spelling-only retardates. Now it is just this sort of spelling error that has been shown to be associated with dysphasia in adult patients with cerebral lesions and that is considered to reflect the underlying language disturbance.

Acquired spelling difficulty is not infrequently associated with dysphasia in adults. For example, Schiller (1947) reported difficulties in 39 out of 46 cases of dysphasia following a bullet wound to the head, and more recently Newcombe (1969) reported significant impairments in spelling from her left hemisphere, dysphasic group of bullet wound patients. The types of spelling errors produced by these patients can often be seen to reflect the underlying language disorders. Although it is very rare, in extreme cases there may be whole word substitutions, the substitutions being on a semantic basis; or the word as written may be an incorrect though related grammatical form of the stimulus word. But what is more frequently observed in the spelling errors of dysphasic patients is an abnormally high incidence of errors involving the omission, addition, or substitution of letters that are phonetically different from those contained in the stimulus word itself. Kinsbourne and Warrington (1964) compared groups of adult patients with cerebral lesions on oral spelling tasks and were able to demonstrate different patterns of spelling errors associated with dysphasia and finger agnosia, respectively. They showed that the pattern of spelling errors of the dysphasic patients was characterized by the high proportion of extraneous letter errors, that is, the addition of letters not found in the stimulus word itself. It is also interesting to note that when spelling impairment is associated with dysphasia in adult patients there is very often a reading impairment as well, the quality of which may also reflect the more widespread language disorder.

Comparisons between acquired impairments in adulthood and developmental difficulties in childhood should only be undertaken with great caution, especially before drawing any conclusions as to the possible involvement of particular cortical structures in these processes. We know that the cognitive effects of lesions in children can be very different from the effects of similarly cited lesions in adults. Partly this can be attributed to the apparent plasticity of the young child's brain—and in the case of specific developmental dyslexia, where there are no abnormal histories of cerebral insult in later life, any supposed "minimal brain damage" must, presumably, have occurred at the neonatal or birth stages. But also, and perhaps more importantly, we must never overlook the fact that different cognitive functions are necessary for the initial acquisition of complex skills such as reading and spelling, than are necessary for the practicing of these skills once they have become well-established habits. Indeed, the skill of reading is a very good example of just how different these requirements may be. Whereas for children, the acquisition of the reading skill is a difficult and complex process, which takes many years to develop to its full extent and which may be adversely affected by many different factors during its development, for adults we have recently been able to show that the reading skill is generally maintained at a high level (indeed often, apparently, at the premorbid level) despite severe degrees of generalized dementia resulting from wide-spread cortical atrophy (Nelson and McKenna, 1975). But having given due consideration to these factors, we feel that it is perfectly valid to argue at the functional level that, just as phonetically inaccurate spelling errors are considered to be related to the underlying language dysfunction in adults, so the phonetically inaccurate spelling errors in children may be considered to reflect a more general, underlying language disturbance.

To summarize, in view of the quality of the disorder itself and in view of the pattern of cognitive strengths and weakness associated with it, we should like to argue that at least some cases of spelling disability when this is associated with a reading disability are best considered as one aspect of a more generalized language retardation. Since the initial acquisitions of reading and spelling skills are such long and complex processes, it should not be surprising that otherwise quite mild language deficits, which do not significantly hinder spoken speech, can produce such severe and apparently specific reading and spelling difficulties.

CHILDREN WITH SPELLING-ONLY RETARDATION

Spelling-only retardation in children seems to occur less frequently than the reading plus spelling disorder (the spelling-only retardates accounted for about a quarter of educational referrals to the National Hospital in a 7-year period), but even approximate estimates of its incidence in the general school population are impossible to make from our data since so many factors affect the probability of the child's difficulties being detected by his teachers or parents, and then his subsequent referral.

Children who are retarded in their spelling ability but have adequate reading ability do not produce an abnormal distribution of Verbal–Performance IQ discrepancies. In our retrospective study there was no significant difference between the mean Verbal and Performance IQs of the spelling-only retardates. Naidoo (1972) showed that spelling-only retardates were not impaired in either Verbal or Performance IQs relative to the controls. We had no systematic records of early language development in our retrospective study, but certainly no qualitative indications of a possible language weakness were noted at the age of testing.

It is currently popular to explain some dyslexic disabilities in terms of an underlying difficulty in dealing with the sequential aspects of material, and certainly the often reported deficits among these children in the Digit Span, Arithmetic, Coding, and Picture Arrangement subtests of the WISC (see, for example, Naidoo, 1972; Nelson and Warrington, 1974) would seem to be consistent with the presence of a sequential disorder, as would the often reported difficulties in rote learning such information as the days of the week and months of the year. Kinsbourne and Warrington (1963b) suggested that the cluster of symptoms found in children with a developmental Gerstmann syndrome, which characteristically involved greater spelling than reading retardation, might all be related to a more basic difficulty in handling units in a linear sequence. If the misspellings of the spelling-only retardates were indeed related in some way to sequential ordering difficulties, then one would expect to find an increased incidence of letter-order errors in these children. And indeed, in the Kinsbourne and Warrington (1964) study of adult patients mentioned previously, it was found that the group whose acquired spelling impairments were accompanied by finger agnosia did produce a relatively higher proportion of errors relating to letter-order than was found in either of the control groups or in the dysphasic group. But in our retrospective study of children there was no significant difference between the two groups in their tendencies to produce letter-order errors; and in any case the absolute numbers of order errors per child (mean of 0.71, range 0–3, out of 10) were too small to provide convincing evidence that the "sequential ordering" explanation of their difficulties is a sufficient one. Furthermore, this notion does not appear to be relevant to explaining the apparent preponderance of phonetically accurate errors.

It is generally accepted by teachers that children make fewer phonetically inaccurate errors as they grow older and their spelling ability improves. These two factors are often confounded but, as part of the standardization of a new graded word spelling test that is being developed in our department, it has been shown that in normal school children the tendency to make phonetically inaccurate errors is related to spelling ability level rather than to chronological age per se. But analysis of the quality of the spelling errors made by the spelling-only retardates showed a different pattern of error tendencies from that produced by the reading plus spelling retardates, even when the two groups were closely matched for spelling level. To recap, the spelling-only retardates made significantly fewer phonetically inaccurate errors than were made by the reading plus spelling retardates.

The method of analyzing errors used in our retrospective study was hierarchical in organization and biased towards the detection of phonetically inaccurate errors, in that words containing both phonetically inaccurate and phonetically accurate errors were allocated exclusively to the "phonetically inaccurate" category. This being so, no definite conclusions can be drawn at this stage concerning the absolute numbers of phonetically accurate errors that were made. However, preliminary analysis of the spelling errors made by a group of normal control children, matched with the retardates for overall spelling ability level, shows a pattern of error tendencies that lies in between those obtained from the two groups of retardates; see Table 1.

Table 1. Comparisons of Children from the Spelling-Only Retarded, the Reading + Spelling Retarded, and the Control Groups, Matched for Schonell Spelling Age

	I Spelling-Only Retardates	II Reading + Spelling Retardates	III Controls	Sig. Levels of t test I & II	Sig. Levels of t test I & III
Phonetically Accurate Errors					
Mean	1.24	2.53	2.27	0.05	0.01
S.D.	0.97	2.24	1.34		
Phonetically Inaccurate Errors					
Mean	8.06	6.47	7.60	0.02	NS
S.D.	1.20	2.24	1.50		

The 15 control children matched for spelling level with the two groups of retardates were spelling at a level commensurate with their chronological age. These results indicate that the spelling-only retardates are better at the phonetical aspects of the spelling task than one would expect from their overall level of performance. Therefore in this respect they behave more like their own, normally spelling peers. In contrast, they have a particular difficulty or set of difficulties that results in the making of phonetically accurate but graphemically inaccurate errors. In our writing system there is often more than one possible graphemic equivalent to a particular phoneme, so in learning to spell a particular word the child has to learn which grapheme is the appropriate one in that particular circumstance. It is just this type of spelling information that the spelling-only retardates appear to find particularly difficult to retain.

Obviously a more detailed analysis is needed in order to identify more precisely the class or classes of words that cause the spelling-only retardates particular difficulty, and that result in these phonetically accurate errors. As a preliminary stage to this investigation, the spelling errors made by normal school children on a longer and more sensitive spelling test than the Schonell have been analyzed in detail. From the 160 words in this test one can select out two groups of words: words that tend to generate phonetically accurate and phonetically inaccurate errors, respectively. One would predict that the spelling-only retardates would have particular difficulty with the former group of words, that is, with those words that are most likely to produce phonetically accurate errors in normal children. If this prediction is upheld, then consideration of the features peculiar to these words could indicate which particular cognitive factors are especially involved in their learning and recall, and hence which particular cognitive system(s) are deficient in this type of specific spelling retardation.

Although the present chapter has concentrated on spelling disabilities, our general approach to the investigation of these disabilities is equally applicable to the wider field of learning disorders. This approach is a move away from the epidemiological type studies, with which the literature already abounds, in favor of a move towards closer analysis of the precise nature of the learning disorders as exhibited by the child. Thus by looking at the actual errors that the child makes we may be able to identify the particular area of cognitive weakness that is responsible; having identified the particular cognitive weakness we should then be in a much better position to help the child develop alternative strategies that by-pass this particular cognitive weakness.

Ocular-Motor Variables in Reading Disorders

Gerald Leisman and Joddy Schwartz

The etiology of reading disorders has been a source of contention among investigators for many years. Although its source is pervasive, Schain (1968) has estimated that these disorders may involve as much as 10% of the general population for whom "subtle brain damage" may be present but not clearly proven. In fact, Ingram, Mason, and Blackburn (1970) noted that the most severe degree of specific reading disability may exist without evidence of central nervous system pathology. Where there is such evidence, reading disability becomes associated with backwardness in other academic areas.

Although the relationship between ocular–motor variables and the ability to read and integrate visual information has been noted (Leisman, 1974, 1975a, 1975b, 1975c, 1975d, 1975e; Leisman and Schwartz, 1975), the nature of the reading process is such that attention must be paid to special features of the individual's higher nervous system in attempting to understand the reading process, and hence its disorders.

A difficulty frequently associated with reading disability in childhood is the inability of the child to attend to and select from various sensory stimuli impinging on him at any given moment. Attentional handicaps, especially those associated with reading disorders, have a marked visual component. Data have been reported that indicate that many children with such disorders demonstrate variable patterns of visual scanning and fixation and do not demonstrate anticipatory saccades[1] (Gittelman-Klein, 1975; Leisman, 1975a, 1975b; Taylor, 1975). By the same token, the child may be unable to expect forthcoming stimuli as demonstrated by the

---

[1] Saccades are rapid flickering eye movements occurring with a latency of approximately 5 min arc to about 10 min arc. The angular velocity averages 10 deg/sec and at times to 800 deg/sec. The duration is about 45 msec and they occur at intervals varying from 0.2 to 3 or 4 sec. These movements are, by definition, termed voluntary. It is during these movements that vision is suppressed or inhibited.

absence of the contingent negative variation (CNV) or expectancy wave[2] in computer-averaged EEG potentials evoked by sensory stimuli paired over time (Sutton et al., 1967; Walter, 1964). When paired presentations of stimuli such as flashes of light are presented over many trials, the interstimulus interval should show the CNV potential. This potential is frequently absent or reduced in these children (Mackworth, 1973). The sequential nature of the reading process, the ability to recognize small differences between similar items visually, the necessity to recognize and remember orientational differences, and the importance of an adequate ocular–motor and visual processing apparatus become important considerations in the development of any model of the reading process.

Mackworth (1971) developed a model of the reading process that is essentially a summary and synthesis of what is presently known. The Mackworth model has several important characteristics. These include input involving selection; attention expectancy and prediction; recognition through comparison to memory; synthesis of multiple inputs to establish context; coding through motor-speech programs into short-term memory, with parallel processing of visual information under the influence of attention; and synthesis of data and storage in long-term memory and all component processes. While Mackworth (1971) addresses herself to the total reading process, it is the specific components of eye movement, information flow, and information processing that are of interest here.

FILTERING AND TRANSMISSION OF INFORMATION

The objective facts of how vision occurs have long been known to be inconsistent with the subjectively experienced temporal continuity. The eye is never completely at rest. In ordinary viewing of the visual world and especially during the reading process, the eye jumps between two and four times a second (Young and Stark, 1963). Each saccadic eye movement or jump displaces the retinal image.

Visual input cannot be continuously presented to the brain as we experience it but is presented in "chunks" (Gaarder et al., 1964, 1966;

---

[2] Contingent negative variation (CNV) or expectancy wave is a slow negative cortical potential in the human brain related to individual differences in the psychological function that involves attention and arousal. CNV typically depends on the association (contingency) or two successive stimuli. The basic experimental paradigm for generating CNV is like that of a constant foreperiod reaction time experiment; S_1 is followed within an invariant time period by S_2 (unconditioned stimulus) to which the subject is to make a motor response. Although the CNV can occur without a motor response, its development is facilitated by a mental or emotional response to S_2.

Leisman, 1975c) at a rate and a time determined by the rate and time of saccadic eye movements. The necessity of a filtering system of information processing can be illustrated by a simple calculation (Jacobson, 1951). If we consider the number of receptor fields and the number of nerve fibers, it appears that the retina can collect information at the rate of 10^7 bits/sec and the million channels in the optic nerve can transmit at a similar rate (see Leisman, 1975c). On the other hand, psychophysical studies on pattern recognition indicate that the information used in recognition of a pattern is seldom more than about 40 bits (Leisman, 1975c). This is a large amount of information since 40 bits enables one out of 10^{12} possible patterns to be distinguished, but it is small compared with 10^7 bits/sec.

Part of the reason for this discrepancy is that 10^7 bits/sec could only be effective in a situation where all patterns viewed consisted of random arrays of small black and white areas. Moreover, for full usage, the random pattern should change in a random way about 20 to 30 times per second. In reading we are concerned with a visual scene in which the length of boundaries between light and dark areas is extremely small compared with the length in a random pattern. Irregular boundaries are extremely rare in comparison with regular boundaries.

Changes in the visual situation during reading occurring within 50 msec are usually small and are seldom completely unexpected. All of these considerations reduce the number of patterns that could possibly be encountered. A decision that confirms what already has a high probability of being true has only a small information content. Most of the visual judgments in reading should be of this nature. Nevertheless, pattern recognition in reading may, and often does, involve very critical judgments. It is also difficult to say in advance which little piece of visual information is going to be critical. The letter "A" may be recognized by "Λ" or by "–" or by "ʌ." Word recognition may work in a similar fashion. In any event, the whole elaborate visual system is needed in order to make available the ten, twenty, or forty bits of information required for a recognition.

Rattle and Foley-Fisher (1968) and Leisman (1975c) have suggested that a person who is performing a critical task summates information during the intervals between saccadic eye movements, but cannot carry forward the precise information from one interval to the next. It has also been demonstrated that if a subject has too frequent saccades he could not make a good vernier setting. A relationship also exists between accuracy on the vernier task and the average time used in making a setting. The results are consistent with the hypothesis that information is summed for times up to 200 msec.

Hubel and Wiesel (1965) noted that information is first filtered and then subjected to a process in which the precision of retinal location is sacrificed for more precise identification of pattern features. The slow movements of the eyes by which the pattern is gradually transferred from one set of retinal receptors to others must be compensated for so that the logical structure of the pattern appears as a constant of the visual scene. The compensation probably breaks down during the involuntary saccades and during the more rapid semivoluntary movements.

There is much evidence in support of the contention that when a rapid movement is initiated a partial block is inserted in the perceptual system so that visual sensitivity diminishes by two or three times (Volkman, Schick, and Riggs, 1968). This block operates a few milliseconds before the movement commences and lasts until it is finished. During this stage, the subject perceives the pattern as being steady and unchanged even when flashing rapidly across his retina. Leisman (1973, 1974, 1975d) has noted that the ability to condition the EEG alpha blocking response, as well as the ability of hemiplegics to recall information, is improved when visual stimuli are retinally stabilized. This indicates that eye movement variables may play an important role in attentional and reading deficiencies. Differences have also been shown to exist in the variability and precision of saccadic eye movements between normal and attentionally handicapped subjects (Leisman, 1975a, 1975b).

SACCADE CHARACTERISTICS
IN CHILDREN AND BRAIN-DAMAGED ADULTS

The clarity of visual perception depends on the precision with which saccadic eye movements are performed. The amplitude of these rotational movements depends on the strength of the muscle contraction and on the properties of the eyes as an inertia system (Gatev, 1968; Robinson, 1964).

Leisman (1975b) reported that with spastic-hemiplegic patients an increase in the amplitude of the saccade results in a concomitant increase in the mean angular velocity, which is consistent with previous studies (Westheimer, 1954; Yarbus, 1956). With a saccade of the same amplitude, the duration is shorter and the velocity greater in hemiplegic as compared to normal subjects. Gatev (1968) reported significantly greater velocities for young normal children than Leisman (1975b), Robinson (1964), Yarbus (1956, 1957), and others have found for normal adults. These results cannot simply be explained on the basis of the immature nature of the nervous system and muscular development (Leisman, 1975a, 1975b). Although no direct evidence exists, it is possible that maturation requires greater precision of saccades with the result being a decrease in saccadic velocity with increasing age. With an increase in the amplitude of the saccade, not only the mean but the maximum velocity increases in both normal and hemiplegic subjects (Leisman, 1975a, 1975b). This indicates that the character of this function and the differences observed between normal and hemiplegic subjects are conditioned, in part, by the differential effects of extra-ocular muscle contractions. One can expect greater velocities and shorter duration if the extra-ocular muscles contract with more force. The reasons for such observed differences have not been determined, but may well be due to spasticity associated with such conditions as hyperreflexia or involvement of inhibitory mechanisms.

Leisman (1975a, 1975b) has reported that the dispersion of the velocity amplitude function increases in brain-damaged subjects. An analogous dependence also exists for the duration/amplitude functions. The increasing variability of these functions in hemiplegics may represent differences between the functioning of their eye control system and that of normals.

The visual-perceptual system must be able to extract information about spatio-temporal changes in the environment from the "stable" and redundant features. This is basic to any theory of information transmission. There is also a necessity for removing information that is not relevant to the immediate situation (Jacobson, 1951).

Each saccade is a controlled quantity upon which the clear reception of visual information depends. The eyes perform each saccade at a maximum velocity, which provides an opportunity for attaining the necessary precision and ensuring the prompt supply of information required.

The existence of duration/amplitude and velocity/amplitude functions permits an exact preliminary program of the duration of future saccadic eye movements. However, the greater variability of these functions in brain-damaged patients makes the preliminary determination of the future saccades more difficult and less exact than for normal individuals.

The above-mentioned differences can be explained in part by differences in the strength of extra-ocular muscle contraction (possibly related to the lack of inhibitory control in hemiplegics), differential effects of inertia and spring stiffness of the eyeball (maturational factors), and learning variables (i.e., deficiencies in the mechanisms of anticipation-learning of saccadic eye movement, control, and precision). This latter possibility is of interest in terms of Mackworth's (1973) finding of an absence of the expectancy wave or anticipatory response in reading-deficient children.

Lindsley (1952) thought that stimuli were coded upon input to aid in perceptual clarity. He conceived of a mechanism in which saccadic eye movements are linked with EEG alpha activity. The saccades occur during an inexcitable phase to avoid retinal discharge impinging on the cortex. Meister (1951) noted a significant relationship between the onset of saccadic eye movements and the alpha rhythm, and Gross, Vaughn, and Valenstein (1967) reported that visual evoked potentials were reduced during eye saccades. The possibility of visually detecting a flash is reduced during a saccade and the ability of a flash to evoke a pupillary response is also greatly reduced (Zuber and Stark, 1966).

Leisman (1974) has shown that when eye movements are recorded by EOG horizontally and binocularly and the EEG alpha rhythm bilaterally, a covariant relationship between the two emerges in both normal and attentionally handicapped subjects. This occurs when the EOG is varied by changes in illumination.

Gaarder, Koresko, and Kropfl (1966) found a component of EEG alpha activity that was temporally related to the occurrence of saccadic eye movements. They found phase locking to be present before the onset of saccade. It was thought, therefore, that the saccade does not serve as a stimulus which locks the alpha activity into phase, but that alpha activity reflects the driving of the saccades. This points to a discontinuous nature of visual perception, with the discontinuities related to the characteristics of saccadic eye movements (see Leisman, 1975c). In summary, then, the alpha rhythm is related to saccadic eye movements, and the differences that exist in the duration and velocity of saccadic eye movements in subjects with attentional and information processing deficits are related to the ability to perceive and integrate visual information in the cortex.

Given such findings, it becomes feasible that the manipulation of the eye movement variable (i.e., deviant characteristics of eye movements that are counteracted by techniques that stabilize images on the retina) should result in changes in the alpha rhythm related to attentional states and improvement in the ability of these subjects to recall information. Leisman (1973, 1974, 1975a) has reported data consistent with these notions; see Figure 1.

John, Herrington, and Sutton (1967) noted that when generalization occurs, a stored representation of prior experience is recalled by a novel stimulus. The neural activity underlying the recall of this prior experience is reflected by the evoked potential components. The essence of John's thesis is that slow waves can reflect the storage and retrieval of information. The neural representation of information stored in the brain is not, in his opinion, the activity of certain hypothetical coded cells that stand for specific items of information, but consists of certain spatio-temporal patterns of organized activity.

What can be concluded from this review is a picture of visual perception as a discontinuous process with the discontinuities temporally and

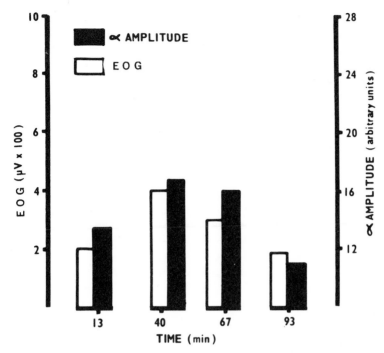

Figure 1. Covariance of the mean alpha and EOG amplitudes among spastic-hemiplegic subjects under nonstabalized image conditions. This figure illustrates the covariance of the mean alpha and EOG amplitudes among hemiplegic subjects while viewing an oscilloscope target moving independent of their eye movements.

phase linked with saccadic eye movements. Information is transmitted in bursts linked in time to the saccade when visual sensitivity diminishes. Saccades of short duration and high velocity may be related to information summation deficits and to difficulties in performing critical judgments. These difficulties have been significantly improved by techniques that manipulate the variable of saccadic eye movements. It is not thought that ocular—motor deficit is the direct cause of reading impairment, but that it is reflective of a more basic inhibitory deficit.

THE ROLE OF SACCADES
IN PATTERN RECOGNITION AND READING

Mackay (1967) proposed a model in which stimulus intensity was encoded logarithmically at a peripheral stage. At a more central stage the organism generates a "matching response" to incoming neural signals. Mackay noted that an internally generated matching response to signals from sensory receptors would "amount logically to an internal representation of the features to which it is adaptive," and proposed the matching response as a physiological correlate of perception (Mackay, 1956, 1966, 1967).

Central to Mackay's model of perception is an active "updating" process, a view which, because of its generality, would be difficult to disprove. It is a comprehensive model of perception only to the extent that perception can entirely be described in terms of action and readiness for action or anticipation of action. In terms of the original problem of perceptual stability maintained in the presence of continually moving eyes, we had inferred a discontinuous model of vision with the discontinuities linked to saccadic eye movements. Several models of CNS activity, however, are concerned with this stability and involve the notion of corollary discharge that is initiated in the motor region of the brain simultaneously with the motor signals, which will result in motor activity (Teuber, 1960). This discharge is then compared with subsequent incoming messages from the sensory system. The difference between the corollary discharge (representing the intended action) and the messages from the eye (which represent the action achieved) can either influence further action, or ascend to a higher center and produce a perception. In Mackay's model, the matching response does not cancel incoming signals, but evaluates them.

Some results (Rattle and Foley-Fisher, 1968) alluded to earlier suggest that a subject who is performing a critical task summates information during the intervals between saccadic eye movements but cannot carry forward the precise information from one interval to the next. These investigators have performed detailed studies of the accuracy of vernier-acuity judgments. In one experiment, a subject was required to move one straight line until it formed a continuation of a fixed line, kinesthetic and proprioceptive cues being excluded. This involved a judgment of whether the movable line was to the right or left of the fixed line, and subjects with good acuity could detect a misalignment of less than 5 sec of arc. A highly significant correlation was found between accuracy of the vernier setting and the intersaccadic interval (i.e., if a subject has very frequent saccades, he cannot make a good setting). These results are consistent with the hypothesis that information is summed for times up to 200 msec but that the summation has to be restarted after each saccade or word scan. The importance of saccade duration and velocity for information processing has been noted earlier, as well as how deviant patterns of scanning and fixation, when controlled by stabilized image techniques, can result in the transmission of greater amounts of visual information. Figure 2 illustrates the stages of visual discrimination related to the reading process based on the model of visual information transmission being developed.

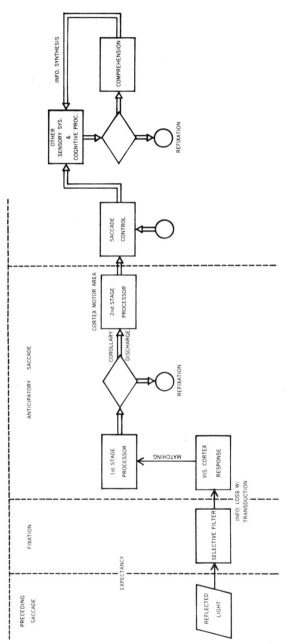

Figure 2. Model or visual information transmission in the reading process.

At the conclusion of a saccade, during reading, the eye is conditioned to assume an angular position, allowing for continuity in what is being read. Eye movements of fixation allow for the maximal activation of foveal receptors. thus providing the best visual acuity. At the same time reflected light from the printed page, while stimulating the receptors, is selectively filtered by a mechanical process. During this process the eye is oriented in such a way as to allow critical line and edge information to align with the central fovea. However, as the foveal area accounts for approximately one-third of the total area of central vision, the eye must oscillate within a range of no more than 20 deg (Yarbus, 1967). This effectively and mechanically reduced the acuity of bits of information in the periphery of central vision, thereby creating a selective filter (Broadbent, 1958; Leisman, 1975a) which emphasizes (a) the boundaries of letters and words and (b) new features. The information carried by the reflected light must be transduced by the receptors into potentials that are then transmitted through the visual system. However, as in other systems requiring transduction, there is an accompanying information loss (Leisman, 1975c).

Mackworth (1973) noted that the anticipatory brain response known as the contingent negative variation is frequently reduced or absent in children with reading impairment. The implication that follows is that the mechanism of expectancy requiring an individual to match a word pattern with a template in the first-stage processor is disrupted. In the same way, the angular position of saccades during reading is conditioned (anticipates) by the position of the preceding saccade. This is consistent with the findings noted earlier that, while normal adults demonstrate a predictable relationship between amplitude/duration and amplitude/velocity of saccades, this relationship is less marked in normal children and is still more variable in hemiplegic patients with attentional and information processing disorders.

Gaarder et al. (1964, 1966) and Leisman (1975a) have noted that the visual evoked response carries information and that the transmission of this information is phase and temporally related to the saccade. It is during the saccade, then, that visual information is transmitted to the visual cortex, which responds to the features of the visual stimuli (Gaarder, 1967; Hubel and Wiesel, 1965).

The first-stage processor then matches bits of line and edge information from the visual cortex with templates, in order to complete initial encoding. This reduces the information to a form that can be processed further. Depending on whether effective matching has occurred at this stage, a decision is then made for the regression of eye movements or for further processing. This regression occurs by influencing the eye position of subsequent saccades mediated by saccade control.

With the effective matching of patterns in the first-stage processor, corollary discharge in the motor cortex allows for the comparison of subsequent incoming activity from the visual cortex and first-stage processor. At the second-stage processor, a recognized pattern is analyzed as being similar to an existing template in memory, or forms a new pattern consisting of component items previously stored (i.e., new templates stored in memory).

Saccade control, which is integral to the model, is maintained through the fields of adversion, which are also centers for visual attention (Leisman and Schwartz, 1975). Saccades are controlled quantities and, hence, specific words are viewed by the establishment of a ratio between the amount of visual information needed and the amount of processing time needed. As we had previously noted, a controlled functional relationship exists between the amplitude of a saccade and its duration and velocity (Leisman, 1975b; Robinson, 1964; Yarbus, 1967). The fields of adversion, then, can influence the processing of visual information by influencing the amplitude of the next saccade. With high information levels to be scanned, one would expect saccades of relatively short duration and greater velocity. The system, as it relates to reading, may be stopped by head movement directing eye movement away from the page scan or by defocusing.

With the conclusion of primary processing, a decision is made for either refixation or forward scanning mediated by the saccade control system. With a decision for further scanning, "higher" processing through other sensory systems and linguistic and cognitive processes (Mackworth, 1971) will occur. If comprehension is achieved, the information is then synthesized for storage; if not, refixation occurs.

Figure 2 may suggest implicitly that the system of visual perception related to reading is like a rather simple computer that receives information, processes in various stages according to built-in programs, and finally transfers it to "higher centers" that have a one-to-one correspondence with consciousness. This, of course, is a gross oversimplification—useful in a limited context, but misleading if naïvely accepted. If we must then liken the visual system to a computer, we must imagine one in which the final processor is able to call for many different analyses or parts of the information or even for some of the original data. It uses many different complex programs in order to produce a decision that results in action. Reading is only one aspect of the activity.

One implication of general systems theory that is of importance to our discontinuous model of visual information transmission as it relates to the reading process is the concept of hierarchy or organization. Shannon and Weaver (1963) have described this concept as it relates to language. A language at its lowest level is made of a set of symbols (letters) and the size of the set (usually small) may be expressed in bits, as indicated earlier. At the next hierarchical level, the letters eventually become redundant concepts, although redundancy still exists on this level in frequently occurring words such as "the." Still higher levels include phrases, sentences, chapters, and so on.

Assuming the visual perception is a discontinuous process linked to saccadic eye movements and occurring in bursts, then these bursts may represent hierarchically higher units of visual information. It can also be seen that, over time, vision consists of a chain of these units, as reading consists of a chain of words.

IMPLICATIONS AND APPLICATIONS

The model of reading described in this chapter involves complex interactions between visual information processing and ocular-motor function. Ocular-motor deficits are not thought to be the cause of reading impairment. Rather, visual information processing is, to a certain extent, reflected in the pattern of ocular-motor activity. Thus, ocular-motor deficits may well be reflective of some central transmission-processing dysfunction. Investigations of the nature of reading and its impairment, employing ocular-motor variables, would therefore prove fruitful.

However, as one studies the reading process, one is impressed by the fact that the cognitive aspects of processing, including coding, are apparently contributed by the individual in an idiosyncratic fashion. As these processes become more complex, the contribution from within the individual, about which little is known, is greater than that which is provided by external stimulation. Therefore, studying higher-order processing is an area that is at best poorly understood. Initially, studies are required that examine the most basic components of such situations. Studies of eye movement that are reflective of higher-order processing would be of little value without attempts to physiologically differentiate brain structures activated during reading so that universals may be derived. For it is only by understanding the total process that its dysfunction may be understood and effective remediation planned. These tactics have not been effectively employed in the field of education.

One of the problems with the approach suggested is that while an experimenter could have good control over the transmission of stimulus events, it is difficult to predict the effect of such stimulation in classroom performance. This brings up a secondary problem, that of stimulus object versus the effect of the stimulus. Educational research focuses on a different class of problems from those stressed in this chapter, namely, the kind of behaviors that the subject undergoes in order to change the stimulus object into an effective stimulus. While the foci of the two approaches are different, albeit with some overlap, it is necessary to combine the two. Besides understanding the basic processes one would also need to know why there exists, for example, such phenomena as "good" readers who can read one or two paragraphs and find their eyes wandering across the page to the bottom, at which time they realize that they have not comprehended anything at all on that page. It would also be important to know, therefore, the events that control whether children translate the printed words on the page into effective stimuli.

As an example of the utility of combining the two approaches, Rothkopf (1965) had identified the process of segmentation, a phenomenon markedly noticeable in beginning readers who inflect downwards at the end of phrases. They segment strings of phrases and sentences. Further parallels can be drawn from trigram learning in that when nonsense syllables are learned in trochees[3] the stressed term can be recovered from the unstressed term within a trochee. It is possible to record eye movements during reading and infer something about the nature of the perceptual span and intervening cognitive processes. It is also possible to draw parallels between the discontinuous nature of visual perception and the discontinuities linked to saccadic eye movements. While there is no empirical evidence to draw such a conclusion, perhaps discontinuous visual reception and transmission may be related to segmentation in reading with the size of the perceptual span governing the boundaries of segmentation. As it is known that with increasing age the precision of saccades increases (Gatev, 1968; Leisman, 1975a, 1975b), it would not be difficult to connect the accuracy and amplitude of the fixation and saccade with a reduction of segmentation and an increase in fluency. Should further study indicate this to be so, reading remediation might incorporate these notions.

The area of computer-assisted instruction would be adaptable to the use of a reading model such as that presented here. One application would be to develop a data base and to design test material that would account for the size of the minimum perceptual span during a fixation while maintaining age-appropriate interest level in the content material. A

---

[3] A trochee is a metrical foot consisting of one long syllable followed by one short syllable or of one stressed syllable followed by one unstressed syllable.

second application would involve the automatic presentation of reading material for times that would account for the varying characteristics of saccadic and fixation eye movement in different groups of children. Both of these applications might be accompanied by individual–computer interaction.

Hochberg (1970) made the point that we have a vocabulary of visuomotor expectancies somewhat like the phonemes and morphemes of speech. Each fixation is checked against an inner plan or set of expectancies. The structure of visuo-motor expectancies provides the basis for selective perception of letter features in much the same way that linguistic expectancies provide the basis for the selective perception of speech. A schema of a word represents the anticipated features that would be seen if particular eye movements were made.

Neisser and Beller (1965) presented subjects with lists of nonmeaningful words that they had to scan. The subjects were required to identify the word containing some specified letter or letters, or the word from which a given letter was absent. The speed of accomplishing such a task was a function of the nature of the materials involved. For our purposes there are two related points to be made. First, the ease with which a search task can be accomplished is related to the distinctiveness of the item being searched for. Thus an angular letter in a background of round letters will be detected more quickly than would a round letter in a background of round letters. The second point derives from the fact that Neisser's observers could, with sufficient practice, detect ten different targets as rapidly as they could one target. This was interpreted as indicating that observers were processing features of letters in parallel and not in a sequential manner.

Gibson (1969) suggested that Neisser's observers may have been learning to get along with fewer features in detecting target words. Gibson's suggestion is supported by the fact that Neisser's observers made more errors with the increase in speed. This would be expected if fewer features were used to identify a target letter. What appears to be acquired in perceptual learning is a greater ability to differentiate features from the mass of stimulation impinging on the child. It is here that visual perception, feature analysis, expectancy, selective attention, and learning disabilities come together. As indicated in some of the other chapters, learning disability children demonstrate a deficit in selective attention, making them less able to formulate schema and extract significant letter and word features. This may be reflected by frequent reversals in reading and by the reduction or absence of the expectancy wave. The instructional approach, which is initially based on the training of cognitive schemas, word building, phonics, etc., might also include the training of pattern detection, employing the methods of visual psychophysics.

As selective attention for significant features must be trained, perhaps studies to determine the suprathreshold features of letters are necessary to reduce the total number of features available to the child for processing, in an attempt to reduce the confusion.

The reading model presented here also brings to light another important consideration. In children with reading difficulties, frequent reversals, transpositions, and other orientational errors of both letters and words are found. Furthermore, reading rate is impaired, at times, even into adulthood.

At least two hypotheses have been proposed to explain specific reading disorders. One view holds that the cells in the visual cortex of many of these children may lack orientational selectivity. An alternative position, which could be consistent with many of the views expressed in the other chapters, is that the visual cortical cells may overly respond to orientational differences, with the result being the spontaneous transformation of text. Both of these views have been discredited (Kolers, 1969). It has been found that with geometrically transformed text the same number and type of errors are noted. Likewise, the pattern of errors is similar to that found among normal readers, including the presentation of the linguistic features. Thus, it would seem that these difficulties must involve something other than disorder of the visual system or of impairment in the processing of language.

In summary, this chapter indicates the utility of employing basic approaches in combination with classroom studies in order to examine the role of various brain structures active during reading and other visual processing. One objective of this type of research may be to predict a child's classroom performance. Hence, further studies of ocular-motor function might be usefully directed towards educational assessment and early prediction of reading disability.

Second, the discontinuous model of vision with the discontinuities linked to saccadic eye movements suggests that visual processing is linked to saccade duration. Besides the diagnostic implications, reading remediation might incorporate these data in selecting appropriate presentation times of text. Also, data obtained through psychophysical experiments might be incorporated in the design of reading remediation material.

Finally and most importantly, this chapter presents evidence to implicate deficits in ocular-motor function, reflective of visual processing, as a component in some reading disorders. By the same token, it also indicates that specific reading disability does not involve disorders of the visual system or impairment in the processing of language as previously thought. What appears to be a strong possibility is that saccades of short duration and high velocity do not allow enough time for effective transmission with consequential effects on visual processing. This could lead to segmentation, inability to achieve fluency, transpositions, and the skipping of words, sentences, and paragraphs. Reversals and other orientational errors may result either from a deficit in orientational selectivity of visual cortical cells or from either insufficient or overstimulation of visual cortical cells.

In conclusion, the need for the development of an adequate model of reading has been stressed before reading disabilities can be understood. Furthermore, this development could be augmented with greater communication between the disciplines.

Part VI

Implications of Drug Studies for the Origins of Learning Disabilities

Drugs and Dosages: Implications for Learning Disabilities

Robert L. Sprague and Esther K. Sleator

Certain limitations and basic definitions apply to this chapter. Only psychotropic medication is considered. There are many drugs prescribed by physicians that have behavioral effects, but this paper is concerned only with those drugs that are prescribed by the physician to produce a behavioral effect rather than a biochemical or physiological one.

There is a distinct emphasis on the learning performance of the child. Because by their very nature learning disabilities are defined by the school environment, the authors strongly believe that school-oriented criteria should be used to assess therapeutic interventions for learning disabilities, especially the interventions that involve prescription of drugs; thus we emphasize learning performance. Since it is quite difficult to accurately monitor learning performance in a typical classroom, the experimenters have relied heavily on laboratory tests of learning that are firmly rooted in behavioral theory and have a broad base of empirical information.

Another school-oriented criterion is that of the social behavior of the child in the classroom as perceived and rated by his regular teacher. Although the ability of the child to perform adequately on scholastic learning tasks is separate and distinct from his social behavior toward the teacher and his peers, these two facets of the child's behavior are, nevertheless, closely related and to some extent mutually dependent on each other. Routinely throughout this series of studies the Conners' Teacher Rating Scale (Conners, 1969) has been utilized. It is a four-point scale with 39 items developed by Conners from an analysis of teachers' comments about 103 hyperactive children. Quite often a shortened version of this scale that consists of 10 items (Conners, 1970a, 1972b; Conners et al., 1972) has been utilized. We have developed normative data on these scales in our geographic area (Sprague, Christensen, and Werry, 1974) and have repeatedly found that the scale is sensitive to psychotropic drug manipulations (Sprague and Sleator, 1973; Sprague and Werry, 1974).

All of the children, ranging in age from about 6 to 12 years of age, who have participated in the series of studies we are reporting have been diagnosed as hyperactive or as minimally brain dysfunctioned (a term commonly used in the United States) using a standard procedure. The child must be rated on the Conners' Teacher Rating Scale above a mean item rating of 1.5, which is more than two standard deviations above the mean for the normal control group in our community. After passing this initial screening test, the child is evaluated with a pediatric examination, a neurological examination, receives a number of clinical laboratory tests, and a social history is obtained from the family. On the basis of all this information, the diagnosis is made. Our operational definition of learning disability is rather simple-minded, i.e., a child of normal intelligence exhibiting learning difficulties and who is academically retarded by a year or more as measured by achievement testing (Sprague, 1972).

TESTS OF COGNITIVE ABILITY

It has been repeatedly pointed out that there are insufficient empirical data in pediatric psychopharmacology to answer the major, pressing questions (Di Mascio, 1971; Sprague and Sleator, 1973; Sprague and Werry, 1974; Sroufe and Stewart, 1973) and an almost complete absence of theoretical models, especially models based upon psychological and behavioral theory (Russell, 1960). This lack of theoretical models has been aptly described:

> "What is missing from most experiments that involve the use of tranquilizers with children, and also adults for that matter, is a theoretical explanation of how or even where these drugs do what they are purported to do. The staunch advocate of tranquilizing medication is very much akin to the head of a house who fixes the family radio by shaking it vigorously" (Rosenblum, 1962, p. 651).

In our laboratory the authors have attempted to avoid the above pitfalls by utilizing measures that have been thoroughly tested by others and firmly rooted in behavioral theory. The careful, systematic empirical work and theoretical model-building of Dr. David Zeaman and Dr. Betty House, from the University of Connecticut, have had a strong impact in our laboratory. Perhaps the best statement of their position was published 12 years ago (Zeaman and House, 1963). Before their work, it was commonly assumed and generally believed that the major difficulty with the mentally retarded was their slow learning, or, in experimental terms, the longer and flatter learning curve obtained by plotting learning performance of retarded subjects against number of trials or exposures of the task to be learned. Typically this plotting was done for groups of subjects, and it was commonly interpreted that the subjects slowly, gradually, and systematically built up some kind of habit (habit strength) that eventually enabled them to give consistently correct responses on the experimental task. "The curve is gradually rising with overall negative acceleration. From this we might erroneously infer a single gradual underlying process similar to the growth of habit strength in Hull's system" (Zeaman and House, 1963, p. 160).

Zeaman and House took a new approach and plotted the learning curves of retarded children backward from the point at which the children reached a criterion of learning, and a remarkably different interpretation was possible; rather than the habit slowly building up over a number of trials, the habit (even in retarded children) developed almost instantaneously, and the major variable influencing performance was their inability to attend to or select out relevant dimensions of the objects to be discriminated. "The difference between fast and slow learning is not so much the rate at which improvement takes place once it starts, but rather the number of trials for learning to start" (Zeaman and House, 1963, p. 162). So retarded children perform more poorly in a simple discrimination task not because of their inability to learn (to associate the correct response with a certain stimulus) but to their inability to selectively concentrate or control their attention.

Another major contribution of these researchers is in the area of experimental design. In a chapter entitled "Miniature Experiments in the Discrimination Learning of Retardates," House and Zeaman (1963) enumerate the distinct advantages of using cross-over (repeated measures) design in situations where a limited number of subjects is available. It should be pointed out that the problems associated with repeated measures in learning experiments are quite similar to the potential problems of repeated measures in psychopharmacology. The basic problem of this design is that exposure to one condition in a learning study may alter the subject (his memory) in some way so that he is not the same person when exposed to a subsequent learning condition. In a similar fashion, the basic problem of repeated measures in psychopharmacology is that a person exposed to a drug in one part of a study may not be the same person because of a carry-over of an active chemical in his blood when exposed to another drug later in the experiment. It is our opinion that these carry-over problems have been given undue emphasis. It is possible to handle these difficulties in a variety of ways; e.g., statistical tests are made to ascertain whether carry-over, in fact, does occur, and if it does not, the study is conducted as planned; if it does occur, the researcher waits a sufficient amount of time to "wash out" the effect and/or the active chemical remaining in the organism. Sensitive tests for minute quantities of metabolites may be eventually developed to assess any carry-over as we have done for methylphenidate (Milberg et al., 1975).

Following the research of Zeaman and House, Scott developed a picture recognition task of short-term memory that we have repeatedly used in pediatric psychopharmacology. Scott's work is directly relevant because: (1) theoretical underpinnings of this task have been developed and (2) a large amount of empirical data has been accumulated on the task, which is necessary in making appropriate interpretations of the data derived from it. Scott describes his work as follows:

> "The general procedure we adopted is to show a child . . . a set of one or more to-be-remembered pictures. This is followed by a memory probe where a single picture is presented, identified by a bell ring. The child responds to the single probe picture by pushing one lever to indicate if the picture came from a set to be remembered or by pushing the other lever if the probe did not" (Scott, 1971, p. 91).

There are a number of features of this task that make it useful for studying cognitive performance in children. (1) It is sensitive to information load; i.e., the greater the number of stimuli in the presented matrix, the lower the accuracy on the test (probe) trial, which allows the experimenter to set appropriate levels of accuracy for widely varying intellectual levels of children. (2) After initial pretraining of a few days, accuracy of performance reaches a plateau, and there is little subsequent change over many experimental sessions, making this an ideal kind of task for repeated measures. (3) There is relatively little change within an experimental session. (4) The obtained measures of accuracy of responding and latency of responding seem to represent almost two independent measures of performance of the task, as Scott clearly indicated with his data from a matrix of intercorrelations and a factor analysis.

Because this laboratory task has been directly related to memory theory, and because there is an impressive amount of empirical data on it, we have selected and used this task in a large number of pediatric psychopharmacological investigations (Sprague and Sleator, 1973; Sprague and Werry, 1971, 1974). The task is completely automated so that there is limited opportunity for the examiner to bias the results.

A schematic of the equipment that the child sees when he participates in the laboratory learning experiment is shown in Figure 1. In the lower part of Figure 1 is a schematic of what the child sees when he sits in front of the screen. The pictures shown to the child are pictures from children's books which children enjoy viewing. Each time they give a correct

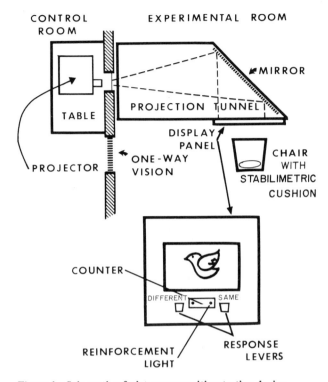

Figure 1. Schematic of picture recognition testing device.

response a green reinforcement light flashes, and the counter adds one to their total score. After the end of the session, they are taken to a small store where they can select one toy, depending upon the total score they obtained, to take home with them. The combination of interesting pictures, a reasonably brief interval of time (about 10–15 minutes), and rewards for cooperating ensures that almost all children like to participate in this task. Modular control equipment automatically programs and automatically records each trial: the number of wiggles made on the stabilimetric cushion, the latency of the response in one-tenth second from the onset of the probe slide until the child presses either the "same" or "different" key, and the trial number of the probe. All of these data are automatically printed out and punched on paper tape. The paper tape can be taken to the computing center for processing.

A similar design has been used throughout this series of studies. Each study is a within-subject or cross-over design, which means that every child participates in every dosage or drug condition. In the early part of the series, a Latin square procedure was used to balance the order of the presentation of the drug or dosage condition, but more recently order has been assigned on a random basis. Although this is not the most commonly used design in pediatric psychopharmacology, there are a number of distinct advantages (Sprague and Sleator, 1975; Sprague and Werry, 1971). Since each subject acts as his own control, typically the error variance is smaller, which means that one has a more sensitive test for drug effects if they are present. From an ethical perspective, parents are more willing to accept this kind of design because it means that their child will receive several forms of treatment during a period of time rather than being placed exclusively on a drug or on placebo for several months duration as sometimes is the case with the between-subjects design.

Once the decision is made to accept the child into the study after the extensive evaluations are completed and the parents have volunteered and signed written consent forms, very close contact is maintained with the family for the duration of the initial study, which is usually 3 or 4 months. Three or four dosage conditions are used; thus three dosages of 4 weeks duration each equal 3 months. The child's regular teacher is contacted, and she is asked to, at least weekly (sometimes even daily), complete the Conners' Abbreviated Teacher Rating Scale. The parents also fill out the same scale on a weekly basis. At the end of each dosage condition, the parent brings the child back to the laboratory for testing, for examination by the pediatrician, for interviews by the social worker, and for prescription refills.

Great care is taken to ensure that the child receives the medication as prescribed. All medication is dispensed in orange opaque capsules, thus concealing the tablets from sight and from taste. A local pharmacist places 5-mg tablets of methylphenidate and/or 5-mg placebo tablets in the capsule to make up any given dose. For a particular child, each capsule always contains the same number of tablets and is always rounded off to the nearest 2.5 mg for each mg/kg condition; i.e., if a child's highest dosage was 25 mg (five 5-mg tablets), then all the other dosages would contain five tablets with X tablets of methylphenidate and Y tablets of placebo.

Each parent is given a file box with a supply of medicine in individually dated envelopes. Parents are told that forgetting to open an envelope and giving the capsule to the child is not a catastrophe, and they are instructed to return unopened envelope(s) so that missed days can be recorded. Each parent usually returns a few unopened envelopes. Medication is always given in the morning before school by one parent.

Strict double blind procedures are always used. Only one member of the investigative team, a person who does not have direct contact with the child, knows the drug sequence code. The pediatrician can obtain this information from that team member any time that an emergency arises. It has been our experience that in times when the code has been broken by the pediatrician for what seemed an emergency, the child was on placebo more often than methylphenidate.

Although it will not be described in detail in the summary below, considerable care is given to the statistical analysis. A multivariate analysis of variance is now used to analyze the data, but during the first few years of the project, analyses of variance were used for repeated measures, since the multivariate analysis was not available. But more important than statistical analysis, in our opinion, is replication of the findings in another group of subjects at a different time (another year) or at the same time in another country (Dr. John S. Werry, Department of Psychiatry, University of Auckland, Auckland, New Zealand, collaborates with us).

REVIEW OF PSYCHOTROPIC DRUG STUDIES

Methylphenidate and Thioridazine

The first study in this series involved an investigation of the effects of methylphenidate and thioridazine in 12 boys who were attending special education classes for the emotionally disturbed (Sprague, Barnes, and Werry, 1970). They had a mean age of 7.9 years with a mean IQ of 98.6.

Both drug (methylphenidate, placebo, and thioridazine) and dosage (low and high) were manipulated. The dosages for methylphenidate were 0.25 mg/kg (low) and 0.35 mg/kg (high) and for thioridazine 0.75 mg/kg (low) and 1.00 mg/kg (high). The dosages were acute in the sense that the children only received the drug at that particular dose for one day about 1.5 hours before testing on the experimental task.

The results of the picture recognition task are shown in Figure 2. The drug significantly influenced accuracy ($F = 9.08$, df = 2/22, $p < 0.01$), but dosage did not significantly influence accuracy ($F = 1.22$, df = 1/11). Post hoc Neumann–Keuls tests indicated that methylphenidate produced significantly higher accuracy scores than either placebo or thioridazine. Thioridazine fell just short from being significantly lower than placebo at the .05 level.

This initial study encouraged us to embark upon our long series of studies because it indicated that the test of short-term memory could clearly differentiate between drugs. Dosage was not significant in this study, but it is also important to note that the absolute range of the dosages used was quite small.

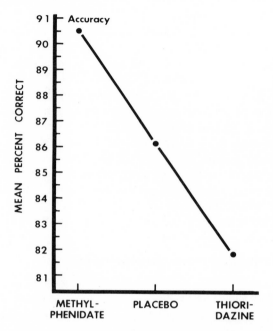

Figure 2. Mean accuracies of methylphenidate, placebo, and thioridazine.

Just as important as the significant finding on the experimental learning task was the pattern of findings obtained from observers in the classroom. Methylphenidate significantly increased attention to the task in the classroom in comparison with placebo and thioridazine, whereas thioridazine did not differ significantly from placebo.

The First Methylphenidate Dosage Manipulation

Sixteen emotionally disturbed children from special education classes received several dosage conditions of methylphenidate (no drug, placebo, 0.10, 0.20, 0.30, and 0.40 mg/kg) about 1.5 hours after ingestion in an acute study (Sprague and Werry, 1971). The subjects were randomly assigned to four orders of drug administration. An analysis of variance for dosage indicated only the large matrix size of three stimuli was significant ($F = 3.20$, df $= 5/75$, $p < 0.025$). The mean percent correct at each dosage level for the matrix with three stimuli is shown in Figure 3.

This was our first study in which we experimentally manipulated dosage of methylphenidate, and the analysis indicates a significant effect. Furthermore, the peak effect is observed at 0.3 mg/kg.

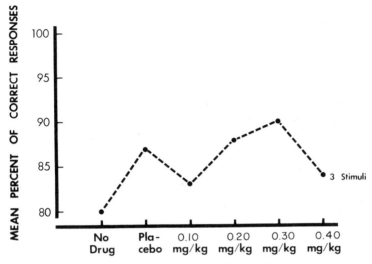

Figure 3. Methylphenidate dosage effects.

Dosage Effects on Teacher Ratings

This study involved the first attempt to ascertain the effects of dosage manipulation of methylphenidate on clinical ratings including the Conners' Teacher Rating Scale (Werry and Sprague, 1974). A total of 36 children participated in the study; 20 children with a mean age of 9.0 years participated in the study at the US (United States) laboratory, and 16 children with a mean age of 8.8 years participated in the NZ (New Zealand) laboratory. Each child was given one of four dosage levels for a total of 4 weeks each for a grand total of 16 weeks. The dosage levels were US: placebo, 0.1, 0.3, and 1.0 mg/kg and the same in NZ, except the highest dose there was 0.5 mg/kg. The Conners' Teacher Rating Scale was completed by the teacher at the end of each dosage month. The mean item rating on the Conners' Scale is shown in Figure 4. The effect of dosage was significant in the US sample (F = 8.78, df = 3/48, $p < 0.001$), in the NZ sample (F = 6.86, df = 3/45, $p < 0.001$), and, as could be expected, in the combined data from both countries (F = 14.30, df = 3/96, $p < 0.001$).

This is a difficult distinction we are asking the teachers to make; rather than rating the often obvious behavioral effects of different drugs, they are asked to rate the small behavioral effects of varying dosages of the same drug representing very small increments, 0.1 mg/kg in some instances. Again, it was clearly demonstrated that manipulation of dosage produced significant changes in ratings by teachers in two different countries. The

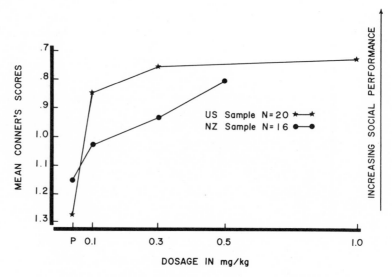

Figure 4. Methylphenidate dosage effects on teacher ratings.

other interesting aspect of this data is that the peak enhancement as seen by the teacher did not occur at 0.3 mg/kg as was observed in the previous study when the criteria were based on the laboratory learning test.

Dosage Effects on Combined Learning and Rating Measures

Although dosage had been manipulated as a variable in the previous studies, we had not used both experimental laboratory measures of learning performance and clinical measures (teacher ratings) on the same subjects at the same time. By this time in this series of studies, there was a strong hint that the different target behaviors, namely, learning performance or social performance in the classroom, produced different dose-response curves. In an attempt to ascertain whether there were two different dose-response curves and in an attempt to replicate previous data by conducting the same study in another year, a new study was conducted. A total of 23 children participated in this study. Their mean age was 7.9 years; mean IQ was 93.0. The following dosages of methylphenidate were used: placebo, 0.1, 0.3, and 0.7 mg/kg. The child received each dosage condition for a period of 4 weeks. A large number of both clinical and laboratory measures was obtained on the children, but our discussion will be limited to the data from the picture recognition task and the Conners' Teacher Rating Scale.

Results of the study are shown in Figure 5. Again, the effect of dosage on number of correct responses in the laboratory tests of learning was significant (F = 7.55, df = 3/57, $p < 0.001$) with 0.3 producing the most accurate performance. Also, dosage manipulations significantly influenced teacher ratings as measured by the Conners' Scale (F = 7.25, df = 3/57, $p < 0.001$) with the ratings continuing to improve as dosage increased as can be seen in Figure 5.

Two main points can be ascertained from this experiment. (1) Significant dose-response curves are again replicated in another population for both learning performance and teacher ratings. (2) When these two dose-response curves are combined in the same graph as was done in Figure 5, it certainly appears that the peak enhancement of performance—cognitive performance as measured by learning or social performance as measured by teacher ratings—seems to be occurring at different dosages.

Comparison of Dextroamphetamine and Methylphenidate

The procedures described above can be readily utilized if one desires to compare two or more different drugs. The clinical lore in our area states that dextroamphetamine is twice as potent as methylphenidate; conse-

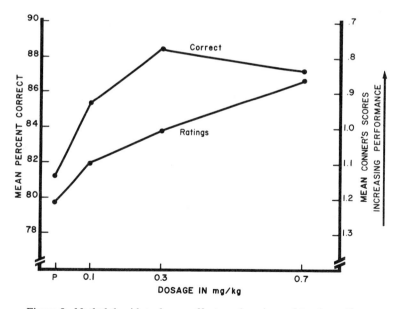

Figure 5. Methylphenidate dosage effects on learning and teacher ratings.

quently many physicians will prescribe a dosage of methylphenidate that is twice the dosage of dextroamphetamine.

Over the past three years (Sprague, 1972), data from 19 children have been collected in a study comparing these dosages: dextroamphetamine 0.1 and 0.25 mg/kg and 0.5 mg/kg of methylphenidate. The dosages were administered for 3 weeks each. Numerous clinical and laboratory measures were taken, but only the picture recognition task will be discussed. In Figure 6 the results of the study are shown. Methylphenidate at 0.5 mg/kg produces a significantly higher accuracy score ($F = 5.62$, df = 2/36, $p <$ 0.01) than either dose of dextroamphetamine.

THEORETICAL IMPLICATIONS

All of the data previously presented have shown mean or average accuracies and/or ratings over a number of different subjects. This procedure has been criticized because it is subject to errors of averaging; i.e., when the data from a number of different children are added together and divided by the number of children to obtain a mean for the group, the mean may not reflect very accurately the performance of a particular subject. This is particularly true if there are one or even a few very deviant scores on any measure. This difficult problem of how to handle averaging errors that may conceal individual differences has been well studied in the area of learning (Estes, 1960), and in fact was the basis for the use of backward learning curves refined by Zeaman and House (1963) as described above in the section on cognitive tests. Since the technique of a backward learning

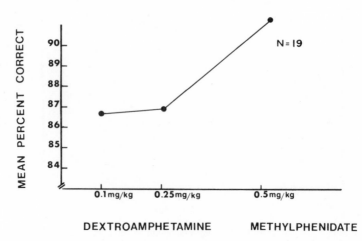

Figure 6. Comparison of dextroamphetamine and methylphenidate dosages.

curve cannot be used in this situation because we do not have a specific point at which a criterion of learning is established, we have elected to present the data from all of our dosage studies in a different manner.

Figure 7 shows the absolute number of subjects who displayed their peak performance on the picture recognition task at each dosage level (since one study had a dose of 0.15 mg/kg and 0.45 mg/kg, these two have been combined with 0.20 mg/kg and 0.40 mg/kg points). When ties in scores occurred, i.e., a subject showed the same accuracy of performance at 0.10 and 0.20 mg/kg, one-half of that subject was assigned to each dosage; in this case one-half to 0.10 and one-half to 0.20 mg/kg in counting the absolute number of subjects. The total number of subjects studied at each dosage point is indicated by the width of the bar under the curve. It is abundantly clear from Figure 7 that most of the subjects showed their peak performance at 0.30 mg/kg, although there is some variance around this median. It should be apparent from Figure 7 that there is little to substantiate the argument that our interpretation of a peak performance on a learning measure at 0.30 mg/kg of methylphenidate is due to an artifact of the averaging error.

In an attempt to summarize all of the above issues in one set of theoretical curves, we have prepared Figure 8. In Figure 8 is a set of theoretical dose-response curves for stimulant medication based primarily on the empirical data outlined above. The three dose-response curves are

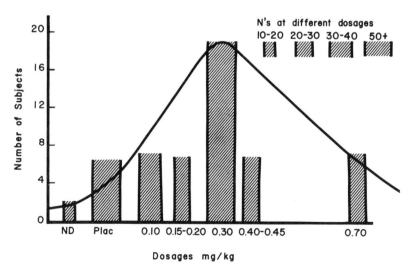

Figure 7. Numbers of subjects showing peak effect at various dosages of methylphenidate.

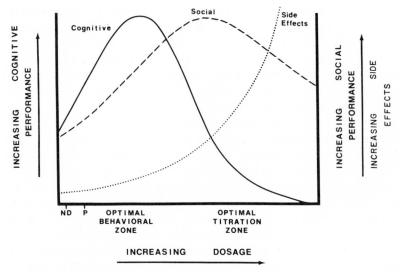

Figure 8. Theoretical dose-response curves.

generated on the basis of three different target behaviors under investigation. One target behavior is labeled cognitive performance and refers to the learning performance of children on the picture recognition task. The second curve is labeled social performance and is based primarily on data obtained from teacher ratings as given by the Conners' Teacher Rating Scale. Our laboratory has shown repeatedly that the teacher ratings show an increasing performance in ratings up to about 0.70 and 1.00 mg/kg of methylphenidate, which is a peak enhancement at a dose about two or three times the dose producing the peak enhancement of cognitive performance (Sleator and von Neumann, 1974; Sprague and Sleator, 1973). The third dose-response curve is based upon the target behavior of side effects. It is postulated that the side effects do not reach an unacceptable level until the dose is increased somewhat beyond the level of the peak enhancement of the social performance.

All of these curves have been generated by plotting either cognitive performance, social performance, or side effects on the ordinate against dosage on the abscissa. The scale of the respective ordinance has been adjusted so that the peaks of each curve would be the same height and the starting point of the cognitive and social curves would be at the same point; the starting point of the side effects curve is zero for the no-drug condition. In the case of the cognitive and social curves, an improvement in performance is seen as one moves from no drug to placebo to low dosages with the peak reached at some point and decline in performance beyond that peak, with the decline continuing below the placebo and no-drug levels. For the side effects curve, it is postulated that it starts at zero, slowly increases in a monotonic fashion as dosage increases, and reaches an unacceptable level at some point at a higher dosage than that obtained for the peak social enhancement.

These theoretical curves demonstrate three very important points: (1) There is a zone of peak enhancement based upon the dosage, whether the target behavior is cognitive performance or social performance. On either side of this zone, i.e., at the low dose and high dose ends, there is less enhancement of the performance or actual deterioration of the performance at the high dose end. (2) The zones of peak enhancement are not the same for both target behaviors. Thus, if one were to enhance the cognitive performance of a hyperactive, distractible child, one would prescribe a dose of stimulant medication that falls within the optimal cognitive performance zone (labeled optimal behavioral zone in Figure 8). But if one wanted to enhance the mental health of the child's teacher in terms of optimizing the teacher's rating of the child, which is based, we believe, largely on the child's social behavior in the classroom, one would prescribe a higher dose that falls within the optimal social performance zone (labeled optimal titration zone) in Figure 8. These two zones overlap some but definitely peak at different points. (3) If one increased the dose of medication until unacceptable side effects appeared, then reduced the medication somewhat as recommended (Klein and Davis, 1969), one would be somewhere in the area between where the side effects curve crosses the social performance curve and the peak of the social performance curve. "... The practice of increasing drug dosage until mild toxic manifestations appear and then decreasing it slightly is feasible only for some drugs and can be uncomfortable and hazardous" (Koch-Weser, 1972, p. 228). The potential hazards of titrating to side effects has been all too dramatically illustrated in pediatric psychopharmacology with one documented death with imipramine (Saraf et al., 1974).

Obviously, no researcher or practitioner is recommending doses that occasionally produce death. But that is not the point of our theoretical speculation. The point is that using high doses to produce a social effect that can be readily observed by teacher, parent, and doctor in a learning disabled child, we postulate, can and does in many cases produce deleterious effects, particularly in the area of cognitive learning, and raises some questions about cardiovascular effects (Ballard, 1975; Sprague and Boileau, 1973) and growth suppression (Safer, Allen, and Barr, 1972, 1975).

CONCLUSIONS

Several conclusions can be drawn from this series of studies. (1) Dosage is a very important variable in pediatric psychopharmacology although it is often functionally ignored. (2) Standardized dosage in the form of mg/kg is a useful index in managing psychotropic drug therapy of MBD children because meaningful dose-response curves can be generated using this index. (3) Dose-response curves differ for different target behaviors. These differences seem important both theoretically, as discussed in this chapter, and clinically in determining the cost–benefit ratio for the individual child. (4) Although the empirical data presented in this chapter are limited to stimulant medication and learning-disabled children, we believe the theoretical dose-response curves also apply to other areas of pediatric psychopharmacology such as the use of the neuroleptics for retarded children, the use of antidepressants for enuresis, etc.

Drugs to Improve Learning in Man: Implications and Neuropsychological Analysis

Stuart J. Dimond

The technology of drug use to change the nature of the mental function of man is, of course, no new phenomenon. Each society seems to have possessed its own psychoactive substances affecting the mind to make the human condition more tolerable and to provide the taker with a sense of well-being. Drug use and abuse extends to those areas of man's conscious activity where perceptions are radically changed and feelings of well-being heightened or depressed. The myth often encountered is that feelings of well-being carry with them an increased capacity for performance and an extension of human abilities. The reverse is unfortunately usually the case.

Perhaps the most profound technological revolution in the use of drugs was introduced by the medical profession itself, where drugs are used for the chemical therapy of emotional and psychological disturbance (Lasagna, 1969). The medical use of tranquilizers, stimulants, or antidepressants can be pointed to, not only as a twentieth century miracle of a kind, but also as one of the major ways in which the individual's mental state and behavior are brought under control. The exercise of pharmacological control over behavior is something that causes the alleviation of much suffering; however, society must consider the broader implications which such controls may have. How far and to what limits should the conduct and mental make-up of man be changed as the result of pharmacological control? Where do the limits of individual freedom lie in this respect?

"INTELLECTUAL DRUGS"

What has happened in the treatment of emotional disorders could well be followed by similar developments in the treatment of intellectual disorders

367

(Conners, 1971b). The concern in the present chapter is with yet another facet of drug use which the author believes will prove to be important in the clinical treatment of learning disorders as well as having ramifications extending well beyond this particular clinical application. Such new developments concern the production of "intellectual drugs," i.e., substances that affect the animal and the human brain and cause improvement of intellectual functions. It will be noted that we are not concerned with drugs that produce a deluded sense of well-being, but with substances that induce a real and genuine change in intellectual performance that can be assessed in measurable terms. We ask whether it is possible to improve man's capacity for mental action through the use of drugs? Is it possible to change the individual into a more effective and efficient being? The capacity to modify human conduct and mental action is a powerful and important tool in medical practice. It would be foolish, however, to pretend that the possibilities inherent in the use of the so-called intellectual drugs have as yet been anywhere near fully attained, or that anything more than a beginning has been made in tackling the important questions of their use. Research to date indicates that drugs can be used to improve selected intellectual functions of the brain. Our task now is to consider the significance of this in practical terms and in terms of the neuropsychological organization of the brain. In this interest, research has been carried out with an "intellectual drug" called Piracetam (UCB 6215) 2 Pyrrolidone acetamide. In animals such drugs have been shown to facilitate the transfer of information from one side of the brain to the other as measured by the transcallosal response (Guirgea, 1971, 1973), implying that each half of the brain functions as a recipient of a stronger signal from its opposite partner. The brain, in other words, seems to be superconnected.

The purpose of the present investigation was to see if these same results applied to man and if superconnection could be established in the human brain to study what the effect of this would be upon the action of the human intellect. The original aims of this study and the results in relation to them are something to which we can return in a later section. In fact, the original aims proved to be secondary in importance to other results of our study which suggested that there is chemical facilitation of specific intellectual functions.

EXPERIMENTAL PROCEDURE

The subjects were 16 students from University College, Cardiff, 12 male and 4 female. All were in their second and third year of the psychology course. The subjects were medically examined before and after the study, and all were healthy, well-adjusted individuals at the top level of their health. The daily dosage was 3 X 4 capsules at 400 mg Piracetam, or the equivalent quantity of placebo.

As a test of verbal learning the subjects were presented with a series of words presented as stimuli upon a memory drum. There were nine words of six or seven letters each, matched for frequency of use. The results of this study are seen in Figure 1. The first points of the graph indicate the performance points before any drugs were given. After the first week of drug taking, the subjects were tested again; the drug is known to be relatively slow acting and it is noteworthy here that there are no significant differences between drug group and controls. After 14 days of drug administration, however, there is a major difference and the drug group shows a large and significant improvement over the controls ($p < 0.01$) (Dimond, 1975a). This improvement occurred not only when direct recall

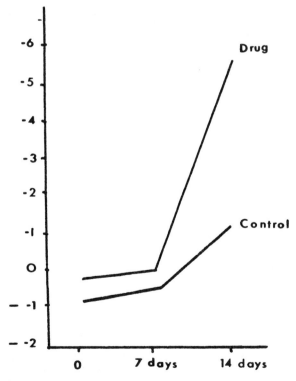

Figure 1. Effects of Piracetam on verbal learning, when direct recall of learned material was required.

was required of that which had been learned, but also when a delay was introduced during which time the subjects were prevented from rehearsal by counting backwards in steps of three starting from a given number (Figure 2). As a contrast to this improvement in the powers of verbal memory, studies of other types of learning were also conducted. For example, pursuit rotor studies were done in which the individual was required to follow a moving point with a stylus. On these, no effect of the drug was found. Tests were also carried out to determine if the individuals themselves were aware of the fact that they were taking the drug, and these in fact also proved to be negative. We had shown that the drug acts to improve verbal learning in normal man, and thus it is possible to enhance learning in the verbal sphere, but not learning of other types.

RESULTS AND CONCLUSIONS

It appears that Piracetam is a substance that acts upon the higher levels of the brain. The point to be emphasized in the drug studies that we have conducted to date is the potential that exists for the possible treatment of disorders in which the intellectual functions are seriously depleted. The action of the brain is clearly modifiable only within specific limits, and no drug can institute functions in a brain in which the basic machinery for such functions is largely absent, or seriously damaged as the result of injury or invading pathology. At the same time, if a substance can be shown to facilitate one or more aspects of intellectual function, then it is a reasonable hope that such a substance will seek employment for this purpose in clinical practice and be used widely to assist individuals towards normal levels of intelligent behavior. In this respect we could see an extension of the use of drugs in psychiatric practice to include, not only the control of emotional or disturbed conduct, but also the amelioration of disorders occurring in the intellectual sphere.

Insofar as learning disorders lie at the root of psychiatric disturbance or contribute substantially to it, it may be important to facilitate new learning—new modes of behavior—to establish an adequate rehabilitation. The question must be asked as to whether drugs that operate in the intellectual sphere could be expected to contribute significantly toward this?

It is clear that if the present finding is confirmed and the results verified across a wide range of abilities and conditions of man, then there is potential in the use of substances of this kind to improve learning under a variety of conditions. Substances that act specifically upon verbal learning could prove to be important where the facility for language has been

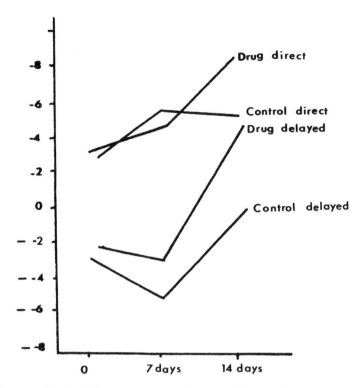

Figure 2. Effects of Piracetam on verbal learning, when a delay was introduced.

disturbed by damage to the brain, minimal brain damage, or birth trauma and so on. If, for example, a person with language difficulties could be provided with only a 10% increase in the capacity for verbal learning, and the indications are for a higher level than that, then such an increase could well give the necessary impetus for him to begin functioning at a higher level and could perhaps bring many individuals within the range of normal function. We do not as yet have the appropriate clinical evidence to present on these particular points, but the research is in progress.

Because the intellectual abilities of man follow a developmental course, and nowhere is this more apparent than in the case of language development, the successful completion of the early stages is a prerequisite for progress to the more advanced stages. It may be, therefore, that if we wish to talk about an increased potential for verbal learning, the indications are for use with the younger rather than with the older patient: pediatric rather than geriatric use. However, be that as it may, animal and human research indicates that intellectual performance can be improved through the use of drugs.

In the future, drugs that affect the intellect will not, of necessity, act in this same restricted range of mental ability. Indeed, different acting substances can be envisaged whose seat of mental action is quite different from substances studied to date.

TARGET FUNCTIONS OF DRUGS

The fact that it is possible to improve the facility for verbal learning without at the same time improving other facets of the individual's performance testifies to a certain uniqueness of the language mechanism and functions as they are organized within the brain. The stage has been reached, the author believes, where it is possible to talk about drugs, not only as having a target site within the brain upon which they act, but also within the constellation of intellectual abilities—a target function. That is, we are witness to the development of drugs that have a unique action on certain neuropsychological abilities and in this sense the manipulation of the level of that ability can be regarded as the target for the drug. A given neuropsychological organization does not exist separately and apart from the brain in which it resides. In talking about an ability as a target for a drug we are almost certainly talking also about a brain system that is particularly sensitive to that drug. With respect to verbal learning, there is good reason to support such a claim. Investigations have been undertaken of the functioning of local regions of the brain through substances that act to suppress function for relatively short periods of time. Procaine and sodium amytal can be quoted as a case in point. Speech is disturbed in a typically aphasic manner if the substance enters the hemisphere containing the speech system. This method has, of course, been used to determine the lateralization of the speech system and to demonstrate its location in the left hemisphere in the large majority of cases (Milner, 1974).

In the studies reported here there is clear evidence that the left hemisphere plays a special role in the production of the speech functions. The drug that promotes verbal learning and increases the capacity for language registration in all probability has its action upon a cerebral system of the left hemisphere and thus could be described in short as a left-hemisphere drug.

This location of verbal learning is also suggested by other studies. In tests of learning performance of the normal individual in which paired associate learning was performed by normal subjects on material flashed by means of a divided visual field to the right or the left hemisphere

(Dimond and Beaumont, 1973), there is a marked superiority when the information is flashed to the left hemisphere, which holds true for both right and left handers (Dimond and Beaumont, 1973). Apperceptive learning, however, showed no direct relationship to hemisphere specialization (Dimond and Beaumont, 1974a) but paired associate learning of an effortful kind showed a distinct relationship to and association with the functions of the left hemisphere.

Further evidence of a similar nature comes from our studies in which contact lenses were employed to restrict visual information to the left or right visual field and hence to a specific cerebral hemisphere. The contact lenses were occluded apart from a clear strip placed towards the periphery. In addition the subjects wore spectacles, again occluded apart from a small strip that allowed vision displaced away from the center. To see, the subject had to align the visual strip of the contact lens with that on the spectacle, and visual information was in this way directed away from central vision (Dimond et al., 1975). It was found that with left hemisphere vision the subjects could type, copy, and read written language at a quick pace. With vision to the right hemisphere there was a gross deterioration and the subjects reached a state approaching word blindness: although in fact simple words could be effectively read slowly, the reading of complex material was painstaking, ineffective, and extremely slow. There is strong evidence, therefore, not only for left hemisphere specialization for verbal registration but also of verbal learning. We carried out studies of pursuit rotor performance similar to those conducted while the subjects were on the drug, but here we found no superiority of one hemisphere over the other. The evidence therefore is strong that facility for verbal registration and verbal learning, as opposed to other types of learning, is something associated with the left half of the brain, and that a drug which works to improve verbal registration and verbal learning could be presumed to do so by virtue of its actions upon the brain systems of the left hemisphere. The concept of a left hemisphere drug is something that the author believes to be new. Insofar as functions are known to be lateralized, the fact that a drug works upon them should, however, occasion no unnecessary surprise. If, as we suggest, that there are intellectual drugs that have as their target of action the abilities and functions of the left hemisphere, then the question naturally arises as to whether there may be other drugs which, although different in kind, have a corresponding action upon the workings of the right hemisphere. In other words are there right hemisphere and left hemisphere drugs? Harshman et al. (1974) report that habitual marijuana users under the influence of the drug show deterioration in verbal and analytic capacities and at the same time show a remarkable improvement in certain aspects of visuo-spatial function concerned with Gestalt perception. The suggestion is that this drug acts in a fairly specific way to improve the functions of the right hemisphere following the report that Gestalt-type perceptions are related to the functioning of the right hemisphere in split-brain man (Levy, Trevarthen, and Sperry, 1972). This research is quoted to illustrate the principle that facilitation of the lateralized functions not only of the left but also the right hemisphere by drugs indicates the possibility and that there can be an induced increase in right hemisphere participation in cognitive-perceptual activities as a result. In facilitating the Gestalt-like perception, marijuana also diminishes verbal and analytic ability and it has a serious debilitating influence that counterbalances any potential benefits it may have. Piracetam, in contrast, appears to be a relatively harmless substance capable of enhancing some aspects of mental ability without seriously debilitating others.

SUPERCONNECTION OF THE BRAIN

As has been stated, the original intention behind our studies was to employ Piracetam in studies of interhemispheric transfer in man. It had been discovered that Piracetam facilitated the transcallosal potential in the animal brain. In other words the drug appeared to interconnect the two halves of the brain in a powerful physiological way, and the questions of interest were: What implications would such superconnections have for man? What behavioral effects would follow as a consequence of the possession of a brain more powerfully connected than is usually the case? Subjects were tested for intermanual transfer by means of a task in which the individual was required to learn the location of objects in a series of boxes with one hand, and then demonstrate the position of those objects with the opposite hand (Dimond et al., 1975). The results of this study were equivocal and did not fully support the view of an increased transfer of information across the corpus callosum.

Evidence of superconnection of the brain as the result of drug administration was obtained, however, on a dichotic listening task in which two verbal messages were played simultaneously on a stereo tape recorder through headphones, one message to the right and the other to the left ear. At the conclusion the subject was asked to write down as many words as he could remember beginning with the ear indicated by the experimenter. The notable effect of the drug was that it increases verbal capacity and subjects are able to increase their ability to report the words of the task, whereas the controls are not. The increase of verbal capacity is of the order of 15% or more (Figure 3).

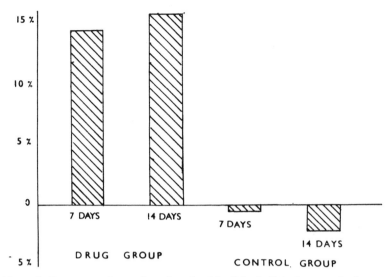

Figure 3. Percentage change from base level in dichotic listening score in drug group and control.

That there is a major improvement in the capacity of the brain to handle verbal information is clear from this result. This change in capacity can in large measure be attributed to increased response to information presented to the left ear (Figure 4). Piracetam is known to facilitate interhemispheric transfer in animals and we can interpret the drug as having much the same effect in man. If information arriving in the left ear via the right hemisphere is to be linked to speech in the left hemisphere, then that information must be transmitted across the interhemispheric commissures. The drug acting upon the corpus callosum would therefore promote the connection of the right hemsiphere message to the speech system and thus act to enhance performance of the left ear.

If, as is suggested, the brain is superconnected by the drug, then we have to ask what the effects of this are in terms of psychological function. There appears to be no effect upon the individual's awareness of himself or his abilities. There may be an effect upon general intelligence, as has been noted in cases of organic deterioration. What does seem well established is that there is an increase in the capacity for learning and that the registration of verbal information is increased.

The exact relationship that the capacity for increased learning holds to the superconnection of the brain is unclear. The two indeed may be unrelated. It is tempting, however, to speculate that superconnection not only leads to increased registration but also plays a part in integrating the

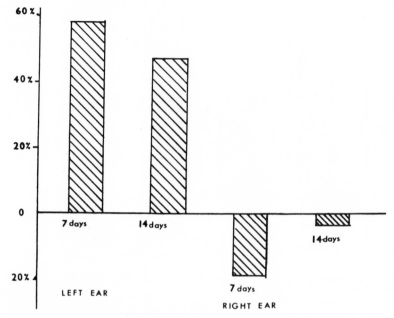

Figure 4. Percentage change from base level in the drug group analyzed by left and right ear scores.

different brain areas, thus leading to a greater capacity for learning (Guirgea, 1971, 1973).

Whatever the explanation, the result raises the prospect that it is possible through reversible chemical means to superconnect the brain by virtue of the action that substances have upon the corpus callosum.

It should be stated that the effective limits of the action of the so-called intellectual drugs are at present unknown. An effect has been demonstrated upon verbal capacity and upon verbal learning, but how far these improvements extend into the fabric of man's ability and into the realms of higher mental action is unclear. Is the power of the thought process increased? Is there an increase in the creative use of language? Is man capable of acting more intelligently as the result of facilitation of verbal learning? These are the relevant questions, the answers to which will determine the course of future development of the intellectual drugs.

IMPROVEMENT OF INTELLECTUAL ABILITIES

The question of the improvement of intellectual abilities, irrespective of any pathology that may exist in the brain, is worthy of consideration. Is it possible that there could be an evolution of intellectual abilities in an upward direction as a consequence of the fact that man is able to take a chemical step to enhance the working of his own brain? Improvement of intellectual abilities can occur, as, for example, fortuitiously where there is an increase in the nutritional well-being of a population which results in additional intellectual power and vigor being available to the community. Drugs that can act to enhance the range and capacity of human abilities might be expected to have such an effect, and contribute to change and evolution of the intellectual functions of man. These are speculations, however, beyond the scope of our present subject.

DRUGS AND LEARNING DISORDERS

Disorders of learning take many forms. They occur throughout the range of intellectual functions and ages, and can potentially affect any of the abilities with which the individual is endowed. One of the tasks that lie ahead is to produce an adequate taxonomy that sufficiently characterizes the nature and the varieties of learning disorders which are seen. In some respect, extended categorization is necessary; many disorders of social conduct not usually classified as learning disorders at all could well be the result of disorder characterized by an inability to learn the ordinary codes of social conduct. Examples could be multiplied, and no doubt many of the categories of clinical disorder have at their base fundamental disorders of the learning process. Failure to assimilate scholastic material should not be regarded as the only area where true and fundamental disorders of learning are to be encountered.

The author is concerned, however, with the educational process and the failure to show adequate learning, despite the presence of normal intellectual potential. Insofar as this can be described as a disorder that has its roots in the neurological action of the brain, disorders represent failures at the highest level of intellectual function. Drugs that act upon learning and in particular verbal learning could have considerable potential in precisely this area because this is their medium. The need is clearly indicated for studies in the effect of the intellectual drugs upon learning disorders to assess the potential benefits they might bring. The types of learning we discuss are those that demand an engagement over a protracted period of time. It must not be assumed that what we see over a brief period of time necessarily characterizes the individual's mental function over the longer span. The theatre that is lively, entertaining, and filled with people on one occasion cannot be presumed to be always so. I believe that the phenomenon of the learning disorders does not, by and large, involve disorders of immediate perception; neither are intelligence, personality, or general behavior necessarily affected. It is perfectly possible that individuals who respond adequately and at the top level of efficiency are sometimes capable of doing this only for a relatively brief period of time (Dimond, 1975a). In such cases the appearance given is often that of relative normality on neurological and perhaps psychological examination, and yet gross depletion can at the same time coexist. Even the Intelligence Quotient as measured by conventional tests need reveal no abnormality. This may not occasion undue surprise because patients, following the removal of the frontal lobes (Hebb and Penfield, 1940), or of a complete hemisphere after cerebral hemispherectomy, have been shown to be remarkably unchanged in the level of their IQ performance.

What is suggested is that there is no relevant disorder of immediate perception, but that there is a change of performance that comes about as the result of a failure to maintain performance for any length of time (Douglas, 1972). It would certainly seem that the capacity to persevere in tasks that are mentally taxing remains low. There are gaps or holes in the individual's mental life that make it difficult and at times impossible to sustain mental action over those periods of time essential for concentrated mental effort to take place. Such a disorder need not be accompanied by neurological abnormality, nor need it be diagnosed as the result of tradi- tional psychological testing procedures. The author believes that here we are dealing with discontinuities of mental action, and it is this that sets the individual at such a severe disadvantage.

That there are problems of lateral balance has been revealed in a number of studies of the learning disorders (Bakker, 1970a; Cernáček et al., 1974; Olson, 1974; Witelson et al., 1972). It is likely that the difficulties associated with cerebral dominance arise because of a disorder in those systems that sort out the rival claims of the competing systems of the brain. In the absence of suitable schema, gaps of consciousness appear because the individual is no longer able to regulate claims and order them in a smooth flowing sequence. If, as the author believes, there is a disorder of this sort, then demands are made at those times in the learning program at which there is no consciousness to be allocated and to support them.

The view can also be expressed that while inadequacies in the working machinery at each side of the brain may not be expected to figure prominently in the individual's difficulties, a failure to regulate the activi- ties at each side will nonetheless result in disorders of sustained action because a functioning hemisphere could well be disengaged at those times at which appropriate function was demanded of it. It need hardly be said that a consideration of the problems of lateral balance is particularly apposite in light of the results of our drug study which suggest that the level at which learning is conducted is dependent in some way upon the extended system by which the two halves of the brain are integrated and linked together. If learning can be improved as the result of the modification of this system then the implication is that learning disorders in their classic form can result from anomalies or distortions of this system. The present results therefore implicate that part of the consciousness mechanism which bears a responsibility for the integration of activity between the cerebral hemispheres, as well as the special language mechanisms of the left hemisphere, and attribute learning disability to disorders of this system.

Whatever the theoretical speculations, it may yet be that an ounce of drug rather than the collected weight of libraries of theoretical speculation will prove itself the most effective agent for therapy of learning disorders. Certainly a productive course of action has opened up over the years to be pursued in research programs. The effects of those substances that have been shown and will be shown to have the power to promote the action of the intellect must be studied in order that the effects and in particular the benefits that these substances have for therapy can be established for mankind.

ACKNOWLEDGMENTS

E.Y.M. Brouwers received a grant from the European program for training in brain and behavior research. We are grateful to Dr. Bodger, Student Health Centre, University College, Cardiff for his help in conducting the medical examination of our subjects.

Effects of Stimulant Drug Therapy on Learning Behaviors in Hyperactive/MBD Children

H. John van Duyne

The guiding a priori assumption, for many clinicians, is that stimulant drug therapy affects the hyperactive child's general cognitive style but not specific learning behaviors (Gollin and Moody, 1973). Although there is still no specific agreement on a definition of hyperactivity, a general behavioral description has emerged. The most common behavioral disorders are high distractibility, short attention span, impulsiveness, over-activity, restlessness, and disruptiveness (Campbell, Douglas, and Morgenstern, 1971; Clements and Peter, 1962; Paine, 1962; Sykes et al., 1971; Wender, 1971; Werry, Weiss, and Douglas, 1964). Both clinical findings and partially controlled experimental results have led to the conclusion that stimulant drugs, especially methylphenidate, are particularly useful in treating behavioral disorders of hyperactivity in children (Campbell, Douglas, and Morgenstern, 1971; Cohen, Douglas, and Morgenstern, 1969; Conners, 1970b; Conners, Eisenberg, and Sharpe, 1964; Knights and Hinton, 1969; Sprague, Barnes, and Werry, 1970; Werry, 1970). Specifically, methylphenidate is reported to increase attention span, decrease restlessness and inappropriate behaviors and reduce impulsiveness. Investigators have also indicated that intelligence as measured by a standard IQ test is increased, especially performance IQ; and that visual-motor skills are improved. The general conclusion has been that learning can be faciliated by the effects of stimulant drug therapy that lead to increased attention span, reduction of impulsiveness, and improvements in perception.

While research has shown that methylphenidate has had a positive therapeutic effect on various behavior dysfunctions of hyperactive children, this effect has been examined in relation to fairly specific and isolated tasks and tests. What is needed at the present time is research on complex behaviors that approximate the actual demands placed upon the child in a school setting. More specifically, research should be directed toward an examination of the effects of stimulant drug therapy in conjunction with specific training procedures used to teach complex learning tasks which satisfy school demands. The research question is, Is there a complex interaction between drug condition, training procedures, and complex behaviors? The aim of this chapter is to illustrate the need to investigate these three variables simultaneously. In order to accomplish this aim, the chapter will first discuss a complex behavior related to a critical period of language and thought development in early childhood, and then summarize preliminary research dealing with training normal and hyperactive children in this behavior.

COMPLEX BEHAVIOR

One complex behavior that is essential to achievement and social-emotional adjustment in school, especially the primary grades, is the ability to control behavior by means of verbal instructions alone (Wepman, 1960). Luria has stated that "the accomplishment of a perceptual-motor activity based on verbal instructions can be regarded as the core of higher mental functions which regulate complex behavior" (1961, p. 52). This particular behavior is referred to as the regulatory function of language and/or verbal control of nonverbal behavior.

A basic perceptual-motor task that has been used in studying the regulatory function of language in normal and abnormal adults and children was pressing a key to a red light and not to a green light (Luria, 1961, 1966a; van Duyne, 1972). There are numerous variations of this task, such as pressing a key twice to a red light and not pressing the key when a green light comes on or pressing a square key to a blue light and a round key to a yellow light. The procedure is that subjects are given verbal instructions alone, and then asked to perform the task.

Findings based upon clinical observations and controlled research indicated that the ability to perform the verbal control of nonverbal behavior tasks is related to the regulation of motor activity, attention processes, and especially to orienting reactions (Luria, 1961, 1966a, 1973; Luria and Homskaya, 1970). Luria has concluded that the inability to regulate motor activity by means of verbal instructions is due to a dysfunction of the frontal lobe system. Recent research on the development of the regulatory function of language has suggested that the ability of 4 or 5 year olds to perform a verbal control of nonverbal behavior task is, also, related to cross-modality transfer of information, i.e., the ability to encode auditory verbal information and then recode the information into visual-motor connections (van Duyne, 1975). It was also found that, among 4 and 5 year olds, verbal control of behavior is related to performance IQ, fine and gross motor skills, and auditory and visual perception (van Duyne, 1975).

PRELIMINARY RESEARCH

During the research on the development of regulatory function of language, the question arose as to whether or not 4 year olds could be trained to perform a complex verbal control task. Zaporozhets (1961, 1969; Zaporozhets and Elkonin, 1971) has shown in his research that 4 year olds learn perceptual-motor skills more readily by means of passive movement (tactual-kinesthetic-visual) training than by imitation (visual) training. Learning is greatly improved if verbal instructions accompany the perceptual-motor training. Four year olds were given either passive movement training with accompanying verbal instructions or imitation training with accompanying verbal instruction, and then performed the verbal control of behavior task. Following this initial training and task, the children were given verbal instructions, without any further training, which reversed the color-geometric form association required on the initial task, and were then asked to perform the task. The ability to reverse the color-form associations and perform the task by means of verbal instructions alone was used as a measure of verbal control of nonverbal behavior.

The results indicated that both training procedures enabled 4 year olds to perform the verbal control task (van Duyne, 1971). Passive movement training was a little better procedure than imitation on the initial tasks. The children were able to reverse the color-form association formed by the initial training by means of verbal instructions alone. The scoring for both the initial and reversal conditions of the task was the number of correct responses out of 38 events. The criterion mean scores are given in Table 1.

Since Zaporozhet's methods were successful in training verbal control of behavior with normal children, the question arose as to how successful would the methods be with atypical children (Zaporozhets, 1961; Zaporozhets and Elkonin, 1971). The research question was whether there is a significant interaction between drug condition and training methods in hyperactive 4 year olds related to verbal control of nonverbal behavior? Zara (1973) replicated the aforementioned research. Her sample consisted of three groups of hyperactive 4 year olds: (1) those receiving methylphenidate, (2) those receiving a placebo (off drugs 72 hours), and (3) those who had never had stimulant drugs. The children never on stimulant drugs were those who were newly diagnosed or whose parents refused to have

Table 1. Mean Criterion Scores

	Task Conditions	
Treatments	Initial	Reversal
1. Passive	32.33	34.67
2. Imitation	28.00	31.00

their child receive stimulant drugs. Again, the scoring was based on the number of correct responses out of 38 events.

The results indicated two significant interactions: The subjects receiving methylphenidate and those who never received drug therapy contributed to the three-way interaction (see Figure 1). The drug group receiving imitation training performed better on the initial task than those receiving passive movement training; however, on the reversal task those who originally received passive movement training performed better than those who originally received imitation training. For the children who never received drug therapy, the opposite was true. They performed better on the initial task when they received passive movement training and better on the reversal task when the original training was imitation. The placebo group did better on both initial and reversal tasks when they received passive movement training. In brief, within this study, performance on the initial and reversal task was dependent upon the type of training and drug condition.

The two-way interaction collapsed across training procedures, indicating that children who never received stimulant drug therapy were able to reverse the perceptual-motor associations formed by initial training and task by means of verbal instructions (positive transfer). On the other hand, both the drug and the placebo group were unable to reverse the originally formed perceptual-motor associations by means of verbal instructions and exhibited a significant decrement in performance on the reversal task (negative transfer). Although there was no difference between drug condition groups on the performance of the initial task, the children who were never on drugs performed better on the reversal task than those who were receiving drug therapy and those who were receiving placebos.

CONCLUSION

The three-way interaction illustrates a need to investigate the effects of stimulant drug therapy in relation to specific educational procedures on

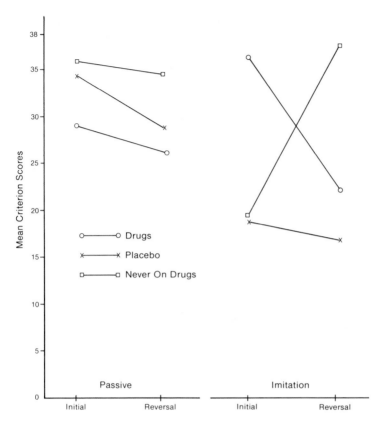

Figure 1. Graph showing the relationship between initial and reversal tasks for initial training using passive movements and imitation with hyperactive children receiving stimulant drug therapy, placebo, and those who never received drug therapy related to verbal control of nonverbal behavior.

various complex behaviors and learning tasks. The statement that stimulant drug therapy remediates various behavioral disorders, and therefore facilitates learning, is perhaps too general for the present stage of the research. This statement may prove to be true. However, it may also be true that, depending upon the type of task and complex behaviors that are required in school, drug therapy may have a differential effect in conjunction with various training procedures upon learning. In brief, the positive effects of stimulant drug therapy may be related to task-specific learning behaviors rather than general cognitive style.

Research is already tending to indicate that there are differential effects of stimulant drug therapy depending upon the behavioral characteristics of the hyperactive child (Conners, 1972a; Millichap, 1974). It may well be that a viable theory of stimulant drug therapy will evolve out of the investigation of a four-way interaction between drug conditions, subject variables, training methods, and learning tasks. The investigation of such a four-way interaction would require interdisciplinary experimental research among medicine, psychology, and education.

The two-way interaction raises a number of interesting research questions. First, if one decides that the group which never received drug therapy is not equivalent to the drug and placebo groups, then how is it that those children receiving methylphenidate behaved similarly to children off the drug for 72 hours? Was it that the drug does not effect verbal control of nonverbal behavior? Or, if one decides the groups were equivalent, then why is it that children off the drug for 72 hours behave similarly to those receiving drug therapy? Is there a latency effect? Is it somehow related to state-dependent learning? If so, how is it related? Whatever specific questions the two-way interaction may raise, it does reinforce the need to investigate the effects of stimulant drug therapy on task specific learning behaviors.

During learning, the normal subject attempts to regulate his cognitive behavior to meet the demands of the specific task. On the other hand, the training method is adjusted to interact positively with cognitive functions in order to facilitate learning of the specific task. In the case of hyperactive children, stimulant drugs may or may not facilitate the regulation of various cognitive functions in relation to the demands of a learning task. On complicated learning tasks, training methods may interact either negatively or positively with drug-related cognitive functions related to the demands of a specific learning task. Therefore, learning a specific complex behavior may be either enhanced or hindered depending upon the unique interaction among drug condition, training method, and specific demands of the task.

Simple laboratory tasks, such as "go, no go" procedures, used to measure the effects of drugs on excitatory and inhibitory processes require little or no training in comparison to reading, mathematics, etc., nor do they require higher mental functioning. Therefore, the problem of drug effects on the complicated interaction among cognitive functions, training methods, and task demands has not been adequately studied. A mature theory of drug therapy must deal with this problem if it is going to be truly useful to the classroom teacher.

One other research problem that needs to be investigated is neurological maturation in both its physiological and biochemical aspects. Wender (this volume) has hypothesized that the drugs most effective in treating

MBD children are those that operate by changing the function of "the biogenic amines." Brante (1949) and Folch-Pi (1955) have found that chemical composition of the human cerebral cortex changes as a function of chronological age. Anokhin (1964) has shown that the effects of various drugs on cerebral function change as a function of ontogenetic development. It is, therefore, highly possible that the effects of stimulant drugs on hyperactive—MBD children may change as a function of neurological maturation. Particular drugs may have quite different effects at different chronological ages.

In summary, there is a need to investigate the a priori assumption that stimulant drug therapy affects the hyperactive MBD child's general cognitive style. Preliminary research indicated a need to study the effects of stimulant drugs in relation to types of training methods and the differing cognitive demands of various learning tasks. Furthermore, since the findings related to 4 year olds did not fully support the positive effects of stimulant drugs, it was suggested that the effects of drugs should be studied in conjunction with neurological maturation.

Learning Disabilities and Stimulant Drugs in Children: Theoretical Implications

C. Keith Conners

Stimulant drugs have been used in the treatment of the hyperkinetic behavior syndrome since the 1930s. The very first observations of Charles Bradley not only noted the increased vigor and drive of the children, but also changes in their academic work and school attitude, with changes in arithmetic being particularly noticeable. (This latter effect may have simply been due to the ease of monitoring the number of problems solved, or it may have reflected the benefits in a task especially sensitive to attention and concentration.)

In any case as stimulant drugs such as benzedrine, dexedrine, and Ritalin became more widely used for hyperkinetic disorders, more frequent reference to the associated learning disorders was made by the treating physicians, and it was generally assumed that changes in academic performance were secondary to the improved behavior. Few have suggested that the sympathomimetic amines influence learning in a direct fashion, although experiments with animals indicate that enhancement of avoidance learning occurs when injections are given in the consolidation phase of learning (Doty and Doty, 1966; McGaugh, 1966). As noted by Barondes and Cohen (1968), "Cognitive information, an intact capacity for cerebral protein synthesis, and an appropriate degree of 'arousal' are all apparently necessary for the establishment of long-term memory."

The generally accepted position, however, is that analeptic drugs improve performance rather than learning, and have their effects largely on simple rather than complex performances (Laties and Weiss, 1967). In animals amphetamine-like stimulants increase arousal and excitability, wakefulness, activity drive, responses to stimuli, active escape-avoidance, fighting behavior and inhibitory control (Irwin, 1968).

The author's concern is whether such stimulants exert effects on learning and behavior that have relevance to the problems of children with learning disabilities. The answer to this question depends upon knowledge (a) of the physiological and behavioral effects of the drugs, and (b) of the physiological and behavioral features of the learning-disabled child. Both problems are complex and require empirical data that are presently limited in scope. However, I believe that enough such data are available to suggest important theoretical links between the mode of action of stimulant drugs and the nature of some learning defects in children.

First, we should clarify the relationship between the clinical group in which stimulants have been studied, and the population of children known as learning disabled. As is well known, the stimulants have been primarily employed in the treatment of the hyperkinetic behavior syndrome, although earlier work in child psychiatry had suggested that the treatment was also useful in psychoneurotic and psychopathic disorders (Bender and Cottington, 1942), sexual preoccupations (Fish, 1960), and postencephalitic behavior disorders (Levy, 1966). Nevertheless, clinical practice has established that it is the hyperkinetic child, first and foremost, who shows the most profound behavioral, cognitive, and academic responses to amphetamine-like drugs. Defects in impulse control and motility are among the cardinal traits of this loosely defined syndrome, and, as originally defined by Laufer (1967), the syndrome is one of several variations or symptom pictures that are the final result of an organically based deviation of function and the way the child adapts to and compensates for this deviation.

This syndrome frequently overlaps with syndromes whose primary defects are in the neuromotor area (cerebral palsy), the neurosensory area (central blindness, deafness, anesthesia), consciousness (epilepsy), communication (dysphasias, aphasias), intelligence (retardation), object relations (psychoses of childhood), and finally in areas of perception, association, conceptualization, and expression (learning disabilities) (Laufer, 1967). These syndromes may vary in severity from mild to gross and frequently overlap with one another. They are best conceived of as flexible class names of related phenomena rather than fixed classes with specific differentiae. To think of a class of "hyperkinetic" children, and a separate class of children with "specific learning disabilities," is an heuristic device, not a factual account of stable relationships. We are dealing, then, with complexly defined and overlapping aspects of cerebral function. Our own approach, like that of Wender, is to consider hyperkinesis and learning disability as partially overlapping entities that are subsets of a larger class of syndromes of cerebral dysfunction. Such a concept is heuristically useful because it directs attention to certain clinical manifestations, forms of treatment, and research questions.

Not all hyperkinetic children suffer from learning disabilities, and in our experience a clinic population will show about 50% of the children referred for hyperkinesis also have specific learning disabilities. This means that generally learning-disabled children without hyperkinesis will not receive treatment with stimulant drugs, and any generalizations about the effects of the drugs are limited to the larger class of hyperkinetics rather than the nonhyperkinetic learning-disabled children. However, it is of interest to note that a recent study by Gittelman-Klein and Klein (1975) found that methylphenidate significantly improved a number of psychometric tests, and seemed to specifically enhance visual-motor function in learning-disabled children who were not hyperkinetic, though verbal functions were not affected in the 12-week trial.

Because hyperkinesis and learning disabilities are not synonymous concepts, it is not necessarily true that one can generalize from the effects of stimulants in the former group to those in the latter; and it is not necessary that theoretical explanations in hyperkinetics elucidate processes involved in learning disabilities. However, it is our belief that there are in fact a number of points at which the two classes of behavior share common processes. If we are to have a unified theory of behavioral dysfunction in children, some attempt at extrapolating the results from drug studies to general features of cognitive and behavioral development, including learning and its disorders, must take place. As the great French physiologist Claude Bernard once remarked, drugs are an "exquisite scalpel" for dissecting the functions of the mind and the body. Drugs are basically a form of chemical alteration of the nervous system, and, insofar as the latter is itself a delicately arranged electrochemical system, we stand to learn from our knowledge of drug–brain interactions about all of human behavior.

Our own experiments have been guided to some extent by the familiar information-processing model of behavior (Broadbent, 1958; Chalfant and Scheffelin, 1969). We can ask what the effects of stimulant drugs are on processes of orientation and discrimination, selection, storage, retrieval, and output. In addition, we know that the information-processing system is interrelated with systems regulating mood, arousal, and general inhibition, and there are also general "stylistic" features (e.g., "impulsivity") that may be considered as either derivatives of the other processes, or limiting factors of a different kind. In any case, we can ask where in the process of information handling the stimulants work, and how the effects are related to the clinically important changes in behavior. Let us begin with the latter question, since historically the interest in stimulants in children has been focused on the effects upon "hyperactive" behavior.

STIMULANT EFFECTS ON MOTOR BEHAVIOR

At first glance, it would seem to be a truism that the stimulants "reduce hyperactive behavior." But as the author has pointed out elsewhere (Conners, 1971b), the evidence shows that gross expenditure of motor energy is not always or even mostly reduced by stimulants in hyperactive children; in fact, motor behavior itself is complex, being both situationally and response specific. We have suggested that it is the goal-directed or task-specific nature of activity that is primarily affected by the stimulants, and, depending upon task demands, the overall level of activity will be either increased or decreased, depending upon which is more appropriate. For example, in a learning situation, the presence of overflow motor activity or excessive restlessness is inimical to the task demands in most instances, thus explaining the usual reduction of motor activity in such situations (e.g., Sprague et al., 1970; Werry, 1968). In free field activity the drugs may produce an increase in activity (Millichap and Boldrey, 1967). Using a Luria-type tremorgraph, we did not find a reduction in synkinetic movements in hyperkinetic children, either when they were doing a discrimination task (Conners, 1966) or a learning task (Conners and Eisenberg, 1963).

On the other hand, a number of studies have shown that the stimulants lead to more controlled motor behavior in tasks such as motor steadiness testing (Epstein et al., 1968; Knights and Hinton, 1969) where a premium is placed on volitional control over motor response. It is precisely these voluntary movements that are less controlled in hyperkinetic children as compared with neurotic children, as we were able to show in a study examining habituation of voluntary and involuntary startle responses (Conners and Greenfeld, 1966). Dr. van Duyne's results in his chapter may also reflect a similar difference in drug effects due to task specific requirements.

The findings of Gittelman-Klein and Klein (1975) mentioned earlier are important in showing that the stimulants produce changes in cognitive function even when activity level is not the source of impairment. Dr. Sprague's elegant studies of dosage effects may also be interpreted as demonstrating a dissociation between the cognitive and the behavioral effects of stimulant drugs. A simple interpretation that is parsimonious would be that the level of inhibition required for alteration of cognitive (especially attentional) behaviors is less than that required for overt (behavioral) motor inhibition, and the corresponding dosages required are lower in the former than in the latter case.

ORIENTING AND HABITUATION

Evidence from GSR studies of orienting and habituation are contradictory with respect to the question of whether hyperkinetic children habituate more rapidly or more slowly than normals (Rugel and Rosenthal, 1974). However, our previous studies have shown that the effect of dextroamphetamine is to produce more rapid habituation in hyperkinetic children, but relatively little effect on the orienting reaction to novel stimuli (Conners and Rothschild, 1973). In a recent study, conducted by Dr. Eric Taylor in my laboratory (Conners, 1975), we examined habituation responses to auditory stimuli for both finger pulse volume (using photoplethysmography) and GSR. Hyperkinetic children were compared with matched normals, and for both measures there was a clear and significant slower rate of habituation in the hyperkinetic children, once the clinically anxious children were excluded from the sample. This heterogeneity of a putatively "hyperkinetic" group is an important source of variance in all such studies and is usually ignored. When this anxiety-free sample was examined with respect to abnormality of birth history and degree of CNS dysfunction as measured by a special neurological examination, there was a clear relationship: the more neurologically abnormal and suspect the history, the slower the rate of habituation.

After undergoing the habituation trials, the subjects in this experiment were given five high and five low tones, one of which was designated as the positive tone to which they would push a key, and one a negative tone to which they would withold a response. The ten tones were presented in random order at 15-second intervals. The results are shown in Figure 1.

The hyperkinetic children showed very little difference between autonomic responses to the positive and negative stimuli, whereas the normal controls have dramatically larger responses when a positive stimulus occurs. If anything, the hyperkinetics tend to show more arousal when the negative stimulus occurs, as though the process of inhibiting the response required more effort or arousal than making a response.

Although resting autonomic levels are not notably different in the patient and normal groups, both the rate of habituation and the active response to a simple task reveal large and striking differences. Moreover, the more positive the neurological background findings, the less arousal response is noted. Indeed, there is no overlap between the clearly abnormal patients and their matched controls in terms of autonomic responsiveness once we eliminate those patients whose clinical behavior is described by the psychiatrist as anxiety-related.

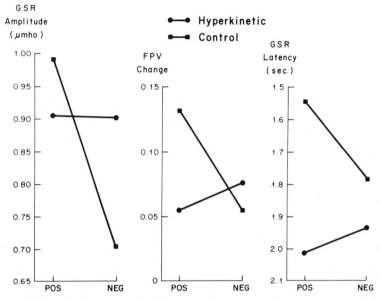

Figure 1. GSR and FPV changes in hyperkinetics and controls in response to positive and negative stimuli. A negative stimulus requires withholding response, a positive stimulus requires a key press.

AROUSAL AND SELECTIVE ATTENTION

The findings just described are compatible with the recent studies of Satterfield and co-workers. They were able to show the following: although skin conductance in hyperkinetic children was higher than normal controls, those hyperkinetics with the most behavioral pathology had the lowest skin conductance, and skin conductance was negatively correlated with response to stimulant medication. In other words, those children who were most likely to benefit from stimulants were the least aroused autonomically (Satterfield et al., 1974). The hypothesis that hyperkinetics are hypo-aroused has an appealing simplicity: it explains the apparent paradox of stimulant improvement of overactive children as a function of increasing their arousal levels to a point where optimal perform-ance can occur. The familiar inverted-U hypothesis relating performance to arousal is invoked as a basis for the apparent paradoxical calming effect of stimulants.

However, an alternative explanation is possible. As noted, much of the impulsivity of the hyperkinetic appears to reflect a primary defect in inhibition or, at a cognitive level, a defect in selective attention. It is true that in order for a child to selectively attend he must have the appropriate degree of cortical and autonomic alertness. But the latter does not guarantee the ability to actively and voluntarily inhibit either conflicting information (distractibility) or impulsive actions.

Experimentally it is difficult to dissociate selective attention from tonic arousal. Porges (unpublished), working in Sprague's laboratory, has reported that hyperkinetics are characterized by directional heart rate changes to stimulation that are associated with active voluntary attention when under the influence of methylphenidate. That is, the pattern of a decrease in heart rate variability, decrease in heart rate, and respiration slowing usually associated with active voluntary attention, became more apparent when the hyperkinetics were treated with a stimulant. Such changes may occur even when the subject is tonically aroused in a task situation.

In one of our studies we sought to demonstrate a separation of arousal and attentional effects by cortical evoked potentials. Subjects were given two conditions: in one condition they heard high and low clicks, with flashes interspersed. They were to press a key when they heard the low click. In the other situation they saw bright and dim flashes, with clicks interspersed, and they were to press the key when they saw the dim flash. Thus, attention was manipulated by having them give a motor response to either the auditory or visual modality, but one modality was stimulating them when they were attending to the other modality. Auditory and visual evoked potentials were measured in this situation for both the bright flashes and high clicks. These measures were taken prior to drug or placebo treatment and while the subjects were on drug or placebo. Figure 2 shows the effect of two stimulants (pemoline and dextroamphetamine) on the amplitude changes in visual evoked potentials. Relative to placebo, both active drugs increase the evoked response amplitudes under relevant (attending) conditions, while pemoline (Cylert) actually decreases amplitudes under nonattending (irrelevant) stimulus conditions. The point to be made here is that general arousal effects are separated from selective attention effects. The results can be interpreted as showing that dexedrine increases arousal under both conditions, while Cylert increases arousal under attending conditions only. In previous studies we had found very little effect of drugs upon auditory or visual evoked potential amplitudes, and only when attention is active do the drugs augment the effect of stimulation.

This point can be made more persuasively by another experiment involving evoked potentials. In this study (Conners, 1973a) use was made of recording from a single site: the vertex. In fact, we were interested in

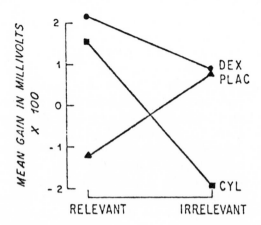

Figure 2. Changes in evoked potential under two conditions of attention in response to Cylert, dexedrine, and placebo.

recording what is known as the "vertex potential," a large evoked response component of polysensory origin that generally shows its maximum amplitude at the vertex. Either auditory or visual stimulation will evoke a component at about 180 msec in children which may be measured in several cortical areas, but which is largest at the vertex. The idea in this study was to deliver both types of stimuli, auditory and visual, at the same time. Since the subject can attend only to one stimulus at a time, the one he attends to should evoke a larger response. Because we can deliver three types of stimuli—auditory, visual, and combined—the subject may attend to either auditory or visual stimuli when presented singly, but can only attend to one of the stimuli when they occur jointly. Thus the singly presented stimuli are control or comparison stimuli that we may use to compare with the combined stimuli. In addition, we may say that since the three types of stimuli are randomly interspersed, any effects of stimulant drugs on arousal levels must apply to all three types of stimuli, but in the combined stimulus situation selective attention will be operative. If the subject randomly switches attention to the single stimuli, attending and nonattending effects will cancel out.

Figure 3 shows the combined, auditory, and visual evoked responses of a subject, in which it may be noted that the combined effect is largely coincident with the visual evoked response, while there is very little effect on the auditory stimulus. Figure 4 on the other hand shows a contrasting result from another subject in which the auditory stimulus appears to be coincident with the combined response. Apparently, then, these two subjects were attending to the visual and auditory dimensions, respec-

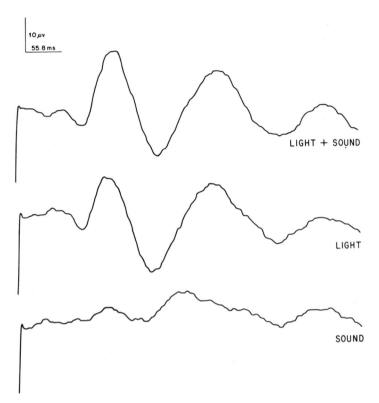

Figure 3. Visual, auditory, and combined AV evoked potentials showing one subject's tendency to attend to the visual dimension.

tively; and when they received the combined stimuli, their evoked response reflected primarily that modality they were attending to. Not all subjects show this phenomenon, of course, although in every subject the combined response is larger in amplitude than either modality taken separately.

What are the effects of stimulants on this situation? If our hypothesis is correct, then we should predict that the drugs will enhance the amplitude of response to the combined stimuli, since the subject will always attend to one or the other of the modalities at that time. The drugs should not, however, affect the single stimulus amplitudes since attention will be randomly deployed and should cancel out over a series of trials. The results are shown in Figure 5, where it may be seen that the prediction is confirmed in this study with 18 hyperkinetic children. Thus, even though

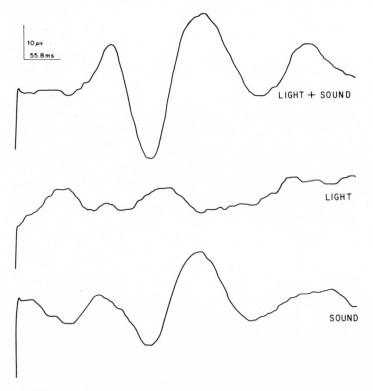

Figure 4. Visual, auditory, and combined AV evoked potentials, showing a subject's tendency to attend to the auditory dimension.

the drugs did not affect the single stimuli, they increased the overall amplitude of the combined response, an effect clearly supporting the hypothesis that the drugs have their main effect on selective attention, not on general arousal level.

EFFECTS OF STIMULANTS ON MEMORY

Careful studies by Sprague and his colleagues have effectively ruled out the possibility that stimulants enhance memory or promote state-dependent learning (Aman and Sprague, 1974); and effects of the drugs on paired associate learning (Conners, Eisenberg, and Sharpe, 1964) and discrimination learning (Sprague, Barnes, and Werry, 1970), though significant, are almost certainly due to drug effects on selective attention rather than learning or memory processes per se. The author has reported elsewhere (Conners, 1972a) that multiple regression analysis shows that a variety of

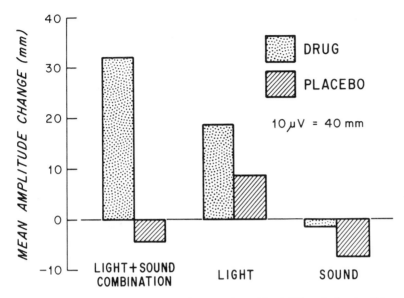

Figure 5. Group changes in visual, auditory, and combined AV evoked potentials as a function of stimulant drug treatment. Changes in the combined stimuli are significant ($p < 0.05$), but drug–placebo differences for separately presented visual or auditory stimuli are nonsignificant.

improvements on tests of visual and auditory perception, discrimination, and learning are largely attributable to attentional factors rather than specific improvements in those functions.

INTERHEMISPHERIC FUNCTION AND DRUGS

Dr. Dimond (this volume) has suggested that psychotropic drugs may differentially affect function in the two cerebral hemispheres. One question to be asked of studies in which improvement occurs in response to drug treatment is whether the improvement in function results from some general alerting or arousing effect, and whether such an effect is simply more apparent in one type of measure than another, e.g., because of differential sensitivity of testing methods for the functions of the two hemispheres, or because only functions related to one hemisphere are sampled. It would have been more persuasive to be able to show that the drug improved verbal but did not improve nonverbal tests, at least as far as the interesting possibility of "hemisphere-specific" drug action is concerned.

In our own studies of hyperkinetic children, the author has found, as mentioned above, considerable evidence to suggest that the stimulant drugs both increase arousal and selective attention. In addition, we have reported (Conners, 1972a) that the stimulants will alter cortical evoked potentials differentially in the two hemispheres, although the effects are of small magnitude. Nevertheless, for caffeine, methylphenidate, and pemoline there is evidence to suggest an alteration in the direction of greater evoked responses in left parietal areas (Conners, 1975).

On the other hand, if subjects are divided into subgroups according to whether their psychological tests show defects in attentional, verbal, or spatial functions, the improvements from stimulant treatment tend to occur in the area of dysfunction. In other words, the drugs appear to remedy defects, rather than improving all functions equally (Conners, 1973a). Another way of looking at this issue is to assume that if stimulants enhance some central attentional or inhibitory system, such a benefit would show up most prominently on a relative basis, in functions most impaired; a defect in visual spatial perception might be partially compensated by greater available selectivity or inhibition in those cortical areas responsible for the defect.

SUMMARY AND CONCLUSIONS

Our review of work with stimulant drugs has been selective and somewhat biased toward those questions that the author has been interested in over the years. A complete review of the evidence from the perspective of alternative explanations might arrive at somewhat different conclusions, but our impression from knowledge of the literature is that:

1. Stimulants produce a variety of changes in behavior, cognition, and perceptual-motor functions.
2. Different stimulants do not necessarily produce the same effects, although generally there are few differences in behavioral, academic, or other measures.
3. Processes involving active inhibition, or voluntary control, are responsible for most of the changes produced by these drugs.
4. Changes in academic function, including changes in spelling, arithmetic, handwriting, and reading, occur whether or not the children are hyperactive, but only for certain children whose learning deficiencies are secondary to defects in active voluntary attention or impulsivity.

The basic implications of the reviewed data with respect to learning disabilities, then, would be that:

1. Certain learning disorders are due to impairments of selective attention or inhibition.

2. Stimulant drugs will be useful in those children whose learning disabilities stem from these defects, but not from defects in memory, basic learning processes (including discrimination and rote learning).

Basically then, inattentive, distractible, and impulsive children who fail certain academic functions despite adequate general intelligence may have secondary learning disabilities that improve with stimulant drug treatment. Other forms of learning disability, e.g., specific dyslexia, are unlikely to show much change except insofar as the drugs simply increase general alertness in bored or fatigued children. The drug literature, we feel, clearly shows the highly important role of central inhibitory mechanisms in certain forms of learning disability.

Part VII

Research Strategies and Models for Learning Disabilities

Evaluation of Two Models of Reading Disability

Donald G. Doehring

The theoretical rationale for two studies of reading problems will be discussed in this chapter. The first began about 15 years ago and the second began four years ago and is not yet completed. At the time of planning these studies the excellent analyses of models of reading disability by Applebee (1971), Guthrie (1973), and Wiener and Cromer (1967) were not available. Applebee and Wiener and Cromer each present six models for conceptualizing reading disability, ranging from a simple model in which reading disability is a unitary disorder resulting from a single antecedent condition to models involving more than one type of reading disability and more than one antecedent condition, with complex inter-relationships among both types of factors. Guthrie contents himself with two categories of models, an Assembly Model, which proposes reading to be an assembly of independent components, and a System Model, which views reading as a system of interdependent components.

An after-the-fact consideration of these possible functional relation-ships between reading disability and antecedent conditions has led me to a more explicit, systematic formulation of the models on which my research was based. I strongly recommend these papers and any others of this type that may appear to anyone who plans to do research on reading disability. The following discussion will attempt to indicate some of the ways in which such theoretical analyses can broaden our perspective regarding reading and learning problems and their relation to brain functioning.

I became interested in studying reading disability while working at Indiana University with Ralph Reitan and Hallgrim Kløve, to whom I am indebted for the neuropsychological model that has served as the basis for my research on reading disability. At that time Reitan had just formulated his method for estimating the location, extent, and type of cerebral lesions in individual patients on the basis of characteristic

The ongoing research reported here is supported by Grants 604-7-858 from the Canadian Department of National Health and Welfare and MA-1652 from the Medical Research Council of Canada.

patterns of impairment on a standard battery of neuropsychological tests (Reitan, 1959). This predictive method can be said to bear some relation to a model of reading disability designated by Wiener and Cromer (1967) as Model 5, which states in part that different forms of reading difficulty may be associated with different syndromes of development cerebral deficit. Since Reitan based his predictions upon relative rather than absolute levels of test performance, his method is also somewhat analogous to Applebee's Model 5, where a reading disorder is determined by relative rather than absolute deficits of underlying abilities (e.g., Reitan's patients with left hemisphere dysfunction would be expected to exhibit deficient verbal abilities relative to their nonverbal abilities and also relative to their presumed level of functioning prior to brain injury) rather than in terms of absolute performance levels.

The remarkably high accuracy of prediction of the location, type, and size of brain lesions provided by Reitan's empirical neuropsychological model led Kløve to speculate that children classified as having specific reading disability might show a definite pattern of neuropsychological impairment similar to that of adults with certain types of left-hemisphere lesions. Preliminary examination of a number of individual profiles that Kløve (1963) had collected suggested that this might indeed be the case. Such a hypothesis was in agreement with some of the earliest workers in this area, who had surmised that "developmental dyslexia" was the result of defective development of the left angular gyrus [see Benton (1975) for a recent historical review].

These considerations led me to carry out, in collaboration with Reitan, Kløve, and A. L. Drew, a quantitative assessment of the neuropsychological test profiles of children classified as having reading disability in comparison with those of normal readers. A carefully selected group of boys aged 10 through 14, two or more years retarded in the oral reading of single words but "otherwise normal," was matched in Performance IQ and other relevant variables with a group of normal readers. The research was, if anything, implicitly based upon reading disability models 1 of Wiener and Cromer and of Applebee in a sense that one form of reading deficit might be associated with a particular pattern of relative strengths and weaknesses on over 100 measures of perceptual, motor, cognitive, and verbal abilities, and this pattern might be similar to that seen in adults with left-hemisphere lesions in the general area of the angular gyrus.

The findings of this study (Doehring, 1968) were somewhat paradoxical. The reading disability model was not appropriate. Clear patterns of deficit similar to those of adults with left-hemisphere lesions did not unequivocally emerge either from statistical comparisons of the experimental and control groups or from evaluation of individual test profiles. The deficit actually encompassed a wide range of visual and verbal skills that would presumably be subserved by a large area of the brain, and some of the deficits that might be expected to occur in association with dysfunction in the area of the left angular gyrus, such as directional confusion, were much less marked than the more general visual-verbal deficits.

However, the results of multiple regression analyses did indicate that reading disability was most highly correlated with visual and verbal tasks that required sequential processing. Kinsbourne and Warrington (1963a) had also reported a relationship between sequential ordering difficulty and a particular form of reading disability, as have a number of subsequent investigators (cf. Bakker, 1970b; Corkin, 1974), and other writers have formulated more general hypotheses concerning sequential processes in relation to cerebral functioning (cf. Cutting, 1974; Das, Kirby, and Jarman, 1975).

If sequencing problems constituted the single underlying basis of all forms of reading disability, Wiener and Cromer's Model 1, which states that reading difficulty "is a class with a single member, this member having a single radical cause" (p. 631) and would be confirmed. I share the skepticism of Applebee, Guthrie, and Wiener and Cromer and many others regarding the plausibility of such a simple model. It is possible that some sort of sequencing difficulty may be basic to one particular type of reading problem. This would, then, conform to Wiener and Cromer's Model 5, which states that reading difficulty "is a class with several members, each member having a single, unique cause" (p. 633). However, the author's previous study did not constitute a rigorous test of this model.

Before passing on to the theoretical considerations of my second study, one might speculate parenthetically that a narrower pattern of deficit could have occurred in the first study if selection criteria had been even more stringent than they were. For example, other investigators might have ruled out any children with a history indicating the possibility of organic pathology, in accordance with Critchley's (1964) strict definition of specific developmental dyslexia. This did not seem necessary in my study, since I was looking for patterns analogous to those of adult brain-damaged patients, but somewhat different selection criteria would probably be used if another study of this type were carried out.

After several years of fruitlessly attempting to derive a "pure" test of sequencing ability (Doehring and Libman, 1974), I decided instead to try to design some research that could lead more directly to useful remedial procedures. The first step was to evaluate the previous design.

One aspect of concern was the possible artificiality introduced by the selective criteria for defining reading disability, which can lead to an unwarranted assumption of homogeneity within the restricted population of disabled readers under study. Applebee contends that specific reading disability must simply be defined as a residual disorder, that part of reading retardation which we have not yet been able to explain, with no implications of unity or specificity until it can be given the kind of rigorous definition necessary to qualify it as a medical syndrome. However, one can, as suggested by Otfried Spreen (1970), be concerned with a very narrowly defined population of specific developmental dyslexia if the purpose is to seek out a rigorous definition of such a syndrome rather than making a prior assumption regarding the existence of a unitary syndrome.

The second aspect of the previous study that concerned me was the use of a single criterion of reading retardation—the accuracy of orally read single words—with the implication that reading acquisition is a unitary process. The preponderance of informed opinion seems to favor the view that reading acquisition involves a number of component skills (cf. Carroll, 1970; Gibson, 1971). If more than one reading skill were measured, more than one form of reading disability might emerge, as has indeed been described by a number of writers (cf. Boder, 1973; Marshall and Newcombe, 1973).

The theoretical model underlying the present research was in part a reaction against the previous model's implications that reading disability is a homogeneous disorder and that reading is a unitary process. The present model postulates that reading acquisition is a complex process involving a number of component skills, and that different forms of reading disability may be associated with different patterns of deficiency in the component skills. Before discussing the potential shortcomings of this model, I will describe progress to date in trying to determine the number and type of different patterns of reading skill impairment that might be found among children with reading problems.

It was first necessary to make a guess as to the identity and the mode of acquisition of the component reading skills. The guess was based upon the views of Gibson (1971), Smith (1971), and La Berge and Samuels (1974). The resulting working model of reading acquisition postulates the acquisition of separate skills for processing letters, letter patterns or syllables, words, and syntactically—semantically related groups of words. At some or all of these levels, separate skills may be acquired for direct processing from print to meaning and for indirect processing via spoken representation. For skills to become functional they must be overlearned to the point where they are rapid and automatic, a process that takes place over a number of years.

Thus, a series of tests was devised that were intended to reflect the acquisition of these rapid reading skills, relying heavily on the 1885 findings of Cattell (Poffenberger, 1947). Speed of letter, syllable, and word reading was assessed by visual scanning, visual matching to a visual sample, visual matching to an auditory sample, and oral reading tasks, with phrase and sentence skills assessed in terms of oral reading only. These tests were given to about 150 children with reading problems, including those associated with hearing, language, and learning disorders, and also to 150 normal readers in all primary and secondary grades.

The results for normal readers (Doehring, 1976) suggest that children begin to acquire skills for the rapid processing of letters, syllables, words, and sentences as early as the first year of reading instruction; that these skills are acquired, usually at different rates, over a number of years; and that skills involving mediation through the speech system play a more prominent part during the early stages of reading acquisition.

The trends for normal readers were sufficiently consistent that we hoped to find characteristic reading skill profiles among the children with reading problems that would serve to define different forms of reading deficit, perhaps at the levels of letter, syllable, and word or phrase processing, or involving auditory-visual association. Thus far, inspection of individual profiles plotted in terms of percentiles derived from the normal readers has not revealed sets of characteristic profiles in children classified as having reading or learning problems, but there is some indication of a specific pattern of letter and word-reading deficit in a group carefully selected by Trites (this volume) to fit a particular criterion of reading disability. Perhaps the paradoxical findings of my first study can be put together with those of the present study to define a form of reading disability in which a sequencing problem is associated with a specific pattern of reading subskill deficit, thus providing partial support for Wiener and Cromer's Model 5.

Before any definite conclusions are drawn regarding the presence or absence of characteristic reading skill profiles, however, one must apply more sophisticated methods of profile analysis, such as those suggested by Knights (1973a). This could involve the factor analysis of reading skills, followed by some form of cluster analysis of the resulting factor scores. Unfortunately, cluster analyses involve subjective decisions that can yield clusters of characteristic profiles even with random data (Applebee, 1971). Applebee suggests that some external criterion may be necessary to define the clusters that appear.

The difficulty of establishing characteristic profiles on the basis of cluster analysis illustrates one of the problems with my present model of reading disability. Although the sampling of a set of different reading skills is a vast improvement over the use of a single measure of reading skill, the types of nonreading measures usually obtained in reading disability studies may also be needed to provide external criteria for clusters of abnormal profiles of reading skill. Without such external criteria the present model is incomplete, since it states, in Wiener and Cromer's terms, that reading difficulty is a class with several members, but it does not specify the antecedent conditions for each member.

There are at least three other difficulties with the present model. First, the results for normal readers revealed differences between component reading skills in terms of differences in their course of acquisition, thus arguing against the possibility that reading acquisition involves a unitary process. However, the skills may be interdependent, thus conforming to the System Model of Guthrie, as contrasted with his Assembly Model, wherein the component skills are independent. If the component reading skills are interdependent, especially during reading acquisition, a deficiency in one or two skills could rapidly lead to a general retardation in all reading skills. This might also be predicted by Wiener and Cromer's final model, Model 6, in which reading acquisition is characterized as involving the development of an ordinal series of interdependent skills. Interestingly enough, however, Guthrie found that his System Model was appropriate for normal readers, whose reading subskills were interdependent, but his Assembly Model was more appropriate for a group with reading disability, whose subskills tended to be independent. This suggested to him that reading disability might actually entail the lack of a normal amount of positive transfer among reading skills. The implicit assumption of my model was that reading skills would be relatively independent for both normal and retarded readers.

Second, reading skill impairment may vary as a function of the stage of development of the perceptual, cognitive, and language skills that presumably underlie the various reading skills. Thus, differences in the pattern of reading skill impairment could result from maturation as well as from the stable influences of different patterns of cerebral dysfunction. This, of course, is exactly what would be predicted by the theory of Satz and his associates (Satz and Sparrow, 1970; Satz and Van Nostrand, 1973) that developmental dyslexia is the result of a lag in the maturation of the left hemisphere which differentially delays the development of perceptual, cognitive, and language skills as a function of their ontogenetic sequence of development. This sohpisticated theory appears to conform to Wiener and Cromer's Model 6, as well as Guthrie's System Model, but there does not seem to be general agreement about the transitory nature of patterns. For example, Satz and Sparrow cite a study by Reed (1967) as demonstrating different patterns of impairment at ages 6 and 10, whereas Applebee cites another study of Reed (1968a) as providing evidence of remarkably stable patterns of impairment in first- and fourth-grade poor readers. In a still later study (Reed, 1970), Reed himself found that a particular pattern of deficit may be an artifact of the criteria used to select groups of poor readers. The longitudinal research of Satz and his associates is shedding further light on these important issues.

The third and final problem, as pointed out by Wiener and Cromer, is that a focus on the components of reading acquisition skills may leave out the end product, reading for some purpose (Gibson, 1972). Some of the component skills may not be needed at all during many forms of skilled reading. In this sense a model in which reading is viewed as a more unitary process involving comprehension might be considered more appropriate for some studies.

Obviously, the model that was formulated for the second study, although an improvement in some ways on the first model, is not without its problems. These problems will be dealt with by assessing nonreading abilities in addition to reading skills, keeping careful track of the age of our subjects, estimating the degree of interdependence of reading skills in normal readers and retarded readers, and thinking of ways to assess more directly the silent reading skills that are the end product of reading acquisition. Since the ideal study that would fully incorporate all these features is beyond our present capacities, one must make the best possible compromises. Our theoretical models must in turn reflect these practical compromises (Hebb, 1974).

The ultimate model or models of reading disability could turn out to be impossibly complex. As Applebee points out, the only sensible approach is to start with the simplest reasonable explanation before moving on to more complex models, keeping in mind that the very simplest models do not seem to fit the problems of reading disability.

I hope that, by reporting these limited experiences with theoretical models of reading disability, readers will be encouraged to peruse my short list of model analyzers (Applebee, 1971; Guthrie, 1973; Wiener and Cromer, 1967), if they have not already done so, and to search out others. Classifications of theoretical models tend to be annoyingly abstruse with respect to the terms in which they are stated, but surprisingly simplistic with respect to the frameworks of explanation that they provide. However, careful study of existing classifications should probably be mandatory for the serious worker, and may prove especially useful if done before rather than after research has irrevocably begun.

Perceptual and Cognitive Factors as Determinants of Learning Disabilities: A Review Chapter with Special Emphasis on Attentional Factors

Virginia I. Douglas

Although I have been working and teaching in the area of "learning disorders" for some time, I have never found a satisfactory definition for the term. To me, it simply means that a child of apparently normal intelligence and opportunity is having trouble learning at school and the cause does not appear to be emotional. Implicit in this definition is the probability that there are many different kinds of learning disability with, presumably, many different causes. Indeed, Dr. Doehring's chapter reminds us that, in the single area of reading disability, one must consider complex models involving many kinds of reading disorder and complex interrelationships among many kinds of causal factors. More important, the chapters by Nelson, Tallal, and Shankweiler demonstrate that we finally are developing the expertise necessary to define and measure specific types of learning and reading disabilities. Surely, therefore, it is time to stop lumping all kinds of learning problems together to form groups of children labeled "learning disabled." Time also has come for journal editors to turn down, automatically, all articles dealing with undifferentiated samples of "learning disabled" children.

To complicate matters further, we have at least two other terms, "minimal brain dysfunction" and "hyperactive syndrome," which we tend to confuse with the "learning disability" label. Indeed, sometimes it seems that the three terms are being used almost interchangeably. Unfortunately, however, like "learning disability," these terms communicate very little about either the cause of a particular child's disorder or possible

413

approaches to treatment. I have suggested previously (Douglas, 1976) that a possible reason for the confusion among these terms is that the three syndromes often share a common constellation of disabilities that include the inability to sustain attention and to keep impulsive responding under control (Douglas, 1972). Usually the syndrome also includes an excessive level of activity, but this is not always so; almost invariably the child will be performing poorly in school. Thus, the ideal neuropsychological theory would have to account for this constellation of symptoms.

I would suggest that this same constellation of disabilities plays a dominant role in the samples of children described in this book by Conners, Ferguson, Sprague, Sheer, Van Duyne, and Wender. The diverse theories presented illustrate that much work is required before arriving at sufficiently accurate definitions of the disabilities under study to support a particular neurological model. The discussions among Dr. Conners, Dr. Sheer, and myself, for example, point up some possible differences among our ways of conceptualizing the deficit. Dr. Conners emphasizes a problem with "selective attention" while I have deliberately avoided this term in favor of "sustained attention." Dr. Sheer, on the other hand, prefers to speak of "focused arousal." Dr. Conners and I also emp, ·size an accompanying deficit that we have labeled "impulse cυ ·trol" or "inhibitory control," while Dr. Sheer, because of the neurological model he has in mind, wishes to emphasize "facilatory" rather than "inhibitory" processes. These are not just semantic differences. Rather, they reflect our struggle to operationalize more clearly the disabilities that we all have been investigating.

This leads to my second reason for concern. Although some of the neuropsychological models that have appeared to explain "hyperactivity" or "minimal brain dysfunction" are intriguing, good neurologizing cannot precede accurate operational definition of symptoms. Some of the neurological models in this area are based on faulty behavioral descriptions and misunderstandings about the effects of the stimulant drugs on children diagnosed as "hyperactive" or "MBD." Like Sroufe (1975), I feel somewhat doubtful that the effects of the stimulants on children in these groups are as "paradoxical" as was originally supposed. Our own research suggests, as well, that hyperactive children are not as unresponsive to reinforcement as has sometimes been postulated and also that they are not as distractible as most clinical descriptions of them suggest. Finally, we are becoming rather confused by the many psycho-physiological studies, including our own (Cohen and Douglas, 1972), that have set out to prove that their "arousal levels" differ from those of normal children.

On the other hand, the evidence does suggest that an acceptable neuropsychological model will have to take account of the inability of these children to sustain attention and to keep impulsive responding under control, and it will have to account as well for the fact that stimulants have a demonstrable therapeutic effect on these problems. Our recent studies on the effect of a variety of parameters in the learning situation on their performance also suggest that the model will have to deal with the fact that these children demonstrate rather unique reactions to several reinforcement contingencies. Some of the evidence behind this point of view follows.

First, a few comments on the problem of defining our samples. In the early days, in order to establish a diagnosis of hyperactivity, we had to rely heavily on interviews with parents and teachers and the diagnostic opinion of psychiatrists and psychologists. This is still partly true but we have been helped considerably by Dr. Conners' development of parents' and teachers' rating scales for hyperactivity. These are reasonably well-researched instruments that have been shown by several investigators to be sensitive to the effects of treatment with the stimulant drugs. As well as asking parents and teachers to complete the rating scales, we interview parents regarding the time of onset of symptoms and the family situation. We include in our samples only children who have demonstrated the symptoms chronically over several years and exclude those whose symptoms appear to be a reaction to a stressful home situation. In view of Dr. Conners' different findings when he excluded "high anxious" children from his sample it is important to note that our original screening procedures tend to exclude "high anxious" subjects. Also excluded are children of below average intelligence, those who show clear evidence of neurological impairment, and those diagnosed by our consultants as neurotic or psychotic. Thus, it could be argued that this group is fairly highly selected and perhaps more homogeneous than some of the samples discussed in the literature. Most of our studies have included children between 5 and 14 years of age, although Dr. Weiss currently is carrying out longitudinal studies on some of these children into adolescence and young adulthood (Weiss et al., 1971).

It was while working with children defined according to these criteria that we became convinced of the importance and interrelatedness of sustained attention and impulse control. This view has been strengthened by correlational studies within our hyperactive subjects, a factor analytic study with normal children (Douglas, 1972), and also by recent studies in which we have been attempting to clarify and extend Kagan's work on the cognitive style of "reflection-impulsivity" (Kagan, 1965).

Following is a brief review of some of the evidence that has encouraged us to focus our effort on sustained attention and impulsivity. One of my doctoral students (Sykes, 1969; Sykes, Douglas, and Morgenstern, 1973) found evidence in two different samples that hyperactive children had difficulty on the continuous performance test, a measure of vigilance that requires the child to react to particular stimuli while ignoring others. The hyperactive group had difficulty with both a visual and an auditory form of the test: they made fewer correct responses and reacted to more of the incorrect stimuli than did the controls, thus suggesting both an attentional and an impulsivity deficit. Their performance also deteriorated more rapidly over time than that of the normal group. Treatment with the stimulants resulted in an increase in correct responses, a decrease in errors, and an ability to sustain attention more effectively over time. All of these drug studies have employed a double blind, cross-over design. In most cases we have used methylphenidate, although we have done some work with dexedrine and have recently completed a small study with caffeine. All of the successful effects we have achieved have been with short-term studies, usually of about three weeks duration: our efforts to prove long-term effects have been discouraging (Weiss et al., 1973).

In three doctoral theses (Cohen, 1970; Parry, 1973; Firestone, 1974), performance of hyperactive subjects and controls has been studied on a reaction time task. A reaction signal is preceded by a warning signal that is meant to help the child develop a set to respond quickly. On this task the hyperactive subjects achieved slower mean reaction times than normal controls, their reaction times were more variable, and their performance fell off more precipitously over time. They also demonstrated several impulsive types of behavior, sometimes pushing in response to the warning signal or before the arrival of the reaction signal; sometimes, too, they made redundant responses to the reaction signal. Cohen's study showed that methylphenidate, a stimulant drug, decreased mean response time, decreased variability of response times, and decreased redundant responding (Cohen, Douglas, and Morgenstern, 1971); Firestone (1974) demonstrated a drop in the three types of impulsive response described above when his hyperactive subjects were being treated with caffeine.

Campbell's dissertation (Campbell, 1969) was concerned with cognitive styles of hyperactive children. One of her measures was Kagan's Matching Familiar Figures Test of Reflection-Impulsivity (Kagan, 1965). In this test the child is asked to search among several alternatives in order to find a picture identical to a standard. Since many of the alternatives are very similar to the target picture, in order to do well the child must study each of the alternatives and compare them carefully with the standard.

Hyperactive children choose significantly more quickly than normals and make more errors. This result now has been replicated in two other doctoral dissertations (Parry, 1973; Peters, 1975). Campbell also found that when the hyperactive children were receiving methylphenidate they took longer to choose and made fewer errors (Campbell, Douglas, and Morgenstern, 1971). It is interesting to note that in this test, where care and caution are necessary, the stimulant drug helped the children slow down and thus increase their reaction times, whereas on the reaction time task, where speed was demanded, the drug enabled them to react more quickly.

Further evidence for a combined attention-impulsivity problem in our hyperactive subjects comes from significantly poorer scores on the Porteus Mazes Test, which requires the child to plan and monitor his own movements in order to avoid blind alleys, and from a higher number of aggressive responses on a story completion test designed to elicit children's reactions to frustrating events (Parry, 1973). Conners and other investigators (Conners, 1972b) have shown that the stimulants improve performance on the Porteus Mazes in children somewhat similar to ours.

To summarize these findings, we believe that they underline the importance of an attentional-impulsivity deficit in these children. We also believe that they provide rather convincing evidence that the stimulant drugs exert a major effect on this deficit.

It is important to point out that, in spite of deficits in sustained attention, we have failed to demonstrate parallel deficits in distractibility in our hyperactive groups. Although clinical descriptions almost invariably portray these children as highly distractible, several efforts to prove that they are more distractible than normal children have been unsuccessful. Attempts have included introducing random white noise while the subjects were performing on the continuous performance test (Sykes, 1969), introducing stimuli of a discrepant color on a choice reaction time task (Sykes, 1969), and comparing their performance with that of normals on the Santostefano and Paley Color Distraction Test (Campbell, Douglas, and Morgenstern, 1971) and on the Stroop Color-Word Interference Test (Cohen, Weiss, and Minde, 1972). Data just analyzed by Peters (unpublished) for his doctoral dissertation also produced no evidence that hyperactives are more distractible than normals on another version of the Color Distraction Test, on a picture-order task of selective attention that assessed both central and incidental memory, or on a selective listening task. It is not suggested that these children cannot be seduced away from a task by novel or exciting events; it is clear, however, that they are not, as some clinicians have suggested, at the mercy of all of the stimuli occurring in their environment.

We have tended to put somewhat less emphasis than other investigators on the activity level of these children. Classroom observations show that much of their behavior is goal-oriented, although their goals often are not those of the teacher (Douglas, 1972). It is true that our "locomotor" measures (e.g., number of times the child is out of his seat) did differentiate younger hyperactives from their classmates, but these differences were not significant in an older group of hyperactives. Although the older group remained in their seats, they were unable to focus their attention successfully on the activities required of them. Similarly, parents' ratings from our longitudinal study (Weiss et al., 1971) showed that, although hyperactivity decreased as the children grew older, problems with attention and impulse control remained. It is for these reasons that we have come to feel that treatment methods, and possibly neuro-psychological theories as well, should put somewhat more emphasis on attention and impulse control than on activity level.

Some of the data from earlier studies also suggest that a neuro-psychological model for these children may have to take account of the fact that they do badly on several measures of fine and gross motor control and eye-hand coordination including the Lincoln–Oseretsky Motor Development Schedule, the Bender Visual-Motor Gestalt Test, and the eye–hand coordination subtest of the Frostig Test of Visual Perception (Douglas, 1974a). It could be argued that their difficulties with these tests are simply evidence of their inability to discipline themselves to look and move carefully; on the other hand, it is conceivable that we are dealing with a neurological link between centers associated with concentration and inhibitory control and those responsible for motor coordination.

Following is a brief review of our studies on the effect of reinforce-ment schedules on the performance of these children. We became inter-ested in this problem because behavior modification techniques are being used with them and also because there has been some suggestion, as in Dr. Wender's biochemical model of the minimal brain dysfunction syndrome (Wender, 1972, 1973b), that they are relatively unresponsive to reinforce-ment. Several years ago Freibergs (Freibergs and Douglas, 1969) com-pleted a doctoral dissertation in which she investigated the effects of continuous and partial reinforcement schedules on concept learning in hyperactive and normal children. Positive reinforcers in this study were marbles that were delivered by a machine when the children made a correct response. The results suggested that the hyperactives were able to cope with the concept problems under a continuous schedule; when reinforcement was reduced to 50%, however, their performance was very poor. Parry (1973) replicated this study using a research design that controlled for the differential effect of information feedback in the two conditions. Once again, the performance of the hyperactives was inferior in the partial reinforcement condition. Cohen (1970), Parry (1973), and Firestone (1974) have shown that social reward (praise) produces improved and less erratic reaction times in hyperactive subjects on the reaction time task described earlier. However, Parry's results also underline the fact that reinforcement exerts its positive effect only when it is delivered contingently, that is, when the child has just given a particularly fast response. Reinforcement delivered randomly actually produced a deterioration in performance in the hyperactive subjects, although in the normal controls it produced improvement (Parry and Douglas, in press). In Firestone's study, the improvement in reaction time in the positive reinforcement condition was accompanied by an increase in the impulsive responses described earlier. Negative reinforcement, on the other hand, produced improved reaction times without increasing impulsive responses (Firestone and Douglas, 1976).

Taken together, these data suggest to us that hyperactive children may be overdependent on positive reinforcement. Although reward can improve performance, it apparently may also induce overexcitement and weaken inhibitory control. Parry's description of the children's behavior during reward suggests that they become more interested in the reinforcement and the person delivering it than in the demands of the task. This behavior is reminiscent of Watson's (1970, 1971) description of the responses of very young children to positive reinforcement. It seems, then, that, rather than being unresponsive, our hyperactive children react to positive reinforcement in unique ways.

It should be noted that our clinic staff feels sure that hyperactive children do not fit the diagnosis of "ahedonia." Tapes of their reactions during our training sessions show that they express great joy when they master a difficult problem and many parents describe the children as loveable and responsive, in spite of their exasperating qualities. We also have investigated their performance on four different measures of "introversion-extroversion" and have found no consistent differences between hyperactives and normal controls.

Attempts to prove that these children function at either an excessively high or excessively low general level of arousal have also raised some questions about theories that describe them as "over-" or "underaroused," although, as Sheer states, the evidence for a defect in "focused arousal" is more convincing. A review of some of the recent heart rate and skin response studies (Cohen and Douglas, 1972; Satterfield and Dawson, 1971; Satterfield, Antonian, Brashears, Burleigh, and Dawson, 1974; Spring,

Greenberg, Scott, and Hopwood, 1974; Sroufe, Sonies, West, and Wright, 1973; Zahn et al., 1975) makes it clear that it is almost impossible to make comparisons among studies from different laboratories. Besides the problem of subject differences mentioned earlier, the various investigators use different indices, measured by different techniques, under different conditions. For example, basal levels may be established during a 2-minute or a 10-minute period; sometimes computations are based on only the last part of the resting period, sometimes on the total time. In some studies subjects are tested in a stimulus-free, soundproof room; in others, measures are taken while the child is watching TV. Sometimes stimuli are delivered through ear phones, sometimes through speakers, and sometimes the method of delivery is not reported.

Perhaps it is not surprising, therefore, that the results across studies are not very consistent. In the reported differences between experimental and control groups on resting levels, for example, three studies report no significant differences, one reports a lower level in the hyperactive group, while one finds a higher level. Results on subjects' responses to nonsignal stimuli are even more scattered, as are the findings on the occurrence of "spontaneous fluctuations" in the records. The greatest consistency occurs in reports of "orienting response" measures taken when the children are required to react to signal stimuli, as in the reaction time task described earlier. Here Zahn et al. (1974) as well as Sroufe et al. (1973) agree with our finding that hyperactive children (or in the case of Sroufe's study, children with learning disabilities) exhibit weaker orienting responses. It should be noted, however, that this shows only that the OR data agree with our reaction time data—and the behavioral data are probably more reliable and considerably less costly!

The differences that have been reported on these autonomic measures between subjects receiving stimulants and those receiving placebos are extremely confusing, partly because of the effects of the stimulants on some of the baseline measures (Cohen, Douglas, and Morgenstern, 1971). Also of considerable interest are reported differences on psychophysiological measures between "good" and "poor drug responders." In order to be convincing, however, these findings will have to be replicated with larger samples in different laboratories; it is also important that we rule out the possibility that statistical artifacts, such as regression to the mean, can account for the findings. Nevertheless, hope springs eternal and I am somewhat optimistic that the more sophisticated EEG measures, such as the evoked potential, contingent negative variation, or Sheer's 40-Hz method, will help us achieve better insight into these issues. Certainly, a valid and reliable measure of "concentration" or, as Sheer would say, of "focused arousal," would help toward a solution of these problems.

Finally, I am somewhat uneasy about the emphasis some psychoneurological theories place on "paradoxical" effects of the stimulants: certainly, the term "paradoxical" represents an oversimplification of the facts. Although the drugs do seem to have a calming and organizing effect on these children, it has long been known that the stimulants also can improve performance in normal adults on some of the very measures used in drug studies with hyperactives. Several medical colleagues have confessed to me, as well, that they have used the drugs, with similar results, with children whose symptoms appear to have emotional rather than "organic" causes. Sroufe (1975) has reached a similar conclusion in an excellent review of the literature on this question. It seems likely that this more conservative interpretation of the effects of the stimulants would influence the neurological model chosen to explain the syndrome.

In closing, it is important to shift emphasis from problems of neurologizing to the problem of finding ways to help the very large number of children who are being diagnosed as learning disabled, MBD, or hyperactive. Here again, it seems that the only hope for progress lies in the kind of detailed empirical analysis of disabilities that have begun to appear at this meeting. I disagree with Dr. Meichenbaum's argument that effective understanding of these children's problems can be achieved only by returning to the "single case analysis" approach; on the other hand, the time surely has come to move beyond what he has labeled "broad band testing." If, however, we can use what we have learned from this approach to develop "specific disability hypotheses" and if we can design clearly operationalized measures to test those hypotheses, we will have taken the first necessary steps toward tailoring treatment techniques to the needs of individual children.

In the case of the "attentional-impulsivity" group that I have postulated, I would have to admit that we could probably arrive at an even more homogeneous group if we were to develop better norms for our measures and then apply more sophisticated statistical methods such as pattern analysis and ipsatization procedures. Nevertheless, we are hopeful that we now know enough to move cautiously into developing training programs for these children, based on our understanding of their specific disabilities. Interestingly enough, in our training approach we have relied rather heavily on a self-verbalization and modeling procedure developed by Meichenbaum (Douglas, 1975; Meichenbaum, 1974; Meichenbaum and Goodman, 1969).

Cognitive-Functional Approach to Cognitive Factors as Determinants of Learning Disabilities

Donald Meichenbaum

This chapter is concerned with strategies used to study the nature of cognitive deficit among children with learning disabilities. Investigators in this area have relied heavily upon two general research strategies. The first of these is a population comparison strategy, which involves comparing the performance of learning-disabled children with a "normal" control group on a comprehensive battery of psychoeducational tests. One infers the nature of a deficit from the differential pattern of performance between learning-disabled and control children. The second general strategy might be described as a specific-deficit analysis strategy: the investigator hypothesizes that a particular type of deficit forms the basis of the learning disability and attempts to assess that specific, hypothesized deficit through a battery of tests. This approach also typically involves the comparison of learning-disabled children with matched controls, but focuses on a test battery designed to assess a specific deficit rather than a more global assessment battery. The first part of the chapter is devoted to a brief critical review of these research approaches. In discussing these research strategies, reference will frequently be made to the schizophrenia literature, since similar methodologies have been used extensively in an attempt to isolate the fundamental deficit of schizophrenia.

The second part of the chapter outlines an alternative research strategy, which might be described as a cognitive-functional approach. This approach involved conducting a psychological analysis of the cognitive requirements of tasks on which the learning-disabled child's performance has been found inadquate. Through a series of converging operations, the performance deficits of each child are investigated on a case study basis,

This research was supported by a grant from the Ontario Ministry of Education.

with the learning-disabled child often serving as his own control. Again, reference will be made to the schizophrenia literature to illustrate this cognitive-functional strategy.

The critical questions that must be addressed are the following. What is the learning-disabled child doing or failing to do that interferes with his performance? What psychological processes are affected? Research methodologies are useful only insofar as they permit these fundamental questions to be addressed. It is the argument of the present paper that the comparison of populations and test battery analysis of a specific postulated deficit are of limited value for addressing these questions. The cognitive-functional approach is proposed as a method of gathering data of greater scientific and clinical significance.

RESEARCH STRATEGIES TO STUDY LEARNING DISABILITIES

Comparative Populations Approach

The comparison of the target population with matched, nonindexed control groups is deeply steeped in the tradition of psychopathological research. This tradition is exemplified by the research on schizophrenia, in which schizophrenics of various levels of pathology have been compared with both hospitalized and nonhospitalized control groups (e.g., see Buss and Lang, 1965; Hunt and Cofer, 1944).

The comparative groups approach to studying learning disabilities has followed the same tradition. In order to understand the nature of children's learning deficiencies, investigators such as Rubin (1971) and Myklebust, Bannonchie, and Killen (1971) have compared learning-disability children with "normal" controls on a comprehensive psychoeducational battery. Rubin employed a battery of cognitive-perceptual-motor tasks that included 41 tests, which provided 59 scores, as well as the Wechsler Intelligence Scale for Children (WISC) and the Metropolitan Achievement Test. Myklebust et al.'s assessment battery reads like a test brochure for a Mental Measurements Yearbook. It included the WISC, the Leiter International Performance Scale, the Oral Emergency Test, Scale D, Healy Picture Completion Test I, Goodenough-Harris Drawing Test, and eight subtests from the Detroit Tests of Learning Aptitude. The children's performance on these tests was then related to a host of academic achievement measures. One must admire the children's endurance in taking so many tests.

A number of clinicians have recommended the inclusion of such a comprehensive assessment battery in the diagnostic workup of children with learning disabilities (Hamill, 1971; Vallett, 1969). Often the test battery or specific tests [e.g., the Illinois Test of Psycholinguistic Ability (ITPA)] are tied to a particular theoretical model, which usually focuses on information processes such as encoding, decoding, etc. However, as Mann and Phillips (1967) have indicated, such attempts to analyze global or molar areas of behavior and functioning into component, information-processing units have little or no empirical basis. Mann and Phillips question the basic assumption that the child's performance may be successfully separated, or, to use their word, "fractionated," into specific entities, units, or functions, each of which is essentially independent and capable of being individually evaluated and/or exercised.

In addition to the Mann and Phillips criticism of a "fractionated" test approach, there remains the fundamental question of the usefulness of a comparative groups approach, with its comprehensive battery of tests (i.e., a sort of "shotgun" approach) for elucidating the precise nature of an individual child's deficit. The experimental design assumes that one or more specific deficits underlie "learning disability" in all cases. Individual variations in performance patterns within the learning-disabled group are often treated as error variance and go unattended to rather than being treated as potentially important data. Unfortunately, given the amount of time and effort required of children and researchers, few data of scientific or clinical significance have been generated by this comparative groups approach.

What we do learn, as in the literature concerning schizophrenics, is that the target population as a group performs more poorly on the assessment devices that do their normal, control counterparts—a rather under-whelming and noninformative finding. Usually, these comparative studies, through a discriminant-function analysis, also indicate which tests were the most sensitive markers of group differences. The intercorrelational matrix of the test performances for the respective groups led one set of investigators to draw the conclusion:

> "A learning disability affects the organization of the intellect: hence, cognition itself is modified. The mental abilities of learning disability children are structured differently" (Myklebust et al., 1971, p. 227).

But such "conclusions" from comparative group studies are of little assistance in revealing the nature of the learning process and how the learning-disabled child is affected. Rather, such an approach tends to lead only to a circularity in which the learning disability is attributed to an inadequate performance on a specific test or set of tests, leaving us still with the problem of what it means to be unable to achieve a certain standard on this measure; what underlies, causes this inability; what can affect a change from incompetence to competence.

Specific Deficits Analysis

A second, related research stragety involves the investigator's proposing that a single deficiency underlies the learning disabilities. A number of specific deficits have been proposed by various investigators. These include an attentional deficit, excessive motoric activity, and memory dysfunction. Each of these hypothetical deficits and the research on which they are based will be discussed briefly.

Dykman and his colleagues (Dykman et al., 1971; Dykman et al., 1970) postulated that an attentional deficit underlies learning disabilities. They employed a battery of tests that assess the various aspects of attention (that is, alertness, stimulus selection, focusing, and vigilance) to study the nature of the learning deficit. Included were tone discrimination, reaction time, conditioning, and orienting tasks. Children with learning disabilities were found to perform less well than normals on these attentional measures. A further comparison of interest was the distinction between hyper- and hypoactive children with learning disabilities. The hyperactive children in the Dykman et al. (1970) study were distractible, impulsive, easily exhaustible, and lacking in ability to concentrate. Furthermore, the movements of the hyperactive children seemed poorly focused and devoid of purpose. The hypoactive children had, in general, characteristics opposite to those of hyperactives: they were unusually slow in movement, speech, thought, and/or affect. The children's performance on the attentional measures paralleled the behavioral profiles, with the hyperactive children having shorter reaction times than hypoactive children and the controls having shorter reaction times than both learning-disabled groups. The results on the remaining attentional measures led Dykman et al. (1970) to conclude,

> "Hyperactive, learning-disability children appear to be over-attentive to their environment, wheras hypoactive ones are under-attentive. The net effect of over- or under-attention on performance is the same" (p. 82).

Note the significance of this conclusion: different underlying processes may result in performance deficits that appear similar. Such a conclusion should caution us against overly facile interpretations of performance deficits without exhaustively investigating the underlying psychological processes, as will be described below, such exhaustive analysis is the essence of the cognitive-functional approach.

The role of an attentional deficit was further implicated in a study by Ackerman, Peters, and Dykman (1971), who found that learning-disabled children versus normal controls differed on the WISC, with learning-disabled children doing most poorly on the mental arithmetic and digit span subtests. Ackerman et al. suggested that the primary deficiency among learning-disabled children might be an inability to hold several bits of information until these bits could be synthesized into a whole, which would then guide a course of action. They indicated that teachers characterize this inability to hold and synthesize bits of information as a short attention span for mental work, especially mental work requiring sustained, independent effort. Thus, the attentional deficit Dykman and his colleagues have identified in learning-disabled children is viewed as a major contributor to their poor performance on the psychoeducational measures used in comparative studies.

Further supporting evidence for an attentional deficit explanation was offered by Bryan and Wheeler (1972) and Bryan (1974), who conducted an observational study of the classroom behaviors of children with learning disabilities. They sought to determine how often, how much, and under what conditions a set of behaviors must be demonstrated by children in order for the child to be characterized as learning-disabled. In short, they asked, "What do learning-disabled children do in a classroom setting?" Bryan and Wheeler (1972) and Bryan (1974) found that learning-disabled children spent significantly less time engaged in task-oriented behaviors (e.g., reading) and more time in non-task-oriented behaviors (e.g., "fooling around"). Moreover, the learning-disabled children seemed less responsive to changes in situational demands, in that their attentional behavior was not dependent upon the subject or content area, as it was in the control group. This was further evident in their poor peer relations. Added to this clinical picture is the finding by Larsen, Parker, and Jorjorian (1973) that children with learning disabilities have a poorer self-concept than normal controls.

The results of these studies on attentional deficit suggest that learning-disabled children are distractible, unable to pay attention, or prone to focus upon irrelevant aspects of the learning situation. But even these conclusions must be tempered. As Tarver and Hallahan (1974) have indicated, whether learning-disabled children are found to be more highly distractible than normal children seems to depend upon the investigator's concept of distractibility and the resulting measures employed. They believe the evidence indicates that learning-disabled children are not more highly distractible by flashing lights or extraneous color cues, but that they do seem to be deficient in ability to focus their attention on tasks involving embeddedness.

The developmental aspects of the attentional deficit have been noted by Rourke (1974) and Douglas (1972). Rourke (1974) reported that the attentional deficit is more characteristic of younger children with learning disabilities, but that this deficit decreases at or about the time of puberty. Similarly, Douglas (1972) and her colleagues observed two groups of hyperactive children (7 and 12 year olds). They found that the most consistent differences between hyperactive children and controls were "purposive behavior not related to classroom behavior" (p. 262). The younger children showed more disorderly behavior, attracted more of the teacher's attention, moved about the room more, and vocalized more than their controls. Behavior of the older hyperactives was less disrupting, but they, too, engaged in more purposive behavior not related to classroom activity. Some suggestions will be offered below concerning the nature of the psychological mechanisms that lead to lack of control of attentional processes and inefficient inhibition.

An interesting observation is that the research on attentional deficits bridges the literatures on learning disabilities and schizophrenia, especially when we learn that a measure of attentional vigilance is a most sensitive indicator of attentional deficit in both schizophrenics (Orzack and Kornetsky, 1966) and hyperactive, learning-disabled children (Sykes, Douglas, and Morgenstern (1973). The attentional vigilance task was the Continuous Performance Task (CPT, Rosvold, 1965). The CPT requires the subject to watch letters that appear one at a time on a memory drum or similar presentation device. The subject is to press a key when he sees an "X" that immediately follows an "A," and not to press the key for any other letters. As mentioned, both schizophrenics and impulsive children have difficulty in maintaining attention on this vigilance task over a prolonged period of time, such as 15 minutes. We will come back to this task and the role of attentional processes momentarily. But we must keep in mind that the term attention is a summary term, referring to such psychological subprocesses as vigilance or maintenance of attention, as well as selective attention and the ability to shift attention from one stimulus to another. Thus, to say that children with learning disabilities or schizophrenics have attentional deficits is far from an explanatory statement.

Related to the attentional focus of Dykman and his colleagues is the view of Keogh (1971) that learning problems, especially among hyperactive children, are a result of increased motor activity. Such motor activity disrupts attention to the task and prevents accurate intake of information. A hasty, impulsive, decisional style further contributes to the learning deficit. Supportive of this view is the finding by Grinsted (1939) of a significant negative correlation ($r = -0.52$) between measures of intellectual ability and activity level for groups of normal children in grades one through seven and grade eleven. Other investigators have confirmed this relationship in various retardate samples (Cromwell, Polk, and Foshbee, 1961; Foshbee, 1958). Maccoby et al. (1965) suggest that a successful problem-solver "modulate[s] or regulate[s] his activity, so that expressive activity is inhibited during crucial points of problem solving where it might . . . interfere with the accurate intake of information" (p. 763). Keogh (1971) indicates that whenever effective therapeutic intervention occurs, whether medication or behavioral management, a decrease in motor activity results, allowing more accurate intake of information, and therefore an accompanying increase in successful learning.

As in the case of attentional control, the nature of a number of different psychological processes involved in fostering motoric control requires explication. Activity level, as attention, should not be viewed as a single or homogeneous phenomenon. Morgan and Stellar (1950) specified three bipolar descriptions of activity level: locomotor versus diffuse, relevant versus irrelevant, and goal-directed versus non-goal-directed. Loo and Wenar (1971) have delineated three qualities of activity: activity level—the quantitative amount of motoric movements; motor inhibition—the degree of ability to inhibit motor impulses; and impulsivity—the lack of self-control in modes other than motoric. In the light of such classificatory schemes, Salkind and Poggio's (1975) suggestion of the development of a careful taxonomy or psychological analysis of activity level, would probably prove to be a purposeful venture. They state,

> "The most popular practice, and perhaps most lacking in construct validity, is the assignment of synonyms that reflect behaviors similar to that descriptive of the hyperactive child but which in no way broaden or advance the applicability of the definition" (p. 6).

Similarly, Keogh (1971) has commented, "most investigators focus on the symptomatology of the condition without defining the construct" (p. 102).

Rather than either an attentional or motoric deficit, Kleuver (1971), in examining learning disabilities among poor readers, proposed a memory deficit as a central problem. Using the Guilford (1967) structure of intellect as a model for studying learning-disabled children, Kleuver (1971) assessed poor readers on 16 memory tests taken from the Guilford test battery. He found that "normal" readers were superior to poor readers on several aspects of memory, especially on more meaningful (semantic), rather than less meaningful (figural) materials, and especially when tasks involved systems and transformations. This led Kleuver to conclude,

> "The structure of memory in children with reading disabilities essentially is similar to that of normal readers even though they are deficient on some factors" (p. 211).

Such conclusions are not uncommon in the specific-deficits literature. However, the questionable value of such broad conclusions is demonstrated by Myklebust et al.'s (1971) having reached, from a similar sort of test approach, the opposite conclusion. It will be recalled that Myklebust et al. had concluded that the structure of intellect among learning disability children was different than for normal children. Whether the structure is the same or not may have more to do with the method of analyses and the nature of the tests than the psychological processes of the children studied. The nature of the psychological processes that contribute to a poor memory performance remains unspecified. This question takes on particular significance when we take into consideration Meachem's (1972) analytic approach to memory. Meachem conceptualized memory as an epiphenomenon consisting of various cognitive activities such as classifying, rehearsing, labeling, visual imagery, and sentence elaboration. Kleuver's results tell us that learning-disabled children who are poor readers have a "memory" deficit relative to a control group, but do not lead to further specification of the nature of the psychological deficit. Moreover, it is unlikely that comparative research investigations, which include a montage of different tests, will be very useful in answering such questions. A different research approach is required.

Consequences of Following the
Comparative Groups and Specific Deficits Research Strategies

Going back to our comparison with the research literature on schizophrenia, we may consider the consequences of using a comparative research strategy, whether one is employing a "shotgun" or a deficit-specific test battery. The failure to conduct a systematic task leads to premature model building and neurologizing. For example, a variety of constructs have been proposed to explain the schizophrenic's performance deficit. A major source of such theorizing has been Broadbent's (1958) model of the human mind as an information channel of limited capacity. This model has led various investigators to hypothesize that schizophrenic behavior is a consequence of (1) a deficient attentional filter (Chapman and McGhie, 1962); (2) an input dysfunction (Venables, 1964); (3) a deterioration in channel capacity (Pishkin, Smith, and Leibowitz, 1962); (4) a failure in scanning processes (Silverman, 1964); (5) a slowness of processing data in the primary channel (Yates, 1966); (6) defective programs (Callaway, 1970). The schizophrenic deficit has also been conceptualized in terms of neurological models. Thus, for instance, it has been hypothetically explained in terms of (1) a primary defect in central nervous system organization (Belmont et al., 1964); (2) a defect in the cortical regulatory system (Venables, 1963); (3) a defect in excitatory modulation (Claridge, 1967), and others. One sees a similar trend toward premature hypothesis-construction developing in the area of learning disabilities, as evidenced in the specific deficits research strategy and in the development of "fractionated" assessment instruments based on information-processing models.

Meichenbaum and Cameron (1973) argued that such hypothetical speculation, whether derived from an information-communication model or a neurological model, seems premature and essentially nonproductive. They suggest that at present the focus of theorizing and empiricism may be more productively directed at a cognitive-functional approach to the schizophrenic's maladaptive behavior. It is argued that a similar conclusion can be applied to the study of learning-disabled children.

Before leaving the example of schizophrenia it is worthwhile to share the observations of Kinsbourne (1971). He notes that schizophrenics are often unusually distractible and responsive to cues that are irrelevant to the task set before them in the test situation. This distraction is easy to demonstrate, and schizophrenics often do not focus their attention normally. (This is reminiscent of Dykman's statements about learning-disabled children.) Kinsbourne raises the question: "Is this because they are unable to do so?" He proceeds:

> "Subjects fail to focus attention on a task or situation if they lack interest in it, if they have emotional resistance demands on their abilities, or if they are otherwise preoccupied. In the mere demonstration of a failure of selective attention, there is no discrimination between primary physiological causation and distractibility secondary to other causes, any or all of which might be applicable to a schizophrenic subject . . . rather than an independent manifestation of disturbed neuronal activity" (Kinsbourne, 1971, p. 309).

Kinsbourne's comments obviously apply equally to children with learning disabilities. These comments do not deny the fact that neurological deficits may contribute to both schizophrenia and learning disabilities. For there is some evidence of the role of neurological impairments in children with learning disabilities (e.g., see Hughes, 1971; Myklebust, 1968). However, as Myklebust (1968) has indicated, the evidence for dysfunction of the brain is most difficult to establish diagnostically; therefore, such evidence for a neurological etiology frequently is "presumptive."

COGNITIVE-FUNCTIONAL APPROACH
TO STUDY OF LEARNING DISABILITIES[1]

A cognitive "hyphen" functional analysis of a psychological deficit, whether conducted on schizophrenics or on children with learning disabilities, emphasizes both a task analysis and an accompanying, psychological analysis of the cognitions (i.e., self-statements and images) that subjects employ in order to perform a task. The tradition of a functional analysis of behavior emphasizes an examination of environmental antecedents and consequences, as related to a given response repertoire. A functional analyst carefully defines the specific response class, notes its naturally occurring topography and frequency within various situational settings, and then systematically manipulates environmental events in order to describe a causal relationship. A cognitive-functional approach to psychological deficits is in the same tradition, but includes and emphasizes the role of the subject's cognitions (i.e., self-statements and images) in the behavioral repertoire. In short, a functional analysis of the subject's thinking processes and a careful inventory of his cognitive strategies are conducted in order to determine which cognitions (or failure to produce key cognitions), under what circumstances, are contributing to or interfering with adequate performance. The cognitive-functional approach is based upon a systematic task-analysis. Most cognitive tasks, especially such formal conceptual tasks as are administered in the comparative-group studies, are complex, and should be analyzed in terms of the behavioral requirements they make on a subject. The task-analysis involves a logical analysis of the psychological demands of a particular task and an analysis of the sequentially organized set of cognitive processes that the subject must emit to perform adequately on a task. Consider, for instance, the following examples of task analysis of concept identification tasks. Price (1968) noted that his concept identification task not only measured the subject's ability to form or identify a particular concept, but also required the following from the subject: (1) experimentally demonstrable understanding of the task instructions, (2) discrimination of the dimensional properties of concept stimuli, (3) the ability to use symbolic information relevant to the concept, and (4) the retention of information relevant to the concept. As Price indicated, a failure of the subject to meet any one of these task requirements would result in a gross but unspecifiable performance deficit. Gholson and McConville (1974), working within a develop-

---

[1] As in most instances, when one completes a chapter he then discovers a host of related references. Similarity to a cognitive-functional approach is found in Scheerer (1945), Estes (1974), and Wozniak (1975).

mental learning theory framework, described a child's performance on a concept identification task as requiring such processes as stimulus differentiation, attention, verbal mediation or verbal coding, visual imagery, memory storage and retrieval, and forms of logical deduction or inference.

The cognitive-functional approach is concerned with the sequential psychological processes required to perform a particular task. The cognitive-functional diagnostician asks the question, "What psychological processes must the successfully learning child engage in and which of these is the child with learning disabilities failing to engage in?" Let me illustrate the approach with the Continuous Performance Task (CPT), on which, as described above, both schizophrenics and hyperactive children perform poorly. Recall, the task ostensibly requires the subject to maintain his attention to a set of letters that are presented on a memory drum and to signal each time the sequence of letters "A," then "X," occurs. The diagnostician who is following a cognitive-functional approach goes about studying the deficit in a two-part manner.

First, in order to speculate about what leads to a poor performance on the CPT, the diagnostician or therapist does the task himself. Upon completion of the CPT, the therapist introspects about the thoughts, images, and behaviors he employed in order to maintain attention and perform adequately. The therapist may wish to take the CPT once again, focusing on the cognitive and behavioral strategies he is employing.

The second step is to have other individuals examine their strategies following performance on the CPT. During each performance the therapist is carefully watching for cues that may indicate the use of particular strategies. The clinical concern is with the "process" variables, and "how" rather than merely the performance outcome.

Subjects who do well on the CPT report that they attempt to monitor their performance and note when attention is waning. This recognition of their attention wandering from the task triggers a variety of cognitive and behavioral strategies, such as trying to visualize the A–X, setting more stringent response standards and self-instructing, or producing motor responses, such as shaking themselves, in order to remain vigilant. In other words, the therapist performs an analysis of not only the behaviors, but also the thinking that is necessary to perform adequately on the task. Thus, inadequate performance on the CPT may result (1) from the subject's failure to engage spontaneously and appropriately in task-relevant, cognitive, and behavioral strategies and/or (2) from a number of subject-generated task interruptions and distractions and the way in which the subject notices and copes with these interruptions. In short, a failure in the internal dialog of the subject, what he says to himself before, accompanying, and following his performance on a task, becomes the focus of analysis. It is suggested that an analysis of such cognitions will help elucidate the nature of the psychological deficit.

Someone who is performing poorly on a task may be producing negative self-statements, task-irrelevant thoughts, and/or anxiety-engendering ideas, which interfere with adequate performance. In addition, the client's affective state may be a source of interruptive, task-irrelevant ideation. What the subject says to himself about his feeling tone will substantially affect performance. As mentioned earlier, Larsen, Parker, and Jorjorian (1973) found that children with learning disabilities had a poorer self-concept that "normal" children. This difference in self-concept is reflected in the child's internal dialog as he approaches a task and while engaging in it, especially when confronted with frustration and failure. Such negative self-statements have the impact of a self-fulfilling prophecy, which further confirms the child's initial internal dialog. Thus, a deteriorating performance cycle is established and reinforced. In addition to producing task-irrelevant cognitions, the learning-disabled child may fail to spontaneously produce task-appropriate cognitive strategies. [See Meichenbaum (1975a, 1975b) and Meichenbaum and Cameron (1974) for a further discussion of the role of negative self-statements in contributing to inadequate performance.]

Meichenbaum (1975b) has theorized that making subjects aware of such self-statements is a necessary but not sufficient condition for achieving behavioral change and performance improvement. For improved performance to occur, the self-recognition must come to act as a cue for the subject to engage in task-relevant cognitions and behaviors that are incompatible with the maladaptive behavior(s). The occurrence of negative self-statements or task-irrelevant thoughts must come to be the reminder to use the task-appropriate strategies taught in therapy. Meichenbaum (1974; 1975a) has described how this training process can be achieved.

Central to a cognitive-functional analysis approach to psychological deficits is the role of the subject's cognitive strategies. Gagne and Briggs (1974) have characterized cognitive strategies as a special kind of skill that governs the individual's own learning, remembering, and thinking behavior. Characterized thus, cognitive strategies are similar to Skinner's (1968) self-management behaviors.

> "A cognitive strategy is an internally organized skill that selects and guides the internal processes involved in defining and solving novel problems. In other words, it is a skill by means of which the learner manages his own thinking behavior. . . . Cognitive strategies have as their objects the *learner's own thought processes.* Undoubtedly, the

efficacy of an individual's cognitive strategies exerts a crucial effect upon the quality of his own thought" (Gagne and Briggs, 1974, p. 48, emphasis added).

A cognitive functional approach is designed to ascertain the nature of the subject's cognitive strategies and the role they play in contributing to the psychological deficit. Cognitive strategies are not "mythical" or merely hypothetical processes, but rather can be viewed as sets of self-statements and images that subjects emit while engaged in a task, and which may be automatic.

A number of alternative theoretical frameworks have been proposed to describe and explain the subject's internal dialog. Some view the thoughts and images as instances of executive routines (Neisser, 1967), which supposedly organize and control various cognitive subprocesses (subroutines). Others have used an information-processing model, characterizing the subject's thinking by such terms as encoding, integration, and decoding (Chalfant and Scheffelin, 1969; Kirk, 1968; Warner, 1973). Regardless of the language system that we employ, it is the description of the subject's cognitive processes, a kind of ethological approach to thinking, that is the goal of a cognitive-functional approach.

In sum, the "cognitive" portion of this hyphenated approach comprises describing the nature of the cognitive strategies required to perform a task. By means of a logical analysis of the task demands, by taking the task oneself and introspecting on one's cognitive strategies, by observing and interviewing others who take the task, and finally, by systematically manipulating the task demands, one can better appreciate the sequential psychological processes required. This latter approach of manipulating the task demands leads us into our discussion of the functional aspects of the recommended diagnostic approach.

Just as the operant conditioner studying psychological deficits conducts a functional analysis by systematically manipulating environmental consequences, the cognitive-functional analyst notes the behavioral and performance changes that result from environmental manipulations. From such alterations in performance the investigator can readily infer the presence or absence of particular cognitive strategies. Three types of manipulations may be employed in a cognitive-functional approach. The task itself may be manipulated, thus affecting the psychological demands. These may be in the form of speeded performance requirements: increasing the rate of stimulus presentation, thus not permitting rehearsal processes to occur; presenting the task through another modality in order to infer at what particular phase of operation the deficit occurs; or making important cues in the stimulus array more salient, in an attempt to elicit the solution strategy on a simpler task, then gradually returning to the more difficult tasks to see whether the child generalizes the solution strategy. Through this approach one can assess both the subject's capabilities as well as his deficits. Under which task parameters is the subject able to demonstrate competence and under which conditions does the subject's performance begin to deteriorate? By systematically manipulating the task demands, one can pinpoint the aspect of his response repertoire that is deficient.

A second type of manipulation that can aid in investigating cognitive strategies is altering nontask, environmental variables. Assessment may be carried out in a room with few distracting stimuli present, or interpersonal factors may be arranged so as to reduce anxiety, and so on. Through such means one can learn whether the subject is able to elicit adequate cognitions "spontaneously" under ideal environmental conditions, and then proceed to determine what aspects of the situation cause a reinstatement of the "deficit."

The third manipulation employed by the cognitive-functional analyst is providing the subject with supports in the form of (1) direct task aids, such as memory prompts, descriptions of the task demands by breaking the stimuli into components, explicit feedback, opportunities for note taking, etc.; (2) instructional aids given to the subject to help him appraise the task, focus attention, self-evaluate performance, etc. Some investigators (Anderson, 1965; Crovitz, 1966; McKinney, 1973) have studied the improvement of performance that follows from having subjects employ overt self-verbalizations. Vygotsky (1962) suggested that a most useful way to assess a child's capabilities was to have the child perform a task and then to note the degree and kind of improvement that derive from the administration of instructions. For Vygotsky, the child's ability to employ and benefit from instructions was the best reflection of intellectual capabilities. This tradition of assessing capabilities as well as deficits, of testing limits, of systematically determining the conditions under which a particular deficit is manifested, has not been fully exploited by investigators of psychopathology in general and, more specifically, by those studying children with learning disabilities.

Two examples of a cognitive-functional approach will be offered: one with schizophrenics, the second with children with memory deficiencies. Price (1968) sought to understand the poor performance of schizophrenics on a concept identification task. Using an analysis of task requirements, he systematically (1) determined that the schizophrenics understood the task instructions by means of pretraining on sample concept identification tasks; (2) controlled the amount of information given subjects about the concept by providing all relevant concept information on a cue-card preceding each test trial; (3) measured the subjects' ability to discriminate and manipulate the concept symbols by introducing experimental conditions in which cue stimuli presented the concept dimensions separately and combined; (4) assessed the amount of performance deficit due to inability to retain the relevant concept information by both simultaneous and successive presentation of cue and test stimuli.

Thus, a cognitive analysis of the concept-identification task led Price to identify the sequence of psychological processes involved (viz., discrimination, symbol manipulation, retention of concept information). Then he could assess how each process contributed to inadequate performance by conducting functional manipulations and noting alterations of performance when each support was introduced and removed.

The potential of such a task-analysis or cognitive-functional approach to children with learning disabilities was illustrated in an experiment by Belmont and Butterfield (1971), analyzing the memory deficiency of mental retardates. Although retardates are distinguished from children with learning disabilities, the Belmont and Butterfield study nicely illustrates a cognitive-functional approach. In order to understand how learning strategies affect recall accuracy, they manipulated the rate of presentation of a serial list of letters that were to be recalled. They permitted the retarded subjects to employ spontaneous strategies and noted that they did not demonstrate primacy and they had poor recall accuracy. However, when the experimenters controlled stimuli presentation and required that the retardates rehearse and use a strategy, their recall accuracy significantly improved. In contrast, normal subjects, when given freedom to proceed as they wished, manifested increased pauses in the presentation rate as they went deeper into the list, thus indicating the spontaneous use of rehearsal strategies. However, when the normals were forced to abandon rehearsal by means of the experimenter's pacing the presentation more quickly, they demonstrated decreased primacy and inferior performance. Thus, by studying performance under conditions of spontaneous and forced strategies, Belmont and Butterfield were able to discern the psychological process (viz., the disposition not to rehearse) that contributed to inferior recall in retardates.

An important specific implication of the Belmont and Butterfield study should be highlighted: their findings suggest a reasonably simple way of mitigating short-term memory deficiencies in retardates by means of altering the stimulus presentation rate, which in turn affects the disposition to rehearse. The more general implication is that in a cognitive-functional approach to performance deficits the distinction between diagnosis and treatment becomes obscure. A systematic, experimental approach to a particular deficit will permit the investigator to make specific suggestions for remediation. Throughout the assessment the cognitive-functional analyst is providing different external and cognitive supports and noting changes in performance. Assessment of deficiencies and capabilities goes hand-in-hand with remediation.

Each candidate for assessment, whether a schizophrenic or a child with a learning disability, becomes the subject of an experimental investigation. Each case is a separate experiment. The administration of a comprehensive psychoeducational battery, if included, should represent the beginning, not the end-product, of our inquiry. The child's profile on the WISC or some such test may serve as a clue for where to begin the experimental work, the exciting detective investigation, in order to pinpoint the nature of the deficit. The adoption of a cognitive-functional approach would have the impact of changing the way we write our diagnostic reports. At present, reading a case folder of children with learning disabilities, as well as other clinical cases, is usually a tedious task. We can just imagine the impact this has on those who have to write such reports.

> "Test A was given; the scores indicated. . . . This is consistent with Test B . . . and the teacher's report . . . etc., etc."

Such reports usually include a list of tests and a "cookbook" interpretation of each. Imagine instead a report in which the diagnostician shared with the reader his thinking processes, hypotheses, and attempts to test each of them, that is, the detective work. For example:

> "The child was referred for this reason. . . . After an examination of school records, interviews with teachers, parents and the child, the following test was administered because. . . . The performance level and profile were surprising in that the child demonstrated. . . . In order to assess the reliability of these findings another test . . . which seems to assess the same psychological processes was administered under highly supportive conditions in order to assess the child's full capabilities. These supportive conditions included. . . . The performance deficit was still evident and seemed reliable, especially in light of the referral comments. . . . A situational analysis of the deficit revealed the following. . . . In order to determine why the child did poorly on this task, the following functional operations were conducted sequentially. . . . The logic and rationale for each of these are offered and the changes in the child's performance in response to each are described . . . ."

One other example of a cognitive-functional approach to a performance deficit is informative. Goodman (1973) examined the scanning behavior of impulsive school children while they were doing a Matching Familiar Figures test (MFF), developed by Kagan (1966). The task requires the child to identify from an array of six figures one that is identical to a standard figure. The impulsive children, compared to reflective children, performed inefficiently, making many errors and responding quickly. This was confirmed by the impulsive children's eye movements, which Goodman recorded. However, when the task was over, Goodman asked all of his subjects how they went about doing the task and what advice they would offer another child who wanted to make very few errors on the MFF. Many of the impulsive children reported that they first carefully looked at the standard figure, then looked at each of the alternatives in turn, checking back to the standard in order to eliminate alternatives, and that this is what other children should do. Interestingly, the strategies offered by reflectives who made few errors and had lengthy decision times did not differ from those offered by impulsive children. But what the impulsive children said they did and what they actually did with their eyes were not correlated. In fact, the analysis of the impulsive children's eye movements revealed that they rarely looked at the standard nor searched all of the alternatives. Their visual scanning was global, nonanalytic, and unsystematic. Several other investigators (Drake, 1970; Siegelman, 1969) have obtained similar results. Thus, soliciting the children's post hoc strategies was informative, for it suggested that the correct strategy was within their repertoires, but that they did not seem to spontaneously call it forth and/or comply with it. This has obvious implications for treatment.

When one looks at the literature on children with learning disabilities, one infrequently, if ever, hears anything from the child. His perception of the task, his description of his strategy, his appraisal of his performance, and his assessment of his own situation (will he go to a separate class; does he think that people feel he's crazy; is he ridiculed as he goes for assessment, etc.) are absent. It is suggested that the children have something to tell us, if we would only ask and then listen. Soliciting such material is most helpful in conducting a cognitive-functional analysis.

COGNITIVE STRATEGIES DEFICIENCY SYNDROME IN CHILDREN WITH LEARNING DISABILITIES

It should be apparent that a cognitive-functional approach leads one away from searching for one underlying deficit as the contributor to inadequate performance in children with learning disabilities. Instead, it had been argued that each deficiency, whether attentional, memory, or other, can be viewed as a complex process consisting of psychological subprocesses. A deficiency in any one of these subprocesses could contribute to an inadequate performance. Each child's deficit has to be analyzed separately. Communalities and principles will then emerge.

However, if one had to summarize this diagnostic process under one rubric, or apply a label, then perhaps the summary term "cognitive strategies deficiency syndrome" could be applied to children with learning disabilities. This label places immediate emphasis on cognitive strategies: the means by which the subject manages his own thinking. The term "deficiency" underscores the failure of the child with learning disabilities to produce and emit task-relevant cognitions and his likelihood to emit task-irrelevant cognitions and behaviors that contribute to inadequate performance. The term "syndrome" is offered to note the constellation of signs and symptoms, the interdependence of the various psychological processes that are involved in any given task. The association between the different deficiencies in psychological processes is probabilistic and not invariant. As Kinsbourne (1971) has indicated, partial syndromes abound, and often it is not clear how many ingredients have to be present to justify the diagnosis of learning disability. This is particularly true because not all ingredients of a syndrome are of equal importance. A process-oriented, cognitive-functional approach places much emphasis on the role of thinking, or inner speech mechanisms, in controlling behavior and in contributing to adequate performance. It is suggested that children with learning disabilities significantly differ from "normals" in their thinking processes, cognitive strategies, and in the quantity and quality of their inner speech, or what they say to themselves when confronted with a task. Meichenbaum (1975a) has demonstrated how adaptive, task-facilitative thinking processes are teachable by means of self-instructional training; that is, by means of teaching a child to talk to himself differently, one can alter his thinking processes.

FINALLY, A FOOTNOTE ON
THE COGNITIVE-FUNCTIONAL APPROACH

Some years ago, Shapiro (1951) offered a clinical assessment approach which has received insufficient attention, except for the efforts of Inglis (1966) and Yates (1970). In contrast to a test battery approach, Shapiro offered an experimentally oriented approach in which the client's problems were formulated and specified into certain hypotheses. The clinician was encouraged to ask himself what effect the confirmation of each of his hypotheses would have on the treatment and disposal of the patient. As

Shapiro indicated, if any of these hypotheses is not likely to have an effect on treatment or disposal, the diagnostician should be disinclined to test it. The task for the clinician is to formulate and sequentially test various hypotheses. The patient becomes the object of an experimental investigation, with the patient often acting as his own control. The present cognitive-functional approach is in the tradition of Shapiro.

A somewhat different tradition of converging operations, offered by Garner, Hake, and Eriksen (1956), also provides a model for the cognitive-functional approach. Although the concept of converging operations was offered in the context of a debate about the nature of perception, the logic of the approach is applicable to any experimental investigation that is designed to elucidate the nature of psychological processes. By converging operations, Garner et al. meant any set of two or more independent experimental procedures that could explain or allow the selection or elimination of alternative hypotheses or concepts (i.e., establish a concept by ruling out alternative interpretations). The value of a set of operations depends less on the nature of the operations themselves than on the quality of the alternative hypotheses that are being considered.

Kinsbourne (1971), in his examination of neuropsychological disorders, nicely illustrates this approach. Once the patient demonstrates a reliable incapacity or deficit, for example on an aphasia test, Kinsbourne "pounces": he does a systematic sensitive analysis of the client's capabilities by presenting the test items in a different format or a different modality. Is the deficit central or does it involve specifiable subprocesses? Thus, by systematically manipulating the modality and form in which the test is administered, Kinsbourne can infer the nature of the psychological deficit and the neurological involvement.

One important caveat must be underscored as the cognitive-functional analyst compares the patient's performance (whether he is brain damaged, schizophrenic, or a child with a learning disability) with a normal control group on the same task under different conditions. Consider, for example, a study of schizophrenics or children with learning disabilities versus matched normal controls on an attentional task administered under neutral and distraction conditions. The inferior performance under the distraction condition, relative to the neutral condition, may be due to a differential deficit that mediates performance such as attention, *or* it may be attributable to the psychometric properties of the measurement instruments employed. Should the inferior performance of the patient group on the distraction versus neutral condition, relative to a matched control group, be attributed to an ability characteristic of the patients, or to the differential discriminating power of the test? Chapman and Chapman

(1973) have pointed out that the magnitude of the performance deficit obtained by any generally less able group in comparison to another group is a direct function of the discriminating power of the test employed. A more discriminating test will reveal a larger discrepancy. Discriminating power is primarily a function of test reliability and mean and variance of item difficulty. Oltmanns and Neale (1974) have indicated that previous studies of the effects of distraction on schizophrenic performance have not equated the neutral and distractor tasks on these variables. On the contrary, the distraction task has consistently been more difficult and quite likely more discriminating than the neutral task. They demonstrated that the differential deficit obtained may reflect a statistical artifact of the measurement procedures rather than a specific deficit characteristic of schizophrenics.

The caveat for the cognitive-functional analyst is to be as concerned with the characteristics of his instruments as with the nature of the psychological deficit of the patient. With this in mind, we can begin to search for the nature of the psychological deficit.

Finally, it is suggested that only by conducting a systematic analysis of the learning process into its functional components, only by employing converging operations and a cognitive-functional approach, will we be able to fully understand the nature of children with learning disabilities. Remediation and theory will then readily follow.

ACKNOWLEDGMENT

The author is grateful to Myles Genest and Roy Cameron for their helpful editorial comments.

Part VIII

Post-Conference Summary

Neuropsychology of Learning Disorders: Post-Conference Review

Otfried Spreen

In this review I will try to highlight some of the major points made without attempting to review every individual paper in detail. In particular, I would like to focus on the main purpose of the conference, the theoretical models and the implications of the data for a neuropsychology of learning disorders. I hope that the authors will forgive me if I do not mention details of many of the experimental studies presented.

This conference has had a wide scope. It included psychologists of widely differing orientations, psychiatrists, and neurologists. If I seem to pay less attention to an individual's work than it deserves, this merely will be a reflection of my inability to integrate everything, and of my lack of knowledge in some areas.

I am planning to make a few comments about neuropsychology and learning disorders first. I will then turn to the topic of definition and prevalence, as well as the question of subforms of learning disabilities. These subforms of learning disabilities have been a continuing theme throughout this conference that not only provides a handle on the question of nosology but also of the treatment of learning disorders. I will then turn to the etiologic factors. The various models of causation presented range from the genetic and maturational causes to the physiological and biochemical correlates. Particularly the concept of maturational lag has found considerable attention. I will touch only briefly on drug studies and their implications for etiology. After that, I will turn to the descriptive core of the learning disabilities: cerebral dominance stands somewhere between etiology and description, the perceptual and cognitive factors deal directly with the manifestations of learning disabilities with special atten-

This chapter was prepared during Study Leave granted by the University of Victoria and supported by Canada Council. The Victoria studies referred to in the manuscript were supported by National Health and Welfare Canada and by the Medical Research Council of Canada.

tion to sequencing, to attention, field dependence, speech perception, and so on. The question of appropriate tests for the assessment of learning disabilities has been touched on but will not be a major topic for discussion. Finally, I would like to review the important question of long-term development of the learning disabilities which has been discussed here as a test of theories of learning disability, as a check on the importance of early findings, and as a question of prediction, of early warning signs.

My first question is: Is there such a thing as a neuropsychology of learning disorders? The majority of participants seem to agree that this is a worthwhile topic to discuss—or we would not be here. However, it is a sore topic with many educators and some of the conference participants. Only a few years ago there was no such thing in the education literature and only a few feeble attempts in the neuropsychological literature. To illustrate how the neuropsychology of learning disabilities fares even in the most recent literature: I have just read two volumes on "Child Variance" by Rhodes and Tracy (1974). These books attempt to give a state-of-the-arts account of all aspects of deviance from the norm in children. Closest to a neuropsychology of learning disorders comes what was called the "biophysical model." It is listed next to the behavioral, the psychodynamic, the sociological, the ecological, and the countertheoretical models. The material in these books was presented in conference and in book form to 225 teacher trainers all over the United States, i.e., a fair sampling of all the education faculties in that country. The authors asked for feedback from the teacher trainers and included that feedback in their books. It is perhaps not surprising to you that the biophysical model was least preferred among the models described and had the least influence on the thinking of the conference participants.

As one of the conference participants here put it: should we jump into theory building and neurologizing or is it too early for this?

I am mentioning this because I do not want us to forget that there are other positions, other interpretations for many of our data. The neglect of alternatives shows a blind singlemindedness of purpose and leads to a further split of our disciplines. Perhaps it is too early to look across to other disciplines; perhaps it is necessary to have this blind singlemindedness of purpose at this time. The next conference perhaps can have a go at integration. Education and educational failure are a hotly debated field because of the personal involvement of almost everybody. Everybody has an opinion, as in politics. Solid data are harder to come by. Education and educational failure have been a domain of psychoanalytic theory, of philosophies of education from the three R's to the *mens sana in corpore sano* of Fernald and others, of behavior modification and its rejection of any theorizing beyond the observable response, of the pessimism of the theorists of hereditary gift or hereditary defect. If neuropsychology has anything to say about this topic it has to be careful to avoid the trap of claiming exclusive rights to the arena, of neurological labeling of learning disorders without respect to other aspects of the problem.

I think we should be modest in our attempt at building a neuropsychology of learning disorders. We are building a theoretical model of brain functioning that tries to encompass the normal and the abnormal learner. The model should contribute to our understanding of the normal learning process and it should have pragmatic value, eventually resulting in proven remedies based on that theory.

DEFINITION AND PREVALENCE

I turn to the topic of definition and prevalence. Dr. Gaddes suggests the use of the term "prevalence" instead of "epidemiology" to avoid medical implications. He points out that illness tends to be an "all or none affair" whereas learning disabilities are not. I am ready to endorse the term prevalence and rename our session as a session on prevalence. Perhaps the best demonstration that we are not dealing with an "all or none affair" has been provided by Dr. Yule and also some years ago by Dr. Leon Eisenberg (1966). Reading ability is distributed in the general population like other abilities, i.e., in the shape of a Gaussian distribution. The distribution of learning abilities is without doubt a similar one. It has been argued that genetic variability plus environmental factors produce such a normal distribution. What then is the neuropsychological aspect of learning disabilities? Is there a pathological factor producing a "pathological surplus"? If so, what is the proportion of such pathological cases? Dr. Yule's "excess of underachievers" at the low end of the distribution reminded me of the curves published by Dingman and Tarjan in 1960 for the field of mental retardation (Figure 1). Dingman and Tarjan postulated that underlying the tail end of the normal distribution is another normally distributed range of pathological cases with a mean IQ of 32. It is important to realize that this population again is normally distributed, because it means that even though the majority of these cases are at the very severe end of mental retardation, the full distribution ranges well into what we would otherwise call normal intellectual functioning. Perhaps it is this pathological contingent of the learning-disabled child which causes the unusual hump in the distribution reported by Dr. Yule. In fact, one is reminded of the even earlier speculations of Knobloch and Pasamanick (1959) about the "continuum of reproductive casualty" that is encountered in any survey of

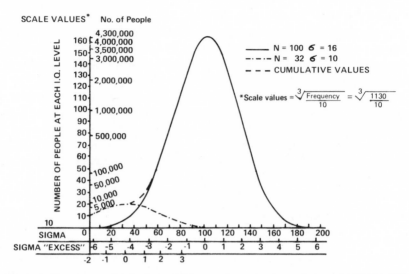

Figure 1. Frequency distribution of IQ assuming a total population of 175,000,000 (from Dingman and Tarjan, 1960).

intellectual functions. We should not forget, however, that Dr. Yule's study showed actually less evidence of neurological pathology in severe cases of reading retardation without general backwardness.

Does it follow then that only in such "pathological cases" the neuropsychology model applies? Or are there other neuropsychological factors contributing? Certainly our knowledge about brain functioning is not applicable to the pathological case only. Variance in cerebral dominance, for example, does not necessarily imply pathology that may be a valid subject of neuropsychological study. However, even here we have to make a distinction between the normal variance of cerebral dominance and its pathological variations.

Dr. Gaddes has tried to determine the proportion of children with learning disabilities as reported in various prevalence studies. The estimates appear to range from 10 to 16% even though only a fifth of that figure is actually found in classes for slow learners, special education, etc. The U. S. Office of Education (1970), on the other hand, talks about only seven hundred thousand learning-disabled children, 28% of whom are served in special programs (Hobbs, 1975). The quoted figures also sometimes include gross mental retardation; in other reports they are restricted to specific learning disabilities.

It is quite obvious that any prevalence estimate is dependent on the definition used. Dr. Gaddes has criticized the 2-year lag as a suitable cutoff point since it produces grossly different figures depending on the age of the child and the tests used. The Myklebust learning quotient (reading age divided by expected age plus correction) is perhaps a better formula. The multiple regression estimate of academic competence by Rutter and Yule attempts an even closer estimate of true learning retardation or deficit that deserves to be more frequently used. Any measurement-based definition, however, will have to consider the fact that in the eyes of parents or teachers only a small portion of "potential" learning problems deserves serious remedial work. The discrepancy between the number of potential learning problems and the number of actually referred or treated cases probably does not stem only from inadequacies in the school system, but from a large number of "survivors," as Dr. Meichenbaum called them, who are able to pull through without remedial help, and from a fair number of children with "temporary" problems that may in the opinion of the teacher clear up within the school year, and that usually do clear up.

The proliferation of terms and the difficulty of agreeing on definitions have been reiterated many times during this conference, especially by Dr. Douglas. In a light vein, E. Fry (1968) a few years ago published a "Do-It-Yourself Terminology Generator" (Table 1) in which a choice of 13 qualifiers such as "minimal," "mild," "organic," "specific" was followed by 13 terms for area of involvement (e.g., nervous, cerebral, reading, perceptual, behavior, CNS) and 13 terms for "problems" such as "retardation, deficit, disability, syndrome, and disorder." Shake well and any number (up to a maximum of approximately 2,000) of fancy new or old terms will emerge. Fry suggested that any number of additional qualifiers, adjectives, or problems could be added to generate another 2,000 terms.

I am not so much concerned with the proliferation of terms as with the adequacy of the description of the group that the term designates. What we call it does not matter so much, but the exact definition of the group under investigation is crucial. In other words, since we will probably not agree on a common definition in the near future, I would settle for less and propose that we at least state clearly what factors were considered in the selection of subjects.

I think it is apparent to all of us that we have to agree at least on some basic rules of description. First, we have to state whether cases of mental retardation (as defined by an acceptable definition) are included or excluded. Second, we have to state whether learning disabilities are strictly a lag in academic progress in the face of normal intelligence or whether maturational lag of other types (i.e., emotional or social) is included. Third, we have to state whether only specific academic skills are retarded, e.g., reading, or whether the learning disability affects a broad range of academic skills. Fourth, we have to state whether our sample is, in

Table 1. Do-It-Yourself Terminology Generator (from Fry, 1968 with permission).

Qualifier	Area of Involvement	Problem
Secondary	Nervous	Deficit
Minimal	Brain	Dysfunction
Mild	Cerebral	Damage
Minor	Neurological	Disorder
Chronic	Neurologic	Desynchronization
Diffuse	CNS	Handicap
Specific	Language	Disability
Primary	Reading	Retardation
Developmental	Perceptual	Deficiency
Disorganized	Impulsive	Impairment
Organic	Visual-Motor	Pathology
Clumsy	Behavior	Syndrome
Functional	Psychoneurologic	Complex

Directions: Select any word from first column, add any word from second column, then add any word from third column. If you don't like the result, try again. It will mean about the same thing. The list will yield approximately 2,000 terms, but if this is not sufficient, add synonyms of your choice, e.g., asthenic, physiological, dyslexic, aphasoid, neurophrenic, etc.

addition, purified by the exclusion of environmental factors, i.e., lack of stimulation and motivation at home, or whether these factors are included. Fifth, we have to state whether neurological damage has been searched for and excluded or whether it has been included or whether it has been left at variance. All these distinctions are very well within our reach at the present time so that there is no excuse for a lack of clarity on these five points. In the area of reading failure, one other distinction should be made. It has been a persistent finding in many studies that populations referred to a reading clinic tend to show more significant results on a variety of measures, from EEG to cognitive performance, while on the other hand findings tend to be marginal or not replicable if the population is drawn directly from the classroom without referral, i.e., is based on reading achievement tests only. This may be related to the error of test measurements, but it may also be related to the fact that only the most serious problems, usually after a lot of experimenting on the part of the teacher, are referred to the experts at the reading clinic. It may be that we are dealing with a more serious "pathological" group in reading clinic populations. At any rate, this distinction between two sources of populations for our studies should be kept in mind.

The list of five factors just made already lends itself to the formation and definition of subgroups. However, before I move on to this point, I would like to raise a question that is often neglected in our studies. All our definitions are centered on success in school, i.e., academic abilities. Whether we use a 2-year cutoff, a learning quotient, or any other type of definition, the criterion usually remains as whether or not the child is doing well in school. We know little about the prognostic value (and I will return to this question later) of any of these lags on later development of the child. We do not know whether a child labeled as a learning problem in grade two will still have a learning problem in grade twelve or whether the child will ever get there. We know even less about what will happen to the child when he leaves school. This is perhaps the most crucial question, which both Dr. Trites and Dr. Yule referred to. It is, of course, a serious handicap for a child to be slow in school. In most cases, it leads to considerable experiences of failure. It also leads often to a lack of a suitable school diploma required for many jobs. Does it automatically lead to failure and unhappiness in life?

The question is not an idle one. Although circumstances may have changed, an older study by Baller and Charles (Charles, 1953) and several other studies in the field of mental retardation have shown that children labeled mentally retarded in school are not necessarily failures in life. In fact, a considerable portion of these children later on slip into a normal, unobtrusive role in our society with income, number of houses owned, size of family, even types of jobs quite similar to those of the "normals" in school. If this is true of the mentally retarded, should this not also be true for the child with learning disabilities or with specific reading disability? We have all seen the occasional doctoral candidate who completes his graduate studies with a serious handicap in reading and writing. However, at the moment we still have hardly any systematic long-term follow-up of this type. We simply do not know. I suspect that we may be overemphasizing academic skills that are not necessarily those required for a successful life in adulthood.

SUBGROUPS

I am turning now to the important question of the finding of subgroups. As I suggested just a moment ago the definition of our sample already provides for some obvious groupings that can be made in the field of learning disabilities: the inclusion or exclusion of the mentally retarded, the inclusion or exclusion of the neurologically handicapped, the inclusion or exclusion of environmentally handicapped (i.e., the distinction between primary and secondary learning disabilities already made by Rabinovitch, 1959), and the inclusion of all academic skills versus the disability in a single skill only (e.g., reading).

During the course of this meeting other subgroups have been suggested. Dr. Yule suggested the distinction between specific reading disability and general backwardness that has been shown to differ in a five-year follow-up study in terms of outcome and has been replicated in other groups. Dr. Tallal suggests a distinction between auditory processing deficit and visual decoding deficit and a third group that has deficits in both areas. Dr. Nelson suggests a distinction between a group that is retarded in spelling and reading (plus low verbal IQ = general language learning deficit) as opposed to a spelling deficit only (without a difference in the two parts of the IQ). Dr. Doehring suggests possible subgroups depending on subskills of reading at the word, letter, oral, and other levels, but does not confirm the distinction between learning disabilities and reading disabilities as used by other authors. Dr. Wender suggests subgroups depending on the response to drugs, with a distinction between those who respond to stimulants and those who respond to depressants. Dr. Ferguson used the distinction of overaroused and underaroused groups. Obviously all these subgroups are somewhat dependent on the investigatory goal of the author. Different groups are likely to suggest themselves, depending on whether we are investigating response to drugs, subskills of reading, cognitive correlates, or outcome over a longer period of time. It is hoped that all these aspects are interrelated in some fashion, although at the moment it does not appear that we are quite ready for such a comparison across the very different interests represented here. It would be a goal for a future conference to attempt an integration between the various models of finding subgroups, since eventually these groups should converge and should provide a better outline of the forms of learning disabilities with the goal of early detection, prognostic implication, and treatment.

The various approaches to the learning disabilities have also led to the suggestion of highly specific terms during this conference. Authors have talked about an attentional reading deficit, an arousal deficit, a focused arousal deficit, a sequencing deficit, a memory deficit, a cognitive strategy deficiency syndrome, and a hypo- and a hyperactive syndrome. Again, these differing terms reflect the special interests and research orientations of the authors and are not necessarily incompatible. The forester, the hunter, the lumberjack, the carpenter, the hiker, the ecologist all have different perceptions of what a forest is. Similarly the geneticist, the experimental psychologist, the educator, and the many other special interest groups studying learning disabilities are likely to have different perceptions of what may turn out to be the same thing.

ETIOLOGY

Let me now turn to the question of etiology. Dr. Hughes has given us a review of the important biochemical and bioelectrical findings in learning disabilities. He was very careful to speak about correlates rather than causes, since changes in the metabolism of a child do not necessarily suggest a cause but may be the result of a functional deficit or even an epiphenomenon of stress in the organism. The routine EEG findings in the field of learning disabilities are quite disappointing as Hartlage and Green (1973) and Burnett and Struve (1974) have shown. The confusing findings with the EEG in learning disabilities allow little speculation about causes, since, as Dr. Hughes implied, an abnormal EEG may actually be a predictor of good success in treatment, i.e., perhaps the result of the brain's reaction to stress in general. The findings with other physiological measures such as GSR, heart rate, and evoked potential are also by no means clear in their implications about the etiology of learning disorders. Dr. Ferguson found only spurious differences in the GSR and heart rate whereas Dr. Levine had more luck with the GSR and heart rate changes in learning-disabled children, which she put into the theoretical context of the orienting reflex model.

Dr. Sheer has limited his research to the 40-Hz EEG band which, when sufficiently isolated, tends to show deficits in learning-disabled children. He has also put his results into the context of a general theory of learning disorders by suggesting that these EEG findings are the result of a deficit in focused arousal. This in turn makes it difficult for the learning-disabled child to maintain sequences in short-term store and to fix memories in long-term store. He suggests that the deficit may be the result of abnormal biochemical mechanisms (of acetylcholine action) at the cortical level, possibly in the angular and supramarginal area, although he also described in detail the role of the reticular activating system as a whole and of the pyroform cortex and the amygdala in particular.

Most of the findings described in the physiological session seem to point to the notion of defective attention or arousal mechanisms in the learning-disabled child. A distinction between the child with lack of attention and the child with excessive attention has been made and confirmed by other findings. At least in the eyes of our physiologically oriented colleagues arousal, regulation, readiness response, and state changes may be at the core of the problem of learning disabilities. As a general theory, this has been expounded for some time. Dr. Douglas has given us a very thoughtful analysis of the attention deficit problem. Future studies, particularly with the new methods for the investigation of blood flow in various areas of the brain (Risberg and Ingvar in Lund, Sweden, 1973) and the evoked response method, may provide the means for yet another promising assessment of the organism in the process of learning.

The locus of disorder in the nervous system has been discussed in some detail by Dr. Sheer. He proposes that the group with a 40-Hz EEG deficit is only one group of the learning disabilities. It is indeed possible that we may have to visualize the physiological locus of the disorder at various different levels. Just for speculation's sake, one could imagine a level of general arousal and resulting general difficulties as found in the hypo- or hyperactive child related to the reticular activating system, a more focused attentional deficit resulting from malfunction at a higher level, e.g., the mid-brain, and one can assume that deficits may result from disorders in the functional development of the neocortex, right or left or specific areas of each. In fact, Dr. Leisman has suggested a basic model of this kind and Dr. Levine has referred to the arousal, activation, and effort three-stage model of Pribram and McGuinness (1975). One is tempted to develop this into a full-blown system of possible deficits also supported by the results of some of the drug studies presented here and as a result have yet another classification system for the learning disabilities. However, I think you will agree that such an interpretation would far exceed what can be based on our data so far.

STRUCTURAL DAMAGE OR PROCESS CHANGE

One basic question of whether we are dealing here with structural damage or process change in learning disabilities has been raised by Dr. Levine, and it is a very important one. It also relates to our conception of the functional asymmetries of the two hemispheres, and it has been specifically discussed in relation to reading disabilities. Are we dealing with structural damage that basically alters brain development and brain functioning for the life span or are we dealing with a functional change, a delayed maturation without tangible damage? Dr. Wender has used the term "biochemical lesion" related to specific neurotransmitters. The investigators of the notion of maturational lag, especially Dr. Satz, have strongly adhered to the position that structural damage is not implied when they talk about a lag in hierarchical development. However, this question may turn out to be a red herring, since it is difficult for me to imagine a gross maturational lag or even moderate changes in psychological functioning without at least some subtle, biochemical substrates for them.

Dr. Satz has stated in one of his theoretical papers (Satz and Van Norstand, 1973) that "the formulation conveniently avoids the use of the term, usually pernicious, which conceptualizes the disorder within a framework of a static disease model (e.g., brain damage)." Dr. Rourke has taken him up on this and postulated that the question of "lag" versus "defect" may be settled on the basis of outcome studies. Indeed, Satz and Friel (1973) have suggested that, since no brain damage is postulated, children with reading disabilities may eventually "overcome" their problem. I have two comments about this issue: (1) I do not agree that an optimistic prognosis is necessarily justified on the basis of the developmental lag theory since the lag may persist or prevent the child from acquiring essential skills during critical periods of his development. Nor do I think that such a prognostic statement is necessarily implicit in or germane to the theory of developmental lag. (2) Rourke's results of a follow-up study between 8 and 12 are important, although his choice of tests does not necessarily meet the expectations of the developmental lag theory for that age. However, they also do not prove lag or deficit, since one could argue that he tested his children either too early or too late in life to be fully convincing—if we accept prognosis as a genuine part of the theory. At any rate, my reading of Dr. Satz's statements is that he would prefer to take no position on the question of brain damage, overt or covert, structural or biochemical, gross or minimal.

The term "minimal brain damage" has fortunately been avoided for the larger part of this conference. My own feeling is that the term is quite useless, since there is nothing minimal about brain damage that causes a serious learning disorder. The term can only refer to our lack of knowledge about the brain damage so that the term "minimal" should be replaced by "unknown" or "undetermined" or "inferred," or, as Dr. Yule called it, "dubious."

In general there are some limits to the information to be gleaned from biochemical and physiological studies. It is perhaps necessary to have a good nosology of the learning disorders before biochemical types can be demonstrated. A genetic hypothesis has also been mentioned by several speakers, and investigated by Dr. Pizzamiglio. The hypothesis is attractive but difficult to untangle because of the well-known nature—nurture issue.

USE OF STIMULANT DRUGS

Dr. Sprague has given us an excellent example of a detailed series of studies investigating the use of stimulant drugs in learning disorders. He has shown that learning improvement and behavioral improvement are two very different things and that dosage of the drug for one purpose may be quite different from that for the other. Dr. van Duyne has also investigated stimulant drugs and described the interaction of the drug effect with training and task conditions. He emphasized initial training as an important variable and led us back to the attentional hypothesis about the learning disabilities. The same position that stimulant drugs affect selective attention was taken by Dr. Conners. His impressive series of studies ranged from the tremograph to the Porteus Maze and the WISC and back again to autonomic measures and the vertex potential. His studies established not only the gain in attention but also opened up the study of individual differences in drug response in that some children tend to improve more in their responses to light than to sound and vice versa. His multiple regression analysis showed the stimulant drugs as facilitators through improved selective attention rather than as "intelligence-specific" drugs for memory or arithmetic or language. A similar position has been taken by Dr. Douglas and her associates in recent studies. Like other speakers she deemphasizes general hyperactivity and distractibility as descriptors of the learning-disabled child and emphasizes specific attention deficits and impulse control. She also reminded us that one cannot expect autonomic or electrophysiologic measures to show improvement if the failure experiences of the child for a given task have already led to a set of nonattending.

To the uninitiated, like myself, in the field of psychopharmacology, the drug therapy in the field of learning disabilities is an area that is only slowly becoming charted. I have heard only a few speculations as to what drugs actually do. But I was fascinated with the gradually accumulating evidence about what drug is useful for what behavior, what dosage is useful and which is harmful, which type of child responds to what drug, and particularly what physiological mechanisms and what structures of the nervous system are being influenced. As in other fields, multiple interactions are to be expected and difficult to untangle.

Enough about this area of which I know very little. I noted, however, that drug intervention has been discussed in some detail here in its implication for a theory of learning disorders while educational and other behavioral intervention has not been a topic of discussion with the exception of the reference by Dr. Douglas to the "strange" response of learning-disabled children to reinforcement. Perhaps it is worthwhile to ask at a future conference what can be learned about the neuropsychological theories of learning disorders from studies of educational or behavioral intervention.

MATURATION

Let me turn now to the concept of maturation and its investigation. The concept of maturational lag in learning-disabled and particularly in reading-disabled children has been forcefully expounded by Satz and Sparrow (1970) after earlier formulations by Money (1966) and De Hirsch, Jansky, and Langford (1966). The notion is deceptively simple. It is postulated that functions involved in language and reading are hierarchically organized and sequentially developed throughout the early childhood, childhood, and early teen years. The development at each age level is age specific, but builds on the functions acquired at earlier stages. In Guthrie's (1973) terms it is not an assembly model of individual components, but a system of associated and interrelated components developed hierarchically. The model allows for the understanding of the seemingly contradictory series of findings with children at different age levels. What appears to be a right–left orientation deficit at one stage in development may appear as a lack of ear, hand, foot, or eye preference at another, and as reading disability in yet another stage in development. A rather impressive amount of supportive findings for the model have been presented over the past few years and this conference is no exception. At the earliest developmental level, Dr. Taylor's demonstration of male–female differences in maturation and hence in development after early lesions can be compared to Wilson's (1970) findings for cerebral hemispherectomy, the report by Buffery and Gray (1972) on sex differences in spatial and linguistic skills, and to Goldman et al.'s (1974) findings of sex-dependent behavioral effects of cerebral cortical lesions in monkeys. Dr. McBurney has reported on the confusing number of switches in handedness, footedness, and eyedness during early childhood and their implications for the further development between the ages of 4 and 6.5 years. She implied that the strongly right-handed person with hand, foot, and eye congruity should fare best in his development. It has been suggested that maturation during the period of reading skill development produces a shift in emphasis from one area of the brain to another, i.e., from the occipital area with primary emphasis on visual sequencing to the temporal area with primary emphasis on auditory information processing. That this shift from one process to another exists has been demonstrated without doubt in many other studies. Whether it really reflects a differential maturation of frontal and occipital areas of the brain or whether it is all in that famous switching station, the parietal lobe, remains speculative of course at this point. Geschwind's arguments about the late myelinizing areas in the parietal lobe may eventually provide an answer here. Other speakers have emphasized the role of the parietal lobe, particularly in relation to language and reading. My own conceptualization of brain maturation favors this area, since in the continued development of the child intersensory integration and a "hookup" of vision, touch, motor activity with language, and audition seem required. This connection between sensory and motor functions with our ability to translate into linguistic modules, i.e., into language, has correctly been described as a "second signal system" by Soviet researchers. Developing written language requires, it seems, almost yet another step of symbolization, a "third signal system," in which the language code is translated into a written code (which has little similarity to spoken language). The obvious area for the integration of all these activities from a purely topographic point of view is the parietal lobe. The results of destructions in the parietal lobe area in man have confirmed this and seem to emphasize the angular and supramarginal areas.

From the study of dyslexic boys and the corresponding control group at age 9, Leong further tried to clarify the maturational lag in retarded readers. He argued that the maturational lag may concern (1) the lateralization of functions in that the symbiotic relationship between the more spatial right hemisphere and the more language oriented left hemisphere is not sufficiently established, and that (2) simultaneous and successive synthesis at the perceptual, mnestic, and intellectual levels (according to Luria's model) are not sufficiently matured.

Leong also presented factor analytic data showing both a divergent and a successive factor space in his experimental groups. As in other studies using factor analytic methodology he found that visual short-term memory and visual sequential memory occupy unique vector space that is disparate from the dimensions in the control group. These findings are quite consistent with earlier findings in Germany by Wewetzer (1959), by Lienert (1961), and by Reinert et al. (1964) that have investigated the so-called divergency hypothesis. Briefly, the divergency hypothesis claims that the factor analytic ability structure in abnormal groups, especially in brain-damaged children and in retarded children, is not necessarily comparable to the factor structure in normal children of the same mental age, but is divergent, i.e., shows different or additional factors compared to control groups. Similar findings have been reported by Baumeister and Bartlett (1962a, 1962b) for retarded populations in the United States. Ellis (1963), in particular, has emphasized the importance of an additional memory or trace factor in retarded groups. Dr. Yule has also referred to the different cognitive structure in children who later developed reading problems.

Witelson also reported a study investigating the developmental lag in dyslexic children between the age of 7 and 16. Bakker follows the same hypothesis in a study of dichotic listening, word naming, masked word naming, and word naming and word matching. He found the repeatedly demonstrated sex difference in favor of girls' earlier development and shows that children at age 8 have two different strategies in reading, the slow but accurate and the fast but sloppy strategy. The importance of these findings is underlined by the fact that at age 11 the more perceptually oriented readers (with a right hemisphere strategy) are at a disadvantage. What appears to be an advantage at age 8 may very well turn out to be a hindrance and possibly a permanent reading problem at a later stage.

A study by Trites finally leads us into the late adolescence in the follow-up study of youngsters with reading disability after 3 years at the age of 15 to 18. His conclusion is rather grim: Dr. Trites tells us that the poor get poorer; the bad get only a little better in spite of remedial help. Of course, Dr. Trites is only investigating the tail end of the reading problem. We do not know what results he would have found if his subjects had been studied from kindergarten or first grade on. His findings do show, however, that it may be too late for successful remediation by the time the child is 12 years old.

Yule's follow-up at a slightly earlier age (from 9 to 14) is also not very encouraging about the future outlook of disabled readers. He found that the prognosis was slightly better if the reading disability occurred in the context of general backwardness and that the specific reading disability students fared worst.

FOLLOW-UP STUDIES

I would like to digress for a moment to look at the general field of follow-up studies in the area of learning disabilities and reading disabilities. We have heard some results presented here and Dr. Trites has summarized others, but, in general, good long-term follow-up studies are hard to come by. A recent literature review of our own showed only a small number of pertinent studies. Many of these were concerned with special groups such as hyperkinetic children, autistic children, children with reading problems, or were concerned with specific effects of treatment or with emotional and behavioral adjustment problems. The well-known study by Balow and

Blomquist (1965) found that of 32 children with severe reading disabilities, all eventually (i.e., 10 to 15 years later) achieved at least a reading level of grade 10 although a variety of related problems were still evident at that time. A similar study by Preston and Yarington (1967) found similar results. A study by Hinton and Knights (1971) found improvement in 75% of children with learning problems in their study if counseling and medication were received. This sounds somewhat more encouraging, but one would have to compare carefully the definitions in these studies before one could arrive at any generalizations.

In children with evidence of brain damage the information is even more sparse. Denhoff (1973), whose study began at infant to preschool age, mentions that over a 10-year span a change in the clinical picture "with diminishing signs of neurological dysfunction and evidence of increasing IQ scores" emerges. Dykman, Peters, and Ackerman (1973) reported on 53 14-year-old returnees who were originally tested in the early grades and reported to have minimal brain damage. In comparison with control subjects they found, not surprisingly, that low IQ scores were predictive of poor academic success and that many of their subjects suffered from poor self-image and dislike of school. The authors speculate that "the younger case, 8 to 9 year olds at the time of the first study, will show greater improvement than the child who is diagnosed as minimally brain damaged at age 10 to 12; the latter case is more apt to carry the scar at age fourteen." Moskowitz (1964) is also somewhat pessimistic about the gain of 25 elementary grade children in classes for brain-injured children after exposure to remedial instruction for 2 to 3.5 years. He reports that their progress was extremely poor with an average IQ around 75. Kaste (1972) examined 116 children including children with established brain dysfunction, with mild brain damage, with minimal brain damage, and controls. These children, originally seen at ages 8 to 12, were followed after a 10-year period and found to show "an even more pronounced degree of patterns which previously have been associated with cerebral dysfunction" for 85% of her subjects. She concludes that "they did not simply grow out of the problem or become more similar to other former child guidance patients with the passage of time." Flach and Malmros (1972) followed 148 children with severe head injury after an 8- to 10-year period and found persisting mental disturbance in 46% and social maladjustment in 27% of these patients. Our own follow-up study with groups of adolescents and young adults originally examined between the ages of 8 and 12 years because of learning problems (with and without definite indications of brain damage and with minor neurological findings) is still in progress but appears to confirm these findings.

The overall impression from follow-up studies is that findings for children identified at an early age are somewhat contradictory and occasionally hopeful, but that findings on children identified at a later age are fairly grim. Moreover, the findings of serious social and emotional maladjustment in these children are rather alarming and should not be neglected. The longer learning disabilities persist the more it is likely that hostility towards school, emotional resistence, and poor motivation occur. If we find that these children do not perform adequately in some of our tasks, we may no longer be justified in attributing this directly to the problem originally identified. In fact, a vicious circle may very well occur: if I am not doing well on the task, I dislike it, and if I dislike it, I am not going to do well on it. Inferences from such performance at a later age must be made with great caution, particularly if we talk about "attention deficit." Furthermore, the studies reviewed here are still rather spotty, leave considerable gaps in the age ranges covered, and are often inconclusive. They suffer frequently from the problem discussed earlier of investigating very small samples from highly selected populations that are often ill-defined.

Fortunately, at the younger age several good follow-up studies are now under way. I have already mentioned a few. A major study by Satz and associates (1973, 1974, 1975) is now on its fifth year and follows the original 21 variables at kindergarten age in their predictive value for reading performance up to grade four with good success. Our own study with 644 children tested three successive years of a total school district population at kindergarten level with four predictor variables and is also moving into its fifth year with all available school achievement tests and grades as criterion variables. One interesting finding is that teacher prediction at kindergarten level only makes successful predictions for performance in grades one and two (as shown before in several other studies) but loses its predictive value in grades three, four, and five. In comparison, our tests, the Peabody Picture Vocabulary Test, the Benton Visual Retention Test, and the Raven Progressive Matrices retain their predictive value up to grade five. Again, a better break-down into specific types of deficits has not been made as yet, but should enhance the value of this as of most other follow-up studies.

Dr. Kalverboer has reminded us that we should include the large bulk of good information on the development from the neonatal to the school age development in our discussion. This has indeed been an omission at this conference and I am glad that he discussed some of his own results and those of others.

Dr. Taylor also referred to lesions probably existing since the prenatal period and showed some information on the Wechsler test in that selected group of individuals who later come to surgery because of epilepsy. The focus naturally is on the school age when we talk about learning disabilities, but the earlier years and the years after school should also be of interest to us.

Dr. Satz has argued forcibly for the need for good longitudinal studies and against the "quick" cross-sectional approach. There is, however, no instant virtue to be regained from the longitudinal approach, although I agree that there is a need for careful planning of research design. The problem has pursued our colleagues in the field of gerontology for some time and they have come up with some rather ingenious solutions in research design. Briefly, they have developed a mixed cross-sectional and longitudinal design that allows an assessment of the cohort effect and of retest and practice effects that are a serious problem in longitudinal studies. Perhaps we could profit from a look at the work of Schaie, Baltes, and Nesselroade on the subject.

Dr. Meichenbaum and also Dr. Kalverboer have argued rather strongly that we should not jump to the general test battery approach or to the investigation of a special deficit model with multivariate methods. Rather, they would prefer to proceed with a systematic task analysis investigating each subject's thinking strategies by manipulating task, nontask, and support conditions. While this resembles the clinical approach many of us practice in the counseling of the individual child, I think the investigation of task variables in the individual can only benefit us all in the long run if some generalizations regarding remediation and/or theory can be derived from the investigation. And Dr. Meichenbaum may yet need a factor analysis to cope with the data generated by a cognitive-functional approach. I am not saying this lightly. Similar to Dr. Kalverboer's "free-field" observation, we have used aphasic free speech in one of our studies. The analysis so far has taken 8 years and has generated numerous variables that can only be handled by multivariate methods.

CEREBRAL DOMINANCE

I need to deal only briefly with the topic of cerebral dominance since it has been summarized by Dr. Satz. Dr. Buffery has very carefully laid out the various factors involved in the study of this topic: the crossed–uncrossed pathways, the eyedness, the earedness, the handedness, the brainedness, and age and sex. These are indeed the variables that have aroused such great attention during the last 15 years, unless you wish to be facetious and add the preference of one nostril over the other. We have heard a number of additional findings in this conference. Dr. Leong reported that dichotic digits are less lateralized to the right ear in dyslexic boys than in his control subjects. Dr. Friedman and Dr. Pizzamiglio added the Witkins field-dependent–independent dimension to the investigations and found that field dependence is frequently found in persons with incomplete dominance of the left side in cognitive behavior. Dr. Pizzamiglio also showed that a genetic linkage can be found for field dependence. The relationship between field independence, verbal ability, and hand awareness has been discussed by Dr. Friedman. It would be interesting to see this variable included in an investigation of developmental trends from 7 to 12 years. Dr. Witelson has added the dichotomous-tactile stimulation and tactile recognition to the more familiar tests of lateral dominance and found atypical asymmetry related to reading disability. She also described some fascinating age-related changes which will need some time for replication and interpretation. I already mentioned Dr. Bakker's important findings on the reading strategies in younger children in relation to the right ear advantage. The finding that older retarded readers retain what Dr. Bakker calls "right hemisphere strategy" with primarily perceptual processing and inadequate language processing shows that in younger children smaller ear differences to the right or the left may actually be an advantage and indicate more maturational flexibility.

The topic of lateral asymmetry and its development will no doubt keep us active for a number of years. What appeared at first as a relatively simple developmental gradient has become increasingly complex. Left handers are no longer the certain candidates for learning disabilities or reading disabilities. Ambilaterality, but only if combined with other indicators of mixed lateralization, may become indicators of the most serious risk group. Even among the left handers, subpopulations may be found. Varney and Benton (1975) have recently emphasized the familial background in respect to handedness and shown that nonfamilial left handedness may be correlated with serious problems. Wilson (1971) at our laboratory showed that the left-handed good reader had no difficulties with visual-auditory integration tasks in comparison to the right-handed good reader. When poor readers were compared, the left-handed poor readers were grossly deficient on these tasks as compared to poor right-handed readers.

Dr. Satz has admonished all of us to be careful not to jump from behavioral observations, e.g., on dichotic listening, into premature speculations about cerebral asymmetry. He showed on the basis of the few data that actually compare dichotic listening with cerebral status that a reversal of ear advantage in most cases does not mean a reversal of cerebral asymmetry. I am happy to endorse his statement: unless we have proof about the state of the brain, it is wise to remain at a descriptive level since nothing can harm us more in this developing field of neuropsychology than unfounded overinterpretation of our data.

He has also called for a high degree of sophistication not only in the formulation of theories, but in the conduction of experiments. That, again, is good advice, also given in a different form by Dr. Meichenbaum. Too often we accept an available method, even from research in adults—as if it were a ready-made "test" and without checking what and how well it measures in a population of children. The 100% and the 0% performance level, the base and ceiling effect, have also plagued many of our studies and have led to nonsignificant or misleading findings. In our own laboratory, we have found it useful to use individual thresholds for each subject. For example, in tachistoscopic half-field studies, ascending and descending threshold determinations are made first, then a 15-practice-trial series is conducted and repeated with a different threshold if the subject does not achieve approximately 50% performance (Maddess, 1975). The result is that the subject performs at optimal level for himself, and that right and left field differences are not confounded by differences in threshold. In the end, the individually determined thresholds for verbal and nonverbal material can serve as separate variables themselves. I think we can invent analogous techniques for other sensory channels.

OTHER PERCEPTUAL AND COGNITIVE FACTORS

Let me now turn briefly to some of the other perceptual and cognitive factors discussed in this conference. Dr. Leisman in his study of saccadic eye movements sees brief fixation pauses as periods of information transmission and processing, essential for storage. During these periods visual sensitivity diminishes; the eye then catches up with renewed sensitivity during the next saccadic movement. He cites evidence that saccadic movements have longer duration and lower velocity in older children and that younger children, hemiplegics, and brain-damaged children show greater velocity and shorter durations. Hence he postulates that in children with attentional and reading problems saccadic movements are less exact, more variable, and that therefore their information transmission may also be ineffective.

Dr. Leisman's findings may eventually contribute to our knowledge of visual processing as the research from the Haskins laboratory has contributed to our understanding of speech perception. Moreover, it would seem to me that both Leisman and Sheer have described a similar deficit in focused attention from very different lines of investigation and have both proposed a deficit in the mechanism of storage as a result. Doehring has attacked the question of subskill patterns important for reading and the pattern of their acquisition from age 6 to 16. Nelson has compared spelling and reading in relation to general language ability and Tallal and Shankweiler have concentrated on the speech perception aspects in relation to language and reading disorders. Tallal has argued that in children with language disorder and reading disorder, temporal order perception is disturbed as demonstrated by the fact that they have difficulties in the perception of short duration of formant transitions in stop consonants. Artificial prolongation of this duration seems to assist these children in this task. Shankweiler investigated the difficulty of segmentation in children with poor reading. He has also provided us with a glance at the Haskins work on how short-term memory works and has argued cogently that a phonetic recoding occurs even for alphabetic material. Confusability at the phonetic level has been shown to be an impairment, especially for the good reader. His findings may well be related to Bakker's findings that the strategy of reading slowly and accurately, i.e., not phonetically confusing, helps in the beginning but may be a hindrance at a later age. The role of verbal mediation and "inner language," i.e., of yet higher-level cognitive skills, has been mentioned in several papers during this conference, but needs perhaps a more detailed treatment at future meetings, since we have been rather preoccupied with the perceptual deficits at this point.

CONCLUDING COMMENTS

Returning to my first question, "Is there such a thing as a neuropsychology of learning disorders?" and looking back at this conference, I believe that we have been quite successful at surveying the field of conceptual hypotheses. The field is becoming staked out. Topics like developmental lag, hemispheric asymmetry and its development, cognitive and perceptual deficits, attention, and arousal clearly form the focus of our present interests and are genuine topics of human neuropsychology.

The theories discussed here deal with differing aspects of the learning-disabled child and are therefore not incompatible. What is studied as a conceptual or perceptual deficit by some of us can, at another level, be perceived as a disorder in the development of hemispheric asymmetry of function, and may, at yet another level, be seen as deficit in sustained attention or focused arousal. Whether these three or four or five different levels represent only different aspects of the same phenomenon, i.e., a unitary form of learning deficit, or whether—what is more likely—we are dealing with distinct subforms relating to these levels or overlapping some of them, remains to be seen in future integrative studies. A first attempt at integrating the attention process hypothesis and the problem of hemispheric asymmetry has been made already in Kinsbourne and Smith's (1974) new book. The maturational lag hypothesis is a longitudinal one and can be seen as occurring in the development of all of these levels. Hence, it would appear to me that we must work on the integration of these basic building blocks of a neuropsychology of learning disorders.

I realize that I am arguing for a rather complex model of learning disabilities. Dr. Doehring has reviewed the models very carefully, but, being a pessimist, I tend to favor a multiple cause—multiple outcome interaction model, which may be most suitable for many of our research efforts. This model, incidentally, lends itself to a canonical method of analysis.

In conclusion I would like to emphasize quite subjectively some points that stand out in their importance to me. First, it is very important that we are precise in our description of the population under investigation and, by implication, in our definition. Second, I have been impressed with our gradual approach to the investigation and description of specific subforms of learning disabilities that stand out not only descriptively but also may be of value prognostically and in their response to treatment. Third, we have made some progress in the investigation of etiological factors; even though they may at the moment perhaps better be described as physiological, biochemical, genetic, or maturational correlates, they are gradually coming into clearer focus and may eventually be related to our purely descriptive subgroups and their treatment and their general outlook for the future. Fourth, we have learned more about perceptual and cognitive factors useful for the description of the deficits found in learning disabilities, namely, in visual or auditory processing, language coding, field dependence, speech perception, and attention, as well as on batteries of tests relating to cerebral dominance and other neuropsychological factors. Fifth, we have made great strides in the investigation of the long-term development of the learning disorders, particularly the investigation of the hypothesis of a developmental lag. This hypothesis is becoming more tangible, details are falling into place, and I hope that we will soon have a solid body of knowledge in this area. Sixth, we have results of a beginning series of follow-up studies that allow us to chart the progress of the learning-disabled child in relation to his future academic development. It was not the purpose of this conference to look at other aspects of development, emotional or social or the long-term outlook for life, but I have suggested that these are important aspects that must be included for a full understanding of the problem.

I hope that this conference is not the last one of its kind.

References

Ackerman, P., J. Peters, and R. Dykman. 1971. Children with learning disabilities: WISC profiles. J. Learning Disabilities 4: 150–166.

Adams, J. 1973. Clinical neuropsychology and the study of learning disorders. Pediatr. Clin. North Am. 20: 587–598.

Adler, S. 1974. Pediatric psychopharmacology and the language-learning impaired child. Am. Speech Hearing Assoc. 16: 299–304.

Agranoff, B.W., R.E. Davis, L. Casola, and R. Lim. 1967. Actinomycin-D blocks formation of memory of shock-avoidance in goldfish. Science 158: 1600–1601.

Allen, I.W., and H.E. Fitzgerald. 1974. Habituation as an index of intra-sensory and intersensory integration of form. J. Gen. Psychol. 124: 131–144.

Alpern, M. 1962. The eye. In H. Davson (ed.), Muscular Mechanisms, Vol. III, pp. 3–299. Academic Press, New York.

Altman, A., L.W. Sutker, and P. Satz. 1974. Hemispheric processing of verbal information in right and left handers. Presented at International Neuropsychology Society Conference, Boston.

Altman, J., and G.D. Das. 1966. Behavioral manipulations and protein metabolism of the brain: Effects of motor exercise on the utilization of leucine-H^3. Physiol. Behav. 1: 105–108.

Aman, N.G., and R.L. Sprague. 1974. The state dependent effect of methylphenidate and dextroamphetamine. J. Nerv. Ment. Dis. 158: 268–279.

Anderson, P., J.C. Eccles, and Y. Loyning. 1963. Recurrent inhibition in the hippocampus with identification of the inhibitory cell and its synapses. Nature 198: 540–542.

Anderson, P.O., and S.A. Andersen. 1968. Physiological Basis of Alpha Rhythm. Appleton-Century-Crofts, New York.

Anderson, R.C. 1965. Can first graders learn an advanced problem solving skill? J. Educ. Psychol. 56: 283–294.

Anderson, W. 1963. The hyperkinetic child: A neurological appraisal. Neurology (Minneap.) 13: 968–973.

Annett, M. 1967. The binomial distribution of right, mixed and left handedness. Q. J. Exp. Psychol. 19: 327–333.

Annett, M. 1973. Laterality of childhood hemiplegia and the growth of speech and intelligence. Cortex 9: 4–33.

Anokhin, P.K. 1964. Systemogenesis as a general regulator of brain development. In W.A. Himwich and H.E. Himwich (eds.), Progress in Brain Research: The Developing Brain, Vol. 9, pp. 54–86. Elsevier, Amsterdam.

Applebee, A.N. 1971. Research in reading retardation: Two critical problems. J. Child Psychol. Psychiatry 12: 91–113.

Arnold, L.E., P.H. Wender, K. McCloskey, and S. Snyder. 1972. Levo-amphetamines and dextroamphetamine: Comparative efficacy in the hyperkinetic syndrome; assessment by target symptoms. Arch. Gen. Psychiatry 27: 816–822.

Baddeley, A.D. 1966. Short-term memory for word sequences as a function of acoustic, semantic and formal similarity. Q. J. Exp. Psychol. 18: 362–365.

Baddeley, A.D. 1968. How does acoustic similarity influence short-term memory? Q. J. Exp. Psychol. 20: 249–264.

Baddeley, A.D. 1970. Effects of acoustic and semantic similarity on short-term paired associate learning. Brit. J. Psychol. 61: 335–343.

Bakker, D.J. 1967. Temporal order, meaningfulness and reading ability. Percept. Mot. Skills 24: 1027–1030.

Bakker, D.J. 1969. Ear asymmetry with monaural stimulation: Task influences. Cortex 5: 36–42.

Bakker, D.J. 1970a. Ear asymmetry with monaural stimulation: Relations to lateral dominance and lateral awareness. Neuropsychologia 8: 103–117.

Bakker, D.J. 1970b. Temporal order perception and reading retardation. In D.J. Bakker and P. Satz (eds.), Specific Reading Disability: Advances in Theory and Method, pp. 81–96. Rotterdam University Press, Rotterdam.

Bakker, D.J. 1971. Temporal Order in Disturbed Reading; Developmental and Neuropsychological Aspects in Normal and Reading Retarded Children. Rotterdam University Press, Rotterdam.

Bakker, D.J. 1973. Hemispheric specialization and stages in the learning-to-read process. Bull. Orton Soc. 23: 15–27.

Bakker, D.J., and P. Satz. 1970. Specific Reading Disability: Advances in Theory and Method. Rotterdam University Press, Rotterdam.

Bakker, D.J., and E. Steenis. 1975. Hemisfeer dominantie en leesstrategie. (In preparation)

Bakker, D.J., T. Smink, and P. Reitsma. 1973. Ear dominance and reading ability. Cortex 9: 301–312.

Bakker, D.J., J. Teunissen, and J. Bosch. 1976. Development of laterality reading patterns. This volume.

Baldessarini, R.J. 1972. Pharmacology of the amphetamines. Pediatrics 49: 694–701.

Ballard, J. 1975. The effects of methylphenidate during rest, exercise, and recovery upon circulorespiratory responses of hyperactive children. Unpublished doctoral dissertation. University of Illinois.

Balow, B., and M. Blomquist, 1965. Young adults ten to fifteen years after severe reading disability. Elementary School J. 66: 44–48.

Balow, I.H. 1963. Lateral dominance characteristics and reading achievement in the first grade. J. Psychol. 55: 323–328.

Balter, M.B., and J. Laine. 1969. The nature and extent of psychotropic drug usage in the United States. Psychopharmacologia 5.

Ban, T. 1969. Psychopharmacology. Williams & Wilkins, Baltimore.

Bannatyne, A. 1971. Language, Reading and Learning Disabilities. Charles C Thomas, Springfield, Ill.

Banquet, J.P. 1973. Spectral analysis of the EEG in meditation. EEG Clin. Neurophysiol. 35: 143–151.

Barondes, S.H., and H.D. Cohen. 1968. Arousal and the conversion of "short term" to "long term" memory. Proc. Natl. Acad. Sci. U.S.A. 61: 923–929.

Basser, L.S. 1962. Hemiplegia of early onset and the faculty of speech with special reference to the effects of hemispherectomy. Brain 85: 427–460.

Basso, A., E. Bisiach, and P. Faglioni. 1975. The Muller-Lyer illusion in patients with unilateral damage. Cortex 11: 26–35.

Bateman, B. 1964. Learning disabilities–yesterday, today, and tomorrow. Except. Child. 31, 4: 167–177.

Bateman, B. 1968. Interpretation of the 1961 Illinois Test of Psycholinguistic Abilities. Special Child Publications, Seattle.

Baumeister, A.A., and C.J. Bartlett. 1962a. A comparison of the factor structure of normals and retardates on the WISC. Am. J. Ment. Def. 66: 641–646.

Baumeister, A.A., and C.J. Bartlett. 1962b. Further factorial investigations of WISC performance of mental defectives. Am. J. Ment. Def. 67: 257–261.

Bayley, N. 1965. Comparisons of mental and motor test scores for ages 1–15 months by sex, birth order, race, geographical location, and education of parents. Child Dev. 36: 379–411.

Beach, F.A. 1971. Hormonal factors controlling the differentiation, development, and display of copulatory behaviour in the ramstergig and related species. In E. Tobach, L.R. Aronson, and E. Shaw (eds.), The Biopsychology of Development. Academic Press, New York.

Beach, G., M. Emmens, D.P. Kimble, and M. Lickey. 1969. Autoradiographic demonstration of biochemical changes in the limbic system during avoidance training. Proc. Natl. Acad. Sci. U.S.A. 62: 692–696.

Beckett, P., R. Bickford, and H. Keith. 1956. The electroencephalogram in various aspects of mental deficiency. Am. J. Dis. Child. 92: 374–381.

Bell, R.Q., G.M. Weller, and M.F. Waldrop. 1971. Newborn and preschooler: Organization of behaviour and relations between periods. Monogr. Soc. Res. Child Dev. 36, Nos. 1, 2.

Belmont, I., H. Birch, D. Klein, and M. Pollack. 1964. Perceptual evidence of CNS dysfunction in schizophrenia. Arch. Gen. Psychiatry 10: 395–408.

Belmont, J., and E. Butterfield. 1971. Learning strategies as determinants of memory deficiencies. Cognitive Psychol. 2: 411–420.

Belmont, L., and H.G. Birch. 1965. Lateral dominance, lateral awareness and reading disability. Child Dev. 36: 57–71.

Bender, L. 1938. A visual motor gestalt test and its clinical use. American Orthopsychiatry Association, Research Monograph 3.

Bender, L., and F. Cottington. 1942. The use of amphetamine sulfate (benzedrine) in child psychiatry. Am. J. Psychiatry 99: 116.

Bender, L., and H. Yarnell. 1941. An observation nursery. Am. J. Psychiatry 97: 1158–1172.

Benson, D.F. 1974. Towards a pathology of reading disorders. Paper presented at the Hyman Blumberg Symposium on Research in Early Childhood Education, Baltimore.

Benson, D.F., and N. Geschwind. 1969. The alexias. *In* P.J. Vinken and G.W. Bruyn (eds.), Handbook of Clinical Neurology, Vol. 4. North-Holland Publishing Co., Amsterdam.

Benton, A.L. 1962a. Behavioral indices of brain injury in school children. Child Dev. 33: 199−208.

Benton, A.L. 1962b. Clinical symptomatology in right and left hemisphere lesions. *In* V. Mountcastle (ed.), Interhemispheric Relations and Cerebral Dominance, pp. 253−263. Johns Hopkins Press, Baltimore.

Benton, A.L. 1962c. Dyslexia in relation to form perception and directional sense. *In* J. Money (ed.), Reading Disability: Progress and Research Needs in Dyslexia, pp. 81−102. Johns Hopkins Press, Baltimore.

Benton, A.L. 1964. Developmental aphasia and brain damage. Cortex 1: 40−52.

Benton, A.L. 1965a. Sentence Memory Test. Iowa City, Iowa. Author.

Benton, A.L. 1965b. The problem of cerebral dominance. The Canadian Psychologist 6a, 4: 332−348.

Benton, A.L. 1970. Cerebral hemispheric dominance. Isr. J. Med. Sci. 6: 2−16.

Benton, A.L. 1973. Minimal brain dysfunction from a neuropsychological point of view. Ann. N.Y. Acad. Sci. 205: 29−37.

Benton, A.L. 1975. Development dyslexia: Neurological aspects. *In* W.J. Friedlander (ed.), Advances in Neurology, Vol. 7, pp. 1−47. Raven Press, New York.

Berdina, N.A., O.L. Kolenko, I.M. Kotz, A.P. Kuzetzov, I.M. Rodinov, A.P. Savtchencko, and V.I. Thorevsky. 1972. Increase in skeletal muscle performance during emotional stress in man. Circ. Res. 6: 642−650.

Berent, S. 1974. Field-dependence and performance on a writing task. Percept. Mot. Skills 38: 651−658.

Berent, S. 1975. Perceptual impairment in psychiatric complaints. Unpublished manuscript.

Berent, S., and A. Silverman. 1973. Field dependence and differences between visual and verbal learning tasks. Percept. Mot. Skills 36: 1327−1330.

Berger, M., W. Yule, and M. Rutter. 1975. Attainment and adjustment in two geographical areas. II. The prevalence of specific reading retardation. Brit. J. Psychiatry 126: 510−519.

Bergés, J., A. Harrison, and G. Lairy. 1965. EEG and speech disturbances in children. EEG Clin. Neurophysiol. 18: 425.

Berkson, G. 1969. Stereotyped movements of mental defectives. V. Ward behavior and its relation to an experimental task. Am. J. Ment. Def. 69: 253.

Berlucchi, G., W. Heron, R. Hyman, G. Rizzolatti, and C. Umiltà. 1971. Simple reaction times of ipsilateral and contralateral hand to lateralised visual stimuli. Brain 94: 419−430.

Berlyne, D.E., and J.L. Lewis. 1963. Effects of heightened arousal on human exploratory behavior. Can. J. Psychol. 17: 398−411.

Berry, J.W. 1967. Matching of auditory and visual stimuli by average and retarded readers. Child Dev. 38: 827−833.

Bettman, J.W., Jr., E.L. Stern, L.J. Whitsell, and H.F. Gofman. 1967. Cerebral dominance in developmental dyslexia. Arch. Ophthalmol. 78: 722−729.

Birch, H.G. 1962. Dyslexia and the maturation of visual function. *In* J. Money (ed.), Reading Disability, pp. 161−169. Johns Hopkins Press, Baltimore.

Birch, H.G. 1964. Brain Damage in Children, the Biological and Social Aspects. Williams & Wilkins, Baltimore.

Birch, H.G. 1970. Nutritional factors in mental retardation. Fifth Annual Neuropsychology Workshop, University of Victoria, Victoria, B.C., Canada.

Birch, H.G., and L. Belmont. 1964. Auditory-visual integration in normal and retarded readers. Am. J. Orthopsychiatry 34: 852−861.

Birch, H.G., and J.D. Gussow. 1970. Disadvantaged Children, Health, Nutrition and School Failure. Grune & Stratton. New York.

Black's Medical Dictionary. 29th Ed. 1971. pp. 321−322. Harper & Row, New York.

Blakiston's New Gould Medical Dictionary. 2nd Ed. 1956.

Block, V. 1970. Facts and hypotheses concerning memory consolidation processes. Brain Research 24: 561−575.

Bloom, S. 1964. Stability and Change in Human Characteristics. Wiley and Sons, Inc., New York.

Bloomberg, M. 1965. Field-independence and susceptibility to distraction. Percept. Mot. Skills 20: 805−813.

Bloomfield, L. 1942. Linguistics and reading. Elementary English 18: 125−130; 183−186.

Bock, R.D., and D. Kolakowsky. 1973. Further evidence of sex-linked major gene influence on human spatial visualizing ability. Am. J. Hum. Genet. 25: 1−14.

Boder, E. 1971. Developmental dyslexia: A diagnostic screening procedure based on three characteristic patterns of reading and spelling. *In* B. Bateman (ed.), Learning Disorders. Vol. 4, pp. 298−342. Special Child Publications, Seattle.

Boder, E. 1971. Developmental dyslexia: Prevailing diagnostic concepts and a new diagnostic approach. *In* H.R. Myklebust (ed.), Progress in Learning Disabilities. Vol. II, pp. 293−321. Grune & Stratton, New York.

Boder, E. 1973. Developmental dyslexia: A diagnostic approach based on three reading-spelling patterns. Dev. Med. Child Neurol. 15: 663−687.

Bogen, J.E. 1969. The other side of the brain II: An appositional mind. Bull. Los Angeles Neurol. Soc. 34, 3: 135−162.

Bogen, J.E., and M.S. Gazzaniga. 1965. Cerebral commissurotomy in man: Minor hemisphere dominance for certain visuo-spatial functions. J. Neurosurg. 23: 394−399.

Bohus, B., and D. De Wied. 1966. Inhibitory and facilitatory effects of two related peptides on extinction of avoidance behavior. Science 1953: 318−320.

Bolinger, D. 1968. Aspects of Language. Harcourt, Brace & World, Inc., New York.

Boydstrum, J.A., P.T. Ackerman, D.A. Stevens, S.D. Clements, J.F. Peters, and R.A. Dykman. 1968. Physiologic and motor conditioning and generalization in children with minimal brain dysfunction. Cond. Reflex 3: 81–104.

Branch, C., B. Milner, and T. Rasmussen. 1964. Intracarotid sodium amytal for the lateralization of cerebral speech dominance. J. Neurosurg. 21: 399–405.

Brandt, S. 1957. EEG findings in 200 children with mental retardation. EEG Clin. Neurophysiol. 9: 735.

Brante, G. 1949. Studies on lipids in the nervous system; with special reference to quantitative chemical determination and topical distribution. Acta Physiol. Scand. 18 (Suppl.): 63.

Broadbent, D.E. 1954. The role of auditory localization in attention and memory span. J. Exp. Psychol. 47: 191–196.

Broadbent, D.E. 1958. Perception and Communication. Pergamon Press, Oxford.

Brown, W.J. 1973. Structural substrates of seizure foci in the human temporal lobe. In M. Brazier (ed.), Epilepsy: Its Phenomena in Man, pp. 339–374. UCLA Forum in Medical Sciences No. 17. Academic Press, New York.

Brus, B.Th., and M.J.M. Voeten. 1972. Een-minuut-test. Berkhout, Nijmegen.

Bryan, T. 1974. An observational analysis of classroom behaviors of children with learning disabilities. J. Learning Disabilities 7: 35–43.

Bryan, T., and R. Wheeler. 1972. Perception of learning disabled children: The eye of the observer. J. Learning Disabilities 5: 484–488.

Bryant, N., and W.J. Friedlander. 1965. "14 + 6" in boys with specific reading disability. EEG Clin. Neurophysiol. 19: 322.

Bryden, M.P. 1970. Laterality effects in dichotic listening: Relations with handedness and reading ability in children. Neuropsychologia 8: 443–450.

Bryden, M.P., and C.A. Rainey. 1963. Left-right differences in tachistoscopic recognition. J. Exp. Psychol. 66: 568–571.

Buchsbaum, M., and P.H. Wender. 1973. Average evoked responses in normal and minimally brain dysfunctioned children treated with amphetamine. Arch. Gen. Psychiatry 29: 764–770.

Buckholtz, N.S., and R.E. Bowman. 1970. Retrograde amnesia and brain RNA content after TCAP. Physiol. Behav. 5: 911–914.

Buffery, A.W.H. 1970. Sex differences in the development of hand preference, cerebral dominance for speech and cognitive skill. Bull. Brit. Psychol. Soc. 23: 233.

Buffery, A.W.H. 1971. An automated technique for the study of the development of cerebral mechanisms subserving linguistic skill. Proc. R. Soc. Med. 64: 919–922.

Buffery, A.W.H. 1974. Asymmetrical lateralisation of cerebral functions and the effects of unilateral brain surgery in epileptic patients. In S.J. Dimond and J.G. Beaumont (eds.), Hemisphere Function in the Human Brain, pp. 204–234. Elek Science, London.

Buffery, A.W.H., and J.A. Gray. 1972. Sex differences in the development of spatial and linguistic skills. *In* C. Ounsted and D.C. Taylor (eds.), Gender Differences: Their Ontogeny and Significance, pp. 123–157. Churchill Livingstone, Edinburgh and London.

Bures, J., Z. Bohdanecky, and T. Weiss. 1962. Physostigmine induced hippocampal theta activity and learning in rats. Psychopharmacologia 3: 254–263.

Burnett, L.L., and F.A. Struve. 1974. The value of EEG study in minimal brain dysfunction. J. Clin. Psychol. 30: 489–495.

Burt, C. 1937 and 1950. The Backward Child. 3rd Ed. University of London Press, London.

Burt, C. 1959. The accomplishment quotient: A reply. Brit. J. Ed. Psychol. 29: 259–260.

Buss, A., and P. Lang. 1965. Psychological deficit in schizophrenia: I. Affect, reinforcement, and concept attainment. J. Abnorm. Psychol. 70: 2–24.

Calfee, R., R. Chapman, and R. Venezky. 1972. How a child needs to think to learn to read. *In* L.W. Gregg (ed.), Cognition in Learning and Memory. Wiley and Sons, Inc., New York.

Callaway, E. 1970. Schizophrenia and interference: An analogy with a malfunctioning computer. Arch. Gen. Psychiatry 22: 193–208.

Cameron, D.E., and L. Solyom. 1961. Effects of RNA on memory. Geriatrics 16: 74–81.

Campbell, S. 1969. Cognitive styles in normal and hyperactive children. Unpublished doctoral dissertation. McGill University.

Campbell, S.B., V.I. Douglas, and G. Morgenstern. 1971. Cognitive styles in hyperactive children and the effect of methylphenidate. J. Child Psychol. Psychiatry 12: 55–67.

Canadian Tests of Basic Skills. 1967. Edited by E.M. King in cooperation with E.F. Lindquist and A.N. Hieronymus. Thomas Nelson & Sons Ltd. (Canada), Toronto.

Cantwell, D.P. 1975. Genetic Studies of hyperactive children: Psychiatric illness in biologic and adopting parents. *In* R.R. Fieve, D. Rosenthal, and H. Bull (eds.), Genetic Research in Psychiatry, pp. 273–280. Johns Hopkins Press, Baltimore.

Capute, A.J., E.F.L. Niedermeyer, and F. Richardson. 1968. The electroencephalogram in children with minimal cerebral dysfunction. Pediatrics 41: 1104–1114.

Carlton, P.L. 1963. Cholinergic mechanisms in the control of behavior by the brain. Psychol. Rev. 70: 19–39.

Carmon, A., and I. Nachson. 1973. Ear asymmetry in perception of emotional non-verbal stimuli. Acta Psychol. 37: 351–357.

Carroll, H.M.C. 1972. The remedial teaching of reading: An evaluation. Remedial Ed. 7: 10–15.

Carroll, J.B. 1970. The nature of the reading process. *In* H. Singer and E. Ruddell (eds.), Theoretical Models and Processes of Reading. International Reading Association, Newark, Delaware.

CELDIC Report. 1970. One million children, a national study of Canadian children with emotional and learning disorders. Leonard Crainford, Toronto.

Celesia, G.G., and H.H. Jasper. 1966. Acetylcholine released from cerebral cortex in relation to state of activation. Neurology 16: 1053–1083.

Cernáček, J., et al. 1974. Relationship between the motor dominance and mental maturity in children. Bratisl. Lek. Listy. 61: 129–134.

Chaffin, D.B. 1969. Surface electromyography frequency analysis as a diagnostic tool. J. Occup. Med. 11: 109–115.

Chalfant, J.C., and F.S. King. 1975. An approach to operationalizing the definition of learning disabilities. J. Learning Disabilities. (In press)

Chalfant, J.C., and M.A. Scheffelin. 1969. Central processing dysfunctions in children. NINDS Monograph No. 9. U.S. Department of Health, Education and Welfare, Bethesda, Md.

Chambers's Encyclopedia. New revised Ed. 1966. Vol. V, pp. 349–351. Pergamon Press, Oxford.

Chapman, J., and A. McGhie. 1962. A comparative study of disordered attention in schizophrenia. J. Ment. Science 108: 487–500.

Chapman, L., and J. Chapman. 1973. Problems in the measurement of cognitive deficits. Psychol. Bull. 79: 380–385.

Charles, D.C. 1953. Ability and accomplishment of persons earlier judged mentally deficient. Gen. Psychol. Monogr. 47: 3–71.

Chatfield, P.O., and E.W. Dempsey. 1942. Some effects of prostigmine and acetylcholine on cortical potentials. Am. J. Physiol. 135: 633–640.

Claridge, G. 1967. Personality and Arousal: A Psychophysiological Study of Psychiatric Disorder. Macmillan (Pergamon), New York.

Clark, M.M. 1970. Reading Difficulties in Schools. Penguin Books, Harmondsworth.

Clements, S.D. 1966. Minimal brain dysfunction in children. NINDB Monograph No. 3. U.S. Department of Health, Education and Welfare, Washington, D.C.

Clements, S.D. 1975. Personal communication.

Clements, S.D., and R.S. Paine. 1969. Minimal brain dysfunction; national project on learning disabilities in children. Public Health Service Publication No. 2015. U.S. Department of Health, Education and Welfare, Washington, D.C.

Clements, S.D., and J.E. Peters. 1962. Minimal brain dysfunctions in the school-age child. Arch. Gen. Psychiatry 6: 185–197.

Cohen, B., S. Berent, and A. Silverman. 1973. Field-dependence and lateralization of function in the human brain. Arch. Gen. Psychiatry 28: 165–167.

Cohen, H.D., and S.H. Barondes. 1968a. Cycloheximide impairs memory of an appetitive task. Commun. Behav. Biol. A-1: 337–340.

Cohen, H.D., and S.H. Barondes. 1968b. Effect of acetoxycycloheximide on learning and memory of a light-dark discrimination. Nature 218: 271–273.

Cohen, J. 1970. A new psychophysiological approach to the diagnostic evaluation of children. Quoted in R.A. Dykman, P.T. Ackerman, S.D. Clements, and J.E. Peters. 1971. Specific learning disabilities: An attentional deficit syndrome. In H.R. Myklebust (ed.), Progress in Learning Disabilities, Vol. II. Grune & Stratton, New York.

Cohen, N.J. 1970. Psychophysiological concomitants of attention in hyperactive children. Unpublished doctoral dissertation. McGill University.

Cohen, N.J., and V.I. Douglas. 1972. Characteristics of the orienting response in hyperactive and normal children. Psychophysiology 9: 238–245.

Cohen, N.J., V.I. Douglas, and G. Morgenstern. 1969. Psychophysiological concomitants of hyperactivity in children. Can. Psychol. 10: 199 (abstract).

Cohen, N.J., V.I. Douglas, and G. Morgenstern. 1971. The effect of methylphenidate on attentive behavior and autonomic activity in hyperactive children. Psychopharmacologia 22: 282–294.

Cohen, N.J., G. Weiss, and K. Minde. 1972. Cognitive styles in adolescents previously diagnosed as hyperactive. J. Child Psychol. Psychiatry 13: 203–209.

Cohn, R., and J. Nardini, J. 1958. The correlation of bilateral occipital slow activity in the human EEG with certain disorders of behavior. Am. J. Psychiatry 115: 44–54.

Coleman, R.I., and C.P. Deutsch. 1964. Lateral dominance and right-left discrimination: A comparison of normal and retarded readers. Percept. Mot. Skills 19: 43–50.

Conners, C.K. 1966. The effect of dexedrine on rapid discrimination and motor control of hyperkinetic children under mild stress. J. Nerv. Ment. Dis. 142: 429–433.

Conners, C.K. 1967. The syndrome of minimal brain dysfunction: Psychological aspects. Pediatr. Clin. North Am. 14: 749–766.

Conners, C.K. 1969. A teacher rating scale for use in drug studies with children. Am. J. Psychiatry 126: 884–888.

Conners, C.K. 1970a. A clinical comparison between magnesium pemoline, dextroamphetamine and placebo in hyperkinetic children. Paper presented at the meeting of the American College of Neuropsychopharmacology, San Juan.

Conners, C.K. 1970b. The use of stimulant drugs in enhancing performance and learning. In W.L. Smith (ed.), Drugs and Cerebral Function. Charles C Thomas, Springfield, Ill.

Conners, C.K. 1971a. Cortical visual evoked response in children with learning disorders. Psychophysiology 7: 418–428.

Conners, C.K. 1971b. Drugs in the management of children with learning disabilities. In L. Tarnapol (ed.), Learning Disorders in Children: Diagnosis, Medication, Education, pp. 253–301. Little, Brown & Co., Boston.

Conners, C.K. 1971c. Recent drug studies with hyperkinetic children. J. Learning Disabilities 4(9), 12–19: 476–483.

Conners, C.K. 1972a. Stimulant drugs and cortical evoked responses in learning and behavior disorders in children. In W.L. Smith (ed.), Drugs, Development, and Cerebral Function, pp. 179–199. Charles C Thomas, Springfield, Ill.

Conners, C.K. 1972b. Symposium: Behavior modification by drugs. II. Psychological effects of stimulant drugs in children with minimal brain dysfunction. Pediatrics 49: 702–708.

Conners, C.K. 1973a. Attentional defects in hyperkinetic children: A study of the effect of stimulant drugs on the vertex potential of the cortical evoked response. Proceedings American Psychological Association, Montreal.

Conners, C.K. 1973b. Psychological assessment of children with minimal brain dysfunction. Ann. N.Y. Acad. Sci. 205: 283–302.

Conners, C.K. 1975. Minimal brain dysfunction and psychopathology in children. *In* A. Davids (ed.), Child Personality and Psychopathology Current Topics. (In press)

Conners, C.K., L. Eisenberg, and L. Sharpe. 1964. Effects of methylphenidate (Ritalin) on paired-associate learning and porteus maze performance in emotionally disturbed children. J. Consult. Psychol. 28: 14–22.

Conners, C.K., and D. Greenfield. 1966. Habituation of motor startle in anxious and restless children. J. Child Psychol. Psychiatry 7: 125–132.

Conners, C.K., and G.H. Rothschild. 1973. The effect of dextroamphetamine on habituation of peripheral vascular response in children. J. Abnorm. Child Psychol. 1: 16–25.

Conners, C.K., L. Eisenberg, and L. Sharpe. 1964. Effects of methylphenidate (Ritalin) on paired-associate learning and porteus maze performance in emotionally disturbed children. J. Consult. Psychol. 28: 14–22.

Conners, C.K., E. Taylor, G. Meo, M. Kurtz, and M. Fournier. 1972. Magnesium pemoline and dextroamphetamine: A controlled study in children with minimal brain dysfunction. Psychopharmacologia 26: 321–336.

Conrad, R. 1964. Acoustic confusions in immediate memory. Brit. J. Psychol. 55: 75–84.

Conrad, R. 1972. Speech and reading. *In* J.F. Kavanagh and I.G. Mattingly (eds.), Language By Ear and By Eye: The Relationships Between Speech and Reading. MIT Press, Cambridge, Massachusetts.

Cook, L., A.B. Davidson, D.J. David, H. Green, and F.J. Fellows. 1963. Ribonucleic acid effect on conditioned behaviour in rats. Science 141: 268–269.

Corah, N.L. 1965. Differentiation in children and their parents. J. Personality 33: 300–308.

Coren, S. 1974. The development of ocular dominance. Dev. Psychol. 10: 304.

Corkin, S. 1974. Serial-ordering deficits in inferior readers. Neuropsychologia 12: 347–354.

Corning, W.C., and E.R. John. 1961. Effect of ribonuclease on retention of conditioned response in regenerated plonorians. Science 134: 1363–1365.

Corson, S.A., E.O. Corson, and V. Kerelcuk. 1973. Normalizing effects of *d*- and *l*-amphetamine on cerebrovisceral pathology. Proc. Soc. Neuroscience, Third Annual Meeting, p. 341.

Crane, A.R. 1959. An historical critical account of the accomplishment quotient idea. Brit. J. Educ. Psychol. 29: 252–259.

Cravioto, J. 1972. Nutrition and learning in children. *In* N.S. Springer (ed.), Nutrition and Mental Retardation, p. 37. Institute for the Study of Mental Retardation and Related Disabilities, Ann Arbor.

Cravioto, J., E.R. DeLicardie, and H.G. Birch. 1966. Nutrition, growth and neurointegrative development: An experimental and ecologic study. Pediatrics 38 (Suppl. 2): 319—372.

Critchley, M. 1964. Developmental Dyslexia. Heinemann, London.

Critchley, M. 1970. The Dyslexic Child. Heinemann, London.

Cromwell, R.L., A. Baumeister, and W.F. Hawkins. 1963. Research in activity level. In N.R. Ellis (ed.), Handbook of Mental Deficiency. McGraw-Hill, New York.

Cromwell, R.L., B. Polk, and I. Foshbee. 1961. Studies in activity level. V. The relationship among eyelid conditioning, intelligence, activity level and age. Am. J. Ment. Def. 65: 744—748.

Crovitz, E. 1966. Reversing a learning deficit in the aged. J. Gerontol. 21: 236—238.

Cruickshank, W.M. 1966. The Teacher of Brain-Injured Children. Syracuse University Press, Syracuse.

Culton, G.L., and L.G. Mueller. 1971. Changing concepts of cerebral dominance, handedness, and language function. Acta Symbol. 2(1): 37—41.

Cutting, J.E. 1973. Parallel between degree of encodedness and the ear advantage: Evidence from an ear monitoring task. J. Acoust. Soc. Am. 53: 368.

Cutting, J.E. 1974. Two left-hemisphere mechanisms in speech perception. Percept. Psychophys. 16: 601—612.

Czudner, G., and B.P. Rourke. 1972. Age differences in visual reaction time of "brain-damaged" and normal children under regular and irregular preparatory interval conditions. J. Exp. Child Psychol. 13: 516—526.

Darby, R. 1974. Ear asymmetry phenomenon in dyslexic and normal children. Unpublished Master's Thesis. University of Florida.

Das, J.P. 1972. Patterns of cognitive ability in nonretarded and retarded children. Am. J. Ment. Def. 77, 1: 6—12.

Das, J.P. 1973a. Structure of cognitive abilities: Evidence for simultaneous and successive processing. J. Educ. Psychol. 65, 1: 103—108.

Das, J.P. 1973b. Cultural deprivation and cognitive competence. In N.R. Ellis (ed.), International Review of Research in Mental Retardation, Vol. 6, pp. 1—53. Academic Press, New York.

Das, J.P., J. Kirby, and R.F. Jarman. 1975. Simultaneous and successive syntheses: An alternative model for cognitive abilities. Psychol. Bull. 82: 87—103.

Das, N.N., and H. Gastaut. 1955. Variations de l'activite electrique du cerveau, du coeur, et des muscles squellettiques au cours de la meditation et de l'extase yogique. EEG Clin. Neurophysiol. 6(Suppl): 211—219.

Davie, R., N. Butler, and H. Goldstein. 1972. From Birth to Seven. Longmans, London.

Davis, R.D., and A. Cashdan. 1963. Specific dyslexia. Brit. J. Educ. Psychol. 33: 80—82.

DeFazio, V. 1973. Field articulation differences in language abilities. J. Personal. Soc. Psychol. 25: 351—356.

DeHaas, A. 1972. Oor dominantie bij LOM-kinderen. Doctoral Thesis. Free University, Amsterdam.

De Hirsch, K., J.J. Jansky, and W.S. Langford. 1966. Predicting Reading Failure: A Preliminary Study. Harper & Row, New York.

Dejerine, J. 1892. Contribution à l'étude anatomo-pathologique et clinique des disférentes variétés de cécité verbale. Mémoires de la Société de Biologie 4: 61.

Delacato, C. 1963. The Diagnosis and Treatment of Speech and Reading Problems. 6th Ed. Charles C Thomas, Springfield, Ill.

Delacato, C. 1967. Neurological Organization and Reading. 2nd Ed. Charles C Thomas, Springfield, Ill.

De La Cruz, F.F., B.H. Fox, and R.H. Roberts. 1973. Minimal brain dysfunction. Whole volume. Ann. N.Y. Acad. Sci. 205.

Denhoff, E. 1973. The natural life history of children with minimal brain dysfunction. Ann. N.Y. Acad. Sci. 205: 188–205.

Department of Education and Science. 1964. Pamphlet No. 46. H.M.S.O. London.

Department of Education and Science. 1972. Children with specific reading difficulties: Report of the advisory committee on handicapped children. H.M.S.O. London.

Department of Education and Science. 1975. A language for life: Report of the Committee of Inquiry under the Chairmanship of Sir Allan Bullock, H.M.S.O. London.

De Renzi, E. 1967. Deficit gnosici, prassici, mnestici e intellettivi nelle lesioni emisferiche unilaterali, Atti XVI Congresso di Neurologia, Roma.

De Renzi, E., and H. Spinnler. 1966a. Facial recognition in brain damaged patients. Neurology 145–152.

De Renzi, E., and H. Spinnler. 1966b. Visual recognition in patients with the unilateral cerebral disease. J. Nerv. Ment. Dis. 142: 515–525.

De Renzi, E., and L.A. Vignolo. 1962. The token test: A sensitive test to detect receptive disturbances in aphasia. Brain 85: 665–678.

De Renzi, E., P. Faglioni, and F. Scotti. 1970. Hemispheric contribution to exploration of space through the visual and tactile modality. Cortex 6: 191–203.

Deutsch, J.A. 1971. The Cholinergic synapse and the site of memory. Science 174: 788–794.

Di Mascio, A. 1971. Psychopharmacology in children. In S. Chess and A. Thomas (eds.), Annual Progress in Child Psychiatry and Child Development, pp. 479–491. Bruner/Mazel, New York.

Dimond, S.J. 1975a. Piracetam (UCB 6215) and increase in the capacity for verbal memory and learning in normal man. Medicina Psicosomatica. (In press)

Dimond, S.J. 1975b. Depletion of attentional capacity following total commissurotomy in man. (In preparation)

Dimond, S.J., and J.G. Beaumont. 1973. Hemisphere function and paired associate learning. Brit. J. Psychol. 65: 275–278.

Dimond, S.J., and J.G. Beaumont. 1974a. Experimental studies of hemisphere function in normal and brain damaged individuals. In S.J. Dimond and J.G. Beaumont (eds.), Hemisphere Functions of the Human Brain. Elek Science, London.

Dimond, S.J., and J.G. Beaumont. 1974b. Hemisphere Function in the Human Brain. Elek Science. London.

Dimond, S.J., L. Farrington, J. Bureš, and E.Y.M. Brouwers. 1975. The use of contact lenses for the lateralization of visual input in man. Acta Psychol. (In press)

Dingman, H.E., and G. Tarjan. 1960. Mental retardation and the normal distribution curve. Am. J. Ment. Def. 64: 991–994.

Dingman, W., and M.B. Sporn. 1961. The incorporation of 8-azaguanine into rat brain RNA and its effects on maze learning by the rat: An enquiry into the biochemical basis on memory. J. Psychiatric Res. 1: 1–11.

Doehring, D.G. 1968. Patterns of Impairment in Specific Reading Disability. Indiana University Press, Bloomington, Indiana.

Doehring, D.G. 1972. Ear asymmetry in the discrimination of monaural tonal sequences. Can. J. Psychol. 26: 106–110.

Doehring, D.G. 1976. Acquisition of rapid reading responses. Monograph of the Society for Research in Child Development. (In press)

Doehring, D.G., and R.A. Libman. 1974. Signal detection analysis of auditory sequence discrimination by children. Percept. Mot. Skills 38: 163–169.

Doty, B.A., and L.A. Doty. 1966. Facilitative effects of amphetamine on avoidance conditioning in relation to age and problem difficulty. Psychopharmacologia 9: 234–241.

Douglas, V.I. 1972. Stop, look, listen: The problem of sustained attention and impulse control in hyperactive and normal children. Can. J. Behav. Sci. 4: 259–282.

Douglas, V.I. 1974a. Sustained attention and impulse control: Implications for the handicapped child. Psychology and the handicapped child. U.S. Department of Health, Education and Welfare Office of Education 6: 149–164, Washington, D.C.

Douglas, V.I. 1974b. Differences between normal and hyperkinetic children, clinical use of stimulant drugs in children. In C. Keith Conners (ed.), Excerpta Medica, pp. 12–23.

Douglas, V.I. 1975. Are drugs enough?–To treat or to train the hyperactive child. Int. J. Ment. Health 199–212.

Douglas, V.I. 1976. Effects of medication on learning efficiency. Research findings review and synthesis. In Robert P. Anderson and Charles G. Halcomb (eds.), Learning Disability/Minimal Brain Dysfunction Syndrome: Research Perspectives and Applications. Charles C Thomas, Springfield, Ill.

Drachman, D.A., and J.R. Hughes. 1971. Memory and the hippocampal complexes, III. Aging and temporal EEG abnormalities. Neurology (Minneap.) 1–14.

Drachman, D.A., and M.A. Leavitt. 1974. Human memory and the cholinergic system. Arch. Neurol. 30: 113–121.

Drachman, D.A., and M.A. Leavitt. 1975. Are neurotransmitter systems specific for cognitive functions? Neurology (Minneap.) 25. (In press)

Drake, D. 1970. Perceptual correlates of impulsive and reflective behavior. Dev. Psychol. 2: 202–214.

Drake, W.E. 1968. Clinical and pathological findings in a child with a developmental learning disability. J. Learning Disabilities 1 (9): 486–502.

Duane, D.D. 1974. A neurologic overview of specific language disability for the non-neurologist. Bull. Orton Soc. 24: 5–36.

Dumenko, V.N. 1961. Changes in the electroencephalogram of the dog during the formation of a motor conditioned reflex stereotype. Pavlov Journal of Higher Nervous Activity 11 (2): 64–68.

Duncan, D.G. 1955. Multiple range and multiple F tests. Biometrics 11: 1–42.

Dunn, L.M. 1965. Expanded Manual for the Peabody Picture Vocabulary Test. American Guidance Service, Minneapolis.

Dykman, R.A., J.E. Peters, and P.T. Ackerman. 1973. Experimental approaches to the study of minimal brain dysfunction: A follow-up study. Ann. N.Y. Acad. Sci. 205: 93–108.

Dykman, R.A., P.T. Ackerman, S.D. Clements, and J.E. Peters. 1971. Specific learning disabilities: An attentional deficit syndrome. In H.R. Myklebust (ed.), Progress in Learning Disabilities, Vol. II, pp. 56–93. Grune & Stratton, New York.

Dykman, R.A., R. Walls, T. Suzuki, P. Ackerman, and J. Peters. 1970. Children with learning disabilities. V. Conditioning, differentiation, and the effects of distraction. Am. J. Orthopsychiatry 40: 776–781.

Eccles, J.C. 1964. The Physiology of Synapses. Springer-Verlag, New York.

Eccles, J.C. 1965. The control of neuronal activity by postsynaptic inhibitory action. In 23rd International Congress of Physiological Sciences. 84. Excerpta-Medica Foundation, Amsterdam.

Edwards, R.P.A., and V. Gibbon. 1964. Words Your Children Use. London.

Efron, R. 1963. Temporal perception, aphasia and déjà vu. Brain 86 (3): 403–424.

Egyhazi, E., and H. Hydén. 1961. Experimentally induced changes in the base composition of the ribonucleic acids of isolated nerve cells and their oligodendroglial cells. J. Biophys. Biochem. Cytol. 10: 403–410.

Eimas, P.D., E.R. Siqueland, P. Jusczyk, and J. Vigorito. 1971. Speech perception in infants. Science 171: 303–306.

Eisenberg, L. 1962. Introduction. In J. Money (ed.), Reading Disability. Johns Hopkins Press, Baltimore.

Eisenberg, L., 1966. Reading retardation. I. Psychiatric and sociologic aspects. Pediatrics Vol. 37, No. 2: 352–365.

Eisenson, J. 1972. Aphasia in Children. Harper & Row, London.

Elkonin, D.B. 1973. U.S.S.R. In J. Downing (ed.), Comparative Reading. Macmillan, New York.

Elliot, R. 1961. Interrelationships among measures of field dependence, ability, and personality traits. J. Abnorm. Social Psychol. 63: 27–35.

Ellis, N.R. 1963. The stimulus trace and behavioral inadequacy. In N.R. Ellis (ed.), Handbook of Mental Deficiency. McGraw-Hill, New York.

Encyclopedia Canadiana. 1970. Vol. 4: 32. Grolier, Toronto.

Englemann, S. 1967. Relationship between psychological theories and the act of teaching. J. School Psychol. 5: 93–100.

Entus, A.K. 1975. Hemispheric asymmetry in processing of dichotically presented speech and nonspeech sounds by infants. Abstract. Presented at the meeting of the Society for Research in Child Development, Denver.

Epstein, L.C., L. Lasagna, C.K. Conners, et al. 1968. Correlation of dextroamphetamine excretion and drug response in hyperkinetic children. J. Nerv. Ment. Dis. 146 (2): 136−145.

Erickson, D., I.G. Mattingly, and M.T. Turvey. 1973. Phonetic activity in reading: An experiment with kanji. Haskins Laboratories Status Report on Speech Research 33: 137−156.

Essman, W.B. 1966. Facilitation of memory consolidation by chemically induced acceleration of RNA synthesis. Fed. Proc. 25: 208.

Essman, W.B. 1972. Neurochemical changes in ECS and ECT. Semin. Psychiatry 4: 67−79.

Essman, W.B., and S. Nakajima. 1973. Current Biochemical Approaches to Learning and Memory. p. 205. Wiley and Sons, Inc., New York.

Estes, W.K. 1974. Learning theory and the new "mental chemistry." Psychol. Rev. 67: 207−223.

Estes, W.K. 1974. Learning theory and intelligence. Am. Psychologist 29: 740−749.

Ewing, A.W. 1930. Aphasia in Children. Oxford Medical Publications, Oxford.

Fagan-Dubin, L. 1974. Lateral dominance and development of cerebral specialization. Cortex 10: 69−74.

Faglioni, P., G. Scotti, and H. Spinnler. 1969. Impaired recognition of written letters following unilateral hemispheric damage. Cortex 5: 120−133.

Falconer, M.A. 1953. Discussion on the surgery of temporal lobe epilepsy. Proc. R. Soc. Med. 46: 971−974.

Falconer, M.A. 1973. Reversability by temporal lobe resection of the behavioural abnormalities of temporal lobe epilepsy. N. Engl. J. Med. 289: 451−455.

Falconer, M.A., and E.A. Serafetinides. 1963. A follow-up study of surgery in temporal lobe epilepsy. J. Neurol. Neurosurg. Psychiatry 26: 154−165.

Falconer, M.A., and D.C. Taylor. 1968. Surgical treatment of drug resistent temporal lobe epilepsy due to mesial temporal sclerosis. Arch. Neurol. 19: 353−361.

Falconer, M.A., E.A. Serafetinides, and J.A.N. Corsellis. 1964. Etiology and pathogenesis of temporal lobe epilepsy. Arch. Neurol. 10: 233−248.

Falconer, M.A., D. Hill, A. Meyer, W. Mitchell, and D.A. Pond. 1955. Treatment of temporal lobe epilepsy by temporal lobectomy: A survey of findings and results. Lancet 827−835.

Firestone, P. 1974. The effects of reinforcement contingencies and caffeine on hyperactive children. Unpublished doctoral dissertation. McGill University. Montreal.

Firestone, P., and V.I. Douglas. 1975. The effects of reward and punishment on reaction times and autonomic activity in hyperactive and normal children. J. Abnorm. Child Psychol. (In press)

Fish, B. 1960. Drug therapy in child psychiatry: Psychological aspects. Comp. Psychiatry 1: 55.

Fish, B. 1971. The "One child, one drug" myth of stimulants in hyper-kinesis. Arch. Gen. Psychiatry 25: 193–205.

Flach, J., and R. Malmros. 1972. A long-term follow-up study of children with severe head injury. Scand. J. Rehab. Med. A (1): 9–15.

Flexner, J.B., L.B. Flexner, and E. Stellar. 1963. Memory in mice as affected by intracerebral puromycin. Science 141: 57–59.

Flexner, L.B., J.B. Flexner, and R.B. Roberts. 1967. Memory in mice analyzed with antibiotics. Science 155: 1377–1381.

Folch-Pi, J. 1955. Composition of the brain in relation to maturation, *In* H. Waelsch (ed.), Biochemistry of the Developing Nervous System, pp. 121–136. Academic Press, New York.

Foshbee, J. 1958. Studies in activity level. I. Simple and complex task performance in defectives. Am. J. Ment. Def. 62: 823–836.

Frankfurter, A., and R.P. Honeck. 1973. Ear differences in the recall of monaurally presented sentences. Q. J. Exp. Psychol. 25: 138–146.

Franzen, R.H. 1920. The accomplishment quotient. Teachers College Record cited by A.R. Crane (op. cit).

Freeman, W.J. 1963. The electrical activity of a primary sensory cortex: Analysis of EEG waves. Int. Rev. Neurobiol. 5: 53–119.

Freibergs, V., and V.I. Douglas. 1969. Concept learning in hyperactive and normal children. J. Abnorm. Psychol. 74: 388–395.

Frierson, E.C., and W.B. Barbe. 1967. Educating Children With Learning Disabilities, Selected Readings, p. 4. Appleton-Century-Crofts, New York.

Fries, C.C. 1963. Linguistics and Reading. Holt, Rinehart and Winston, New York.

Fry, D.B., A.S. Abramson, P.D. Eimas, and A.M. Liberman. 1962. The identification and discrimination of synthetic vowels. Language and Speech 5, (4): 171–189.

Fry, E. 1968. A do-it-yourself terminolody generator. J. Reading 11: 428–430.

Fugslang-Frederiksen, V. 1961. The EEG in mental deficiency. EEG Clin. Neurophysiol. 13: 481.

Fujisaki, H., and T. Kawashima. 1970. Some experiments on speech perception and a model for the perceptual mechanisms. Ann. Rep. Engineering Res. Inst. (University of Tokyo) 29: 207–214.

Fuller, G.B. 1969. The Minnesota percepto-diagnostic test (Rev.). J. Clin. Psychol. (Monogr. Suppl.) 28.

Fuller, G.B. 1974. Three diagnostic patterns for children with reading disabilities. Presented at the International Conference of the Association for Children with Learning Disabilities, Houston, Texas.

Furth, H. 1966. Thinking Without Language: Psychological Implications of Deafness. The Free Press, New York.

Fuxe, K., and U. Ungerstedt. 1970. Histochemical, biochemical, and functional studies on central monoamine neurons after acute and chronic amphetamine administration. *In* E. Corta and S. Garrattini (eds.), International Symposium on Amphetamines and Related Compounds, pp. 257–288. Raven Press, New York.

Gaarder, K. 1967. Interpretive study of evoked responses elicited by gross saccadic eye movements. Percept. Mot. Skills 27: 683–703.

Gaarder, K., R. Koresko, and W. Kropfl. 1966. The phasic relation of a component of alpha rhythm to fixation saccadic eye movements. EEG Clin. Neurophysiol. 21: 544–551.

Gaarder, K., J. Krauskopf, V. Graf, N. Kropfl, and J.C. Armington. 1964. Averaged brain activity following saccadic eye movements. Science 146: 1481–1483.

Gaddes, W.H. 1968. A neuropsychological approach to learning disorders. J. Learning Disabilities 1: 523–534.

Gaddes, W.H. 1969. Can educational psychology be neurologized? Can. J. Behav. Sci. 1 (1): 38–49.

Gaddes, W.H. 1972. Learning disorders in the neurologically handicapped. Brit. Columbia Med. J. January, 13–16.

Gaddes, W.H. 1975. Neurological implications for learning. In W.M. Cruickshank and D. Hallahan (eds.), Perceptual and Learning Disabilities in Children. Vol. 1, Chapter 6. Syracuse University Press, Syracuse.

Gagne, R., and L. Briggs. 1974. Principles of Instructional Design. Holt, Rinehart and Winston, New York.

Gaito, J. 1961. A biochemical approach to learning and memory. Psychol. Rev. 68: 288–292.

Galambos, R. 1958. Electrical correlates of conditioned learning. In M. Brazier (ed.), The Central Nervous System and Behavior. Josiah Macy, Jr. Foundation, New York.

Gallagher, J.J. 1957. A comparison of brain-injured and non-brain-injured mentally retarded children on several psychological variables. Monogr. Soc. Res. Child Dev. 22: (2, Serial No. 65).

Gallagher, J.J. 1966. In W.M. Cruickshank (ed.), The Teacher of Brain-Injured Children. Chapter 2. Syracuse University Press, Syracuse.

Garfield, J.C. 1964. Motor impersistence in normal and brain-damaged children. Neurology 14: 623–630.

Garg, M., and H.C. Holland. 1968. Consolidation and maze learning: The effects of post-trail injections of a stimulant drug (Picrotoxin). Psychopharmacologia 12: 96–103.

Garner, W., H. Hake, and C. Eriksen. 1956. Operationism and the concept of perception. Psychol. Rev. 63: 149–159.

Gates Basic Reading Tests. 1958. Bureau of Publications, Teachers College, New York.

Gates-McKillop Reading Diagnostic Tests. 1962. Bureau of Publications, Teachers College, New York.

Gatev, V. 1968. Studies on the temporal characteristics of the saccadic eye movements of normal children. Exp. Eye Res. 7: 231–236.

Gazzaniga, M. 1974. Cerebral dominance viewed as a decision system. In S. Dimond and J. Beaumont (eds.), Hemispheric Functions in the Human Brain, pp. 367–382. Halstead Press, London.

Geffen, G., J. Bradshaw, and G. Wallace. 1971. Interhemispheric effects on response time to verbal and non-verbal stimuli. J. Exp. Psychol. 39: 425–436.

Gentry, J.T., E. Parkhurst, and G.V. Bulin. 1959. An epidemiological study of malformations in New York State. Am. J. Public Health 49: 497–513.

Gerard, R.W. 1961. The fixation of experience. *In* A. Fessard, R.W. Gerard, J. Konorski, and J.F. Delafresnaye (eds.), Brain Mechanisms and Learning, pp. 21–32. Blackwells, Oxford.

Geschwind, N. 1962. The anatomy of acquired disorders of reading. *In* J. Money (ed.), Reading Disability: Progress and Research Needs in Dyslexia, pp. 115–129. Johns Hopkins Press, Baltimore.

Geschwind, N. 1968. Neurological foundations of language. *In* H.R. Myklebust (ed.), Progress in Learning Disabilities, Vol. I, pp. 182–198. Grune & Stratton, New York.

Geschwind, N. 1974. Selected Papers on Language and the Brain. D. Reidel Publishing Co., The Netherlands.

Geschwind, N. 1974. The anatomical basis of hemispheric differentiation. *In* S.J. Dimond and J.G. Beaumont (eds.), Hemisphere Function in the Human Brain, pp. 7–24. Elek Science, London.

Geschwind, N., and W. Levitsky. 1968. Human brain: Left-right asymmetries in temporal speech region. Science 161: 186–187.

Gesell, A., and L.B. Ames. 1947. The development of handedness. J. Genet. Psychol. 70: 155–175.

Gholson, B., and K. McConville. 1974. Effects of stimulus differentiation training upon hypotheses, strategies, and stereotypes in discrimination learning among kindergarten children. J. Exp. Child Psychol. 18: 81–97.

Giannitrapani, D. 1969. EEG average frequency and intelligence. EEG Clin. Neurophysiol. 27: 480–486.

Gibson, A.R., S.J. Dimond, and M.S. Gazzaniga. 1972. Left field superiority for word matching. Neuropsychologia 10: 463–466.

Gibson, E.J. 1969. Principles of Perceptual Learning and Development. Appleton-Century-Crofts, New York.

Gibson, E.J. 1971. Perceptual learning and the theory of word perception. Cog. Psychol. 2: 351–368.

Gibson, E.J. 1972. Reading for some purpose. *In* J.F. Kavanagh and J.G. Mattingly (eds.), Language by Ear and by Eye, pp. 3–19. MIT Press, Cambridge.

Gittelman-Klein, R. 1975. Psychopharmacological approaches to the treatment of learning disabilities: Implications for visual processes. *In* G. Leisman (ed.), Basic Visual Processes and Learning Disability. Charles C Thomas, Springfield, Ill. (In press)

Gittelman-Klein, R., and D.F. Klein. 1975. Methylphenidate effects in learning disabilities: I. Psychometric changes. Arch. Gen. Psychiatry. (In press)

Glasky, A.J., and L.N. Simon. 1966. Magnesium pemoline: Enhancement of brain RNA polymerase. Science 702–703.

Glasser, A., and I. Zimmerman. 1967. Clinical Interpretation of the Wechsler Intelligence Scale for Children. Grune & Stratton, New York.

Glasser, W. 1969. Schools Without Failure. Harper & Row, New York.

Gleitman, L.R., and P. Rozin. 1973. Teaching reading by use of a syllabary. Reading Res. Q. 8: 447–483.

Goldman, P.S., H.T. Crawford, L.P. Stokes, T.W. Galkin, and H.E. Rosvold. 1974. Sex-dependent behavioural effects of cerebral cortical lesions in the developing rhesus monkey. Science 186: 540–542.

Goldstein, D.M. 1974. Learning to read and developmental changes in covert speech and in a word analysis and synthesis skill. Ph.D. Dissertation. University of Connecticut (Psychology).

Gollin, E.S., and M. Moody. 1973. Developmental psychology. Ann. Rev. Psychol. 24: 1–52.

Goodenough, D.R., G. Krupp, J. Freund, and S. Starker. 1971. Eye dominance and field dependence. Tech. Rep. Princeton: ETS.

Goodenough, D.R., E. Gandini, T. Olkin, L. Pizzamiglio, D. Thayer, and H.A. Witkin. 1975. A study of x chromosome linkage with field dependence and spatial visualization. Behav. Genet. (In press)

Goodglass, H., and M. Barton. 1963. Handedness and differential perception of verbal stimuli in left and right visual fields. Percept. Mot. Skills 17: 851–854.

Goodman, J. 1973. Impulsive and reflective behavior: A developmental analysis of attentional and cognitive strategies. Ph.D. Dissertation. University of Waterloo, Waterloo, Ontario.

Goodman, K.S. 1968. The psycholinguistic nature of the reading process. In K.S. Goodman (ed.), The Psycholinguistic Nature of the Reading Process, pp. 15–26. Wayne State University Press, Detroit.

Gordon, B. 1953. An experimental study of dependence-independence in a social and laboratory study. Doctoral Dissertation. University of Southern California.

Graham, F.K., and R.K. Clifton. 1966. Heart rate change as a component of the orienting response. Psychol. Bull. 65: 305–320.

Granit, R. 1963. Recurrent inhibition as a mechanism of control. In A. Moruzzi, A. Fessard, and H.H. Jasper (eds.), Brain Mechanisms. Vol. 1: Progress in Brain Research. Elsevier, New York.

Green, J.B. 1961. Association of behavior disorder with an EEG focus in children without seizures. Neurology (Minneap.) 11: 337–344.

Grinspoon, L., and S.B. Singer. 1973. Amphetamine in the treatment of hyperkinetic children. Harvard Educ. Rev. 43: 515–555.

Grinsted, A.O. 1939. Studies in gross bodily movement. Unpublished doctoral dissertation. Louisiana State University.

Gross, E.G., A.G. Vaughn, and E. Valenstein. 1967. Inhibition of visual evoked responses to patterned stimuli during voluntary eye movements. EEG Clin. Neurophysiol. 22: 204–209.

Gruenberg, E.M. 1964. Epidemiology. In H.A. Stevens and R. Heber (eds.), Mental Retardation, pp. 259–306. University of Chicago Press, Chicago.

Grunewald-Zuberbier, E., G. Grunewald, and A. Rasche. 1975. Hyperactive behavior and EEG arousal reactions in children. EEG Clin. Neurophysiol. 38: 149–159.

Gubray, S.S., E. Elles, J.N. Walton, and S.D.N. Count. 1965. Clumsy children. A study of apraxic and agnosic defects in 21 children. Brain 88: 295–312.

Guilford, J. 1967. The Nature of Human Intelligence. McGraw-Hill, New York.

Guirgea, C. 1971. The pharmacology of Piracetam (UCB 6215): A Nootrapic drug. Report UCB Pharm. Division, Brussels, Belgium.

Guirgea, C. 1973. The Nootrapic approach to the pharmacology of the integrative action of the brain. Conditional Reflex 8: 108–115.

Guirgea, C., and F. Mouravièff-Lesuisse. 1971. Pharmacological studies on an elementary model of learning: The fixation of an experience at spinal level. Arch. Int. Pharmacodyn. Ther. 191: 279–291.

Guirgea, C., and F. Moyersoons. 1972. The pharmacology of cortical evoked potentials. Arch. Int. Pharmacodyn, Ther. 199: 67–78.

Guthrie, J.T. 1973. Models of reading and reading disability. J. Educ. Psychol. 65: 9–18.

Guttman, E. 1942. Aphasia in children. Brain 65: 205–219.

Guyer, B., and M. Friedman. 1975. Hemispheric processing and cognitive styles in learning disabled and normal children. Child Dev. (In press)

Haggard, M.P. 1971. Encoding and the REA for speech signals. Q.J. Exp. Psychol. 23: 34–45.

Hallahan, D.P., and W.M. Cruickshank. 1973. Psycho-Educational Foundations of Learning Disabilities. Prentice-Hall. Englewood Cliffs.

Halperin, Y., S. Nackshon, and A. Carmon. 1973. Shift of ear superiority in dichotic listening to temporally patterned nonverbal stimuli. J. Acoust. Soc. Am. 53: 46–50.

Halwes, T. 1968. Comment. In J.F. Kavanagh (ed.), Communicating by Language, p. 160. NICHD, Bethesda, Md.

Hamill, D. 1971. Evaluating children for instructional purposes. Acad. Ther. 6: 343.

Hardy, W.G. 1965. On language disorders in young children: A reorganization of thinking. J. Speech and Hearing Dis. 8: 3–16.

Harris, A.J. 1947. Harris Tests of Lateral Dominance: Manual of directions for administration and interpretation. Psychological Corporation, New York.

Harris, A.J. 1958. Harris Tests of Lateral Dominance. The Psychological Corporation, New York.

Harshman, R.A., H. Crawford, and E. Hecht. 1974. Marijuana, cognitive style and cerebral dominance. Progress Report. Dept. of Psychology, University of California, Los Angeles.

Harter, M.R. 1967. Excitability cycles and cortical scanning: A review of two hypotheses of central intermittency in perception. Psychol. Bull. 68: 47–58.

Hartlage, L.C. 1970. Sex-linked inheritance on spatial ability. Percept. Mot. Skills 31: 610.

Hartlage, L.C., and J.B. Green. 1973. The EEG as a predictor of intellective and academic performance. J. Learning Disabilities 6: 239–242.

Head, H. 1926. Aphasia and Kindred Disorders of Speech. Cambridge University Press, London.

Hebb, D.O. 1949. The Organization of Behavior. Wiley and Sons, Inc., New York.

Hebb, D.O. 1974. What psychology is about. Am. Psychologist 29: 71–79.

Hebb, D.O., and W. Penfield. 1940. Human behavior after extensive bilateral removal of the frontal lobes. Arch. Neurol. Psychiatry 44: 421–438.

Heber, R. 1970. Epidemiology of Mental Retardation. Charles C Thomas, Springfield, Ill.

Hécaen, H., and R. Angelergues. 1963. La Cécité Psychique. Masson, Paris.

Hécaen, H., and J. Sauguet. 1971. Cerebral dominance in left-handed subjects. Cortex 7: 19–48.

Heron, W. 1957. Perception as a function of retinal locus and attention. Am. J. Psychol. 70: 38–48.

Herz, A. 1959. Effects of atropine on early stages of learning in the rat. Arch. Exp. Pathol. Pharmacol. 236: 110–111.

Hess, R., Jr., W.P. Koella, and K. Akert. 1953. Cortical and subcortical recordings in natural and artificially induced sleep in cats. EEG Clin. Neurophysiol. 5: 75–90.

Hill, R.T. 1974. Neurochemical mechanisms in rat behavioral models of the euphoregenic and antihyperpenetic actions of psychomotor stimulants. Presented at the 13th annual meeting of the American College of Neuropsychopharmacology. San Juan, P.R. (Unpublished)

Hines, D., and P. Satz. 1974. Cross-modal asymmetries in perception related to asymmetry in cerebral function. Neuropsychologia 12: 239–247.

Hinton, G.G., and R.M. Knights. 1971. Children with learning problems: Academic history, academic prediction and adjustment 3 years after assessment. Except. Child. 37 (7): 513–519.

Hintzman, D.L. 1967. Articulatory coding in short-term memory. J. Verb. Learning Verb. Behav. 6: 312–316.

Hirsh, I.J. 1959. Auditory perception of temporal order. J. Acoust. Soc. Am. 31: 759–767.

Hobbs, N. 1975. The Futures of Children, Categories, Labels and Their Consequences. Jossey-Bass, San Francisco.

Hochberg, J.E. 1970. Attention, organization and consciousness. In D.I. Mostofsky (ed.), Attention: Contemporary Theory and Analysis, pp. 99–124. Appleton-Century-Crofts, New York.

House, B.J., and D. Zeaman. 1963. Miniature experiments in the discrimination learning of retardates. In L.P. Lipsitt and C.C. Spiker (eds.), Advances in Child Development and Behavior, Vol. I. Academic Press, New York.

Hubel, D.H., and T.N. Wiesel. 1959. Receptive fields of single neurons in the cat's striate cortes. J. Physiol. 148: 574–591.

Hubel, D.H., and T.N. Wiesel. 1962. Receptive fields, binocular interaction and functional architecture in the cat's visual cortex. J. Physiol. 160: 106–154.

Hubel, D.H., and T.N. Wiesel. 1965. Receptive fields and functional architecture in two non-striate visual areas (18 and 19) of the cat. J. Neurophysiol. 28: 229–289.

Huey, E.B. 1908. The Psychology and Pedagogy of Reading. Macmillan, New York.

Hughes, J.R. 1965. A review of the positive spike phenomenon. In W.E.

Wilson (ed.), Applications of the Electroencephalography in Psychiatry, pp. 54–101. Duke University Press, Durham.

Hughes, J.R. 1967. Electroencephalography and learning. In H.R. Myklebust (ed.), Progress in Learning Disabilities, Vol. I, pp. 113–146. Grune & Stratton, New York.

Hughes, J.R. 1971. Electroencephalography and learning disabilities. In H.R. Myklebust (ed.), Progress in Learning Disabilities, Vol. II, pp. 18–55. Grune & Stratton, New York.

Hughes, J.R., and G.E. Park. 1968. The EEG in dyslexia. In P. Kellaway and I. Petersen (eds.), Clinical Electroencephalography of Children, pp. 307–327. Almqvist and Wiksell, Stockholm.

Hunt, J.McV. 1961. Intelligence and Experience. Ronald Press, New York.

Hunt, J.McV., and C. Cofer. 1944. Psychological deficit. In J.McV. Hunt (ed.), Personality and the Behavior Disorders, Vol. II. Ronald Press, New York.

Hurst, P.M., R. Raslow, N.C. Chubb, and S.K. Bagley. 1969. Effects of d-amphetamine on acquisition, persistence and recall. Am. J. Psychol. 82: 307–319.

Hutt, C., S.J. Hutt, and C.A. Ounsted. 1965. The behavior of children with and without upper C.N.S. lesions. Behavior 24: 246.

Hydén, H. 1961. Biochemical aspects of brain activity. In S. Farber and R. Wilson (eds.), Control of the Mind. Part 1. McGraw-Hill, New York.

Hydén, H. 1961. Satellite cells in the nervous system. Scientific American 205 (6): 62–70.

Hydén, H., and E. Egyhazi. 1964. Changes in RNA content and base composition in cortical neurons of rats in a learning experiment involving transfer of handedness. Proc. Natl. Acad. Sci. U.S.A. 52: 1030–1035.

Hydén, H., and P.W. Lange. 1970. Protein synthesis in the hippocampal pyramidal cells of rats during a behavioral test. Science 159: 1370–1373.

Immergluck, L. 1966. Resistences to an optical illusion, figural aftereffect, and field dependence. Psychonom. Sci. 6: 281–282.

Inglis, J. 1966. The Scientific Study of Abnormal Behavior. Aldine, Chicago.

Ingram, T.T. 1959. Specific developmental disorders of speech in childhood. Brain 82: 450–467.

Ingram, T.T.S., A.W. Mason, and I. Blackburn. 1970. A retrospective study of 82 children with reading disability. Dev. Med. Child Neurol. 12: 271–281.

Irwin, S. 1968. A rational framework for the development, evaluation, and use of psychoactive drugs. Am. J. Psychiatry (Suppl. Drug Ther.) 124: 1–9.

Irwin, S., and A. Benuazizi. 1966. Pentylenetetrazol enhances memory function. Science 152: 100–102.

Itil, T.M. 1970. Digital computer analysis of the electroencephalogram during rapid eye movement sleep state in man. J. Nerv. Ment. Dis. 150: 201–208.

Jackson, J.H. 1874. On the duality of the brain. Medical Press, 1874, 1: 19. Reprinted in J. Taylor (ed.), Selected Writings of John Hughlings Jackson, Vol. II, pp. 129–145. Hodder and Stoughton, London, 1932.

Jackson, J.H. 1876. Case of large cerebral tumour without optic neuritis and with left hemiplegia and imperception. Royal London Ophthalmological Hospital Report 8: 434. Reprinted in J. Taylor (ed.), Selected Writings of John Hughlings Jackson, Vol. II, pp. 146–183. Hodder and Stoughton, London, 1932.

Jacobson, H. 1951. The informational capacity of the human eye. Science 113: 292–294.

Jasper, H.H., and C. Stefanis. 1965. Intracellular oscillatory rhythms in pyramidal tract neurones in the cat. EEG Clin. Neurophysiol. 18: 541–553.

Jasper, H.H., C. Bradley, and P. Saloman. 1938. EEG analysis of behavior problem children. Am. J. Psychiatry 95: 641–658.

Jastak, J.F., and S.R. Jastak. 1965. The Wide Range Achievement Test. Guidance Associates, Wilmington.

Jastak, J.F., S.W. Bijou, and S.R. Jastak. 1965. The Wide Range Achievement Test. Guidance Associates, Wilmington.

Jensen, A.R. 1969. How much can we boost IQ and scholastic attainment? Harvard Educ. Rev. 39: 1–123.

John, E.R., R.N. Herrington, and S. Sutton. 1967. Effects of visual form on the evoked response. Science 155: 1439–1442.

Johnson, D.J., and H.R. Myklebust. 1967. Learning Disabilities, Educational Principles and Practices. Grune & Stratton, New York.

Kagan, J. 1965. Impulsive and reflective children: Significance of conceptual tempo. In J.D. Krumboltz (ed.), Learning and the Educational Process. Rand McNally, Chicago.

Kagan, J. 1966. Reflection-impulsivity: The generality and dynamics of conceptual tempo. J. Abnor. Psychol. 71: 17–24.

Kalverboer, A.F. 1975. A Neurobehavioral study in pre-school children. Heinemann, London.

Kass, C.E. 1964. Auditory closure test. In J.J. Olson and J.L. Olson (eds.), Validity Studies on the Illinois Test of Psycholinguistic Abilities. Photo Press, Madison, Wisconsin.

Kaste, C.M. 1972. A ten-year follow-up of children diagnosed in a child guidance clinic as having cerebral dysfunction. Dissertation Abstracts International 33 (4-B): 1797–1798.

Keele, S.W. 1973. Attention and Human Performance. Goodyear Publishing Co., Inc., Pacific Palisades.

Kellaway, P., J.W. Crawley, and N. Kagawa. 1959. A specific electroencephalographic correlate of convulsive equivalent disorders in children. J. Pediat. 55: 582–592.

Kellmer Pringle, M.L., N.R. Butler, and R. Davie. 1966. 11,000 Seven-year-olds, studies in child development. Quoted in Celdic Report 56. Longmans, London.

Keogh, B. 1971. Hyperactivity and learning disorders: Review and speculation. Except. Child. 38: 101–109.

Keogh, B. 1973. Perceptual and cognitive styles: Implications for special education. In D. Mann and D. Sabatino (eds.), Review of Special Education, Vol. I. Journal of Special Education Press.

Keogh, B., and G. Donlon. 1972. Field-dependence, impulsivity, and learning disabilities. J. Learning Disabilities 5: 331–336.

Kephart, N.C. 1960. The Slow Learner in the Classroom. Merrill, Columbus.

Kershner, J.R. 1971. Children's acquisition of visuo-spatial dimensionality: A conservation study. Dev. Psychol. 5: 454–462.

Killam, K.F., and E.K. Killam. 1967. Rhinencephalic activity during acquisition and performance of conditional behavior and its modification by pharmacological agents. In W.R. Adey and T. Tokizane (eds.), Progress in Brain Research, Vol. 27, Structure and Function of the Limbic System. Elsevier, New York.

Kimura, D. 1961a. Cerebral dominance and the perception of verbal stimuli. Can. J. Psychol. 15: 166–171.

Kimura, D. 1961b. Some effects of temporal-lobe damage on auditory perception. Can. J. Psychol. 15: 156–165.

Kimura, D. 1963. Speech lateralization in young children as determined by an auditory test. Cortex 56: 899–902.

Kimura, D. 1967. Functional asymmetry of the brain in dichotic listening. Cortex 3: 163–178.

Kimura, D., and M. Durnford. 1974. Normal Studies on the function of the right hemisphere in vision. In S.J. Dimond and J.G. Beaumont (eds.), Hemisphere Function in the Human Brain, pp. 25–47. Elek Science, London.

Kinsbourne, M. 1967. Effect of focal cerebral lesions on perspective and movement reversals. J. Nerv. Ment. Dis. 2: 144.

Kinsbourne, M. 1971. Cognitive deficit: Experimental analysis. In J. McGaugh (ed.), Psychobiology. Academic Press, New York.

Kinsbourne, M. 1972. The neuropsychology of learning disabilities. Seventh Neuropsychology Workshop, University of Victoria, Victoria, B.C., Canada.

Kinsbourne, M. 1973. Minimal brain dysfunction as a neurodevelopmental lag. Ann. N.Y. Acad. Sci. 205: 268–273.

Kinsbourne, M. 1974. Mechanisms of hemispheric interaction in man. In M. Kinsbourne and W.L. Smith (eds.), Hemispheric Disconnection and Cerebral Function, Chapter 8. Charles C Thomas, Springfield, Ill.

Kinsbourne, M., and W.L. Smith. 1974. Hemispheric Disconnection and Cerebral Function. Charles C Thomas, Springfield, Ill.

Kinsbourne, M., and E.K. Warrington. 1963a. Developmental factors in reading and writing backwardness. Brit. J. Psychol. 54: 145–156.

Kinsbourne, M., and E.K. Warrington. 1963b. The developmental Gerstmann syndrome. Arch. Neurol. 8: 490–501.

Kinsbourne, M., and E.K. Warrington. 1964. Disorders of spelling. J. Neurol. Neurosurg. Psychiatry 27: 224–228.

Kinsbourne, M., and E.K. Warrington. 1966. Developmental factors in reading and writing backwardness. In J. Money (ed.), The Disabled Reader: Education of the Dyslexic Child, pp. 59–72. Johns Hopkins Press, Baltimore.

Kintsch, W. 1970. Learning, Memory, and Conceptual Processes. Wiley and Sons, Inc., New York.

Kintsch, W., and H. Buschke. 1969. Homophones and synonyms in short-term memory. J. Exp. Psychol. 80: 403–407.

Kirk, S.A. 1968. Illinois test of psycholinguistic abilities: Its origin and implications. *In* J. Hellmuth (ed.), Learning Disorders, Vol. 3. Special Child Publications, Seattle.

Kirk, S.A., and B. Bateman. 1962. Diagnosis and remediation of learning disabilities. Except. Child. 29: 73–78.

Kirk, S.A., and W. Becker. 1963. Conference on children with minimal brain impairment. University of Illinois (mimeo.), Urbana.

Kirk, S.A., J. McCarthy, and W. Kirk. 1968. Examiner's Manual: Illinois Test of Psycholinguistic Abilities. (Rev. Ed.). University of Illinois Press, Urbana.

KIT of reference test for cognitive factor. 1963. Educational Testing Service, Princeton.

Klein, D.F., and J.M. Davis. 1969. Diagnosis and Drug Treatment of Psychiatric Disorders. Williams & Wilkins, Baltimore.

Kleuver, R. 1971. Mental abilities and disorders of learning. *In* H. Myklebust (ed.), Progress in Learning Disabilities, Vol. 2. Grune & Stratton, New York.

Klinkerfuss, G.H., P.H. Lang, W.A. Weinberg, and J.L. O'Leary. 1965. EEG abnormalities of children with hyperkinetic behavior. Neurology (Minneap.) 15: 883–896.

Kløve, H. 1963. Clinical neuropsychology. *In* F.M. Forster (ed.), The Medical Clinics of North America. Saunders, New York.

Knights, R., and G.G. Hinton. 1969. The effects of methylphenidate (Ritalin) on the motor skills and behavior of children with learning problems. J. Nerv. Ment. Dis. 148: 643–653.

Knights, R.M. 1970. A review of the neuropsychological research program. Special Educ. November: 9–27.

Knights, R.M. 1973a. Problems of criteria in diagnosis: A profile similarity approach. Ann. N.Y. Acad. Sci. 205: 124–131.

Knights, R.M. 1973b. The Effects of Cerebral Lesions on the Psychological Test Performance of Children. Carleton University, Ottawa.

Knights, R.M., and A.D. Moule. 1967. Normative and reliability data on finger and foot tapping in children. Percept. Mot. Skills 25: 717–720.

Knobel, M., M.B. Wolman, and C. Mason. 1959. Hyperkinesia and organicity in children. Arch. Gen. Psychiatry 1: 310–321.

Knobloch, H., and B. Pasamanick. 1959. Syndrome of minimal cerebral damage in infancy. JAMA 170: 1384–1387.

Knopp, W., L.E. Arnold, R.L. Andras, and D.J. Smeltzer. 1973. Predicting amphetamine response in hyperkinetic children by electronic pupillography. Pharmakopsychistries Neuro-Psychopharmakologie 6: 158–166.

Knott, J.R., S. Muehl, and A.L. Benton. 1965. Electroencephalograms in children with reading disabilities. Electroenceph. Clin. Neurophysiol. 18: 513–533.

Knox, C., and D. Kimura. 1970. Cerebral processing of nonverbal sounds in boys and girls. Neuropsychologia 8: 227–237.

Koch-Weser, J. 1972. Serum drug concentrations as therapeutic guides. N. Engl. J. Med. 287: 227–231.

Kolers, P.A. 1969. Reading is only incidentally visual. *In* K.S. Goodman and J.T. Fleming (eds.), Psycholinguistics and the Teaching of Reading. International Reading Association. Newark, Delaware.

Koppitz, E.M. 1971. Children with Learning Disabilities: A Five Year Follow-up Study. Grune & Stratton, New York.

Kornblum, S. 1973. Attention and Performance IV. Academic Press, New York.

Krnjevic, K. 1969. Central cholinergic pathways. Fed. Proc. 28: 113–120.

Krnjevic, K., and J.W. Phillis. 1963. Acetylcholine-sensitive cells in the cerebral cortex. J. Physiol. 166: 296–327.

Kuhn, G.M. 1973. The phi coefficient as an index of ear differences in dichotic listening. Cortex 9: 450–457.

Kurland, L.F., and D. Colodny. 1969. Psychiatric disability and learning problems. *In* L. Tarnopol (ed.), Learning Disabilities: Introduction to Educational and Medical Management. Charles C Thomas, Springfield, Ill.

La Berge, D., and S.J. Samuels. 1974. Toward a theory of automatic information processing. Cog. Psychol. 6: 293–323.

Lacey, J.I., J. Kagan, B.C. Lacey, and H.A. Moss. 1963. The visceral level: Situational determinants and behavioral correlates of autonomic response pattern. *In* P.H. Knapp (ed.), Expression of the Emotions in Man. International University Press, New York.

Lairy, G.C., and A. Harrison. 1968. Functional aspects of EEG foci in children: Clinical data and longitudinal studies. *In* P. Kellaway and I. Petersen (eds.), Clinical EEG of Children, pp. 197–212. Almqvist and Wiksell, Stockholm.

Lackner, J.R., and H.L. Teuber. 1973. Alterations in auditory fusion thresholds after cerebral injury in man. Neuropsychologia 11: 409–415.

Landucci, L., and G. Piantossi. 1961. EEG and psychometric researches in children suffering from mental deficiency. Acta Paedopsychiatrica 28: 161–171.

Lansdell, H. 1964. Sex differences in hemispheric asymmetries of the human brain. Nature 203: 550.

Lansdell, H. 1968. The use of factor scores from the Wechsler-Bellevue Scale of Intelligence in assessing patients with temporal lobe removals. Cortex 4: 257–268.

Larsen, S., R. Parker, and S. Jorjorian. 1973. Differences in self-concept of normal and learning disabled children. Percept. Mot. Skills 37: 510.

Lasagna, L. 1969. The pharmaceutical revolution. Science 166: 1432.

Laties, V.G., and B. Weiss. 1967. Performance enhancement by the amphetamines: A new appraisal. *In* H. Brill, et al. (eds.), Neuropsychopharmacology. Excerpta-Medica Foundation, Amsterdam.

Laufer, M.W. 1967. Brain disorders in children. *In* A.M. Freedman and H.I. Kaplan (eds.), Comprehensive Textbooks of Psychiatry. Williams & Wilkins, Baltimore.

Laufer, M.W., and E. Denhoff. 1957. Hyperkinetic behavior syndrome in children. J. Pediatr. 50: 463–473.

La Veck, G., and F. De la Cruz. 1963. EEG and etiologic findings in mental retardation. Pediatrics 31: 478–485.

Leisman, G. 1973. Conditioning variables in attentional handicaps. Neuropsychologia 11: 199–205.

Leisman, G. 1974. The relationship between saccadic eye movements and the alpha rhythm in attentionally handicapped patients. Neuropsychologia 12: 209–218.

Leisman, G. 1975a. The role of visual processes in attention and its disorders. *In* G. Leisman (ed.), Basic Visual Processes and Learning Disability. Charles C Thomas, Springfield, Ill.

Leisman, G. 1975b. Characteristics of saccadic eye movements in attentionally handicapped patients. Percept. Mot. Skills 40: 803–809.

Leisman, G. 1975c. The neurophysiology of visual processing: Implications for learning disability. *In* G. Leisman (ed.), Basic Visual Processes and Learning Disability. Charles C Thomas, Springfield, Ill.

Leisman, G. 1975d. Electro-oculographic and alpha rhythm relationships in spastic-hemiplegic patients: Building a model of visual information transmission. Presented at Third Annual Meeting International Neuropsychological Society, Tampa, Florida.

Leisman, G. 1975e. Functional cortical anatomy in relation to visual processes and learning disability. *In* G. Leisman (ed.), Basic Visual Processes and Learning Disability. Charles C Thomas, Springfield, Ill.

Leisman, G., and J. Schwartz. 1975. Ocular-motor function and information processing: Implications for the reading process. *In* M. Kling (ed.), Promising New Methodological Approaches in Understanding the Reading/Language Process. International Reading Association. Newark, Delaware. (In press)

Lenneberg, E.H. 1967. Biological Foundations of Language. Wiley and Sons, Inc. New York.

Leong, C.K. 1975a. Laterality patterns in disabled and non-disabled nine-year-old readers. Presented at the Boerhaave International Conference on Lateralization of Brain Functions, Leiden, The Netherlands.

Leong, C.K. 1975b. An Efficient Method for Dichotic Tape Preparation. Behav. Res. Meth. Instrument. 7: 447–451.

Leong, C.K. 1975c. Lateralization in severely disabled readers in relation to functional cerebral development and syntheses of information. This volume.

Leong, C.K. 1975d. Spatial-Temporal Information-Processing in Children with Specific Reading Disability. (In press)

Levine, M., and G. Fuller. 1972. Psychological, neuropsychological and educational correlates of reading deficit. J. Learning Disabilities 5: 50–58.

Levy, J. 1969. Possible basis for the evolution of lateral specialization of the human brain. Nature 224: 614–615.

Levy, J. 1974. Psychobiological implications of bilateral asymmetry. *In* S.J. Dimond and J. Beaumont (eds.), Hemisphere Function in the Human Brain, pp. 121–183. Elek Science, London.

Levy-Agresti, J., and R.W. Sperry. 1968. Differential perceptual capacities in major and minor hemispheres. Proc. Natl. Acad. Sci. U.S.A. 61: 1151.

Levy, J., C. Trevarthen, and R.W. Sperry. 1972. Perception of bilateral chimeric figures following hemispheric deconnexion. Brain 95: 61–78.

Levy, S. 1966. The hyperkinetic child—a forgotten entity: Its diagnosis and treatment. Int. J. Neuropsychiatry 2: 330–336.

Liberman, A.M. 1973. The specialization of the language hemisphere. *In* The Neurosciences: Third Study Program. MIT Press, Cambridge.

Liberman, A.M., I.G. Mattingly, and M.T. Turvey. 1972. Language codes and memory codes. *In* A.W. Melton and E. Martin (eds.), Coding Processes in Human Memory. Winston, Washington.

Liberman, A.M., F.S. Cooper, D. Shankweiler, and M. Studdert-Kennedy. 1967. Perception of the speech code. Psychol. Rev. 74: 431–461.

Liberman, I.Y. 1971. Basic research in speech and lateralization of language: Some implications for reading disability. Bull. Orton Soc. 21: 71–87.

Liberman, I.Y. 1973. Segmentation of the spoken word and reading acquisition. Bull. Orton Soc. 23: 65–77.

Liberman, I.Y., D. Shankweiler, F.W. Fischer, and B. Carter. 1974. Reading and the awareness of linguistic segments. J. Exp. Child Psychol. 18: 201–212.

Liberman, I.Y., D. Shankweiler, A.M. Liberman, C. Fowler, and F.W. Fischer. 1976. Phonetic segmentation and recoding in the beginning reader. *In* A.S. Reber and D. Scarborough (eds.), Reading: Theory and Practice. Erlbaum Associates. Hillsdale, New Jersey. (In press)

Libet, B., W.W. Alberts, E.W. Wright, Jr., and B. Feinstein. 1967. Responses of human somatosensory cortex to stimuli below threshold for conscious sensation. Science 158: 1597–1600.

Lienert, G.A. 1961. Ueberpruefung und genetische Interpretation der Divergenzhypothese von Wewetzer. Vita Humana 4: 112–124.

Lindsley, D.B. 1952. Psychological phenomena and the electroencephalogram. EEG Clin. Neurophysiol. 4: 443–456.

Lombroso, C.T., I.H. Schwartz. D.M. Clark, H. Muench, and J. Barry. 1966. Ctenoids in healthy youths: Controlled study on 14- and 6-per second positive spiking. Neurology (Minneap.) 16: 1152–1158.

Loo, C., and C. Wenar. 1971. Activity level and motor inhibition: Their relationship to intelligence test performance in normal children. Child Dev. 42: 967–971.

Loranger, A.W., H. Goodell, J.E. Lee, and F. McDowell. 1972. Levadopa treatment of Parkinson's syndrome: Improved intellectual functioning. Arch. Gen. Psychiatry 22: 163–168.

Lowe, A.D., and R.A. Campbell. 1965. Temporal discrimination in aphasoid and normal children. J. Speech Hearing Res. 8: 313–314.

Lukianowicz, M.S. 1975. Sex differences in verbal skills, and their relationship to hand and ear preference in the deaf child. Manuscript submitted for publication.

Luria, A.R. 1961. The Role of Speech in the Regulation of Normal and Abnormal Behavior. Liveright, New York.

Luria, A.R. 1966a. Higher Cortical Functions in Man. Basic Books, New York.

Luria, A.R. 1966b. Human Brain and Psychological Processes. Harper & Row, New York.

Luria, A.R. 1970. Traumatic Aphasia: Its Syndromes, Psychology and Treatment. Mouton, The Hague.

Luria, A.R. 1973. The Working Brain: An Introduction to Neuropsychology. Penguin, London.

Luria, A.R., and E.D. Homskaya. 1973. Frontal lobes and the regulation of arousal processes. In D.I. Mostofsky (ed.), Attention: Contemporary Theory and Analysis. Appleton-Century-Crofts, New York.

Lykken, D.T., and P.H. Venables. 1971. Direct measurement of skin conductance: A proposal for standardization. Psychophysiology 8: 656—672.

Maccoby, E., E. Dowley, J. Hagan, and R. Degerman. 1965. Activity level and intellectual functioning in normal school children. Child Dev. 36: 761—770.

Mach, E. 1959. The Analysis of Sensation. Dover, New York.

Mackay, D.M. 1956. Towards and information flow model of human behavior. Brit. J. Psychol. 47: 30—43.

Mackay, D.M. 1966. Cerebral organization and the conscious control of action. In J.C. Eccles (ed.), Brain and Conscious Experience, pp. 422—445. Springer, New York.

Mackay, D.M. 1967. Ways of looking at perception. In W. Walten-Dunn (ed.), Models for the Perception of Speech and Visual Form, pp. 25—43. MIT Press, Boston.

Mackworth, J.F. 1971. Some models of the reading process: Learners and skilled readers. In F.B. Davis (ed.), The Literature of Research in Reading With Emphasis on Models. 8: 67—101. Rutgers University, Graduate School of Education, New Brunswick, N.J.

Mackworth, N.H. 1973. Personal Communication.

MacMahon, B., and T.F. Pugh. 1970. Epidemiology, Principles and Methods. Little, Brown & Co. Boston.

Maddess, R.J. 1975. Bilateral tachistoscopic presentation of letters and line orientations in the bisected visual fields at three visual angles. Ph.D. Dissertation. University of Victoria.

Malmquist, E. 1958. Factors Related to Reading Disabilities in the First Grade of Elementary School. Almqvist and Wiksell, Stockholm.

Mann, L., and W. Phillips. 1967. Fractional practices in special education: A critique. 33: 311—319.

Marcel, T., L. Katz, and M. Smith. 1974. Laterality and reading proficiency. Neuropsychologia 12: 131—139.

Marshall, J.C., and F. Newcombe. 1973. Patterns of paralexia: A psycholinguistic approach. J. Psycholinguistic Res. 2: 175—199.

Marshall, J.C., D. Caplan, and J.M. Holmes. 1975. The measure of laterality. Neuropsychologia 13: 315—321.

Masamoto, F., K.L. Bost, and H.E. Himwich. 1971. EEG arousal sites of amphetamine and its psychotomimetic methoxy derivatives in rabbit brain. Biol. Psychiatry 3: 367—377.

Masland, R.L. 1967. Lacunae and research approaches to them, III. In F.L. Darley (ed.), Brain Mechanisms Underlying Speech and Language, pp. 232—235. Grune & Stratton, New York.

Mattingly, I.G. 1972. Reading, the linguistic process and linguistic aware-
ness. *In* J.F. Kavanagh and I.G. Mattingly (eds.), Language By Ear and
By Eye: The Relationships Between Speech and Reading. MIT Press,
Cambridge.

Maxwell, A.E. 1959. A factor analysis of the Wechsler intelligence scale for
children. Brit. J. Educ. Psychol. 29: 237–241.

Maxwell, A.E. 1972. The WPPSI: A marked discrepancy in the correlations
of the subtests for good and poor readers. Brit. J. Math. Stat. Psychol.
25: 283–291.

McCall, R.E., and M.I. Appelbaum. 1973. Bias in the analysis of repeated-
measures designs: Some alternative approaches. Child Dev. 44: 401–415.

McConnell, J.V. 1962. Memory transfer through cannibalism in planaria. J.
Neuropsychiatry 3(Suppl. 1): 42–48.

McCready, E.B. 1910. Biological variations in the higher cerebral centres
causing retardation. Arch. Pediatr. 27: 506–513.

McGaugh, J.L. 1966. Time dependent processes in memory storage. Science 153: 1351–1358.

McGaugh, J.L., and L. Petrinovich. 1959. The effects of strychnine sul-
phate on maze learning. Am. J. Psychol. 72: 99–102.

McGlone, J., and A. Kertesz. 1973. Sex differences in cerebral processing
of visuospatial tasks. Cortex 9: 313–320.

McGraw-Hill Encyclopedia of Science and Technology. 1971. Vol. 5, pp.
37–39. McGraw-Hill, New York.

McGrew, W.C. 1972. An Etiological Study of Children's Behavior. Academic Press, New York.

McKeever, W.F., and M.D. Huling. 1970. Lateral dominance in tachistoscopic word recognitions of children at two levels of ability. Q. J. Exp.
Psychol. 22: 600–604.

McKinney, J.A. 1973. Developmental study of the effects of hypothesis
verbalizations and memory load on concept attainment. Unpublished
manuscript. University of North Carolina, Chapel Hill.

McLardy, T. 1969. Ammon's horn pathology: An epileptic dyscontrol.
Nature 221: 877–878.

Meachem, J. 1972. The development of memory abilities in the individual
and society. Hum. Dev. 15: 205–228.

Meichenbaum, D. 1974. Therapist manual for cognitive behavior modification. Unpublished manuscript. University of Waterloo.

Meichenbaum, D. 1975a. Self-instructional methods. *In* F. Kanfer and A.
Goldstein (eds.), Helping People Change. Pergamon Press, New York.

Meichenbaum, D. 1975b. Toward a cognitive theory of self-control. *In* G.
Schwartz and D. Shapiro (eds.), Consciousness and Self-Regulation:
Advances in Research. Plenum Press, New York.

Meichenbaum, D., and R. Cameron. 1973. Training schizophrenics to talk
to themselves: A means of developing attentional controls. Behav. Ther.
4: 515–534.

Meichenbaum, D., and R. Cameron. 1974. The clinical potential of modi-
fying what clients say to themselves. Psychother. Theory, Res. Pract. 11:
103–117.

Meichenbaum, D., and J. Goodman. 1969. Reflection-impulsivity and
verbal control of motor behavior. Child Dev. 40: 785–798.

Meister, R.K. 1951. A hypothesis concerning visual alpha rhythm with reference to the perception of movement. Unpublished Ph.D. Thesis. University of Chicago.

Meldrum, B.S., and J.B. Brierley. 1972. Neuronal loss and gliosis in the hippocampus following repetitive epileptic seizures induced in adolescent baboons by allylglycine. Brain Res. 48: 361–365.

Meyer, V., and H.G. Jones. 1957. Patterns of cognitive test performance as functions of the lateral localization of cerebral abnormalities in the temporal lobe. J. Ment. Sci. 103: 758–772.

Meyer, V., and A.J. Yates. 1955. Intellectual changes following temporal lobectomy for psychomotor epilepsy. J. Neurol. Neurosurg. Psychiatry 18: 44–52.

Michelson, M.J. 1961. Effects of atropine on an auditory discrimination task in the cat. Activatis Nervosa Superior 3: 140–147.

Milberg, R.M., K.L. Rinehart, R.L. Sprague, and E.K. Sleator. 1975. A reproducible gas chromatographic-mass spectrometric assay for low levels of methylphenidate and Ritalinic acid in blood and urine. Biomed. Mass Spect. (In press)

Miles, T.R. 1974. The Dyslexic Child. Priory Press, London.

Miles, W.R. 1929. The A-B-C Vision Test. Psychological Corporation, New York.

Miller, B.F., and C.B. Keane. 1972. Encyclopedia and Dictionary of Medicine and Nursing, p. 326. Saunders, Toronto.

Miller, E. 1971. Handedness and the pattern of human ability. Brit. J. Psychol. 62: 111–112.

Millichap, J.G. 1974. Neuropharmacology of hyperkinetic behavior: Response to methylphenidate correlated with degree of activity and brain damage. In A. Vernadakis and N. Weiner (eds.), Drugs and the Developing Brain. Plenum Press, New York.

Millichap, J.G., and E.E. Boldrey. 1967. Studies in hyperkinetic behavior. II. Laboratory and clinical evaluation of drug treatment. Neurology 17: 467.

Milner, B. 1954. Intellectual function of the temporal lobes. Psychol. Bull. 51: 42–62.

Milner, B. 1962. Laterality effects in audition. In V.B. Mountcastle (ed.), Interhemispheric Relations and Cerebral Dominance, pp. 177–195. Johns Hopkins Press, Baltimore.

Milner, B. 1969. Residual intellectual and memory deficits after head injury. In E. Walker, W. Caveness, and M. Critchley (eds.), The Late Effects of Head Injury. Charles C Thomas, Springfield, Ill.

Milner, B. 1971. Interhemispheric differences and psychological processes. Brit. Med. Bull. 27: 272–277.

Milner, B. 1974. Hemispheric specialization: Scope and limits. In F.O. Schmitt and F.G. Warden (eds.), The Neurosciences: Third Study Programme. MIT Press, Cambridge.

Milner, B. 1975. Psychological aspects of focal epilepsy and its neurosurgical management. In D.P. Purpura, J. Kiffin Penry, and R.D. Walter (eds.), Advances in Neurology, Vol. 8, pp. 299–322. Raven Press, New York.

Milner, B., and L. Taylor. 1972. Right-hemisphere superiority in tactile pattern-recognition after cerebral commissurotomy: Evidence for non-verbal memory. Neuropsychologia 10: 1–15.

Milner, B., L. Taylor, and R.W. Sperry. 1968. Lateralized suppression of dichotically presented digits after commissural section in man. Science 161: 184–186.

Minskoff, J.G. 1973. Differential approaches to prevalence estimates of learning disabilities. Ann. N.Y. Acad. Sci. 205: 139–145.

Molfese, D.L., R.B. Freeman, Jr., and D.S. Palermo. 1975. The ontogeny of brain lateralization for speech and nonspeech stimuli. Brain and Language 2: 356–368.

Money, J. 1962. Reading Disability: Progress and Research Needs in Dyslexia. Johns Hopkins Press, Baltimore.

Money, J. 1966. The Disabled Reader, Education of the Dislexic Child. Johns Hopkins Press, Baltimore.

Money, J. 1972. Studies on the function of sighting dominance. Q. J. Exp. Psych. 24: 454–464.

Monroe, M. 1932. Children Who Cannot Read. University of Chicago Press, Chicago.

Monsees, E.K. 1961. Aphasia in children. J. Speech Hearing Dis. 26: 83–86.

Montplaisir, J.Y. 1975. Cholinergic mechanisms involved in cortical activation during arousal. EEG and Clin. Neurophysiol. 38: 263–272.

Morgan, C., and E. Stellar. 1950. Physiological Psychology. McGraw-Hill, New York.

Morin, S. 1965. EEG correlates of stuttering. EEG Clin. Neurophysiol. 18: 425.

Morrell, F. 1961. Lasting changes in synaptic organization produced by continual neuronal bombardment. In J.F. Delefresnaye (ed.), Brain Mechanisms and Learning. Blackwell, Oxford.

Morrell, F., and H.H. Jasper. 1956. Electrographic studies of the formation of temporary connections in the brain. EEG Clin. Neurophysiol. 8: 201–215.

Morris, J.M. 1966. Standards and Progress in Reading. New York University Press, New York.

Morrison, R.S., and E.W. Dempsey. 1943. Mechanisms of thalmocortical augmentation and repetition. Am. J. Physiol. 138: 297–308.

Moskowitz, S. 1964. The program for brain injured children in the NYC Public Schools—an appraisal. NYC Board of Education. N.Y. Bureau of Educational Research.

Motokizawa, F., and B. Fujimori. 1964. Fast activities and DC potential changes of the cerebral cortex during EEG arousal response, EEG Clin. Neurophysiol. 17: 630–637.

Mountcastle, V.B. 1961. Duality of function in the somatic afferent system. In M.A. Brazier (ed.), Brain and Behavior, Vol. 1. American Institute of Biological Sciences, Washington, D.C.

Muehl, S., J. Knott, and A. Benton. 1965. EEG abnormality and psychological test performance in reading disability. Cortex 1: 434–440.

Myklebust, H.R. 1963. Psychoneurological learning disorders in children.

In S.A. Kirk and W. Becker (eds.), Conference on Children with Minimal Brain Impairment. University of Illinois, Urbana.

Myklebust, H.R. 1965. Development and Disorders of Written Language: Picture Story Language Test. Grune & Stratton, New York.

Myklebust, H.R. (ed.), 1967. Progress in Learning Disabilities, Vol. I. Grune & Stratton, New York.

Myklebust, H.R. 1968. Learning disabilities: Definition and overview. *In* H.R. Myklebust (ed.), Progress in Learning Disabilities, Vol. I. Grune & Stratton, New York.

Myklebust, H.R. (ed.). 1971. Progress in Learning Disabilities, Vol. II. Grune & Stratton, New York.

Myklebust, H.R., and B. Boshes. 1969. Final report, minimal brain damage in children. Department of Health, Education and Welfare. Washington, D.C.

Myklebust, H.R., M.N. Bannonchie, and J.R. Killen. 1971. Learning disabilities and cognitive processes. *In* H.R. Myklebust (ed.), Progress in Learning Disabilities, Vol. II. Grune & Stratton, New York.

Naidoo, S. 1972. Specific Dyslexia. Pitman. London.

Nakajima, S. 1969. Interference with relearning in the rat after hippocampal injection of actinomycin D. J. Comp. Physiol. Psychol. 67: 457–461.

National Advisory Committee on Handicapped Children. 1967. United States Office of Education, Washington, D.C.

Neale, M.D. 1958. Neale Analysis of Reading Ability Manual. Macmillan, London.

Nebes, R.D. 1971. Superiority of the minor hemisphere in commissurotomized man for the perception of part-whole relations. Cortex 7: 333–349.

Nebes, R.D. 1972. Dominance of the minor hemisphere in commissurotomized man on a test of figural unification. Brain 95: 633–638.

Neisser, U. 1967. Cognitive Psychology. Appleton-Century-Crofts, New York.

Neisser, U., and H.K. Beller. 1965. Searching through word lists. Brit. J. Psychol. 56: 349–358.

Nelson, H.E., and P. McKenna. 1975. The use of current reading ability in the assessment of dementia. Brit. J. Soc. Clin. Psychol. (In press)

Nelson, H.E., and E.K. Warrington. 1974. Developmental spelling retardation and its relation to other cognitive abilities. Brit. J. Psychol. 65: 265–274.

Newbrough, J.R., and J.G. Kelley. 1962. A study of reading achievement in a population of school children. *In* J. Money (ed.), Reading Disability, pp. 61–72. Johns Hopkins Press, Baltimore.

Newcombe, F. 1969. Missile Wounds to the Brain. Oxford University Press, London.

Nickel, T. 1971. The reduced size Rod and Frame Test as a measure of psychological differentiation. Educ. Psychol. Measurement 31: 555–559.

Nissen, T., H.H. Roigaard-Petersen, and E.J. Fjerdingstad. 1965. Effect of ribonucleic acid extracted from the brain of trained animals on learning in rats. II. Dependence of the RNA effect on training condition prior to RNA extraction. Scand. J. Psychol. 6: 265–270.

Norman, D.A. 1969. Memory and Attention: An Introduction to Human Information Processing. Wiley and Sons, Inc., New York.

Obrist, P.A., R.A. Webb, and J.R. Sutterer. 1970. Cardiac-deceleration and reaction time: An evaluation of two hypotheses. Psychophysiology 6: 569–587.

Oldfield, R.C. 1971. The assessment and analysis of handedness: The Edinburgh inventory. Neuropsychologia 9: 97–113.

Olds, J. 1974. The creation of learning and memory. Engineering and Science 37: 12–17.

Olson, M.E. 1974. Laterality differences in tachistoscopic word recognition in normal and delayed readers in elementary school. J. Nutr. Sci. Vitam. (Tokyo) 20: 343–350.

Oltman, P.K., and F. Capobianco. 1967. Field dependence and eye dominance. Percept. Mot. Skills 26: 503–506.

Oltmanns, T., and J. Neale. 1974. Schizophrenic performance when distractions are present: Attentional deficit on differential task difficulty. Unpublished manuscript. State University of New York at Stony Brook.

Orton, S.T., 1928. Specific reading disability-strephosymbolia. JAMA 90: 1095–1099.

Orton, S.T. 1937. Reading, Writing, and Speech Problems in Children. W.W. Norton and Co., Inc., New York.

Orton, S.T. 1966. "Word-Blindness" in School Children and Other Papers on Strephosymbolia (Specific Language Disability–Dyslexia). The Orton Society, Inc., Pomfret, Conn.

Orzack, H., and C. Kornetsky. 1966. Attention dysfunction in chronic schizophrenia. Arch. Gen. Psychiatry 14: 327–326.

Ostfeld, A., X. Machme, and K. Unna. 1960. The effects of atropine on the electroencephalogram and behavior in man. J. Pharmacol. Exp. Ther. 128: 265–272.

Ounsted, C. 1970. Some aspects of seizure disorders. In D. Hull and D. Gairdner (eds.), Recent Advances in Paediatrics, pp. 363–400. Churchill Livingstone, London.

Ounsted, C., and D.C. Taylor. 1972. Gender Differences: Their Ontogeny and Significance. Churchill Livingstone, Edinburgh.

Ounsted, C., and D.C. Taylor. 1972. The Y chromosome message: A point of view. In C. Ounsted and D.C. Taylor (eds.), Gender Differences: Their Ontogeny and Significance, pp. 241–262. Churchill Livingstone, Edinburgh.

Oxford English Dictionary. 1933. Clarendon Press, Oxford.

Pagano, R.R. 1966. The effects of central stimulation and nasal airflow on induced activity of olfactory structures. EEG Clin. Neurophysiol. 21: 269–277.

Paine, R.S. 1962. Minimal chronic brain syndromes in children. Dev. Med. Child Neurol. 4: 21–27.

Paine, R.S. 1965. Organic neurological factors related to learning disorders. *In* J. Hellmuth (ed.), Learning Disorders, Vol. 1, pp. 1–29. Special Child Publications, Seattle.

Palmer, R.D. 1964. Development of a differentiated handedness. Psychol. Bull. 62: 257–272.

Paré, W. 1961. The effect of caffeine and seconal on a visual discrimination task. J. Comp. Physiol. Psychol. 54: 506–509.

Park, G.E., and K.A. Schneider. 1975. Thyroid function in relation to dyslexia (reading failures). (In press)

Park, G.E., M. Bieber, and E.A. Zeller. 1975. Functional dyslexia: Abnormal pattern in platelet monoamine oxidase. (In press)

Parmeggiani, P.L., and G. Zanocco. 1963. A study on the bioelectrical rhythms of cortical and subcortical structures during activated sleep. Arch. Ital. Biol. 101: 385–412.

Parry, P. 1973. The effect of reward on the performance of hyperactive children. Unpublished doctoral dissertation. McGill University, Montreal.

Parry, P.A., and V.I. Douglas. 1975. The effects of reward on the performance of hyperactive children. J. Abnorm. Child Psychol. (In press)

Pavy, R., and J. Metcalfe. 1965. The abnormal EEG in childhood communication and behavior abnormalities. EEG Clin. Neurophysiol. 19: 414.

Penfield, W., and L. Roberts. 1959. Speech and Brain Mechanisms. Princeton University Press, Princeton.

Perez-Borja, C., F.A. Tyce, C. McDonald, and A. Uihlein. 1961. Depth electrographic studies of a focal fast response to sensory stimulation in the human. EEG Clin. Neurophysiol. 13: 695–702.

Perry, N. 1975. Neural predictors of performance in grades K, 1, 2. Read at the Third Annual Meeting, International Neuropsychology Society, Tampa, Florida.

Peters. 1976. Personal communication, being written for publication.

Piaget, J. 1926a. Judgment and Reasoning in the Child. Harcourt, Brace & World, Inc., New York.

Piaget, J. 1926b. The Language and Thought of the Child. Routledge & Kegan Paul, London.

Piaget, J. 1928. Judgment and reasoning in the child. Routledge & Kegan Paul, London.

Pilliner, A.E.G., and J.F. Reid. 1972. The definition and measurement of reading problems. *In* J.F. Reid (ed.), Reading: Problems and Practices. Ward Lock Educational, London.

Pishkin, V., T. Smith, and H. Leibowitz. 1962. The influence of symbolic stimulus value on perceived size in chronic schizophrenia. J. Consult. Psychol. 26: 323–330.

Pizzamiglio, L. 1974. Handedness, ear preference and field dependence. Percept. Mot. Skills 38: 700–712.

Pizzamiglio, L., and R. Carli. 1974. Visual, tactile and acoustic embedded figures test in patients with unilateral brain damage. Cortex X: 238–246.

Pizzamiglio, L., and M. Cecchini. 1971. Development of hemispheric dominance in children from 5 to 10 years of age and their relations with the development of cognitive processes. Brain Res. 31: 1361–1378.

Poffenberger, A.T. 1947. James McKeen Cattell: Man of Science. Vol. 1. Psychological Research. Science Press. Lancaster, Pennsylvania.

Polanyi, M. 1964. Personal Knowledge: Towards a Post-Critical Philosophy. Harper & Row, New York.

Poppen, R., J. Stark, J. Eisenson, T. Forrest, and G. Wertheim. 1969. Visual sequencing performance of aphasic children. J. Speech Hearing Res. 12: 288–300.

Population 1921–1971, revised annual estimates. Statistics Canada. Catalogue 91–512, 55.

Porges, S.W. 1972. Heart rate variability and deceleration as indexes of reaction time. J. Exp. Psychol. 92: 103–110.

Porter, R.J., Jr., and C.I. Berlin. 1975. On interpreting developmental changes in the dichotic right-ear advantage. Brain and Language 2: 186–200.

Posey, H. 1951. The EEG in mental deficiency. Am. J. Ment. Def. 55: 515–520.

Preston, R.C., and D.J. Yarington. 1967. Status of fifty retarded readers eight years after reading clinic diagnosis. J. Reading 11: 122–129.

Pribram, K.H., and D. McGuinness. 1975. Arousal, activation and effort in the control of attention. Psychol. Rev. 82: 116–149.

Price, R. 1968. Analysis of task requirements in schizophrenic concept identification performance. J. Abnorm. Psychol. 73: 285–294.

Porges, S.W., G.F. Walter, R.J. Korb, and R.L. Sprague. 1975. The influence of methylphenidate on heart rate and behavioral measures of attention in hyperactive children. Child Dev. 46: 727–733.

Quiros, J. De. 1964. Dysphasia and dyslexia in school children. Folia Phoniatrica 16: 201–222.

Rabinovitch, R.D. 1959. Reading and learning disabilities. In S. Arieti (ed.), American Handbook of Psychiatry, pp. 857–869. Basic Books, New York.

Rabinovitch, R.D. 1962. Dyslexia, psychiatric considerations. Chapter 5. In J. Money (ed.). Reading Disability, pp. 73–79. Johns Hopkins Press, Baltimore.

Rabinovitch, R.D., A.L. Drew, R. De Jong, W. Ingram, and L.A. Withey. 1954. A research approach to reading retardation. Assoc. Res. Nerv. Ment. Dis. 34: 363–396.

Rabinovitch, R.D., A.L. Drew, R.N. De Jong, W. Ingram, and L. Withey. 1956. A research approach to reading retardation. In Neurology and Psychiatry in Childhood, Vol. 34. Research Publications of the Association for Research in Nervous and Mental Disease. Williams & Wilkins, Baltimore.

Rall, W., and G.M. Shepherd. 1968. Theoretical construction of field potentials and dendrodentritic synaptic interactions in the olfactory bulb. J. Neurophysiol. 31: 884–915.

Ramirez, M., and A. Castaneda. 1974. Cultural Democracy, Bicognitive Development and Education. Academic Press, New York.

Rasmussen, T., and C. Branch. 1962. Temporal lobe epilepsy: Indications for and results of surgical therapy. Postgrad. Med. 31: 9–14.

Rattle, J.D., and J.A. Foley-Fisher. 1968. A relationship between vernier acuity and intersaccadic interval. Optica Acta 15: 617–620.

Rawson, M. 1968. Developmental Language Disability: Adult Accomplishment of Dyslexic Boys. Johns Hopkins Press, Baltimore.

Read, C. 1971. Pre-school children's knowledge of English phonology. Harvard Educ. Rev. 41: 1–34.

Reed, H.B.C. 1963. Some relationships between neurological dysfunction and behavioral deficits in children. *In* Conference on Children With Minimal Brain Impairment, pp. 54–70. University of Illinois Press, Urbana.

Reed, H.B.C. 1968. Biological intelligence. Unpublished paper. Tufts Medical School, Boston.

Reed, J.C. 1967. Reading achievement as related to differences between WISC verbal and performance IQ's. Child Dev. 38: 835–840.

Reed, J.C. 1968a. The ability deficits of good and poor readers. J. Learning Disabilities 1: 44–49.

Reed, J.C. 1968b. The ability deficits of good and poor readers. J. Learning Disabilities 2: 134–139.

Reed, J.C. 1970. The deficits of retarded readers—fact or artifact. The Reading Teacher 23: 347–352.

Reger, R. 1965. School Psychology. Charles C Thomas, Springfield, Ill.

Reid, J.F. 1969. Dyslexia: A problem of communication. Educ. Res. 10: 126–133.

Reinert, G., P.B. Baltes, and L.R. Schmidt. 1964. Faktorenanalytische Untersuchungen zur Differenzierungshypothese der Intelligenz: Die Leistungsdifferenzierunghypothese. Psychologische Forschung 28: 246–300.

Reitan, R.M. 1959. The Effects of Brain Lesions on Adaptive Abilities in Human Beings. Indiana University, Medical Center (mimeo.).

Reitan, R.M. 1964. Relationships between neurological and psychological variables and their implications for reading instruction. *In* H.A. Robinson (ed.), Meeting Individual Differences in Reading. University of Chicago Press, Chicago.

Reitan, R.M. 1966. The needs of teachers for specialized information in the area of neuropsychology. Chapter 15. *In* W. Cruickshank (ed.), The Teacher of Brain-Injured Children. Syracuse University Press, Syracuse.

Reitan, R.M. 1967. Psychological assessment of deficits associated with brain lesions in subjects with and without subnormal intelligence. *In* J.L. Kharma (ed.), Brain Damage and Mental Retardation: A Psychological Evaluation. Charles C Thomas, Springfield, Ill.

Reitan, R.M. 1974. Psychological testing of epileptic patients. *In* P.J. Vinken and G.W. Bruyn (eds.), Handbook of Clinical Neurology, Vol. 15, The Epilepsies, pp. 559–575. North Holland Publishing Co., New York.

Reitan, R.M., and L.A. Davison. 1974. Clinical Neuropsychology: Current Status and Applications. Winston, Washington.

Reitan, R.M., and C.E. Heinemann. 1968. Interactions of neurological deficits and emotional disturbances in children with learning disorders:

Methods for differential assessment. *In* J. Hellmuth (ed.), Learning Disorders, Vol. 3, pp. 93–135. Special Child Publications, Seattle.

Rhodes, W.C., and M.L. Tracey. (Eds.). 1974. A study of Child Variance. Vol. 2. University of Michigan Press, Ann Arbor.

Ridgley, B., and B.P. Rourke. 1970. The neuropsychological abilities of young normal and retarded readers. Presented at the meeting of the Canadian Psychological Association, Winnipeg.

Risberg, J., and D.H. Ingvar. 1973. Patterns of activation in the grey matter of the dominant hemisphere during memorizing and reasoning. Brain 96: 737–756.

Robinson, D.A. 1964. The mechanics of human saccadic eye movements. J. Physiol. 174: 245–264.

Robinson, H.M., and H.K. Smith. 1962. Reading clinic–ten years after. The Elementary School Journal 63: 22–27.

Rosenblum, S. 1962. Practices and problems in the use of tranquilizers with exceptional children. *In* E. Trapp and P. Himelstein (eds.), Readings on the Exceptional Child, pp. 639–657. Appleton-Century-Crofts, New York.

Rosenzweig, M.R., D. Krech, and E.L. Bennett. 1960. A search for relations between brain chemistry and behavior. Psychol. Bull. 57: 476–492.

Rosenzweig, M.R., D. Krech, E.L. Bennett, and M.C. Diamond. 1962. Effects of environmental complexity and training on brain chemistry and anatomy: A replication and extension. J. Comp. Physiol. Psychol. 55: 429–437.

Rosner, J., and D.P. Simon. 1971. The auditory analysis test: An initial report. J. Learning Disabilities 4: 40–48.

Rosvold, H. 1965. A continuous performance test of brain damage. J. Consult. Psychol. 20: 343–350.

Rothkopf, E.Z. 1965. Some theoretical and experimental approaches to problems in written instruction. *In* J.D. Krumbholtz (ed.), Learning and the Educational Process, pp. 193–221. Rand McNally, Chicago.

Rourke, B. 1974. Brain-behavior relationships in children with learning disabilities: A research programme. Presented at the Annual Meeting of the American Psychological Association, New Orleans.

Rourke, B.P. 1975. Brain-behavior relationships in children with learning disabilities: A research program. Am. Psychol. 30: 911–920.

Rourke, B.P., and G. Czudner. 1972. Age differences in auditory reaction time of "brain-damaged" and normal children under regular and irregular preparatory interval conditions. J. Exp. Child. Psychol. 14: 372–379.

Rourke, B.P., and M.A.J. Finlayson. 1975. Neuropsychological significance of variations in patterns of performance on the Trail Making Test for older children with learning disabilities. J. Abnorm. Psychol. 84: 412–421.

Rourke, B.P., D.M. Dietrich, and G.C. Young. 1973. Significance of WISC verbal-performance discrepancies for younger children with learning disabilities. Percept. Mot. Skills 36: 275–282.

Rourke, B.P., R.R. Orr, and B.A. Ridgley. 1974. Neuropsychological abilities of normal and retarded readers: A three-year follow-up. Presented at the meeting of the Canadian Psychological Association, Windsor.

Rourke, B.P., D.W. Yanni, G.W. MacDonald, and G.C. Young. 1973. Neuropsychological significance of lateralized deficits on the Grooved Pegboard Test for older children with learning disabilities. J. Consult. Clin. Psychol. 41: 128–134.

Rowland, V. 1958. Discussion in Morrell, F. Electroencephalographic studies of conditioned learning. In M. Brazier (ed.), The Central Nervous System and Behavior. Josiah Macy, Jr. Foundation, New York.

Rozin, P., and L.R. Gleitman. 1976. The structure and acquisition of reading. In A.S. Reber and D. Scarborough (eds.), Reading: Theory and Practice. Erlbaum Associates, Hillsdale. (In press)

Rubin, E. 1971. Cognitive dysfunction and emotional disorders. In H. Myklebust (ed.), Progress in Learning Disabilities, Vol. II. Grune & Stratton, New York.

Ruble, D., and C. Nakamura. 1972. Task orientation vs. social orientation in young children and their attention to relevant social cues. Child Dev. 43: 471–480.

Rugel, R.P., and R. Rosenthal. 1974. Skin conductance, reaction time and observational ratings in learning disabled children. J. Abnorm. Child Psychol. 2 (3): 183–192.

Russell, R.W. 1960. Drugs as tools in behavioral research. In L. Uhr and J.G. Miller (eds.), Drugs and Behavior, pp. 19–40. Wiley and Sons, Inc., New York.

Russell, R.W., and M.L.E. Espir. 1961. Traumatic Aphasia. Clarendon Press, Oxford.

Russo, M., and L.A. Vignolo. 1967. Visual-figure ground discrimination in patients with unilateral cerebral disease. Cortex 3: 113–127.

Rutter, M. 1969. The concept of dyslexia. In P.H. Wolff and R. MacKeith (eds.), Planning for Better Learning. Clinics in Developmental Medicine No. 33. Heinemann, London.

Rutter, M., and W. Yule. 1973. Specific reading retardation. In L. Mann and D. Sabatino (eds.), The First Review of Special Education. Buttonwood Farms / J.S.E. Press.

Rutter, M., and W. Yule. 1975. The concept of specific reading retardation. J. Child Psychol. Psychiatry. 16: 181–197.

Rutter, M., P. Graham, and W. Yule. 1970. A Neuropsychiatric Study in Childhood. Clinics in Development Medicine Nos. 35/36. Heinemann, London.

Rutter, M., P. Graham, and W. Yule. 1970. A Neuropsychiatric Study in Childhood. Lippincott, Philadelphia.

Rutter, M., J. Tizard, and K. Whitmore (eds.), 1970. Education, Health and Behaviour. Longmans, London.

Safer, D.J. 1973. A familial factor in minimal brain dysfunction. Behav. Gen. 3: 175–186.

Safer, D.J., and R.P. Allen. 1971. The central effects of scopolamine in man. Biol. Psychiatry 3: 347–355.

Safer, D.J., R.P. Allen, and E. Barr. 1972. Depression of growth in hyperactive children on stimulant drugs. N. Engl. J. Med. 287: 217–220.

Safer, D.J., R.P. Allen, and E. Barr. 1975. Growth rebound after termination of stimulant drugs. Pediatr. Pharmacol. Ther. 86: 113–116.

Sakakura, H., and R.W. Doty. 1969. Bizarre EEG of striate cortex in blind squirrel monkeys. EEG Clin. Neurophysiol. 27: 734–735.

Sakhiulina, G.T. 1961. EEG manifestation of tonic cortical activity accompanying conditioned reflexes. Pavlov Journal of Higher Nervous Activity 11 (3): 48–57.

Salkind, N., and J. Poggio. 1975. Hyperactivity: Theoretical and methodological concerns. Unpublished manuscript. Kansas University.

Sameroff, A.J. 1974. Early influence on development: Fact or fancy? Presented at Merrill-Palmer Conference on Infancy, Detroit.

Saraf, K.R., D.F. Klein, R. Gittelman-Klein, and S. Groff. 1974. Imipramine side effects of children. Psychopharmacologia 37: 265–274.

Satterfield, J.H., and M.E. Dawson. 1971. Electrodermal correlates of hyperactivity in children. Psychophysiology 8: 191–197.

Satterfield, J.H., G. Antonian, G.C. Brashears, et al. 1974. Electrodermal studies in minimal brain dysfunction children. In C.K. Conners (ed.), Clinical Use of Stimulant Drugs in Children. Excerpta Medica, Amsterdam.

Satterfield, J.H., D. Cantwell, L.I. Lesser, and R.L. Podosin. 1972. Physiological studies of the hyperkinetic child. Am. J. Psychiatry 128: 1418–1424.

Satterfield, J.H., L.I. Lesser, R.E. Saul, and D.P. Cantwell. 1973. EEG aspects in the diagnosis and treatment of minimal brain dysfunction. Ann. N.Y. Acad. Sci. 205: 274–282.

Satterfield, J.H., G. Antonian, G.C. Brashears, A.C. Burleigh, and M.E. Dawson. 1974. Electrodermal studies in MBD children. In C.K. Conners (ed.), Report on the Clinical Use of Stimulant Drugs in Children. Excerpta Medica, Amsterdam.

Satz, P. 1968. Laterality effects in dichotic listening. A reply. Nature 218: 277–278.

Satz, P. 1972. Pathological left-handedness: An explanatory model. Cortex 8: 121–135.

Satz, P. 1975a. Developmental parameters in the lateralization of brain functions. Presented at Boerhaave Conference on Lateralization of Brain Functions, Leiden, The Netherlands.

Satz, P. 1975b. Hits and myths in reading disability: A time perspective. Presidential address. International Neuropsychological Society, Tampa, Florida.

Satz, P. 1976. Laterality tests: An inferential problem. Cortex. (In press)

Satz, P., D.J. Bakker, J. Teunissen, R. Goeber, and H. Van der Vlugt. 1975. Developmental parameters of the ear asymmetry: A multivariate approach. Brain and Language 2: 171–185.

Satz, P., and J. Friel. 1973. Some predictive antecedents of specific learning disability: A preliminary one-year follow-up. In P. Satz and J.J. Ross (eds.), The Disabled Learner. Rotterdam University Press, Rotterdam.

Satz, P., and J. Friel. 1974. Some predictive antecedents of specific reading disability: A preliminary two-year follow-up. J. Learning Disabilities 7: 437–444.

Satz, P., J. Friel, and R. Goebel. 1975. Some predictive antecedents of specific reading disability: A three-year follow-up. Bull. Orton Soc. 25: 91–110.

Satz, P., J. Friel, and F. Rudegeair. 1974. Differential changes in the acquisition of developmental skills in children who later became dyslexic: A three-year follow-up. *In* D. Stein, J. Rosen, and N. Butters (eds.), Plasticity and Recovery of Function in the Central Nervous System. Academic Press, New York.

Satz, P., J. Friel, and F. Rudegeair. 1975. Some predictive antecedents of specific reading disability: A two-, three- and four-year follow-up. *In* J.T. Guthrie (ed.), Aspects of Reading Acquisition. Johns Hopkins Press, Baltimore. (In press)

Satz, P., D. Rardin, and J. Ross. 1971. An evaluation of a theory of specific developmental dyslexia. Child Dev. 42: 2009–2021.

Satz, P., and S. Sparrow. 1970. Specific developmental dyslexia: A theoretical formulation. *In* D.J. Bakker and P. Satz (eds.), Specific Reading Disability: Advances in Theory and Method, pp. 17–39, Rotterdam University Press, Rotterdam.

Satz, P., and G.K. Van Nostrand. 1973. Developmental dyslexia: An evaluation of a theory. *In* P. Satz and J.J. Ross (eds.), The Disabled Learner: Early Detection and Intervention, pp. 121–148. Rotterdam University Press, Rotterdam.

Savin, H.B. 1972. What the child known about speech when he starts to learn to read. *In* J.F. Kavanagh and I.G. Mattingly (eds.), Language by Ear and by Eye: The Relationships Between Speech and Reading, pp. 319–329. MIT Press, Cambridge.

Schain, R.J. 1968. Minimal brain dysfunction in children: A neurological viewpoint. Bull. Los Angeles Neurol. Soc. 33: 145–155.

Schain, R.J. 1972. Neurology of Childhood Learning Disorders. Williams & Wilkins, Baltimore.

Scheerer, M. 1945. Problems of performance analysis in the study of personality. Ann. N.Y. Acad. Sci. 46: 653–678.

Schell, A.M., and J. Catania. 1975. The relationship between cardiac activity and sensory acuity. Psychophysiology 12: 147–151.

Schiller, F. 1947. Aphasia studies in patients with missile wounds. J. Neurol. Neurosurg. Psychiatry 10: 183–197.

Schonell, F.J. 1935. Diagnostic tests for specific disabilities in school subjects. Yearbook of Education. Evans, London.

Schonemann, P.H. 1966. A generalized solution of the orthogonal procrustes problem. Psychometrika 31: 1–10.

Schulman, J.L., J.C. Kaspar, and F.M. Throne. 1965. Brain damage and behavior. *In* A Clinical-Experimental Study. Charles C Thomas, Springfield, Ill.

Scott, K.G. 1971. Recognition memory: A research strategy and a summary of initial findings. *In* N.R. Ellis (ed.), International Review of Research in Mental Retardation, Vol. 5, pp. 84–111. Academic Press, New York.

Scrimshaw, N.S., and J.E. Gordon. (eds.). 1968. Malnutrition, Learning and Behavior. MIT Press, Cambridge.

Semmes, J. 1968. Hemispheric speculation: A possible clue to mechanisms. Neuropsychologia 6: 11–26.

Semmes, J., S. Weinstein, L. Ghent, and H-L. Teuber. 1960. Somatosensory Changes After Penetrating Brain Wounds in Man. Harvard University Press, Cambridge.

Senf, G.M., and P.C. Freundl. 1971. Memory and attention factors in specific learning disabilities. J. Learning Disabilities 4: 36–48.

Serra, A., L. Pizzamiglio, and A. Boari. 1976. Cognitive characteristics of subjects with eterosomic aneuploidia. Tech. Rep.

Shankweiler, D.P. 1963. A study of developmental dyslexia. Neuropsychologia 1: 267–286.

Shankweiler, D., and I.Y. Liberman. 1972. Misreading: A search for causes. In J.F. Kavanagh and I.G. Mattingly (eds.), Language by Ear and by Eye: The Relationships Between Speech and Reading, pp. 293–317. MIT Press, Cambridge.

Shankweiler, D., and I.Y. Liberman. 1976. This volume.

Shannon, C.E., and W. Weaver. 1963. The Mathematical Theory of Communication. University of Illinois Press. Urbana.

Shapiro, M. 1951. An experimental approach to diagnostic psychological testing. J. Ment. Sci. 97: 748–764.

Shaywitz, B.A., R.D. Yager, and J.H. Klopper. 1976. Selective brain dopamine depletion in developing rats: an experimental model of minimal brain dysfunction. Science 191: 305–308.

Sheer, D.E. 1970. Electrophysiological correlates of memory consolidation. In G. Ungar (ed.), Molecular Mechanisms in Memory and Learning. Plenum Press, New York.

Sheer, D.E. 1972. Neurobiology of memory storage processes. Winter Conference on Brain Research, Vail, Colorado.

Sheer, D.E. 1973. Children with minimal brain dysfunction: Neural processes. Winter Conference on Brain Research, Vail, Colorado.

Sheer, D.E. 1974. Electroencephalographic studies in learning disabilities. In H. Eichenwald and A. Talbot (eds.), The Learning Disabled Child, 37–43. University of Texas Health Sciences Center, Dallas.

Sheer, D.E. 1975. Biofeedback training of 40 Hz EEG and behavior. In N. Burch and H. Altschuler (eds.), Behavior and Brain Electrical Activity. Plenum Press, New York.

Sheer, D.E., and N.W. Grandstaff. 1970. Computer-analysis of electrical activity in the brain and its relation to behavior. In H.T. Wycis (ed.), Topical Problems in Psychiatry and Neurology. Karger Press, Basel/New York.

Sheer, D.E., and L. Hix. 1971. Computer-analysis of 40 Hz EEG in normal and MBI children. Society for Neuroscience Meeting, Washington, D.C.

Sheer, D.E., V.A. Benignus, and N.W. Grandstaff. 1966. 40 c/sec electrical activity in the brain of the cat. V. Pattern relations between visual cortex and the behavioral response in learning. Symposium on Higher Nervous Activity, IV World Congress of Psychiatry, Madrid.

Shepherd, G.M. 1970. The olfactory bulb as a sample cortical system: Experimental analysis and function and implications. In F.P. Schmidt (ed.), The Neurosciences Second Study Program. Rockefeller Press, New York.

Sherrington, C. 1951. Man On His Nature. 2nd Ed. Cambridge University Press, Cambridge.

Shipley, T., and R.W. Jones. 1969. Initial observations on sensory interaction and the theory of dyslexia. J. Commun. Dis. 2: 295−211.

Shute, C.C.D., and P.R. Lewis. 1967. The ascending cholinergic reticular system: Neocortical, olfactory and subcortical projections. Brain 90: 497−520.

Siegelman, E. 1969. Reflective and impulsive observing behavior. Child Dev. 40: 1213−1222.

Silver, A.A., and R.A. Hagin. 1964. Specific reading disability: Follow-up studies. Am. J. Orthopsychiatry 35: 95−102.

Silver, A.A., and R.A. Hagin. 1966. Maturation of perceptual functions in children with specific reading disability. The Reading Teacher 253−259.

Silver, A.A., and A. Hagin. 1975. Search, a Scanning Instrument for the Identification of Potential Learning Disability, Experimental Edition. New York University, Bellevue Medical Center, New York.

Silverman, J. 1964. The problem of attention in research and theory in schizophrenia. Psychol. Rev. 71: 352−379.

Silverman, L.J., and A.S. Metz. 1973. Number of pupils with specific learning disabilities in local public schools in the United States: Spring 1970. Ann. N.Y. Acad. Sci. 205: 146−157.

Silverman, A.J., G. Adevais, and W.E. McGough. 1960. Some relationships between handedness and perception. J. Psychosom. Res. 10: 151−158.

Sinclair, C. 1971. Dominance patterns of young children, a follow-up study. Percept. Mot. Skills 32: 142.

Skakun, E., T.O. Maguire, and A.R. Hakstian. 1972. An application of inferential statistics to the factorial invariance problem. Research and information report. University of Alberta, Division of Educational Research Services, Edmonton.

Skinner, B.F. 1968. The Technology of Teaching. Appleton-Century-Crofts, New York.

Skinner, H.A. 1961. The Origin of Medical Terms. 2nd Ed. Williams & Wilkins, Baltimore.

Sleator, E.K., and A. Von Neumann. 1974. Methylphenidate in the treatment of hyperkinetic children. Clin. Pediatr. 13: 19−24.

Smith, F. 1971. Understanding Reading: A Psycholinguistic Analysis of Reading and Learning to Read. Holt, Rinehart and Winston, New York.

Smith, F. 1973. Psycholinguistics and Reading. Holt, Rinehart and Winston, New York.

Sokolov, E.N. 1963. Perception and the Conditioned Reflex. Macmillan, New York.

Sommers, R.K., and M.L. Taylor. 1972. Cerebral speech dominance in language-disordered and normal children. Cortex 8: 224−232.

Sorel, F.M. 1974. Prevalences of Mental Retardation. Tilburg University Press, Groningen, Netherlands.

Sparrow, S. 1969. Reading disability and laterality. Proceedings of the

77th Annual Convention of the American Psychological Association, pp. 673–679.

Sparrow, S., and P. Satz. 1970. Dyslexia, laterality and neuropsychological development. *In* D.J. Bakker and P. Satz (eds.), Specific Reading Disability: Advances in Theory and Method, pp. 41–60. Rotterdam University Press, Rotterdam.

Special education memorandum EH 72-3 (Buff), 1972. Department of Education, State of California, Sacramento, Calif.

Spehlman, R. 1971. Acetylcholine and the synaptic transmission of nonspecific impulses to the visual cortex. Brain 94: 139–150.

Sperling, G. 1963. A model for visual memory tasks. Hum. Fact. 5: 19–31.

Sperry, R.W. 1968. Hemispheric disconnection and unity in conscious awareness. Am. Psychol. 23: 723–733.

Sperry, R.W. 1970. Cerebral dominance in perception. *In* F.A. Young and D.B. Lindsley (eds.), Early Experience and Visual Information Processing in Perceptual and Reading Disorders, pp. 167–178. National Academy of Sciences, Washington, D.C.

Sperry, R.W., M.S. Gazzaniga, and J.H. Bogen. 1969. Interhemispheric relationships: The neocortical commissures; syndromes of hemisphere disconnection. *In* P.J. Vinken and G.W. Bruyn (eds.), Handbook of Clinical Neurology, Vol. 4. Wiley and Sons, Inc., New York.

Sprague, R.L. 1972. Psychopharmacology and learning disabilities. J. Op. Psychiatry 3: 56–67.

Sprague, R.L., and R.H. Boileau. 1973. Are drugs safe? *In* R.L. Sprague (chm.), Psychopharmacology of children with learning disabilities. Symposium presented at the American Psychological Association, Montreal.

Sprague, R.L., and E.K. Sleator. 1973. Effects of psychopharmacologic agents on learning disorders. Pediatr. Clin. North Am. 20, 3: 719–735.

Sprague, R.L., and E.K. Sleator. 1975. What is the proper dose of stimulant drugs in children. Int. J. Ment. Health. (In press)

Sprague, R.L., and J.S. Werry. 1971. Methodology of psychopharmacological studies with the retarded. *In* N.R. Ellis (ed.), International Review of Research in Mental Retardation, Vol. 5, pp. 147–219. Academic Press, New York.

Sprague, R.L., and J.S. Werry. 1974. Psychotropic drugs and handicapped children. *In* L. Mann and D.A. Sabatino (eds.), The Second Review of Special Education, pp. 1–50. J.S.E. Press, Philadelphia.

Sprague, R.L., K.R. Barnes, and J.S. Werry. 1970. Methylphenidate and thioridazine: Learning, reaction time, activity, and classroom behavior in disturbed children. Am. J. Orthopsychiatry 40: 615–628.

Sprague, R.L., D. E. Christensen, and J.S. Werry. 1974. Experimental psychology and stimulant drugs. *In* C.K. Conners (ed.), Clinical Use of Stimulant Drugs in Children, pp. 141–164. Excerpta Medica, The Hague.

Spreen, O. 1970. Postscript: Review and outlook. *In* D.J. Bakker and P. Satz (eds.), Specific Reading Disability: Advances in Theory and Method, pp. 1–15. Rotterdam University Press, Rotterdam.

Spring, C., L. Greenberg, J. Scott, and J. Hopwood. 1974. Electrodermal activity in hyperactive boys who are methylphenidate responders. Psychophysiology 11: 436–442.

Sroufe, L.A. 1975. Drug treatment of children with behavior problems. Rev. Child Dev. Res. (In press)

Sroufe, L.A., and M.A. Stewart. 1973. Treating problem children with stimulant drugs. N. Engl. J. Med. 289: 407–413.

Sroufe, L.A., B.C. Sonies, W.D. West, and F.S. Wright. 1973. Anticipatory heart rate deceleration and reaction time in children with and without referral for learning disability. Child Dev. 44: 267–275.

Stafford, R.E., 1961. Sex differences in spatial visualization as of sex-linked inheritance. Percept. Mot. Skills 13: 428.

Stark, J. 1966. Performance of aphasic children on the ITPA. Except. Child. 33: 153–158.

Stark, R., P. Tallal, and B. Curtiss. 1975. Speech perception and production errors in dysphasic children. J. Acoust. Soc. Am. 57: 524.

State of California. Special Education Memorandum. EH 72-3 (Buff). 1972.

State of Iowa, Department of Public Instruction. 1974.

Statistics of special education for exceptional children. Dominion Bureau of Statistics (Canada). Catalogue 81-537, 1966, Table 5, pp. 60–61.

Steele, W.G., and M. Lewis. 1968. A longitudinal study of the cardiac response during a problem solving task and its relationship to general cognitive function. Psychon. Sci. 11: 275–276.

Stefanis, C., and H. Jasper. 1964. Recurrent collateral inhibition in pyramidal tract neurons. J. Neurophysiol. 27: 855–877.

Stegnick, A.J. 1972. The clinical use of Piracetam; a new Nootrapic drug. The treatment of symptoms of senile involution. Arzneimittel Forschung (Drug Research) 22: 975–977.

Stein, L., J.D. Belluzzi, and C.D. Wise. 1975. Memory enhancement by central administration of norepinephrine. Brain Res. 84: 329–335.

Stevens, D.A., et al. 1967. Presumed minimal brain dysfunction in children. Arch. Gen. Psychiatry 16: 281–285.

Stevens, H.A., and R. Heber, R. 1965. Mental Retardation: A Review of Research. University of Chicago Press, Chicago.

Stevens, J.R., K. Sachdev, and V. Milstein. 1968. Behavior disorders of childhood and the electroencephalogram. Arch. Neurol. 18: 160–177.

Stewart, R.J.C., and B.S. Platt. 1968. Nervous system damage in experimental protein-calorie deficiency. In N.S. Scrimshaw and J.E. Gordon (eds.), Malnutrition, Learning and Behavior, pp. 168–180. MIT Press, Cambridge.

Stoch, M.B., and P.M. Smythe. 1968. Undernutrition during infancy, and subsequent brain growth and intellectual development. In N.S. Scrimshaw and J.E. Gordon (eds.), Malnutrition, Learning and Behavior, pp. 278–289. MIT Press, Cambridge.

Storey, P.B. 1967. Psychiatric sequelae of subarachnoid haemorrhage. Brit. Med. J. 3: 261–266.

Stratton, L.O., and L. Petrinovich. 1963. Post-trial injections of an anticholinesterase drug and maze learning in two strains of rats. Psychopharmacologia 5: 47–54.

Strauss, A.A., and L.E. Lehtinen. 1947. Psychopathology and Education in the Brain-Injured Child. Grune & Stratton, New York.

514   References

Studdert-Kennedy, M., and D. Shankweiler. 1970. Hemispheric specialization for speech perception. J. Acoust. Soc. Am. 48: 579–594.

Subirana, A. 1964. The relationship between handedness and language function. Int. J. Neurol. 4: 215–234.

Sutton, S., P. Tueting, J. Zubin, and E.R. John. 1967. Information delivery and the sensory evoked potential. Science 155: 1436–1439.

Sykes, D.H. 1969. Sustained attention in hyperactive children. Unpublished doctoral dissertation. McGill University.

Sykes, D.H., V.I. Douglas, and G. Morgenstern. 1972. The effect of methylphenidate (Ritalin) on sustained attention in hyperactive children. Psychopharmacologia 25: 262–274.

Sykes, D., V.I. Douglas, and G. Morgenstern. 1973. Sustained attention in hyperactive children. J. Child Psychol. Psychiatry 14: 213–220.

Sykes, D.H., V.I. Douglas, G. Weiss, and K.K. Minde. 1971. Attention in hyperactive children and the effect of methylphenidate (Ritalin). J. Child Psychol. Psychiatry 12: 129–139.

Tallal, P. 1976a. An investigation of rapid auditory processing in normal and disordered language development. J. Speech Hearing Res. (In press)

Tallal, P. 1976b. A reevaluation of auditory sequencing abilities of children with reading disorders. Submitted to Brain and Language.

Tallal, P. 1976c. Impairment of auditory perception and acquisition of phonic skills in children with reading disorders. Submitted to Brain and Language.

Tallal, P., and F. Newcombe. 1976. What can computer-synthesized speech tell us about the language comprehension impairment of adults with residual dysphasia? J. Acoust. Soc. Am. 59: 585.

Tallal, P., and M. Piercy. 1973a. Defects of non-verbal auditory perception in children with developmental aphasia. Nature 241: 468–469.

Tallal, P., and M. Piercy. 1973b. Developmental aphasia: Impaired rate of non-verbal processing as a function of sensory modality. Neuropsychologia 11: 389–398.

Tallal, P., and M. Piercy. 1974. Developmental aphasia: Rate of auditory processing and selective impairment of consonant perception. Neuropsychologia 12 (1): 83–94.

Tallal, P., and M. Piercy. 1975. Developmental aphasia, the perception of brief vowels and extended stop consonants. Neuropsychologia 13: 69–74.

Tallal, P., R. Stark, and B. Curtiss. 1976. The relation between speech perception impairment and speech production impairment in children with developmental dysphasia. Brain and Language 3: 305–317.

Tarver, S., and D. Hallahan. 1974. Attention to deficits in children with learning disabilities: A review. J. Learning Disabilities 7: 36–45.

Tatsuoka, M.M. 1971. Multivariate Analysis: Techniques for Educational and Psychological Research. Wiley and Sons, Inc., New York.

Taylor, D.C. 1969. Differential rates of cerebral maturation between the sexes and between the hemispheres: Evidence from epilepsy. Lancet ii: 140–142.

Taylor, D.C. 1972. Mental state and temporal lobe epilepsy: A correlative account of 100 patients treated surgically. Epilepsia 13: 727–765.

Taylor, D.C. 1974. Influence of sexual differentiation on growth, development and disease. *In* J. Davis and J. Dobbin (eds.), Scientific Foundations of Paediatrics, pp. 29–44. Heinemann, London.

Taylor, D.C. 1975. Factors influencing the occurrence of schizophrenia-like psychosis in patients with temporal lobe epilepsy. Psychol. Med. 5: 249–254.

Taylor, D.C., and M.A. Falconer. 1968. Clinical, socio-economic and psychological changes after temporal lobectomy for epilepsy. Brit. J. Psychiatry 114: 1247–1261.

Taylor, D.C., and C. Ounsted. 1972. The nature of gender differences explored through ontogenetic analysis of sex ratios in disease. *In* C. Ounsted and D.C. Taylor (eds.), Gender Differences: Their Ontogeny and Significance, pp. 215–240. Churchill Livingstone, London.

Taylor, E.A. 1975. Ocular-motor processes and the act of reading. *In* G. Leisman (ed.), Basic Visual Processes and Learning Disability. Charles C Thomas, Springfield, Ill.

Taylor, L.B. 1972. Perception of digits presented to right and left ears in children with reading difficulties. Presented at meeting of Canadian Psychological Association, Hamilton, Canada.

Teuber, H-L. 1960. Perception. *In* T. Field, H.W. Magoun, and V.E. Hall (eds.), Handbook of Physiology, Section I: Neurophysiology, pp. 1595–1669. American Physiological Society, Washington, D.C.

Teuber, H-L. 1962. Effects of brain wounds implicating right or left hemisphere in man. International Symposium on Cerebral Dominance. Johns Hopkins Press, Baltimore.

Thiebauld, C. 1971. Improvement of intellectual performance: Contribution of a specific cortical therapy. Delivered to the 38th Congress of Medicine, Beyrouth.

Thorndike, R.L. 1963. The Concepts of Over-and-Under-Achievement. Bureau of Publications, Teachers College, Columbia University, New York.

Thurstone, L.L. 1955. The Differential Growth of Mental Abilities. University of North Carolina Psychometric Laboratory, Chapel Hill.

Tobach, E., L.R. Aronson, and E. Shaw (eds.). 1971. The Biopsychology of Development. Academic Press, New York.

Torres, F., and F.W. Ayers. 1968. Evaluation of the electroencephalogram of dyslexic children. EEG Clin. Neurophysiol. 24: 287.

Touwen, B.C.L., and H.F.R. Prechtl. 1970. The Neurological Examination of the Child with Minor Nervous Dysfunction. Heinemann, London.

Tschirgi, R. 1958. Spatial perception and central nervous system symmetry. Arquivas de Neuro-Psiquiatria 16: 364–366.

Tymchuk, A.J., R.M. Knights, and G.C. Hinton. 1970a. Neuropsychological test results of children with brain lesions, abnormal EEGs, and normal EEGs. Can. J. Behav. Sci. 2: 322–329.

Tymchuk, A.J., R.M. Knights, and G.C. Hinton. 1970b. The behavioral significance of differing EEG abnormalities in children with learning and/or behavior problems. J. Learning Disabilities Nov.: 1–4.

Tymchuk, A.J., R.M. Knights, and G.C. Hinton. 1970c. The behavioral significance of differing EEG abnormalities. J. Learning Disabilities 3: 548–551.

Umilta, C., G. Rizzolati, C.A. Marzi, G. Zamboni, C. Franzini, R. Camarda, and G. Berlucchi. 1974. Hemispheric differences in discrimination of line orientation. Neuropsychologia 12: 165–174.

U.S. Office of Education. Number of pupils with handicaps in local public schools: Spring 1970. U.S. Government Printing Office, Washington, D.C.

Vallett, R. 1969. Programming Learning Disabilities. Fearon Publications. Palo Alto, California.

van Duyne, H.J. 1971. The facilitating effects of various training methods on the development of verbal control of nonverbal behavior in four year old children. Psychon. Sci. 22: 345–346.

van Duyne, H.J. 1972. The development of the control of adult instructions over nonverbal behavior. J. Genet. Psychol. 120: 295–302.

van Duyne, H.J. 1975. Age and intelligence factors as predictors of the development of verbal control of nonverbal behavior. J. Genet. Psychol. (In press)

van Duyne, H.J., and D. Scanlan. 1975. Gender differences in the development of regulatory function of language. J. Genet. Psychol. (In press)

van Duyne, H.J., D.C. Scanlan, and M. Faltynski. 1975. The effects of quantity of information on monaural stimulation related to verbal control of nonverbal behavior. (In preparation)

Van Egeren, L.F. 1973. Multivariate statistical analysis. Psychophysiology 10: 517–532.

Varney, N.R., and A.L. Benton. 1975. Tactile perception of direction in relation to handedness and familial handedness. Neuropsychologia. (In press)

Venables, P. 1963. Selectivity of attention, withdrawal, and cortical activation. Arch. Gen. Psychiatry 9: 74–78.

Venables, P. 1964. Input dysfunction in schizophrenia. In B. Maher (ed.), Progress in Experimental Personality Research, Vol. 1. Academic Press, New York.

Vernon, M.D. 1971. Reading and Its Difficulties. Cambridge University Press, London.

Volkman, F.C., A Schick, and L.A. Riggs. 1962–1968. Time course on visual inhibition during voluntary saccades. J. Opt. Soc. Am. 58.

Vygotsky, L. (1962) Thought and Language. Wiley and Sons, Inc., New York.

Wada, J. 1969a. Interhemispheric sharing and shift of cerebral function. International Congress of Neurology. Excerpta Medica 193: 296–297.

Wada, J. 1969b. Presentation at 9th International Congress of Neurology, New York.

Wada, J.A., R. Clarke, and A. Hamm. 1975. Cerebral hemispheric asymmetry in humans. Cortical speech zones in 100 adult and 100 infant brains. Arch. Neur. 32: 239–246.

Wada, J. 1975. Human cerebral asymmetry in a hundred adult and a hundred infant brains. Arch. Neurol. (In press)

Wada, J., and T. Rasmussen. 1960. Intracarotid injection of Sodium Amytal for the lateralization of cerebral speech dominance. Experimental and clinical observations. J. Neurosurg. 17: 266–282.

Wada, J., R. Clarke, and A. Hamm. 1975. Cerebral hemispheric asymmetry in humans. Arch. Neurol. 32: 239–246.

Waddington, C.H. 1971. Concepts of development. *In* E. Tobach, L.R. Aronson, and E. Shaw (eds.), The Biopsychology of Development. Academic Press, New York.

Waites, L. (recording secretary). 1968. World Federation of Neurology: Research group on developmental dyslexia and world illiteracy. Report of Proceedings 22.

Walker, S. 1974. We're too cavalier about hyperactivity. Psychology Today Dec.: 43–48.

Walter, R., C. Yeager, and H. Rubin. 1956. An EEG survey with activation techniques of "undifferentiated" mental deficiency. Am. J. Ment. Def. 60: 785–791.

Walter, W.G. 1964. Slow potential waves in the human brain associated with expectancy, attention and decision. Archiv für Psychiatrie und Nervenkrankheiten 206: 309–322.

Walter, W.G. 1967. Slow potential changes in the human brain associated with expectancy, decision, and intention. EEG Clin. Neurophysiol. 26 (Suppl.): 123–130.

Walzer, S., and J.B. Richmond. 1973. The epidemiology of learning disorders. Pediatr. Clin. North Am. Vol. 20, 3: 549–565.

Warner, J. 1973. Learning Disabilities: Activities for Remediation. The Interstate Printers. Danville, Ill.

Warrington, E.K. 1967. The incidence of verbal disability associated with reading retardation. Neuropsychologia 5: 175–179.

Wary, W.G. Supervisor of Special Education and Learning Disabilities. Bucks County Public Schools, Pennsylvania. Personal communication.

Watson, P. 1970. Individual differences in children's reactions to frustrative non-reward. J. Exp. Child Psychol. 10: 216–234.

Watson, P. 1971. Individual differences in children's reactions to reward and non-reward. J. Exp. Child Psychol. 12: 170–181.

Wechsler, D. 1949. Wechsler Intelligence Scale for Children (Manual). Psychological Corporation, New York.

Weckroth, J., and H. Mikkonen. 1972. On the effect of UCB 2615 on certain intellectual, perceptual, psychomotor performance traits of subjectively rested mental state. Communication of the 30th International Congress on Alcoholism and Drug Dependence, Amsterdam, The Netherlands.

Weiss, G., E. Kruger, V. Danielson, and M. Elaman. 1973. The effect of long-term treatment of hyperactive children with methylphenidate. Presented at the American Neuropsychopharmacology Conference, Palm Springs, Florida.

Weiss, G., K. Minde, J.S. Werry, V.I. Douglas, and E. Nemeth. 1971. Studies on the hyperactive child: A five year follow-up. Arch. Gen. Psychiatry 24: 409–414.

Wender, P.H. 1971. Minimal Brain Dysfunction in Children. Wiley-Interscience Inc., New York.

Wender, P.H. 1972. The minimal brain dysfunction syndrome in children. J. Nerv. Ment. Dis. 155: 55–71.

Wender, P.H. 1973a. Minimal brain dysfunction in children: Diagnosis and management. Pediatr. Clin. North Am. Vol. 20, 1: 187–202.

Wender, P.H. 1973b. Some speculations concerning a possible biochemical basis of minimal brain dysfunction. Ann. N.Y. Acad. Sci. 205: 18–28.

Wender, P.H. 1974. Some speculations concerning a possible biochemical basis of minimal brain dysfunction. Life Sci. 14: 1605–1621.

Wender, P.H. 1975. The Hyperactive Child–Handbook for Parents. Crown Publishers Inc., New York. (In press)

Wender, P.H., R.S. Epstein, I.J. Kopin, and E.K. Gordon. 1971. Urinary monoamine metabolites in children with minimal brain dysfunction. Am. J. Psychiat. 127: 1411–1415.

Wepman, J.M. 1951. Recovery From Aphasia. Ronald Press. New York.

Wepman, J.M. 1960. Auditory Discrimination, speech and reading. Elementary School Journal 60: 325–333.

Wepman, J.M. 1964. Discussion of "the modality concept". In H.A. Robinson (ed.), Meeting Individual Differences in Reading. University of Chicago Press, Chicago.

Werry, J.S. 1968. Studies of the hyperactive child: An empirical analysis of the minimal brain dysfunction syndrome. Arch. Gen. Psychiatry 19: 9–16.

Werry, J.S. 1970. Some clinical and laboratory studies of psychotropic drugs in children: An overview. In W.L. Smith (ed.), Drugs and Cerebral Function. Charles C Thomas, Springfield, Ill.

Werry, J.S., and R. L. Sprague. 1970. Hyperactivity. In C.G. Costello (ed.), Symptoms of Psychopathology. Wiley and Sons, Inc., New York.

Werry, J.S., and R.L. Sprague. 1974. Methylphenidate in children–effect of dosage. Aust. N.Z. J. Psychiatry 8: 9–19.

Werry, J.S., G. Weiss, and V. Douglas. 1964. Studies on the hyperactive child. I. Some preliminary findings. Can. Psychiatric Assoc. J. 9: 120–130.

Westheimer, G. 1954. Mechanism of saccadic eye movements. Arch. Ophthalmol. 52: 710–724.

Wewetzer, K.-H. 1959. Das Hirngeschaedigte Kind. Thieme, Stuttgart.

Whitehouse, J. 1964. Effects of atropine on discrimination learning in the rat. J. Comp. Physiol. Psychol. 57: 13–15.

Whitfield, J.C. 1965. "Edges" in auditory information processing. In 23rd International Congress of Physiological Sciences. Excerpta Medica Foundation, Amsterdam.

Whitman, M.A., and R.C. Sprague. 1968. Learning and distractability in normals and retardates. American Institute for Mental Studies–The Training School Bulletin 65: 89–101.

Wiener, M., and W. Cromer. 1967. Reading and reading difficulty: A conceptual analysis. Harvard Educ. Rev. 37: 620–643.

Wikler, A.W., J.F. Dixon, and J.B. Parker. 1970. Brain function in problem children and controls: Psychometric, neurological and electroencephalographic comparison. Am. J. Psychiatry 127: 634–645.

Williams, M., and K. Jambor. 1964. Disorders of topographical and right-left orientation in adults compared with its acquisition in children. Neuropsychologia 2: 55–69.

Wilson, R.F. 1971. Assessment of the cerebral dominance theory of dyslexia as measured by a visual-auditory integration task. Ph.D. Dissertation, University of Victoria.

Wilson, P.J.E. 1970. Cerebral hemispherectomy for infantile hemiplegia, a report of 50 cases. Brain 93: 147–180.

Winer, B.J. 1962. Statistical Principles in Experimental Design. McGraw-Hill, New York.

WIRT Stereopsis Test. 1960. Titmus Optical Co. Petersburg, Va.

Witelson, S.F. 1962. Perception of auditory stimuli in children with learning problems. Unpublished Master's (Appl.) Thesis. McGill University.

Witelson. S.F. 1974. Hemispheric specialization for linguistic and nonlinguistic tactual perception using a dichotomous stimulation technique. Cortex 10: 3–17.

Witelson, S.F. 1976. Sex and the single hemisphere: right hemisphere specialization for spatial processing. Science. (In press)

Witelson, S.F. 1975. Left and right hemisphere functional specialization in developmental dyslexia. This volume.

Witelson, S.F., and W. Pallie. 1973. Left hemisphere specialization of language in the newborn: Neuroanatomical evidence of asymmetry. Brain 96: 641–646.

Witelson, S.F., and M.S. Rabinovitch. 1971. Children's recall strategies in dichotic listening. J. Exp. Child Psychol. 12: 106–113.

Witelson, S.F., and M.S. Rabinovitch. 1972. Hemispheric speech lateralization in children with auditory-linguistic deficits. Cortex 8: 412–426.

Withrow, F.B. 1964. Immediate recall by aphasic, deaf and normally hearing children for visual forms presented simultaneously or sequentially in time. Am. Speech Hearing Assoc. 6: 386.

Witkin, H.A. 1962. Psychological Differentiation. Wiley and Sons, Inc., New York.

Witkin, H.A. 1967. A cognitive style approach to cross-cultural research. Intern. J. Psychol. 2: 233–250.

Witkin, H.A., and D. Goodenough, and S. Karp. 1967. Stability of cognitive style from childhood to young adulthood. J. Personal. Social Psychol. 7: 291–300.

Witkin, H.A., R.B. Dyk, H.F. Faterson, D.R. Goodenough, and S.A. Karp. 1962. Psychological Differentiation. Wiley and Sons, Inc., New York.

Wolff, P.H., and I. Hurwitz. 1973. Functional implications of the minimal brain damage syndrome. In S. Walzer and P. Wolff (eds.), Minimal cerebral dysfunction in children. Semin. Psychiatry 5: 105.

Wolthius, O.L. 1971. Experiments with UCB 6215, a drug which enhances acquisition in rats: Its effects compared with those of methamphetamine. Eur. J. Pharmacol. 16: 283–297.

Wozniak, R. 1975. Psychology of the learning disabled child in the Soviet Union. In W.M. Cruikshank and D.P. Hallahan (eds.), Research and Theory in Minimal Cerebral Dysfunction and Learning Disability. Syracuse University Press, Syracuse.

Wusser, M., and A. Barclay. 1970. Dominance, linguistic skills and reading. Percept. Mot. Skills 31: 419–425.

Yarbus, A.L. 1956. The motion of the eye in the process of changing points of fixation. Biofizika 1: 76–78.

Yarbus, A.L. 1957. Eye movements during a change in stationary points of fixation in space. Biofizika 2: 698–702.

Yarbus, A.L. 1967. Eye Movements and Vision. Plenum Press. New York.

Yates, A. 1966. Data processing levels and thought disorder in schizophrenia. Aust. J. Psychol. 18: 103–117.

Yates, A. 1970. Behavior Therapy. Wiley and Sons, Inc., New York.

Yeni-Komshian, G.H., S. Isenberg, and H. Goldberg. 1975. Cerebral dominance and reading disability: Left visual field deficit in poor readers. Neuropsychologia 13: 83–94.

Young, L.R., and L. Stark. 1963. Variable feedback experiments testing a sampled data model for eye tracking movements. IEEE Trans. HFE-4: 38–51.

Yule, W. 1967. Predicting reading ages on Neale's analysis of reading ability. Brit. J. Educ. Psychol. 37: 252–255.

Yule, W. 1973. Differential prognosis of reading backwardness and specific reading retardation. Brit. J. Ed. Psychol. 43: 244–248.

Yule, W. 1976. Dyslexia. Psychol. Med. (In press)

Yule, W., M. Rutter, M. Berger, and J. Thompson. 1974. Over-and-under-achievement in reading: Distribution in the general population. Brit. J. Educ. Psychol. 44: 1–12.

Yule, W., M. Berger, S. Butler, V. Newham, and J. Tizard. 1969. The WPPSI: An empirical evaluation with a British sample. Brit. J. Educ. Psychol. 39: 1–13.

Zahn, T.P., F. Abate, B. Little, and P. Wender. 1974. MBD, stimulant drugs and Ans activity. Unpublished manuscript. University of Maryland.

Zangwill, O.L. 1960. Cerebral Dominance and its Relation to Psychological Function. Oliver and Boyd, London.

Zangwill, O.L. 1962. Dyslexia in relation to cerebral dominance. In J. Money (ed.), Reading Disability, pp. 103–113. Johns Hopkins Press, Baltimore.

Zaporozhets, A.V. 1961. The origin and development of the conscious control of movements in man. In N. O'Conner (ed.), Recent Soviet Psychology. Liveright, New York.

Zaporozhets, A.V. 1969. Some of the psychological problems of sensory training in early childhood and the preschool period. In M. Cole and I. Maltzman (eds.), A Handbook of Contemporary Soviet Psychology. Basic Books, New York.

Zaporozhets, A.V., and D.B. Elkonin. (eds.). 1971. The Psychology of Preschool Children. MIT Press, Cambridge.

Zara, M. 1973. Effects of mediation on learning in hyperactive four year old children. Unpublished doctoral dissertation. Northern Illinois University.

Zeaman, D., and B.J. House. 1963. The role of attention in retardate discrimination learning. In N.R. Ellis (ed.), Handbook of Mental Deficiency, pp. 159–223. McGraw-Hill, New York.

Zimmerman, F.T., and S. Ross. 1944. Effect of glutamic acid and other amino acids on maze learning in the white rat. Arch. Neurol. Psychiatry 51: 446–451.

Zuber, B.L., and L. Stark. 1966. Saccadic suppression: Evaluation of visual threshold associated with saccadic eye movements. Exp. Neurol. 16: 65–79.

Zurif, E.F., and G. Carson. 1970. Dyslexia in relation to cerebral dominance and temporal analysis. Neuropsychologia 8: 351–361.

Index